ALSO BY ERIC RUTKOW

American Canopy: Trees, Forests, and the Making of a Nation

THE
LONGEST LINE
ON THE MAP

The United States,
the Pan-American Highway,
and the Quest to Link the Americas

ERIC RUTKOW

SCRIBNER

New York   London   Toronto   Sydney   New Delhi

Scribner
An Imprint of Simon & Schuster, Inc.
1230 Avenue of the Americas
New York, NY 10020

First Scribner hardcover edition January 2019

SCRIBNER and design are registered trademarks of The Gale Group, Inc., used under license by Simon & Schuster, Inc., the publisher of this work.

For information about special discounts for bulk purchases, please contact Simon & Schuster Special Sales at 1-866-506-1949 or business@simonandschuster.com.

The Simon & Schuster Speakers Bureau can bring authors to your live event. For more information or to book an event, contact the Simon & Schuster Speakers Bureau at 1-866-248-3049 or visit our website at www.simonspeakers.com.

Interior design by Jill Putorti

Manufactured in the United States of America

10 9 8 7 6 5 4 3 2 1

Library of Congress Cataloging-in-Publication Data
Names: Rutkow, Eric, author.
Title: The longest line on the map : the United States, the Pan-American Highway,
    and the quest to link the Americas / Eric Rutkow.
Description: New York : Scribner, [2019] | Includes bibliographical references.
Identifiers: LCCN 2018043679 | ISBN 9781501103902 (hardcover) |
    ISBN 9781501103919 (pbk.) | ISBN 9781501103926 (ebook)
Subjects: LCSH: Pan American Highway System. | Roads—America—History. |
    United States—Foreign relations—America.
Classification: LCC HE358 .R88 2018 | DDC 388.1/22097—dc23
LC record available at https://urldefense.proofpoint.com/v2/url?u=https-3A__lccn
    .loc.gov_2018043679&d=DwIFAg&c=jGUuvAdBXp_VqQ6t0yah2g&r=ATh3bu
    79KSZJC2mHobPsF7IIIi28o-UPyxJ5n0kknw29qy141ZQdEWou5Xio05RJ&m
    =uJIOt4JhGQ0-UqpO8XQrByMSZplj5H7TX_g4CsGzFFw&s=QVGgynWu_
    HxKdBbQMwlGB9Rl_ImWanUvu6jWq97Euk4&e=

ISBN 978-1-5011-0390-2
ISBN 978-1-5011-0392-6 (ebook)

For my sister

Contents

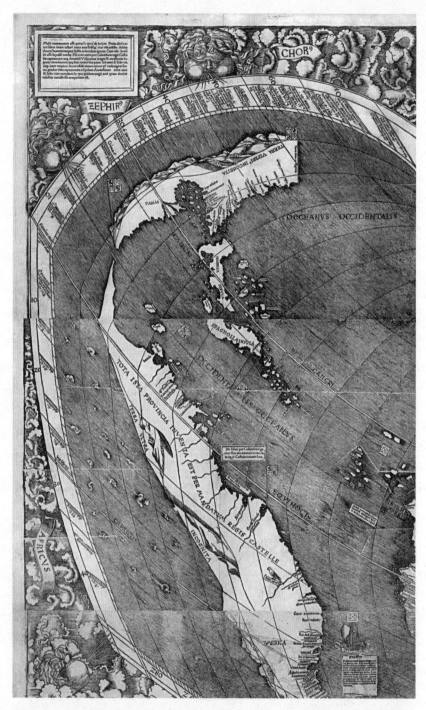

Two panels in the *Universalis Cosmographia Secundum* (c. 1507) showing the first European depiction of the Americas. Note the gap between the two continents, signifying an initial belief that North and South America were unconnected.

Introduction

The highway unfolded before Sal Paradise. It was the spring of 1949, and Paradise, the narrator of Jack Kerouac's *On the Road*, had decided to head in a new direction. For the past several years, he had vagabonded across the United States in an endless chase of freedom, but now the road was leading him and his friend Dean Moriarty beyond the nation's borders for the first time. "I couldn't imagine this trip," said Paradise. "It was the most fabulous of all. It was no longer east-west, but magic *south*. We saw a vision of the entire Western Hemisphere rockribbing clear down to Tierra del Fuego and us flying down the curve of the world into other tropics and other worlds." The last word went to Moriarty: "Man, this will finally take us to IT!"

Soon they entered Mexico on the Pan-American Highway.

The Pan-American Highway is the longest road in the world, running the length of the Western Hemisphere from Prudhoe Bay in Alaska to Tierra del Fuego in South America. It represents a dream of friendship, commerce, mobility, of the Americas united. Our collective imaginations have been forged along its path: Ernesto "Che" Guevara, the iconic Argentine revolutionary, traveled it northward in *The Motorcycle Diaries*; Kerouac, the voice of the beat generation, followed it southward in *On the Road*. Many adventurers have journeyed the highway's distance, but the road itself still remains shrouded in mystery. Why was it built? And why does it remain unfinished, with a sixty-mile-long break, the famed Darien Gap, between Panama and Colombia?

*   *   *

I first encountered the Pan-American Highway a decade ago as a tourist traveling through Latin America. Like Paradise, I spent little time thinking about how the road came to be. It seemed as though it had always formed part of the landscape, carving a path to connect the hemisphere's capitals, skirting volcanoes and coastal deserts and teeming jungles along the way. Life in the New World almost appeared to have arisen along the route of the ever-present highway. The road became easy to take for granted, an indelible fixture of the region.

The Pan-American Highway only piqued my historical curiosity several years later, after I read in an obscure volume that its construction in Central America and Panama had once been the largest foreign development project attempted by the United States. This assertion surprised me, as I had never before heard that the United States had played any role in the Pan-American Highway, let alone such a significant one. Why, I wondered, did the United States seek to build a foreign highway through half a dozen sovereign nations?

Soon I began searching through histories of US–Latin American relations for more information on the highway. But my early investigations proved unsatisfying. The road rarely received more than a passing mention in any of those works. And the more I searched, the more elusive the road seemed to become. While hundreds of histories have been written on the hemisphere's other great infrastructure project, the Panama Canal, none has ever been published on the Pan-American Highway.

The terms "North America" and "South America" are fictions created by geographers and mapmakers. The United States may seem separated by an ocean from South America, but in truth they both form part of the same American supercontinent. The American landmass is shaped like an hourglass, with Central America as the connecting link. Overland travel is theoretically possible along the entirety of the Western Hemisphere.

The historical relationship between the United States and Central and South America is rarely seen as one of overland neighbors. But this is a mistake. The shared dream of overland connectivity—originally as a Pan-American Railway and later as a Pan-American Highway—exerted a profound influence on hemispheric development and relations over the course of a century.

The two infrastructure projects were the material embodiment of Pan-Americanism, an ideology birthed in the early 1800s and given modern form late that same century, insisting that the Americas shared a common destiny and mutual interests. For Pan-Americanists throughout the New World, no project better reflected their aspirations—and frustrations—than this monumental quest to link the Americas.

Both hemispheric initiatives began through the efforts of the United States, where the ideals of Pan-Americanism intersected with an expansionist compulsion to reach new, foreign markets. And the United States—through both private and public measures—subsequently nurtured each massive project with direct, extraterritorial actions. The story of the United States and its quest to link the Americas, a forgotten drama that played out over the course of nearly one hundred years, is the subject of *The Longest Line on the Map*. It is a story of grand visions and fraught politics, of engineering marvels and unyielding nature. It is a story of remarkable perseverance and of eventual failure. It is a story of an imagined geography, Pan-America.

In telling this story, the book charts a course through more than a century of US–Latin American relations. The United States that emerges from this "Pan-American" history is a study in contradictions, torn between goodwill and self-interest, cooperation and control, pragmatism and paranoia. Indeed, Pan-Americanism was something of a paradox for the United States: while it elevated Latin American nations to stand as geopolitical equals and aimed at fraternal cooperation, it simultaneously cleared a path, through the explicit exclusion of Europe from the alliance, for the "Colossus of the North" to exert its dominion over the region.

A second theme of the story, along with Pan-Americanism, concerns road building and its relationship to US visions of international development. Like Pan-Americanism, this subject has been the victim of scholarly neglect. The countless histories of US automobiles and roads that have been written tend to stop at the nation's borders. The role of the US government in promoting highway development abroad is thus rarely considered. But the United States, the world's largest producer of cars for much of the twentieth century, actually played quite an active role in exporting automobile highways, thereby creating an infrastructure that encircled the globe over the last hundred years and ushered in the world's contemporary, oil-dependent transportation regime. *The Longest Line on the Map* traces how the US federal government grew to be a major road builder in the first place and then follows its evolution into an international operation through the

Pan-American Highway, a shift that marked the beginning of modern over-seas development for the nation.

The Pan-American Highway ultimately commanded the interest of every US president from Calvin Coolidge to Richard Nixon, though none was able to witness its completion. The highway's enduring appeal spoke to a persistent—if not always paramount—strain of presidential senti-ment favoring hemispheric connectivity, an imagined community forged in asphalt and concrete.

The highway, however, is no longer the great hemispheric infrastruc-ture project of the age for the United States. That distinction now rests with a planned wall to run along the US-Mexican border. The old dream of connectivity has ceded to a new one of separation, of a shielded fortress physically blockaded from the rest of the Americas. But the expansive his-tory of the US quest to link the Americas—reconstructed here for the first time—reveals just how incongruous this recent vision of partition truly is.

The Longest Line on the Map is driven by individuals more than unseen forces, by drama more than statistics, by storytelling more than analysis. The dream of connecting the hemisphere has captured the imagination of mil-lions during the past century and a half. *The Longest Line on the Map* finally gives this dream a history.

PART I
The Rail

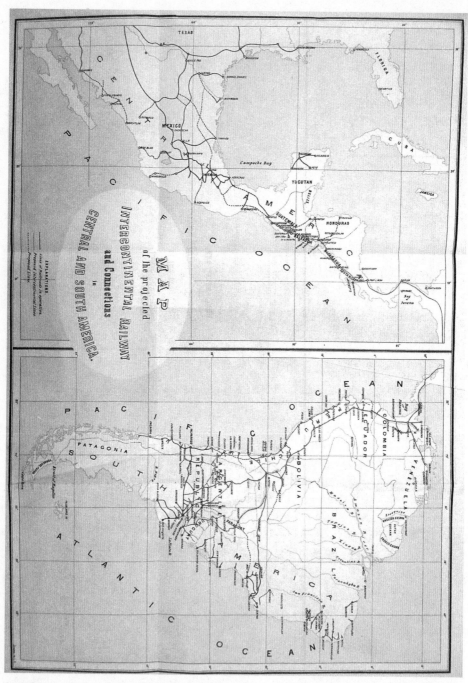

An 1891 Intercontinental Railway Commission map, the first depiction of the route for a hemispheric railway.

CHAPTER ONE

The Magnificent Conception

"Why Not by Rail?"

The swells of the southern Atlantic Ocean pummeled the sailing ship *Lord Clarendon*, splashing the decks and straining the riggings. Four days earlier, on November 26, 1866, the British-flagged passenger vessel had departed under calm skies from Buenos Aires, destined for New York City, but conditions had soured quickly once the *Lord Clarendon* veered into the path of an "unusually violent" Argentine pampero, a polar wind blowing off the fertile plains of lower South America. Belowdecks, supine in his bunk, thirty-six-year-old Hinton Rowan Helper, the outgoing US consul to Buenos Aires, contemplated his fate.

Helper tossed and fretted, wracked by what he described as "the torture of seasickness" and "Neptunian nausea." The physical distress mixed with feelings of impatience and disgust as he wondered how long the *Lord Clarendon*'s ceaseless rocking might endure and when he might reach the United States. Then, according to Helper, in the midst of the fourth day of punishment, "[at] about 2 o'clock in the afternoon, taxing my mind with redoubled duty to devise a means for others, if not for myself, to travel more pleasantly and expeditiously between far-distant points of our sister continents, the distinct answer to my mental inquiry, a sort of Yankee answer, came like a flash, 'Why not by rail?'"[1]

For an ordinary man, such an outlandish insight might have dissipated, along with the nausea, as soon as the pampero abated. But Helper was anything but ordinary. At the outbreak of the Civil War, shortly before he had departed for Buenos Aires, he was considered "the best known and most widely hated man in America."[2]

*   *   *

Helper's life had begun unremarkably enough in December 1829. He was the youngest of five children in a middle-class family of mixed English and German origin that had settled in the North Carolina Piedmont. His father had made cabinets and found enough success to afford four slaves but died from the mumps when Helper was barely nine months old. The surviving Helper clan avoided penury through the support of relatives. A teenaged Helper even spent several years at an elite local private school and was developing into what one admirer later described as "a very athletic man, above six feet in height, straight as an arrow, and broad-shouldered as a giant." At seventeen, he started apprenticing as a store clerk but soon grew restless and, in a moment of desperation, stole $300 from his employer. The theft, which Helper eventually acknowledged and tried to repay, would haunt him for the rest of his life, though his crime likely provided the funds for his first great adventure outside of North Carolina.[3]

In early 1851, Helper determined to set out for California, a land that the United States had wrested from Mexico three years earlier. A settlement rush had been sweeping California following the discovery of gold at Sutter's Mill in 1848, and Helper had found this excitement irresistible. However, like the countless other easterners trying to get west, he faced a transportation dilemma: no developed overland route connected the settled portions of the United States with its new western holdings. One possible solution for Helper was to join a schooner caravan and risk his life crossing any of several continental trails with origins older than the nation. A second option combined ocean travel with shorter overland crossings through the malarial tropical lowlands of Mexico or Central America. The longest, but seemingly least precarious, itinerary involved an unbroken fifteen-thousand-mile ocean voyage around the entirety of South America.

Helper selected this last alternative. His decision appeared wise until midway through the journey, with his ship rounding Cape Horn, when a violent storm struck and, according to Helper, "for seven successive days and nights kept us almost completely submerged." A weary Helper finally disembarked at his destination in May 1851, nearly four months after his departure.[4]

Life in the newly settled lands of California, where ethnicities mixed and licentious behavior flourished, differed radically from that of North Carolina. For Helper, who possessed a healthy dose of both southern propriety and racism, moral offense quickly proved easier to find than gold. Moreover, the hard work of prospecting suited his tastes less than the joys of literary pomposity and self-promotion. He returned to North Carolina in 1854, choosing this time to risk an overland crossing in Nicaragua rather than face the potential fury of Cape Horn once more.

Helper arrived home short of funds and soon authored a critique of California, *Land of Gold: Reality Versus Fiction*. The book sold poorly, but the experience left Helper determined to find success as an author, and soon his focus turned to the defining issue of his age, the "peculiar institution" of slavery, which Helper had recently begun to question. He feared that the forced labor of blacks had both undercut the economic prospects of poor southern whites and impeded the South's ability to industrialize. The dehumanizing treatment of the actual slaves, however, mattered little to Helper, whose racism equaled that of any plantation master.[5]

By the spring of 1857, he had drafted a polemic over four hundred pages long built around data drawn from the last national census. The manuscript, titled *The Impending Crisis of the South: How to Meet It*, sought to provide an economic counterweight to the moral case put forth five years earlier in Harriet Beecher Stowe's *Uncle Tom's Cabin*. Or, in Helper's words, "it is all well enough for women to give the fictions of slavery; men should give the facts." Helper's approach blended abolitionism with racism and used economic reasoning to discard with the ethical and religious argument against slavery popular in New England. Others had previously discussed some of the economic criticisms that Helper employed, but never so systematically and almost never when the author was a proud southerner. The twenty-seven-year-old Helper, a bona fide son of Dixie, child of a slaveholder, had dared to challenge the central institution of his homeland in print.[6]

The northern publishing establishment, worried about offending southern readers, shut out Helper entirely until a minor New York book agent agreed to publish *The Impending Crisis* for an upfront fee.

When the book finally appeared in the summer of 1857, scandals came as fast as sales. Across the South, rumors spread of people being lynched or imprisoned on mere suspicion of ownership, and the Dixie press pilloried both the book and its author. One writer even managed to discover Helper's juvenile theft of $300 and painted him as an untrustworthy vagrant.

Soon the fracas over Helper spilled into Congress. The controversy there began when a group of nearly seventy northern Republican congressmen signed a petition of support for the beleaguered Helper. This pro-Helper document predictably enraged many southern legislators, who viewed their colleagues' action as an unpardonable capitulation to radical sentiments. In late 1859, one of the petition's signatories, Representative John Sherman of Ohio, lost his leading campaign for House Speaker after southerners disqualified anyone who had endorsed Helper's work.[7]

During the subsequent presidential campaign of 1860, an abridged version of Helper's *Impending Crisis* flooded hotly contested counties throughout the border states. Election results suggested that Lincoln, whose early views on slavery shared more with Helper than with Harriet Beecher Stowe, did particularly well in areas that saw heavy distribution of this abridgment. By the close of 1860, Helper's book had sold over 140,000 copies, and his name had become among the best-known and most divisive in the nation.[8]

For Helper, however, fame brought little success. He earned virtually nothing from *The Impending Crisis*, and his pariah status left him unemployable throughout the South. He soon appealed directly to Lincoln, seeking a patronage position as reward for his role in the president's victory. Lincoln balked at first, likely fearing the repercussions of a Helper appointment among southern politicians, but in November 1861, seven months after the shelling of Fort Sumter and the outbreak of the Civil War, Helper received a minor appointment as US consul to Buenos Aires, Argentina, then a city of about a hundred thousand people.[9]

Only two US-flagged sailing ships at the time offered passenger service from New York to Buenos Aires. The few easterners who traveled to South America typically detoured first through Europe upon foreign-flagged steamers. The Old World powers—Great Britain especially—controlled commercial and passenger shipping throughout the Western Hemisphere and had created a sort of hub-and-spoke system anchored on the far side of the Atlantic. The patriotic Helper nonetheless insisted that as consul he ought to travel on a US-flagged vessel, even if that meant forgoing the faster and more reliable European steamers.

Helper initially anticipated a sea voyage of approximately two months' duration, but, as he later explained, "prolonged calms ... and an immoderate superfluity of kelp in the brine" turned the journey aboard a US-flagged sailing ship into a ninety-eight-day-long nightmare. The ocean had again betrayed him. He finally landed in Argentina on April 12, 1862.[10]

The inauspicious start to his official tenure nonetheless gave way to one of the happiest times in Helper's life. The European-inspired architecture and culture of Buenos Aires delighted him, and he began courting an Argentine woman reportedly of "pure Spanish descent," who had spent five years in the United States and was, according to Helper, "as thoroughly American as if she had been born in the Capitol at Washington." They married in early 1863.[11]

Helper's time in Buenos Aires also convinced him of the enormous potential that Latin American markets held for US manufacturers. He spoke of "an immense demand" and pleaded in dispatches to Washington for the establishment of subsidized steamer service between the New World's two continents. But these entreaties garnered little response, and the same could be said of his frequent requests for a salary increase, a situation that grew increasingly dire as Helper assumed several thousand dollars in debts. Finally, in late 1866, with the Civil War over, his debts increasing, and his salary demands summarily unmet, he tendered his resignation to the State Department.[12]

The prospect of a return sea voyage, however, created a new dilemma for Helper. The two US-flagged ships that earlier traveled to Buenos Aires had disappeared, casualties of a Civil War that had wholly disrupted the meager north–south sea trade of the United States. Eventually Helper decided to ride a British-flagged sailing ship named *Lord Clarendon*, but his oceanic transit turned disastrous for a third time when the pampero struck shortly after his departure from Buenos Aires. This latest misfortune led Helper to imagine his wild alternative, a fantastical vision, a futuristic reverie that seemed ripped from the pages of a Jules Verne novel: a ten-thousand-mile-long hemispheric railway between North and South America.[13]

Helper's outlandish insight stemmed not merely from his personal discomfort and fear, but also from his grandiloquent patriotism. The railway's greatest benefit, in Helper's view, related to a potential impact on US commerce, on helping his nation to gain market share in Latin America. "From the very first," Helper later explained, "it has been . . . my object to acquire (because geographically and politically and socially and otherwise it belongs to us) the bulk of that vast and rapidly augmenting business. . . . The time has now come for us to reach out into distant lands, and to open avenues abroad for our merchants and manufacturers."[14]

Helper's railway idea aligned with his earlier diplomatic pleas for increased steamship service, but a railway offered benefits to the United States that steamers could never match: an overland travel corridor impervious to European competition; and access to the southern continent's great, resource-rich interior. One newspaper later compared this strategy with "the piercing to the centre of the nut at once, extracting the kernel while foreign nations are looking for an opening on the outside."[15]

The broader geopolitical objectives that Helper hoped to advance through his hemispheric railway had a history of their own, one that first gained voice in the United States during the late 1810s. At that time, a dispute was under way among the nation's leaders over diplomatic recognition for a wave of independence movements that had spread throughout Spain's colonies in Mexico, Central America, and South America. Those US politicians opposing recognition feared upsetting the Spanish empire or abandoning the nation's professed commitment to neutrality, while those in favor saw a moral imperative to aid potential democracies. But in the opinion of the liberation movements' greatest congressional champion, House Speaker Henry Clay of Kentucky, far more than principle stood to be gained.[16]

Clay saw the potential autonomy of Spain's New World colonies through the prism of his own nation's struggle for greatness. When the anti-Spanish agitation had first started to gain international attention around 1810, the United States was already several years into a dispute with England and France over their refusal to let US merchants trade neutrally and safely with all parties. This commercial conflict had sparked a war with England in 1812 that lasted thirty months before the United States emerged victorious. Following this, Clay had become convinced that Spain's rebellious colonies held the key for the United States to forge a new trading system that could replace the one the War of 1812 had largely dismantled.[17]

As he explained in an 1820 speech, "It is in our power to create a system of which we shall be the centre, and in which all South America will act with us. . . . Our citizens engaged in foreign trade . . . must take new channels for it, and none so advantageous could be found as those which the trade with South America would afford." The liberated Spanish territories, in Clay's view, would allow the United States to transform from an agrarian satellite of England into the manufacturing and commercial hub of the New World.[18]

The European powers, however, had their own designs for the future of a potentially liberated Spanish empire. Merchants both in England and on the Continent intended to compete aggressively for the Western Hemisphere's trade and to fold any freed Spanish colonies into a European-centered commercial system. Moreover, the proposed Holy Alliance among the Russian

Empire, the Austrian Empire, and the Kingdom of Prussia seemed disposed to attempt a conquest of any freed Spanish territories during their vulnerable chrysalis from colony to nation.

The European political threat troubled Clay as well as many US leaders, including President James Monroe. His administration had started recognizing some of the independence movements in 1822, and the president had no desire to see a fading Spanish empire replaced with rising European powers. Monroe finally addressed this issue directly in a December 1823 speech before Congress. As he explained,

> [W]e should consider any attempt on [the part of European powers] to extend their system to any portion of this hemisphere as dangerous to our peace and safety.... [W]e could not view any interposition for the purpose of oppressing [the former Spanish colonial possessions], or controlling in any other manner their destiny, by any European power in any other light than as the manifestation of an unfriendly disposition toward the United States.

This soon-to-be-famous Monroe Doctrine, though practically unenforceable given the nation's limited naval power, inaugurated a new approach to the hemisphere that diverged from the United States' general foreign policy of neutrality toward all. The federal government, according to Monroe, would consider any new conquests in the Americas an overt act of aggression against the United States. The nation, at least on paper, now stood as the protector for American independence *writ large*. However, Monroe's address left unanswered the question of whether the independent New World nations ought to band together for commercial or other purposes, as Clay had long advocated.[19]

Clay's idea for a hemispheric alliance nonetheless resonated with some of the elites leading the anti-Spanish independence movements. As far back as 1815, Simón Bolívar, a South American–born aristocrat who would soon spearhead the liberation movement across much of his home continent, had advocated the convening of an "august assembly" of the New World's nations during "some happier period of our regeneration." Over the next decade, the "happier period" that Bolívar awaited seemed to grow closer with each military victory, and in late 1824 the "Great Liberator," as Bolívar had come to be known, formally called for an international congress at Panama City to "sketch the mark of our relations with the universe." Bolívar's proposal at first extended strictly to the former Spanish territories, but pressure from other independence leaders convinced him to invite the United States as well as an observer from Great Britain.[20]

Bolívar's begrudging invitation soon provoked a new round of debate in Washington over the nation's relationship with the rest of the Americas. The staunchest support for attendance came from Clay, who had recently been appointed secretary of state and who saw the conference as a starting point for his US-led hemispheric commercial system. Clay's antagonists, however, insisted that participation would compromise US neutrality, especially since Spain had yet to concede defeat against some of the liberation movements. Additional hostility emerged from southern congressmen worried about how the slavery question might be handled in Panama. The congressional impasse, which stretched out for several weeks, became "one of the most bitter controversies ever waged" in the estimation of a historian reflecting back from a century's distance. Clay ultimately prevailed, but his success hardly mattered: one of the US delegates died en route to Panama and the other arrived too late to participate.[21]

Only eight delegates had actually managed to attend Bolívar's 1826 Panama Congress, and the solitary treaty of union that this quorum negotiated gained approval nowhere besides Bolívar's home realm, a sprawling but unstable state known as Gran Colombia (present-day Colombia, Ecuador, Panama, Venezuela, and parts of Brazil, Guyana, and Peru).[22] The congress ended up a near-total failure.

In the years that followed, the hope for a true hemispheric alliance dimmed further. The former Spanish colonies, for their part, confronted political instability that hampered any serious attempts at internationalism. By the late 1830s, internal divisions had broken apart both Gran Colombia and the Federal Republic of Central America (present-day Guatemala, El Salvador, Honduras, Nicaragua, and Costa Rica). In the United States, meanwhile, the all-consuming fight over slavery and the sectionalism that resulted quashed any hopes for overseas leadership.

Clay's vision for a US-led, New World system to compete against Europe languished as long as the nation remained divided against itself. Perhaps it was appropriate that Hinton Rowan Helper, the same man whose explosive anti-slavery screed helped launch the Civil War, would seek to restore Clay's long-abandoned dream.[23]

Upon Helper's return from Buenos Aires in early 1867, the sight of a decimated and defeated southern landscape seemed to overwhelm the famed agitator and temporarily superseded any interest he had in promoting a hemispheric railway. He once more turned to his pen, producing a trilogy of racist tracts during the next five years. These books, all commercial failures, contained some of the more grotesque sentiments ever published in the country and represented the leading edge of an intense racism that would sweep the South in the decades after emancipation. The severity of his work also related to an almost pathological need to rebuff charges that *The Impending Crisis* had contained "pro-negro sentiments." Helper's brutal campaign of racist invective, which assuaged few of his critics, summarily eviscerated any prewar legacy as an abolitionist.[24]

Only at the close of this execrable decade did Helper make his first utterance on the railway. At the time, he was working under contract to resolve a festering dispute between the estate of a deceased US shipping merchant and the Brazilian government. In a typical flare of disproportionate resolve, Helper determined to gain a personal audience with the Brazilian emperor, Dom Pedro II, and thus traveled to Paris, a stop on the monarch's prolonged European tour. On May 9, 1877, after checking into the stately Hotel du Rhône, Helper penned a lengthy letter requesting an interview. The communication restated the facts of the legal case at length and then, buried in the eleventh paragraph, cryptically noted:

> if Brazil will now but do simple justice to my client, that act [will] place me in possession of a fee which ... I shall expend ... in perfecting plans [that will] give her back at least one hundred dollars for every dollar she will pay me. This large and feasible scheme of development has been locked exclusively in my own breast ever since 1866.

Helper managed to secure a short audience with Dom Pedro, but the emperor refused to discuss governmental affairs. Undeterred, Helper headed to Rio de Janeiro, the Brazilian capital, and petitioned Dom Pedro's daughter Izabel along with several high-ranking officials, using similarly vague yet bombastic language about his mysterious "feasible scheme." His machinations and fantastic promises, however, failed to convince anyone in Brazil to reconsider his client's legal claim.[25]

The Brazilian episode seemed only to encourage Helper's railway promotion efforts and to strengthen his convictions. After returning to the United States, he began discussing his project openly for the first time, trying to raise seed money among some of the same men who had supported him before the Civil War. But few expressed any interest. Former

New York governor Edwin Dennison Morgan, one of the firmest backers of *The Impending Crisis*, questioned Helper's sanity and supposedly declared that "under no circumstance or consideration whatever would I myself ever invest in the endeavor one dollar, or even one dime."[26]

The force of Morgan's denunciation convinced Helper to abandon eastern capital entirely. He turned west and selected as his new base of operations St. Louis, a fast-growing Missouri metropolis of soaring ambition, where overland commerce held more appeal than along the Eastern Seaboard and where Helper's views on race might prove less of a liability.[27]

Upon reaching St. Louis in late 1878, Helper deposited $5,000 that he had somehow amassed in the city's Bank of Commerce. The money was to finance an essay contest in furtherance of his scheme, which he had named "The Three Americas Railway." To judge this contest, he recruited two local railway men and the city's school board president, rumored to be "the only man in America who understands Hegel." Nearly fifty people, including eleven women, submitted essays or poems, most of them panegyrics devoid of substance. Helper hoped that the essays and a subsequent published volume, *The Three Americas Railway*, would generate sufficient interest to spur initial construction, with the goal of a completed route by 1892, to coincide with the four hundredth anniversary of Christopher Columbus's encountering the New World.[28]

But Helper's faith in himself as a charismatic promoter in the style of his contemporary P. T. Barnum far exceeded his capacities, at least in the eyes of some in the eastern press establishment. The *New York Times* labeled his quest "as astonishing as it is inexplicable" and scorned his supporters as "a band of lunatics." The *Baltimore Sun* titled its coverage of Helper's essay contest "Money to Throw Away," quipping that the submissions "were intended to be written in an elevated style, and it is quite possible that Mr. Helper's railroad from Alaska to Patagonia is meant to be an elevated railroad."[29]

Not everyone, however, dismissed Helper so easily. Words of encouragement arrived from numerous politicians, especially those in landlocked, interior states. Helper's early supporters included the governors of Illinois, Kansas, and Missouri. Representative James B. Belford of Colorado approved so heartily of the scheme that he presented Congress an unsuccessful resolution calling for 150,000 copies of Helper's *Three Americas Railway* to be printed at federal expense. Even John Sherman of Ohio, whose political ambitions had suffered so greatly from his earlier association with Helper, wrote, "No greater enterprise has been suggested during our time; nor does the difficulty seem so great to me."[30]

The emergence of these political backers encouraged Helper to transform from promoter to lobbyist. He soon drafted a bill requesting that Congress appoint and fund a three-man commission to visit Latin America, where they could locate support for his railway and gather data on the true scope of hemispheric trade. Representative Belford and Francis Cockrell, the Democratic senator from Helper's adopted state of Missouri, each agreed to sponsor the legislation. Versions appeared simultaneously before the House and Senate in late April 1882, but both failed.[31]

Helper's legislative proxies introduced bills anew at every session, until finally, in early 1884, the Cockrell bill gained a hearing in the Senate's Committee on Foreign Relations, whose ranks included John Sherman, now a senator. Helper soon wrote an open letter to the *Washington Post* pleading with Sherman to ensure the bill's "speedy passage." Three months later the law gained approval in both the Senate and House, its substance little changed from the original draft. A House report on the final bill—in a moment of staggering credulity that likely stemmed from Helper's exhaustive propaganda—noted, "While it may be true that a railroad from the United States to the Argentine Republic is of greater magnitude [than the transcontinentals], yet it is believed that the obstacles to its completion are no more formidable than were encountered eighteen or twenty years ago in the construction of our first trans-continental line."[32]

Helper had triumphed, but it was a brief-lived victory. The selection of commissioners fell to Republican president Chester A. Arthur, who ignored Helper's attempts to shape the three-man body. The president's choices likely owed more to patronage than qualifications, as only one of the commissioners actually understood Spanish. None of the men even knew Helper, a slight that left the railroad promoter's many friends and supporters "very much puzzled." Helper had been pushed aside from his own project and would never quite manage to claw his way back. Nonetheless, the famed southern firebrand had started the wheels turning not only for his envisioned railway, but also for a much bigger political movement, one tied to the era's most powerful statesman.[33]

The Plumed Knight Rides an Iron Horse

Helper's legislation had passed in the midst of a shake-up in Republican Party leadership. The party's nominal head, President Arthur, had owed his position to the assassination of President James A. Garfield and, in consequence, had lacked the broad support of an elected commander in chief.

Several rival Republican politicians had been eagerly awaiting the chance to challenge Arthur, and the 1884 Republican National Convention, held in Chicago during early June, had provided them the opportunity. After a few tense days, a fourth round of balloting finally produced a new nominee: James G. Blaine of Maine, silver-tongued, silver-haired, an indomitable force in post-Reconstruction US politics.[34]

Blaine accepted the nomination in a letter sent from his home in Bar Harbor, Maine. The missive largely featured familiar Republican cant but nonetheless included an unusual declaration, one almost unknown in presidential politics since the days of Henry Clay: "We have not improved our relations with Spanish America as wisely and as persistently as we might have done. For more than a generation the sympathy of those countries has been allowed to drift away from us. We should now make every effort to gain their friendship." A Blaine victory would quite likely mean a historic shift in hemispheric relations, a reigniting of the program that Clay had envisioned more than sixty years earlier.[35]

Blaine's novel pronouncement on Latin America, however, generated little initial attention. Most voters cared less about his policies than about his charisma and his mystique as a master politician. Born in 1830 to a middle-class Pennsylvania family, Blaine had moved to Maine in his early twenties to be closer to his wife's relatives and their finances, using a perch as the editor of a local paper to launch into politics. His legislative career began with the Whigs, an antebellum party of infrastructure development, elite rule, and increased federal authority, but Blaine soon shifted to the newly formed Republican Party of "free soil, free labor, free men." The Republicans and Blaine subsequently gained strength in tandem. He became Speaker of the Republican-dominated Congress in 1869, won a Senate seat seven years later, and then developed into a quadrennial contender for the party's presidential nomination, coming up short in 1876 and 1880.

Those who admired Blaine displayed unwavering loyalty. Those who opposed him seethed with contempt. In the words of Senator George Hoar of Massachusetts, "There has probably never been a man in our history upon whom so few people looked with indifference. He was born to be loved or hated. Nobody occupied a middle ground as to him." Blaine's divisiveness arose, in large part, because beneath his facade of competence, of witty retorts, of prodigious memory, of unflagging industriousness, of beguiling hypochondria, rested a murky layer of corruption and self-dealing that penetrated down to the very bedrock.[36]

Blaine often transcended the constant charges of corruption through obfuscation, intimidation, or charm. A friend famously described him as a "plumed knight" who threw "his shining lance" at "every maligner of his fair reputation." Nonetheless, the interminable allegations became impossible to ignore during his 1884 presidential campaign. Shortly after Blaine received his party's nomination, charges resurfaced that he had once used his influence to secure railroad grants that he later profited from. Blaine, as always, demurred, but a railroad clerk named James Mulligan produced incriminating correspondence upon which Blaine had scrawled, "Burn this letter." The phrase followed Blaine throughout the 1884 campaign. Roscoe Conkling—a lawyer, former Republican Senate rival, and power broker in New York politics—refused to endorse Blaine's candidacy, reportedly declaring, "I don't engage in criminal practice." [37]

Scandalous pasts seemed to be a calling card for those closest to Blaine. The Plumed Knight's top campaign operative and frequent business associate, Stephen B. Elkins, had made his early fortune in New Mexican land grants that many considered among the most brazen acts of graft in the history of the West. After Elkins in the 1884 campaign hierarchy came Richard Kerens of St. Louis, a onetime stagecoach driver who had garnered riches through fraudulent federal postal contracts that Blaine had supposedly helped authorize—when President Arthur tried to investigate these so-called Star Route frauds, Blaine played defense and helped shield Kerens and others from prosecution. [38]

The besmirched reputations of Blaine and those in his inner circle, however, could not derail his campaign. He performed strongly against Democratic nominee Grover Cleveland, a popular New York politician who struggled to contain his own scandal involving a supposed illegitimate child. The election results were so close that the final outcome remained unknown for days, until New York announced that Cleveland had carried the state by less than 0.3 percent. Conkling had been vindicated. Blaine was out. [39]

Defeated, he retired temporarily from the national spotlight, but his presence still loomed over the Capitol. Many Republican congressmen assumed he would receive the 1888 presidential nomination. And almost in anticipation of this outcome, a movement was building among legislators for closer relations in the hemisphere, following a path that Blaine himself had first plotted seven years prior. [40]

Blaine's devotion to hemispheric unity originated under circumstances almost as hazy as his personal fortune, buried beneath the sediment of subsequent hagiography and self-promotion. A preliminary step seemed to have occurred in the late 1870s, when he enlisted an associate to conduct "a study of the resources, needs, aspirations, [and] possibilities of the southern hemisphere." Blaine's concerns at the time paralleled those of both his political hero Henry Clay and his contemporary Hinton Rowan Helper: a desire to strengthen the US economy through increased manufacturing exports, and a recognition that such ends might be accomplished by snatching Latin American trade from Europe. But Blaine, during his Senate tenure, took few steps to facilitate this outcome, aside from occasionally advocating expanded Latin American steamship commerce as a way to compete against Great Britain.[41]

In many respects, the subject of Latin American relations only impressed itself upon Blaine in early 1881 after newly elected President Garfield, in need of seasoned counsel, appointed him secretary of state. At the time, a long-standing border dispute between Mexico and Guatemala threatened to turn violent, and a debate over valuable nitrate deposits in the Atacama Desert, which straddled the borders of Chile, Peru, and Bolivia, had already thrown all three of those nations headlong into the War of the Pacific. The weaker parties in both of these cases, Guatemala and Peru, respectively, had appealed to the United States for aid, and Blaine, out of simple inexperience or naive faith, agreed to provide assistance, only to find himself ensnared in two diplomatic imbroglios. Some in the press would take to calling him "Jingo Jim."[42]

Both of the Latin American disputes remained unresolved when, in early July 1881, a crazed office seeker shot Garfield and incompetent doctors effectively condemned the president to a slow and painful death. Vice President Arthur replaced Garfield in the fall of 1881 and soon determined to jettison Blaine, a political rival and constant threat. "And so," in the words of one Blaine scholar, "in a last and brilliant effort characteristically imaginative and ingenious Blaine placed in his brief record as secretary of state a new and striking proposal that would smooth over if not rub out his past mistakes."[43]

The "new and striking proposal" called for a gathering of representatives from all the independent states of the hemisphere for an international conference. Blaine seemed to be grasping for the mantle of Simón Bolívar, but the Plumed Knight's plan, unlike that of the Great Liberator, placed the United States in a central leadership role. Above all, Blaine sought to combat "the existence or the menace of these wars" that had plagued his tenure as secretary of state. This utopian end, he believed, could be achieved through an agreement requiring that all potential disputes first face mandatory arbitration, a process in which a neutral third party (or parties) listens to both sides and offers a judgment. Arbitration would be the only official item on the conference's agenda. Blaine's proposed hemispheric conference offered an internally oriented complement to the half-century-old Monroe Doctrine, which had focused strictly on external threats, and it thus marked the potential start of a new era in US political leadership throughout the New World.[44]

On Blaine's urging, President Arthur issued official invitations in December 1881. The president's support, however, soon eroded for what increasingly seemed like a conference designed to boost the reputation of his presumptive presidential rival. In early 1882, Arthur instructed the State Department to withdraw the invitations on the grounds that Blaine had lacked congressional approval for his conference. Blaine's effort to salvage his reputation and his time as secretary of state had achieved little but national embarrassment for the moment.[45]

The matter now shifted to Congress, which could still authorize a conference through legislation. Blaine's numerous allies there offered a reason for the ousted secretary of state to remain optimistic, and even those outside Blaine's northern Republican power center, particularly southern Democrats, had begun to view overseas commercial expansion in Latin America as a key to the nation's economic health. Within days of Arthur's announcement, Alabama senator John Morgan, a Democrat and ally of Blaine's, started the campaign for the conference's reinstatement, though his bill soon died in committee.[46]

On the same day that Morgan introduced his bill, Helper's unrelated railroad commission legislation had first appeared. The dual efforts to create an international conference and an intercontinental railroad subsequently reinforced one another. A few failed bills simply combined both initiatives. The mid-1884 approval of Helper's commission had arisen, in part, because Arthur and his new secretary of state saw the measure as a way to delay Blaine's conference.[47]

Blaine's narrow 1884 presidential loss hampered congressional momentum further, but a recession in the mid-1880s, which some blamed on overproduction and a lack of export markets, increased calls for improved overseas trade with Latin America. These appeals intensified as optimistic reports began to appear from Helper's commission. By early 1885, the commissioners had concluded that the scope of trade exceeded prior estimates by several hundred million dollars, and all three members of the commission testified on the value of a conference. As one of the commissioners noted, "Every country favored [a commercial convention]. They wanted the United States to take the initiative, however, and call the convention, naming the topics that would be considered."[48]

Gradually, the commission's concerns over commerce and Blaine's original, limited plan for arbitration merged. When Republican senator William Frye from Blaine's home state of Maine proposed a revised international conference in 1886, the bill included a greatly expanded agenda: a customs union, direct steamship communication, standardized commercial and legal regulations, common silver currency, and universal arbitration. Frye's legislation offered a breathtaking combination of proposals that, if somehow enacted, would turn the entire non-European-controlled portion of the hemisphere into one economic federation. The long-departed dream of Henry Clay had finally returned to the fore.

Versions of Frye's bill surfaced repeatedly, and the conference finally gained approval in 1888, after a six-year struggle, on the eve of a new election.[49]

All eyes once more turned to Blaine. For many in his party, he represented the best hope to reclaim the White House from Cleveland and to restore the reign of Republican presidents that had stretched unbroken from 1860 to 1884. However, few knew that their potential savior was suffering the early stages of Bright's disease (now known as nephritis), a malady that had recently killed former president Arthur. Officially, Blaine averred that he would only accept the nomination if his party insisted upon it.[50]

Blaine's conspiratorial cabal of lieutenants, Elkins and Kerens foremost among them, maneuvered to produce this outcome, but at the Republican convention, Senator John Sherman, the same man who had lost the 1859 House speakership over *The Impending Crisis*, refused to withdraw his candidacy. Sherman's obstruction forced the Blainites to abandon their cause, and Elkins switched his energies to Benjamin Harrison, a Civil War general, ex-senator, and grandson of a former US president. Harrison soon carried the Republican nomination, though, as one delegate acknowledged, "I think it is only the truth to say that the nomination was . . . made by the friends of Blaine."[51]

The news about Harrison's nomination reached Blaine while he vacationed and convalesced in Scotland with his dear friend Andrew Carnegie, the steel baron. Blaine then watched from afar as his carefully selected replacement triumphed in November, buoyed by a commitment to strong tariffs that would protect domestic manufacturers against European rivals. When the election ended, Harrison, like Garfield before him, appointed Blaine as secretary of state. Once more the presidency had slipped from Blaine's grasp, but he had returned to diplomacy with the groundwork fully laid for a vastly enlarged hemispheric conference.[52]

Blaine quickly realized that Harrison, despite owing his presidency to the influence of the Plumed Knight's men, was neither a puppet nor willing to pay the tab for his secretary of state's innumerable political debts. However, the new president initially gave Blaine wide latitude when their policies aligned, as with Latin America and the upcoming conference. In January 1889, Harrison wrote Blaine: "I am especially interested in the improvement of our relations with the Central and South American States. We must win their confidence by deserving it. It will not come upon demand."[53]

Blaine, operating within the bounds of Harrison's loose oversight, used the approaching conference in part to repay personal and political favors. Of the ten US delegates selected in the spring of 1889, eight came from the Republican Party, including the presidents of the last two national conventions as well as Blaine's intimate friend Andrew Carnegie. Of the two Democratic delegates, one spot went to former senator Henry Gassaway Davis of West Virginia, a coal and railway baron whose connections to Blaine were as thick as soured milk and whose company boards invariably included the Plumed Knight himself, the old Star Router Richard Kerens, and Stephen Elkins, who also happened to be Davis's son-in-law.[54, 55]

While the profound interrelations that the conference delegates shared with the new secretary of state drew little attention, the conspicuous number of businessmen nonetheless worried some members of the Latin American press. They felt that Blaine's choices were part of an underlying agenda of economic expansion and not merely a reflection of a compromised Gilded Age culture that drew few lines between commerce and politics. José Martí, a Cuban patriot, future revolutionary, and profound literary talent, covered the conference for an Argentine paper and considered the entire enterprise a swindle pushed by a nation "glutted with unsalable merchandise and determined to extend its dominions in America."[56]

The conference finally convened in Washington, DC, during early October 1889 and benefited from a moment of unprecedented peace among the hemisphere's nations. The countries of South America were, at last, without major international conflicts after having endured several bloody decades that featured both the War of the Pacific (1879–1883) in the Atacama Desert and the War of the Triple Alliance (1864–1870), in which the combined forces of Argentina, Brazil, and Uruguay decimated Paraguay. Mexico, meanwhile, was nearly fifteen years into strongman Porfirio Díaz's regime of "order and progress," and the small nations of Central America enjoyed relative calm following the 1885 death of Guatemalan caudillo Justo Rufino Barrios, who had tried unsuccessfully to reunify the isthmus through force. Additionally, several weeks after the 1889 conference began, the Empire of Brazil, the hemisphere's only independent monarchy, underwent a revolution that birthed a republic.

All of these political developments nonetheless could not prevent the conference from stumbling hopelessly from one minor controversy to another. The prickly atmosphere owed much to the vast cultural distance between the United States and the rest of Latin America. Three hundred years of separated histories had yielded distinct languages, legal systems, religions, racial identities, and elite comportment. As one US delegate lamented, "I don't understand those people."[57]

But politics and economics still lay at the heart of the conference's tension. The delegates from Argentina, a nation with close ties to several European powers, feared, like Martí, that the entire initiative served as a US power grab, and they sought to assert their own leadership. When Blaine tried to install himself as conference president, a move that many saw as a sign of US commitment, the Argentines tried to block him on procedural grounds, only to abstain from the eventual vote that granted Blaine the title. Meanwhile, the Chileans, whose government Blaine had affronted in 1881 during the War of the Pacific, worked assiduously to water down an arbitration agreement.

Many of the difficulties, however, rested squarely within the United States' own delegation. The nation's ten representatives, unlike most of their Latin American counterparts, lacked authority to speak for official national policy and, consequently, produced a cacophony of conflicting opinions.

The possibility loomed large that the conference might be unable to reach a single accord, even as a hortatory message.[58]

Helper's Three Americas Railway idea started out on the margins of the conference it had helped to inspire. Blaine had alluded briefly to the railway in his opening remarks, and a subcommittee had been assigned to the topic of railroad communications, though its agenda lacked any particular reference to a hemispheric route. Helper himself had no official role in the conference, but he nonetheless arrived at one point from St. Louis to plead his case personally. Less expected but perhaps more consequential was the appearance of Colonel H. C. Parsons of Virginia.[59]

Parsons was a prominent Republican entrepreneur and an intimate associate of both Blaine and Davis. His investments included the land containing the famed Natural Bridge, which once belonged to Thomas Jefferson and was among the most popular eastern tourist attractions of the nineteenth century. Parsons announced to the conference attendees in Washington that he was in the process of forming a corporation with an astounding $100 million in capital to build a railroad through South America and connect the line via steamship to the United States. Parsons's ambitious plan seemed to resonate with his friend Davis, who, along with Carnegie, represented the United States on the railroad committee.[60]

Davis undoubtedly had more practical railroad experience than anyone else present on the committee, and his subsequent support for an intercontinental railway project helped to extract a rare moment of consensus from the delegates. By late February 1890, nearly five months into the gathering, the railroad committee had agreed upon a series of resolutions calling for the formation of an Intercontinental Railway Commission, composed of representatives from each nation, to study the hemispheric route further.[61]

The official conclusion of the conference, which some in the press had dubbed the "Pan-American Conference," finally arrived in mid-April 1890. Depending on one's perspective, the gathering that Blaine helped inspire— and the idea of Pan-Americanism that it now represented—had been either a glorious success or an unmitigated failure.

The Argentines, for their part, criticized the proceedings in all the Buenos Aires papers. In the words of Victor Ernesto Quesada, an Argentine delegate and future president of that nation, "the Yankees are immensely and genuinely proud . . . : criticisms don't even reach them, because they are all intimately and sincerely convinced of the superiority of their *manifest destiny*; but lively as they are, they know how to appreciate those that look at them with eyes wide open."

Matías Romero, the long-serving Mexican foreign minister with close ties to US capital, felt more charitable, writing, "it might appear that the results of the Conference have been disappointing; but . . . its success has been greater than there was any reason to expect."

Elihu Root, the future US secretary of state under President Theodore Roosevelt, more hopeful still, considered the delegates "the advance guard in the greatest movement since civilization began towards the brotherhood of man and the federation of the world."

In terms of actual substance, however, the delegates in Washington had managed only three tangible results: a weak arbitration agreement that no government ratified; a commercial bureau for gathering trade information that the US Congress would reluctantly fund; and the formation of the Intercontinental Railway Commission.[62]

Blaine and Harrison subsequently nurtured the proposed Intercontinental Railway Commission like it was the lone ember of a once-mighty bonfire. Blaine declared, "No more important recommendation has come from the International American Conference. . . . In no other way could the Government and people of the United States contribute so much to the development and prosperity of our sister Republics and at the same time to the expansion of our commerce." Harrison, in a message to Congress requesting $65,000 in commission funding, said, "The work contemplated is vast but entirely practicable. . . . I do not hesitate to recommend that Congress make the very moderate appropriation . . . suggested by the conference." Harrison's request soon sailed through a Republican-controlled legislature.[63]

While the official conference resolutions granted each country three spots for engineers, Blaine and Harrison determined to fill the positions for the United States instead with the most prominent railway men in the nation. The first opening went to Alexander Cassatt, the recently retired vice president of the Pennsylvania Railroad, the country's largest corporation. The aristocratic Cassatt, brother of impressionist painter Mary Cassatt, enjoyed a stellar reputation, having successfully introduced George Westinghouse's revolutionary air brake throughout the vast Pennsylvania system. Blaine believed that Cassatt "would enlist the confidence & interest of [railroad] men in a remarkable degree." For the second spot, Harrison recruited George Pullman, the foremost producer of railway passenger cars. The final place, in Blaine's view, needed to go to a southern Democrat for balance, and former senator Davis lobbied successfully to claim this last US seat on the commission as his own.[64]

The initial meeting was soon set for late 1890.

Almost exactly twenty-five years after Helper's flash of insight aboard the *Lord Clarendon* and ten years after Blaine first announced a hemispheric conference, the dream of an intercontinental railway had finally, improbably, become an official, US-sponsored project.

An Imaginary Red Line

At noon on Thursday, December 4, 1890, fifteen men gathered at the diplomatic reception room of the Department of State for the first meeting of the Intercontinental Railway Commission. Secretary of State Blaine himself called the meeting to order, declaring: "I hope that this [day] is to mark the beginning, the auspicious beginning, of a very great enterprise, that shall draw closer together South America, Central America, and North America; that shall ... be a benefit to the present generation and the millions yet unborn. I am ready for business, gentlemen."[65]

With those hopeful words commenced the career of the Intercontinental Railway Commission, the pioneer organization for international relations in the hemisphere. The dream of the railway had ushered in a new age, before a single rail had been laid, before an official route even existed.[66]

Blaine's hopes for an "auspicious beginning" nonetheless clashed with the room's general air of unreadiness. Aside from the United States, only five of the sixteen nations involved had managed to send delegates in time. The scant attendance owed more to circumstance than to principle, as most Latin American leaders at the time equated railroad building with progress, future prosperity, and the expansion of state control. Political disorganization and the general paucity of local engineers accounted for many of the missing people. The commission's inaugural meeting lasted just long enough to elect Cassatt as president and adjourn until the following Thursday.[67]

The laughable participation rate stretched out week after week, leaving the commission effectively hamstrung. A frustrated Davis, professing "no disposition to be discourteous," finally insisted in late January that "the work should proceed."[68]

With Davis now stoking the embers, the commission began to confront its responsibilities using the limited resources available. Their main priorities, according to the Pan-American Conference resolutions, were to "study the possible routes, determine their true length, estimate their respective cost, and compare their reciprocal advantages." To accomplish these goals, the delegates soon organized subcommittees that could plan a route and could organize three field surveys, the most that the meager budget seemed to allow.[69]

Cassatt's efforts during these early weeks focused on locating a principal engineer for the project. The success or failure of the railway, after all, would ultimately rest on the competency of its lead engineer as much as on anything the commission did directly. Soon an ideal candidate emerged in the form of Virgil Bogue, a Union Pacific Railroad engineer who spoke Spanish fluently and had spent several years in Peru building one of the spectacular Andean lines that the commission hoped to incorporate into its grand system. In mid-February, Cassatt excitedly told the other delegates of his plans to hire Bogue, but then the engineer rejected the offer, which left Cassatt scrambling to find a replacement. In panic, the commission quickly settled on sixty-year-old William Shunk, a New York railroad engineer with strong credentials but no firsthand knowledge of Latin America. Upon learning of the selection, Helper dashed off a flurry of ineffective letters protesting this "injudicious appointment" of a man "enfeebled and superannuated and almost totally deaf."[70]

The long-delayed Argentine delegation finally arrived shortly before Shunk joined the commission. Their presence immediately shifted the tenor of commission meetings from cordial to contentious. All three Argentines had engineering backgrounds, a qualification that the original conference resolutions had expressly called for but that few other delegates possessed. This professional distinction only heightened the deep political and cultural divisions that had earlier surfaced at the Pan-American Conference: the wary attitude toward US intentions; the desire to assert leadership; and the admirable, if occasionally slavish, devotion to procedure. Soon the Argentine engineers determined to focus all these concerns on the nature of the railway's proposed route.[71]

The history of the route predated the commission by a decade. Several of the essays in Helper's contest had spoken of potential paths, and Helper himself had addressed the issue in a single paragraph tucked among the four hundred pages of his 1881 *Three Americas Railway* duodecimo. Helper's brief description, however, had offered little serious insight, advocating a route "as rectilineal as the straightest street in the most quadrangular city," a somewhat preposterous suggestion given the strong features of Latin American geography and the limitations of railway design. Several years later a Uruguayan professor had plotted a far more developed, geographically precise route for the South American portion, and this professor's sketches had informed a hastily drafted 1890 report, which Davis and Carnegie had requested, authored by First Lieutenant George A. Zinn of the US Army Corps of Engineers.[72]

Zinn, per official instructions, aimed to "unite the principal cities lying in the [route's] vicinity" and to utilize existing railroads "as far as is possible." His report, drawn from several dozen books and maps, proceeded country by country and, while little more than a mandarin's fantasy, outlined several fundamental decisions and obstacles that any future planner would inevitably confront.[73]

The imagined route presented few apparent challenges in Mexico, where rail lines from the United States already reached Mexico City and where previously conducted surveys pushed almost to the country's southern edge. From the Mexican border to Guatemala City, a distance of roughly 120 miles, Zinn weighed equally one option that passed through the densely populated Maya highlands and another that crossed the lower-elevation coffee fincas. From Guatemala City southward for nearly 400 miles, the existence or promise of several short-haul rail lines and the appearance of two major geographic features—the 3,000-square-mile Lake Nicaragua and the Gulf of Fonseca, where a deepwater port could be constructed in the Pacific Ocean—dictated a general line through El Salvador, Honduras, and Nicaragua. South from Nicaragua for the 600 miles that comprised Costa Rica and Panama, Zinn offered little more than the suggestion that "the general line may take either [the Atlantic or Pacific side of the isthmus]."

Upon reaching South America, the landscape widened dramatically, from about 50 miles in the Darien region of southern Panama to over 3,000 miles along the Amazon's central latitude. Zinn acknowledged that several general routes could succeed but favored a specific approach that cleaved the heart of the Andean plateau, along the far west of the continent. In this way, Zinn speculated, the railroad "would reach throughout its length the most thickly settled portion of the continent; it would reach all its mineral wealth and connect with nearly all the railways so far projected, and besides there are but a few points where great difficulty would be found in the location."

Geography dictated that the railroad must enter the lower continent in Colombia, a nation divided by three branches of the Andes. These great north–south ranges gradually converged near the southern colonial city of Popayan, about 400 miles south of Colombia's Caribbean coastline. Zinn advocated a route along the more western of the two interior Andean valleys, a fertile region known as the Cauca. After traversing the Cauca valley, the railroad would enter the convergence zone of Colombia's three mountain chains, an area labeled "the Knot of the Andes," which Zinn imagined to be the "one difficult portion of the proposed line." From this crossing south, a number of rail lines planned or already constructed for mineral extraction helped set a rough path for over 2,000 miles through Ecuador, Peru, and Bolivia, including Lake Titicaca and the lands near the legendary silver mine at Potosí. Finally, Zinn's line connected with the planned railway network of Argentina, which would cover the last 1,000 miles to Buenos Aires. Several spurs would then provide connections to Brazil, Chile, Paraguay, Uruguay, and Venezuela.

Zinn estimated the total distance between the constructed Mexican and Argentinian lines at 4,900 miles. This distance, according to Zinn, contained within its length 230 usable rail miles and 1,800 more under survey. All that remained, he declared, were "2,870 miles to be located in order to complete the line that will eventually unite the republics of the Western Hemisphere." Zinn's pronouncement, however, lacked several vital caveats about which he seemed wholly ignorant or indifferent. For starters, most of the 230 "preexisting" miles of rail used a narrow one-meter gauge instead of a "standard" four-foot-eight-inch gauge, and compatibility would require reconstruction. Furthermore, many of the supposed 1,800 miles of surveyed line were no less imaginary than Zinn's route. And finally, the total estimated distance of 4,900 miles swelled inexorably without his ridiculous fiction of nearly straight lines connecting all the major cities.[74]

The Zinn Report, despite its weaknesses, had guided the early work of the Intercontinental Railway Commission's survey committee. Davis, who represented the United States on this body, had pushed hard to certify a preliminary route as fast as possible and had found support from the Colombian minister who served as committee chairman. Soon the survey committee had produced a map that showed the route as a bright red line, like a hemispheric aorta. In Central America, the line followed Zinn's coastal option through Guatemala and then the Atlantic side through Costa Rica and Panama. In South America, it corresponded with Zinn's plan entirely. The survey committee had given copies of this map for comment to all the delegates present.

In the meantime, plans had commenced to prepare the three field parties for exploration of the projected path.[75]

*   *   *

When the Argentine delegation arrived and learned of all that had been done in their absence, they objected to the proposed route immediately, condemning the commission's work as hasty and capricious. As one Argentine observed, "To adopt a line on the map without any sufficient foundation does not answer any practical purpose. . . . How can [the commission] determine that the surveying parties will follow a line, if it has not been first ascertained whether that line is acceptable topographically and economically and is in accordance with the general interests of the countries to be connected?"[76]

This question highlighted a central conundrum, one the early meetings had indeed ignored: A survey based on an uninformed route without full consent risked being useless if not harmful, but such a survey seemed the only way to set a route with any precision through lands unknown in places to even their home governments. Many on the commission nonetheless defended the route as the only way forward, imperfect as it was. The Colombian survey committee chair, who led this defensive campaign, further noted that the three field parties would focus on Central America and Colombia, "forced points no matter where the rest of the line should go." But none of these justifications satisfied the Argentines, whose ultimate consent arrived under a shadow of protest after weeks of debate.[77]

Their cause lost, the Argentine delegation moved to suspend the commission's operations temporarily. The other delegates quickly concurred with this motion since the survey parties were already set to depart and plans had previously been made for a Cassatt-led executive committee to handle any ongoing activities.

Before suspending their operations formally, the commissioners took time to thank Cassatt for his leadership and also approved a special resolution applauding Davis's "constant attention." Davis, without doubt, had influenced the commission's work profoundly. He had not only attended meetings religiously and helped designate the railway's route, but had also recruited several intimates to fill commission ranks. His friend and business partner, the Star Router Richard Kerens, had assumed George Pullman's spot when the railcar magnate declined to serve, and Davis had installed as commission secretary another of his sons-in-law, forty-five-year-old R. M. G. Brown, a naval officer who had earned fame for his heroics during the great 1889 hurricane that struck the US fleet stationed at Samoa.[78]

The full commission entered its indefinite hiatus less than five months after its first meeting commenced. The future of the Intercontinental Railway now lay in the field.

"A White Man Ought to Laugh at It"

The survey parties all departed from New York City in mid-April 1891 with plans to spend approximately one year abroad.

Corps One headed to Guatemala with instructions to survey the several possible routes in that country as well as a four-hundred-mile-long stretch southward through Nicaragua. Almost all its members came from within the ranks of the US Army, whose leadership had provided this staffing as a way to offset the commission's overall budget shortfalls. To oversee the group, the army had designated a veteran surveyor of high rank, though a severe illness struck as he made final preparations, and Corps One ended up beneath the control of an assistant engineer with little survey experience, a thirty-eight-year-old army lieutenant named Montgomery Macomb.[79]

Corps Two and Three, staffed with civilians, traveled together to Guayaquil, a city on the Ecuadoran coast. They planned to split in opposite directions after arrival at Quito, the Ecuadoran capital. Shunk led Corps Two, which would go north into Colombia, navigate the imposing Knot of the Andes, and continue upward along the Panamanian isthmus to Costa Rica if time permitted. The third team, under the leadership of engineer J. Imbrie Miller, aimed to cover the thousand-mile-long mountainous section from central Ecuador to Cuzco, Peru.

Each team brought along assistant engineers, topographers, draftsmen, rodmen, and one surgeon per squad. More than twenty men were involved in total. The United States had sent exploratory parties abroad before, but nothing approached this operation in terms of overland geographic sweep.[80]

All three groups and their equipment reached their destinations promptly. Officials in Guatemala received Macomb and his team "very kindly" and reportedly extended "every facility," including the assignment of four local engineers as assistants. The Ecuadoran government, meanwhile, provided the other two survey teams with official transportation and a military escort to assist with the ten-day inland journey from Guayaquil to Quito. The surveyors entered the Ecuadoran capital in an official procession, while a committee of leading citizens welcomed them and hosted a grand banquet. The country's president received the surveyors a few days later, offering them free use of his personal carriage and ensuring them that "the asking only was necessary for anything [they] wanted." The various receptions grew so elaborate and prolonged that Shunk felt some relief when his men finally "detach[ed themselves] from these rather embarrassing and impeding hospitalities."[81]

The initial burst of enthusiasm fizzled once the teams left the cities and faced the perilous conditions in the field. Macomb's team had arrived just as the prolonged Guatemalan rainy season began—a fact that no one on the commission appeared to have foreseen, likely owing to the near absence of Central American delegates—and, consequently, Corps One found fieldwork almost impossible for the first few months. Illnesses of all sorts also incapacitated many of the surveyors. Shunk wrote from his first encampment, "We might name our present station Camp Convalescence." The toll of foreign disease left Shunk himself nearly bedridden for several months, and a persistent type of malarial fever compelled Miller, the leader of Corps Three, to retire altogether from the survey. Miller's responsibilities soon passed to assistant engineer William D. Kelley, though problems with the mails left Kelley uncertain of his new status for more than six months.[82]

The crews, enfeebled, inexperienced, soaked, and almost helpless in the strange environment, depended upon the aid of guides and native communities, but these locals displayed noticeably less excitement than their governmental representatives. The surveyors' expensive equipment, unknown motivations, lack of language skills, and stockpiles of cash made them easy targets for abuse. One member of Shunk's team complained, "So soon as we arrive at any considerable place and pay off our peons they fly by night and we find ourselves without help in the morning. They always carry away some trifling article [and the] police can never catch them." Another of the surveyors explained in a letter, "our approach to a town is the signal for the formation of 'food trusts' as it were, to take the stranger in." His letter concluded, "for general cussedness . . . these people can't be beat." The United States' entrenched and expanding culture of "scientific racism" only exacerbated these conflicts. When native doctors informed Shunk's surgeon that a certain valley might prove deadly, he asserted, "if one of these abortions can pass through [then] a white man ought to laugh at it."[83]

The surveyors' racial theories of superiority, however, had apparently been explained inadequately to Latin America's natural landscape, which thwarted the men at every step, far more so than anyone on the commission had seemed to anticipate. Shunk, whose dispatches always displayed literary grace and unflagging optimism, wrote, "The Andine Brotherhood of Mountains did not admit us to fellowship without inductional exercises beforehand." The route that had seemed so simple as a red streak on a map yielded to a reality that in many places, as Kelley explained, offered "no practicable line," merely a series of "precipitous mountains" that were "cut deep by gorges." Even redoubtable Shunk lost his patience, complaining at one point,

> What seems fair, green ground, at a distance, proves to be covered with a matted growth of ferns and thorny vines, shoulder deep, the former half green, half grown, dead and stiff, as if beaten out of thin copper. It is worse than the worst Allegheny mountain laurel. . . . Even knee deep it is fully as tiresome to wade through as snow of like depth.

The conditions plagued not only the men but also their hired mules and horses, whose deaths reached such alarming numbers that it would have been fair to wonder if the surveyors had a vendetta against pack animals.[84]

Due to these setbacks, costs spiraled and progress slowed. All three teams remained mired in their arrival countries as late as Thanksgiving, more than six months after they had disembarked in Latin America.

Shunk only reached Colombia's imposing Knot of the Andes, the heart of his mission, in early 1892. Difficult conditions there limited actual field-work, leaving Shunk to imagine several possibilities without establishing a definite line. His subsequent dispatch suggested that a six-hundred-foot tunnel might provide a suitable passageway through this "most difficult" section, where the headwaters of the continent's eastbound and westbound rivers divided. He requested that this corridor be named for Helper, whom Shunk considered "the honored Gentleman who first conceived the enterprise, who urged it forward to general acceptance, and who, I hope, may live to be the chief guest at its inauguration to the World's service." If Shunk knew of Helper's prolonged campaign against him for superannuation, he didn't seem to take offense.[85]

With the end of the first year's fieldwork approaching and the survey's completion nowhere in sight, the fears the Argentines had expressed back in Washington seemed increasingly borne out. Lieutenant Macomb remained encamped in Guatemala, collecting triangulations and other measurements that far exceeded his mandate, either out of fastidiousness or what Shunk simply labeled "enchantment." Shunk himself had covered only two-thirds of his route, as far as central Colombia, where tropical pests caused a "cease-less, unwinking, comprehensive and diversified itch" that left him sleepless. Only Kelley's crew remained close to the original timetable, though they had largely abandoned extensive survey methods—Kelley had resorted to "forced marches" for days on end during the final leg of their journey.[86]

The Macomb and Shunk teams remained in the field after Kelley completed his route. The survey budget, however, had not been designed to cover such a long expedition, and with each passing week the commission's coffers shrank further.

Davis and Cassatt, acting on behalf of the Intercontinental Railway Commission's executive committee, struggled to resolve this funding crisis from back in the US capital. They faced not only the rising cost of the fieldwork, but also the general resistance of Latin American nations to contribute their promised shares. The terms established during the Pan-American Conference had required each nation to contribute in proportion to its population, $1,000 per million inhabitants. A half dozen nations had honored their commitments, a few twice over, but just as many remained derelict, and Argentina, Mexico, and Uruguay had all refused outright with the justification that they already possessed developed national rail networks and would not tax their citizens twice for the cause of railroad communication. Davis at one point suggested to Cassatt that they might cover the shortage personally, but Cassatt replied, "I am not at all prepared to say that I am willing to do that."[87]

The matter soon ended up before Congress. The Intercontinental Railway Commission had already received one supplemental round of funding the year prior, but conditions in Washington had turned less favorable in recent months. The Republican Congress that had rubber-stamped the earlier appropriations without debate had lost their House majority in the last election, and the Democrats in the lower chamber, though they had earlier championed the Pan-American Conference, showed decidedly less appetite for the Intercontinental Railway. Even worse, Blaine, the railway's patron and protector, announced his resignation as secretary of state in June 1892 during the Republican National Convention—the rivalry between the Plumed Knight and the president for the future of their party had made their ongoing partnership untenable as a new election neared.[88]

The railway appropriation question landed on the floor of Congress shortly after Blaine's resignation. Congressman James McCreary of Kentucky, a Democrat who had championed both the Pan-American Conference and the previous railway appropriations, led the fight and appealed to national pride. As he explained, "At the start we could have refused to ratify [the railway's funding bill], but Congress at two different times appropriated money under that contract, and having thereby induced the sister republics to contribute their money, I hold that, as a matter of honor, it is our duty now to make this last appropriation in order to finish the preliminary survey."[89]

McCreary's words sparked a flurry of protest, especially from within his own party, and, for the first time, Congress engaged in a genuine and long-overdue debate on the nature and purpose of the Intercontinental Railway. The first major question concerned the constitutional basis for funding such overseas actions. The opposition pointed to the century-old Jeffersonian policy of "friendly relations towards all" but "entangling alliances with none." This venerated principle, as several congressmen noted, seemed threatened by the Intercontinental Railway, especially its "permanent neutrality" clause—in their view, the threat to or violation of the railway's neutrality would force the United States "to send an army to these foreign countries to protect the neutrality of that line of road." Other representatives raised concerns over the railway's future ownership, which was generally assumed to rest with a private corporation. In one exchange, two southern congressmen traded barbs that would have fit comfortably on a vaudeville stage:

The road may never be built.
If you do not propose to build a road, what is the use of making the survey?

I have no doubt it will eventually be built, but I do not propose to build it.
Who proposes to build it?

Nobody, that I know of, just now. Do you propose to build it?
Well, if I did not suppose that it would be built, I certainly would not be willing to enter upon any preliminary survey. . . . And if it is to be done through an organized corporation, is not this appropriation for a preliminary survey simply a step by this Government in aid of that corporation?

All I say is that if there is any corporation now in existence for that purpose, I have no knowledge of it.[90]

The stream of inquiries and objections generated few compelling counterarguments on the House floor, and the appropriation appeared doomed. But Davis and his son-in-law R. M. G. Brown worked tirelessly behind the scenes—especially in the more supportive, Republican-controlled Senate—to build consensus, promising that this appropriation would be the absolute last. Eventually they found the necessary votes, and the $65,000 appropriation passed in mid-July 1892, with the caveat that "this sum shall be in full of the share of the United States for the expense of said preliminary survey." An ecstatic, and possibly deranged, Helper declared, "Truth and justice have been fully vindicated. Prudence prevails, and right is still in the ascendant. . . . Jubala! Jubalo! Jubalum! Heighho! Hey! Hem! Bismillah! Cockadoodledoo! Hooplah! Up goes the hat! He laughs best who laughs last. Ha! Ha! Ha!"[91]

The new funds kept the long-suffering parties that Shunk and Macomb commanded in the field, where they still needed to tackle more than fifteen hundred miles between southern Guatemala and northern Colombia, a distance greater than their combined total efforts to date. Hundreds of these miles remained practically uninhabited and empty of trails. These stretches promised painfully slow progress, but the surveyors' pace had to increase lest the stream of money run dry again.

Shunk had already started to favor simple forward progress over actual surveying. His dispatches suggested, with resignation, that tricky passages "be studied by our successors" or "be provisionally 'constructed' from authoritative documents." Meanwhile, Lieutenant Macomb, still in Guatemala, refused to expedite his progress until an irate Cassatt cabled him personally in December 1892: "Executive Committee orders discontinuance of triangulation. Confine yourself to preliminary railroad survey."[92]

The revised plan, in an effort to approximate coverage of the remaining route, called for Macomb to proceed at all speed over six hundred miles south to San José, Costa Rica, and for Shunk to sail five hundred miles north from Colombia to San José as well and then bushwhack south. The engineering survey was transforming into little more than an elaborate through-hike.

Even as a hike, however, conditions south of Nicaragua stymied the engineers at every turn. As Shunk wrote, "We thought we had seen in South America the worst roads in the world. They were bad enough. . . . [But] the sun in his circuit, visiting planetary and astral worlds innumerable . . . does not see in all the holy heaven a worse thing to be called road than [this]." The two-hundred-mile stretch from San José, Costa Rica, to David in northern Panama required fifty-three days to cross. Along the way, much of Shunk's equipment sank in a canoe accident and at least five mules died. He and his men were all "half invalid" by the end of the journey, and they avoided tough interior treks for the rest of their passage southeast along Panama and its wild Darien region, doing little more than "rush work" for the final stretches. Macomb's men fared little better. An assistant who scouted passages in northern Costa Rica lost one mule to a "tiger" (likely a jaguar) and "eked out his supplies by turtle meat," while the main Macomb party "relied upon iguana" to sustain them in the "uninhabited wilderness." The two survey corps, depleted and haggard, finally completed their itineraries in April 1893 and headed back home.[93]

By the time they all returned, the original enthusiasm seemed to have evaporated altogether. Blaine, the Intercontinental Railway's most prominent backer, had finally succumbed to Bright's disease in late January and died while in Washington, where, according to reports, "the surging wave of public interest . . . made his private funeral one of the most impressive of public demonstrations in honor of the dead." Congress, meanwhile, had soured on the project and seemed more interested in the possibility of constructing an interoceanic canal in Nicaragua, especially as it became clear that France's much-discussed effort to build a rival canal through Panama had collapsed entirely, bankrupting much of the French populace. Moreover, any possibilities for private funding of the railway had fallen apart with the 1893 depression—Colonel Parsons, the Virginian businessman with the $100 million plan to construct a South American railroad, had made scant progress and would be fatally shot by a half-crazed train conductor in mid-1894.[94]

Even the members of the commission, with the possible exception of Davis, appeared to be losing interest. Cassatt, though always diligent, paid far more attention to his six-hundred-acre horse farm outside Philadelphia and his prized hackney stallion Comet. And Davis's son-in-law R. M. G. Brown, who had handled much of the routine survey supervision, would lessen his involvement after receiving an official naval retirement in late 1894.[95]

Nonetheless, the reports still needed to be published. Cassatt pushed for completion as fast as possible, but Macomb refused to rush his team's calculations. The endless delays convinced Cassatt to publish the work piecemeal. Volumes on the South American routes appeared in 1895 and 1896, while the commission's summary report and the work of Macomb only emerged as completed drafts in mid-1898, more than five years after the survey had concluded. By that point, Cassatt had lost all faith, admitting privately to the man who had assumed Brown's responsibilities, "The fact is we have not only not made a final location, but it can hardly be said that we have made a preliminary one. . . . [We] are not now prepared to say even that in all cases the general route adopted is the best."[96]

The long-delayed, completed report finally arrived late in 1898. Its seven folio volumes—four filled with text and three containing 311 maps—weighed a staggering thirty-two pounds in total. The immense size and weight prompted Secretary of State John Hay to caution Cassatt that his department "has no present means of receiving and distributing so great a bulk." Helper, for his part, assured Cassatt that "the long-lasting and arduous labors . . . have been ably performed, and with absolute and unfaltering fidelity." Cassatt himself seemed mostly relieved to finally unload the burden of such "unfaltering fidelity," instructing the commission's secretary in mid-March 1899, "the office shall be closed and the accounts of the Commission finally audited, and I desire that this shall be done by the first of April."[97]

Nearly a decade had passed since the original post–Pan-American Conference mandate in 1890. The early, limited momentum that Davis, Blaine, and Harrison created had been squandered upon the shoals of an ambitious survey with no clear objective. During these same years, in comparison, the Russian Empire had conceptualized, authorized, and half completed the great five-thousand-mile Trans-Siberian Railroad from Moscow to Vladivostok. The domestic US press and many politicians, reflecting a major shift in national priorities, showed far less interest in the commission's final publications than in a one-volume report on the proposed Nicaraguan Canal that appeared almost concurrently.[98]

Thoughts about Latin America and US power generally were moving away from the iron highways of the land and toward the foam-flecked lanes of the sea. And an unconquerable personality in US politics would steer this new course.

The Rough Ride to Empire

Shortly after midday on July 1, 1898, several months before the release of the long-delayed Intercontinental Railway report, a phalanx of US soldiers amassed in the tropical heat around bullet-strewn lowlands beneath Kettle Hill, a rise along the San Juan Heights near Santiago, Cuba. The ranks included a volunteer cavalry outfit of skilled horsemen drawn mostly from the Southwest, dubbed the "Rough Riders." Their commander, a barrel-chested, bespectacled, beaver-toothed thirty-nine-year-old named Teddy Roosevelt, rode through the lines, encouraging his men. Finally, in a pitched falsetto, he reportedly screamed, "Gentlemen, the Almighty God and the Just Cause are with you. Gentlemen, Charge!" Hooves pounded the ground like thunder as the men followed Roosevelt up the hill toward a cluster of Spanish troops controlling the high ground.[99]

When the gunfire and shouting ceased and the smoke cleared, each and every Spaniard had surrendered or died. The Rough Riders and Roosevelt had triumphed, their minor victory part of a decisive battle in the United States' first major armed conflict since the Civil War.[100]

The hoofbeats of this new war had first started to clatter in the United States several years earlier in response to a Cuban independence movement. The great sugar-producing Caribbean island, barely ninety miles from the base of Florida, had sought to free itself from the rule of a deflated and limping Spanish empire. In 1895, patriots in the island's eastern lands had sparked a widespread rebellion that quickly descended into prolonged violence and brutality. The cause of a free Cuba had found sympathy throughout the hemisphere, and, as the months and then years accumulated, some in the United States had begun to demand intervention. Resistance from US isolationists had held this bellicose urge in check until February 1898, when a mysterious explosion sank the USS *Maine*, a warship stationed in Havana Harbor. Many rushed to blame Spanish agitators, and US war hawks seized the momentum. Two months later Congress formally declared war against Spain. The navy then began a blockade of Cuba, but the conflict quickly escalated beyond Cuba to Spain's other two remaining imperial island possessions, Puerto Rico and the Philippines.[101]

The joint efforts of native and US forces repulsed the once-mighty Spanish empire with a swiftness and decisiveness that few fully foresaw. Spain surrendered provisionally in August, barely ten weeks after the conflict began. The New World was finally free, after more than four hundred years, of its oldest European conqueror. And a war that had started with mixed political support in the United States ended with wild enthusiasm at home.

The Rough Riders, upon their return to the United States, rode this wave of enthusiasm as expertly as they had ridden their mounts. Reporters trailed them through the halls of hotels and theaters in New York City as the heroes traded war stories while clad in their pressed khaki uniforms. In the words of journalist Charles M. Pepper, who covered the war from Cuba and then encountered the Rough Riders back home, "Everybody makes room for them. They can collect a crowd wherever they please. . . . They lionized the war. . . . I have no doubt that in a few years the tradition . . .

will be that the fighting at Santiago was done by the Rough Riders, while the regular army carried their packs and looked after the mules." By far the most popular of these dashing, self-mythologizing figures was their leader, Colonel Roosevelt. He became a nationally recognized personality virtually overnight.[102]

Roosevelt's emergence as a war hero and fearless adventurer would have surprised those who knew him during his earliest years of privilege in New York City. As he himself acknowledged, "I was a sickly, delicate boy, suffered much from asthma, and frequently had to be taken away on trips to find a place where I could breathe." These physical weaknesses troubled young Roosevelt enormously. He longed to emulate his father, a patrician New Yorker of steadfast resolve and rigid self-control, infallible in his son's eyes, "the best man I ever knew." Roosevelt worked tirelessly to overcome his limitations, fortifying himself through rugged activities like boxing, hunting, and horseback riding. But physical strength alone left Roosevelt unsatisfied. In his words, "I had to train myself painfully and laboriously not merely as regards my body but as regards my soul and spirit." By the time he entered Harvard at seventeen, he not only possessed the foundations of a stoutly robust physique but a capacious intellect, a profound knowledge of natural history, a stern moral compass, and an endless well of self-assurance, if not self-righteousness.[103]

Immediately upon graduation, Roosevelt had developed an interest in politics and joined the Republicans, the only party that "a young man of my bringing up and convictions could join." Months of dues paying in smoke-filled Republican parlors eventually yielded him a spot as the youngest member of the New York State Legislature, and in 1884 his party even sent their rising star as a delegate to the presidential convention in Chicago. During the convention, Roosevelt aligned himself with the party's reformist wing, which sought to replace patronage with a merit system, but his faction lost out to the hard-charging, pro-patronage Blainites. Roosevelt reluctantly fell in line, though the subsequent Blaine campaign left him disillusioned. And to this political crisis of faith, fate soon added an all-consuming personal one in the nearly simultaneous deaths of his mother and beloved first wife.[104]

Following these tragedies, Roosevelt announced his retirement from politics and left New York for a cattle ranch that he had recently purchased near the South Dakota badlands. His life effectively began anew, remolded in the virile image he had first crafted for himself as a boy, "a free and hardy life, with horse and with rifle." He might have remained out west permanently but for a blizzard that destroyed his stock, and for a chance encounter with a childhood friend from New York whom he would marry in 1886.[105]

Once more, Roosevelt grabbed hold of the political ladder and began climbing, rung over laborious rung. His first attempted comeback, a bid for New York City mayor as a sort of cowboy reformer, ended in failure. A series of political appointments followed, and Roosevelt built a checkered reputation as a combative crusader, especially during two years as police commissioner of New York City. As he confided to a friend, "This is the last office I shall ever hold. I have offended so many powerful interests and so many powerful politicians that no political preferment in future will be possible for me." Despite Roosevelt's histrionics, in 1897 Republican president William McKinley himself offered Roosevelt the post of assistant secretary of the navy, which he accepted.[106]

Naval affairs had long captivated Roosevelt. His interest reached back at least to his time at Harvard, when he began working on a history of naval battles in the War of 1812. Roosevelt published the completed book in mid-1882, shortly before his twenty-fourth birthday. The precocious volume, with its anodyne title *The Naval War of 1812*, earned its wunderkind author widespread acclaim, launching his side career as a writer and historian—his prodigious output would eventually include over ten distinct books and countless essays. Roosevelt's broader interest in sea power was also influenced by the ideas of his contemporary Alfred Thayer Mahan, a US naval officer who published a transformational book in 1890 on the relationship between sea power and national strength.

Mahan's epic study, titled *The Influence of Sea Power Upon History*, had struck with the force of a Whitehead torpedo fired at close range when it first appeared. As Mahan alleged in his preface, "Historians generally have been unfamiliar with the conditions of the sea ... and the profound determining influence of maritime strength upon great issues." Around the globe, policy makers consumed the lessons of *The Influence of Sea Power*, and Roosevelt was no exception. He first set forth his thoughts on the subject in a fawning review written for the *Atlantic Monthly*. In the piece's conclusion, Roosevelt shifted suddenly from third person to first and issued a prescient exhortation that extended Mahan's own careful historical analysis to its logical conclusion: "[O]ur greatest need is the need of a fighting-fleet. . . . We need a large navy . . . able to meet those of any other nation. It is not economy—it is niggardly and foolish short-sightedness—to cramp our naval expenditures."[107]

Roosevelt brought this attitude to his new role in the Navy Department, where the prospect of war with Spain already loomed. The nation's fleet, central to any overseas combat, had been growing throughout the previous decade but only "timidly and hesitatingly" as far as Roosevelt was concerned. He soon aligned himself with those in the navy who saw war as inevitable— if not a rationale to boost naval expenditures further—and used "all the power there was in [his] office" to hasten preparations.[108]

His enthusiasm quickly spilled over the department's gunwales and into the public sphere, as he openly favored the need to free Cuba. When hostilities commenced, he raced to find a spot at the front. As he explained, "a man ought to be willing to make his words good by his deeds. . . . He should pay with his body." Fortune, however, felt no need to collect fully on the debt, and Roosevelt escaped his Rough Rider days without serious injury. "There are," he later wrote, "no four months in my life to which I look back with more pride and satisfaction."[109]

Once hostilities ceased in September, Roosevelt returned to his home state of New York, where his newfound popularity radically transformed the political landscape. The Republican Party machine, though wary of their unpredictable and uncontainable war hero, begrudgingly accepted that he represented their best chance to claim the governorship in the upcoming November election and offered him the nomination. Roosevelt accepted, cruised to victory, and then proceeded to champion a reformist agenda, just as the machine operatives feared.

Top state Republicans soon decided he needed to go, but public affection protected him like the armor of Achilles. It seemed the only way to force him out was to push him higher up, from New York to the national stage. State party leaders thus hatched a plan to make Roosevelt the running mate in President William McKinley's 1900 reelection bid. Roosevelt, with eyes on the presidency himself, consented to their proposal, and the scheme succeeded despite objections from McKinley's top adviser, the Republican kingmaker Mark Hanna, who reportedly said with a gasp, "Don't any of you realize that there's only one life between that madman and the Presidency? . . . What harm can he do as Governor of New York compared to the damage he will do as President if McKinley should die?"[110]

*   *   *

The election of 1900 reprised the matchup of four years prior, with McKinley squaring off against Democrat William Jennings Bryan. Their last contest had revolved around the future of the gold standard, an almost mystical economic belief system that controversially required a rigid correspondence between the nation's total money supply and its physical stockpile of gold. Bryan favored a bimetal monetary system that incorporated silver, and he had nearly triumphed in 1896, arguing, "You shall not crucify mankind upon a cross of gold." This impassioned plea still remained important in 1900, but a strong economy and recent gold rushes in both the Canadian Klondike and South Africa diminished its urgency. The election's second great issue concerned, in Roosevelt's words, "the need . . . of meeting in manful and straightforward fashion the extraterritorial problems arising from the Spanish War."[111]

Victory had left the United States with a moral quandary over the future of Spain's former possessions Cuba, Puerto Rico, and the Philippines. The chaos of war and centuries of colonial rule had shackled all three island regions with inadequate political infrastructure, but prolonged US control in the name of administration and nation-building risked turning a war of liberation into an act of conquest. McKinley wrestled mightily with this dilemma, especially regarding the far-distant Philippines. As he explained, "I walked the floor of the White House night after night until midnight; and . . . I went down on my knees and prayed Almighty God for light and guidance more than one night." He ultimately decided to maintain control—the Almighty, apparently, favored US expansion. A vote for McKinley meant an explicit endorsement of this decision.

In the end, the contest wasn't even close, and McKinley returned to the White House with Roosevelt in tow.[112]

The American body politic had formally and enthusiastically sanctioned a new overseas empire through their decision in the 1900 election. Whether this move marked a break with the past or a logical extension of the nation's history depended on one's perspective. The annals of the prior century, after all, were filled with episodes of territorial expansion: Thomas Jefferson's Empire of Liberty, the Louisiana Purchase, the countless takings of Native American lands, Manifest Destiny, the 1848 Treaty of Guadalupe-Hidalgo that gave the nation half of Mexico, to name several. The distinction between these precedents and the new empire risked collapsing if pressed too far, but most Americans, cognizant of their own past, believed that they were entering a new imperialist phase after 1900, one meant to be temporary but with no clear end in sight and, of course, with need for an even stronger navy.[113]

The new empire, in conjunction with the nation's seemingly limitless economic expansion, heightened long-standing fears across Latin America concerning US power and influence. Spanish-speaking intellectuals, in particular, promoted an agenda of anti-Americanism. In 1900, the Uruguayan writer José Enrique Rodó captured this phenomenon in a widely read, rambling essay that used two characters from Shakespeare's *The Tempest* to illustrate his point. Latin Americans, he implied, possessed the creativity and passion of the enslaved but rebellious spirit Ariel, while the United States displayed the crass materialism and utilitarianism of the scarcely mentioned, honorless Caliban.

Rodó's antipathy toward the United States, however, hardly represented a universal feeling, just as imperialism remained divisive in the United States. As Rodó reluctantly acknowledged, "Admiration for [the United States'] greatness, its strength, is a sentiment that is growing rapidly in the minds of our governing classes, and even more, perhaps, among the multitude, easily impressed with victory or success."[114]

McKinley and Roosevelt, like many of their constituents, saw little contradiction between their new Caribbean imperialism—justified as a limited intervention to support a "civilizing mission"—and the goal of closer Latin American relations. McKinley's administration even took several concrete steps to promote Pan-Americanism. One of these had occurred in late 1899, with the initial ten-year term of the fledgling Commercial Bureau of American Republics set to expire, when the president issued calls for a new Pan-American Conference to be held in the near future. The McKinley administration also offered financial and political support to a proposed world's fair in Buffalo, New York, oriented around the theme of hemispheric unity, to be called the Pan-American Exposition.[115]

When this Pan-American Exposition finally opened in the spring of 1901, it proved the major tourist event of the year, with millions arriving to enjoy the innumerable spectacles. McKinley himself visited the exposition in early September and gave a sanguine speech on hemispheric relations. His words echoed Blaine's earlier idealism and made no mention of Cuba or the Monroe Doctrine. His concluding paragraph asked, "Who can tell the new thoughts that have been awakened, the ambitions fired, and the high achievements that will be wrought through this exposition?" But the answers to these questions would never be known to McKinley, for soon after delivering his speech, while standing before the exposition's Temple of Music and shaking hands with a throng of admirers, he fell victim to a gunshot that a crazed anarchist fired from point-blank range. Eight days later, the president, like Lincoln and Garfield before him, died while in office from an assassin's bullet.[116]

The news of McKinley's death reached Roosevelt while hiking with his family on Mount Marcy, New York's highest peak and part of the Adirondack Park. He immediately headed for Buffalo, then swore the oath of office in a makeshift ceremony, and thus became at age forty-two the youngest president in the nation's history. Upon hearing the news, Mark Hanna reportedly groused, "Now look! That cowboy is President of the United States."[117]

Roosevelt, cowboy or not, didn't want to spook the herd of politicos like Hanna. His new administration, he explained, aimed "to continue, absolutely without variance, the policy of President McKinley, for the peace and prosperity and honor of our beloved Country." But Roosevelt's professed intentions could endure only so long. New problems required leadership, arriviste or otherwise, and Roosevelt struggled to restrain himself.[118]

One of the first major issues that Roosevelt confronted involved the proposed Central American canal, a potential centerpiece of future naval strategy. The dream of connecting the world's two great oceans had captured the European imagination soon after Columbus reached the New World, and the upstart United States had joined this conversation in a serious way after gaining control of California and its broad Pacific coastline in 1848. Great Britain, the world's dominant sea power, had formally recognized the United States' newfound interest through an 1850 bilateral treaty that forbid either nation from constructing a canal without the other's express consent. This treaty, however, grew increasingly problematic as the United States' naval strength increased and Great Britain's hemispheric interests decreased. Cries to invalidate the treaty had swelled in Washington after the emergence of the new overseas US empire.

In mid-1900, McKinley's secretary of state John Hay had managed to negotiate a new treaty in which Britain ceded their canal claims if the United States agreed to keep any future project neutral and unfortified. The new treaty, in Hay's view, marked a masterstroke of diplomacy, but Roosevelt, while New York governor, had aligned himself with the majority of senators who rejected Hay's efforts for being too weak. As Roosevelt wrote to the naval strategist Mahan, "I do not see why we should dig the canal if we are not to fortify it so as to insure its being used for ourselves and against our foes in time of war." Roosevelt, upon ascending to the presidency, impressed this view upon Hay, who returned to England and successfully extracted this final concession on fortifications. The new treaty was signed in November 1901, finally clearing a diplomatic path for a US-controlled canal.[119]

In little more than three years, the circumstances that had once made the Intercontinental Railway the nation's leading international infrastructure project had all but disappeared. The United States had created an overseas empire and positioned itself diplomatically to command the most important strategic ocean crossing in the Western Hemisphere, if not the world. Moreover, the nation's new president, who championed the canal as part of his overall naval strategy, saw few limits to his executive power, believing that "it was not only [the president's] right but his duty to do anything that the needs of the Nation demanded unless such action was forbidden by the Constitution or by the laws."[120]

Against this backdrop arose the Second Pan-American Conference, the first referendum on hemispheric relations in twelve years.

Cannibals, Carnegie, and a Permanent Commission

Most of the plans for the Second Pan-American Conference had been arranged before Roosevelt ascended to the presidency. Hosting duties lay with Mexico, where the long-standing regime of Porfirio Díaz maintained order through force and progress through the investments of US capitalists, especially railroad men. The selection of the five US delegates—half the number from the First Pan-American Conference—had been overseen personally by McKinley, who had favored men with experience in diplomacy and journalism. The only holdover from the first conference—and the only businessman—was Henry Gassaway Davis, whose agenda of Intercontinental Railway promotion conflicted somewhat with the new president's prioritization of sea power and canal building.[121]

Roosevelt issued instructions to the delegates in early October 1901, barely two weeks before the second conference's scheduled opening. His message stressed friendliness more than leadership, reflecting the president's deeply held skepticism of international law and his belief that the responsible use of power, not treaties, preserved global order. The delegates needed primarily "to disabuse [Latin American] minds of any false impres-

sions, if they exist, regarding the attitude and purpose of the United States."
As long as friendly relations endured, US economic expansion and com-
mercial integration with Latin America could continue unhampered. As
Roosevelt's instructions explained,

> [W]e may assume that . . . the volume of our trade with South Amer-
> ica will soon grow to large proportions. These means are: Adequate
> transportation facilities, such as steamship lines, railroads, and an isth-
> mian canal; reciprocal trade relations; participation in the business of
> banking, and a corps of commercial travelers specially equipped for
> Latin-American trade. It is not impossible that, following such devel-
> opment, *the magnificent conception* of an international railroad connect-
> ing the United States with the remotest parts of South America may
> at last be realized.

The above-mentioned language, buried deep in Roosevelt's instructions
to the delegates, not only laid out the contours of the president's plan for
US economic activity in the hemisphere, but also captured the essence of
his attitude toward the Intercontinental Railway. The vision of Helper and
Blaine and Davis was indeed a "magnificent conception," but nonetheless a
faraway dream to be realized only, if at all, once a long list of more pressing
projects had been successfully implemented.[122]

Roosevelt's assessment, however, clashed with the general sentiments of
the Mexico conference. What seemed a long-distant fantasy to the US president had been routinely promoted—by boosters and eager governments
alike—as the foundation, the trunk line, of a much-desired hemispheric system. Railroads symbolized progress, even if they inevitably relied on foreign
investment and tended to produce narrowly channeled economic growth
more than broad social development. Encouraging their construction practically constituted a stand-alone ideology for leaders like President Díaz.[123]

The Mexican delegation's official report to the second conference
argued, "It would be useless and tiring to enumerate the extensive efforts
and sacrifices . . . that Mexico has made to carry into practice the dream of
an intercontinental railway." One of Costa Rica's delegates, noting Mexico's
apparent prosperity, assured that the Intercontinental Railway offered "great
benefits" and was "greatly favored." The project's popularity even led delegates to push for Davis's nomination as conference chairman, an honor he
refused, partly to respect Roosevelt's express instructions against displays of
leadership.[124]

*   *   *

Among this chorus of Intercontinental Railway enthusiasm in Mexico City, one Latin American voice spoke the loudest, that of Colombian delegate General Rafael Reyes. He cut a striking figure with his broad shoulders, wide midsection, regal attire, partly paralyzed left arm, and glorious mustache, which pointed outward several inches like two tiny bloodhounds sensing prey. His legendary exploits in several minor Colombian civil wars had earned him widespread admiration, and his ambition matched his bravery. Many assumed he sought greater political power. His views on leadership and progress shared much with those of Díaz, especially the need to stimulate transportation infrastructure.[125]

Reyes's efforts to promote development years earlier in Colombia had already cost him dearly, far more than all his military campaigns combined, and the painful memories left him reticent to even discuss what had occurred. But rumors of a story too incredible to be believed, a journey worthy of Odysseus, swirled through the hallways of the Mexico conference, and finally Reyes—seeking to strengthen consensus for the Intercontinental Railway and impressed by the assemblage of hemispheric plenipotentiaries—agreed to tell his long-guarded story at a banquet in late December.[126]

The assembled crowd hushed and listened "with profound attention" as Reyes began to recount the remarkable tale of several explorations he'd made a quarter century earlier, into the unsettled heart of South America. His maiden trek commenced near the same Andean Knot that Shunk later surveyed, only Reyes and his small party turned eastward, descending through treacherous vertical drops, into the headwaters of the Putumayo River, which snaked a thousand miles through Colombian territory before joining the Amazon. Along the Putumayo's wild verdant banks lived warring nomadic tribes, including some that practiced cannibalism. Reyes had worried initially about native hostilities but instead encountered "kindness and generosity" along the Putumayo. The tribes provided steady assistance and even taught Reyes how to "dig a sort of grave" to bury himself at night when insects swarmed so thick that "on clapping the hands together, there remains between them a solid mass of mosquitoes."[127]

Reyes navigated the Putumayo successfully and decided to bring his younger brother Nestor along for a follow-up mission, but at that point his good fortune ran short. Nestor lost his way in the forest and wandered into the territory of Putumayo cannibals, who took him captive and devoured his body—as Reyes told the stunned crowd of hemispheric delegates, "We could only recover his bones." Reyes subsequently lost his older brother Henry to a "malignant fever" while exploring another interior river. The pursuit of progress—of expanding Colombian influence into the unsettled interior—had cost Reyes both his brothers, but thanks to their efforts, as he assured, "we discovered some unknown rivers, we established steam navigation in others, [and] we communicated by means of overland routes the river navigation with the towns of the Andes."[128]

The link between these feats of exploration and the proposed Intercontinental Railway existed largely in Reyes's own progress-obsessed mind. Hundreds of miles or more separated the navigable portions of most Atlantic-oriented rivers from the surveyed rail route. Nonetheless, as Reyes explained toward the end of his talk, "I must call attention . . . to the important fact that the Inter-Continental Railway . . . could easily . . . be connected with the immense system of river communications formed by the Amazon and its tributaries."[129]

Reyes implored his audience to lend their support to this vision of continental development. Their advocacy, Reyes seemed to imply, could ensure that his brothers had not died in vain. When Reyes finally concluded his lengthy speech, the crowd broke into a vigorous applause, and Davis, according to reports, "heartily congratulated him and thanked him."[130]

Reyes had provided the pathos, and Davis presented a path forward.

Roosevelt's warnings about exerting leadership had not ultimately dissuaded Davis from taking charge of the Mexico conference's committee on the Intercontinental Railway. And Davis, as committee chair, advocated two new initiatives: a second US-led survey of Latin America to focus on the railway's commercial aspects; and a new five-person permanent commission to reside in Washington. Davis also favored replacing the adjective "intercontinental" with "Pan-American" to better reflect the project's intimate relationship with the broader political and economic movement.

Davis's recommendations passed with little debate, and before the Mexico conference concluded in late January 1902, a Permanent Pan-American Railway Committee had been organized under his watchful gaze. Davis assumed the new committee's chairmanship personally, then added three compliant ministers, from Guatemala, Mexico, and Peru. For the final spot, he attached the name of his old colleague from the First Pan-American Conference, Andrew Carnegie.[131]

Carnegie's influence, as Davis well knew, had recently increased to incomparable levels. Barely one year earlier, the steel baron had agreed to sell his eponymous company to financier John Pierpont Morgan, a man Carnegie personally disliked but who was among the only people in the world able to meet the nonnegotiable asking price of $400 million. After closing the deal at Carnegie's home, Morgan reportedly grasped the tycoon's hand and said, "Mr. Carnegie, I want to congratulate you on being the richest man in the world." Carnegie had subsequently begun using his fortune to embark on one of the greatest runs of philanthropy the world had ever seen, and the mere mention of his name stirred thoughts of spectacular financial largesse. This mystique of unchecked generosity had induced Davis to incorporate Carnegie into the new commission without even acquiring the philanthropist's full consent first.[132]

Davis's triumph at the conference left him newly energized. He soon secured Carnegie's involvement and then arranged an audience with Helper, where he supposedly bragged that "Andrew Carnegie was himself able to build the whole road, from one end to the other." But official support also mattered greatly to Davis, and he petitioned both Roosevelt and Secretary Hay for their endorsements as well. After repeated urgings, Roosevelt relented and requested that Congress appropriate $20,000 for two surveyors to "investigate and report upon the means of extending the commerce of the United States with [Central and South America]."[133]

For the first time in a decade, the subject of funding for the Pan-American Railway reappeared before Congress. The appropriation request easily passed the Senate, where several of Davis's allies held key committee positions, but strong resistance emerged once more in the House.

Davis's lobbying there continued unabated until late in the year, when, at seventy-nine years old, he lost within a six-week span both his spouse of nearly fifty years and his forty-six-year-old daughter, the wife of R. M. G. Brown. The losses devastated Davis, but during his formal period of mourning, he nonetheless alighted upon a solution to the appropriation dilemma. After conferring with Carnegie in January 1903, he presented his plan to his old Senate ally and longtime railway booster Francis Cockrell of Missouri: "If you cannot consistently appropriate the money, Mr. Carnegie and myself feel such deep interest in the subject and in the advantages to be given our country that we will furnish the necessary expenses of the commissioner." Each man, Davis explained, agreed to contribute a tiny sliver of his vast personal fortune if Congress provided a nominal amount to ensure the air of legitimacy.[134]

This new proposal, a private subsidy of public internationalism, managed to extract $2,500 from Congress in early March 1903. The resulting contributions of Davis and Carnegie amounted to $3,750 each, for a total of $10,000, half of Roosevelt's initial request but enough to send one person abroad.[135]

Carnegie's seed money also produced a bountiful crop of rumors about the future of the railway. Davis had helped initiate this speculation when he attended a Washington gathering of hemispheric diplomats shortly after the appropriation passed and intimated, according to reports, that Carnegie "might be prepared to take financial interest" in the railway's construction. Days later, the *Washington Post* described "the offer of Andrew Carnegie to head a big syndicate of Anglo-American capitalists" to finance the entire project. The gossip surrounding Carnegie's involvement led Helper—convinced that his Three Americas Railway should be financed strictly through public funds—to complain that "there was perceptibly something ... that smacked loudly of a trick, if it did not smell strongly of a trust." According to several papers, J. P. Morgan, the "central figure" in financing this Carnegie syndicate, had conducted a secret meeting on the matter with General Rafael Reyes of Colombia at the Hotel de Inglaterra in Havana, Cuba. This conjecture, however, ignored a more likely explanation for the Reyes-Morgan meeting: the potential funding of a canal in Colombia's Panama Province, which had displaced Nicaragua as the front-running location—Reyes had fatefully told the local press after his supposedly "secret" meeting, "Whatever the American government may [do], it will do as the agent and in the name of the Colombian republic."[136]

The flurry of speculation and excitement surrounding Carnegie's involvement overshadowed the actual news that another Pan-American Railway survey had been authorized. By some accounts, the survey's announcement attracted less attention in the United States than in Europe, where merchants feared the possibility of losing trade to a hemispheric rail route.[137]

The new survey, in stark contrast to the work that Shunk had overseen a decade prior, required little planning. The only preliminary matter of substance was the selection of the sole surveyor. A seventy-three-year-old Hinton Rowan Helper tried to convince Congress to give him this role, but the position, on Davis's recommendation, went to Charles M. Pepper, the journalist who had followed the Rough Riders and who had later served as one of Davis's codelegates at the Mexico conference. Once this appointment had been finalized, the State Department issued letters of endorsement to the various countries involved. Pepper then departed in mid-April 1903, barely one month after Congress had first authorized the trip.[138]

But Pepper, by this point, was not the only one peddling a plan for a hemispheric railway in Latin America. In the far south of Mexico, a small group of US capitalists had recently started construction on a rival Pan-American Railroad. The three-hundred-mile-long line sat at the southern end of a rail network that reached all the way to the United States. For this Mexican project, the promotional activities of men such as Davis and Pepper ultimately mattered less than a rival process of development, one that predated modern Pan-Americanism.

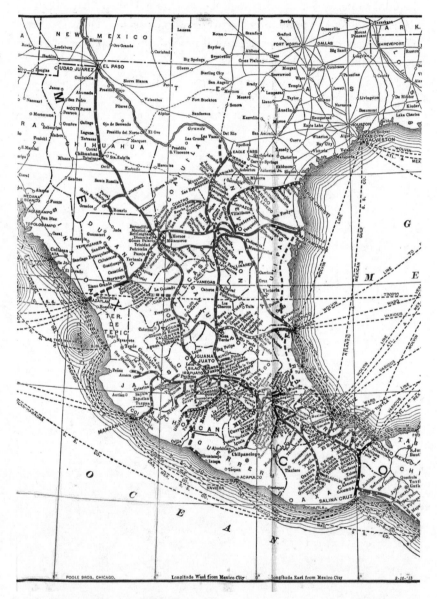

A 1911 National Railways of Mexico map depicting the government-owned network soon after the outbreak of the Mexican Revolution. The three lines connecting Mexico City with Texas all began as extensions of US transcontinental systems.

CHAPTER TWO

The Eagle and the Octopus

The Transcontinental Turn

On a Thursday evening in mid-November 1880, several months before Helper published *The Three Americas Railway*, a score of men who controlled most of the United States' transcontinental rail network assembled around a private table at Delmonico's, the most fashionable restaurant in New York City. Clad in top hats and dark frock coats and wing-collar starched shirts, they dined that night on Gilded Age delicacies, on canvasback duck and aspic of foie gras, on Neapolitan ice cream and *croûte aux ananas*. The sole attendee from outside the United States was Mexico's Matías Romero, who had personally convened the dinner and who was one of Mexican president Porfirio Díaz's closest confidants.

Upon the completion of the meal, Romero rose to address the assemblage on the reason for their brief union. "For many years past," he declared, "I have been convinced that the prosperity of the United States must inevitably be extended to Mexico. . . . I shall feel that I have done my country a very great service if I can happily contribute in any way to decide the capitalists of this Metropolis seriously to engage in [Mexican railway] enterprises."

At the time of the dinner, almost no rails had yet crossed the southern US border into Mexico. However, the men around the Delmonico's table clamored to remedy this situation, and Romero's words simply reinforced their convictions.[1]

Mexico had become the new frontier in a railroading contest that had started when Congress authorized the transcontinentals during the Civil War. Over the course of twenty years, the quest to bridge the continent with bands of steel had transformed into a rivalry among several gigantic rail systems for supremacy, and their initial east–west orientations had expanded into more extensive visions that included north–south development into Mexico. At the center of this process sat Romero's dinner guest Collis P. Huntington, the president of the Southern Pacific Company. His career mirrored the entire transcontinental era and its ultimate turn south, a reorientation that had the potential to spread US corporate influence beyond the nation's borders on a scale never before witnessed.[2]

Huntington, born in 1821 to modest circumstances in northwestern Connecticut, had set out as a teenager with little besides his ambition and work ethic. The golden promise of California eventually lured him west, and he established a successful hardware store in Sacramento that provisioned the endless stream of emigrants seeking quick riches in the Gold Rush. His interest in western railroading first emerged in 1860 after a prominent engineer approached him about contributing funds in support of a potential transcontinental route east from California.[3]

The dream of a transcontinental railroad, by that point, stirred the imagination of the whole country. Many saw it as the natural continuation of Manifest Destiny, and serious support for the transcontinental railroad emerged shortly after the United States acquired political control of California in 1848 at the close of the Mexican-American War.

"Transcontinental," however, was really a term of art. The actual distance contemplated ran about 1,750 miles from the Pacific Coast to the Missouri River, where the nation's more established rail network would soon reach.

Various proposals to bridge this distance appeared during the 1850s, but the ultimate power to launch transcontinental construction rested with Congress. The federal government not only controlled much of the territory along the proposed routes, but also had the constitutional authority to oversee interstate commerce and, perhaps more consequentially, to incentivize construction.[4]

Without congressional aid, the transcontinental project made little economic sense. The United States' new western territories contained meager populations, with much of the land under the effective control of native tribes that shared relatively few commercial ties with the East. Huntington observed of one proposed route, the "road might as well be a thousand miles in the air so far as any local business is concerned."[5]

In the years preceding the Civil War, Congress discussed a range of subsidies that it might authorize to accompany any actual charter granting a right-of-way (generally known as a concession). The contemplated subsidies included guaranteed loans, government-backed bonds, and massive grants of federal land containing some of the best timber and mineral resources in the country. These unprecedented financial incentives were intended to outweigh the equally unprecedented challenges, which included construction across hundreds of miles of inhospitable desert as well as the Rocky Mountains and the High Sierras. As one prominent developer advised Huntington, "[T]he risk is too great, and the profits, if any, are too remote."[6]

This advice nonetheless failed to deter Huntington. In 1861, as much of the nation descended into the Civil War, he, along with several colleagues (known collectively in the press as the Associates), organized the Central Pacific Railroad Company to pursue a transcontinental route. The new company's need for congressional support soon compelled Huntington to travel to Washington, DC, and there he demonstrated a flair for manipulating politicians at the highest levels. His efforts in the capital helped push through the wartime legislation that officially authorized the transcontinental project in 1862. His Central Pacific then received the subsidized concession to build the western portion of this route, from San Francisco to the eastern border of California. The concession for the longer but less difficult stretch east from California went to the Union Pacific Company, a corporation that Congress itself had created as part of the transcontinental project.[7]

Upon receiving the concession, one of Huntington's partners reportedly telegraphed the other Associates, "We have drawn the elephant. Now, let us see if we can harness him up." And so, like mighty Hannibal crossing the Alps, Huntington worked to master this great new beast. His company, however, nearly collapsed before the first fifty miles of rail were laid, the project beset by internal conflicts and financing demands that exceeded the cushion that the original subsidies provided.

Huntington and his partners soon lobbied Congress successfully for even more generous political terms, including 1864 legislation that increased their subsidies and relaxed federal oversight. Over the next several years, an army of fourteen thousand laborers, mostly Chinese immigrants, worked for the Central Pacific to drive rails across the mountains of the High Sierras, where freezing temperatures, four-story snowdrifts, frequent cave-ins, and some of the toughest terrain in the country made every mile of progress a major victory. Huntington held this whole operation together, preserving his company's credit through desperate, often deceptive, financial practices and through, in his words, "untiring perseverance that works twenty-four hours a day."[8]

The threat of bankruptcy nonetheless loomed over these Sierra activities like the edge of an approaching thunderstorm, and Huntington convinced his Associates that survival required a new, expansionist strategy. The more lines they controlled, Huntington argued, the more access he would have to fresh capital and the less they would have to worry about competition for traffic. The additional lines would also serve as "feeders" to their Central Pacific route, functioning like tributaries to a great transcontinental river.

In 1868, shortly after the Central Pacific finally ran trains over the spine of the Sierras, the Associates implemented Huntington's strategy in earnest with the purchase of the Southern Pacific Railroad Company. This acquisition gave Huntington construction rights along a five-hundred-mile coastal route between San Francisco and San Diego as well as a minor interest in the California portion of a southern transcontinental route from Los Angeles to New Orleans. California's entire coastal and southern trade suddenly lay within their grasp.[9]

By the time the Associates completed their original Central Pacific line in 1869, they had transformed from railroaders into veritable empire builders. Soon their holdings swelled to include a host of smaller California rail concessions and a major interest in the largest steamship line on the Pacific Coast. Much of this activity was eventually consolidated into a parent corporation, known as the Southern Pacific Company.[10]

Critics would liken the Southern Pacific to an octopus for the way it seemed to stretch in all directions at once, its iron tentacles invading nearly every corner of California's economic and social life. A widely read 1901 novel lambasting the early days of western railroading was simply titled *The Octopus*. Its author described Huntington's fictional analogue with a mixture of terror and admiration: "[N]o one individual was more constantly in the eye of the world; no one was more hated, more dreaded, no one more compelling of unwilling tribute to his commanding genius, to the colossal intellect operating the width of an entire continent."[11]

The real-life Huntington, throughout the early 1870s, faced financial strains so great that he frequently contemplated selling out altogether. His position, however, stabilized once the Great Panic of 1873 subsided and his Central Pacific line began to see increased traffic. Soon he embarked on another run of lobbying in Washington, where his influence increased steadily through persuasion, strong-arm tactics, and a cavalier use of payoffs. In Huntington's view, the Congress that revolved around James Blaine contained the "hungriest set of men that ever got together," and most of them lined up like pigs to Huntington's trough of goodies. At one point, with desired legislation seemingly stalled, he confided to an associate, "I believe with $200,000 I can pass our bill." The few congressmen who refused to consume his handouts—out of principle or, more often, commitments to competitors in the railroading game—were labeled by Huntington as "wild hogs," and he worked assiduously to "fix" them or drive them out of office altogether.[12]

Among Huntington's greatest triumphs in this period was an expansion of his Southern Pacific's claims to the coveted, yet-to-be-built southern transcontinental line from Los Angeles to New Orleans. The Southern Pacific originally had rights only to the California portion of this transcontinental route, but Huntington had gradually found political support to push his legal claims more than five hundred miles farther east, across Arizona and New Mexico, at least as far as El Paso, a small trading outpost in western Texas on the Rio Grande.[13]

Huntington's newly expanded portion of the southern transcontinental route, throughout most of its length, skirted close to the nation's border with Mexico. Below that border stretched an arid territory rich in minerals but untouched by rails. As a contemporary US government report noted, "Mexico has been likened unto a cornucopia, with its mouth turned towards the United States." Congress had long touted the appeal of Mexican trade as a reason to authorize the southern transcontinental concession, and Huntington appreciated these arguments. Mexico, it appeared, now lay within reach of his tentacular grasp.[14]

The size of the border created many potential crossing points, but geography and the limitations of railroad engineering shrank the options dramatically. If Huntington entered too far west, his only route to Mexico's great interior plateau and to the population-rich capital farther south would involve crossing the Western Sierra Madres, a range as imposing as the Rocky Mountains. The most desirable entry point for Huntington by far was at El Paso, which had once been an important stop on the Spanish empire's great north–south Camino Real trail that ran fifteen hundred miles from Mexico City to Santa Fe, New Mexico. An entry at El Paso would allow Huntington to capitalize on the preexisting Camino Real route. Thus, every mile that Huntington built from California toward El Paso brought him not only closer to a second transcontinental line but also to a gateway for Mexico City.[15]

However, in the midst of Huntington's great drive east, he butted up against a man every bit his equal, the notorious Jay Gould.[16]

*   *   *

Gould, born in 1836, was fifteen years Huntington's junior, but the two shared a surprising amount in common, as though the Fates had cast a new Romulus and Remus for the industrial age. Their roots in America both reached back to notable families in colonial New England. Gould grew up on a farm in upstate New York located less than ninety miles from Huntington's birthplace and, like Huntington, started working outside the home at fourteen in search of better economic prospects. The early exploits of each man, stories of small fortunes gained and lost, took on legendary qualities that filled later biographies. And as the two men matured, they both displayed implacable demeanors, their emotions hidden beneath robust beards, Gould's a jet black that matched his piercing eyes, Huntington's rounded with gray and white.[17]

Their differences nonetheless defined them. As a business associate once opined, "Take the very reverse of Jay Gould and you have Huntington." "Old Collis," as Huntington was sometimes known even in his thirties, stood more than six feet with a bulky frame and avuncular mien. Gould, in contrast, was spare, sallow-cheeked, and short. The press liked to call him the "Napoleon of finance." Another honorific, the "Little Wizard of Wall Street," reflected his deep association with the New York stock market. Huntington once noted, "I wouldn't go into the stock market against Gould, for he could whip me at that game. [But w]hen it comes to building and operating railroads in the most efficient and economical way, I can whip him, for that is my business."[18]

Gould decided to enter Huntington's western railroading business in 1873. At the time, mismanagement, inadequate traffic, and mounting debt loads had pushed both halves of the original transcontinental line to the brink of bankruptcy. Gould was already quite experienced in railroad securities speculation, having risen to national prominence during the 1860s through gambles on Erie Railway stocks that kept entire industries on edge, and he sensed that the Union Pacific's weakness had created a new opportunity for an easy profit. His agents soon purchased enough depressed Union Pacific stock on the open market to grant Gould a dominant position. Gould then installed his own men on the board and subsequently sold off excess shares from his controlling portion at a profit to small investors who trusted the Wizard of Wall Street. The nation's only completed transcontinental route suddenly belonged half to Gould and half to Huntington.[19]

Gould next pursued the same imperialistic strategy that Huntington had pioneered. As Gould claimed in testimony to Congress, "I had passed the time when I cared about mere money-making. My object . . . was more to show that I could make a combination and make it a success."[20]

While the far west already rested beneath Huntington's thumb, opportunities remained farther inland. Gould decided to focus on a stretch of territory fanning out southwest from St. Louis. This broad region contained a dense network of speculative concessions and completed rail lines, and Gould, taking advantage of the easy credit that a strong national economy produced in the late 1870s, absorbed many of these routes in a spectacular two-year spree, creating his own octopus. By late 1880, his holdings had expanded to nearly ten thousand miles, even more than what Huntington possessed. One St. Louis paper observed late that year, "[Gould] seems to almost have found the lever of Archimedes."[21]

Among Gould's new acquisitions was a concession covering the eastern half of the southern transcontinental route. More than four hundred miles of this line had already been completed in eastern Texas, but financing challenges had halted construction in the west of the state and, during the years of inactivity, Huntington had secured overlapping claims for the region around El Paso. Gould aimed to revive the project and wanted to reach El Paso before Huntington could. Whoever arrived there first would hold a major advantage in the contest for Mexico City, its three hundred thousand citizens, its coastal rail connection, and the countless resources that could be cultivated or mined along the route.[22]

Gould and Huntington, however, were not the only ones racing for El Paso and Mexico by this point.

A competition for rail access to El Paso from the north had emerged in parallel with the fight over the southern transcontinental.

One side of this north–south rail battle was led by a group of Boston capitalists who shared Huntington's philosophy on the importance of combinations. The Boston men had been building another railroad octopus that grew from a trunk line connecting Atchison, Kansas, with Santa Fe, New Mexico. Their spreading network, sometimes labeled the "Atchison system," sat between Huntington's Southern Pacific system to the west and Gould's empire to the east. The Atchison men lacked a completed transcontinental line, but their geographic position provided great leverage in the competition for the Southwest and for Mexico. One of their concessions covered the distance from Santa Fe to El Paso, along the northernmost four hundred miles of the old Camino Real.[23]

The Atchison men's competitor for this northern approach to El Paso was William Palmer, another powerful railroader interested in Mexico. Palmer, a Quaker engineer from Philadelphia, had risen to the rank of general during the Civil War before joining the transcontinental frenzy early on. He eventually settled in Colorado and, beginning in the 1870s, built an independent rail system around Denver that exclusively used a narrow-gauge track, which could be built at less cost and with simpler engineering in difficult terrain than the standard-gauge tracks of his main competitors. The independent-minded Palmer also broke away from east–west railroad orthodoxy and began to think north–south, influenced by his Civil War mentor General William Rosecrans, who served as US minister to Mexico in 1868.[24] Palmer's vision ultimately reached as far as Mexico City, and the shortest potential rail route there from Colorado entered at El Paso, which was located due south of Denver. Palmer, like the Atchison men, had acquired a concession that reached El Paso from the north.

Legal rights aside, the only suitable north–south railroad corridor to El Paso had to pass through the Royal Gorge, a ten-yard-wide canyon in Colorado that was too narrow for two competing lines. This quirk of geography had forced Palmer and the Atchison men into a frantic contest for control during the late 1870s. They had fought with lawyers and with private militias until finally, in 1879, Palmer conceded defeat. One journalist, with little embellishment, later declared, "there will probably never be another railroad war to compare with the battle . . . for the possession of . . . the Royal Gorge." Nonetheless, the crushing loss of the El Paso route did not dissuade Palmer from pursuing a Mexican concession, and he maintained an agent in the foreign capital.[25]

By mid-1880, the simmering of competition to build toward Mexico City reached a boiling point, adding urgency to a debate over US railroad construction already roiling Mexican politics.[26]

"Between Strength and Weakness, the Desert"

Like all nations in Latin America, Mexico lagged far behind the United States and Western Europe in railroad development. Mexico's first major rail project, a British-financed 265-mile line from the capital southeast to the port of Veracruz, only opened in 1873 after more than thirty years of setbacks. As late as 1876, the entire country contained a meager 416 miles of track—in comparison, the United States that year possessed nearly 77,000 miles. Most of the leading Mexican politicians favored railroad development, but they differed sharply over the role that the United States should play in the process.[27]

Some, like Matías Romero, who had served as foreign minister to the United States during the 1860s, believed that their northern neighbor held the key to their country's future. In Romero's view, railroads connected to the booming markets in the north could function like a cable upon which Mexico winched itself toward prosperity. He treated the proposed Mexican lines as "extensions and feeders of the great system of American railways." Moreover, eager US capitalists seemed likelier to succeed than local businessmen, with their limited access to financial markets and scant knowledge of railroads.[28]

Others in Mexico remained circumspect, with much of their concern stemming from anxieties over US aggression. The Mexican-American War had seared a deep wariness into Mexico's foreign policy that endured for more than a generation. A leading Mexican congressman insisted, "It is a natural law of history that border nations are enemies. . . . We should always fear the United States." Miguel Lerdo de Tejada, the Mexican president from 1872 to 1876, was reported to have offered the trenchant observation, "Between strength and weakness, the desert."[29]

Many politicians worried equally about long-term threats to Mexico's financial stability. Rail construction would likely saddle the Mexican government with new debts, especially since developers from the United States wanted performance-based cash subsidies to incentivize construction. Under that type of arrangement, each new mile of track completed would drain thousands of dollars from the federal treasury, regardless of whether the promised prosperity materialized. Imported development carried a high cost, and the financial reckoning could lead to economic servitude and the partial loss of sovereignty. As one Mexican congressman famously warned, "[W]ould you exchange your beautiful and poor liberty of the present for the rich subjection which the railroad could give you?"[30]

Conflicts over how to answer this question had long produced ambivalence and inconsistency in the Mexican government's handling of US-sponsored railroads. A number of US-backed projects had withered in the years after the Civil War, and a general frustration over President Lerdo's failure to develop railroads had helped to bolster the 1876 revolution that Díaz led. Díaz, however, had done little at first to resolve the issue, due in large part to congressional resistance and a recondite bureaucracy. At one

point in late 1877, the Mexican Congress, citing concerns over an invasion of Yankee capital, had invalidated by fiat a concession that Palmer had
painstakingly organized to link El Paso with Mexico City.[31]

In the ensuing three years, as Díaz strengthened his grip over his country, a series of failed attempts at locally organized railroad development
helped accelerate the Mexican leader's embrace of the US transcontinentalists and of subsidies. According to Romero, Díaz had decided by 1880
that it would be "worth while to spend large sums of money for the purpose
of having railways built without delay, . . . trusting, at the same time, that
the material development of the country promoted by the railroads would
yield revenue enough to pay all the subsidies granted." Díaz seemed finally
willing to gamble the economic future of his country on the success of
US-built railroads, an aggressive policy for a nation already mired in debt.
Díaz's plan, however, required that he first consolidate control over the
diffuse bureaucracy that handled concessions, with authority split among
individual states, Congress, ministers of the executive branch, and the president.[32]

In early 1880, Díaz gained a powerful and unanticipated advocate for
his development plans when Ulysses S. Grant, the former Civil War general and two-term US president, arrived in Mexico City for an extended
tour. Grant loved Mexico almost as much as he loved cigars, horses, and
whiskey. His fascination with the country reached back to his service in the
Mexican-American War, and he had spent decades advocating for closer
union between the two nations. According to Grant, his tour served both as
a family vacation and another opportunity to promote "relations of friendship and commerce." Grant's critics, however, insisted that the trip was the
calculated move by a potential 1880 presidential candidate to escape Washington, DC, and avoid the sorts of scandals and bad press that seemed to
cling to Grant like burrs in wool.[33]

During Grant's visit, Romero, who had long known the former president, worked with several other "leading men of the country" to persuade
their guest that Mexican progress depended, above all, on international rail
development. As Romero observed seven years later, Grant "saw at once,
with his great foresight, that the material resources of Mexico could not be
developed in large scale except by the construction of railroads, which would
really be extensions of the railway system of the United States." Romero
subsequently urged Grant to use his influence to hasten this outcome. Grant
acquiesced, but cautioned that his presidential ambitions might limit his
efforts. He soon gave several statements endorsing US railroad expansion

into Mexico, and the major papers of both nations provided him extensive coverage.[34]

Grant's efforts helped finally break the stalemate in Mexico over US investment. As one British diplomat observed, "General Grant may ... be considered as having been instrumental in bringing about ... a more liberal policy in Mexico." Two months after his departure, the Mexican Congress, which had increasingly fallen under Díaz's control, passed legislation providing the Mexican president direct authority to issue rail concessions. The new law allowed Díaz to finally end the decades of failure and half measures in railroading.[35]

In early September 1880, the Mexican president took his first major step in this direction, awarding the Atchison men a massive subsidized concession to connect Mexico City with El Paso. Díaz's selection of the Atchison men seemed to grow out of a confidence he had developed with them three years earlier, when they had acquired a four-hundred-mile-long, less politically sensitive concession in northern Mexico. The new 1880 concession, however, dwarfed this earlier deal, authorizing more than two thousand miles of rail construction in total, centered around a twelve-hundred-mile standard-gauge line that roughly followed the old Camino Real route north from Mexico City.[36]

Once more, the Atchison men had outflanked Palmer. Their new concession covered the route he had all but acquired before the Mexican Congress denied him in 1877. But Palmer still had powerful friends in Mexico City as well as potential legal challenges that could hold up Díaz's new concession.

Díaz moved quickly to pacify Palmer by granting him a heavily subsidized concession as well. This consolation prize, awarded five days after the Atchison deal was signed, involved thirteen hundred miles of rails, including a narrow-gauge line to run eight hundred miles from Mexico City to Laredo, a small trading outpost on the Rio Grande in eastern Texas. This Laredo line, though less direct than the El Paso route, would provide Palmer another chance to realize his dream of a narrow-gauge empire that stretched from Denver to Mexico City. In the meantime, Mexico would gain a rail line along its eastern flank and another connection to its northern neighbor.[37]

With a few strokes of his pen Díaz had remapped the future of his nation and its relationship with US capital.

* * *

The two new concessions, however, only affected Mexico's northern and central regions. The south, including the state of Oaxaca, the home of both Díaz and Romero, remained untouched. And Romero, for his part, saw no reason why the power of US capital ought to stop at the rail depots of Mexico City.

In the five-day window between the issuance of Díaz's twin concessions, Romero secured permission to promote a 250-mile route from Mexico City to Oaxaca, with potential spurs extending to both coasts. This southern concession lacked subsidies, but in Romero's view possessed great value thanks to its "triple character [as] an interoceanic route of importance, a local route of great power, and a trunk line between Mexico and Central America."[38]

Romero soon traveled to New York to recruit Grant, whose political hopes had crumbled after Garfield secured the 1880 presidential nomination. Grant's cooperation, according to Romero, "would be almost indispensable for obtaining a good outcome." The two men met in October 1880. Grant listened to Romero's pitch—as well as his blandishments—and before the meeting concluded the former president had agreed to organize a company to construct the line through southern Mexico.[39]

Despite this triumph, Romero still needed to find men with both the practical experience and the funds that Grant lacked. Unfortunately, the best-equipped candidates, most notably Gould and Huntington (who both had yet to receive concessions from Díaz), remained bitterly divided around the fight for Mexico City. Romero concluded, shortly after securing Grant's support, that if he could convene everyone, he could perhaps "procure the conciliation of all the existing interests, with the object that those in the process of construction, as much as those seeking concessions, would support each other mutually instead of fighting one another." Harmony would hopefully reign thereafter, perhaps allowing Mexico to escape from the darker urges of capitalistic competition and overbuilding that already plagued the US West. On November 8, 1880, six days after the election that placed Garfield in the White House with Blaine as his secretary of state, invitations for a dinner at Delmonico's went out under Romero's name.[40]

The hastily arranged meal brought together all the major players, a rogues' gallery of Gilded Age excess. Alongside Gould and Grant and Huntington and Palmer and the Atchison men also sat their top lieutenants, collaborators, and brokers, many of them household names in their own right, known for their feats as well as their physiognomies. Gould's allies alone at the dinner included Grenville M. Dodge, the Civil War general who had personally selected Omaha as the transcontinental's starting point and who donned a mustache that would have intimidated a bull walrus; Sidney Dillon, the financier who helped lay the last rail in the first transcontinental and who sported glorious muttonchops that cascaded several inches below his cheeks; and Russell "Old Straddle" Sage, a powerful speculator who shared an office floor with Gould and, as a *Washington Post* reporter sniped, carried "a long crooked nose that might have been slightly warped in following some elusive rumor around the Wall Street corners."[41]

The evening's meal eventually yielded to speeches from Romero and then Grant. The former president, in remarks intended for the national press as much as his audience, pled for cooperation and assured that Mexico's promise offset any need for subsidies. After Grant's remarks concluded, the assemblage appointed a ten-man committee from their ranks to meet shortly in Huntington's home to determine if cooperation was in fact possible.[42]

Numerous precedents existed for cooperation in western railroading. The first transcontinental line itself demanded some collaboration between Gould and Huntington, the owners of its eastern and western halves, respectively, and all the US players held overlapping financial interests in various companies. However, cooperation generally emerged from weakness, a half measure when an opponent's strong position blocked monopoly control or when the threat of competitive shipping rates proved unpalatable for all involved or when the scale of a project demanded collective financing and risk spreading. These alliances rarely endured very long.[43]

For Romero's plan to succeed, each party needed to believe that coordinated development offered meaningful advantages over unrestricted competition, at least for the time being. Gould and Huntington, lacking Mexican concessions, quickly assented and soon convinced the Atchison men that joint action would ultimately benefit all of the lines meeting at El Paso. Palmer, in contrast, seemed little inclined to endorse any cooperative agreement, especially as he no longer held interests in the joint El Paso crossing thanks to the Atchison men's victory in the battle over Royal Gorge. Palmer's resistance increased further when Gould, days after the Delmonico's dinner, nearly engineered a takeover of Palmer's entire Denver system and, shortly thereafter, snatched up the sole rail concession that covered the distance between Palmer's US system and his new Mexican concession.[44]

By Christmas 1880, newspapers reported that the commission created at Delmonico's, regardless of prolonged efforts, had "found it impossible to harmonize all the interests involved."[45]

The Many Roads Through Mexico

Romero's failed attempt at coordinated, rational railroad development had not been entirely in vain. The appeal of his southern concession, despite its lack of subsidies, had helped to align everyone but Palmer, and the remaining three major players, according to Romero, all attached the "greatest importance" to the potential of controlling a route to Central America. Gould, Huntington, and the Atchison men each soon invested in the new southern company. Their power—in combination with that of Grant, whose name, Romero felt, "alone equaled" all the others in value—seemed to ensure success. And as a further precaution, to "represent the Mexican element in the company," Romero brought in Porfirio Díaz, who had voluntarily stepped down from power for the time being to preserve a facade of Mexican democracy. By late March 1881, Romero considered his promotional work completed successfully and felt assured of a future railroad into southern Mexico, if not into Central America.[46]

Grant, now formally running Romero's new company, returned to Mexico the following month to pursue additional rail connections toward Central America. His efforts quickly yielded an unsubsidized concession from Oaxaca to Mexico's southern border with Guatemala. Subsequently, the president of Guatemala gave Grant permission to continue his prospective line another 250 miles south.[47]

The route Grant assembled corresponded with a portion of the project that Hinton Rowan Helper had been advocating for in his recently published *Three Americas Railway* volume. Grant, however, never seemed to endorse Helper's plan, and Helper himself hardly mentioned Grant or any of the businessmen involved in Mexico. In Helper's view, businessmen could only corrupt a project meant to be public and government-led. But Helper's concerns belied the nearly total indifference that transcontinentalists showed toward his project in its earliest incarnation. Gould openly opposed Helper's plan, supposedly declaring that the hemispheric route could never pay, even if the trains hauled nothing but diamonds.[48]

From Gould's perspective, talk of a hemispheric road distracted from the more pressing issue of connecting his own system with the Mexican capital. This goal, which Huntington also shared, faced resistance from Mexican politicians who felt that the two concessions already granted in 1880 had addressed any traffic needs in the near term. Huntington eventually offered to forgo subsidies entirely, just as Grant had earlier counseled. Gould, for his part, refused to compromise but pushed equally hard. By the fall of 1881, their intense lobbying had won them each an independent, standard-gauge concession from Mexico City to the Rio Grande: Gould's subsidized line would cross at or near Laredo, in direct competition with Palmer; Huntington's unsubsidized line would connect a hundred miles farther upriver, at a settlement called Eagle Pass.[49]

The new concessions not only strengthened the positions of Gould and Huntington against Palmer and the Atchison men in Mexico, but also amplified a long-building tension between Gould and Huntington over the impending clash of their dueling southern transcontinental lines in the United States. Gould, at the time, trailed Huntington by ninety miles in the race to El Paso, still considered the premier standard-gauge gateway to Mexico City. Huntington, however, required that Gould not block the Southern Pacific system's entry into Texas and its connection to the newly approved Mexican line at Eagle Pass. The only paths forward, according to newspapers, appeared to be cooperation or what the *New York Times* called a "Southern railroad war."[50]

In mid-November 1881, shortly after their Mexican concessions had been finalized, Gould and Huntington met face-to-face to discuss their next steps. Newspapers subsequently reported that the two men had agreed upon several basic terms: they would cooperatively build and share, as equal partners, the ninety-mile stretch east of El Paso; they would grant each other reciprocal privileges over the rails that they had already constructed toward El Paso; and Gould would not block Huntington's path across southern Texas. The potential collision had been avoided, the stalemate over Mexican entry points had disappeared, and the nation received its long-awaited southern transcontinental line. The *Atlanta Constitution* considered the agreement "one of the most important events of this railroad era," explaining further that "the entire compact relates to a southern line to Mexico and California."[51]

The alliance of Gould and Huntington gave them nearly full control of the nation's two completed transcontinental lines. Their duopoly, however, faced a challenge from the Atchison men, who had already built a connection to Huntington's Southern Pacific and had also acquired a fifteen-year-old transcontinental concession to link St. Louis with San Francisco, two thousand miles away. This competing San Francisco line's completion appeared inevitable, but two months after Gould and Huntington reached their El Paso accord, they jointly took over a near-bankrupt company that held enough interest in the Atchison's concession to block any progress west. One of the ousted directors from the acquired company declared, "It means negation—prevention. . . . Gould and Huntington will maintain their monopoly on Texas and California." The Atchison men, suddenly squeezed from east and west, had few directions in which to expand besides south.[52]

By this point, the Atchison's Mexican line already contained several hundred miles of fully constructed rails, a promising sign given the special challenges that US rail corporations confronted below the Rio Grande. These obstacles included language and culture barriers that confounded US engineers; a landscape that offered fewer forest resources than large portions of the US West; and a fledgling industrial base that produced almost none of the necessary manufactured components. Construction needs in the first two years alone required the Atchison men to import nearly forty thousand tons of rails from England and countless cargoes of lumber from the United States.[53]

The only resources that the Atchison men seemed to find in sufficient quantities were native laborers, but initial company reports described these employees as "entirely inexperienced . . . and unaccustomed to railroad work." The Atchison's lead engineer, as one of his contemporaries noted, felt that the Mexicans "could not so much as pilot a mule to water along a beaten trail." Nonetheless, accommodation from both labor and management outpaced animosity. The engineer's same chronicler explained, with racist awe, "In less than a month the line was literally alive with these human ants. Red ants, fleece-clad, from the mountains, naked ants from the Terre Coliente, and black ants from Sonora . . . swelled the army." By mid-1883, nearly fifty thousand Mexicans were reportedly employed on the line, laying down rails and ties imported from abroad, expanding the system two miles per day.[54]

The rapid pace of construction allowed the Atchison men to finish their line in early March 1884, almost exactly fifteen years after the driving of the last spike in the original US transcontinental at Promontory Summit, in the Utah territory. On the actual day of completion, a "considerable crowd" gathered in a barren stretch of desert to watch the laying of the final rail and the meeting of two trains, one from Mexico City, the other from the US border, each draped with the flag of its respective nation. Two weeks later, a special train departed Mexico City for a six-day, twenty-five-hundred-mile voyage to Chicago. The passengers on board, fifty Mexicans and twenty-five Americans, each paid $150 for the privilege of being the first to experience the route. The Atchison men soon arrived to great acclaim in Mexico City, where, according to reporters, their path "was literally strewn with roses."[55]

This enthusiasm nonetheless failed to convert some skeptics. An article in the *Washington Post* announcing the opening of the line cautioned, "As to the probable financial success of the road ... there are ... some serious doubts." Within months complaints circulated that "the freight charges are too high ... so high on [certain] classes of merchandise as to be a partial embargo on trade." A general depression beginning in 1884 and the Mexican government's temporary suspension of subsidy payments the following year only amplified these problems.[56]

Despite these limitations, the Atchison men had at least managed to complete their line. The same could hardly be said of their early rival General Palmer. He had struggled from the outset to overcome the hurdles of Mexican construction, and Gould's constant meddling only worsened the problems. Within the first year, subscriptions in Palmer's line began selling at a discount. Soon thereafter he took measures to increase his company's capitalization without corresponding equity, a questionable practice known as "watering stock." When a newspaper reporter in early 1882 asked one of Palmer's codirectors if the line was "progressing very rapidly," he simply answered, "No." Palmer finally began to sell out his position to a syndicate of British capitalists the following year. His responsibilities thereafter gradually shrank to figurehead and adviser.[57]

By the time Palmer sold out, Grant had also abandoned his Mexican line entirely. Construction in the south had been particularly complicated, with seasonal rains inhibiting work, but Grant's withdrawal owed almost everything to the swift collapse in 1884 of his son's financial firm, which held most of the former president's capital. Grant found himself suddenly indebted several hundred thousand dollars as various loans came due. During this period, doctors also diagnosed Grant, a lifetime cigar addict, with a likely fatal form of throat cancer. Grant, his time suddenly limited and his debts mounting, turned all his energy toward writing his memoirs, which offered a way to cement his legacy and raise funds. A completed draft emerged several months later, by which point his death appeared imminent.

In his final days, when he could no longer speak and barely left his bed, he continued to dream of Mexico's bright future, writing, "I hope Mexico may now begin an upward and prosperous departure. She has all the elements of success."[58]

Grant's death and financial troubles created numerous headaches for Gould in Mexico. The relationship between the two men had grown especially close, with Grant often acting as promoter for Gould's Mexican interests, leading some papers to suggest that the former US president was nothing "but the agent of Jay Gould." In 1883, the two men had even managed to merge their separate concessions into one subsidized super route that extended through all of Mexico. This move had given Gould the dominant position over all his rivals, but he had also linked his fate to Grant through invisible bonds as strong as the chains of Hephaestus. In consequence, Gould's railroad claims all evaporated when, in mid-1885, the Mexican government finally invalidated the concession the two men shared for failure to reach mandated construction minimums on time. Gould suddenly appeared to be out of the race for Mexico, though his scheming, like a thirst that could not be slaked, continued unabated.[59]

Huntington, during this fractious period of the mid-1880s, had avoided Gould's meddling as well as the pitfalls that time-based subsidies created in Mexico. His unsubsidized line south from Eagle Pass, supported with funds from his Southern Pacific network, progressed steadily toward a junction with the Atchison line roughly five hundred miles north of Mexico City. In early 1888, Huntington finally reached this junction, providing a second de facto international line with the Mexican capital. Huntington's route reduced the distance to eastern markets in the United States by roughly seven hundred miles, and he immediately began to siphon Atchison traffic. The competition grew even fiercer several months later, when the syndicate handling Palmer's narrow-gauge line completed their route to Laredo, which further reduced the total distance to the US border.[60]

Seven years had now passed since Díaz granted the original concessions. In the interim, Mexico City had gained three lines north at a cost to the federal treasury of approximately $40 million. While Díaz's investment had produced some domestic returns, they flowed most directly to the elites and "speculative investors" who owned or acquired land along the routes. Their property values rose, and the rail lines offered a new means to transport agricultural products or minerals. For the majority of the nation, however, the promised prosperity remained slow in arriving, glimmering somewhere on the far-off horizon, beyond sight of the tracks. The best jobs that the railways created, including engineer and conductor, remained almost exclusively with workers brought in from the United States.[61]

Gould seemed to have finally lost interest in the route to Mexico City by the time all three rival international lines began operating. When a reporter asked him in 1890 about rumors that he might try to buy the Atchison line south from El Paso, he insisted that he was "not extending in that direction." His son George, whom Gould was grooming as his business heir, reaffirmed these sentiments. Gould nonetheless continued visiting the border region. He insisted that these trips simply benefited his health, which had begun to decline noticeably, but his appearances still triggered rumors about his Mexican intentions. These speculations reached a crescendo in April 1892, when he and Huntington conducted a private summit in El Paso. The two men shared no news publicly of what, if anything, had transpired, but reports suggested an agreement that included permission for Gould to build a line from El Paso to a point in Mexico on the Pacific, potentially gaining a dedicated transcontinental route of his own at long last, after a decade butting up inexorably against Huntington.[62]

However, before the year was out, Gould had died from consumption. The rabble of Wall Street, upon learning the news, gasped as though a seam had ripped open temporarily in the metaphysical fabric of the nation's economy. Gould's closest associates guessed his net worth at somewhere between $70 million and $150 million, though no one felt confident that they knew where all the Wizard's money lay. The titans of US capital, including Huntington, lined up to pay respects.[63]

Of the many traits that Gould and Huntington shared throughout life, the last might have been a mutual admiration and respect for one another. Huntington, shortly after Gould's death, said of his great rival, "I have known him intimately for thirty years. . . . I found Mr. Gould to be a man who always did exactly what he agreed to do. He was certainly a man of ability . . . [and] a genial and pleasant man to meet socially." Gould's family, acknowledging the two men's close relationship, even requested that Huntington serve as one of the pallbearers at the funeral.[64]

The sudden absence of Gould nonetheless benefited Huntington immensely, fraternal sentiments aside. The two rivals had long held joint control of the valuable Pacific shipping trade, but Huntington soon wrested this shared company away from Gould's son George. In conjunction with this victory, Huntington began exploring the possibilities of extending his

Mexican line over the Sierra Madres and of constructing a transcontinental line across Guatemala, with both lines designed to connect with his Pacific shipping interests.[65]

Huntington's unflagging ambitions, however, belied his advanced age. As the century came to a close, he was approaching his eightieth year, his beard had turned snow white, and he suffered from a weak heart. His various projects kept him active, but on August 13, 1900, while relaxing with his family in the Adirondacks, he dropped dead just before the stroke of midnight. His family buried him in a mausoleum worthy of an ancient king that Huntington had constructed in the Bronx's Woodlawn Cemetery. Down one of the cemetery's pathways, in an equally impressive tomb modeled after the Parthenon, lay the remains of his old rival Jay Gould. For the two men, even death had been a competition.[66]

The passing of Huntington concluded an era of railroading that had transformed much of the continent. This forty-year period had begun with the building of the first US transcontinental line, then evolved into a contest among railroad combinations for control of the West, and eventually produced three major international lines to Mexico City and numerous smaller routes throughout Mexico. By the close of the century, Mexico had more railroads than any Latin American nation save Argentina, where an equally ambitious rail building program had been financed by British capital, especially the Baring Brothers Bank.

The Mexican railways built during this twenty-year period provided the foundation for an unprecedented influx of US capital below the border and a corresponding growth in trade. Commercial exchange between the two nations increased fourfold between 1880 and 1900. Total US investments in Mexico reached $500 million in 1900 and would soon expand to $1 billion. Of this amount, roughly 70 percent related to the railroads. The "railway invasion of Mexico" marked the start of the United States' international industrial expansion, just as the War of 1898 had initiated a new, formal overseas empire. President Díaz, who controlled Mexico throughout most of this period, reportedly lamented sometime after 1900, "Poor Mexico, so far from God and so close to the United States," but, in reality, his own support of US capitalists had greatly hastened this very outcome.[67]

Remarkably, this profound expansion of US railroad investment in Mexico rested on a record of nearly constant failure. Romero had failed in his quest for cooperation, Grant had gone bankrupt, Palmer had lost control of his own concession, Gould had tormented his rivals while building almost nothing himself, Huntington never managed to conquer the Western Sierra Madres or extend his line to Mexico City, and the Atchison men struggled to turn a profit. A historian summarizing the Mexican activities of US railroaders in 1921 concluded, "The mistake made was in assuming that what could be done in the southwestern part of the United States could be done with equal speed south of the Rio Grande, where conditions were more essentially different than they appeared." Or perhaps it was simply that a paradoxical type of failure that still produced growth followed the railroads south from the United States. Historian Richard White's recent observation of the behavior of the US transcontinentals applied equally well to the lines toward Mexico City: "Hauling something, even at a loss, was better than hauling nothing. In attempting to cut economic losses, the railroads helped create . . . what might be called dumb growth."[68]

The many frustrations in Mexico nonetheless failed to intimidate a new generation of US capitalists, who soon heard Mexico's siren call and hungered to surpass their departed predecessors. Gould's son George had learned much about Mexico through travels with his father and displayed what Russell Sage described as "a laudable ambition to become a great railroad magnate." The potential of Mexican railroads also appealed greatly to oil tycoon Henry Clay Pierce, who wanted to expand his Missouri- and Texas-based distribution operation south. But the loftiest aspirations seemed to lie with E. H. Harriman, a short, energetic financier who donned a mustache "as unkempt as if [it] had been worn by a Sky terrier," in the estimation of one colleague. Some felt that Harriman evoked memories of Gould, both for his "mental alertness and financial audacity" and, less admirably, for his practice of utilizing "the devices of lawyers and technicalities" to achieve desired outcomes. Huntington, ever astute, had advised a reporter in 1898, "Keep your eyes on Harriman. He is bound to be a big man in railroad affairs."[69]

Harriman aimed to reinvent the rules of railroad building, just as Huntington had done the generation prior. The entire industry, in Harriman's view, needed to be modernized. Harriman's most recent biographer explained,

> [T]o make money, a road had to haul greater loads at lower rates as cheaply as possible. . . . Bigger payloads required longer trains with larger cars and heavier engines, which in turn needed a straighter line,

lower grades, heavier rails, better ballast, sturdier bridges, updated sig-
nals, more sidings, and newer facilities. . . . To undertake the whole
package at once meant a huge investment from which most rail managers shrank.

As Harriman once noted, "I have more imagination than [other rail
managers]. . . . I see what they [see], but I see it larger, because I see its possibilities." [70]

Harriman had first applied his modernizing philosophy in the late 1890s
when, at nearly fifty years old, he gained control of the Union Pacific. The
former Gould property had fallen into receivership during the depression
that began the year after Gould's death and, although management maintained the line's basic infrastructure, numerous reports maligned the Union
Pacific as "two streaks of rust and a right-of-way." Harriman soon invested
millions to improve and straighten the line, bringing in a workforce that
swelled to more than a hundred thousand men, who rapidly carried out
engineering feats that his predecessors had deemed functionally and fiscally
impossible, such as boring an eighteen-hundred-foot-long tunnel through
solid granite. [71]

Tales of Harriman's remarkable achievements soon floated through the
corridors of Wall Street and the Capitol, but his growing legend could
hardly keep pace with his actual activities. Shortly after Huntington's death
in 1900, Harriman took over almost all of the Southern Pacific system,
which included the Central Pacific. The purchase placed the nation's original transcontinental route under unified control for the first time, thirty-
one years after its completion. As Harriman declared, "We have bought not
only a railroad, but an empire." Harriman also inherited Huntington's great
rivalry with the Gould system, now under George's control. [72]

The new rivalry between Gould and Harriman quickly spilled into
Mexico, where the death of Huntington had helped trigger a chain reaction of ownership changes. Both the Laredo line and Huntington's Mexican line were purchased in mid-1901 by James Speyer, the banker who had
handled much of Huntington's construction project and who maintained
such a selective clientele that even his firm's address was an insider secret.
Speyer seemed to view the moves as a way to protect his prior investments
in Huntington, a custodial function more than that of an empire builder.
Speyer's purchases also coincided with the Atchison men's decision to sell
their underperforming El Paso–Mexico City line to Henry Clay Pierce. The
purchase gave Pierce an automatic distribution network for his oil products

throughout most of northern Mexico as well as access to the Gulf of Mexico through a spur connection with the port of Tampico. As for Harriman, according to the *Mexican Herald*, he had been "caught asleep" during this rapid mid-1901 shake-up.[73]

Harriman nonetheless soon found an entry point into Mexico through the old western line that the Atchison men had received from the Díaz administration in 1877. The four-hundred-mile route began in Nogales, Arizona, and continued through the arid state of Sonora along the western slopes of the Sierra Madres before reaching the Pacific. This Sonora line had never received the same attention as the three Mexico City routes, but Harriman saw potential and decided to rehabilitate the rail bed and then extend it farther south along hundreds of miles of Pacific Coast. Ultimately, Harriman's imagined system extended far into Central America.[74]

Harriman, however, was hardly the only US railroader looking south beyond Mexico City at this point. By the time he had acquired a Mexican foothold, Díaz had already awarded a major new southern concession to a small syndicate of US capitalists. The men composing this syndicate were all but unknown to Harriman, Gould, Speyer, Pierce, or any of the other titans of railroading who controlled the rest of the Mexican system. Nonetheless, under this small group's leadership, the material construction of an international railroad would finally merge with the idea of Pan-Americanism.[75]

"The Greatest Chance I Ever Saw"

Distance accounted for only part of the separation between Mexico's far southern region and the rest of its territory. Before the Spanish conquest, much of the central latitudes, including the capital, had belonged to the Aztec empire, but large parts of the south fell within the ambit of the Mayas, whose cultural reach extended deep into Guatemala and Honduras. Southern Mexico and Central America also shared a tropical climate, with prolonged rainy seasons and the potential to produce countless agricultural products. Foreign capitalists, including US railroaders, had long been interested in Mexico's southern zone, but at the dawn of the new century, their efforts had yet to bear much tropical fruit. The region remained, in the words of one paper, "a virgin country full of splendid opportunities [where] the land is very cheap."[76]

The largest completed rail project south of Mexico City ran 130 miles across the Isthmus of Tehuantepec. Known as the Tehuantepec Railroad, the line lay about three hundred miles south of Mexico City and linked the nation's two coasts at their closest point. The strategic and commercial importance of the Tehuantepec line had drawn the interest of both Huntington and Gould, but Díaz had rebuffed them, preferring that his government exert direct control over its shortest transcontinental crossing. The Mexican government officially inaugurated the Tehuantepec Railroad in 1894, though poor construction and inadequate port facilities made the line, in the opinion of many, "not fit for transisthmian service," if not completely useless.[77]

South of Tehuantepec the rail situation deteriorated even further. Grant's 1884 bankruptcy had shuttered the first major attempt at a route to the Guatemalan border, and his British successors only managed to grade eighty miles of roadbed before the great Baring Bank Crisis of 1890 wiped out much of their financing as well as the entire Argentine economy. When news of the Baring crisis reached workers on the southern Mexican line, "they were panic-stricken," according to one uncharitable contemporary, "and they abandoned the job in about the same manner that burglars would leave the cracking of a safe at the sound of a policeman's rattle." The ten years that followed saw much of the construction materials "ruined by the action of time, climate and vandals."[78]

The three-hundred-mile line from Tehuantepec to Guatemala awaited someone who knew how to navigate the challenges of southern Mexico and who appreciated the route's many special advantages. A savvy promoter would understand that President Díaz wanted to see the route completed, desiring a faster way to move troops to the volatile Guatemalan border, and that an eventual extension into Central America could reach a future US-built canal. The climate also offered its own attractions to the right investors. In the words of John M. Neeland, a rail promoter eyeing the concession and the lands around it, "Some portions . . . are a tropical paradise. . . . [D]ate and cocoa palms grow all over the coast. . . . Oranges and lemons are produced plentifully at little expense. Corn produces two crops a year without plowing the ground."[79]

Neeland, born in the cold of Ontario, Canada, in 1857, had learned the railroad business long before his arrival in tropical Mexico. His education included time in Kansas, where the corrupt railroad battles of the 1880s produced seven competing lines, giving the state more track mileage than either New England or New York by the decade's close. Neeland eventually settled in Los Angeles and then developed an interest in Mexico as a land ripe for business schemes if not outright plundering. As one paper joyously declared, "At his home [in California] may be seen a rare and valuable collection of antique curios gathered on his travels [throughout Mexico], and in some instances unearthed by his own hands, from where they had lain hidden possibly for generations."[80]

Over the course of the 1890s, Neeland's knowledge of Spanish improved and he cultivated powerful friends in the Mexican capital. His network centered around the American colony of Mexico City, an expatriate community whose leadership included several men who had made fortunes as agents for Gould, Huntington, and Palmer. One historian of the American colony has described some of these leaders as a "tropical mafia," and Neeland earned their favor through his ability to charm foreign investors toward various local projects and his reputation for uncompromising management tactics, including a terrifying episode when he had ordered unruly laborers locked up overnight inside makeshift coffins that bore the words "Here lies one without shame." The *Mexican Herald*, an English-language newspaper closely associated with the colony, described Neeland as "well and favorably known." Neeland also ingratiated himself with several Mexicans closely tied to Díaz, most notably Joaquín Casasús, a prominent lawyer, and Enrique Creel, the nation's leading banker, both of whom would eventually serve as ambassadors to the United States.[81]

As the decade came to a close, Neeland's success in networking bolstered his business aspirations and railroad dreams. One of his colleagues said, "His initiative and imagination were marvelous. He would conceive of schemes so great and daring that it made an ordinary man catch his breath." And the greatest rail dream of the age, from Neeland's perspective in Mexico City, was the Pan-American Railway.[82]

Mexico, like the United States and Argentina, fell outside the route recognized by Henry Gassaway Davis's Permanent Pan-American Railway Committee because its rail network was considered sufficiently developed. Díaz nonetheless had designated a Pan-American route within its territory. The line began in Laredo and ended with the unbuilt three-hundred-mile concession south of Tehuantepec that had lain fallow since the 1890 Baring Crisis.

The rights to this unbuilt, southernmost portion of the Pan-American route had come to rest with a speculative proprietor, "a rather shrewd old Mexican" in the estimation of one US contemporary. Neeland eventually tracked this man down and, in 1900, secured permission from him to act as the line's new promoter.[83]

Neeland now needed capital and began traveling to Los Angeles to recruit investors. His appeals soon caught the attention of the Everetts, a close-knit family of businessmen visiting from Nebraska. The Everetts had built a small fortune back home through corn farming, local banking, and a sober temperament, but had traveled to Los Angeles in search of new opportunities for their capital. One of the Everetts later recalled,

> Neeland drew rosy pictures of how easily he would make all participants "rich beyond the dreams of avarice" if [we] would finance the scheme.... [H]is vivid imagination and great command of language enabled him to convince his hearers that the success of the plan was at least possible.... "You fellows put up the money and I will put on my overalls and go down and build the road," was his airy statement.[84]

The Everetts, acting out of prudence, insisted on seeing the project first-hand before opening their wallets. Neeland, in response, offered to accompany them through Mexico and, in early 1901, orchestrated a tour designed to quell any doubts. The group traveled the route through the southern state of Chiapas, and Neeland's guests, thoroughly entranced, took to imagining "the wonderful opportunities the country seemed to offer." When the tour concluded, the Everetts' patriarch, a man considered by his family to be "always wise, far-seeing and cautious," declared the project to be "the greatest chance I ever saw."[85]

Neeland used the tour to sell the Everetts not simply on the value of his Mexican route, but on the potential for a larger hemispheric railway. Their itinerary had continued south beyond Chiapas as far as Honduras, and Neeland assured that "it is our purpose to push on through Central America." The Everetts, as Neeland's words and actions suggested, would be participants in the greatest project of the age, the dream of James G. Blaine, the headline story from the First Pan-American Conference, the inspiration for the US government's recent seven-volume report, and the subject of a special committee at the Second Pan-American Conference, scheduled for later that year in Mexico City. The importance of hemispheric thinking to Neeland's project resonated in the name that he and the Everetts chose when incorporating their new venture in June 1901: the Pan-American Railroad Company.[86]

Neeland's Mexican contacts Creel and Casasús, who both eventually joined this company, helped arrange especially generous terms from Díaz. The concession, issued in September 1901, included financial subsidies as well as the right to incorporate a new bank in Chiapas. Díaz was literally granting Neeland the right to print his own money. The *Mexican Herald* noted, "The concession stands foremost among the best railway charters ever given by the Mexican government."[87] The company's success seemed so assured, its subsidies and perquisites of such remarkable value, that a man claiming to have connected Neeland with the Everetts soon filed a lawsuit against both of them and demanded $3 million in damages for their failure to include him in the project. Neeland mocked the claim as a "pipe dream," though the legal fight would not finally disappear for another nine years.[88]

As construction got under way in early 1902, the firm's leadership gathered to fete someone almost as central to their success as Díaz himself: José Limantour, Mexico's finance minister, a man one US secretary of state described as possessing "all the finish and dignity of a French gentleman of the old school." Limantour had replaced Romero, who died in 1898, as Díaz's most influential adviser on rail development, but Limantour's views had evolved somewhat from those of his deceased predecessor. The potential of US capitalists like Harriman to monopolize Mexico's railways worried Limantour to the extent that he contemplated the nationalization of the entire system. However, like Romero, he recognized the importance of first completing the national rail network through the south and warmly supported Neeland. Limantour's remarks at the dinner, according to press reports, emphasized that his nation would "use every endeavor to contribute as far as Mexico was concerned to the completion of the '*Ferrocarril Panamericano.*'"[89]

Nothing exemplified Mexico's commitment to Neeland's project better than the unprecedented bank charter, but in practice this special privilege produced problems much faster than pesos. At the time of the Limantour dinner, difficulties locating the initial capitalization of $250,000 in Mexican silver threatened to undermine the entire operation. Neeland lamented, "The merchants here have scraped their tills to sell us every cent of silver money they had." The provisional bank charter would have expired except that, at the last minute, one of the Everetts' associates arrived after a long overland journey with the final $50,000 in Mexican silver, "his face ... covered with two weeks' growth of beard; his hair ... matted with dust, his clothing in rags." The bank soon created its own paper currency, each note engraved with images of the Everetts, several of whom had moved to Mexico to manage operations personally. This curious money was intended to serve as compensation for workers on the line, but the employees refused to accept what seemed like little more than company scrip. By August 1902, barely six months after opening, the bank ceased operating temporarily.[90]

The bank closure, however, seemed like a trifling inconvenience compared to the difficulties that the Everetts felt they faced with Neeland. One of the Nebraskans later groused, "Experience proved to us that [Neeland] was [as] incompetent, where executive ability was required, as a child of ten years. He was a promoter, pure and simple, and a very good one."[91]

The first rails had hardly been laid in Mexico when Neeland began traveling around cities in the US Midwest to promote a new, related venture that would soon be known as the Pan-American Land and Colonization Company. This scheme involved undeveloped properties along the railway's planned route that Neeland had acquired or intended to acquire as lots to unload on middle-class US families, dubbed "prospective settlers [to] the promised land." The US consul in Mexico City would later describe this as "one of the biggest fakes on record," but the tales Neeland told of the Pan-American Railway and of tropical agriculture made his unimproved plots, offered at outrageously inflated prices, sound like unbeatable opportunities for anyone seeking easy returns or a slice of paradise.[92]

The Everetts, the first midwesterners to actually purchase a version of Neeland's fantasy, gradually realized that they, at least, had been sold a mirage. Within a few years, the difficulties of daily life in southern Mexico led them to contemplate abandoning their project entirely. One of the Everetts explained, "we were tired of Mexico, its hardships, its privations, and I may add, its dangers. . . . More than half of the white men who went from the north to assist in this work went to their graves within three years." Several of these deaths stemmed from "natural" causes that the Everetts considered "undoubtedly induced by the tropical climate," but violence took the lives of others, including one man "literally chopped up with an ax" by an unknown assailant. The multiple tragedies compounded "the tremendous strain of financing the project" that they had felt after their bank venture failed. The Everetts' patriarch even appealed in vain to Carnegie in early 1903, shortly after the rumors emerged of the steel baron's interest in the Pan-American Railway.[93]

When an opportunity to sell their interests arose the following year, the Everetts eagerly accepted. The new purchasers comprised a syndicate of investors from St. Louis, where Jay Gould had long fueled dreams of commercial expansion into Mexico and where the city's 1904 World's Fair had generated a great deal of interest in Pan-Americanism. The arranging of this syndicate was one of the first major business deals for a young, ambitious St. Louisan named George Herbert Walker, forebear of the Bush family political dynasty that would produce two US presidents a century later. Walker, however, played only a supporting role in the operating of the new venture, whose leading spirit was David Perry Doak. A midwestern railway man, Doak had moved to California in the 1890s as a Gould agent and charmed both the Los Angeles business community and its social set.[94]

Once the sale of the Pan-American Railroad had been consummated, the Everett clan headed back to Nebraska. In the end, they had successfully completed 125 miles of rail line, about 40 percent of the concession. One of the Everetts later wrote wistfully, "We were all glad to return to our native land . . . [but] there is no period of our lives to which we look back with so much pleasure as the three years in which we struggled with all sorts of difficulties in the wildest part of Mexico."[95]

While the Everetts' departure terminated their relationship with Neeland, the promoter himself remained in Mexico. The sale of the company had been arranged under his auspices and only increased his authority. Doak, as president, appeared sympathetic to Neeland's style of management, promotion, and general flimflam. The new board soon elevated Neeland from general manager to vice president.[96]

For all his faults, Neeland had successfully promoted the construction of a portion of the Pan-American Railway and continued its advancement. Many others, from Helper to Colonel Parsons of Virginia, had tried in vain to accomplish these same tasks during the prior twenty-five years. Several companies had even been incorporated specifically to exploit the synergies between Pan-Americanism and railroad building, but they had all given up as well. Only Neeland remained.[97]

"Six Battleships Against a Railway Connection to Buenos Aires"

Just as Neeland finalized the sale of his Pan-American Railroad Company to the Doak syndicate, newspapers in Washington, DC, announced the return of Charles Pepper, the journalist whom Henry Gassaway Davis had appointed to survey Latin America. Pepper's whirlwind, yearlong tour on behalf of Davis's committee and the Pan-American Railway had reportedly touched twenty-one countries and covered twenty-five thousand miles.[98]

Pepper had found progress almost everywhere he looked and laid out his conclusions in a report released immediately after his return. In Mexico, according to Pepper's report, the north–south rail network approached completion and the government attached "supreme importance" to this undertaking. The nations of Central America, he further explained, had linked numerous agricultural zones to the coasts through a host of small lines that "will be the encouragement to north and south roads, for which they will serve as feeders." Peru had also recently passed a new railroad law that was, in Pepper's view, "decidedly favorable to the Pan-American idea." Bolivia had gone even further, its president urging his Congress to "complete the network of international highways which will form the grand intercontinental system proposed by the United States of America."[99]

These encouraging developments made it easy to overlook the statement buried deep within Pepper's report that 4,825 miles remained to be constructed between Mexico and Argentina. This figure was a mere 75 miles less than the number Lieutenant Zinn had calculated in his 1890 report for Carnegie and Davis. The work of fifteen years had, so far, reduced the estimated gap by less than 2 percent.[100]

One additional factor, however, convinced Pepper of a bright future for the railway. He had begun his tour with the prospects for an isthmian canal uncertain, hung up in treaty negotiations between the United States and Colombia. But in November 1903, six months into his trip, revolutionaries in Panama declared independence from Colombia, and the United States provided just enough naval support to ensure their success. Roosevelt later boasted in his autobiography that he "took Panama," a controversial decision that cleared the path for a US-controlled canal. Pepper noted in his report, "The influence of the Panama Canal on railroad construction is both a moral and a material one. . . . [T]he value of the Panama Canal as a factor in Pan-American railway development can not properly be omitted."[101]

Pepper's report brought the Pan-American Railway favorable coverage in periodicals throughout the nation and hemisphere. Even the *Wall Street Journal*, whose business readership had previously displayed little interest in the imagined route, soon declared the railway "an enterprise which excites the imagination of all, and has commended itself to the wisdom of many who have studied it on its economic, engineering, and financial sides."[102]

Pepper intended for his report to jump-start another round of railway promotion in the nation's capital, but politics quickly intervened. A presidential election loomed in November, and the Democrats gave the vice presidential spot on the ticket to Pepper's patron, Henry Gassaway Davis. The West Virginian had recently turned eighty, making him the oldest candidate ever nominated in a presidential contest. His selection, according to many involved, reflected the desperation of his party, faced with the unenviable task of opposing Roosevelt and hoping that the octogenarian Davis might provide funds from his vast fortune—estimated at $30 million—to boost the meager prospects of the party's compromise presidential nominee, the rather dour and uninspiring Judge Alton Parker. In August, the month after Davis received the nomination, his personal secretary wrote apologetically to Pepper, "I know that you will realize how pressed [Davis] will be, in the meantime, with matters of an imperative nature."[103]

The 1904 campaign featured few of the substantive disagreements that had defined the prior two elections. A booming economy had quashed the long-standing debate over the gold standard, and concerns over imperialism had ceded to wild enthusiasm for Roosevelt's proposed Panama Canal. The Democrats—outside the South, where a racist Jim Crow regime produced de facto one-party rule—had little to offer voters besides simple party loyalty and a historical association with populism.[104]

But even the claims to populism (already suspect with a railroad tycoon like Davis on the Democratic ticket) faced challenge from Roosevelt. In 1902, his administration had signaled a break from big business, specifically from railroad men, with the filing of an antitrust suit against a gigantic railroad holding company called Northern Securities. The company controlled the entire transcontinental network of the Pacific Northwest and had formed several years earlier as a cooperative measure between Harriman and rival railroad titans. Roosevelt shared a personal friendship with Harriman, but the scale and imperious behavior of Northern Securities had prompted Roosevelt to, in his own words, "take[] down the fences of a very great and very arrogant corporation." Roosevelt's decision, and the lawsuit's eventual success, captured the spirit of a reformist age that witnessed the ascent of muckraking journalism and critical novels like *The Octopus*. According to some papers, "it was the northern securities case that clinched Roosevelt's nomination for President." The nation's leader had become a "trust buster," a reputation he carried into his 1904 election bid.[105]

Despite this, the titans of industry, recognizing the likelihood of a Roosevelt victory, lined up to fill his campaign coffers, and the president accepted their tributes. Harriman personally contributed $50,000, while Gould gave a staggering half million dollars. These vast sums led a fading and desperate Judge Parker in the final weeks of the election season to accuse Roosevelt of either blackmailing corporations or promising special favors to secure their contributions. A furious Roosevelt responded, "I would ask all honest men whether they seriously deem it possible that the course this Administration has taken in every matter, from the Northern Securities suit [onward], is compatible with any theory of public behavior save the theory of doing exact justice to all men without fear and without favoritism." [106]

Roosevelt's impassioned defense helped secure him a landslide victory several days later. The pugnacious leader who had first gained the White House through tragedy finally had a mandate. His campaign had triumphed nearly everywhere outside the former Confederacy, even in Davis's home state of West Virginia.

The inglorious end of Davis's vice presidential run freed the aging West Virginian to once again focus on the railway and Pepper's report. He soon began arranging a celebratory dinner to honor Pepper and, hopefully, his old colleague Andrew Carnegie.

Scheduling conflicts ultimately prevented Carnegie's attendance, but in his absence, on Davis's urging, Carnegie submitted a brief letter to be read aloud at the dinner. "Against the big navy programme [of Roosevelt]," Carnegie wrote, "let us put the Pan-American Railway, which would cost less money in the next twenty years.... If the United States gave the $100,000,000 toward the railway now spent yearly on the navy ... we should do more to eliminate the element of danger, which at best is small, than we shall with all the warships we can build." When the dinner finally took place, in March 1905, the reading of Carnegie's surprisingly combative letter trumped any of the actual speeches from the numerous diplomats and politicians in attendance. [107]

Carnegie's attack had placed the Pan-American Railway suddenly at the center of a debate that he had been waging for years with Roosevelt over the future of the United States' role in the world. Their clash, at its core, asked whether the United States stood for idealism (a faith in international institutions and legal structures) or realism (a belief that power dictates outcomes or, put simply, might makes right). Neither man held absolutist views, but Carnegie favored the former and Roosevelt the latter. Carnegie also insisted that US projections of power, to the extent they occur, remain in the Western Hemisphere, while Roosevelt held global ambitions. As Carnegie once explained to Roosevelt, "I see grave complications probable in the unfair attempt, as I think it, of enforcing the Monroe Doctrine on our own continent, and yet claiming the right to interfere in other continents. 'America for Americans' implies Europe for Europeans, Asia for Asiatics." [108]

Each of them used their considerable personal influence to advance their perspective. Roosevelt, as president, furthered his agenda through an expansive naval program, the "taking" of Panama, and his December 1904 declaration that the United States would behave as a police power in the hemisphere, a policy soon known as the Roosevelt Corollary to the Monroe Doctrine. Carnegie, as the world's richest man, typically spoke loudest through his wallet, funding peace initiatives around the country and abroad.

In the weeks leading up to the Pan-American Railway dinner, Roosevelt and Carnegie had been arguing passionately in correspondence over the suppression of the Philippines and over a proposed international arbitration treaty, which the president had not supported to Carnegie's satisfaction. Carnegie's letter to Davis's dinner guests reframed their debate anew: a large navy stood for endless and expensive militarism, the Pan-American Railway for peace and hemispheric harmony.[109]

Several days after the dinner, Carnegie elaborated on his views in an editorial that the *New-York Tribune* had solicited.

> I need not enlarge upon the security which direct railway connection would give to the Monroe Doctrine, compared to a fleet of warships. . . . What territory worth having could combined Europe hold in South America against forces which we could send . . . if we had direct railway communication and the invaders had to transport their armies by sea? . . . The proposition really is: Six battleships added to our navy and provision made for their maintenance, against a railway connection with Buenos Ayres; the cost of a great navy being perpetual and without cessation, year after year, the cost of the railroad ceasing soon after it is put in operation. . . . The ships are always subject to attack by foes, the railway is immune . . . thus settling this Monroe Doctrine for all time.

The forceful editorial seemed like a potential shot across the bow of Roosevelt's naval fleet. However, Carnegie failed to back his words with his millions. His commentary, if anything, only managed to bind the idea of the Pan-American Railway with the opinions of someone Roosevelt increasingly viewed as an impractical and naive meddler in his presidency.[110]

But Carnegie represented only one perspective on the Pan-American Railway. His colleague Davis chose to frame the project instead in economic terms. Davis noted that, according to recent government figures, US trade with Mexico had grown in parallel with the development of the rail systems connecting the two countries. The commerce in the rest of the hemisphere remained dominated by European nations, just as had been the case when Helper dreamed up his railway idea in 1866 or when Blaine convened the First Pan-American Conference in 1889. The economic evidence from Mexico suggested that the Pan-American Railway could remedy this problem in each country it touched.[111]

Davis personally reached out to Roosevelt once more several months after the Carnegie dinner. As he explained, "The increased volume of our trade with Mexico shows some of the advantages we derive from railroad communication with that country. This leads me to ask you to consider, in connection with your forthcoming [State of the Union] message to Congress, the importance to the United States of the proposed Pan-American Railway."

Roosevelt, however, saw his upcoming address as a chance to highlight an agenda that included canal construction, naval buildup, and railway regulation. None of these goals aligned well with the Pan-American Railway, especially given Carnegie's recent editorial and Harriman's ongoing expansion into Mexico. In late October 1905, Roosevelt wrote to Davis, explaining, "I am fully awake to the importance of the All-American Railway, but I do not know quite what can be done about it now. I have to deal with so many matters in my message, that I do not want to add another unless there is something immediate that I can gain by it." As long as Roosevelt remained in the White House, the possibility of the US government working to further the Pan-American Railway seemed remote at best.[112]

Despite Roosevelt's demurral, the subject of the Pan-American Railway soon appeared before Congress, though not in a guise that Davis would have preferred. The Pan-American Railway's original promoter, Hinton Rowan Helper, quite likely in the throes of dementia, had concluded that "distant and despicably dishonest schemers" intended to "perpetrate grossly guilty and ghastly and ghostly and ghoulish games of greed" through the railway. An urgent letter he drafted on the matter reached Congress in December 1905. "I ardently request you," he wrote, "with well pondered and sincere views of immensely promoting the mental and moral and material interests of our entire Western Hemisphere, to do nothing at all . . . until after you shall have heard from me again on the subject." Helper never explained exactly what lay behind his concerns, but his protests only added to the challenges that Davis already faced.[113]

Davis, his path to congressional action stalled, turned his attention to the upcoming Third Pan-American Conference, scheduled for July 1906 in Rio de Janeiro, Brazil. The prior two conferences had played central roles in developing the Pan-American Railway idea, and this new gathering offered a similar opportunity to reignite popular and diplomatic interest in the project. Davis's lobbying began in January with a letter to Roosevelt's secretary of state Elihu Root that politely asked if "attention could be specifically called to the Pan-American Railway" at the Brazil conference. Davis then authored an article for the widely read *North American Review*, titled "The Pan-American Railway: Its Business Side," which again presented his economic arguments related to Mexican railway expansion.[114]

But his efforts once more butted up against an indifferent administration. Though Roosevelt, as always, endorsed the project on paper, he failed to appoint Davis or anyone else connected with the Pan-American Railway as a delegate to the Brazil conference. The United States, for the first time, would have no one directly advocating for what had once been the nation's boldest hemispheric initiative.[115]

Roosevelt's indifference, however, could not ultimately smother the project. Though the US government would never again take serious interest in the Pan-American Railway, the idea and the physical project continued to expand. Support for the Pan-American Railway was becoming particularly strong in Central America, especially with the route almost complete to the Guatemalan border and with the Panama Canal promising unprecedented trade opportunities; but six international border crossings stood in the way, each one the site of low-lying conflicts waiting to explode.

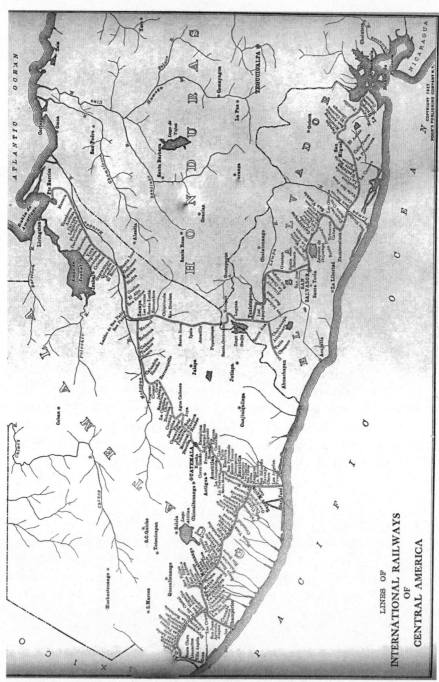

A 1926 map from the International Railways of Central America, a US corporation, depicting its multinational system.

CHAPTER THREE

The Route of Volcanoes

"To Crush Out Revolutions and Introduce Evolution"

On May 11, 1906, a small band of Guatemalan political exiles living in Mexico City boarded a northbound train heading to El Paso, twelve hundred miles away. Their fares authorized passage all the way to the US border, but their journey lasted just long enough to escape the Mexican capital and the watchful gaze of the Guatemalan government spies stationed there. Under cover of darkness, the exiles hastily disembarked and transferred to a private, southbound Pullman sleeper car, one equipped with rifles, saddles, and even medical dressings. This specially equipped car soon passed back through Mexico City without triggering the attention of the Guatemalan spy network. The exiles then continued along the sole rail route that traversed southern Mexico, first toward the port of Veracruz, next along the Tehuantepec Railroad, and finally to Neeland's Pan-American Railroad, which almost extended to the Guatemalan border.[1]

Upon their arrival in the far south of Mexico, the exiles, seeking to allay suspicions of their true intentions, posed as a group of potential investors. Such groups appeared fairly often along the route of the Pan-American Railroad thanks to the efforts of promoters like Neeland, though most came from the US Midwest or California. Nonetheless, the exiles, led by sixty-one-year-old former Guatemalan president Manuel Lisandro Barillas, bore "a very good resemblance to a high-class land prospecting group," according to a subsequent *Mexican Herald* report. Over the next two weeks, their small band grew to two hundred as sympathizers joined the clandestine plot.[2]

Finally, on May 27, 1906, Barillas and his two hundred men crossed the southern border and stormed into Guatemala. Additional forces simultaneously entered Guatemala from neighboring El Salvador and British

Honduras (current-day Belize). A revolution had erupted in the land of volcanoes.[3]

The forces behind this uprising had been building since 1898, when Manuel Estrada Cabrera assumed the presidency of Guatemala. Estrada Cabrera considered himself a farsighted leader in the mold of Mexico's Porfirio Díaz, but his detractors viewed him as an intolerable tyrant even by the debased standards of Central American despots. William Sands, a US diplomat in the region, described Estrada Cabrera as "astute, cold-blooded, and pitiless." Estrada Cabrera had initially gained his position following a presidential assassination that many suspected he had arranged personally. Soon, power and paranoia consumed him in equal parts and, as Sands observed, the dictator "lost all ideas except that of defending himself against his ubiquitous enemies." According to rumors that most accepted as incontrovertibly true, Estrada Cabrera only ate meals prepared by his own mother and slept in a different bed each night to avoid his enemies. Under his tenure, a network of government spies honeycombed the country. Anyone suspected of disloyalty faced torture; murder; or, if they were fortunate, mere confiscation of their property and exile.[4]

Estrada Cabrera's obsession with his own protection left him well prepared for the Barillas-led revolution, despite its broad scope and element of surprise. Guatemala's national army reportedly counted seven thousand full-time professional soldiers with thirty thousand more in reserve, and Estrada Cabrera kept his generals complacent, allowing them to grow rich selling native Indian labor and terrorizing planters for tribute. The dictator himself remained safely ensconced in the capital, Guatemala City, nestled five thousand feet above sea level among mountainous terrain, far inland and geographically protected against any of the rebel entry points.

Facing such defenses, the rebellion never managed to threaten the capital. However, along the Salvadoran frontier, both sides locked in a tense stalemate, and Estrada Cabrera seemed poised to pursue a military campaign against his neighbor, whose president was one of the Guatemalan strongman's "ubiquitous enemies." The revolution begun along the Pan-American Railroad was threatening to transform into international war at any moment.[5]

*   *   *

Into the midst of this chaotic situation suddenly appeared J. M. Neeland. He had been dreaming of extending his Pan-American Railroad into Central America for years and, with construction almost complete in southern Mexico, finally decided to act. The threatened war between Guatemala and El Salvador seemed only to inspire him. He believed that his railroad might well resolve the region's political instability, offering a foundation for the sort of development and interconnectivity that could free Central America from revolutionary violence. Many of the region's diplomats, politicians, and businessmen agreed with this assessment. The same day Neeland departed for Guatemala, one prominent member of the American colony in Mexico City authored an article arguing, "To crush out revolutions and introduce evolution along healthy lines is the mission of the Pan-American Railway."[6]

Neeland headed to Central America carrying a "big box" reportedly "filled with blue prints that show every curve and gradient of the road . . . from the northern boundary of Guatemala to a connection with the Panama railway." His first stop, in Estrada Cabrera–controlled Guatemala, yielded few definitive results, but on the next stop, in El Salvador, the government greeted him warmly, promising a subsidized concession as soon as hostilities ceased. The faster the conflict subsided, the faster Neeland could embark on part of his next great project: the Pan-American route south of Mexico.[7]

By this point, six weeks since Barillas first launched his revolution, the threatened war between Guatemala and El Salvador began to gain the attention of President Roosevelt. Soon the US president sent a direct cable to his Salvadoran counterpart that cautioned, "Disturbance of the peace of Central America inflicts grievous injury upon the United States and causes the gravest concern to the United States, whose sole desire is to see its neighbors at peace."

In Roosevelt's view, instability anywhere in Central America threatened the security of his planned Panama Canal, the centerpiece of his foreign policy. Moreover, his robust interpretation of the Monroe Doctrine, the so-called Roosevelt Corollary, had committed the United States to acting as a sort of police power in the region. Failure to restore peace in Central America would, therefore, not only undermine Roosevelt's international leadership but also risk opening the door for European nations to exert stronger influence in the United States' geopolitical backyard.[8]

Roosevelt, however, felt that he could not act without cooperation from

Porfirio Díaz. Central America and Mexico shared strong cultural, social, and political ties that reached back to the era of Spanish conquest, and Díaz, already in power for more than a quarter century, loomed as the single largest political figure in the region. Roosevelt had long admired Díaz's surefooted leadership and had previously suggested that the Mexican president should assert more authority over his unstable southern neighbors. In 1901, Roosevelt had gone so far as to declare, "For Mexico there are but two roads; to absorb the small republics of Central America as far as Panama, because they are always at war; or to belong to the United States." While neither of these stark options interested Díaz, he strongly favored stability, and, in the wake of the threatened war between Guatemala and El Salvador, soon agreed to cooperate with Roosevelt in seeking peace.[9]

Even with Díaz's assistance, Roosevelt nonetheless faced a diplomatic situation that appeared hopeless. On July 10, two days prior to their agreement, the US minister handling negotiations in Guatemala had cabled the secretary of state, "all efforts for peace are useless." However, a diplomatic window quickly opened thanks to one well-placed bullet that a sniper fired at El Salvador's preeminent military leader, a former president who had entered the conflict without civilian authorization and had almost single-handedly maintained the Salvadoran campaign. The loss, according to US diplomats, left El Salvador "anxious for peace." Soon Guatemala's Estrada Cabrera consented to a mediated peace process as well, reportedly to ensure that "the United States government guarantee[d] that further hostilities against Guatemala will cease."

During a flurry of telegrams that followed, both sides (as well as neighboring Honduras, which had entered the fray in defensive alliance with El Salvador at the last moment) agreed to meet aboard the US cruiser *Marblehead* to hash out peace terms in the presence of US and Mexican observers.[10]

On July 19, 1906, representatives from all the nations involved boarded the *Marblehead*, which promptly carried them nine miles from shore. The hope for peace lay inside a conversation unfolding in the Pacific Ocean. According to a widely spread story that diplomat Sands later recounted, "It was charged that the Yankee officer in command of the Marblehead had laid her broadside against the long rollers of the Pacific and had let her wallow there until the conferees were ready to sign anything." The delegates only escaped the punishing conditions after reaching an agreement that both concluded the hostilities and mandated joint US- and Mexican-led arbitration of any future disputes.[11]

For Roosevelt, the treaty signed aboard the USS *Marblehead* marked a major diplomatic victory. He had proven his leadership in Central America before the entire international community. The *Marblehead* accords also complemented work he had recently done helping to negotiate the end of the Russo-Japanese War, a feat that soon garnered him the 1906 Nobel Peace Prize. The stain of his having "taken" Panama three years earlier seemed to have lifted somewhat.[12]

Roosevelt's triumph, however, only strengthened Estrada Cabrera's tyrannical grip over Guatemala. The United States, the strongest nation in the hemisphere, had given the dictator the official stamp of approval in the eyes of his nation and the world. Estrada Cabrera had accepted limited US involvement in his affairs for de facto protection against the externally supported revolutionary movements that posed the greatest threat to his regime. One Guatemalan dissident complained to the State Department the next year, "The signing of peace was instrumental in affirming Estrada Cabrera's power and ever since he has given broader vent to his policy of rigor and cruelty."[13]

Neeland, meanwhile, benefited in his own right from the *Marblehead* accords. The day the *Marblehead* summit commenced, El Salvador confirmed plans to issue him a railway concession, reportedly "on the same conditions as those granted by Mexico." The *Mexican Herald* soon asserted that Neeland's new project was "looked upon with favor from a financial viewpoint." The potential extension of the Pan-American Railway as far as the Panama Canal had never before seemed more viable.[14]

In a remarkable coincidence, the *Marblehead* treaties had been signed the day before the long-awaited Third Pan-American Conference was scheduled to open in Rio de Janeiro, Brazil.

Brazil had never before hosted an international gathering of such magnitude, and an air of anticipation suffused Rio's downtown streets. When the delegates finally arrived for the opening ceremonies, they encountered huge, jubilant crowds. According to witnesses, warships in the city's harbor cast their searchlights against the conference's main pavilion, "making it almost as light as day" as the first session began at 8:00 p.m. on July 21, 1906.[15]

The conference provided the first hemispheric forum in five years, a period that had witnessed the US-backed Panamanian Revolution as well as the United States' taking over of Santo Domingo's customs receipts, two events that had inflamed critics of the "Colossus of the North." As Sands noted, many Latin Americans felt that Roosevelt "was indeed one of their own most characteristic types of politician, the *cacique* or *caudillo*, the uninhibited tribal or party Chieftain, with his own private gunmen or his own private army paid by the government." However, Roosevelt's sudden diplomatic success in Central America, achieved without the landing of marines or any overt show of naval force, softened such anti-Americanism significantly. Roosevelt's cooperative work with Díaz even prompted a special resolution of thanks from a delegate representing Argentina, a nation that had historically locked horns with the United States over hemispheric affairs.[16]

This newfound goodwill received an additional boost in Rio through the personal appearance of Elihu Root, the secretary of state in Roosevelt's second term. Root, a corporate lawyer and consummate Republican insider, displayed greater commitment to hemispheric affairs than any of his predecessors save James G. Blaine or Henry Clay, and his trip to Brazil marked the first time that someone holding his office had conducted an official visit to a foreign nation. "We all feel happy that the first visit was to Latin America," declared the Brazilian ambassador to the United States. In order to "perpetuate the memory" of Root's visit, Brazil named the Rio conference's central building the Monroe Palace. Root, for his part, amplified these fraternal sentiments through speeches filled with soaring rhetoric and high-minded appeals to hemispheric unity and economic integration, a velvet-gloved hand holding Roosevelt's proverbial "big stick." The lead US delegate at the conference, William Buchanan, who possessed broad experience in Pan-American affairs, noted, "[T]he visit of the Secretary of State to South America has resulted in greater good to our relations with Central and South America than any one thing that has heretofore taken place in our diplomatic history with them."[17]

Root, like the president he served, insisted that the Rio conference aimed not to advance concrete political agendas but rather to promote ideals "the full realization of which may be postponed to a distant future." His efforts along these lines helped to delay resolution of the most pressing political issue, a proposal known as the Drago Doctrine, which prohibited the use of foreign military intervention to enforce payment of delinquent sovereign debt. Root focused instead on strengthening the fledgling Bureau of American Republics, the almost stillborn child of the First Pan-American Conference, and the Rio delegates gave the beloved Root nearly unanimous support. The secretary of state subsequently appealed to Carnegie for $750,000 to fund a new building in Washington, DC, that could house what would now be known as the Pan-American Union.[18]

Carnegie quickly consented, but stressed that he ultimately considered his philanthropy in service of the great intercontinental railroad. As he wrote to Root,

> You very kindly mention my membership of the first Pan-American Conference and advocacy of the Pan-American Railway, the gaps of which are being slowly filled. The importance of this enterprise impresses itself more and more upon me, and I hope to see it accomplished. I am happy, therefore, in stating that it will be one of the pleasures of my life to furnish to the Union of all the Republics of this hemisphere, the necessary funds ($750,000) from time to time as may be needed for the construction of an international home in Washington.[19]

Root favored the Pan-American Railway as well. As he noted at the Rio conference, "Nothing polices a country like a railroad. Nothing material so surely discourages revolution." The secretary of state, however, never pushed for the Pan-American Railway as he had the expanded Pan-American Union.[20]

The sudden lack of US leadership on the Pan-American Railway question after more than fifteen years had left the other nations at the Rio conference unsure how to proceed with its development. While the topic commanded widespread attention from the delegates, the few substantive proposals put forward gained little traction. In the end, the Rio conference simply passed resolutions reaffirming the conclusions of the prior Pan-American Conference of 1901 and confirmed the "existence" of a permanent committee whose US members—Davis, Carnegie, and Pepper—were wholly absent from the proceedings thanks to Roosevelt.[21]

The Pan-American Conference system, so instrumental in developing the Pan-American Railway idea since the first meeting in 1889, no longer seemed a useful mechanism for advancing the project. Ideals alone did not build railroads. Nor could they ensure the peace so essential to the Pan-American Railway's southward expansion.

In Central America, almost as soon as the Rio conference concluded, the shortcomings of the *Marblehead* accords began to surface. The terms agreed upon at sea had only applied to the three belligerent nations (Guatemala, El Salvador, and Honduras), leaving Costa Rica and Nicaragua unaffected by the new accords. Costa Rica, historically the most peaceful and stable nation in the region, had soon agreed to host a follow-up conference aimed at expanding the *Marblehead* provisions to all of Central America, but Nicaragua refused to attend altogether.[22]

Decision-making authority in Nicaragua rested almost entirely with President José Santos Zelaya, who had held power continuously since 1893. Zelaya viewed himself as another liberal progressive like Porfirio Díaz, a personal friend of the Nicaraguan leader. Zelaya's ideas on progress included not only the development of railroads—in his words, "arteries spreading our agricultural and mineral riches, our vital energy, throughout the nation"— but also the restoration of the defunct Federal Republic of Central America (1823–1838), a dream of many liberals throughout the isthmus.[23]

Zelaya's progressive rhetoric, however, obscured a rank tyranny every bit as merciless as that of Guatemala's Estrada Cabrera. In the words of Sands, the US diplomat, "the difference between Zelaya and Estrada [Cabrera] was about the difference between a jaguar and a bushmaster snake." Sands's diplomatic colleague William Merry, the US minister to Nicaragua, laid out his thoughts on Zelaya in a December 1906 letter he sent to Secretary of State Root, written in longhand because "confidential typewriting" was "hard to obtain." As Merry observed, "Zelaya admits no personal neutrality." Merry's list of complaints, which he assured were "publicly known to all intelligent men in Nicaragua," stretched out for ten pages. The dictator, Merry observed, tortured his enemies with "enemas of chile peppers," sexually exploited teenaged girls at his whim, and had gone "crazy on graft." Merry insisted that Zelaya had personally assured him of a desire someday to retire to Europe, where, the handwritten letter noted, "his money awaits him."[24]

Zelaya and Guatemala's Estrada Cabrera, despite their similarities, viewed one another as mortal enemies. The frequent revolutionary attempts they each faced stemmed in part from their own international meddling. Zelaya, for instance, had openly supported the 1906 Barillas-led aborted revolution, even sending a gunboat to Guatemala's largest Atlantic port, reportedly to intercept Estrada Cabrera should he have attempted "to elude his pursuers and escape in that direction."[25]

The two men's rivalry destabilized the entire region, especially El Salvador and Honduras, which each had the unfortunate geographical fate of being sandwiched between the feuding dictators. The two middle countries served both as staging grounds for revolutionary movements led by exiles and as scenes for de facto proxy wars between Estrada Cabrera and Zelaya.

El Salvador, with its small territory and dense population, preserved some degree of political autonomy and effective military defense in spite of these exogenous challenges. But the larger and less densely populated Honduras faced a hopeless situation, with the contest between dictators overtaxing an already weak government besieged by foreign capitalists. As historian Walter LeFeber noted of this period, "Honduras was less a nation than a customs house surrounded by adventurers."[26]

The resolution of the most recent spurt of Central American violence aboard the USS *Marblehead* in July 1906 had infuriated Zelaya. The accords had not only spared Estrada Cabrera from a prolonged conflict, but had also brought US diplomatic oversight into the region for the first time. And the Nicaraguan dictator, unlike his Guatemalan rival, displayed an unabashed anti-Americanism as profound as his tyrannical excesses. Zelaya's grievances against the United States included bitterness over the US decision to select Panama over Nicaragua as a canal site after years spent cajoling the dictator. However, the anti-Americanism of Zelaya went deeper than mere scorn, to the very core of his ideas about sovereignty, power, and pride. According to Merry, Zelaya boasted that he was "not afraid of the United States" and considered the *Marblehead* accords a "farce." Nicaragua's refusal to join the follow-up Central American peace conference at San José, Costa Rica, in September 1906 had stemmed mainly from Zelaya's opposition to the *Marblehead* resolution requiring mandatory arbitration under US-led authority of any future disputes.[27]

The US State Department only learned that Zelaya officially "decline[d] to be bound" by the *Marblehead* accords in early January 1907, six months after their enactment. The timing of this announcement had appeared somewhat arbitrary until a telegram arrived later that day from Honduras. It announced the outbreak of a new revolutionary movement along that nation's border with Nicaragua, "believed to be aided by President Zelaya." According to numerous sources, the purpose of this revolt was to help Zelaya remove Honduran president Manuel Bonilla, an ally of Estrada Cabrera. Soon the rebels drew the Honduran military into a firefight that crossed into Nicaragua.[28]

This violation of Nicaraguan sovereignty created an ideal pretext for Zelaya, who continued to insist publicly that he played no role in the rebellion. He quickly declared the trespass tantamount to a declaration of war and then brushed off US attempts to invoke arbitration along the lines of the *Marblehead* accords. As he defiantly informed Roosevelt, "I must say that public sentiment in Nicaragua is in the same state as that of the American people when the S.S. *Maine* was blown up."

Zelaya's military soon launched a full-scale campaign into Honduras. In late March, the Honduran capital of Tegucigalpa fell. The United States appealed for peace, but Zelaya truculently resisted until mid-April, by which point it was clear that the government of Honduras had been fully ousted. A US chargé d'affaires then mediated a peace treaty, completed on April 23, 1907, in Amapala, Honduras.[29]

Once more, Roosevelt had achieved a diplomatic peace in Central America—a vital precursor to any southern advancement on the Pan-American Railway—but peace, as with the *Marblehead* accords nine months prior, had arrived only through the strengthening of a ruthless dictator.

The signing of the April 1907 peace treaty at Amapala coincided with a new surge in tensions between Guatemala and Mexico. The two countries' relationship had taken a hostile turn two weeks prior to the Amapala ceremony when a knife-wielding Guatemalan murdered Manuel Lisandro Barillas, the leader of the failed 1906 revolution, who was once again residing in Mexico City. Most in Mexico blamed the murder on Estrada Cabrera, but the Guatemalan dictator predictably denied any involvement and then refused to cooperate with Mexico's investigation. Formal relations between the two countries quickly broke down completely. One Mexican paper, summarizing popular sentiment, declared that Estrada Cabrera had "ripped off his mask . . . to reveal the disgusting deformity beneath." Soon, President Díaz began moving tens of thousands of troops to the border along the Pan-American Railroad and urged Neeland to complete the road as fast as possible.[30]

Neeland now joined the chorus of voices demanding the prompt removal of Estrada Cabrera. He had grown tired of being denied by the Guatemalan dictator in his efforts to secure a Pan-American concession. From Estrada Cabrera's perspective, as one observer noted, a railroad connection to Mexico or El Salvador seemed like an invitation to a foreign military invasion, a "drawbridge" that could cross "the moat of his baronial castle." In mid-May 1907, Neeland wrote the US ambassador in Mexico City pleading for some type of Roosevelt-led intervention, adding: "[S]hould we build the railroad through Guatemala (which we will), and should I be fortunate enough to make $1 or a million out of it, I am perfectly willing to sign a guaranteed

contract that I will donate the profits to any orphan asylum or hospital . . .
but it would suit me better to donate it to assist in forming a humane government for that rich little country." [31]

Neeland's contempt for Estrada Cabrera drove the rail promoter straight
into the arms of Zelaya. The goal of building a railroad to Panama aligned
nicely with the Nicaraguan dictator's long-standing ambition of uniting the
isthmus into one republic. Neeland soon explained, "President Zelaya is the
only ruler in Central America who is working honestly and seriously toward
the great end of the confederation and with him we have been willing to
cast our lot, believing sincerely that it is through him, and him only as matters now stand, that the ultimate success of confederation can be hoped for."
A Zelaya-led confederation, however, would require the forceful removal of
leaders in Guatemala, El Salvador, and possibly Costa Rica. [32]

By June 1907, Neeland was meeting regularly with pro-Zelaya revolutionists in Mexico City and reportedly providing them financial support,
including funds that President Díaz funneled to him through ongoing subsidies to the Pan-American Railroad in Mexico. Suddenly, a hemispheric
railway meant to promote peace had become a driving force behind planned
revolutions in multiple countries at once. As the *San Francisco Call* declared
in the subhead of a June 11 article, "Railroad Promoters Said to Be Behind
Great Conspiracy; Diaz is Giving Aid." [33]

The very morning that this *San Francisco Call* article appeared, Zelaya
launched a new military campaign, dispatching several hundred of his soldiers in a gunboat bound for Acajutla, the largest port in El Salvador. The
men soon stormed the Salvadoran city in the name of a pro-union politician, and the poorly defended port fell immediately. The six-week-old peace
treaty signed at Amapala had been shattered. The *Washington Post* declared
the siege of Acajutla "the beginning of the great struggle in Central America which has been so long coming." [34]

The Nicaraguans, however, held Acajutla for only one day before the
Salvadoran military mobilized and drove them out. Following this encounter, tensions in Central America remained elevated but largely nonviolent
for several months. Zelaya, Neeland, and their pro-unionist revolutionaries
continued plotting while Estrada Cabrera aided and sheltered Honduran
president Manuel Bonilla, who was bent on reclaiming his country from a
Zelaya-backed regime. [35]

*　　*　　*

In Washington, Roosevelt and Root hoped to restore peace once more through "moral force," a popular euphemism for high-minded diplomacy in the shadow of US gunboats. But the United States faced a dilemma: the Roosevelt administration had yet to officially recognize the new Zelaya-backed regime in Honduras. This stance made any formal diplomacy between the two nations impossible, and the Honduran regime had spent months in vain pleading for the United States to change its stance. In late August 1907, the Honduran foreign minister once more begged Root to reconsider, insisting that US recognition was now "necessary for the maintenance of [our] neutrality." This latest appeal, set against the background of impending war, finally persuaded Roosevelt, who soon invited President Díaz to join him "in lending friendly influence in the cause of peace and humanity."

Díaz, up to this point, had been persistently fueling the political tension in the region, especially through his involvement with Neeland and the Pan-American Railroad. But Díaz's gaze rarely faced in one direction alone, and he found few advantages in forcing a rift with his northern neighbor. The Mexican president went so far as to call Roosevelt's Central American peace plan "incapable of improvement."[36]

The proposal that Roosevelt and Root were putting forward called for a full-scale, isthmus-wide diplomatic summit. They were hoping to replace the hasty, reactive *Marblehead* accords of the year prior with proper treaties and to establish mechanisms for their enforcement.

Eventually, all the nations of Central America agreed to participate. A conference was then scheduled for mid-November 1907 in Washington, DC, at the Bureau of American Republics (the soon-to-be Pan-American Union), a location the State Department considered "common neutral ground." Mexico and the United States each also agreed to send an official observer. Enrique Creel, the banker and Pan-American Railroad investor, would represent the Díaz regime, while William Buchanan, the lead US delegate from the last Pan-American Conference, in Rio, would attend on behalf of Roosevelt.[37]

Zelaya and Estrada Cabrera could have refused to cooperate at any point and risked a potential, though unlikely, US military response, but they had both already proven an ability to manipulate US diplomacy into increased power.

The Washington Conference—the informal name given to this Central American gathering—convened on November 14, 1907. Secretary of State

Root personally opened the inaugural session and addressed the delegates with the same lofty cadences heard earlier in Rio de Janeiro. This time, however, his remarks included a plea that the participants "find practical definite methods" to ensure that "the great principles you declare are not violated." Root was alluding to a proposed Central American court of arbitration, a popular idea among international lawyers in which a permanent body of jurists drawn from each isthmian nation would review the merits of any regional dispute impartially.[38]

Root's request enjoyed the support of most of the professional diplomats who filled the delegate ranks, but some in the audience had another, more radical solution in mind to ensure peace.

As soon as discussions got under way, a resolution calling for a full-fledged political union among the five states emerged from the Honduran delegation, which was operating under "special instructions" from their Zelaya-backed government. This surprise resolution immediately gained the backing of the Nicaraguan delegates, who assured that they acted out of principle alone. They even pledged that their controversial president would voluntarily step down if such a gesture advanced Central American union, a bargaining bluff that Zelaya knew no one could call. Suddenly, Roosevelt's peace conference had transformed into a Zelaya-led referendum on the possibility of creating a new nation.[39]

The Guatemalan delegation, caught as much off-guard as the United States, understandably opposed any union program that originated with Zelaya, but Estrada Cabrera's representatives faced an uphill battle to outflank the Nicaraguans. Political union stirred the hearts of Central American diplomats more than any other goal, except perhaps the Pan-American Railway itself. And outright opposition to the principle of union remained diplomatically problematic, especially as most Central American constitutions contained clauses favoring the eventual return to a single republic. Even the delegation from El Salvador, although largely aligned with Estrada Cabrera, inclined toward union "in principle."

While Estrada Cabrera's men had initially approached the Washington Conference with instructions simply to reaffirm the *Marblehead* accords of the year prior, they soon, in desperation, began to vastly expand their original plans in an effort to sidetrack a Zelaya-led union. After intense negotiations, the delegates from El Salvador and Costa Rica agreed to reject the union proposal in favor of the Guatemalans' alternative offer to "harmonize" the "economic, moral, political, and material elements" of all the Central American nations.[40]

The lead Costa Rican delegate in these discussions had long advocated the Pan-American Railway, perhaps more than any other Central American diplomat, and his influence helped ensure that the harmonizing of "material interests" meant advancement of the international route.[41] Soon he leveraged his success from the negotiations with Guatemala into a campaign for a new regional railway accord. His proposed resolutions stipulated that the governments would arrange surveys, subsidies, and special privileges to ensure the Pan-American Railway's speedy completion. Eventually the Costa Rican campaign succeeded, and all five countries agreed to sign the region's first convention on the Pan-American Railway.[42]

News of this newest Pan-American Railway treaty nonetheless attracted few headlines. The press, both in the United States and abroad, focused instead on another great success at the Washington Conference, the authorization of a new permanent court of arbitration, the idea that Root had advocated at the outset. The proposed Peace Court, the first of its kind anywhere in the world, swiftly placed Central America at the vanguard of international law after years of being seen as an uncivilized backwater in the eyes of the world. No longer would treaties be "written in water," to quote Root. Instead, any violation of the agreements signed in Washington would face the scrutiny of five jurists, one from each of the Central American nations. And these jurists would hopefully provide a bulwark to defend Honduran neutrality, something each nation at the Washington Conference had explicitly vowed to respect.[43]

The new court represented the type of institutionalized commitment to peace that men like Carnegie had tirelessly pursued for so many years. The great Pan-American philanthropist himself later agreed to donate $100,000 to fund a lavish, permanent home for the new Peace Court in Cartago, Costa Rica. In the end, Root achieved exactly what he had sought at the Central American summit's outset.[44]

The Washington Conference finally drew to a close on December 20, 1907, after more than a month of labor. The initial fight over union that had split the conference yielded to the glories of international praise showered on the delegates. Central America now had the most advanced peace court in the world, and all the agreements signed in Washington, including the renewed commitment to the Pan-American Railway, would operate beneath the informal guarantees—the "moral force"—of the United States and Mexico. Excitement and congratulations drowned out any concerns over the wholly unresolved tensions between Zelaya and Estrada Cabrera. Secretary Root, who closed the conference personally, declared,

May the poor husbandman who cultivates the fields of your five Republics, may the miner who is wearing out his weary life in the hard labors of your mines, may the mothers who are caring for the infant children that are to make the peoples of Central America in the future, may the millions whose prosperity and happiness you have sought to advance here, may the unborn generations of the future in your beloved countries have reason to look back to this day with blessings upon the self-devotion and the self-restraint with which you have endeavored to serve their interests and to secure their prosperity and peace.[45]

Five months later, on the day the new Peace Court opened in late May 1908, mobs lined the streets of Cartago, Costa Rica. Children tossed flowers at the carriages carrying the newly appointed judges from the train station to the city's central plaza. The entire downtown had been transformed for the celebration, with buntings draping the main buildings, temporary arches crowning the intersections, and Mexican and US flags flying alongside those of the five Central American countries. Buchanan, who had traveled to the inauguration with Creel, announced to the throngs in the central plaza that he and his government "confidently look forward to your complete success."[46]

Buchanan's subsequent report to the State Department, however, displayed a more somber tone. He cautioned that the Central Americans lacked the "underlying necessary stratum" of unity necessary for the Peace Court to function properly.[47]

At the time the Peace Court opened, fissures in this "underlying stratum" were already starting to surface. The deposed Honduran president Manuel Bonilla, exiled in Guatemala, was once again organizing forces to reclaim his country from the Zelaya-backed regime that had been installed the year prior. Bonilla's supporters included both Estrada Cabrera and a legendary US mercenary soldier named Lee Christmas, who had a penchant for chewing glass to intimidate those around him. Word of the pending revolution quickly reached diplomat William Sands, once more in Guatemala on assignment for the State Department. Sands confronted Christmas, asserting that the revolution would violate the newly signed Washington treaties. Christmas supposedly replied, "I've seen plenty of men try to play poker with bad cards, but I'd like to see how you play it without no cards at all." Soon Christmas invaded Honduras from the Atlantic side while another pro-Bonilla force entered through El Salvador.[48]

In Nicaragua, Zelaya prepared for war but also appealed to the new Peace Court on behalf of Honduras. His earlier mockery of US attempts to deploy arbitration in the region seemed to have softened now that his own puppet regime faced a revolution in Honduras.

The court acted promptly, demanding the cessation of all hostilities while the judges reviewed the issues. This order found strong support from the US State Department, and soon the belligerent states all complied. As one Costa Rican paper noted, "Behind the court is the well-fed garrote of Theodore Roosevelt." US "moral force" and the new architecture of peace had outplayed the glass-chewing forces of revolution for the moment.[49]

Almost immediately after the Peace Court issued its order of cessation, Estrada Cabrera announced to great fanfare that he had authorized the completion of the Pan-American Railway in Guatemala, the prize Neeland had been seeking since 1906. The *Los Angeles Times* credulously observed, "No course more conducive to peace and prosperity can be imagined. . . . If [Estrada] Cabrera were as anxious for war and disturbance as some represent him to be, he would hardly be doing as he is."[50]

The new Pan-American contract, however, went to a company more interested in expanding its reach over the Pacific Guatemalan coffee trade paralleling the Pan-American route than in actually connecting the line with the Mexican system, as Neeland and countless Pan-Americanists desired. Some State Department officials confidentially insisted that Estrada Cabrera acted for "political capital only" in response to "exigencies of the political situation" that compelled the dictator to "show progress" on the Pan-American Railway. Estrada Cabrera, savvy as ever, had managed to transform the Pan-American Railway from a project of material progress and of Central American union into a diplomatic facade useful for manipulating the United States into tolerating his regime even while he flagrantly encouraged violations of the Washington Conference.[51]

Estrada Cabrera's decision to grant the Pan-American concession to a company with strictly domestic intentions not only stymied the larger hemispheric project, but also effectively condemned Neeland to failure in Central America. Neeland, in a last desperate effort, had asked the State Department once more to intervene against the dictator, adding, "I . . . hope to be working in Guatemala before the year closes, and should [Estrada] Cabrera still be in power he would unquestionably hire someone to assassinate me." But the State Department showed no interest in assisting Neeland. The promoter's years spent agitating for the Pan-American Railroad and sponsoring revolutions to bring about its southern expansion had all been for naught. Estrada Cabrera was an obstacle he simply could not overcome, and Neeland would never manage to construct a single line of track south of Mexico.[52]

Central America remained relatively quiet throughout the fall of 1908 while the Peace Court reviewed the case that Zelaya had brought, but the fragile balance of forces impeding warfare faced the destabilizing potential of a change in US presidents.

Roosevelt, who had overseen the formation of the region's peace architecture, had decided not to run for reelection and had designated William Howard Taft as his replacement. Taft was a pure product of US empire, having served as governor of the Philippines and then secretary of war under Roosevelt. Even Taft's three-hundred-plus-pound frame, so large that it required a new bathtub installed in the White House, seemed to encapsulate the swollen status of the United States since the War of 1898. In the November 1908 election, Taft defeated perennial Democratic presidential contender William Jennings Bryan, a victory that Roosevelt's strong endorsement helped underwrite.[53]

Taft soon placed responsibility for untangling Latin America's thorny challenges with his new secretary of state, Philander Knox, whose public career had commenced eight years earlier when President McKinley appointed him attorney general. Knox had led the successful prosecution of the Northern Securities case that transformed Roosevelt into a "trust buster," and the new secretary of state seemed to feel that similarly rigid enforcement of laws could succeed internationally in Latin America. According to the State Department's second-in-command, F. M. Huntington Wilson, Knox acted as "a complete autocrat in his domain" and demanded a "much stricter application" of the principles that his predecessor Root had employed flexibly and judiciously, insisting that "the respected must act respectably." The velvet glove holding the big stick had to be removed. Perhaps it was no surprise that, in the words of Huntington Wilson, "there was no love lost" between Knox and Root. Many on Root's diplomatic team, including Sands, quickly received their marching orders, and the gossip mill in Washington felt that the new staff's "ineptitude was colossal."[54]

At the time Taft and Knox assumed power in March 1909, circumstances in Central America appeared once more to be spinning toward violence.

The Peace Court in Cartago had delivered a ruling in December on its first case that satisfied no one. The decision split along predictable political lines, with the only somewhat neutral party, Costa Rica, issuing an intentionally ambiguous deciding opinion. By March, rumors flew that Zelaya was planning to invade El Salvador in revenge for its having hosted pro-Bonilla revolutionaries.[55]

Knox evaluated the Central American situation like a man who stumbled upon a street brawl and assumed that the fighter readying the next blow had been the aggressor all along. Knox's hasty evaluation soon found support from Zelaya's numerous critics, who insisted that all of Central America's problems ultimately stemmed from the Nicaraguan dictator. Mexican diplomats nonetheless urged Knox to continue Root's policy of cooperative engagement using "moral force," but Knox determined that Zelaya had to go, even though the rumored attacks on El Salvador never actually materialized. By early October 1909, the secretary of state had convinced Taft both of the need to take some "positive" action against Zelaya and of their ability to proceed without Mexico.[56]

Within days of Taft agreeing to this policy shift, Knox learned that the governor of one of Nicaragua's lightly populated Atlantic provinces had betrayed Zelaya and declared a revolution, with himself the new provisional president. This breakaway administration, which had support from anti-Zelaya factions within and without Nicaragua, immediately proclaimed its friendship toward the United States.[57]

Zelaya moved to crush the revolution as he had so many others before, but revolutionaries continued to pour in from neighboring states, and the United States took no action to stanch the flow. Many of the munitions the rebels used traveled aboard private US ships that belonged to companies looking to exploit the forests and potential banana lands of the Atlantic. Aid and support also appeared to be channeled through William Merry, the former US minister to Nicaragua who had been reassigned to Costa Rica after Zelaya demanded his removal in 1907.[58]

Three weeks into the revolution, Zelaya's government caught two inveterate US soldiers of fortune setting up a mine attack. Both men confessed to their actions, and the embattled Nicaraguan dictator swiftly authorized their execution, a highly questionable action under the law of war but an unambiguous message to the United States.[59]

Zelaya's bloody statement of defiance finally gave Knox the opportunity he had been awaiting. On December 1, the secretary of state severed all diplomatic relations with Nicaragua, declaring, "[T]he United States is convinced that the revolution represents the will of a majority of the Nicaraguan people more faithfully than does the Government of President Zelaya." Knox's decree suddenly reversed the United States' prior position of defending established regimes against revolutionary challenges. Mexico quickly dispatched Creel to Washington to plead for behavior more reminiscent of the Roosevelt-Root era, but Knox refused, insisting on seeing the revolution succeed, even if that meant direct military intervention. Soon the impossibility of victory impressed itself upon Zelaya. Knox had finally called his bluff.[60]

On December 21, 1909, Zelaya announced his resignation, effective immediately. A Mexican ship then provided Zelaya safe passage to Mexico City, where his old friend President Díaz offered him a warm reception. Zelaya eventually departed for Europe to live in exile and enjoy the riches that he had amassed through the exploitation of his own people. The man who had two years earlier offered to sacrifice his power for the cause of Central American union had instead done so, as he explained in a message to his nation, "in order to avoid harm to my country and desiring to place it in a position to renew friendly relations with the United States."[61]

Zelaya, however, would quickly become one of the world's greatest anti-American propagandists. In several works he subsequently authored, each filled with selective but damning evidence, he painted a disastrous picture of the United States that sympathetic readers across Europe and Latin America consumed with delight. Taft and Knox, according to Zelaya, had trampled the very peace treaties that Roosevelt and Root had worked so earnestly to foster two years prior in Washington. Zelaya insisted that his regime, unlike that of Estrada Cabrera, had never violated the Washington Conference treaties but that the United States decided to depose the Nicaraguan dictator regardless. To many outside the United States, Knox's decision appeared to be intervention for intervention's sake, a new tool for a power-mad nation trying to pick political winners in an endless quest for stability and subservience.[62]

The week after Zelaya announced his resignation, Knox attended a luncheon in Washington, DC, honoring Andrew Carnegie. The great philanthropist, distraught over the reports about the revolutionary violence in Nicaragua, announced unexpectedly that he would give $20 million to have peace in Central America. The only project under consideration that could have required such a massive sum was the Pan-American Railway, the great dream that Carnegie had been advocating for since the early 1890s.

Carnegie's proposal, however, left Knox visibly angered. The secretary of state seemed to feel that Carnegie intended for his offer to serve as a direct challenge to Knox's recent actions toward Nicaragua. According to newspaper reports, Knox curtly informed Carnegie that Central America "did not require money, but simply the use of a 'big stick.'"[63]

Relations between the United States and Central America had taken a destructive turn, with no resolution in sight. And Knox's diplomacy had also begun to spawn tensions with Mexico, home of the first thirteen hundred miles in the Pan-American Railway's route south of the United States.

A Tiger on the Tracks

During the summer of 1906, while Díaz and Roosevelt first collaborated to pacify Central America, Mexico's finance minister, José Yves Limantour, was traveling around New York City on a cooperative mission of his own. Limantour's trip resembled the one his mentor Matías Romero had taken in 1880, when the famous Delmonico's dinner occurred. Once again, a top Mexican governmental official was seeking to harmonize the interests of all north–south rail lines connecting with the United States. However, one major distinction separated Limantour's position from that of his deceased predecessor: Limantour wanted his own government, not US corporations, to have ultimate control.[64]

The Mexican government had long worried about the potential power of US corporations, and the issue had grown more pronounced following Collis P. Huntington's death in 1900. The rise of E. H. Harriman and a simultaneous mania for mergers that gripped Wall Street produced new behemoth combinations, such as Northern Securities, on scales unthinkable a generation prior. As one US railroad expert told the *Mexican Herald* in early 1901, "It is economically logical that the railroads of Mexico will be absorbed by some of these systems."[65]

The specter of Harriman, in particular, haunted Limantour. In early 1902 Harriman had made his interests in Mexico clear when he traveled to the capital and spoke with Díaz and Limantour together. Accounts of their conversation suggested that Harriman expressed the desire both to expand his Southern Pacific far below the northern state of Sonora and to spearhead a "community of interests" for all the north–south trunk lines connecting at Mexico City. Shortly after that trip, James Speyer, the financier controlling the Laredo and Eagle Pass lines to Mexico City, announced a restructuring of his Mexican rail holdings that placed Harriman on the board.[66]

Limantour finally decided during the spring of 1902 to "intervene in the fight" for control of his nation's transportation infrastructure using the "same tools" as the railroad companies themselves. His campaign began when his treasury department outbid Speyer for effective control of a line that would have provided Speyer's Mexican rail system a much-desired outlet to the gulf. According to Limantour, "[T]he entire world was shocked to see the government get involved."[67]

The surprise purchase compelled Speyer to entertain Limantour's appeals for greater involvement from the Mexican government. As Sands later noted, "Speyer was the sort of businessman who knew precisely what he wanted and precisely how much trouble and expense he was willing to suffer in getting it." Soon Speyer agreed to a complicated arrangement that granted the government of Mexico a controlling interest in his system's voting stock in exchange for Limantour's recently purchased gulf-outlet route as well as $4.5 million in cash and a few construction privileges. The deal, completed in July 1903, gave the Mexican government a degree of control over more than three thousand miles of track, about one-third of the nation's total, including two of the three trunk lines that linked the capital with the US border. State Department officials observing the arrangement from afar cautioned that Limantour's actions had been "of more importance than a mere business transaction." But Limantour insisted he had no need to expand government control any further, having successfully blocked the menace of US trusts generally and of Harriman specifically.[68]

Limantour largely maintained this position at the outset. By 1906, however, a sharp decline in the financial health of the Mexican Central, which controlled the prized El Paso–Mexico City route, moved Limantour to consider abandoning his earlier promises of governmental restraint. Limantour soon began recruiting Speyer to aid the Mexican government in purchasing the Mexican Central from US oil merchant Henry Clay Pierce, who had acquired the company during the 1901 shake-up following Huntington's death. Speyer, who himself held some Mexican Central debt, had long viewed Pierce as a rival and eventually agreed to join Limantour. But Pierce, stubbornly independent, resisted all initial efforts from the two men.

Negotiations dragged out over the summer of 1906, until Pierce's desperation for additional funds to cover debts from an ambitious expansion program eventually forced his capitulation.[69]

The final deal created a new state-owned company, the National Railways of Mexico. This company would include two boards of directors, one in New York City that Pierce would chair, and another in Mexico that Limantour would guide and that would handle most of the domestic management questions. The agreement also required that the new company's debt, held primarily by Pierce and Speyer, would carry a guarantee from the Mexican government. Limantour later observed of this guarantee, "I hesitated before the fear of a political crisis that might someday wipe out the colossal edifice I was trying to raise."[70]

In December 1906, Limantour proudly presented the National Railways plan to the Mexican Congress for approval. As he explained, his foresight and shrewd negotiations since 1902 had put his nation in a position to finally arrest the threat of US trusts, and governmental control had required little more than a debt guarantee and less than $10 million in total cash. The Mexican Congress quickly approved Limantour's plan. Fourteen months later, in March 1908, the National Railways finally began operations.[71]

Limantour had achieved a stunning success. The Mexican government now controlled all the trunk lines built during the Huntington era as well as their subsequent extensions, a system that included more than five thousand miles. After thirty years playing the risky game of externally led development, Mexico appeared to have shown that subservience to and dependence on foreign capitalists were not inevitable outcomes.[72]

In early May 1908, shortly after the inauguration of the National Railways, the final forty-mile section of Neeland's Pan-American Railroad opened for business. The governor of Mexico's southernmost state of Chiapas presided over the official ceremonies, and enthusiastic crowds rejoiced at the news. Every station on the three-hundred-mile-long line bore special decorations to honor the moment. After nearly seven years, Neeland's Pan-American Railroad was finally complete. Rail travel was now possible from the United States all the way to the last inhabited outpost in southern Mexico.[73]

Completion, however, denoted a technical accomplishment more than an actual delivery of service. Neeland had paid only for the barest construction necessary. One local Chiapas paper griped several months before the inauguration, "[T]he rail ties are all rotted or broken [and] the bridges are almost entirely provisional. . . . When it rains, water seeps into the cars and it's necessary to use an umbrella." The Mexican paper *Dictamen* added, "The service is among the worst known; from the first rails to the last, it has all been a chain of accidents and harms that have caused personal misfortune and loss." Hugh Pollard, an Englishman who traveled through Mexico, described his experience aboard with unsparing contempt:

> No English workman would care to use the Pan-American first-class accommodation for half an hour's ride, but we are condemned to have two days of it! . . . The heat soon gets unbearable, and the passengers lie inert on the blistering seats, drinking tepid beer, too slack to read or smoke, and almost unconscious of the attacks of clouds of venomous mosquitoes and coffee flies. . . . The journey drones on through the same scenery, and the train slows down to cross the little culverts and bridges. Everybody looks anxious. You feel the bridge sink and tremble beneath you.

Pollard's train, predictably, suffered a minor accident along its route north.[74]

Despite the Pan-American's many shortcomings, its strategic location helped maintain a steady stream of takeover rumors. As a *Los Angeles Times* correspondent observed in 1905, "'All roads lead to Rome' is a saying that can safely be paraphrased in Mexico [as] all roads lead to the Pan-American, the steel wedge that is entering the heart of Central and South America, from the heel of Mexico."[75]

One potential buyer was Limantour. His recently opened National Railways of Mexico controlled all the major lines north from Mexico City, and the Mexican government additionally held independent control of the main through route into southern Mexico that traveled along the Tehuantepec Railroad before reaching the Pan-American. The purchase of Neeland's three-hundred-mile-long rail line would thus give Limantour control over his nation's entire north–south rail corridor.[76]

However, many in "financial circles" believed that the likeliest purchaser was Harriman. Neeland's recently completed line stood in the path of a through route to Panama that Harriman hoped to build along the Pacific side of the Western Sierra Madres. The *Mexican Herald* bluntly asserted in mid-November 1908, "Harriman Is After Railroad to Panama." According to the article, Neeland "refused to either affirm or deny the story."[77]

Several factors seemed to favor Neeland's selling his recently finished line to one of these potential suitors. To begin with, the trials of day-to-day management had never suited Neeland as well as promotion, and any proceeds earned from selling the Pan-American could help finance new ventures, above all the Central American extension he had been working feverishly to realize. Additionally, the value of the Pan-American depended in large part on Mexican political stability, which seemed increasingly fragile. President Díaz, who was approaching eighty, had spoken of retiring, and serious challenges to his leadership had started to emerge. A further touch of urgency came from Neeland's lead investor and company president, David Doak, whose wife had recently discovered that her husband had been living a secret life with another woman while supposedly away on "business trips" related to the Pan-American. The news shocked Los Angeles society and left Doak scrambling to contest the costly divorce petition his wife planned to file. With each passing month, Neeland's motivation to effect a sale only appeared to increase.[78]

Neeland and Doak continued to play coy with the press throughout the spring and summer of 1909. But finally, in mid-August, news that they had decided to sell the Pan-American Railroad leaked out despite the "utmost secrecy and precaution" of everyone involved. The long-awaited announcement nonetheless provoked both surprise and scandal, for the supposed new owner was neither Harriman nor the Mexican government. Instead, at a purchase price of nearly $10 million gold, the Pan-American had "virtually been sold" to David E. Thompson, the sitting US ambassador to Mexico.[79]

Thompson, despite his diplomatic position, possessed broad knowledge of both the railroading business and Mexican investing. Born in Nebraska, he had shot through the ranks of the Burlington Railroad and then built a small investment empire, including properties in Mexico. Alongside his fortune grew a reputation for questionable business ethics, but he found enough supporters to consider politics. A failed Republican Senate bid in 1900 soon led to an appointment as minister to Brazil, and after several years Thompson lobbied successfully for a transfer to Mexico, where his earlier investment activities had yielded a warm relationship with Díaz.

Díaz and Thompson grew steadily closer throughout the latter's tenure as US ambassador. Thompson supported Díaz without fail or folly, whether that meant aiding the cooperative work to contain the crises of Central America, or helping to facilitate Limantour's National Railways, or providing diplomatic cover for the countless US-backed ventures that Díaz supported. Díaz, however, was not able to spare Thompson from the diplomatic ax that Secretary of State Knox wielded against Roosevelt-appointed men, and in July 1909 Thompson announced that he planned to resign at the start of the next year. A month later leaked the news of his Pan-American Railroad purchase.[80]

The announcement of the sale set off a frenzy of speculation about Thompson's true motives. One *Mexican Herald* editorial imagined that Thompson sought a "reassuring effect" at a time when US investors expressed concern over the ongoing strength of the Díaz regime: "No other single act, in our opinion, could so forcibly impress the fact that those who are best acquainted with Mexican conditions have full confidence in the present situation, as well as the future development of the country." The overwhelming majority of press coverage, however, assured that Thompson served as a mere middleman, a facilitator for an ultimate transfer to Harriman. On the same day the *Mexican Herald* praised Thompson's "reassuring effect," the *Los Angeles Herald* fumed: "[N]othing more humiliating to the people of the United States has ever happened than the Harrimanization of the United States diplomatic service in Mexico. The prostitution of the office of ambassador to the Harriman interests is without precedent or parallel."[81]

Thompson himself immediately denied the sale and insisted that he was "in no way connected with Mr. Harriman." But his refutations had little impact on the rumors. The claims of a secret Harriman deal poured forth for another two weeks, fueled by a consular report describing Harriman's apparent plans for "through cars from Seattle to Panama." Then, on September 9, 1909, the rumors suddenly ceased. That afternoon, at 1:30 p.m., E. H. Harriman, the source of all this speculation over southern Mexico, died quietly in his home in New York, the victim of complications from an inoperable stomach cancer that he had diligently hid from the public. The greatest railroad builder of them all, only sixty-one years old, was no more. His railway to Panama—and the even larger globe-spanning transportation system he envisioned it being a part of someday—died with him.[82]

Shortly after Harriman's death, Thompson confirmed publicly for the first time that he had indeed purchased the Pan-American and then laid out an ambitious plan for his new acquisition. The entire road would need to be rebuilt, Thompson explained, with permanent steel bridges, concrete stations, and "rolling stock of the latest type." Moreover, he intended to construct a two-thousand-foot-long railroad bridge over the Suchiate River, which divided Mexico from Guatemala. This international bridge would finally connect the two nations' rail systems (even if the gauges did not align). All of this work, according to the *Los Angeles Times*, was "to be done at once." [83]

The following month, Thompson named a new board of directors. Not a single seat went to men associated with Harriman's Southern Pacific, but the new board's membership included several leading names from Limantour's National Railways, among them Porfirio Díaz's son. Either Harriman's death had changed Thompson's strategy dramatically or, more likely, he had planned this approach all along. As Thompson well knew, Limantour preferred to purchase well-built, completed trunk line roads than to have his government invest directly in construction. The rehabilitation of the Pan-American thus offered Thompson a chance to earn a tidy profit with relatively little risk. [84]

But the dream of expanding the Pan-American into Central America seemed to quickly overshadow Thompson's interest in improving the existing Mexican trackage. He soon traveled to Guatemala to personally petition Estrada Cabrera for a concession and hopefully succeed where Neeland had failed. While the dictator had already issued a Pan-American concession eighteen months earlier, the Guatemalan leader still consented to Thompson's request, and Thompson walked away from his encounter with Estrada Cabrera feeling triumphant, though diplomat William Sands, who had attended the conference as Thompson's Spanish translator, warned him shortly thereafter,

> I am inclined to think ... that Mr. Estrada Cabrera has intentionally attempted to make discord and if possible create litigation between two American concerns in order to prevent the connection being made across the Mexican border. . . . I should hate to see Mr. Estrada Cabrera succeed in playing off one american against another for a point in his own private game. . . . Do not (if you will let me advise you) put to [*sic*] much faith in Mr. Estrada Cabrera. He is working entirely in his own interest. [85]

Thompson, however, chose to ignore Sands's advice entirely. Construction on the Suchiate Bridge started in early 1910 and proceeded at great expense despite continuous protest and threats of litigation from the rival Pan-American Railway concessionaire, whose Pacific coffee trade risked being siphoned off to competing Atlantic ports once a rail link to Mexico existed. Outfoxing his opposition, Thompson completed the bridge in late 1910, but quickly discovered just how correct Sands had been all along. A

US traveler who attempted to walk across the bridge into Guatemala after its inauguration described the experience as follows:

> Scarcely had we set foot on the bridge when there came racing out of a palm-leaf hut on the opposite shore three male ragamuffins in bare feet, shouting as they ran. One carried an antediluvian, muzzle-loading musket, another an ancient bayonet red with rust, and the third swung threateningly what I took to be a stiff piece of telegraph wire. "No se pasa!" screamed the three in chorus, spreading out in skirmish line like an army ready to oppose to the death the invasion of a hostile force. "No one can pass the bridge!" "But why not?" I asked. "Because Guatemala does not allow it.... The Pope himself cannot cross this bridge."[86]

In late August 1910, shortly before the Suchiate Bridge opened and when the possibility of continuing farther into Guatemala already appeared hopeless, Thompson sold out his position to the Mexican government. Thompson's board already contained so many National Railways men that the sale required few changes to the Pan-American's directorship. Nonetheless, the transfer carried great symbolic value. The government, which already owned nearly all the trunk lines radiating from Mexico City, finally controlled the entire rail system connecting the US border with Guatemala. The consolidation marked a height in state power and a triumph for Limantour's circle of pragmatic, technocratic *científicos*. Thompson's Pan-American was the final piece in an elaborate jigsaw puzzle that Limantour had started assembling nearly a decade earlier, a fitting capstone to crown the massive nationwide celebrations of September 1910 that honored both the centenary of Mexican independence and President Díaz's eightieth birthday.[87]

On the same morning that the National Railways' board met to ratify the purchase of the Pan-American, several of the company's own workers smuggled Mexico's most influential political prisoner, Francisco I. Madero, across the US border to safety and freedom.[88]

Madero, scion of one of northern Mexico's wealthiest families, had challenged Díaz for the 1910 presidency and had amassed a huge popular following around the slogan "Valid Voting, No Reelection." Díaz had only staved off Madero's challenge through massive electoral fraud and had subsequently imprisoned his rival on trumped-up charges. But Díaz's control of the situation collapsed once Madero escaped to the United States inside the National Railways baggage car. The political exile soon began coordinating a full-scale revolution, which he launched in late November 1910.[89]

Madero's revolution swept across Mexico like a crown fire, fueled by pent-up populist frustrations and by the ambitions of powerful men seeking greater influence in a post-Díaz world. Much of the nation's northern rail network fell to the revolutionists during early 1911, and they finally entered the capital that April. The following month Díaz agreed to resign, a humbling conclusion to a thirty-five-year-long reign, a political feat without parallel in post-colonial Latin America. "Madero has unleashed the tiger," Díaz warned as he prepared to board a ship carrying him to exile. "[L]et us see if he can control him."[90]

Díaz's dire warning, however, appeared unfounded at first. Political tensions rarely turned violent throughout the summer of 1911, and Madero peacefully gained the presidency that November following the freest elections the nation had ever seen. Additionally, the all-important, government-owned National Railways performed well throughout this period, despite suffering damage during Madero's revolution. Profits accrued steadily and the company faithfully serviced the government-backed debt that Pierce and Speyer controlled. The vice president of the National Railways declared shortly before Madero's election, "[T]here is a general feeling of satisfaction with Senor Madero, who has shown great ability and wisdom in his leadership of the nation. . . . In time I look for railroad connections not only between St. Louis and Panama, but between St. Louis and Buenos Aires."[91]

Among those happiest to see Madero in power was Henry Clay Pierce, the former owner of the Mexican Central. Pierce had long opposed Díaz and the inner circle of *científicos*, who had not only nationalized his rail line during Limantour's daring 1906 consolidation but had also arranged a major Mexican oil concession for Weetman Pearson, an Englishman whom Pierce considered a corrupt rival for the future of Mexico's booming oil products business. Porfirio Díaz's son once confided to Pearson that Pierce "has been the cause of all the troubles in Mexico since the year 1910."[92]

Madero largely shared Pierce's views that the *científicos* had become irredeemably corrupt and that Pearson, if unchecked, threatened to exert a monopoly over Mexican oil production. The new Madero administration soon purged most of the *científicos* from the National Railways board and replaced them with Pierce men. Even more dramatic action came nine months later, in June 1912, when Madero authorized a major new oil concession for Standard Oil, the massive US trust, whose leadership shared an uneasy alliance with Pierce.

The awarding of an oil concession to a Pierce ally predictably enraged Pearson, and the British mogul began contemplating dramatic action, possibly overthrow.[93]

Pearson was not alone in considering such action. Several power-hungry revolutionary leaders had grown disaffected with Madero, whom they considered weak and ineffective. Foremost among this group was Victoriano Huerta, a fearsome general with command of several thousand soldiers near the capital. These anti-Madero plotters also found a willing conspirator in US ambassador Henry Lane Wilson, who had replaced David E. Thompson and disliked Madero on both personal and political grounds. Ambassador Wilson assured that he would support regime change should the circumstances warrant.

Soon Pearson began funneling money to Huerta and his co-conspirators, and in February 1913 Huerta managed to take Madero prisoner. One of Huerta's co-conspirators then completed the coup with a single gunshot to Madero's neck. The revolution had its first martyr, and Mexico soon had a new dictator in Huerta.[94]

General Huerta had abandoned Madero's democratic ideals for military authority but still aimed to be seen as continuing the revolution. His solution to this dilemma was anti-Americanism, one of the revolution's secondary themes. Madero, for his part, had often downplayed this quality of the revolution, but anti-Americanism resonated with many in the laboring classes who had witnessed an unprecedented influx of US capital during the last thirty years. And the single greatest symbol of Mexican independence in the face of US economic domination remained the National Railways.[95]

Huerta soon began working aggressively to strip all the foreign elements from the National Railways, which maintained a corps of US workers, especially for the high-pay, high-skill jobs such as engineer and conductor. Under Limantour, a program to train Mexicans for these highly sought positions had begun, but Huerta accelerated this transition to the point of chaos. E. N. Brown, the US engineer who had run the National Railways since its inception, observed of Huerta's mandate, "[T]he officials were flooded with requests from mayors, governors, and other officials to give positions to their friends, many of whom had no railroad experience." The rail situation grew even more disordered in mid-1913 when Huerta suspended debt payments altogether, a move that most harmed Pierce, the single biggest bondholder.[96]

Pierce had been scheming for Huerta's removal since the moment the dictator assumed power, and this latest insult only hardened his resolve. He and others fearful of what further Huerta rule would mean for their investments in Mexico began to contemplate the radical step of direct US military intervention. The United States, after all, had already shown a willingness to topple dictators four years prior in Nicaragua, and this time a homegrown democratic movement existed under the leadership of Venustiano Carranza, a general who headed the Constitutionalist faction of the Mexican Revolution.[97]

Pierce soon appealed to the new US president, Democrat Woodrow Wilson. The idealist president opposed intervention in principle but nonetheless displayed sympathy for "the great movement of the [Mexican] people" under Carranza. Pierce and his cohort subsequently worked to convince Wilson that intervention was the morally correct response to Huerta's parade of injustices. Their arguments resonated, though Wilson reportedly informed his personal physician, "I sometimes have to pause and remind myself that I am president of the whole United States and not merely of a few property holders in the Republic of Mexico."

Finally, in April 1914, Wilson authorized the military intervention that Pierce had long been seeking. Soon US troops invaded the port of Veracruz to seize large caches of arms that Huerta had stored there. But the intervention failed to topple Huerta, and the dictator responded by immediately removing all US workers from his nation's railroads, a swift if chaotic completion to the nationalization of railway labor in Mexico.[98]

While Huerta was struggling to defend his regime, Pierce secretly reached out to Carranza with a bold proposal about his old Mexican Central line. Pierce's former rail network technically belonged to Huerta's government, but in practice the twelve-hundred-mile trunk line from Mexico City to El Paso was largely held by anti-Huerta revolutionaries, with Carranza covering the stretch above Mexico City and with Pancho Villa, Carranza's ally and rival, controlling the northernmost section. Pierce wanted to reclaim control of this entire line and restore order, a move that he assured Carranza would both help the greater anti-Huerta revolutionary cause and diminish

Villa's strength in the north. The proposal intrigued Carranza, who offered his potential support. But then, in late June 1914, their secret correspondence was leaked to the press.

The scandal embarrassed Carranza. He subsequently grew more stridently anti-American. And his contempt for the United States remained resolute when his revolutionary forces finally defeated Huerta in August 1914.[99]

The month after he gained victory, Carranza commandeered the entire National Railways outright. In so doing, Mexico finally assumed control of every aspect of the rail system that US capital had first started building in 1880. The process of nationalization, which had begun in 1902 with a series of audacious financial maneuvers, had been completed twelve years later through a combination of presidential force, wartime necessity, and defaulted loans. The idea that a rail route might somehow remain neutral in time of prolonged war, a founding tenet of the Pan-American Railway movement, had proven no less fantastic than the belief that arbitration courts alone could eliminate military conflicts altogether.[100]

While Carranza's government now owned and ran the National Railways outright, the revolution had left the company in such poor shape as to be almost unrecognizable. The steady profits had disappeared entirely by 1914, and the trackage had suffered too much damage to be usable in many places. The former US president of the National Railways estimated that the Carranza government faced a situation where "one-half of the rolling stock is not serviceable, . . . some 15,000,000 ties are necessary to be replaced[, and] sixty-five or seventy million dollars United States money would be required [for further rehabilitation]." The pre-revolution news editor of the *Mexican Herald* guessed that the actual extent of National Railways operations taking place under Carranza was so small as to "seem trifling and unbelievable." And Carranza had little chance to improve upon these challenges, for the month after he took over the railroad, the two other most powerful revolutionary generals, Pancho Villa and the charismatic land reform champion Emiliano Zapata, broke away from the Constitutionalists and refused to submit to Carranza's authority.[101]

The bloodiest years were still ahead. But the violence of the Mexican Revolution was about to be eclipsed by an even greater conflict, one with global implications that would impact the entire Western Hemisphere. The nations of Europe, which had collectively played such a profound role in shaping the Americas since 1492, were fast descending into total war.

The War and William McAdoo

The effects of the war on the far side of the Atlantic immediately struck across the entire Western Hemisphere. European banks, which had long financed development throughout the region, swiftly retreated to the safety of gold and the demands of wartime financing. The threat of German U-boat submarines also decimated the European-led steam shipping trade that had long directed both commercial exchange and passenger travel throughout the Americas. And the flow of European-manufactured goods upon which South American states in particular depended shrank to a trickle. As one US politician noted, "The South Americans were like the customers of a store that has burned down."[102]

For the United States, however, the war's impact on Latin America created an opening for its corporations to finally displace their European rivals as the fulcrum of economic life in the hemisphere. "Wake up United States!" declared one of New York's leading financial journalists just as the war began. "The United States now has the opportunity, not of a lifetime, but of a century."[103]

US-based Pan-Americanists had long been dreaming of this moment. Clay had seen the conquest of Latin American markets as crucial to the success of his American System. Helper had spoken of these markets as the inspiration for his Three Americas Railway. Blaine and Root had both urged closer commercial relations during their speeches before Pan-American Conferences in 1889 and 1906, respectively. And the mantle of this deep tradition in US foreign affairs was about to be claimed by William Gibbs McAdoo, the nation's powerful Treasury secretary, whose influence exceeded that of nearly every public official in the country save McAdoo's own father-in-law, President Woodrow Wilson.[104]

McAdoo, born in 1863 to a middle-class family living near Marietta, Georgia, had developed a national reputation long before he entered politics or embraced Pan-Americanism. His fame stemmed from a single great triumph that finally arrived after years of toiling at law in New York City, of failing catastrophically at a scheme to build an electric rail in Knoxville, Tennessee, and of helplessly watching his first wife battle against a debilitating melancholy that would lead to her death. In the midst of these difficulties, McAdoo decided to attempt the seemingly impossible: construction of a long-sought rail tunnel beneath the Hudson River to link New York City with New Jersey and the rest of the US mainland. Few schemes so enlivened the imagination of those living in the nation's great island metropolis, which remained cut off from the national rail network. For millions of New Yorkers at the turn of the century, the only way to reach the mainland was aboard crowded, rickety ferries.[105]

Several prior attempts to tunnel the Hudson had collapsed, in both the metaphorical and literal senses, but McAdoo remained as undaunted as he was inexperienced. He confronted the project's innumerable challenges through a combination of boundless energy, organizational brilliance, teetotalist focus, exceptional mastery of detail, and good fortune. After six years of highly publicized work, the $70 million "McAdoo Tunnel" finally opened in early 1908. President Roosevelt personally activated the first train, and a reported crowd of twenty thousand spectators greeted the inaugural passengers when they arrived safely eight minutes later at Hoboken, New Jersey. The *New York Times* declared the project "one of the greatest engineering feats ever accomplished, greater perhaps than the Panama Canal will be when opened, considering the obstacles which had to be overcome."[106]

McAdoo and Woodrow Wilson first met the year after the triumphant opening of the Hudson tunnel. Wilson, a onetime professor of history originally from Virginia, was then serving as president of Princeton University in New Jersey, where McAdoo's son was enrolled. The paths to success that each man had traveled diverged radically, but they nonetheless shared much in common as transplanted southerners and as committed progressives dedicated to monopoly reform, organizational efficiency, and social justice—McAdoo's rail tunnel company would soon adopt the earnest, if easily mocked, slogan: "The public be pleased." McAdoo later wrote that he immediately found Wilson "gracious and unpretentious in manner, [possessing] to an unusual degree, the indefinable quality of charm."[107] When McAdoo learned the following year that Wilson had received the 1910 Democratic nomination for governor of New Jersey, he quickly volunteered his support. Their friendship and political alliance then blossomed as Wilson won the governorship and quickly set his eyes on the presidency.

Wilson's 1912 presidential campaign benefited from a Republican Party split between two candidates, incumbent Taft and former president Roosevelt. The Rough Rider had decided to run as an independent after determining that Taft had drifted too far from Roosevelt's positions. This Republican split, more than any single issue, helped sway the election toward Wilson, who became the first southerner to win the presidency since before the Civil War. Wilson soon appointed southerners—Democratic progressives but ardent segregationists—to a number of high-ranking posts, including McAdoo, who became secretary of the Treasury.[108]

McAdoo's Treasury Department was poised to play an outsized role in Wilson's administration. The need for banking and currency reform had become a national and congressional obsession following the Panic of 1907, and Wilson had campaigned on the promise to finally resolve the system's structural problems and put an end to the J. P. Morgan–led "money trust." "I don't want a banker or financier," Wilson supposedly explained to McAdoo. "What I need is a man of all-round ability." Wilson's promised reforms had finally arrived in December 1913 with the passage of the Federal Reserve Act, comprehensive legislation that gave the Treasury Department tools to manage the nation's money supply. McAdoo quickly became so integral to Wilson's administration that the president insisted his Treasury secretary remain in the cabinet even after learning in late 1913 of McAdoo's plans to marry one of Wilson's daughters, a woman more than twenty-five years his junior.[109]

The wisdom of Wilson's decision to retain McAdoo was confirmed soon thereafter, when the arrival of war in Europe brought unexpected challenges to the nation's financial system. The first gunshots of August 1914 had sent European investors holding US securities scampering to the safety of British pounds, and another US panic loomed. But McAdoo, working with leading Wall Street financiers, took the bold and unprecedented step of shutting down the stock market altogether for a period of four months in 1914, until the threat subsided. McAdoo's mandate subsequently expanded even further to encompass the stability of the shipping trade, which transported the gold the entire international financial system relied upon. The war played to McAdoo's natural tendency to arrogate authority, prompting him to think in broader terms than ever before, and his attention soon landed on Latin America and, eventually, on the Pan-American Railway.[110]

The outbreak of war had delayed the next Pan-American Conference, originally scheduled for 1915 in Santiago, Chile. McAdoo determined to capitalize on this Pan-American political vacuum and convinced Wilson to authorize a special ad hoc conference focused specifically on McAdoo's intertwined fiefdoms of finance and shipping.

The subsequent gathering, known as the Pan-American Financial Conference, took place over one week in May 1915, shortly after a German U-boat sank the US-flagged *Lusitania* and triggered a new wave of war panic. Representatives from eighteen Latin American countries attended the conference, which convened in the new, Carnegie-financed, marble-clad Pan-American Union building on Washington's National Mall. McAdoo had been suffering from nervous exhaustion during the weeks prior, but he recovered in time to direct the conference and assert himself as the new US apostle of Pan-Americanism.[111]

The next year, McAdoo, like Root before him, traveled to South America for a follow-up conference. The concerns from the prior May had only deepened as the war in Europe raged with no end in sight, and the Latin American delegates pleaded with McAdoo for increased US banking facilities and, above all, improved shipping. Some prominent voices also felt that discussions of trade needed to focus just as centrally on the Pan-American Railway, a topic that had received little attention the previous year. Santiago Marín Vicuña, a Chilean engineer, asked, "Is not the present occasion of the meeting in Buenos Aires the most suitable in which to propound and settle the problem of the Pan American railroad!"[112]

The magnitude of the Pan-American Railway appealed greatly to McAdoo, who owed his career to the pursuit of the comically ambitious Hudson River rail tunnel project. Upon returning to the United States, McAdoo declared to the press,

> Outside of ocean transportation, no other undertaking is more essential to the future development of North and South America than the construction of this great railroad. It is not a visionary idea; it is a very practical idea and one that can be realized at much less cost than the Panama Canal. This is the kind of constructive enterprise that appeals to the imagination and spirit of our people. There are no people to whom a great and daring development of this character appeals so strongly as the people of the United States.... "ALL ABOARD FOR BUENOS AIRES!," when shouted in the railroad stations of New York City, will be a thrilling announcement.[113]

McAdoo's railway endorsement resonated with traditional Pan-American idealists as well as with those in the United States who feared that German U-boats might eventually compromise access to the recently completed canal. Roosevelt's great engineering project had formally opened for service on August 15, 1914, just as the war began, and fears about canal security had increased dramatically after the sinking of the *Lusitania* in May 1915. Germany's subsequent refusals to curtail its U-boat campaign ensured that these fears continued to grow. "Should we lose command of the sea, how are we going to defend the Panama Canal?" asked journalist Frederick Palmer in early 1916. "It will be almost impossible to march troops overland.... Why not, though the seas should be closed to us, have a line of steel running to Panama itself?" Even Roosevelt, who had long stymied US support for the Pan-American Railway, now seemed to embrace this view, arguing in late 1916, "A railroad extending to the Panama Canal would give us access by land to [that] with which the future of the United States is so bound up."[114]

Plans to advance the Pan-American Railway anew had been drafted in Buenos Aires with McAdoo's approval. They called for new field surveys and economic studies, all to be carried out by the Permanent Pan-American Railway Committee that former senator Henry Gassaway Davis had created fifteen years earlier.[115]

The Permanent Pan-American Railway Committee had struggled to stay relevant after 1906, when Roosevelt failed to send any of its members to the Third Pan-American Conference in Rio. Davis's occasional entreaties to Roosevelt thereafter had drawn barely a response, and the octogenarian Davis began to lament in private correspondence the committee's lack of "younger and more active men." Davis's own vigor, however, remained surprisingly high for his advanced years. In early 1908 the eighty-five-year-old even married one of his daughter's close friends, a woman less than half his age.[116]

Davis's role as chief Pan-American Railway advocate only grew more difficult with the arrival of President Taft and Secretary Knox, neither of whom showed much interest in Pan-Americanism. It hardly seemed a coincidence that two weeks after Taft's inauguration, in March 1909, the railway's original champion, Hinton Rowan Helper, half mad and living in a run-down boardinghouse near the White House, finally accepted defeat and took his own life. The *Washington Post*'s front-page obituary declared, "His life's work void of fruition and dissipated into emptiness; his fondest hopes and ambitions crumbled and scattered; shunned as a fanatic, and unable to long wage life's battle, Hinton Rowan Helper . . . sought the darkest egress from his woes and disappointments."[117]

Despite grim prospects for success, Davis refused to accept failure and found hope in the prospect of the Fourth Pan-American Conference, scheduled for midsummer 1910 in Buenos Aires. Several months after Helper's death, Davis began drafting plans for a syndicate of his own, one he hoped to organize in time for the conference. The moment for direct action, he felt, had finally arrived, after twenty years of advocacy, with Davis pushing ninety. Soon he recruited his son-in-law and former Blaine operative Stephen Elkins, now a West Virginia senator who had grown rich through the bloody trade in Alaskan seal furs, and then Davis pitched the syndicate to Carnegie in January 1910. The great philanthropist, whose $20 million offer for peace in Central America had been rejected by Knox barely one month prior, consented, adding, "You cannot engage in a nobler work and we youngsters all take heart when we see the old veteran with his coat off." [118]

Davis next brought his proposal directly to the men who formed the core of the much-despised "money trust." The bankers listened with interest, and Davis walked away convinced that they "not only favored" the syndicate but that "they would join in building the road" as well. However, two weeks later, Henry Davison, the right hand of J. P. Morgan, politely informed Davis that the banks could not make a "definite commitment . . . as one of the incorporators." Davis felt that their hesitation owed to the uproar in Congress over banking and currency reform, but his advanced age may have been just as strong a factor.

The money trust's refusal to provide financing effectively snuffed out any momentum for Davis's syndicate, which collapsed entirely by the time the Fourth Pan-American Conference finally met in July 1910. And, once more, none of the US members in Davis's railway committee received an invitation to the hemispheric gathering. [119]

Over the next several years, Davis's interest in the Pan-American Railway gradually waned. He only managed to arrange one more official Pan-American Railway dinner, and the meal seemed more swan song than strategy session. Committee member Charles Pepper tried to encourage Davis thereafter, but Davis's private secretary informed Pepper in August 1913, "I regret to say that I could not enlist his interest [in the railway]. . . . [H]e is now beyond the years when it might be expected that he would personally enter further into this important affair." Davis himself rejected Pepper's request for funding shortly after war broke out in Europe, asserting, "I do not consider the matter of sufficient importance at this time." [120]

A brief illness that Davis contracted in early 1916 led to his death in mid-March of that year at the age of ninety-two. He had been born the same year as the Monroe Doctrine and had lived to see the United States gain influence in the hemisphere greater than anything Monroe had likely imagined, but the Pan-American Railway that Davis had spent a quarter century promoting still remained a distant dream.[121]

The death of Davis left the railway committee he had created without leadership for the first time. Had he lived two months longer, he would have learned about McAdoo's newfound enthusiasm for the Pan-American Railway. Instead, McAdoo returned from Buenos Aires with instructions for a committee that had all but collapsed and with the most stalwart US proponent of the Pan-American Railway recently deceased.

The disintegration of the Davis committee was hardly the only obstacle that McAdoo encountered when he arrived back in Washington. McAdoo's political patron, President Wilson, held mixed feelings about his Treasury secretary's increasing involvement with foreign affairs and expressed little interest in the railway idea. Moreover, the Pan-American idealism that McAdoo propounded, and that Wilson supported in principle, bumped up against a serious crisis in relations with Mexico.[122]

The United States' southern neighbor had been mired in a bloody civil war since the break in late 1914 between Constitutionalist Venustiano Carranza and his rivals Pancho Villa and Emiliano Zapata. President Wilson had formally recognized Carranza's government in October 1915, but Wilson's decision had infuriated Villa, who had ultimately responded with a deadly raid into Texas in March 1916 that had prompted Wilson to authorize military intervention once more. McAdoo's dream of a railroad to South America made little practical sense with the US military pursuing a "punitive expedition" inside the first country along the route.[123]

The upcoming 1916 US presidential election also diverted the attention of both Wilson and McAdoo from foreign affairs. The already overcommitted Treasury secretary had to travel the country stumping for Wilson, stressing the reelection campaign's main slogan: "He kept us out of war." This antiwar theme would help Wilson secure a convincing victory from an electorate divided over the two-year-old European conflict and largely favoring neutrality.

Wilson retained McAdoo for a second term as Treasury secretary, but McAdoo's Latin American projects soon fell victim to preparations for a war that increasingly seemed inevitable. Despite the Wilson reelection rhetoric, few in the administration had believed that US neutrality could be preserved for long, especially with Germany escalating its U-boat campaign and with the Allies increasingly dependent on US loans and supplies.[124]

The last hope for US neutrality evaporated shortly after the election when Wilson learned that Germany had secretly attempted to form an alliance with Mexico. The proposal, which British intelligence had discovered after intercepting a coded telegram, asked for Carranza's aid in exchange for Germany supporting a reconquest of the lands Mexico had lost to the United States in 1848. Carranza, despite his anti-Americanism, rejected the offer, but Germany's actions nonetheless played into US fears of European belligerence expanding into the hemisphere. As McAdoo later observed, "After Europe had settled its gigantic row—with Germany, in all probability, on the top of the heap—the United States would have become the target of universal contempt. Our rights would have been trampled on everywhere and the Monroe Doctrine would have gone the way of Belgium's historic 'scrap of paper.'"

In April 1917, Wilson received permission from Congress to finally declare war against Germany in order to, in the president's words, "make the world safe for democracy."[125]

The declaration of war allowed Wilson to implement a program of industrial and military mobilization on a scale unknown in US history, and McAdoo was soon placed in charge of the financing for this effort. His Treasury Department would subsequently raise billions of dollars through the sale of Liberty Bonds to the general public, with much of the funds going to support a $2.5 billion shipbuilding program that ultimately produced twelve million tons of vessels.[126]

The militarization of the nation's economy, however, placed great strain on the nation's privatized rail system. The profit motive clashed inexorably with military necessity, and policy makers gradually began to call for nationalization of what was the country's largest industry, a radical step but one that all other belligerents had already taken. By late December 1917, even financier James Speyer, who held a massive portfolio of railroad securities, was suggesting that Wilson appoint an administrator "who would have broad powers over all the roads [and] could insist on the necessary harmony and co-operation."

The president finally nationalized the railroads shortly after Christmas 1917 and granted "paramount authority" over the system to McAdoo, whose earlier work tunneling the Hudson had familiarized him with railroad management and who seemed to revel in the accretion of bureaucratic power. The three-hundred-thousand-mile system that barely a decade earlier had appeared destined to fall under the control of Harriman and a handful of other tycoons now belonged to Uncle Sam in the guise of McAdoo. The *New-York Tribune* labeled McAdoo "the Most Powerful Man in America Next to [the] President."[127]

Railroad nationalization marked one of the final steps in the militarization of the US economy. Eleven months later, on November 11, 1918, the combined forces of the United States and the Allies finally compelled Germany to surrender. The war cost over a hundred thousand US lives, more than any conflict since the Civil War but a small amount compared with the millions who perished from each of the great European powers. The US government ultimately spent more dollars prosecuting the war than the combined total of all federal spending from 1789 to 1916.[128]

The war left Europe in tatters but transformed the United States into the undisputed power center within the Western Hemisphere. The United States had gone from a debtor nation to the globe's largest creditor, thanks in part to McAdoo's decisive financial actions during 1914. The nation's improved financial position also turned the dollar into the world's strongest currency, one backed by enormous stockpiles of gold. Moreover, US national banks, which had gained the right to open overseas branches as part of the 1913 Federal Reserve Act, began to penetrate Latin America in earnest starting in 1915, shortly after McAdoo's Pan-American Financial Conference. And many of the ships constructed during the mobilization were soon decommissioned and converted into a commercial merchant marine that gave the United States control over oceangoing trade in the Western Hemisphere. The dream of Clay and Helper and Blaine and Root and McAdoo to displace Europe as Latin America's dominant commercial partner had at last been realized.[129]

All of this, however, had been achieved without the Pan-American Railway. The hemispheric ascendance of the United States quashed the long-standing arguments that the Monroe Doctrine could only be fully realized through construction of the railway. Perhaps it was fated that Andrew Carnegie, who had long advocated this position, should die three months before the Armistice, at the age of eighty-three.

McAdoo, meanwhile, tendered his resignation to Wilson four days after hostilities ceased. As he informed the president, "Now that ... peace is assured, I feel at liberty to apprise you of my desire to return, as soon as possible, to private life." McAdoo soon reentered private law practice, though his high profile brought numerous public opportunities. At one point in late 1920, the government of Mexico, which hoped to restore its decimated rail system to former glory, flirted with placing McAdoo in charge, but the deal never transpired. McAdoo, who would die in 1941, eventually settled in California and returned to public office as a one-term US senator. However, he never again reached the heights of influence he had achieved during the war years, when he had dreamed of completing the Pan-American Railway.[130]

The Greatest Ambition of an Uncrowned King

At the end of the Great War much had changed in the Western Hemisphere, but the potential expansion of the Pan-American Railway below Mexico still faced the same confounding obstacle that had stalled its progress a dozen years earlier: President Manuel Estrada Cabrera of Guatemala. He had outlasted the war just as he had outlasted so much else beforehand, and Guatemala remained trapped inside a regime that seemed to grow more paranoid and unpredictable with each passing year. But then, in March 1920, a group of assemblymen representing a newly energized unionist movement took the floor of the Guatemalan Congress, declared Estrada Cabrera insane, and seized power. The dictator was finally ousted, after more than two decades in charge.[131]

The downfall of Estrada Cabrera arrived too late to benefit most of the Pan-American Railway's former boosters in the United States. Neeland, who had worked so diligently to depose Estrada Cabrera, had long ago ceased investing in southern Mexico. Former ambassador Thompson, who had succeeded Neeland, had fled Mexico during the revolution, retired several years later, and was about to wed a woman thirty-seven years his junior. McAdoo, the railway's leading spirit in the war years, had recently departed the national stage. And Davis and Carnegie had both died.[132]

However, on a Long Island estate named Babylon lived one man, Minor C. Keith, for whom the Pan-American Railway dream remained very much intact. Keith also happened to know more about building railroads in Central America than anyone else alive. As the editor of *Forbes Magazine* wrote in 1917, "He is the uncrowned king of the tropics, ... a demigod in the eyes of half a dozen republics."[133]

*   *   *

Keith, born in Brooklyn in 1848, had been raised on stories of Latin American railroad construction. His uncle, Henry Meiggs, had started laying rails in South America before the Civil War and had earned fame after erecting the highest standard-gauge line in the world across the Peruvian Andes. Meiggs's biographer dubbed his subject the "Yankee Pizarro," a nod to the Spanish conquistador who had defeated the Incan Empire in the 1530s.

Initially, Keith sought to forge his own path through several business ventures in Texas, but he changed his mind when his uncle's firm recruited him in 1871 to assist with a recently acquired rail contract from the Costa Rican government that Meiggs could not oversee personally. The new contract involved constructing Central America's first major railroad, an approximately hundred-mile route from the capital of San José to Puerto Limón on the Atlantic coast. As Keith later reflected, "[They] told me that I would make more money in Costa Rica in three years than I could make in Texas all my life. Perhaps there was a railroad tinge in the family blood."[134]

The promises of quick riches, however, soon ceded to a series of daunting challenges. Neither the financing nor the labor needs had been fully arranged, which left twenty-three-year-old Keith scrambling to resolve both issues. These trials only increased the strains Keith faced when confronting the railroad engineering nightmare he found in Costa Rica's rugged landscape, from the teeming jungle lowlands near the coasts to the vertiginous slopes of the central cordillera. But the greatest test came from exposure to the tropical climate itself. Within a year, malaria and yellow fever killed more than half of the seven hundred laborers he had imported from the United States to supplement an immigrant Jamaican labor force in Limón. Disease soon also claimed the lives of Keith's brother and cousin, who had joined him on the project. Keith nonetheless rarely took ill and seemed to thrive in the rough, semilawless environment around Limón. Diplomat William Sands, who eventually met Keith, observed, "He was the sort of American entrepreneur who took his own risks, met his difficulties and dangers without asking his government for help, but claimed as his natural right whatever profits came from his enterprise."[135]

Constant financial shortfalls gradually forced the entrepreneurial Keith to reinvent the rules of railroading, just as Collis P. Huntington had done several years earlier in California. Keith, however, could not follow Huntington's expansionist strategy since no other rail lines yet existed. He needed a strategy adapted to the tropics and at first focused on his firm's steamships.

They primarily hauled building materials and labor south, but Keith realized that they could also yield steady profits as northbound carriers for tropical agricultural products. Even greater profits stood to be earned if Keith could control the production of the export crops his ships carried. This insight led him to an interest in bananas, cream-fleshed fruits that thrived in humid jungle lowlands and displayed resilience in transport but that remained virtually unknown in the United States. Keith concluded that a constant supply of bananas, brought to port in his train cars and then shipped north in his steamers, could allow his uncompleted route to the Costa Rican capital to "pay for itself." In 1872, he established Central America's first industrial banana plantation near Limón.[136]

Keith's banana strategy had taken on a life of its own by the time his Costa Rican railroad opened to great acclaim eighteen years later. His industrial plantations had expanded well beyond Limón into other parts of Costa Rica as well as into Nicaragua, Panama, and even Colombia. Keith had become the largest banana planter in Latin America, and the robust US demand he had helped create spawned aggressive imitators across the Caribbean. "In a way the banana is to Central America what coal is to Great Britain," noted one popular US author who had traveled through the tropics. "It provides the shipping and the trade grows out of the shipping."[137]

In 1899, Keith persuaded his main Caribbean banana rival to consolidate their interests as a way to spread geographic risk and eliminate their lesser competition. Their new company, United Fruit, immediately became one of the largest enterprises in Latin America, controlling not only the banana plantations but also the rails and ships that transported them to market. The company's multinational dominance—and at times ruthless labor practices—soon led to widespread resentment throughout Latin America. Many referred to United Fruit as *El Pulpo*, Spanish for The Octopus. Keith assumed the new company's vice presidency, but, in the words of his biographer (who was also his nephew), "[f]irst and foremost Keith remained a railroad builder."[138]

Keith soon set his sights on a railway project in Guatemala that equaled, if not exceeded, the challenges he had overcome earlier in Costa Rica. The scope of the project attracted the "kind of man who likes enterprises more than profit," to borrow a phrase that columnist Walter Lippmann had once used to describe William McAdoo. The proposed 275-mile-long route ran from the inland capital of Guatemala City to Puerto Barrios on the Atlantic coast, descending over 5,000 feet through thick tangles of tropical wilderness along the way. If completed, the line would not only link the capital with the Atlantic for the first time, but also intersect with the railway that Collis Huntington had earlier built from Guatemala City to the Pacific, thus giving Guatemala both a valuable transcontinental route of its own and a means to transport its Pacific-oriented coffee crop directly to eastern markets.[139]

The Guatemalan government had attempted to build this 275-mile line itself but had abandoned the work partway through under financial duress. The line's completion nonetheless remained vitally important to Estrada Cabrera, and in 1904, after prolonged negotiations, he granted Keith the rail concession as well as rights for vast banana plantings, which would once again help surmount the inevitable financial hurdles. Keith soon placed the banana plantations in the hands of United Fruit but formed a new independent company to handle the rail work. The completed line opened less than four years later, in early 1908, shortly after the conclusion of the 1907 Washington Conference.[140]

Keith had again triumphed. There appeared to be no railroad that Keith could not construct in Central America should he so desire.

The Pan-American Railway had been little more than a delirious secret locked within Hinton Rowan Helper's breast at the time Keith began his Central American career. But three decades later, when Keith decided to enter Guatemalan railroading, the Pan-American Railway idea had blossomed. Keith's interest in the Pan-American Railway seemed to emerge in earnest during this period. The idea resonated with his self-perception as a benevolent visionary bringing progress to backward lands. Keith, like Neeland and many others, also saw the Pan-American Railway as essential to achieving a new union of Central American republics. As he once noted, "[O]nly railroads can bring [union] about. . . . There must first be commercial and social intercourse. The railroad will make that possible." The goal of constructing the portion of the Pan-American Railway from Guatemala to the Panama Canal soon became, in the words of Keith's family biographer, "the greatest ambition of his lifetime."[141]

Keith had laid the foundation for this great ambition in 1904 when he formed his new Guatemalan rail company. The company's charter, filed in the notoriously business-friendly state of New Jersey, permitted the acquisition and operation of railroads not only in Guatemala but also throughout all of Central America. In 1908, Keith first tapped this expansive power with the acquisition of a concession to build a rail spur from his recently fin-

ished Puerto Barrios–to–Guatemala City line into El Salvador via the Guatemalan town of Zacapa. This new Zacapa concession, though not on the
official Pan-American route, would form the first rail link between the two
nations, and soon the government of El Salvador granted Keith's company
a corresponding concession that ran the entire length of that country. By
mid-1908, Keith had acquired concessions that potentially allowed through
travel from the United States all the way to the El Salvador/Honduras border and also secured him an Atlantic-oriented rail route for El Salvador's
valuable coffee crop, which could then be transported directly to eastern
markets aboard his United Fruit ships.[142]

For several years, Keith largely held these new concessions in reserve as
he pursued a strategy of further consolidation in Guatemala. Most of that
country's railroads, including the one that corresponded with the official
Pan-American route, belonged to the rail company that Collis Huntington
had formed the century prior. After prolonged negotiations, in early 1912,
Keith finally reached a deal to purchase this entire enterprise outright. Soon
he renamed his own firm the International Railways of Central America.
All the pieces seemed to have finally fallen into place for a bold new construction program.[143]

Keith's swift consolidation, however, had alarmed Estrada Cabrera. While
the dictator had initially benefited from Keith's relentless entrepreneurial-
ism, he had begun to worry in the years prior to the consolidation about
Keith gaining "greater power and influence . . . than he already possesse[d],"
according to diplomat Sands. Moreover, Estrada Cabrera's opposition to the
Pan-American Railway and to international railroad connections generally
remained steadfast—even the granting of the 1908 Zacapa concession to
Keith had likely been little more than a by-product of the dictator's post–
Washington Conference attempt to, in the State Department's words, "show
progress" for "political capital only." Estrada Cabrera's compliant ministers
soon threw enough spurious legal delays in the path of the International
Railways to halt almost any construction toward El Salvador.[144]

Keith had already spent decades overcoming the entrenched challenges
of Central American nature, financing, and labor, but the Guatemalan
government's sudden change of heart confounded him. Keith's in-country
manager, Frederick Williamson, complained to the dictator personally in
early 1913 of apparent "systematic obstruction." Two months later, Williamson told the State Department that he "believ[ed] his life in danger"

after a campaign by government-affiliated papers to stir up labor resentment against United Fruit and the International Railways. A widely read editorial declared of the two companies, "The one strikes the face and the other gives the spear thrust at the side."[145]

Guatemalans needed little prodding to turn on Keith's men. The company's US-born employees often displayed contempt and unveiled racism toward local workers, many of whom had been forced into the rail work through a peonage system the Estrada Cabrera regime required. One US roadmaster griped, "most of the section force are Jamaican niggers and Guatemalan Indians and are, as a rule, a dishonest, unreliable, drunken and lazy lot." Popular sentiment throughout Central America had also turned sharply against the issuance of blanket concessions that gave foreign corporations leverage over national development.[146]

Estrada Cabrera's prolonged campaign against the International Railways ultimately compelled Keith to seek US governmental assistance, a step he had managed to avoid previously. In 1914, he convinced President Wilson to send a special emissary to investigate the situation officially. Wilson's agent, after visiting Guatemala, concluded that its government had indeed violated the International Railways' legal rights. This determination induced Estrada Cabrera to promise compliance moving forward, but the dictator returned to his delay tactics soon after Wilson's agent departed. So long as Estrada Cabrera remained in power, Keith's Pan-American Railway ambitions, like those of Neeland before him, seemed hopeless.[147]

The long-awaited downfall of Estrada Cabrera finally arrived in 1920, and the pro-unionist Guatemalans who deposed him aligned with a political tradition that had previously supported the Pan-American Railway. The new Guatemalan president, however, soon canceled the International Railways' Zacapa concession outright, a move that stunned Keith. State Department officials believed that the Guatemalan president had been bribed by the Pacific Steamship Company, a US-owned firm that had once belonged to Huntington and that stood to lose much of its Central American coffee trade if Keith provided El Salvador with a rail outlet to the Atlantic. Keith fought the decision, but before his campaign had progressed very far the new president's regime collapsed in the face of a coup d'état that several of Estrada Cabrera's military officers had arranged. The general who subsequently seized power displayed less hostility to an international rail connection, though he still felt that any capitulation to Keith might result in his overthrow.[148]

Keith, by this point, had grown increasingly comfortable relying on US governmental assistance. His firm had retained the services of Robert Lansing, the US secretary of state during World War I, and Keith had convinced the State Department to act as courier for all essential International Railways correspondence out of fear that the Guatemalan government would otherwise read his communications. Eventually the State Department stepped in to mediate directly on Keith's behalf, "not only because the [International Railways] is an American company," according to department dispatches, but also "because of the importance of the projected new line as a link between Salvador, Honduras and Nicaragua and the United States." At the end of this link also lay the Gulf of Fonseca's deepwater Pacific port, a strategic naval asset that the United States considered vital for defense of the Panama Canal.

After months of tortuous negotiations, in May 1923, Guatemala finally agreed to restore the Zacapa concession. The Pan-American Railway could progress south once more, after a delay of more than fifteen years.[149]

Just as the Zacapa negotiations were concluding, the long-delayed Fifth Pan-American Conference convened in Santiago, Chile. The US delegation had not intended to devote much attention to the Pan-American Railway, but the host nation's delegates had included Santiago Marín Vicuña, the same engineer who had helped convince McAdoo of the Pan-American Railway's importance in 1916. During the Santiago conference, Marín Vicuña worked with other railway supporters to craft a new resolution calling for the Pan-American Union to reorganize the committee that had lain fallow since Henry Gassaway Davis's death. Several months later, the Pan-American Union board announced the appointment of seven committee members, and one of the US spots went to Keith, who, by that point, had spent nearly two decades working to advance the Pan-American Railway in Central America.[150]

The reorganized committee soon began to hold regular meetings once again. Charles Pepper, the only returning member, became the new chair and served as a sort of éminence grise, a link back to the hopeful days of Davis and Carnegie. The balance of power, however, shifted away from the United States and toward Latin America, whose four new committee members constituted a functional majority for the first time. This change, in turn, reoriented the committee away from discussions about ways to secure US political support and toward a dispute over the location of the railway in South America.[151]

The South American route, first established in 1890, ran along the Andean range in the far west of the continent. Concerns about the route in general had plagued the original Intercontinental Railway Commission but had seemed to disappear once the Shunk-led survey departed for Latin America in 1891. The official route had subsequently guided railway plans throughout South America, even if little of the Andean portion had yet been constructed. However, in 1919, a debate over the South American route had reemerged when Juan Briano, an Argentine engineer and university professor, published a manifesto titled *The Pan-American Railway: Its New Orientations.*[152]

Briano's polemic argued that the established route sat too far west and that the limited progress in the Andes proved the route's fundamental shortcomings. He proposed instead that the railway cut through the Amazon en route to Buenos Aires. Briano's proposal garnered the attention of railway engineers throughout South America, including Marín Vicuña, and played a role in the 1923 decision to reorganize the Permanent Pan-American Railway Committee. Soon thereafter the Pan-American Union recognized the significance of Briano's efforts by appointing him as one of the seven members of the reorganized committee.[153]

Briano's presence ensured that the committee's meetings rarely strayed from the South American route question for long. The debate gradually overshadowed all other potential topics or pragmatic concerns, and those on the committee who felt that Briano's proposal had created more problems than solutions grew increasingly embittered. The third US committee member, engineer Verne L. Havens, became so frustrated after several years that he declared,

> I have no hesitancy in saying that I see no purpose whatsoever in the study of a route through the Amazon River valley such as has generally been referred to as Mr. Briano's route. . . . I am personally thoroughly satisfied that the so-called Briano route is absolutely impossible within the field of finance, continuity of operations or even construction of the line within any ordinary lifetime.

But the intellectual Briano never seemed to accept that engineering challenges and geographic consensus ultimately mattered less than political will and the commitment of railroad capitalists. After more than thirty-five years, the reorganized Pan-American Railway Committee seemed to be mired in the same debates as at the very start, at least as far as South America was concerned.[154]

The only meaningful construction advances the committee could note during the years following the 1923 conference took place under Keith's International Railways. In late 1925, with the South American route debate still raging, the Pan-American Railway Committee declared, "In view of the satisfactory progress in Central America it was the sentiment of the members of the Committee that this section of the general line could be left to the interests represented by Mr. Keith to complete to the Isthmus of Panama." The road to Panama, officially, now rested solely with Keith.[155]

Keith had many reasons in the mid-1920s to feel optimistic about his chances of realizing his portion of the Pan-American Railway. To begin with, the profits of both the International Railways and United Fruit were growing year over year as a surging US economy and savvy marketing campaign bolstered the demand for his bananas. Additional revenue was also coming from western-grown Guatemalan coffee, which increasingly traveled along his transcontinental rail route to Puerto Barrios thanks to a controversial rate structure that Keith had implemented earlier. Moreover, Keith had started negotiations with the Guatemalan government to construct the southern section of the official Pan-American route and spoke of finally completing the rail connection with Mexico at the Suchiate River.[156]

By 1925, an army of six thousand laborers was working on Keith's lines in El Salvador and Guatemala. The following year their efforts produced 120 miles of new track, a remarkable feat given the geography they faced. The toughest construction stretch, which remained to be completed, sat just west of Zacapa, where the road climbed 2,500 feet through difficult terrain and volcanic ash, "the most undesirable material imaginable for a roadbed, [standing] up almost like hard pan in the dry season, simply flow[ing] away during the wet season," according to one of Keith's associates. Keith described the conditions near Zacapa as "exceedingly heavy" and demanding of "a great deal of engineering skill." The most daunting stretch required half a dozen meandering switchbacks, the same number of tunnels, and two viaducts, more than five miles of physical rails for each mile of distance gained.[157]

These geographic challenges forced Keith to push back his estimated 1927 completion date for the Zacapa–to–El Salvador line, but he remained confident of eventual success there and beyond. In mid-1928 he boasted, "We contemplate building 480 more miles of line and purchasing the Pacific Railroad of Nicaragua. When this is done it will be possible to travel by rail from the States to Colon, Panama." One of Keith's associates in this period went even further in his postulations, asserting in the *Bulletin of the Pan American Union* that the International Railways was "the only one destined some day to realize Bolivar's Pan American ideal of bridging the distance between the capitals of Washington and Buenos Aires."[158]

The greatest obstacle that Keith faced no longer seemed to be geography or politics but his own mortality. He had turned eighty in 1928, a profound accomplishment for someone who had logged so many years in the disease-filled tropics, and his health was starting to decline noticeably. In late November that year, the International Railways announced that Keith had resigned the presidency and accepted the role of company chairman, a "comparatively uninfluential position," according to the State Department. Keith died the following June, six months before his long-awaited Zacapa–to–El Salvador line would finally open for international traffic.[159]

Encomiums for Keith poured forth from across Central America. One editorial that the *New York Times* republished from the *Panama Star Herald* declared, "[Keith] has done more for [Central America] than any other single man. . . . [H]is intimates were Presidents and Cabinet Ministers, native peons and American negroes. His good works will live many years after him and will be the finest kind of a monument to his memory."[160]

The news of Keith's passing prompted one reporter to ask the new International Railways president about the future of the Pan-American Railway. Keith's successor bluntly described the project as "impractical," adding, "Each Central and South American country should build its own railroad system with a single object—the opening of quick routes to the sea so that freights may readily be carried to the ships." Soon the International Railways' planned extensions beyond El Salvador disappeared from the company's annual reports. Over the next several years, the company fell under complete control of United Fruit, Keith's former creation, whose management now showed no interest in the Pan-American Railway.[161]

Keith's death concluded the United States' fifty-year-long odyssey with the Pan-American Railway. The rail titans who once saw no geographic limits to their empires had all disappeared. No one remained with the skills, capital, and passion necessary to advance the line any farther. In the end, the synergy of hemispheric visions and railroad capitalism had failed to build a railroad the length of the Americas, but these forces had nonetheless produced a route stretching nearly two thousand miles below the Texas border as far as the Gulf of Fonseca at the southern end of El Salvador, an imperfect, indirect transportation corridor built largely under US corporate leadership and passable everywhere except for the dilapidated bridge at the Mexico-Guatemala border.

In the years after Keith's death, a handful of additional links in the Pan-American Railway route would be constructed, but these sections were largely built for local commercial purposes and not for reasons of larger hemispheric dreams. The only real evidence of the hemispheric route's ongoing existence in the political imaginary was the wholly ineffective Pan-American Railway Committee, which would endure until 1950, when the largely forgotten group was finally disbanded under orders from the Pan-American Union's successor, the Organization of American States.[162]

The underlying dream of hemispheric connectivity, however, never died. Rather, the senescence of the Pan-American Railway had corresponded with the birth of a new, rival vision for long-distance connection. As one Chilean paper observed in 1927,

> To think of constructing a railroad of such magnitude [as the Pan-American], of fantastic expanse and fabulous cost, in an epoch of cars and planes is to think very little of modern progress. Thirty years ago, the train was the fastest and easiest form of rapid overland transport. Today the rails are starting to be an obstacle and an anachronism. Rail lines are difficult to construct in territory like that found in the Americas, demanding enormous costs and not producing economic value for routes of enormous distance. . . . It would be far more rational and in accord with the ideas of our time to think of a [long-distance highway], a work much simpler to execute and of a cost infinitely smaller . . . which would resolve continental communication economically for the automobile.

Ultimately, "All aboard for Buenos Aires" had come to sound antiquated during the age of the motorcar.[163]

This new dream of a hemispheric highway had first emerged in the mid-1920s, while Keith was still building his Zacapa line. It was a dream born not only of Pan-Americanism but also of a powerful social crusade, the US "good roads" movement.

The same men who had led the fight to bring "good roads" to the United States would be the ones who would first champion Latin American highway development. And the same system of federal aid road building that they had devised at home would soon be exported abroad in support of this hemispheric highway. For these men, the dream of the highway grew not simply from the Pan-American movement, but more directly from a longer struggle within the United States to build modern "good roads." It was a struggle that ultimately reached back to a debate over national road building at the Constitutional Convention.

INTERLUDE

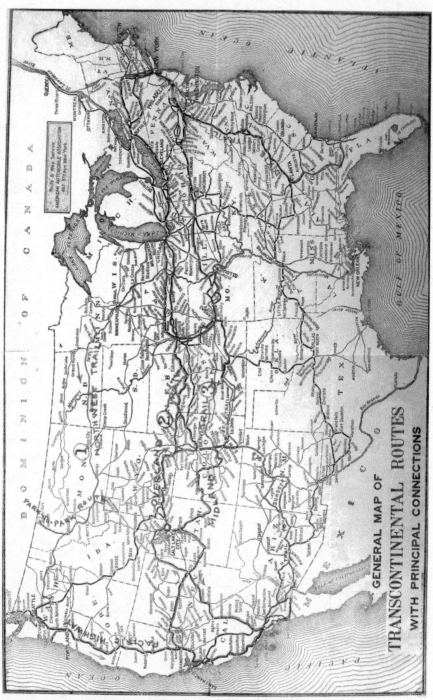

A map (c. 1912) showing two years of promotional automobile journeys that the chairman of the American Automobile Association took on behalf of good roads.

CHAPTER FOUR

Out of the Muck

The Other Monroe Doctrine

The Founding Fathers disagreed over the responsibility that a federal government should have in building highways. Some felt that a strong country would need centrally planned roads, while others feared the consequences of vesting such an expansive power with a national authority instead of with the states. For both sides of the debate, support could be found in the legendary roads of Rome, a product of the much-admired republican era but also a tool for unpopular military control during the subsequent imperial phase.

At the Constitutional Convention of 1787 in Philadelphia, the roads question formed part of a broader conversation concerning "internal improvements," a blanket term that also covered canal and harbor development. The debate over internal improvements lingered in the background of the convention until its final days, when the polymath senior statesman Benjamin Franklin finally offered a concrete proposal, urging that specific authority be granted Congress "to provide for cutting canals, where deemed necessary." This suggestion found immediate backing from the lead constitutional draftsman, James Madison, who soon used the opening Franklin had created to push for a generalized congressional power that could include road building "to secure an easy communication between the states." Both of these propositions, however, ultimately wilted before concerns about states' rights and national monopolies, and the final version of the Constitution said nothing about internal improvements nor about highways.[1]

But constitutional silence could not mute cries for federal highways. Advocates of such projects sought reliable communications both among the existing states and with the unsettled western lands around the Great

Lakes that the recent Northwest Ordinance had brought under congressional control. National authority, after all, mattered little if the government and its citizens had no easy means to reach large portions of the new country. President George Washington's powerful Treasury secretary Alexander Hamilton, who supported nationally sponsored public highways, observed, "The improvement of the communications between the different parts of our country is an object well worthy of the national purse."[2]

One of the most popular ideas along these lines was the construction of a great east–west road to reach the northwestern territories. This proposal even appealed to Thomas Jefferson, the most prominent critic of federal overreach in the 1790s and the president from 1801 to 1809. Despite his fears that too much centralized power would lead to tyranny, Jefferson believed that the nation's future prosperity and the survival of its democracy demanded western agrarian expansion, an "Empire of Liberty" in his words, and a developed western overland route promised to facilitate this outcome.[3]

The push to authorize this western road became one of the features of Jefferson's administration. A specific proposal first emerged in 1802, the year after Jefferson became president, when a congressman called for a western road to be built as part of the process of granting Ohio statehood. The next several years witnessed prolonged deliberations in Congress over both the plan's constitutionality and the road's proposed route and financing, but in 1806 Jefferson and Congress managed to secure an initial authorization for what would soon be known as the National Road. Its route would follow a course that George Washington himself had originally helped survey during the French and Indian War, beginning in the Maryland tidewater, crossing the Cumberland Valley, and then reaching the new northwestern territories.[4]

As part of the debates over this National Road, the Senate had also requested the first full-scale study of internal improvements throughout the United States. Responsibility for this landmark investigation fell to Jefferson's Treasury secretary Albert Gallatin, a gifted Swiss-born politician who might have risen to the presidency but for his foreign origin. Gallatin's report finally appeared in 1808 and laid out an elaborate network of several dozen canals and "artificial roads . . . of gravel or pounded stone" that would link the entire nation east of the Mississippi River. His plan, which included the already authorized National Road, promised a means to forge physical bonds of union that would complement the legal bonds that the Constitution had created two decades earlier. Gallatin further suggested that the states amend the Constitution to authorize his program and, consequently, resolve the festering concerns over the legality of federally sponsored internal improvements.[5]

Lurking behind Gallatin's program, unstated but omnipresent, were also concerns about the United States' commercial dependence on Europe. The nation's reliance on European trading partners had been coming under heightened scrutiny after England and France, as part of the Napoleonic Wars, had both violated US merchants' ability to trade neutrally with all parties, sometimes through impressment; and in 1807, the year before Gallatin's report appeared, Jefferson had gone so far as to authorize the first of a series of Embargo Acts that forbid US exports to Europe. The Gallatin plan thus offered a long-term blueprint to shift development away from Europe and toward the nation's vast interior. Nonetheless, the tensions with Europe took political precedence over his report in the near term, and the ongoing behavior of England eventually led the United States into a two-and-a-half-year-long war with its former colonizer that crushed any immediate hope for the realization of an ambitious plan of internal improvements.[6]

Interest in Gallatin's report, however, was subsequently reanimated by the surge of nationalism that followed the War of 1812. Especially strong support came from House Speaker Henry Clay and his congressional colleague John C. Calhoun. Together they championed a new program for national development, known as the American System, built upon the three pillars of internal improvements, a national bank, and a strong tariff. (Clay would soon also internationalize this vision through his advocacy of New World independence movements: a hemispheric American System that would provide the necessary markets for the increased manufacturing his domestic program aimed to achieve.) Congressional enthusiasm for internal improvements grew steadily over the next several years, and in late 1816 Congress passed new legislation to fund the construction of a communications system that included the National Road and other parts of Gallatin's decade-old report. As Calhoun declared, "Let us, then, bind the Republic together with a perfect system of roads and canals."[7]

The age of systematic, federally sponsored overland communication seemed finally to have arrived. But then, in March 1817, President James Madison stunned Clay, Calhoun, and the rest of Congress with a veto of their legislation as his final presidential action.

Madison's opposition seemed to cut against the entire record of his eight-year presidency. He had begun his administration with support for the nationalist policies that helped trigger the War of 1812, had subsequently allowed Congress to continue funding Jefferson's slowly expanding

National Road, and in 1815 had even specifically asked Congress to authorize "roads and canals which can best be executed under national authority." Madison's sudden about-face, as he explained in his veto message, arose from the "insuperable difficulty" he felt trying to reconcile Clay's legislation with the Constitution itself. The president remembered well the original fight over internal improvements at the Constitutional Convention and, in his final days of office, felt a profound need to defend the charter he had helped author against the latitudinarian impulses of men like Clay and Calhoun.[8]

Madison's presidential successor James Monroe, a fellow Founding Father, endorsed this strict interpretation and, like Gallatin before him, urged a constitutional amendment to permit internal improvements.

The stance of Monroe and Madison, however, failed to convince many in Congress that they lacked the requisite authority. The congressional champions of internal improvements pointed both to precedents such as the National Road and to several broad constitutional provisions, including the "general welfare" clause. Soon Clay and Calhoun spearheaded a new congressional campaign that culminated with an 1822 bill authorizing the federal government to administer tollgates along the National Road as a way to fund its ongoing maintenance and construction.[9]

Monroe, as expected, vetoed the tollgate measure as unconstitutional, but the relentless pressure in Congress for internal improvements and the absence of any moves toward a constitutional amendment compelled the president to reconsider his earlier view. He soon issued a novella-length memo that concluded in somewhat woolly prose that Congress might have the authority under the "general welfare" clause to fund improvements if the federal government never exercised jurisdiction directly and only pursued projects that were truly national in character.[10]

A clearer affirmation of this policy finally appeared in December 1823, during the same congressional address in which the president introduced the famed Monroe Doctrine. As he explained, "Congress possess[es] the right to appropriate money for . . . a national object (the jurisdiction remaining to the states)." Thus, at the same moment that Monroe had created the nation's first hemispheric foreign policy, he had also put forth a constitutional theory of road building that would allow the federal government to play a direct role in the construction of highways as long as the states maintained ultimate control.[11]

The emergence of Monroe's road doctrine helped to bring about a large amount of new legislation for internal improvements in the mid-1820s, and millions would be appropriated for roads and canals. Monroe's approach was also largely subscribed to by President Andrew Jackson, who rode to office in 1828 on a wave of discontent with the federal government. Jackson's support helped further enshrine the legitimacy of Monroe's carefully argued doctrine, bringing something of a conclusion to the road building debate that the Constitution itself had failed to settle.[12]

The fervor for national road building, however, lasted barely half a decade before serious congressional concerns emerged. Surfaced highways demanded constant, costly upkeep, and Monroe's rejection of federal tollbooths had forced Congress to appropriate new funds continuously to maintain the National Road and other federal projects. By 1829, Congressman James Buchanan of Pennsylvania was lobbying to have the states along the National Road assume full control over the route since only they had the required authority to operate tolls. Buchanan's proposal gained traction through the early 1830s, and Congress finally began to enact this transfer in 1835. The Panic of 1837 then helped shut the flow of Washington money for road building entirely. The federal government by that point had spent roughly $7 million on the National Road and another $7 million on other highways, a combined amount approximate to what Jefferson had paid for the Louisiana Purchase.[13]

But the National Road's expense was hardly the only reason why Congress withdrew its support from the project. For southern slaveholders, the National Road and other federal highways were setting a dangerous precedent: the same liberal reading of the Constitution's "general welfare" clause that Monroe had used to sanction internal improvements could potentially allow federal interference with the South's "peculiar institution" as well. One influential southern congressman sounded the alarm in 1824, declaring, "If Congress possesses the power to [make internal improvements] . . . they may emancipate every slave in the United States."[14]

The slaveholding South's contempt for federal projects subsequently progressed in near lockstep with its zeal for states' rights during the next quarter century. By 1848, the official platform of the southern-dominated Democratic Party abandoned Monroe's view entirely and stated that "the Constitution does not confer upon Congress the power to commence and carry on a general system of internal improvements." An exasperated Henry Clay, in one of the last speeches he gave before succumbing to tuberculosis in 1852, wondered when "the people would rise up en masse and trample down your little hairsplitting distinctions about what is national and state and demand what is fair and just." [15]

Southern resistance critically injured federal efforts to provide long-distance communication networks in the generation before the Civil War, but the final nail in the coffin of national road building took the form of an iron spike. Starting around 1830, commercial steam trains had begun appearing in the United States, and their arrival had immediately threatened the wagon road's timeless monopoly on overland travel. Railroads moved goods and people faster than even the swiftest horse-drawn carriages. With each passing year, the disruptive technology's range and reliability increased. The growing rail network gradually provided a challenge to the many turn-pikes and toll roads that had been built through state, federal, and private funds but whose high maintenance costs had proved dispiriting. [16]

By the time the Civil War finally broke the southern blockade on federal spending, the railroad had fully displaced the wagon road as the preferred means for long-distance overland travel. The once-mighty National Road that had caused so much uproar in the nation's early years became a relic of a former age, its spiritual and practical standing replaced by the federally sponsored transcontinental rail project. State governments similarly raced to invest in the new "iron highways" and abandoned their road obligations, which they viewed as redundant, as unnecessary burdens on the public treasury. The role that the government played in long-distance travel thus shifted from the creation of public thoroughfares to the support and promotion of privately owned routes, and the policy that Monroe had crafted redounded to the advantage of men such as Jay Gould and Collis Huntington. The existing long-distance roads either collapsed or remained with private corporations that held tollbooth monopolies and showed only minimal concern for maintenance. [17]

Rural roads, in the popular imagination, now existed primarily to cover the gaps that separated the nation's railroads and harbors from the sites of agricultural production, a "farm to market" function, fundamentally local in character. [18]

"A Slough of Despond"

Traditions inherited from centuries-old English common law placed default responsibility for US rural roads with the communities they served. Most typically, a "working out" tax required each adult male to devote one or two days a year to road upkeep under the supervision of a rotating community supervisor, who received some compensation. This system aimed to ensure continual maintenance, but farmers treated their obligations more as holiday than hard labor. As one nineteenth-century observer griped,

> Arriving on the ground long after the usual time of beginning work, the road-makers [banter] until slow-acting conscience convinces them that they should be about their task. They then with much deliberation take the mud out of the road-side ditches . . . and plaster the same on the centre of the road. A plough [next] destroys the best part of the road, that which is partly grassed and bush-grown, and the soft mass is heaped up on the central parts of the way. . . . An hour or two is consumed at noon-day by lunch. . . . A little work is done in the afternoon, and at the end of the day the road-making is abandoned until the next year.[19]

Farmers behaved in this lackadaisical fashion less out of indolence or indifference than out of resignation. Their young nation had a character far wilder than England in terms of both geography and climate. One nineteenth-century road builder noted, "In many parts of the United States the roads are torn up with the outcoming frost in the spring, soaked with the autumn rains, frozen into ridges in winter, and buried in the dust in the summer, making four regular seasons of bad roads, besides innumerable brief 'spells.'" Moreover, few parts of the United States had been settled long enough or with sufficient population density to benefit from the slow, imperceptible compaction effect that hooves and wagon wheels exerted on roadbeds over generations. Many farmers simply doubted that better-quality roads could be achieved without incredible expense, if at all.[20]

The situation's seeming inevitability left US farmers largely unresponsive to several crucial innovations in road building techniques that had arisen in Europe during the early nineteenth century. The developments there centered around the efforts of John Loudon McAdam, a Scottish road supervisor. McAdam, after years of experimentation and consultation with engineers, had devised a technique that produced hard-surfaced roads that could compete in terms of durability with the far more expensive Roman style, which had treated roads almost like mason walls turned horizontal. McAdam's approach required that the ground be properly drained and graded and then covered with a six-to-eight-inch layer of compacted "walnut sized" stones. This type of surface, unlike ones composed of gravel or larger "mischievous" stones, actually grew stronger through use and regular maintenance. As one writer explained, "Under the constant passing of wagons equipped with iron-tired wheels, the roads not only lived, but improved, the wheels crushing a percentage of the rock and the dust particles sifting their way into the interstices and forming a cemented, bonded, impervious, water-shedding shell." The virtually impermeable barrier that resulted— soon known as a "macadamized surface" or, simply, macadam—prevented rain or winter frosts from compromising the subsoil's integrity and ensured long-term resilience.[21]

McAdam's reforms extended beyond technical innovation to also include the need for both rigorous supervision and maintenance. As he noted in the 1823 edition of his landmark treatise on road building, "my labours have been as constantly directed towards the introduction of a wise and well-regulated system of management for the roads, as towards their mechanical construction."[22]

The impact of McAdam's ideas on management and technical construction helped transform the British landscape over the course of several generations. A mid-nineteenth-century US traveler observed of England, "The first thing [the American] discovers is that England is a land of Roads, new Roads, and that every body there, as here, is in motion. The whole map of the island is covered with a fine net work of rails and macadamized Roads."[23]

The disparity between local British and US roads could easily scandalize English visitors touring their former colonies. Charles Dickens, who traveled along backcountry Ohio roads during his famous 1842 visit to the United States, wrote of his journey,

> At one time we were all flung together in a heap at the bottom of the coach, and at another we were crushing our heads against the roof. Now, one side was down deep in the mire[, and then the coach] was rearing up in the air, in a frantic state. . . . The drivers on these roads . . . so twist and turn the team about in forcing a passage, corkscrew fashion, through the bogs and swamps, that it was quite a common circumstance on looking out of the window, to see the coachman with the ends of a pair of reins in his hands, apparently driving nothing. . . . Never, never once, that day, was the coach in any position, attitude, or kind of motion to which we are accustomed.

A portion of Dickens's trip, equally unpleasant, also included so-called corduroy roads, which were built by laying down logs one after another. This style of road building, which experienced something of a craze in the United States during the 1840s, was favored in areas with plentiful wood but little gravel or suitable stones. No one, however, considered corduroy roads equal to macadam ones.[24]

In the decades after Dickens's visit, the shortcomings with the United States' rural road network only deepened. Many farmers and immigrants eschewed intensive development of established agricultural regions and their wagon roads, preferring instead the promise of new, fertile lands that railroads helped open. And in the more heavily settled eastern regions, railroad networks grew dense enough to provide cheap, easy connections between most towns and cities. The faster the nation's railroad network expanded, the worse the rural roads seemed to become.

The US commissioner of agriculture asserted in 1868, some two dozen years after Dickens's trip, that "good [roads] are the exceptions in all the States." The few instances of "good roads" that could be found tended to appear in wealthy towns near major urban areas. Everywhere else had roads so bad as to almost defy belief. Contemporary observers described the situation as a "crying evil" and a "slough of despond." One frustrated late-nineteenth-century US professor stated, "Whether on the gravelly soil of Massachusetts, the clays of New York and Indiana, or the prairies of the Mississippi Valley, our common roads are worse than in any other civilized country." An 1888 federal government report added, "While our railway system has become the most perfect in the world, the common roads of the United States have been neglected and are inferior to those of any other civilized country in the world. They are deficient in every necessary qualification that is an attribute to a good road; in direction, in slope, in shape and service, and, most of all, in want of repair."[25]

The nation's torturous roads inconvenienced everyone, but farmers suffered the most. In muddy months, the rural roads of many regions worked about as well as New England canals in the depths of winter, when the rivers froze over, and farmers bore the costs of spoiled crops, overtaxed horses, and ruined wagons. As one jingle explained, the farmer "cannot haul to market when the market is high; he must haul to market when the roads are dry."

These burdens faced scant interrogation until the 1880s, a period when farmers started to organize around a range of grievances, most notably excessive rail rates, low crop prices, and the inflexible gold standard. An 1883 editorial in the *Southern Cultivator* explained, "Bad roads, like bad whisky, not only make bad morals, but . . . impose upon the people taxes heavy, onerous, and . . . perfectly appalling. . . . It is a tax on mind, muscle, morals and material—on man, beast and vehicle, upon time and sense, upon all things animate and inanimate that travel the highways." Throughout the 1880s, a small number of farmer congresses met to discuss the subject, but the twin weights of tradition and tax fears dragged down virtually every attempt at reform.[26]

During these same years, pockets of northeastern elites, often gentlemen farmers with country estates, began to champion good roads as well. One of the most prominent such good roads advocates was Pennsylvania's Alexander Cassatt, the railroad executive who would soon chair the Intercontinental Railway Commission. Cassatt had personally assumed the position of road supervisor in his hometown, a novel step that prompted one journalist, while writing on "the indifference of the general public" for good roads, to suggest that Cassatt must have accepted the responsibility "partly as a joke." But Cassatt's behavior likely owed more to a sense of noblesse oblige and, above all, a desire to trot his prized horses through the lands around his estate.[27]

In New Jersey, meanwhile, a serious campaign for good roads was coalescing around Chauncey Ripley, a prominent lawyer with large holdings in Union County. Ripley and his well-connected cohort wanted to reform the traditional laws that placed all power with individual towns and that inhibited systematic improvement of county through routes. As one of Ripley's coagitators explained,

> The law of the middle ages regarding the maintenance of public roads is still in force ... generally throughout the State.... As the matter now stands every township ... is at liberty to patch and repair general public highways in as many different ways as there are districts. That is why nine-tenths of the roads in this State are well-nigh impassable during certain seasons of the year.

In mid-1889, Ripley's group finally convinced the New Jersey Legislature to reform the state's laws to permit the designation of "county roads" whose upkeep could be funded through bonds. Following the legislative victory, Ripley crowed, "This act is the practical outcome of long-growing dissatisfaction [wherein public roads] are kept in a state of wretched unrepair by the spasmodic and utterly inefficient system of township control."[28]

Ripley's victory marked the first time that a state had acknowledged the impracticality of leaving road management, at a general level, strictly with the smallest unit of government. The long descent into intolerable roads that had begun in the 1830s with the arrival of steam trains, with the despair over costly turnpike upkeep, and with the collapse of federal involvement beneath southern resistance had, quite possibly, started to rebound from its nadir.

And at this same moment, a powerful movement was forming to launch a national crusade for good roads. The men behind it would bring a new-found fervor and organization, and they would arrive on two wheels, as missionaries of a revolution in personal transport.

The Gospel of Good Roads

The bicycle had first pedaled into the US imagination with a public display at the 1876 Philadelphia Exposition, a grand affair commemorating the nation's centennial. The self-propelled transportation device, with its large front wheel and spoked rubber tires, had evolved gradually in France and England before debuting in Philadelphia alongside other modern marvels such as the typewriter and Alexander Graham Bell's telephone.[29]

The throngs amassed at Philadelphia had included Colonel Albert A. Pope, a young Civil War veteran and entrepreneur from Boston who quickly grasped the bicycle's revolutionary potential. Pope soon began importing bicycles from England and, in 1878, manufactured the nation's first domes-tic model, known as the Columbia. During the subsequent few years, a large portion of total US bicycle sales originated directly from Pope, who mixed an aggressive pursuit of patents with a host of manufacturing advances and a flair for promotion. As one contemporary admirer noted, "With one hand he had to create a demand and with the other create the supply."[30]

Pope, like other vendors, sold most of his products to affluent young and middle-aged men. The rest of the population tended to balk at the bicycle's high cost and at the inherent risks of traveling on a contraption that could launch a rider headlong over its tall front wheel upon striking any small obstacle or pothole in the nation's notoriously poor roads. Mark Twain, who sampled an early model, quipped, "Get a bicycle. You will not regret it, if you live."[31]

The new technology's danger and expense soon produced a distinct cul-ture built around elite masculinity, sport, and daredevilry. For the average farmer or merchant, however, bicycles represented a rich man's plaything, a nuisance that spooked horses. And the conflicts between these competing road users quickly prompted numerous municipalities to pass ordinances against bicyclists.

*   *   *

In March 1880, the editor of the nation's first bicycle magazine finally responded to these mounting restrictions with a call for a new lobbying organization. His announcement asked dedicated riders from around the country to gather two months later in Newport, Rhode Island, the epicenter of Gilded Age opulence. The resulting meeting brought together 150 riders, "good-looking, gentlemanly, and easy-going," according to the *Providence Journal*. Together they formed the League of American Wheelmen "to protect and to further [their] general common rights and interests." Pope attended as a Massachusetts delegate and helped fund some of the campaigns that followed.[32]

Initially, the Wheelmen's efforts focused on the Northeast, where their numbers were strongest, but their influence began to swell dramatically in the late 1880s, following the arrival of the "safety bicycle." This newer design, with two equal-sized wheels that decreased the peril from spills, expanded the technology's appeal to broad segments of society, especially women. By 1888, the Wheelmen had successfully overturned nearly all the legal obstacles they faced, and at their annual meeting that year the group's leadership decided to turn their attention to a new cause, the scourge of bicyclists: bad roads.[33]

The new campaign started out targeting state law reform directly, but staunch resistance from farmers fearing increased taxation compelled the Wheelmen to shift tactics by 1890. Soon they focused on good roads education, assigning control of this task to Isaac Potter, a New York lawyer who had previously secured for his compatriots the much-sought-after right to pedal through Central Park.[34]

Potter subsequently used his position to guide the Wheelmen's evolution from a group blatantly pursuing its own interest to one purporting to act for the common man, the farmer above all. As Potter declared in his widely distributed 1891 polemic *The Gospel of Good Roads*, "Every other civilized nation on the face of the globe has repented its shamefaced imposition upon the farmer." Potter identified a host of reasons why the nation needed to take action: good roads would revitalize rural life, ensuring that even in rainy months children could attend school and families could travel to church; the current system wasted countless millions on ineffective supervisors with no knowledge of road building techniques or maintenance; and improved roads would ultimately pay for themselves through increased productivity and reduced transportation costs. Potter stressed,

It is a reform that benefits all and injures none; makes you broader and better in your person and in your possessions; helps and hastens the happiness of your family; shields and saves the patient friend that drags your wagon so many miles from year to year; puts you on better terms with yourself and all mankind and leaves you wondering what sort of a farmer that was who lived and labored in a sea of mire.[35]

Loyal Wheelmen began preaching Potter's *Gospel* around the country. In lectures and through dozens of other pamphlets, they spread the message that good roads meant prosperity for all. Pope, the organization's largest donor, even financed a five-year educational program in highway engineering at the Massachusetts Institute of Technology.[36]

The Wheelmen's instructional work in this period provided the glue that strengthened the numerous individual good roads reform movements around the country. The bicyclists also directly contributed to the success of several campaigns for state reform, including Chauncey Ripley's ongoing labors in New Jersey, which helped produce the nation's first state aid law in 1891. The *New York Times* observed of the Wheelmen the following year, "It is novel to find so philanthropic a motive underlying the efforts of an amateur athletic organization."[37]

By mid-1892, the most important verse in the Wheelmen's gospel dealt with the restoration of federal involvement to US road building. This radical idea, practically unspoken for almost three generations, had been revived within Wheelmen circles through the agitation of Pope. He first broached the subject publicly during an October 1889 speech to the Carriage Builders' National Association. As he explained, "The high point to be aimed at is the recognition . . . by the national government, and the establishment by Congress of a national system. . . . A commissioner of highways might be provided for, in the Agricultural Department, with a corps of consulting engineers, and suitable appropriations made, for the prosecution of a general supervising work."[38]

Pope's proposal resonated not only with many Wheelmen, but also with Roy Stone, a Civil War general and prominent New York engineer. Stone displayed a penchant for oversized projects, and nothing seemed larger than a national road network. Soon the New Yorker put together a proposal intended to be submitted as a bill in Congress that pleased both Pope and the Wheelmen leadership. It called for the creation of a National Highways

Commission whose duties would include conducting studies toward the realization of a federal system of roads. The Wheelmen leadership subsequently arranged to have sympathetic legislators submit Stone's proposal in early July 1892, the same month as the bicycle organization's annual convention, scheduled that year for Washington, DC.[39]

The Wheelmen, whose ranks had reached an estimated twenty thousand, championed Stone's bill with greater intensity than any prior effort. During the July convention, a river of Wheelmen flowed through the streets of the capital, and letters of support rained down on Congress. Pope pushed with particular zeal and corresponded directly with countless national leaders, including President Benjamin Harrison. At the height of the summer campaign, Harrison said of the Wheelmen, "[Y]our body deserves a medal in recognition of its philanthropy." By late July, the bicyclists' prodigious efforts had secured Senate approval of the Highways Commission bill, and Stone bragged to the press the following month: "[T]he current of public opinion is setting strongly toward a return here to the ideas of Clay and Calhoun and the legislation of the era, when it was declared the duty of the Government 'to bind the Republic together with roads,' and many National roads were begun."[40]

Stone's public optimism, however, belied the difficulties remaining in the House, where newly enacted rules demanded unanimous consent within the committee overseeing his bill. One of Stone's coagitators confided to him in late July, "[T]hese gentry [representing agricultural interests] are openly boasting that they will prevent unanimous consent."[41]

Despite the Wheelmen's prolonged efforts, many farmers and their representatives continued to be wary of good roads and of the potential taxes involved. The newly formed Populist Party, which brought together many of the regional agricultural groups that had emerged in the 1880s, had largely refused to prioritize road building. The party's Omaha Platform, a landmark statement of principles that appeared almost simultaneously with Stone's bill, had ignored good roads entirely, defying both the Wheelmen and an unrelated appeal from a wealthy Ohio businessman named Jacob Coxey for a $500 million national highway system.[42]

Stone and his Wheelmen allies nonetheless pushed relentlessly to persuade reluctant congressmen, and by late summer 1892 much of the farmer-aligned congressional opposition had retreated beneath their ongoing efforts. But Stone's quest for unanimity ultimately collapsed in the face of opposition from House Speaker Charles Crisp, a Georgia Democrat who had pledged that July to defend "the plain people of the country who are burdened with unjust taxation." Stone later lamented that his bill had failed through "the determination of one man who had it in his power to put his foot on it."[43]

The surprise defeat following such a dramatic and widespread campaign convinced Stone to revise his strategy entirely. He concluded that his National Highways Commission bill could only succeed and restore federal involvement to the road problem if he first decoupled the good roads movement from the very bicyclists who had been its greatest proponents. The movement, he felt, needed to become more inclusive and less dependent on an athletic organization that many farmers continued to regard with skepticism.

Soon Stone determined to form a new organization, a National League of Good Roads. This league would allow the formal unification of the nation's various good roads advocates: progressive farmers, bicyclists, road builders, carriage makers, and even railroaders, some of whom had come to accept that better roads would facilitate the delivery of farm products to their train depots. Stone's proposal found support from Pope and Potter, who also recognized that the prominence of the Wheelmen in the movement was acting to limit agricultural support for good roads. By late September 1892, Stone had arranged for the *New-York Tribune* to publish the announcement of an inaugural league congress to be held in Chicago the following month during the "dedication week" of the Columbian Exposition, where the massive anticipated crowds would offer a wide pool of potential attendees.[44]

The congress officially convened on October 19, 1892, and drew an impressive showing several hundred strong. The founding members included not only Stone and Pope and Potter but also Chauncey Ripley, Alexander Cassatt, the railcar magnate George Pullman, and a host of prominent politicians and businessmen devoted to good roads. Stone, who would soon be appointed to head the league, introduced the grand gathering, declaring, "Columbus discovered America in vain, if after four hundred years we are still behind the Ancient [Incas] and are not ashamed of it."[45]

Nearly all the people in attendance agreed that the nation needed major reforms of its road laws. Nonetheless, the potential return of direct federal aid, which many considered the ultimate goal, remained a divisive subject. Even Stone, who desperately sought financial support from Washington, assured publicly that "so bold and radical a departure ... will bring a cold shiver, like a plunge into unknown waters ... and it may even be found that direct national aid is not needed at all." The league, Stone felt, should primarily nurture grassroots support lest it alienate farmers, if not the broader population. The dreams of Clay and Calhoun would have to wait for a later day.[46]

Throughout the duration of the October congress, the views of Stone and Pope seemed bound as tightly as two neighboring rocks in a macadam road. But their consensus crumbled in early November 1892, when Pope declared publicly that he sought far more than what Stone's congress had seemed to agree upon. Pope insisted that the country needed a National Road Department with a cabinet-level officer at the helm, and soon he began heavily promoting a petition demanding this outcome.[47]

Pope's rogue behavior infuriated Stone, who feared that this new proposal would tarnish his league while achieving nothing so long as Speaker Crisp retained his power in the House. Stone assured the press that he had been caught by "complete surprise" and that "many of us disagreed with [Pope's] views very decidedly." Several weeks later, the league forced Pope to resign from its executive committee.[48]

While Pope labored to drum up popular support for his petition, the league leadership began working quietly on a rival strategy that one of Stone's congressional allies devised. According to this congressman, the House's problematic unanimity rule did not apply to the Committee on Agriculture, which meant the league might find success by transforming Stone's earlier bill into an Agricultural Department rider. Such a transfer also seemed likely to help bolster the support of farmers, who trusted that department more than any other federal body. Soon the league presented this plan to President Harrison's secretary of agriculture, who had previously expressed his adamant support for good roads, and in mid-January 1893 the agriculture secretary formally requested a $15,000 appropriation from Congress.[49]

The new request provoked little fanfare—no bicycle parades, no letter writing campaigns, no boastful proclamations to the press. Instead, Stone simply testified before Congress along with other league members and insisted that the measure sought ends that were "purely educational" and was not a scheme for national aid. Stone's assurances succeeded in persuading many of the congressmen involved to support his bill, but ongoing resistance forced the Department of Agriculture to strip down the measure further until all that remained was $10,000, primarily to fund "inquiries in regard to the status of road management" and "investigations in regard to the best method of road-making." This reduced request finally satisfied enough congressmen to allow its passage in early 1893.[50]

A yearlong battle that had captivated the capital in the summer of 1892 culminated in a meager $10,000 appropriation to support road building education. But this modest measure had finally brought the subject of roads back to the federal government's purview after an absence longer than the life span of many of the men involved. Soon the Department of Agriculture would use the funds to create an Office of Road Inquiry and appoint Stone to be its director.[51]

Pope, meanwhile, continued his vainglorious petition drive with little concern for the actions of his semi-estranged friend Stone. As he explained to a reporter in March 1893, "over 100,000 petitions were sent out ... and all signed petitions should be mailed to me at once." The following month, Pope finally presented Congress with the incredible results of his labors. His gargantuan petition, laid out as a single scroll, reportedly contained 150,000 signatures and measured nearly a mile in length. This profound show of support for good roads nonetheless left Congress wholly unmoved, just as Stone had anticipated five months earlier.[52]

Pope, the man many considered the "Father of the modern American good roads movement," had failed utterly in his bold gambit, but a glimmer of his dream still lived on through Stone's new Office of Road Inquiry.[53]

The Quiet Reign of Stone

Stone entered the fall of 1893 like a man trying simultaneously to ride two horses drawn toward different ends. His National League, which he continued to lead, remained the nucleus of US good roads agitation, but his new federal position demanded conformity with the policies of President Grover Cleveland, who had returned to the White House in March 1893 after a four-year absence and whose Democratic Party had led the opposition to Stone's National Highways Commission. Cleveland's new agriculture secretary, J. Sterling Morton, famed as the founder of Arbor Day, cautioned Stone repeatedly to act along "conservative lines" that would not be "officious or intrusive."[54]

Stone's plight only deepened as the nation entered a prolonged economic malaise following the Panic of 1893. The trying financial circumstances dissuaded lawmakers from increasing appropriations anywhere, and the good roads movement received particular scrutiny thanks to Jacob Coxey, the Ohio businessman who had unsuccessfully pushed a road building program on the Populist Party in 1892. Coxey had decided that the widespread unemployment unleashed through the 1893 Panic required government intervention and in early spring 1894 had commenced a march from his home state to the capital, where he planned to demand a $500 million federally sponsored road building initiative as a way to put unemployed laborers to work. His march, largely following the route of the old National Road, drew massive press attention and a corps of colorful supporters. Coxey's 350-person "army of the poor" finally reached the Capitol on May 1, 1894. Coxey tried to deliver a rousing speech before the assembled crowd, but police arrested him for trespassing before he could utter a word. The spectacle discomfited many in Washington and tarnished the cause that Stone had worked so assiduously to insulate from all prior displays of exuberance. Good roads reform suddenly seemed entangled with the actions of a dangerous man.[55]

Three months after Coxey's humiliating arrest, Stone's National League finally convened for its first convention since the formation of the Office of Road Inquiry. The meeting, held in Asbury Park, New Jersey, brought together many of the central figures in the good roads movement, and few could ignore Stone's altered demeanor. The formerly sanguine leader appeared chastened, no longer acting as a visionary engineer pursuing the revival of national road building. As Stone explained to the delegates,

> The Secretary [of Agriculture] does not believe in paternal policies, but [rather] in the policy Congress has adopted of making a very careful investigation ... of the condition of the roads of the country.... [The] one thing that we can do here ... is to gather some very definite information as to what is being done in the various States.... I do not desire to speak on the general question [of good roads] because I want to get information from those that are here.

Several days after this speech, Stone assured an anxious congressman that "absolutely nothing [was] being done in the name of the National League," which was "practically dead" moving forward. The federal office, Stone promised, now "answer[ed] all the purposes of the headquarters."[56]

During the subsequent few years, Stone and his small office staff pursued a range of initiatives that conformed to Morton's mandate. Much of their work consisted of gathering data and compiling information from states, more than half of which had passed road building aid legislation by 1895. And gradually, a federal-level institutional knowledge began to coalesce from the fog of uncoordinated developments taking place around the nation.[57]

The strictures of being a federal officer, however, weighed heavily on

Stone. He had long been a man of action, not a bureaucrat, and the temptation of good roads lobbying proved impossible to resist when several of his old colleagues began pushing to revive the National Highways Commission bill. In February 1896, Stone endorsed this resurrected measure publicly and contended that national work "could advantageously be broadened and extended."

The campaign soon stumbled, but Stone's prospects to "broaden and extend" his own office's work nonetheless improved shortly thereafter when Republican William McKinley won the 1896 presidential election and appointed James Wilson as his secretary of agriculture. Upon reaching Washington, Wilson encouraged Stone to "push the practical side of our work instead of the Academic."[58]

Wilson's directive allowed Stone to finally try implementing a program that he had long viewed as essential: object-lesson roads. These had first been employed at a state level as far back as 1889, but almost nothing had been attempted by Stone's office during Morton's tenure. Following Wilson's arrival, however, Stone began shifting resources toward this new program. An office memorandum of that year explained,

> The lecturer on good roads . . . is listened to like one who tells fairy stories or travelers' tales of distant lands; but put down a piece of well-made Macadam road as an illustration and let the people try it in all weathers and no lecturer is needed, the road speaks for itself, all doubts disappear, and the only question raised is how fast can it be extended and how soon can the improvement become general.[59]

Wilson also suggested that the object-lesson program stretch beyond macadam surfacing to include steel roadways, an unproven concept that Stone had been desperately hoping to test for the past several years. Stone's basic design resembled a set of railroad tracks that had been widened to about ten inches and set flush against the ground. The durability of such a system, Stone felt, would make macadam roads obsolete. As he told a reporter in mid-1896, "I believe that the ultimate solution of our good roads problem for all great thoroughfares lies in the steel highway." Stone appealed to Wilson for a few thousand dollars to cover the costs of manufacturing special rolled steel for what he hoped would be a revolutionary development in highway building, but the new secretary, despite his support, soon proved unwilling to expend political capital fighting for increased road appropriations.[60]

Before Wilson's first year as secretary had concluded, the ongoing limitations of the Office of Road Inquiry drove Stone again toward outside advocacy. The paradox of possessing an authority that made him powerless had simply become intolerable. By November 1897, he was traveling to St. Louis to lend his name to a good roads convention that had been arranged by W. H. Moore, a charismatic promoter who seemed interested in restoring a national movement. The following month Stone offered "every possible support and encouragement" for plans from a resurgent Wheelmen's organization to distribute a million pamphlets endorsing state aid. And the Wheelmen heard from Stone once more several months later when he urged their backing for a transcontinental highway, something he assured "the Government could well afford."[61]

Throughout this period, Stone continued attending faithfully to his office responsibilities, but his priorities shifted altogether in mid-1898 after the United States declared war on Spain. The old Civil War veteran, more than thirty years removed from his last military campaign, volunteered without hesitation. Soon the army placed him at the head of a scouting mission in Puerto Rico locating roads for troop movements.[62]

Once the war ended, military leaders asked that Stone remain behind to oversee the construction of roads and other public projects. Of this work, he observed,

If the change to American possession can be made to bring the blessings of good roads to this island, the lesson may react upon the continent itself and aid the work of road improvement at home; and this is one thing which encourages me in my local work here and consoles me for my absence from the greater field.

Stone, however, gradually came to find his overseas activities so engrossing that he decided to tender his resignation to the secretary of agriculture in mid-1899. In the end, building roads for the federal government abroad brought fewer headaches than trying to accomplish the same back home.[63]

"A Zeal More Offensive Than Discreet"

Stone's resignation created a leadership void at the Office of Road Inquiry. The opening quickly drew interest from within Stone's staff, but the McKinley administration let politics prevail and handed control of the office to forty-nine-year-old Martin Dodge, a lawyer and state senator from the president's home of Ohio.[64]

Dodge had previously led Ohio's Highway Improvement Commission and saw his new appointment as an opportunity to expand his state-level good roads reform work to the national stage. Shortly after taking control of the federal road office, he declared, "The time has now come [for better] common highways.... And in order to make sure of [their] rapid and permanent improvement ... we should appeal to the original system of internal improvements advocated by Clay and Calhoun." The enthusiasm for national reform Dodge displayed at the outset of his Washington tenure matched, if not exceeded, that of Stone in the months before the outbreak of the Spanish-American War.[65]

But Dodge had reason to feel more optimistic than his predecessor about the possibilities for reform. His arrival had practically coincided with a major change in federal postal delivery that left rural communities clamoring for good roads. The new policy, the result of a decade-long debate in Washington, offered free mail service to all communities that had roads passable year-round. The government was finally offering rural populations the same free services that their urban counterparts had enjoyed for more than a generation: daily newspapers, catalogs, letters from relatives. The caveat about roads, however, disqualified almost everyone. The nation's farmers desperately wanted their newly granted free mail services, but they first needed improved roads. The assistant postmaster general declared in mid-1900, "With well-built agricultural roads traversing every part of this great country, and the free delivery of the mails brought to nearly every farmer's home, I confidently believe that a social revolution will be effected the benefits of which will be felt for generations to come."[66]

Dodge hoped to channel this incipient energy from rural districts toward national road reform and soon found a kindred spirit in W. H. Moore, the charismatic promoter who had earlier convinced Stone to visit St. Louis. Moore had recently formed the Interstate Good Roads Association specifically to push federal involvement with road building. His new organization aimed to revive the work of Stone's defunct National League. Moore himself lacked the financial means of earlier promoters like Pope but had nonetheless devised an ingenious way to both finance his movement and help stretch the federal road office's budget.[67]

Moore's scheme sought to capitalize on the dilemma that the postal service had created. Some rural communities, Moore speculated, would pay to host a good roads convention if the gathering included an engaging speaker and an object-lesson road demonstration that a federal official oversaw. It was akin to a tent revival for the gospel of good roads, and the funds raised would cover construction materials as well as speaker fees, leaving the federal government only responsible for its engineers' expenses.[68]

The plan soon received its first test when a federal engineer set out to accompany Moore's loyal apostle Rella Harber, supposedly the only "[female] good roads missionary in the country." Together they visited a hundred towns on a tour that reportedly covered thirty-five thousand miles spread across the Midwest. The tour's efficacy impressed Dodge, and in mid-1900 he began traveling personally to some of these conventions. His subsequent reports to the secretary of agriculture boasted of "very successful" results from his appearances, though he generally downplayed Moore's central role in organizing the events.[69]

After two years of these federally assisted conventions, Moore's group had expanded far beyond its Missouri roots. The promoter formally acknowledged this evolution at a November 1900 convention in Chicago during which he rechristened his strengthened group as the National Good Roads Association, a name that evoked Stone's widely admired former organization.[70]

Soon Secretary Wilson agreed to meet with Moore, who now appeared to be the dean of the national good roads movement. The promoter used the occasion to press one major objective: a $150,000 appropriation for Dodge's office. This amount, which represented a tenfold increase over the current expenditures, corresponded precisely with a recently revised budget that Dodge himself had submitted to Wilson after returning from one of the convention trips. Dodge and Moore, at times, seemed willing to scratch one another's back until blood flowed.[71]

Their bold appropriation request never reached Congress, but brighter prospects still awaited Moore in New York City. He headed there from Washington to meet with Stuyvesant Fish, the president of the Illinois Central Railroad. Fish had first offered his "hearty cooperation" to the good roads movement in 1892 and had recently written Moore to again express his support. During their meeting, the two men spoke of the problems Fish's railroad had experienced with an "inland mud blockade" that separated the port of New Orleans from one of his rail depots. Moore then suggested a proposal he had prepared beforehand: a "good roads train" that would carry road building equipment, speakers, and federal engineers to communities across the country. The cost, Moore estimated, would be $50,000. "That is a large amount of money to throw in the mud," the Illinois Central president observed, "but we will consider it." Three weeks later, Moore received the answer he had been hoping for.[72]

Fish's assent allowed Moore and Dodge to transform their earlier conventions into even grander affairs. The first good roads train, which traveled from Chicago to New Orleans in the spring of 1901, featured half a dozen weeklong gatherings. "The numbers attending these conventions," Dodge wrote Wilson, "were very large in every instance, being about 1,000 persons, and they were composed of leading citizens and officials of the state and local government." A second Fish-sponsored effort followed several months later, covering the distance from Chicago to Buffalo, where Moore arranged for a major convention and a special "Good Roads" day to coincide with the Pan-American Exposition. Following this, the Southern Railway and the Great Northern Railway both offered Moore funds to continue his campaign throughout their regions.[73]

The supposed public-spiritedness of these good roads trains helped to obscure the more questionable actions of Dodge and Moore. In addition to blurring the lines between private advocacy and government support, the two men were rumored to be accepting advanced payments for object-lesson roads that could only be funded if Dodge's office secured dramatically larger appropriations. One frustrated federal engineer complained privately,

> Moore always conveyed the impression that this was a government commission at large in the land to redeem the people from bondage to the mud. As the countenance of Dodge always beamed "Amen" to the most grotesque promises, pretenses, and philippics of these confidence artists the communities were prone to accept them at face value.... Only the mighty Dodge, representing the majesty of this supreme government and its beneficent Dept. of Agriculture, enabled this crafty gent to work his schemes upon honest people and avoid jail.

Dodge's participation in these trains lasted until Secretary Wilson decided to halt federal involvement altogether after 1902. By that point, however, Dodge had already discovered a new way to advance his agenda.[74]

*   *   *

In November 1902, Dodge had learned that Colonel W. P. Brownlow, a popular Republican congressman from Tennessee, was willing to sponsor a federal aid measure for good roads. This welcome news had reached Dodge through his second-in-command, Maurice Eldridge, who had recently enjoyed a chance encounter with Brownlow that included a discussion of the nation's atrocious highways. According to Eldridge, an imperious Brownlow had declared, "[Y]ou go back to Washington, consult with your chief and prepare a bill, submit it to me, and I will introduce it in Congress."[75]

Brownlow's words moved Dodge to take swift action, and within days he produced a new bill. The measure he drafted resembled New York's popular state aid law, which had been passed four years earlier and allowed Albany to fund half the costs of local highway construction if a state engineer approved the plans first. Dodge wanted to replicate New York's system on a national level, replacing the state engineer's function with a new federal bureau that would hopefully grow from the office he already controlled. His proposal suggested an initial outlay of $24 million over three years, enough to test the program in all the states.[76]

Brownlow found Dodge's work so compelling that he insisted the bill be the first measure introduced when the House reconvened in December. The congressman also decided to act as the bill's author, a move that suited his aggrandizing style and insulated Dodge from scrutiny for having injected politics into the federal road office.[77]

The bill's subsequent introduction in Congress seemed to finally unleash the momentum that had been building for good roads over the past decade. Brownlow considered the measure to be "the most popular . . . ever introduced in the House of Representatives since the Civil War." Support quickly poured in from farmers seeking their improved postal roads and from all the organizations that Dodge and Moore had helped build over the last several years. Even the South, which had led the fight against federal road building in the antebellum period, now displayed what Dodge described in correspondence as a "newly-revived and enlightened energy." As one eighty-year-old southerner explained,

> From Puget Sound to Cape Canaveral the people cry out for better country roads. In 1898 any one who put his ear to the ground could hear the coming of the Spanish-American War. . . . Now, if you put

your ear to the ground you can hear the on-coming of the good roads movement.... The Brownlow bill ... is demanded by more people than cried out for Cuba's deliverance, and more than are calling for the Panama Canal.[78]

The bill became the newest battlefront in Dodge's multiyear campaign for national reform. He soon reoriented much of his office toward advocacy, trampling the limits of his official mandate. As one federal engineer explained in private correspondence, "We are the ammunition and [Brownlow] is the cannon, and one could not get along without the other." Before long, Dodge turned some of this ammunition over to his longtime collaborator Moore, who had greater freedom of action than a federal official and who, as usual, had a clever plan.[79]

Moore's new scheme paralleled the one that Stone had employed ten years prior when his National League's inauguration piggybacked on the Columbian Exposition's dedication week. A similar opportunity, Moore had realized, awaited in his hometown of St. Louis, which was hosting the dedication ceremonies for the upcoming Louisiana Purchase Exposition in late April 1903. Moore had long been preparing to hold an annual meeting during this window, but the sudden appearance of the Brownlow bill—combined with Dodge's support—raised the event's profile dramatically. Eventually some of the most prominent men in the country agreed to attend and give talks. The final list included Democratic leader William Jennings Bryan and President Roosevelt. By March 1903, Moore was barnstorming the country, promising groups as far afield as Los Angeles, "The convention will be a big affair in every way."[80]

This "big affair" finally opened on April 27, 1903, and proved to be Moore's greatest success to date. Newspapers reported that more than twelve hundred people attended, with every state represented. The convention's main auditorium had been "profusely decorated" and wherever one looked banners preached the good roads gospel: "Your town will prosper in proportion to the improvement of your country roads"; "Good roads are necessary for rural mail delivery"; "There is no more common interest than the common road"; "As the public roads are the property of all and for the use of all, their cost should be shared by all."[81]

Roy Stone, who traveled to St. Louis for the event, could hardly believe how much the movement had grown in ten years. As he explained in a speech to the delegates,

The convention of 1892 was called by a few private enthusiasts, with fear and trembling for the result; this convention was called by a multitude of high officials in perfect confidence of the Nation's interest and participation. In 1892 our delegates were self-appointed; here they are appointed by municipalities, States, and public bodies. In that convention we dared not whisper "National aid to road build" save in secret; now we can shout it on all the highways and byways.[82]

Nearly everyone in attendance agreed with Stone that the time had finally arrived for national aid. Even Roosevelt, who avoided expressing overt support, stated in his closing message to the convention, "The faculty, the art, the habit of road building marks in a nation those solid, stable qualities, which tell for permanent greatness.... [W]e should have a right to demand that such a nation build good roads."[83]

The convention's delegates left St. Louis confident that national aid was near. Most newspapers agreed, and the campaign for Brownlow's bill continued unabated throughout the year, gaining sway across much of the nation. Eldridge wrote Dodge during an October trip to the Pacific Coast, "The idea of national aid is sweeping over the West like a tidal wave." By November, an editorial in the *Los Angeles Times* was declaring, "the advocates of the measure are anxious to develop some active opposition, as this will help them get the subject before the people, and give them an opportunity to show the strength of their case."[84]

Opposition nonetheless existed, and voices unfriendly to Brownlow's bill began to assert themselves more forcefully in 1904 as they became, in Dodge's words, "a little alarmed at the rapid progress of events." Brownlow's measure, according to its detractors, was "[t]he most stupendous example of centralization and fraternalism now on the boards," a "wildly paternalistic project" with "a bountiful output of pork." Foes of the Brownlow bill also believed that the potential scope of national road aid "would make the national debt, the pension account, the Panama programme, and all the rest combined look like a bagatelle." The Democrat-friendly *Washington Post*, which ran a series of scathing editorials against Brownlow throughout 1904, boldly headlined one screed, "Why Not Interplanetary Transportation?"[85]

In Congress, the fiercest resistance arose from the two Democrats respectively chairing the agricultural committees in the House and the Senate. They not only opposed the Brownlow measure in principle, but also personally disliked Dodge, the bill's true author. Their quarrels with Dodge reached back to his repeated attempts with Moore to gain larger appropriations. In the congressmen's view, Dodge had never respected his limited mandate and during the prior two years had foisted the Brownlow bill on both the politicians and public.[86]

The two powerful committee chairs finally concluded in early 1905 that the surest way to stymie national aid was to simply dispatch with Dodge altogether, and soon they inserted a short phrase into the annual agricultural appropriations bill to require that the director of the federal road office "be a scientist" moving forward. Their coup displayed such subtlety and precision that few in Congress even realized what was happening. The *New-York Tribune*, which had long championed national aid, subsequently explained that Dodge had been "quietly legislated out of office [for] exhibit[ing] a zeal more offensive than discreet in [his] propaganda . . . and especially in the direction of missionary work for the [Brownlow] bill."[87]

Secretary Wilson replaced Dodge with Logan Waller Page, a gifted thirty-four-year-old engineer who had spent the prior five years working for the federal government. Page came from one of the most well-respected families in Virginia and displayed the sort of probity that many felt Dodge had compromised.

Upon taking over the office, Page immediately stripped advocacy from its agenda. The whole fracas over the Brownlow bill struck him as a distraction to be avoided. The office, he soon insisted, "can not legitimately be a party to any movement, the direct purpose of which is to influence Congress in favor of National aid." As he explained, "An engineer should not be made a politician nor a politician an engineer." His few early forays into politics served mainly to challenge people such as Moore, who seemed to be exploiting legitimate good roads sentiments for personal gain. As Page later asserted, "I fought [Moore] in the public press and he finally dropped his road work. . . . As you well know, there are a lot of human vultures feasting on the road movement."[88]

Page's sudden withdrawal of his office from politics deprived the Brownlow bill of its greatest asset, and gradually the measure disappeared from the forefront of the national discourse. But Page's promotion would change more than just politics. He represented a new breed, the college-trained highway engineer, and he brought with him a remarkable asset: the world's greatest knowledge of road building materials.

The New Macadam

Page's interest in highway engineering could be traced to his relationship with Nathaniel Shaler, an uncle by marriage and renowned geology professor at Harvard. Shaler was an early proponent of good roads and in 1892 had persuaded his nephew, who was then a student at the prestigious Virginia Polytechnic Institute, to transfer to Harvard, where Shaler was about to inaugurate a pathbreaking program in highway engineering.[89]

When Page reached Cambridge, he became part of a three-man cohort that would be the first group in the United States to ever receive formal college training in road building. "The term 'highway engineer,'" Page later observed, "was [then so little] known [that] my colleagues in college laugh[ed] at me when I would speak of [it]." The pioneering curriculum at Harvard mixed lectures from a local engineer with tours around the community that, according to Shaler, allowed the three students to study "all grades of roads, from the various kinds of pavements used in a great city to the ordinary earth ways of very rural districts."[90]

Page readily distinguished himself in the program as well as in the social life of Cambridge. As one classmate noted, "He was a most interesting and charming companion, a man of wide information and picturesque power of expression. He had the qualities of a Southern gentleman of the best type." Among those taken by Page's genteel charm was Shaler's daughter, Anne, and soon the two cousins embarked upon a consanguineous courtship.[91]

Page's education, like his love life, progressed under Shaler's watchful gaze. The Harvard professor encouraged his nephew to cultivate his "unusual talents" as an investigator. Shaler's particular hope was that Page would specialize in the scientific study of road materials, a subfield of highway engineering that had emerged around 1870 in France but was virtually unknown in the United States. Soon Shaler arranged for Page to spend the beginning of 1893 at France's École des Ponts et Chaussées, then considered "the recognized authority and perhaps the only educational institution in the world created to advance the science of highway engineering." The time abroad gave Page a knowledge of road testing methods exceeding that of any other US highway engineers, and in mid-1893 Shaler invited his protégé to take control of a newly authorized road materials testing laboratory at Harvard, which would be the nation's first such facility. With little delay, Page returned to Cambridge to assume this new responsibility and to continue his courtship of Shaler's daughter, whom he would marry in October 1893.[92]

The work at the new laboratory suited Page's meticulous and thought-ful temperament. In the words of one colleague, Page possessed that "rare scientific patience essential in order to discover the reasons for many of the empirical practices of engineering."[93]

The laboratory's largest initiative was the classification of New England's various minerals as road surfacing materials. As Page explained,

> No one rock can be said to be a universally excellent road material. . . .
> To select a material in a haphazard way, without considering the needs
> of the particular road on which it is to be used, is not unlike an ill
> person taking the nearest medicine at hand without reference to the
> nature of the malady or the properties of the drug. . . . An error in the
> selection of a material means an inferior road and occasionally a com-
> plete failure.

Using machines imported from France and several of his own design, Page soon began systematically analyzing the region's materials for three crite-ria: hardness (resistance against abrasion), toughness (resistance against impact), and cementation (the ability of wet rock dust to bind coarse frag-ments). His investigations finally brought the scientific method to the art of US road building, and his discoveries were eagerly greeted by New England road builders who had long chosen their materials through little more than tradition and guesswork.[94]

The federal government also began to pay attention. Page was providing a valuable service that exceeded anything Stone's Office of Road Inquiry was equipped to handle, and by 1899 Secretary Wilson had concluded that his Department of Agriculture needed a laboratory of its own. The follow-ing year Congress appropriated $7,500 for a national laboratory. The direc-torship was immediately offered to Page, who embraced the opportunity to expand his work to the national level.[95]

Page subsequently allowed his breadth of vision to grow alongside his increased resources. The new federal laboratory offered free testing of road materials from anywhere in the United States, and Page also broadened his work beyond this straightforward analysis into more creative endeavors. In one set of his experiments, Page practiced a type of geological alchemy, blending multiple rock types in an attempt to generate cementation values that exceeded the levels of each material alone. The most impressive dis-covery was a mixture of limestone and granite, which Page liked to boast displayed a binding power "more than seven times their common average."

Page additionally worked to devise solutions for regions that lacked easily accessible macadam materials, a problem across much of the South and Midwest. His proposed replacements included "burnt clay" and a clay-sand composite, both of which approximated the resilience of a macadamized surface under certain conditions.[96]

Page's work in this period ultimately aimed to strengthen McAdam's basic insights from a century prior and adapt them for circumstances in the United States. A new challenge, however, began to command increasing amounts of Page's energy around the time he was promoted to lead the federal road office: the very principles of macadamized construction seemed to be breaking down beneath the wear from a new transportation technology, the automobile. In the words of one journalist, the automobile was "the greatest menace to macadam that has ever made its appearance."[97]

The nation's rural road network had originally been seen more as a barrier to automobiles than as their victim. The dirt pathways that a horse and wagon could tolerate presented the faster-moving automobiles with an obstacle course of ruts, dips, and loose stones. As one of Henry Ford's early engineers noted, "Most of the roads were terrible, which was one reason why we took them; a car which survived them met the acid test." Charles Duryea, whose family firm produced the first US-built car in 1893, once quipped, "[Our] vehicles were built for bad roads and could go on good ones as well."[98]

Concerns about the automobile's impact on rural roads had only emerged in the early 1900s as the number of motorists grew and as touring became more popular.[99]

The first problem to gain notice were the dust clouds produced by fast-moving automobiles. These clouds coated crops and were generally seen as a health nuisance for anyone living nearby. As one newspaper editorial observed, "emerald lawns were taking on the hue of London fog and that box hedge was dove grey rather than green." The severity of the problem even led some in the nation's oil-producing regions to experiment with spraying crude petroleum directly onto their roads. This approach offered some relief, though few thought that it constituted a permanent solution.[100]

A second, related problem—and one of greater concern to the nation's highway engineers—involved the automobile's impact on macadam surfacing. As Page explained in 1907,

Fast automobile traffic has reached such proportions . . . as to shorten the life of the most carefully constructed and expensive macadam roads. . . . The powerful tractive force exerted by the driving wheels of automobiles soon disintegrates the road surface; the fine dust which ordinarily acts as a cementing agent is thrown into the air and carried off by wind or is easily washed off by rains. The pneumatic rubber tires wear off little or no dust to replace that removed by natural agencies. The result is that the stones composing the road become loose and rounded . . . and water is allowed to make its way freely to the foundation of the road.

The automobile, Page observed, was upending the century-old balancing act between wagon traffic and macadam wherein the regular passage of iron wheels and hooves produced rock dust at a rate that maintained surface cementation. This looming crisis was unlike anything the nation's road builders had ever faced. "This is a subject," Page cautioned, "which should engage the earnest attention of the National Government at once."[101]

Page hoped to resolve the predicament using the same scientific approach that he had earlier brought to macadam construction. Soon his office began measuring road decomposition and also constructing experimental roads with a bewildering variety of surface treatments. At one point, federal engineers even tested a road bound with molasses, which the press roundly mocked as a "candy road." The most promising binders, however, appeared to be tar and asphalt, two thick hydrocarbons that could be found in nature or derived from petroleum or coal.[102]

The idea of using asphalt or tar in road building was not entirely new. Some US cities already featured asphalt paving, a hardened mineral stew that blended the bituminous hydrocarbon with gravel, sand, clay, or pebbles. This style of paving had grown popular in the nation's urban areas during the late nineteenth century, following the exploitation of large natural asphalt deposits in Trinidad and Venezuela. Many city dwellers felt that the smoothness and resilience of asphalt paving made it superior to other urban surfaces, such as brick, woodblock, or cobblestone. The novelist Laura Ingalls Wilder's daughter, Rose, captured the experience of encountering asphalt paving for the first time in a passage she wrote describing an 1894 trip to Topeka, Kansas:

In the very midst of the city, the ground was covered by some dark stuff that silences all the wheels and muffled the sound of hoofs. It was like tar, but Papa was sure it was not tar, and it was something like rubber but it could not be rubber because rubber cost too much. We saw [ladies' heels dent] the street, and while we watched, those dents slowly filled up and smoothed themselves out. It was as if that stuff were alive. It was like magic.[103]

Asphalt paving, though ideal for automobile traffic, could not be transferred whole cloth to rural road building. The nation's sprawling road network, including the improved macadam highways, lacked the well-constructed foundations that underlay city streets, and, to make matters worse, the paving industry was controlled by a small number of private companies that guarded as proprietary secrets their processes and mixtures. Early attempts to spray heated asphalt directly onto macadam roads also produced disappointing results, with the bitumen failing to coat individual rocks fully enough to ensure a permanent bond.[104]

Page and his federal office worked tirelessly to overcome these hurdles. They conducted some of the earliest experiments on the application of asphalt to rural roads and soon found success using a variety of premixed compounds of macadamized stones and asphalt or tar, creating a surface known as bituminous macadam, or tarmac. Other road builders and state highway engineers also joined them in these experiments, but Page acted as the binder holding these disparate efforts together. Under Page's direction, the results gleaned from experimental bituminous roads throughout the country were collected and distributed as federal bulletins, helping to bring order and scientific rigor to an exceptionally messy process. Page's office even published the first glossary of bituminous road construction, which gave road builders a common language with which to describe the innumerable mixtures and techniques available.[105]

Alongside these activities, Page also explored the use of concrete as a road building material. Concrete, which some described as "synthetic stone," was created by mixing water with sand, an aggregate (such as pebbles or gravel), and a powerful binder known as cement. This cement, itself another miraculous artificial material, was a manufactured powdery substance derived from kiln-heated limestone and small amounts of other minerals—the dominant cement type, "Portland cement," had been developed in Europe and gained popularity in the United States during the late nineteenth century. Concrete, like asphalt paving, had already started appearing as street surfacing in urban areas, but it showed a problematic tendency to develop cracks that grew wider with time. Soon, however, Page would determine that wet concrete could be mixed with a specific proportion of oils to produce a material with much greater flexibility and water resistance as a road surface. This breakthrough, along with similar innovations performed by other highway engineers and road builders, helped to make concrete a more attractive option for fast-moving automobile traffic.[106]

By mid-1908, Page no longer viewed the automobile as a purely destructive force. As he explained, "[T]he automobile, while tending to destroy macadam road surfaces, has been an important influence not only in the building of many miles of well-constructed highways but also in rendering most urgent the study of road preservatives."[107]

The United States was not alone in facing the macadam crisis. Automobiles were also proliferating in Europe, where a far more expansive network of macadam roads existed thanks to massive investments that several governments had made during the prior century.

Europe's highway engineers, like their US counterparts, had been scrambling to find ways to save their good roads, and in early 1908 Page learned that the French minister of public works had decided to convene an international conference to discuss the matter. The conference's goal, Page explained, would be "that all nations should centralize their efforts [and] exchange information and thus make far more rapid progress toward the common goal" of saving roads from the automobile menace.[108]

The conference was to be held that October in Paris. The French minister invited all the world's highway engineers to attend and also "formally requested" participation from the governments of several nations, including the United States. President Roosevelt, who supported the French initiative, soon appointed Page to chair the nation's official delegation. The conference, Page felt, would be "the most momentous . . . ever convened to deal with any phase of transportation."[109]

When Page finally arrived in Paris, he encountered a scene every bit as grand as he had anticipated, with twenty-four hundred people from twenty-nine countries in attendance. The elaborate opening receptions were hosted in the Élysée Palace, and the French government had arranged for discussion sessions to be held at the Sorbonne and in a building nestled among the famous Tuileries gardens. The delegates were even treated at one point to lunch at Versailles, where they enjoyed the full display of palace fountains, a privilege reserved only for "rare occasions."[110]

Page used his time at the conference to compare notes with the world's

leading highway engineers and found that his country's work in road testing drew universal praise. According to the *Los Angeles Times*, engineers
from both France and England informed Page "that America had stepped
ahead of both those nations in the testing of materials for building macadam roads." Page himself concluded, with much pride, that the United
States "had nothing to learn from the older nations [in] the more scientific
branches of highway construction." The nation's sudden ascendance in this
aspect of road building was little short of remarkable, testament to Page's
fifteen years of laboratory work and his careful stewardship of the federal
road office.[111]

The overall US highway picture, however, remained bleak. According
to figures that Page's office had compiled shortly before the conference,
only 7.14 percent of the nation's 2,150,000-mile road network had been
improved to any degree. France alone possessed as many miles of improved
roads, and her highways were far wider and better maintained than almost
any of the United States' "good roads." Official US estimates also suggested
that it cost the average farmer twenty-five cents per mile to haul a ton
of goods by road, roughly double the rate in Europe. The United States,
Page conceded, trailed Europe to an "amazing degree in the percentage of
improved road mileage and in the jealous care with which their splendid
highways are maintained." The nation still remained hopelessly stuck in the
mud, despite having taken the lead in scientific road building.[112]

The United States' dismal road situation cut against the nation's self-
image as a rising power in the world. One reporter, in summarizing the
results of the conference, observed,

> There are scores of reasons why the United States should lead the
> world in good roads. . . . [F]rom the very dawn of civilization the
> nations which have ruled the world have led all others in road building
> and road maintenance. . . . If America is to maintain rank as the lead-
> ing nation of the world, there is work for highway engineers, and the
> time is short.

Before this dream could be achieved, however, the nation needed first to
address the political issue that most distinguished US road building from
that of its European rivals: the absence of national aid.[113]

The Long-Awaited "Plunge into Unknown Waters"

The good roads coalition that had pushed Brownlow's federal aid bill to the front of the national agenda had come undone over the course of several years. First there was the 1905 withdrawal of the federal road office, which had reoriented itself under Page's leadership to prioritize scientific work and investigations into dustless highways. Next was the decline of Moore's organization, whose vitality had depended upon its active cooperation with the federal government. And alongside these losses also came a subtler, but equally important, shift: the rural support that had grown so vast in favor of federal aid had begun to recede before the rise of the automobile, or, more pointedly, before the speeding motorist, what one writer called the "imbecile rushing by like a grinning idiot." As a February 1906 editorial noted, "The decline of the good-roads movement has practically been coincidental with the increasing racing use of the automobile. . . . What use to expend money to improve the roads, when the best roads are taken possession of by reckless racing automobilists . . . ?"[114]

An organized campaign for federal aid only resurfaced in the summer of 1908, several months before the international roads conference in Paris. The impetus was the impending presidential election, and the campaign's impresario was none other than Martin Dodge, who continued to inform credulous reporters that he represented the federal government. Dodge drew from Moore's old organizational connections and helped rebuild a political network to champion federal aid. His campaign included the convening of two National Good Roads Congresses to coincide with the Democratic and Republican National Conventions, respectively. Following these congresses, both political parties endorsed federal aid, but this ultimately mattered little since Taft, unlike his presidential predecessor, opposed it as a "dangerous experiment."[115]

Concurrent with Dodge's campaign, but away from the political spotlight, a new good roads coalition was also beginning to take shape. At the center of the coalition was the American Automobile Association (AAA), which had been created in 1902 to do for motorists what the League of American Wheelmen had done for bicyclists. Joining the AAA were two other groups: the American Road Builders' Association, a six-year-old body that brought together various interests involved directly with road construction; and the National Grange, an agricultural organization whose leadership, despite the tensions between rural farmers and joyriding motorists, had recommitted themselves to good roads reform in 1908.[116]

This new coalition's first meeting took place over two days in July 1908 at Buffalo, New York, site of the great Pan-American Exposition seven years prior. The AAA's leadership dubbed this meeting "the first national good roads convention," placing the event in a sort of competition with Dodge's two similarly titled congresses, one of which was convening at the exact same moment in Denver. Unlike the Dodge gatherings, however, the Buffalo convention aimed not to advance specific political outcomes, such as federal aid, but rather to start a general dialogue between "road users and road makers." Soon this new coalition eclipsed Dodge's network altogether.[117]

In December 1909, the AAA leadership turned even harder toward good roads advocacy with the election of journalist Amos Batchelder as organization chairman. Batch, as he was known to friends, had learned the gospel of good roads as a young Wheelman in New York State. His subsequent interest in automobiles had grown from the same yearning for risk and adventure that had earlier drawn him to bicycles, and he had turned his passion into a salary in 1903 when media baron William Randolph Hearst hired him to help start a new national monthly magazine called *Motor*. From that point onward, as one newspaper observed shortly after Batchelder's AAA election, "It is doubtful that any one has been a more consistent 'plugger' than Mr. Batchelder, and at the present time he is identified with every movement to promote the interests of the [automobile], and the whole industry respects his opinion and judgment on things of national importance."[118]

Batchelder merged a Wheelmen's missionary impulse for road reform with an automobilist's sensibility. The roads that he wanted were not the macadam or gravel or dirt surfaces of old, but the modern dustless highways finished with asphalt or concrete. The AAA, Batchelder felt, should be on a mission to achieve these goals and bring the nation into the automobile age. As Batchelder observed after taking over the AAA, "Years ago it was the cyclist, looked upon almost as a visionary, who fought for good roads. His place has been taken by the motorist. . . . Now we motorists have no hesitation in working brazenly and openly for good roads."[119]

Batchelder soon turned his focus to federal aid. The national government, he felt, undoubtedly would have to play a role in any system of long-distance roads. Moreover, he believed that the burden of funding such a system ought not land on motorists or local communities alone, but should be spread evenly among all the population. The system that Batchelder envisioned ultimately called for the federal government to help sponsor a network of long-distance, interconnected motor highways that could link all the nation's major cities and national parks. As he explained the year after his election as AAA chairman,

> The government, in the last few years, has spent hundreds of millions of dollars for improving rivers and harbors, an aggregate sum that would build half a dozen trunk highways across the continent. . . . When we can get some such assistance so that the people of the East can comfortably travel westward to the Pacific coast, thousands of tourists who are spending their summers in Europe will remain in America. And these highways, when once acquired, will be as valuable to the agriculturist as to the city man.[120]

Batchelder's advocacy work brought him into contact with Logan Waller Page, who had been giving the matter of road reform increased attention since his visit to Paris. Page agreed with Batchelder that a progressive approach to the nation's road problem required the construction of "connected and systematic" highways, though he viewed the overt championing of federal aid as premature. According to Page,

> The need of the day in road work is to take the administration of the roads away from the influence of politics; to insist on skilled supervision of all road work; to remedy the evils of too much localization, and to substitute uniformity and system for the confusion incident to pure localism as we now find it in some of the States.

Page's position as head of the federal road office gave him broad authority, and in the summer of 1910 he announced plans to form his own organization, one free of "the cheap charlatanism of the professional promoter and the bungling efforts of the well-meaning but uninformed citizen." Page, a reform progressive to his core, had finally decided to enter highway lobbying in order to strip out corruption, self-interest, and unprofessionalism from the good roads movement.[121]

An alliance soon formed between Page and Batchelder over their common ground. Both wanted a national network of dustproof modern automobile roads, even if they held different views on federal aid. Batchelder subsequently helped drum up support for a conference that Page was planning for November 1911 in Richmond, Virginia, once the site of a grand good roads train rally that had featured Dodge and Moore. Aiding Batchelder in the promotional work was A. G. Westgard, a talented driver and the founder of the Touring Club of America. Westgard was another leader in the new automobile-centric good roads movement and spent much of 1911 on a federally endorsed motor trip around the country to advertise both the Richmond meeting and the idea of automobile touring more generally. The *New York Times* noted, "This [was] the first time in the history of automobiling in the country in which a motoring organization [had] the active aid of the Government in effective work for road improvement."[122]

The combined efforts of Page, Batchelder, and Westgard turned the Richmond conference into a landmark summit. The *New York Times* considered the event "the most extensive and important meeting of road experts and highway officials ever held in this country." The official agenda, per Page's instructions, focused on questions of state and local reform, but the conversation inevitably turned toward federal aid, a subject that Batchelder and other motorists deemed the top priority.[123]

By the time Page's conference met, Batchelder had already made arrangements for a dedicated federal aid summit to be held two months later in the capital. "It will be," he explained to the *New York Times*, "the first gathering devoted solely to this one idea." Batchelder's conference subsequently allowed the conversation begun in Richmond to receive a full hearing over the course of three days, and most people in attendance fell into one of two camps. The more conservative and rural participants favored variations on the old Brownlow plan, which would distribute federal funds broadly for local improvement of post roads. The motorists, engineers, and road builders, in contrast, largely wanted a system of interstate automobile highways that would be funded, at least in part, by federal dollars. Both sides found support from congressmen, some three dozen of whom had attended the conference, and in recognition of the likely political impasse, Representative Oscar Underwood of Alabama proposed the creation of a joint congressional committee to study the matter further.[124]

The politicians who attended Batchelder's conference carried the federal aid conversation with them back into the halls of Congress. According to reports, about half of Congress actively supported some form of federal aid, with the strongest enthusiasm in the western and southern states, where roads remained the least developed. Soon after Batchelder's conference, Underwood submitted a bill calling for his joint commission, and the measure, which required little funding, passed unanimously in April. Alongside Underwood's bill came dozens of other proposals for federal aid, but these measures all faced significantly more resistance. They not only exposed the divisions between the two sides of the federal aid movement but also generated opposition both from traditional states' rights defenders and from a number of northeastern congressmen who felt that their districts had already invested in improved roads and should not have to subsidize their less developed neighbors.[125]

Throughout the summer of 1912, the congressmen favoring federal aid worked to build consensus. Eventually they channeled their energy toward a request for $500,000 to begin an experimental program of federal post road construction. This modest approach neutralized many of the financial objections. Some congressmen also felt that linking federal aid to the clause in the Constitution that read, "The Congress shall have the power to establish . . . post roads," would ensure its legitimacy (though this view ran counter to the intentions of most of the Founding Fathers, who had wanted Congress to have the power to designate postal routes but not necessarily to build them). For many of the bill's backers, the ultimate goal was simply to craft a bill that could free up funds so that highway engineers at different levels of government could figure out "how to cooperate and get a good job done." Finally, in mid-August, after months of debate, Congress signed off on the $500,000 appropriation and the measure became law soon thereafter.[126]

The door to federal aid had finally been opened, and the events of 1912 invigorated the broader good roads movement. Most involved with the process felt that significant appropriations were bound to follow. Soon the desire to shape this future legislation prompted an all-out lobbying offensive, one even greater than anything Moore or Dodge had ever attempted.[127]

The motorists led this charge. Batchelder personally spearheaded the AAA campaign and traveled the country to rally his membership, whose ranks had swelled dramatically in the four years since Henry Ford introduced the first car for the masses, the Model T. As Batchelder informed one group in California, "Don't be satisfied with any temporary federal aid which will serve only as a stop-gap, for what you want first of all are transcontinental routes." Batchelder's campaign received help from a host of related motorist organizations, many of which had formed in the prior few years to promote specific national routes. The list included the Dixie Highway Association, the Jefferson Highway Association, the Old Trails Association, and the Lincoln Highway Association, which wanted a transcontinental route that grew in part from the old National Road. Page observed of these groups, "there are so many different roads of this nature proposed, that it is impossible to keep up with them all."[128]

The manufacturers who stood to benefit from federal aid also joined the lobbying chorus. The most extensive campaign along these lines was one carried out by the National Highways Association, a joint initiative of road making equipment mogul Charles E. Davis and Charles Du Pont, whose family owned refining and chemical plants that produced some of the materials used in automobile roads. The National Highways Association's pamphlets, titled *Good Roads Everywhere*, urged "a Nation-wide system of National Highways" and warned that any other system of federal aid would produce "*roads beginning nowhere, ending nowhere.*"[129]

The harder these national highways interests pushed, however, the harder their antagonists pushed back. Congressmen who favored Brownlow-style plans of federal aid condemned the automobilists and manufacturers as a "lobby against good roads." Representative Dorsey Shackleford of Missouri, who was sponsoring a federal aid measure tied to post roads, declared at one point,

> There are in this country a number of road associations made up of men of great wealth who have special interests that they want to promote, and they have undertaken to shape all road legislation that is adopted here or in the States. . . . These associations do not want a road built unless it shall have such magnificent proportions that it calls for the letting of a big contract, out of which great profit may be made by the men who make up these associations. . . . What [do they] want— peacock lanes built at the expense of the taxpayers?[130]

Page, for his part, felt that a way forward could be found if the state highway engineers took control of the process. Their professional authority, he believed, could help to cut through the naked politics that had come to define federal aid. Page's stance was further grounded in his experience administering the pilot program that Congress had authorized in 1912. Working directly with states was far easier than trying to administer aid at the county or local level, a possibility that remained open in some of the Brownlow-style plans.

By 1914, Page had helped persuade Batchelder that assigning ultimate responsibility to state highway engineers would be the surest path to success. A conciliatory Batchelder soon abandoned his doctrinaire demands for national highways in favor of a more nuanced list of requirements for federal aid. As he explained,

These embraced an annual appropriation, to be divided among the states upon the basis of area, population and road mileage, the state to put up a dollar for every federal dollar received, and the joint money to be expended upon whatever roads the state highway department and the secretary of agriculture should agree.

Any legislation that met these requirements would have Batchelder's support as well as that of all the automobilists who looked to him for leadership.[131]

Before such legislation could arise, however, the state highway engineers first needed to organize themselves. Page finally raised this issue in November 1914 at the Fourth American Road Congress, a joint undertaking of his organization and of Batchelder's AAA. According to one witness, Page told a small group of listeners that included several state highway engineers and Batchelder,

If you gentlemen expect to get any federal aid—if you expect the government to help you on road building—you ought to help yourselves. You should organize outside of any material interests. You should form an association of highway commissioners representing all the states. You should [draft] a federal act [that includes] recognition of the highway commissioners of the [various] States, . . . and I will do all in my power to further the association and the scheme.[132]

Page's words inspired several of the engineers present to take immediate action. As one of them remarked, "As good a time to begin as any that has ever presented itself, is now." The very next day, they issued a call for a new organization. Three weeks later the American Association of State Highway Officials was born. Following this, the group's leadership designated a special committee to prepare federal aid legislation, and a working draft emerged early in 1915. The organization then distributed the draft to all the states for comment. A final version, calling for a $75 million initial appropriation over three years, was presented publicly in December 1915 at the group's first annual meeting in Chicago.[133]

The new proposal called for the placing of administrative control over federal aid with state highway departments and required that all states create such departments within three years or risk losing their potential federal allotments. The amount of funds available to each of these state highway departments would be calculated using complicated formulas that factored in population size and geographic area. The state highway commissioners would have discretion to apply these funds for both the interstate roads that automobilists wanted and the post roads that rural districts sought. The ultimate authority, however, would still rest with Page's office, which had the right to approve all projects and to withdraw funds for any "breach of agreement." Batchelder, who supported the proposal as the best path forward, noted, "Federal authority . . . would give a double check, and should prevent the employment of money entirely for trunk line routes or its ineffectual distribution over too great a mileage, for local purposes."[134]

The state highway engineers arranged for sympathetic legislators to submit their proposal in early 1916, prompting yet another round of debate in Congress. The new bill satisfied many of the men who served on the joint committee on federal aid, but nonetheless faced fierce resistance from Shackleford, who continued to insist on a plan tied to post roads only and used his position as head of the House Committee on Roads to gain leverage. Eventually, Shackleford's intransigence forced the sponsors of the state highway engineers' bill to amend it so that federal aid would be restricted exclusively to roads where the mails were actively being carried. Following this concession, the measure gained passage in Congress. In July 1916 President Woodrow Wilson signed the bill into law. After an absence of eighty years, significant federal aid for road building had finally returned.[135]

The president gave the official pen he had used to authorize the legislation to Batchelder, who was invited to witness the signing ceremony. Many considered Batchelder to be the man most responsible for the new law's realization, even though the final version of federal aid ultimately privileged post roads over interstate automobile routes. The *American Motorist* observed, "Take it from me, Uncle Sam, along with you and me, owes a whole lot to [Batchelder] for this happy termination of a fight that [he] has helped wage for more than thirty years, without ever faltering or doubting the eventual victory which now has been won."[136]

The long campaign that began in the late nineteenth century with the Wheelmen had taken a huge leap forward. The national government was finally poised to oversee the planning and funding of road building throughout the country. But the timing of this development could hardly have been worse. Federal aid had arrived just as the nation was drifting hopelessly away from neutrality, and the demands of total war would soon take precedence over road building.

The Horseless Cavalry

The effects of the US mobilization effort were quickly felt throughout the nation's road building industry. As Page explained, "the scarcity of [railroad] cars, the scarcity and high cost of labor, and the high cost of materials operate . . . to very seriously limit road work." [137]

The newly authorized program of federal aid road building confronted not only these war-related challenges but also a host of problems that had slowly surfaced in the months since the bill's passage. One engineer in Page's office complained that the act had "provided for no system of roads, set no definite standards of design and construction, set forth no specifications, and was virtually wide open at both ends." Especially problematic was the act's strict requirement about post roads, which Page felt he had a duty to follow. As a February 1917 editorial in the *Atlanta Constitution* griped, "It would be the height of absurdity to improve a little stretch of road here and skip a few miles and improve another stretch, leaving the part in between unimproved because not now used by a rural mail carrier." By May, the *Constitution* declared of federal aid road building, "there has been nothing but talk and red tape!" [138]

At the state highway engineers' December annual meeting, its first gathering since the outbreak of war, Page apologized for the disappointing results but affirmed his commitment to the program. As he explained to the assembled engineers, "For the most part you have been patient in the face of delays, which however unavoidable, were exasperating, and you have endeavored earnestly and conscientiously to meet all the requirements of the Federal Government. I assure you that I shall reciprocate in every possible way." [139]

After some debate, the state highway engineers pledged their ongoing support to Page, with the caveat that the federal government offer a "more liberal interpretation" of the post roads clause. The official resolutions from the meeting stated, "We reiterate our faith in the Federal-Aid road act, and believe that it has done more for the cause of road improvement than any other one influence has ever done." [140]

For many at the meeting, however, the concerns about federal aid mattered less in the near term than questions about the role of the nation's highway system in the war effort. The conference's report on wartime matters noted, "[T]his association . . . would be derelict in its duty to the country if every member did not use his utmost endeavor to secure and maintain those highways which are necessary to enable the full resources of the country to be made available at all times."[141]

The idea that roads might be crucial to the nation's military effort had received little attention at the war's outset, but the nation's highways had become the subject of increasing discussion throughout 1917 as the railroads struggled to keep up with shipping demands. In November, the month before the state highway engineers' meeting, President Wilson's powerful Council of National Defense had created a four-man Highways Transport Committee in order to achieve "greater use of highways ... to relieve the tremendous burden placed on the railroads by the war." The nation's domestic highways were finally being conscripted, and the man overseeing this transformation was the new committee's chair, thirty-seven-year-old Roy D. Chapin, the wunderkind president of the Hudson Motor Company and one of the most influential good roads advocates in the nation.[142]

Chapin had enjoyed a spectacular rise through the ranks of the automobile industry. His career had commenced in 1901 at age twenty-one when he dropped out of college to pursue a sales job with the pioneering automaker Ransom E. Olds, the founder of Oldsmobile. Shortly after accepting this job, Chapin earned headlines for a daring sales stunt in which he successfully piloted one of Olds's new lightweight models from Detroit to New York, a feat that had never before been accomplished. As the *New-York Tribune* reported, his car arrived "covered with mud and grime," and a triumphant Chapin noted "that his experience has [shown] that the lightweight automobiles are well adapted for such tours." Oldsmobile soon promoted Chapin to sales manager, but the ambitious and well-connected Chapin wanted a company of his own and in 1906 partnered with several others to form a new venture that evolved into the Hudson Motor Company, one of the few independent auto manufacturers to compete effectively against the "Big Three" (Ford, General Motors, and Chrysler) in the first half of the twentieth century. Chapin became Hudson's president in 1909 at age twenty-nine, making him the youngest leader of any major automaker.[143]

The good roads movement had interested Chapin from his earliest years in the auto industry. He understood that better roads would be the key to his industry's growth and sought the day when the nation's rural network would be developed enough so that a trip like the one he had made from Detroit to New York would be neither newsworthy nor dependent on vast reserves of skill and courage. By the time Chapin became president of Hudson Motors, he was already recognized as the auto industry's good roads leader, and in 1914 his colleagues made him chair of the good roads committee for the National Automobile Chamber of Commerce, a new, powerful trade group that covered most of the nation's car manufacturers.[144]

Chapin subsequently played a crucial role alongside Batchelder in the effort to bring the nation's roads into the automobile age. Among the initiatives that Chapin led was a campaign in the spring of 1916 to convince motorists and auto manufacturers to support state taxes on vehicles so long as the funds went to support highways—Chapin's success helped create vast new revenue streams for road building. And though Chapin hoped that federal aid would be used for national auto highways, he nonetheless supported the final bill that Wilson signed in July 1916. As he telegrammed Batchelder the day of the bill's passage, "I am going to buy you a very large drink the next time I see you. The policy of federal aid, which so many have claimed was a myth, is at last effective."[145]

By the time federal aid passed, Chapin's attention was beginning to shift from road reform to military preparedness and to the ways in which highways and automobile transport could impact warfare. That September, seven months before Wilson's declaration of war, he gained a preview of how motorized combat might work in practice during an observational trip he made to the US-Mexican border to witness the nation's first deployment of military supply trucks. The vehicles had been requested by General John "Black Jack" Pershing during his "punitive expedition" against Pancho Villa as a way to supplement the region's dysfunctional train system. Chapin's trip quickly exposed him to both the possibilities and the pitfalls of motorized transport. As he noted in a letter from Mexico sent to his wife, "Truck trains running constantly over any road but a concrete or brick one will wear it out quick—so the army has had no easy job to keep the supply trains going." Chapin returned home convinced that he had glimpsed the future of war. His biographer noted, "in Mexico with Pershing, Roy had seen . . . the necessity for motor equipment wherever rail lines were non-existent, crippled, or inadequate. He felt certain that the motor trucks of the nation could be mobilized into an effective service of supply."[146]

Chapin's Mexican adventure subsequently shaped the way he viewed the war. As he watched the nation's rail system strain beneath the demands of mobilization, he imagined that motor trucks would be able to relieve the supply problem, much like they had done during Pershing's "punitive expedition." By October, Chapin had determined that the time had arrived to do "[his] share in the common good" and soon he landed a consultative meeting with the Council of National Defense's director of transportation. During their conversation, Chapin proposed that the federal government create a special committee tasked with using highways and motor trucks to help relieve the nation's transportation crisis. The following month, the council authorized his proposed committee, and Chapin was appointed its leader. The Detroit automobile capitalist had become a dollar-a-year man in the service of the war.[147]

Chapin's new committee faced an enormous challenge, one that went well beyond transportation logistics. As his biographer explained,

> The project at the outset had to drive against a wall of military skepticism and of public unfamiliarity with organized motor transport on a large scale.... Paris had not yet been saved by the taxicab army rushing to the Battle of the Marne. The British had not yet introduced the tank as a weapon of war. The four and one-half million automobiles in the country were universally referred to as "pleasure cars," and the three hundred and twenty-five thousand motor trucks were for the most part small delivery wagons. There was no body of public opinion, even in the motor industry itself, which visualized motorized equipment as an important adjunct of war.[148]

Chapin's first initiative as chair seemed to grow out of his earlier experience navigating an Oldsmobile from Detroit to New York. He felt that the truck needed initially to "prove itself at home" and thus suggested that vehicles purchased by the military not be shipped east by railcar, as was then standard practice, but instead be piloted overland to Atlantic ports. This scheme would both free up valuable railcar space and provide a thorough demonstration of the truck's durability. Chapin used his influence within the automobile industry to help persuade reluctant manufacturers to embrace this punishing test of their vehicles, and he quickly arranged for Batchelder's AAA to send out volunteer pilots to map out the best routes along the nation's sprawling rural road network. Barely one month after his committee had been formed, preparations were complete. The *New York Times* observed, "It will be the first time in the United States that so large a number of motor trucks have been run over the highways for so great a distance as a unit." The rolling march of vehicles that followed helped introduce the nation to the idea of long-distance truck transport, and official figures suggested that Chapin's plan ultimately freed up twenty thousand railcars.[149]

Chapin next turned his committee's attention to the rail system's "embargo points," the short gaps that separated depots from both producer and consumer. Motor trucks, Chapin believed, could cover these distances, relieving the problem of "corn and potatoes rotting because they cannot be moved." A handful of "rural motor express" services already existed in eastern regions to handle products that spoiled easily, such as milk and fresh vegetables, but Chapin took actions to expand these systems dramatically. Soon his committee helped inaugurate truck delivery in Washington, DC, and other metropolitan areas began to follow suit. As Chapin boasted in August 1918,

> In the last six months there has come to our view an entirely new picture of transportation in America.... We have seen the railroads taken over by the United States government, and, simultaneously, we have seen the highways of the country taken over by the people for the purpose of hauling goods which could not [otherwise] be hauled.... Suddenly the motor truck has come forward and has supplied for the highways what the steam-engines supply for the railroads and the electric car supplies for the interurban systems—rapid transit.[150]

The arrival of motor truck delivery fundamentally transformed the purpose of the nation's highways. They were no longer wagon roads or "peacock lanes" for motorists, but linchpins of a new economy built around automobility, where motorized transport reached to everyone's front door. Chapin noted, "[H]ighway transport by gasoline-propelled vehicles is not only going to revolutionize economic and food conditions, it is going to better living conditions for city and country alike. It is going to break down the barriers of city limits, county lines and state lines as never before."[151]

The nation's highways, however, were hardly equipped to handle this transformation. The macadam surfacing that was already suffering beneath the speeding motorist degraded even faster beneath the weight of motor trucks, and dirt roads rapidly wore out trucks moving at any great speed. The motorized truck instead required modern roads of asphalt or concrete. As Batchelder observed in 1918, "And there is now another reason for pavement highways, for the motor truck is ready and willing to meet its maximum possibilities ... not only of the state, but of the nation itself."[152]

The dustless roads that the touring automobile had forced engineers to devise ten years earlier no longer seemed an unattainable luxury when the future of a truck-based transportation system depended on their construction.

The Zero Milestone

The month after the Armistice, the state highway engineers gathered with the leaders of the automobile industry and of the various motorist organizations for the first US roads conference since the end of hostilities. The thousand delegates who had traveled to Chicago were all eager to resume the work that the war had interrupted, but they anticipated an atmosphere that would be, in the words of one engineer, "charged with high voltage tensions." Another attendee explained, "The Federal-aid principle had not yet had a chance to prove that it could function. . . . The war had intruded and immensely complicated the difficulties. . . . It was inevitable that the battle of Federal-aid versus National Highways would come to a show-down at [the December] convention."[153]

Page was among those who had traveled to Chicago, and he planned to mount a defense of federal aid. He believed that the foundations for success had all been established, even if almost no actual federal aid construction had yet taken place. By the close of the war, Page noted, all the states had finally established highway departments, and the federal road office had organized over a dozen field offices to oversee the anticipated work. Moreover, approximately 750 projects covering nearly eight thousand miles had been approved. As Page explained in late November, "It is quite probable, therefore, that State and Federal funds for construction purposes will, during 1919, run well over $100,000,000."[154]

Despite this optimistic outlook, Page conceded that federal aid needed to be reformed. In his view, the post roads provision remained too restrictive and the total appropriations warranted an increase so that federal aid could serve as an effective bulwark against the unemployment that was expected to accompany demobilization. He observed, "In my judgment no more effective means of insuring employment, particularly to unskilled labor, can be devised. . . . The benefits of improved highways are immediate, to say nothing of the great desirability of having all labor employed and money active." Page ultimately planned to argue for an amendment to the 1916 act that loosened the post roads language and doubled the funding available for federal aid.[155]

But such an amendment did not go far enough for those who favored national highways. The leaders of the motor lobby—including Batchelder and Chapin—instead supported a proposal connected with Senator Charles E. Townsend of Michigan, whose state had become dependent on the success of the automobile industry. Townsend's plan called for a new major appropriation and the creation of a National Highways Commission to directly oversee the construction of an integrated system of automobile highways that would link the entire country together. "I believe," declared Townsend, "that we ought to have a nationalized system of roads. . . . I have not been pleased with the administration of [federal aid thus far]. I think the money has not been as wisely expended as it should have been."[156]

As the delegates were preparing for the expected showdown over federal aid, news arrived of a most tragic nature. Shortly after Page had arrived in Chicago, he had dropped dead of a heart attack. "America has lost one of her worthy men," wrote a longtime colleague, convinced that Page's death owed to the strains of getting federal aid started during wartime. The state highway engineers' association observed in a special resolution several days later, "By word, pen, act and deed, from his early boyhood to his untimely removal, he had contributed unceasingly his entire strength, energies and time toward the establishment of better methods and more scientific statutes for all of the states and the Nation. . . . By the death of Logan Waller Page this association and the road builders of the whole United States have lost one of its members who cannot be replaced."[157]

In the shadow of Page's death, the state highway engineers at the Chicago conference had to decide whether to support the amendment he favored or the ambitious system that Townsend advocated. One participant explained, "On the showdown resolution . . . the convention voted 50–50. It was a tie." Nonetheless, the amendment that Page had supported found enough eventual support to carry the day, allowing the state highway engineers to "cling to [their] ideal of Federal-State cooperation." For the moment, the people tasked with implementing federal aid would remain supportive of the system that the 1916 legislation had created.[158]

But the sudden passing of Page had left the federal aid program's administration in limbo. The entire system had arisen around him, and he lacked an obvious successor. President Wilson and Secretary of Agriculture David Houston knew that the wrong decision for Page's replacement would almost certainly ruin federal aid. After much consideration and consultation, in early 1919, they finally offered the position to Iowa's chief highway engineer, thirty-eight-year-old Thomas H. MacDonald. Moving forward, the hopes for federal aid road building would rest on MacDonald's leadership.

MacDonald had grown up in Montezuma, Iowa, an agricultural community set amidst a landscape of bad roads. As MacDonald's maternal grandfather observed, "if you tried to travel [our roads in wet months] you could expect to go in up to the hubs. Yes sir, those prairie roads were a good bit like Longfellow's little girl with the curl: 'When they were good they were very, very good; but when they were bad they were horrid.'"[159]

MacDonald's romance with road building and highway engineering began during his undergraduate years. He had started out in a teachers' preparatory school but in 1901 had transferred into a new program in highway engineering that had just been introduced at Iowa State College. MacDonald's subsequent training shared much in common with the education that Page had received a decade earlier at Harvard, and MacDonald, like Page before him, developed an appreciation for highway engineering as a disciplined profession with rigorous standards and a contempt for base politics.[160]

Upon graduating in 1904, MacDonald was appointed to serve in his state's newly created, three-person highway department. The limited resources available to the department made the work difficult, but MacDonald responded with a tireless work ethic, both at his desk and in the field. As one newspaper observed, "Through impetus given by [MacDonald], Iowa started pulling her Main streets and farmers out of their Spring and Fall mudholes. He put on his overalls [and] demonstrated first-hand how to build substantial bridges and culverts." Along with this work, MacDonald also pushed hard for state-level road reform, and, after several years spent overcoming what one editorial described as "the bitter opposition of temporizers and political exploiters," he helped secure his department wide control over county planning.[161]

In 1913, MacDonald was promoted to chief highway engineer for the state. The earlier work that he had done to strengthen the department made this position especially powerful, and MacDonald soon began working to implement a progressive system of modern surfaced highways. The annual report that his department published the year of MacDonald's promotion noted that Iowa would be "the first State in the Middle West to establish a State-wide system of main roads."[162]

MacDonald threw himself completely into the work, poring over surveys and personally inspecting the nearly seven thousand miles of roads involved in the system. The road builders of Iowa grew familiar with the sight of his silhouette, short and sturdy, like that of a football tailback. His thinning hair made him seem older than his years, and his intense gaze and stern expression only increased the sense of authority that he easily conveyed. The road builders respected him, and the system grew steadily over the next several years.[163]

By the end of World War I, some felt that Iowa possessed "one of the finest road systems in the nation." An admirer of MacDonald observed, "[T]he State ought to give him a monument [for his] contribution to taking Iowa out of the mud and providing its model highway system."[164]

MacDonald was already a leader in the federal aid movement when Houston offered him the chance to replace Page in early 1919. Three years earlier, he had helped draft the original proposal that the state highway engineers submitted, and he had played a central role in their national association. His popularity among his fellow state highway engineers was part of what made him such an attractive candidate to Houston. As the influential *Engineering News-Record* explained, "The whole highway field has confidence in him and will gladly pledge him hearty and unqualified support." The president of one of the major highway organizations added, "[T]he Secretary of Agriculture [has] made an appointment nobody could criticize with justness." MacDonald's colleagues from other states even successfully petitioned the government to raise his proposed salary by $1,000 to better reflect the importance of the job.[165]

When MacDonald arrived in Washington, DC, he inherited an enormous operation. The program's available funds had more than doubled in size shortly before his arrival thanks to the passage of the amendment that Page had favored. The office had also been redesignated as the Bureau of Public Roads to reflect its newfound status. And as Page had promised, hundreds of projects were ready to begin. The early months of MacDonald's tenure, in consequence, witnessed a vast increase in active construction, and the dream of Henry Clay for a nationally guided system of roads was finally starting to be realized.[166]

This progress, however, failed to satisfy the national highways lobby. Men like Townsend, Batchelder, and Chapin continued to insist that the country needed a National Highways Commission to oversee the construction of interstate automobile roads. They felt that only through direct federal leadership—not state-led cooperation alone—could the nation gain an infrastructure for the automobile age.[167]

Their concerns were shared by the military, which had begun to see automobile highways as part of the nation's defense network. In July 1919, the secretary of war addressed this issue directly with a memo instructing his staff to "make a study of highways within the continental limits of the United States and desirable from a military point of view." This order had also corresponded with the departure of the military's first transcontinental truck convoy, which had started from Washington, DC, in early July and had followed the route of the Lincoln Highway to San Francisco. The seventy-two-vehicle "Army-transport train" needed two months to cross the nation's undeveloped interior road network and, out of necessity, was "always preceded by a road-making and bridge-repairing crew." The *San Francisco Chronicle* noted in the first week of September, "The arrival of the train here means more than just the arrival of a number of trucks and cars. It calls attention of the entire Nation to the need for a national system of highways."[168]

The pressure to build national highways became a preoccupation for MacDonald. He agreed with both the military and the automobile lobby that the nation needed a system of modern interstate roads, but, as a former state highway engineer himself, he wanted to preserve the state-led quality of federal aid cooperation. The easiest solution, MacDonald felt, would simply be to increase appropriations for the existing federal aid system. He felt confident that his office and the state highway departments could put additional funds to use effectively in a way that would satisfy most motorists.[169]

Throughout 1919 and 1920, while Townsend continued to push for his National Highways Commission, MacDonald worked to build consensus among the various factions in the federal aid dispute. Ready support was found from most of the state highway engineers, who saw MacDonald as one of their own. The automobile industry, however, remained more cautious until MacDonald found a crucial ally in Pyke Johnson, a Denver newspaperman who had recently been appointed as the secretary of the good roads committee for the powerful National Automobile Chamber of Commerce. The two men formed a fast friendship, and Johnson's subsequent loyalty helped persuade other industry leaders to trust MacDonald. By July 1920, Chapin was telling the Iowan, "I feel confident that the industry will always be willing to meet you more than half way in any problems which you may have."[170]

MacDonald's position strengthened further with the election of Warren G. Harding to the presidency in November 1920. Harding had followed the federal aid battles during his years in Congress and seemed more inclined to support a modest increase in appropriations than the erection of a whole new bureaucracy, as Townsend's National Highways Commission would require. Of particular importance for Harding was also an assurance that the states would retain responsibility for all maintenance so that federal funds would not ultimately be "wasted" on highways that rapidly deteriorated. As he explained shortly after taking office, "There is nothing Congress can do more effectively to end this shocking waste than condition all Federal aid on provisions for maintenance." While the plans of both Townsend and MacDonald had called for maintenance to remain with the states, MacDonald's proposed amendment had much stricter penalties for noncompliance, which helped increase its attractiveness to Harding.[171]

Shortly after Harding's inauguration, with Townsend still maintaining his resistance, MacDonald introduced a modified proposal that he hoped would finally placate the national highways lobby and end the seemingly interminable fighting over federal aid. It started with the assumption that federal aid should be limited to roads of heaviest use, and, based on his experience as head of the Bureau of Public Roads, MacDonald posited that 7 percent of each state's total mileage "serv[ed] adequately 80 or 90 per cent of the traffic" and ought therefore to compose the entirety of a federal aid system. States, he felt, should retain the rights to design these 7 percent systems so long as 3 percent of the total highways were designated as "primary or interstate roads." As MacDonald explained, "The systems so determined will not fall under a single definition. In one State it will be an intercounty seat system; in another, one or two through roads; in [some], the most important roads will parallel the railroads; in [others] they will radiate from important railroad centers." The states would thus hold on to control, but interstate routes would nonetheless have to form the centerpiece of each system. The plan seemed to embody Monroe's century-old doctrine that federal dollars only go to projects with a clear national purpose and that jurisdiction remain with the states.[172]

The popularity of MacDonald's plan, which reached Congress in mid-1921, compelled Townsend to finally concede defeat. By August, the senator had agreed both to drop his demand for a National Highways Commission and to sign off on a bill that largely followed MacDonald's approach. Congress then passed the measure along with a supplemental $75 million appropriation. MacDonald's revised scheme for federal aid finally became law on November 10, 1921, when Harding happily applied his signature to the bill.[173]

The 1921 legislation seemed at long last to resolve the debate over federal aid. Townsend declared, "I regard this new law as one of the most progressive steps looking toward internal improvement ever taken by the Congress." Chapin noted,

[F]ederal aid can no longer be scattered broadcast. . . . The immediate effect of this act will be to stimulate the construction and maintenance of the trunk highways in those states which because of lack of funds have not thus far, made much progress toward an adequate system of connected highways.... [R]ecognition of interstate roads [is] now a fundamental principle in the national highway law."

Batchelder would likely have also supported the new law in equal measure to Chapin, but five months before its passage, he had died tragically in a plane accident.[174]

Though much work remained to be done, the passage of the 1921 law marked the start of what one federal engineer subsequently labeled "the golden years." As MacDonald explained in April 1922, "Picture a pile of gravel and stone twice as high as the Washington monument and of equal length and breadth, and you will have a fairly accurate notion of the quantity of material required for the Federal-aid roads under construction and completed at the close of last year.... The Federal-aid program has advanced with a rapidity little short of startling." An admiring journalist wrote of MacDonald two months later, "Morgan nor Rockefeller nor Carnegie nor the First Families of Croesus ever had the spending of so much money in so small a time. And he spends it all to the ultimate benefit of the motorist!"[175]

After trailing Europe for well over a century, the United States was finally advancing to the first rank of road building nations. Monroe's doctrine on road building had at long last been put into effect, but its character had been redefined for the automobile age, with roads not of stone or gravel but of asphalt and concrete.

On June 4, 1923, a ceremony was held to commemorate the federal system that had finally been put into place. The outdoor event, convened on the spot near the Washington Monument from where the military truck convoy had departed nearly four years prior, was attended by several thousand people, including the president and much of the cabinet. The focus of the ceremony was the dedication of a stone pillar that would henceforth serve as the Zero Milestone for the nation's planned 180,000-mile system of federal aid automobile highways. Upon accepting this stone gift on behalf of the nation, Harding declared,

My countrymen, in the old Roman forum there was erected in the days of Rome's greatness a golden milestone. From it was measured and marked the system of highways which gridironed the Roman world and bound the uttermost provinces to the heart and center of the empire. We are dedicating here another golden milestone, to which we and those after us will relate the wide-ranging units of the highway system of this country.... To us, coming late in the drama of human development, it was particularly necessary that wonders of highway construction should be accomplished in an almost inconceivably short time.... Within two decades ... marking the beginning of the motor age, our advance in this respect has been phenomenal, making it most fitting that a recognized center of the highway system should at this time be set up.... We may fittingly dedicate the Zero Milestone to its purpose in the hope and trust that it will remain here through the generations and centuries, while the Republic endures, as the greatest institutional blessing that Providence has given to any people.[176]

All roads would now lead to Washington. And though Harding only spoke of a national system, some in attendance were already thinking beyond the nation's borders, to the rest of the hemisphere. As one of the day's speakers observed,

The system of highways radiating from Washington to all the boundaries of the national domain and all parts of the Western Hemisphere will do vastly more for national unity and for human unity than even the roads of the Roman Empire. It would seem that a system of highways that embraces a hemisphere, and that is directly related to the welfare and progress of humanity, should have a definite point of beginning, and that that point should be marked by a suitable milestone.[177]

Meanwhile, in an office not far from that Zero Milestone, plans were already under way to bring about this end. The dream of hemispheric connectivity had begun to inspire a new generation, a motoring generation, and soon some of the same men who had brought automobile highways to the United States would dedicate themselves to exporting their transportation system to the rest of the New World. Latin America had become the new frontier for the infrastructure of the automobile age.

PART II

The Road

A map from early 1929 showing the status of roads along the route of an imagined Inter-American Highway to run from the southern US border to Panama City.

CHAPTER FIVE

Good Roads Make Good Neighbors

The Highway of Friendship

Almost exactly one year after the Zero Milestone ceremony, on June 2, 1924, the nation's preeminent good roads advocates and top federal officials once more gathered in the capital. They had again come together to celebrate the nation's new federal highway system, but the audience this time had changed dramatically. Instead of a cheering crowd several thousand strong, there now stood thirty-seven Latin Americans, all carefully selected for their potential to serve as apostles of the good roads movement in their home countries. Soon the visitors would be whisked on a multiweek tour across some three thousand miles of US highways with Thomas MacDonald as their guide. In welcoming the delegates to the capital, US Secretary of State Charles Evans Hughes declared,

> I wish . . . to congratulate you on the important Pan American service that you are rendering. . . . Your visit to this country . . . indicates one of the most significant phases of Pan American development. . . . The improvement of means of communication is a matter far more closely related to democratic development than we are accustomed to suppose. . . . Highway construction enlarges the market for your products which in turn stimulates production and leads to general economic advance. We in the United States are deeply interested in the progress thus made.[1]

The tour marked the start of a new US initiative to promote highway development throughout Latin America. The same men who had brought about the federal aid system were turning their gaze outward, and, in Pan-

Americanism, they had found a philosophy that offered an ideal vessel for the transmission of the gospel of good roads abroad. The tour's commemorative program reflected this sentiment through its title: "Highways of Friendship."[2]

The roots of the tour reached back fifteen months to the Fifth Pan-American Conference, which had convened in Santiago, Chile, during the spring of 1923. The conference had been delayed nearly a decade on account of the Great War, and by the time it finally arrived, the automobile had fully transformed life in the United States. At the urging of several car manufacturers, the US-led board of the Pan-American Union had decided to introduce the topic of "motor transport" to the conference agenda. For the first time, highways would be a subject of Pan-American relations.[3]

Motorized transport, however, still remained relatively novel throughout Latin America. Fewer than 250,000 automobiles could be found across the entire region, an amount exceeded by the number of vehicles in New York City alone. For Latin Americans, automobiles remained a privilege of the wealthiest, and those fortunate enough to own one tended to restrict their usage to urban areas since improved rural roads were practically unknown anywhere south of the United States. Some countries' rural transportation networks consisted of nothing more than mule trails, impossible terrain for an automobile to navigate. Even where rural routes were wide enough to accommodate a vehicle, drivers still faced a nearly hopeless situation due to the rainy season and the unforgiving topography. One Latin American writer noted in a 1917 article from *Automotive Industries*,

> In the majority of the Latin American countries, and especially in those within the tropics, the highways are in very bad condition, due to the heavy rains which destroy them notwithstanding the large amount of money spent on repairs during the dry season. In all Central America, Panama, Colombia, Ecuador, Bolivia, Venezuela, the southern part of Mexico, Haiti and Santo Domingo, roads during more than half of the year are impassable, even for ox-carts. The topography of those mentioned countries and of Peru, Chile and a large part of Brazil has necessitated the construction of roads through deep ravines, up mountain slopes and rocky hills, crossing rivers and having to climb from the level of the sea to the high plateaus, sometimes 6,000 to 10,000 ft. in the short distance of from 100 to 300 miles.[4]

Most Latin American countries lacked meaningful domestic good roads movements altogether. The discussion of modern highways was largely limited to members of urban automobile clubs, whose numbers remained too small to have much impact. In Mexico, the inaugural national good roads conference had only taken place in 1921, and the first such meeting in Argentina had finally arrived the year after. No national government aside from that of Uruguay had yet embarked on any consequential program of modern road building. A sales manager for General Motors who had toured the hemisphere in mid-1922 observed, "I did not find any general campaign under way over all of Latin-America for better roads."[5]

Unsurprisingly, few of the delegations at Santiago came prepared to discuss the subject of motor transport. The United States, however, was an exception. Its delegation had received instructions to take the matter up from the US State Department, which had first consulted with leading members of the automotive industry. Once the conference got under way, members from the US delegation managed to have introduced a series of three motor-related resolutions, the most consequential of which called for a special conference to be held in the future "to study the most adequate means of developing an effective program for the construction of motor roads in and between the various American countries."[6]

The motor resolutions prompted little discussion and were ultimately accepted without any debate, likely due to general disinterest. The delegates had preferred to spend their time during the conference's plenary session on communications discussing maritime transport, radio broadcasting, and the Pan-American Railway. Nonetheless, the lead US delegate considered the motor resolutions a sign of his nation's bright prospects in the automotive arena, noting, "There is no doubt in my mind that the United States can hold the [automobile] market in South America which this country got during the war, although there will be intense competition.... The relations between the United States and the Pan-American countries are better than ever."[7]

Once the conference concluded, the responsibility for implementing the Santiago resolutions passed to Leo S. Rowe, the director-general of the Pan-American Union. Rowe, who had earlier worked in the State Department and in the University of Pennsylvania's Political Science Department, had recently taken the helm of the organization and sought to expand its influence. The union, he felt, should be exerting leadership on all subjects that held the promise of improving hemispheric relations. For Rowe, the resolution on a proposed motor roads conference seemed especially worthwhile. Leadership on technical issues provoked less backlash than leadership in the political realm, and the United States had valuable experience in road building that could easily be shared with Latin America.[8]

In July, two months after the Santiago conference ended, Rowe arranged for a meeting with Thomas MacDonald and a representative from the Department of Commerce to discuss the Santiago resolutions. The proposed roads conference, Rowe assured, warranted the active support of both the bureau and the Commerce Department. Rowe explained that he felt the conference should be held somewhere in Latin America but that the United States should first arrange "a preliminary conference of technical experts" in Washington. In such a manner, the nation could help shape and benefit from a good roads movement that was sure to spread throughout the New World.[9]

Rowe had little trouble convincing MacDonald of the merits of his plan. The nation's chief road builder saw no reason why the lessons the United States had learned in the past twenty years should not be shared with the country's Latin American neighbors. Such a knowledge transfer, MacDonald felt, would allow those nations to avoid some of the mistakes the United States had made and to profit from the wisdom already gained. MacDonald also seemed to enjoy the prospect of seeing his influence expand from the United States to the entire hemisphere. Soon he began plotting out geographic correspondences between individual states and the countries of Latin America. According to his notes, North Carolina approximated parts of Brazil, while Argentina aligned with Illinois and the Mississippi Valley.[10]

In the Department of Commerce, meanwhile, news of Rowe's proposed technical conference gradually worked its way up the administrative hierarchy. Eventually it reached Secretary of Commerce Herbert Hoover, an ambitious politician who had already gained a national reputation for his administrative success during the Great War. Hoover had selected the secretariat of the Department of Commerce over other, more prominent, cabinet posts because he believed in the department's untapped potential. For Hoover, Rowe's preliminary conference proposal—and the broader idea of overseas automotive expansion it represented—proved immediately intriguing. The automobile industry was already the nation's largest, and Hoover believed that his department had a duty to work for its benefit. He had even created a special automotive division to accomplish this end.[11]

Hoover had recently named as assistant secretary of commerce someone especially well positioned to help develop Rowe's plan, forty-seven-year-old J. Walter Drake. The chairman and cofounder of Hupp

Motor Company, Drake had a reputation in Detroit every bit as large as that of Roy D. Chapin, and he had served for many years as the industry's point person on exports. His firm had been focused on overseas sales since its founding in 1909, a time when most US car manufacturers cared solely for the nation's vast domestic market. In 1910, Drake's younger brother had even embarked on a much-publicized round-the-world trip in one of their Hupmobiles. Drake had long led the National Automobile Chamber of Commerce's export division, and he had started consulting for the government soon after Hoover took over the Department of Commerce. It was Drake who had originally led the push for the inclusion of "motor transport" in the Santiago conference agenda. With his appointment as assistant secretary, he had turned his commitment to automobile exports into an official, full-time duty.[12]

The automobile industry, by this point, had largely reached a consensus on the importance of exports, but a debate still existed over the best way to achieve them. The nation's largest car manufacturer, Henry Ford, felt that automobile sales must precede road building. As he explained,

> The only way to get enthusiasm and money for roads is to have something waiting to run on them. Some people say: "Let us get roads and then our people will use automobiles!" That is not the way it has worked. American experience runs in the opposite direction—let the people get automobiles and the roads will come soon enough.... I suppose the situation in South America is much the same as it was here. They need roads, yes.... These will come with startling rapidity, providing they have something to run on them.

Drake, however, disagreed with Ford. Road building, he felt, could serve as a catalyst to automobile sales, and Rowe's proposed technical conference struck Drake as akin to a seed from which a hemispheric good roads movement could blossom.[13]

Once Hoover gave Drake the authorization to help organize the conference, the export-minded automaker decided to expand the scope of Rowe's proposal dramatically. The United States, in Drake's view, needed to put on a grand display of good roads enthusiasm, taking the invited Latin American delegates on a multiweek tour of the nation's new federal aid road network as well as its automotive industry.[14]

In November 1923, Drake held a meeting with representatives from across the automotive and road building sectors to promote this tour. Private industry, he urged, must take the lead in financing the entire affair, as the anticipated positive effects would invariably benefit US manufacturers directly. Eventually his arguments and his promises of new foreign markets won over the room. Drake told one of the attendees after the meeting, "My impression is that the road machinery people will now go through with the automotive group with every prospect of making the enterprise an outstanding success. The plan itself is bound to have a very important influence upon the Pan American countries in their purchase of automobiles and other commodities related to highway development."[15]

The commercial aspects of the tour, however, were something that Drake sought to downplay lest the delegates misinterpret the gathering as purely a ploy to push US goods on the rest of the hemisphere. Soon Drake's concerns led him to embrace an idea proposed by Chapin, who had attended the November meeting and would prove one of the tour's strongest champions. The entire event, Chapin had suggested, should be handled under the auspices of the Highway Education Board, a public-private partnership that had been established in 1920 through the efforts of rubber baron Harvey Firestone as a way to educate the public on the benefits of truck transport. The Highway Education Board's members included MacDonald, Chapin, Firestone, and Secretary of Education John Tigert. As one of the engineers in the Bureau of Public Roads explained, "It was a high class propaganda agency doing its work openly and having no political affiliations of any kind."[16]

With the preliminary questions of financing and organization settled, attention turned to the selection of the delegates. The entire operation's success hinged on getting these choices right. As one member of the Department of Commerce observed, "The significant point is that if American interests support the preliminary conference they can choose the men from the Latin American countries whom they wish. Otherwise if the delegates should be chosen by the various governments they would inevitably be political and diplomatic." The Commerce Department soon issued instructions to its consuls in the various countries to find suitable men, noting, "It is essential that the opinion of American business interests in your country and the native business element friendly to Americans be completely informed and be given a considerable voice in deciding upon your nominations."[17]

The delegate search encountered few problems aside from an incident involving Haiti, which had proposed to send a black man. Such a possibility had immediately caused panic in the Department of Commerce, which feared "the uncomfortable situation which would result if a colored delegate were taken through the South." After some deliberation, the department concluded that the easiest solution simply omitted Haiti from the list of participating nations. The men justified this decision on the grounds that the US Navy already conducted extensive road building operations there as part of an occupation that had begun in 1915. Road building programs had, in fact, formed part of every US occupation since the days of the Spanish-American War, when Roy Stone had begun laying out highways in Cuba and Puerto Rico. As one Marine Corps commandant observed in 1921, "You can not have good military control; you can not have good business; you can not have good anything in any country without roads." [18]

The delegates that the Department of Commerce had selected for the tour began arriving at Washington in late May 1924 in anticipation of the June 2 opening ceremonies. Among the group were the dean of the engineering faculty at the University of Montevideo, the inspector of streets and sanitation in Buenos Aires, a former Nicaraguan minister of finance, a Guatemalan general, and numerous engineers from various ministries of public works. Some of the men spoke English, others only Spanish. [19]

The welcome the delegates soon received carried all the pomp and celebration of a major state visit. "It was fantastic," noted one of the Argentine delegates. "I had figured that we would receive some official attention, but I never imagined that we would be treated like such important guests." The tour's extensive promotion had been handled personally by Pyke Johnson, MacDonald's close friend who served as the lobbyist for the National Automobile Chamber of Commerce. The official program began with a personal address from Secretary of State Hughes, and afterward the thirty-seven delegates were escorted to the White House, where President Coolidge received them warmly. As Coolidge declared,

> The tour of inspection that you are about to undertake and the studies in which you are about to engage are matters of very real significance to all the republics of the American continent. We see today, more clearly than ever before, that the improved means of communication is not only one of the great forces making for cultural and economic advance, but it is also one of the basic factors in the development of Pan-American unity. . . . There is something inspiring in the thought of the assembling of eminent citizens from the nations of the Americas for

the purpose of exchanging views and profiting by one another's experience in the solution of the great questions of common interest. . . .
As you travel through this country you may be sure that the friendly
feeling for your respective countries extends far beyond the confines of
the national capital. . . . When you return to your respective countries,
I hope that you will take with you this heartfelt message of fraternal
good feeling, for in it is to be found the surest guarantee of peace and
prosperity of the American continent.[20]

The keynote address in Washington was delivered by Hoover. An engineer himself, Hoover encouraged the delegates to think of their work in
grand terms, and during the course of his talk he spoke about the need to
revive the old dream of a hemisphere-long transportation corridor. As he
explained,

> For many years, for perhaps half a century, the engineers have car-
> ried a dream in their minds that they might some day have a railway
> from Canada to Tierra del Fuego. That dream is much more likely of
> realization and is certain of realization through the development of a
> great new form of transportation by automobile, for through that we
> will have the extension of our road system to that point where we shall
> have at last and in reality, and in not many years, real communication
> between all the nations of the American continent.

Hoover's vision would quickly come to serve as inspiration for many of the
Latin American guests. According to one delegate, the promise of a future
highway throughout the Americas was "widely discussed at our dinners and
meetings."[21]

Following the introductory events, the delegates were turned over
to MacDonald, who had planned out a three-week-long itinerary. The
route included multi-day stops in North Carolina, Illinois, and Minne-
sota. According to one witness, everywhere the delegates traveled the local
populations "met [them] with salvos of applause while roses [were] tossed
into the cars, bands play[ed] national anthems, [and] flags and pennons
flutter[ed] from every vantage point." This witness added that in North
Carolina the reception had featured "everything that the generous instincts
of the South could arrange . . . barbecues, negro jubilees, concerts, break-
fasts, luncheons, dinners, Indian lacrosse games, [and] dances." One of the
Argentine delegates observed, "They received us with displays of friendship

and care unmatched by anything that I had ever witnessed back home for any man."[22]

MacDonald had designed the tour to provide the delegates with exposure to a wide range of road building conditions. All the selected sites, however, had been constructed according to the bureau's engineering standards, whether the roads featured the newest in concrete and asphalt surfacing or the older-style, less expensive sand and gravel treatments. Among the delegates, the simplest, cheapest roads commanded the greatest interest. As an article in the *New York Herald* explained, "It was held by the visitors . . . that the immediate demands of their respective countries are for serviceable roads, which can be brought to a higher state of development later as traffic demands increase."[23]

The tour concluded with visits to some of the nation's manufacturing centers, including Detroit, where the delegates met with many of the country's leading automakers. At one point, Henry Ford himself came to speak with the Latin Americans. MacDonald later wrote appreciatively to Chapin,

> We all enjoyed the visit to Detroit. The thing that has impressed me particularly is the personal time and attention which those highest in the motor vehicle industry contributed. Certainly this was not all due to their interest in the delegates. Much, if not most, was due to their desire to cooperate with you, and you are personally responsible for their attitude. I know of nothing that could have taken the place of the personal attention that was given the delegates.[24]

The delegates' itinerary ended with a final celebration back east in Atlantic City. A number of delegates nonetheless decided to carry on toward Washington to plan out next steps. Once in the capital, these delegates worked closely with MacDonald and Rowe to draft an agenda for the proposed Pan-American Highway Conference, which Argentina had recently agreed to host at some time in the following year. Along with the agenda also came plans for a permanent organization. Each country, the delegates concluded, should set up its own highway propaganda body, with the US Highway Education Board serving as the central coordinator for what would be henceforth known as the Pan-American Confederation for Highway Education. Drake soon wrote to Rowe in satisfaction, "I am convinced that we started a fine practical piece of work."[25]

When the Highway Education Board next convened that December, Firestone suggested that the confederation ought to comprise an independent body. Soon the board decided to spin off a separate seven-man executive committee. They assigned leadership responsibility to Rowe and gave committee seats to Drake, Chapin, and MacDonald. The team that had brought about the tour was now, officially, in charge of the incipient Pan-American good roads movement.[26]

The new confederation quickly set to work. Rowe headed to South America, where he endeavored to drum up support for the upcoming highway conference, which, according to Argentine papers, was failing to draw much interest. Back in Washington, the committee members urged Coolidge to ask Congress for a $15,000 appropriation to fund the costs of sending a multiperson US delegation to Buenos Aires for the meeting.[27]

Coolidge agreed to bring the matter to Congress, and in March the request reached the House floor. A short but heated debate then ensued. The leading opposition voice argued, "[T]his is nothing in the world but a proposal in behalf of the automobile industry and the road-building machinery industry to take $15,000 out of the Public Treasury to advertise their business in the South American countries. . . . This is a junket trip mainly and is upon matters connected with private business." Despite these objections, the appropriation request found enough votes in Congress to gain passage, and in mid-April Coolidge named seven delegates for the trip to Buenos Aires, among them Drake and MacDonald.[28]

The announcement of the US delegation added legitimacy to the highway conference, which Argentina had decided to postpone until October after struggling to raise enough funds to cover the hosting expenses. Shortly after Coolidge made his appointments, the Buenos Aires paper *La Acción* declared, "The other countries invited by the Argentine government to the said Roads Congress should not delay in following the action of the United States, but should proceed at once to the designation of their delegates." Soon several other nations followed the US lead, and by midsummer nearly every nation in the Pan-American Union had agreed to send representatives.[29]

In late August 1925, six weeks before the conference was scheduled to begin, the US delegation departed from New York as emissaries for a new type of foreign relations: highway diplomacy. The delegates carried with them a letter from President Coolidge, who had briefly received them before their departure. Coolidge's letter, meant to be read at the conference, stated: "Your mission is an important one. . . . I look forward hopefully to the time when through the efforts of the delegates to these Pan American conferences the two continents of North America and South America will be united in physical fact through modern highways, as they are today united by the bonds of mutual friendship and goodwill. God Speed."[30]

The delegation first stopped in Panama, where an impressive road building program had started two years earlier thanks to a $4.5 million loan that US banks had floated the government. Much of the work was being overseen by thirty-eight-year-old Tomás Guardia, an ambitious and exacting engineer who had trained in England and had participated in the 1924 tour across the United States. The rapid pace of development in and around Panama City made a strong impression upon the delegates. In the words of Pyke Johnson, who had accompanied the delegation as an unofficial representative of the automobile industry,

[H]ere was a country where modern ways are rapidly overtaking the old. . . . Heavy duty trucks vie with native carts in competition for trade. Private passenger traffic is heavy with American cars everywhere. . . . The proceeds from the first [road loan] are about exhausted and the arrangements must soon be made for more money. . . . A large agricultural development awaits only transportation.[31]

The delegates departed from Panama on its Pacific side and then continued their journey by ship southward another fifteen hundred miles before pausing to visit Peru. There they received an elaborate welcome, including two audiences with the nation's president, who informed the delegates, "We are prioritizing highway improvement in Peru. . . . We have already under way 106 projects, . . . our best wish being that in time the triumphant automobile may go from one end of our territory to the other." Johnson wrote of their time in Peru, "Our most important part we were told is to do all we can to provide for closer relations between the engineers of North and South America, see that they have all of our technical material, arrange if possible for scholarship exchanges, [and] send in films and educational materials for popular distribution."[32]

The delegation's itinerary sent them subsequently to Chile, where the reception they received rivaled what had just taken place in Peru. One fancy dinner followed another, and the delegates met with many of the nation's lead engineers as well as the president. Before departing the country, the group also paid a visit to General Pershing, who was there on a special diplomatic mission of his own related to a border dispute between Chile and

Peru that reached back to the days of James G. Blaine. Pershing, a pioneer in the use of motorized vehicles in war, told the delegation, "Transportation is the crying need of the South American countries." In Johnson's view, Pershing's comment "about summ[ed] up the whole story."[33]

The final leg of the US delegation's journey carried them over the Andes and across the Argentine pampas to Buenos Aires. Since no motor roads had yet crossed the Andes, the delegation had traveled aboard the famous Trans-Andine Railroad, which connected Chile with Mendoza, Argentina. From there, a government-controlled railroad had taken them the final six hundred miles, a journey that was, according to Johnson, "disappointingly pleasant if such a thing were possible." The courteous treatment that the delegates received nonetheless contrasted somewhat with the underlying sentiments of the railroad interests in Argentina, who feared that the highway diplomats represented, in Johnson's words, "the beginning of a new order of things."[34]

The conference finally commenced on October 3, 1925, and the delegates soon adopted the slogan "Good Roads, Good Will Towards Mankind." MacDonald held court as a larger-than-life figure and reconnected with a number of the men he had first met during the tour the previous year. For MacDonald, however, the conference ultimately proved disappointing, too focused on technical details. As he later lamented, "The broad principles of highway transport economics, administration and financing were not accorded the relative weight and time consistent with their importance. There was too much confusion of matters of good or recommended engineering practice with the fundamental principles underlying highway transport."[35]

The conference had also tended to focus on domestic concerns at the expense of broader, Pan-American issues, such as the establishment of intercountry linkages. Most of the delegates felt that these international matters were something better taken up at a future date, perhaps at the next conference, which they agreed would convene in Rio de Janeiro. MacDonald and his fellow US representatives nonetheless worked to build support for the Pan-American good roads movement, and their efforts ultimately yielded a resolution recognizing the status of Rowe's confederation and urging a continuing promotional campaign. The subsequent US delegate report to the secretary of state assured that "the feeling that cooperation was essential [was] strong."[36]

This optimistic pronouncement was welcome news to President

Coolidge, who felt that the Pan-American good roads movement held vast potential as a tool for hemispheric solidarity. Over the next several years, Coolidge continued to follow the work of Rowe's confederation as it sponsored two more US tours, one for journalists in 1926 and another for businessmen in 1927. During this period, the president also started to talk about the potential value of a hemispheric highway. Such a project, he felt, could serve as a backbone for a transportation network girding the hemisphere and facilitating inter-American goodwill. By October 1927, newspapers were reporting that the president believed "nothing could be more effective as a means to bring the nations of the Western world into closer and more harmonious relations." [37]

At the time Coolidge expressed these sentiments, relations between the United States and the rest of the hemisphere were as far from harmonious as at any time in the nation's history. The trouble related to a decision by the United States to intervene in Nicaragua during early 1927 in an effort to stabilize a political situation that had remained volatile ever since the departure of José Santos Zelaya seventeen years earlier. The intervention, however, had turned into a guerrilla war after one of the Liberal leaders, General Augusto Sandino, had refused to submit to a US-brokered truce and had taken to the hills with a loyal band of soldiers to fight against what he viewed as a US occupation. The United States had found itself suddenly enmeshed in an unpopular conflict against a charismatic leader whom many in the hemisphere considered a freedom fighter confronting imperialism. [38]

The war in Nicaragua was still raging when the Sixth Pan-American Conference convened at Havana, Cuba, in January 1928. As a gesture of goodwill, Coolidge had decided to take the unprecedented step of attending the conference personally with the hope that his appearance might dampen calls for a resolution prohibiting US interventions. Once in Havana, the president addressed the audience of hemispheric representatives directly. His speech, which conspicuously avoided any reference to Nicaragua, focused on the positive actions the United States could take to promote hemispheric amity, and foremost among Coolidge's proposals were improved communications. In the middle of his speech, he noted, "On the wall of my office hangs a map showing proposed highways connecting the principal points of our two continents." Coolidge assured that the United States was committed to help realize the dream of a hemispheric highway. [39]

When the discussion sessions got under way in Havana, the US delegation moved to give action to Coolidge's words. Eventually they arranged
to have a resolution introduced calling for the upcoming Second Pan-
American Highway Conference in Rio to undertake "the consideration and
adoption of agreements looking to the construction of a road of longitudinal communication across the continent." A second, related resolution then
urged the participating nations "to give [their] full approval to the initiative
for the building of an inter-American highway and to recommend to all
governments, members of the Pan-American Union, that they cooperate,
in so far as possible, in the prompt realization of said project." The general
assembly subsequently authorized both of these resolutions, giving an official imprimatur to the grand scheme. In the end, the US delegation had
pulled off a remarkable performance, advancing Coolidge's pet highway
project and simultaneously fending off a strong campaign from Mexico, El
Salvador, and Argentina to force a vote on a pledge of nonintervention.[40]

The actions taken at the Havana conference marked a triumph for the
multiyear propaganda campaign that had begun with the 1924 tour and
been framed around the idea of friendship. One federal engineer observed
of the Havana resolutions,

> In view of the international situation confronting the delegation from
> the United States at the Havana Conference it may be considered sig-
> nificant that such specific and unqualified approval should have been
> given to the project. It must have been realized by this time by the
> representatives from Central America and the southern continent that
> the commercial and civic interests of the United States, as well as the
> government, would certainly be drawn into active participation by so
> large a construction project as any longitudinal or intercontinental
> road must be. The economic soundness of the proposal for improved
> highways and specifically for an international route . . . had sufficiently
> impressed the Pan American delegates to secure their support on the
> merits of the proposition. . . . Thus was the careful and well planned
> work of the Highway Education Board and its South and Central
> American affiliations beginning to show some effect.

Through the Pan-American good roads movement and Coolidge, the hazy
vision of a hemispheric highway, first publicly suggested by Hoover four
years prior, had transformed into a formally sanctioned initiative for the
Americas.[41]

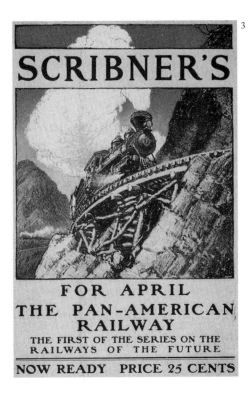

Top left, the logo of the Intercontinental Railway Commission, the Americas' first hemispheric organization, founded in 1890. The commission organized a major US-sponsored reconnaissance survey along the proposed rail route in Latin America between Mexico and Argentina. Top right, Corps One in a clearing in Guatemala, joined by several local engineers who provided additional support. Below, an advertisement for *Scribner's Magazine* featuring the Pan-American Railway. During the early 1890s, the United States seemed more likely to fund a Pan-American Railway than an isthmian canal.

Top left, $1,000 US bond (c. 1903) for the Pan-American Railroad Company of Mexico, a US-funded operation. The original backers sold their position in 1904 to a syndicate arranged partly by George Herbert Walker, namesake and paterfamilias of two future presidents named George Bush. **Top right,** Mexicans watching the passage of a railcar emblazoned with "Ferrocarril Panamericano" (c. 1906). **Below,** a 1908 advertisement in the *Mexican Herald* for the Pan-American Railway.

7

Above, a political cartoon from Mexico's *El Imparcial* in 1909 showing Uncle Sam being strangled by E. H. Harriman, whose specter also loomed over Mexico in this period. Harriman had spent the early 1900s expanding his US system down Mexico's Pacific coast with the rumored goal of sleeper service between Seattle and Panama City, if not beyond to South America. **Below**, J. R. Drake, cofounder of the Hupp Motor Company, during a 1910 around-the-world promotional tour in a Hupmobile. The international expansion into Mexico of US railroads contrasted with the domestic focus of nearly all early automobile manufacturers, save for Hupp. Drake's brother and company cofounder, J. Walter, would later become one of the earliest proponents of the Pan-American Highway.

8

9

10

Though rarely remarked upon, US capital ultimately built more contiguous rail miles south of the nation's border than the distance of the legendary transcontinental route. Minor C. Keith, the founder of United Fruit, considered it his life's mission to complete a through-road from the United States to Panama, though he died before this ambition could be realized. **Top left,** a train from Keith's International Railways of Central America traveling along an unloading pier into the Gulf of Fonseca near the border of El Salvador and Honduras. **Top right,** a railway cut with nearly vertical sides, to mitigate water erosion, one of the many engineering challenges in Central America. **Below,** a map of heavy construction near Zacapa, Guatemala, where five miles of rails were needed for every mile of forward progress.

11

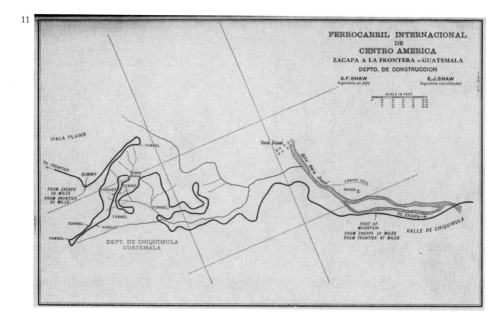

" How cam'st thou in this pickle?"—*Shakespeare.*

12

13

The United States' well-developed rail network of the late nineteenth century stood in stark opposition to the state of its rural roads, which were considered "the worst in civilization." **Top left**, the title-page illustration from *The Gospel of Good Roads* (1891), an influential reformist tract from the League of American Wheelmen, a bicyclists' club. **Top right**, a "good roads" train hauls road building equipment through the south in 1901 on a promotional tour involving the federal government. **Bottom left**, the second chief of the federal road office, Martin Dodge, driving a car along a steel road, an experimental technology that briefly received widespread acclaim as a potential solution to the nation's road problem. **Bottom right**, Thomas MacDonald, the much-admired head of the Bureau of Public Roads from 1919 to 1953, stands near Washington, DC's Zero Milestone, dedicated in 1923 as the starting point for a new system of federal aid roads.

14

15

16

17

The United States began agitating for a Pan-American good roads movement almost as soon as its federal domestic road building program was on solid footing. **Top left**, a scene from North Carolina with locals building a road while Latin American delegates watched as part of a 1924 tour. **Top right**, President Herbert Hoover (center) meets with US delegates before their departure for the Second Pan-American Highway Conference in 1929. **Below**, a reconnaissance team in Guatemala as part of a US-sponsored location survey across Central America and Panama in the early 1930s, a mission that encountered almost as many hardships and missteps as the Intercontinental Railway survey forty years prior.

18

At the urging of President Franklin Roosevelt, the US Congress in 1934 allocated $1 million for construction of the Inter-American Highway in Central America and Panama, a move that would soon inaugurate modern overseas development for the nation. **Top left**, a scene from a 1935 overland automobile trip between Panama and Guatemala—almost certainly the first—undertaken by federal road engineer Edwin Warley James. **Top right**, draft animals (c. 1936) pull an automobile across a future bridge site on Guatemala's Tamazulapa River. **Below**, chief federal road builder Thomas MacDonald (second from right) stands before a globe showing the envisioned Pan-American Highway at the famed Futurama exhibit of the 1939 New York World's Fair.

A 1942 advertisement from White Trucks framing construction on the Inter-American Highway as the munificent work of "ambassadors in overalls."

A 1941 advertisement from Alliance Oil Corporation depicting "flowing profits" from the United States to South America.

24

25

26

The outbreak of World War II prompted newfound interest in the Inter-American Highway, as the United States grew concerned about the lack of an overland route to the Panama Canal. **Top left**, the 1942 opening of El Salvador's Cuscatlan Bridge, the longest bridge on the Inter-American route. **Top right**, laborers hand grading a steep slope in Costa Rica, where the heaviest wartime construction took place. **Above**, a panorama of the access road between Dominical and San Isidro, Costa Rica, built during the war as a step in the ultimate conquest of the daunting Cerro de la Muerte (Mountain of Death). **Bottom left**, the opening stanzas of a wartime song that a Costa Rican wrote to honor US Army–affiliated engineers. **Bottom right**, US congressmen arrive at Cerro de la Muerte during a 1946 inspection trip to investigate charges of widespread wartime fraud.

27

28

The Pan-American Highway and Inter-American Highway began to infiltrate the nation's popular culture long before actual construction neared completion. **Above,** a magazine illustration from 1947 showing an imagined traffic jam of American tourists confronting ongoing work on the Inter-American Highway. **Inset, top right,** a panel from a 1946 comic book relating one of the earliest attempts to travel by road along the entire Western Hemisphere.

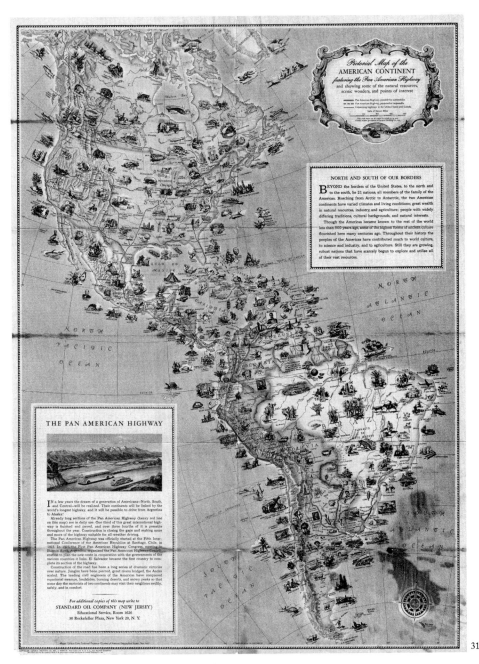

A promotional map of the Pan-American Highway from midcentury that Standard Oil produced, illustrating material or cultural products considered representative of each region.

32

Above, the promotional map from the previous page being discussed by Edwin Warley James, the federal engineer who oversaw the Inter-American Highway project for a quarter century. **Bottom left**, James and three companions (c. 1950) standing at Guatemala's Selegua canyon, a daunting obstacle on the route of the Inter-American Highway. **Bottom right**, Vice President Richard Nixon poses during a 1955 goodwill mission to Central America with Guatemalan president Carlos Castillo Armas. The visit convinced Nixon of the pressing need to finish the Inter-American Highway and led him to call publicly for its completion, an action that prompted Congress to authorize $75 million in funding several months later.

33

34

US participation in the construction of the Inter-American Highway, which had slowed after World War II, accelerated following Nixon's goodwill trip and the subsequent congressional action. **Top left**, a collection of road-grading equipment for the Inter-American Highway in Costa Rica (c. 1955). **Top right**, a scene during the Ninth Pan-American Highway Conference, held in May 1963 in Washington, DC, showing President John F. Kennedy congratulating participants in a ceremonial bus caravan that had traveled there from Panama City. **Below**, a reporter's notes from a southbound trip on the Inter-American Highway in mid-1963.

With the opening of the Inter-American Highway and with a drivable route already built in South America, the last remaining bottleneck in the mid-1960s for the Pan-American Highway was the so-called Darien Gap, positioned at the exact spot where the two continents appeared to meet. **Top left**, bedecked in adventure gear, Richard Tewkesbury, a diminutive North Carolina schoolteacher, prepares to enter the Darien Gap in 1939 as a self-appointed scout for the Pan-American Highway. **Top right**, a panel from a 1942 comic book recounting Tewkesbury's failed first attempt and successful second try in 1940. **Bottom**, Panamanian anthropologist Dr. Reina Torres de Araúz seen reading a *National Geographic* with an indigenous woman in 1958 during an early Panamanian exploratory mission into Darien in service of the future highway.

35 36

US participation in the construction of the Inter-American Highway, which had slowed after World War II, accelerated following Nixon's goodwill trip and the subsequent congressional action. **Top left**, a collection of road-grading equipment for the Inter-American Highway in Costa Rica (c. 1955). **Top right**, a scene during the Ninth Pan-American Highway Conference, held in May 1963 in Washington, DC, showing President John F. Kennedy congratulating participants in a ceremonial bus caravan that had traveled there from Panama City. **Below**, a reporter's notes from a southbound trip on the Inter-American Highway in mid-1963.

37

With the opening of the Inter-American Highway and with a drivable route already built in South America, the last remaining bottleneck in the mid-1960s for the Pan-American Highway was the so-called Darien Gap, positioned at the exact spot where the two continents appeared to meet. **Top left**, bedecked in adventure gear, Richard Tewkesbury, a diminutive North Carolina schoolteacher, prepares to enter the Darien Gap in 1939 as a self-appointed scout for the Pan-American Highway. **Top right**, a panel from a 1942 comic book recounting Tewkesbury's failed first attempt and successful second try in 1940. **Bottom**, Panamanian anthropologist Dr. Reina Torres de Araúz seen reading a *National Geographic* with an indigenous woman in 1958 during an early Panamanian exploratory mission into Darien in service of the future highway.

41

The campaign to close the Darien Gap was spearheaded by a three-man, international Darien Subcommittee composed of representatives from Colombia, Panama, and the United States. **Above**, a subcommittee vehicle driving down a makeshift bridge during the first motorized crossing of the gap in 1960. **Bottom left**, a commemorative stamp from the Eighth Pan-American Highway Conference showing the Pacific highway route that Colombia had approved in 1959 but would then change in 1967 beneath pressure from the United States. **Bottom right**, a meeting of the Darien Subcommittee in the early sixties. The committee was chaired by Panamanian road builder Tómas Guardia (seated center), a veteran engineer known as the "godfather" of the Inter-American Highway. His son Tommy (standing in the photo) oversaw all the Darien explorations and surveys until 1964. Five years later, the United States authorized $100 million to cooperatively build the Darien Highway with Panama and Colombia, but the project stalled in the 1970s.

42

43

44

Above, the footbridge at the current end of the Panamanian highway system in Yaviza, a town that was the terminus of Richard Tewkesbury's trip in 1940—somewhat remarkably, the contemporary Darien Gap bears no overlap with Tewkesbury's route. **Below**, a "zero kilometer" road marker in Panama City, dedicated in the 1930s as the intended center point for the Pan-American Highway, now all but forgotten.

45

"Leaven to the Bread of Progress"

The immediate responsibility for advancing the Havana resolutions rested in principle with the Pan-American Union. However, some US congressmen felt that the federal government ought to exert direct control over the process of developing a "longitudinal highway."

The subject of such a road was already well known in Congress by this point. The federal legislature had initially broached the topic a full year before the Havana conference thanks to the efforts of an engineer named James Dietrick, a former employee of E. H. Harriman. Dietrick had earlier worked in Mexico and had once carried out a survey related to Harriman's planned intercontinental railway. According to Dietrick, his "extensive experience" in building railroads through Mexico had made him particularly suited "to learn and carry out the work" of constructing a hemispheric road. Dietrick's plan, which he developed in the mid-1920s, had called for the US government to create a special commission to oversee the project. By late 1926 he had found two sponsors for his proposed legislation, Senator Ralph Cameron of Arizona and Representative Clarence McLeod of Michigan.[42]

On January 3, 1927, both congressmen had introduced bills calling for the creation of a "Pan-American Peoples Great Highway Commission." The legislation proposed to create a fourteen-man body composed mainly of cabinet-level officials and asked for an appropriation of $200,000 to cover expenses, which would include a $6,000 annual payment to a "consulting engineer" position, a role that Dietrick hoped to fill personally. Cameron, in introducing the measure, explained that the highway would link the capitals of nineteen countries and would also "serve aircrafts as a possible landing place when forced down." The senator had further assured that "President Coolidge has expressed to me his high personal interest in this very important development."[43]

The legislation had immediately drawn support from numerous influential good roads enthusiasts. As the vice president of General Motors declared in a letter submitted to Congress, "it will be a great ideal" that "will have a great influence upon road building generally, long before the highway itself can be completed. In that it will be like our Lincoln Highway 10 years ago." Even Martin Dodge resurfaced to promote the measure, stating that he felt a "duty" to aid in the bill's passage given that he was one of "the only living representatives of the old Pioneer Association—that is, the National Good Road Association."[44]

These endorsements helped to build consensus for the measure in Congress, and in late March 1927 the bill managed to win passage in the Senate. The House, however, concluded its legislative session before the measure reached a vote.[45]

Following the issuance of the Havana resolutions the next February, Representative McLeod decided to reintroduce the legislation. Soon he took to the House floor and delivered a lengthy speech on the matter. As he explained,

> I believe we are ready to take the step in road building which will give us supremacy for all time, namely, the Pan American highway. Just as we opened up counties, then States, and then the continental territories of North America by means of roads and paved highways, so we are now on the verge of opening up the unrevealed splendor of the Western Hemisphere by an artery of trade and travel that will extend into every country of the three Americas. . . . The Pan American highway will act as leaven to the bread of Latin-American Highway progress. It will serve as the backbone for many thousands of miles of side roads. One thing we must remember is that if we do not lend a helping hand in the inevitable development of Latin-America, the efficient and aggressive merchants of Europe will quickly and effectively take our southern neighbors to themselves. . . . This highway will commemorate a different kind of civilization from any heretofore important in the affairs of mankind. It will stand, not for the engineering achievement of a military emperor but for the more advanced genius of mutual cooperation between friendly republics. In other words, this highway is a challenge to the principle of cooperation rather than conquest, to the ability of self-governed peoples to concentrate on a great engineering feat of purely peace-time value. For the first time in the Christian era we have an opportunity to surpass the road-building feats of the Romans, and I am confident that the United States and the . . . friendly republics to our south are capable of meeting the challenge in true American fashion.

For McLeod, the proposed Pan-American Peoples Great Highway Commission seemed to embody nothing less than the dawn of a new age of enlightened hemispheric relations.[46]

McLeod's renewed appeal quickly gained the backing of numerous congressmen and Washington policy makers. As Herbert Hoover noted, "[McLeod's] bill represents a sound proposition, and the sooner it can be enacted into law the better. It is a good-will message to Central and South America." [47]

Not everyone who favored the Pan-American Highway, however, supported the McLeod bill. MacDonald, for one, displayed hostility to any rival road building bureaucracy within the federal government and also felt that "the initiative . . . should come from Latin-American countries." In the State Department, meanwhile, some raised concerns about the danger of creating an independent body that could engage in freelance diplomacy. [48]

The opposition from both MacDonald and the State Department soon found a sympathetic hearing from Cyrenus Cole, an Iowa representative who chaired the subcommittee handling the bill. Cole had reservations of his own about the measure's prospective cost and had concluded that the best way to halt the popular McLeod legislation would be through an alternative proposal. After consulting with MacDonald and the State Department, Cole decided to put forth a resolution allowing the president to "loan" engineers from the Bureau of Public Roads to any nation in Latin America that requested their services. Cole's proposal carried no appropriation and created no new agencies. "I think it is just in the form that we want," observed Cole. "I wish that all big projects could be started off so modestly." [49]

Cole's resolution quickly received the public support of MacDonald, Johnson, Rowe, Chapin, and State Department officials. Their testimonials helped persuade Congress to accept the new measure as a suitable replacement for the Pan-American Peoples Great Highway Commission, and in early May 1928 the Cole resolution gained passage. [50]

Though the resolution had been created as a defensive maneuver, it was nonetheless hailed in Congress as a major step forward in the campaign for a Pan-American Highway. Soon Cole's committee published a special dual-language, English-Spanish report to accompany and promote the matter. The report framed the highway as part of a much longer effort to build a hemispheric transportation corridor, noting, "Many years ago James G. Blaine, conspicuously, proposed a similar project in the form of a Pan American railroad. But at the present time the world is thinking in terms of automobiles and motor trucks." A Pan-American Highway, the report assured, would ultimately bring about a new age of hemispheric fraternity:

> Attention need not be called to the good will and international unity among all the Republics of the two American continents which may be promoted by the projected Pan American Highway. Nations that are now separated will be brought closer together. People that sometimes

now misunderstand each other may be brought into better mutual understandings. Along this highway there will be a constant interchange of ideas as well as interchange of commerce.

More than five thousand copies of this report were subsequently distributed throughout Latin America by the Pan-American Union.[51]

A related promotional effort came later in the year directly from Hoover, who had been elected president in November 1928. Hoover had decided to follow his victory with a goodwill tour of Latin America and had made the Pan-American Highway one of his top discussion topics. As the *Washington Post* explained, "Everywhere he went he took occasion to talk with highway officials regarding the Pan-American highway, and everywhere he discovered the greatest interest." Journalist Will Irwin, who accompanied Hoover on his tour, observed, "I heard no talk whatever of new railroads in South America; every one is talking roads. . . . [I]t is perhaps not likely that any of our generation will ever see a through Pan-American railroad, while on the other hand, within a decade or so the motor bus from Quebec to the Horn may become a commonplace of American life, just as the transcontinental tour is today."[52]

While President-elect Hoover was away on his goodwill trip, Coolidge made one last plea of his own for the Pan-American Highway during his final congressional address, delivered the first week of December 1928. As he explained,

[W]e should lend our encouragement for more good roads to all the principal points in this hemisphere south of the Rio Grande. . . . As those countries enter upon programs for road building we should be ready to contribute from our abundant experience to make their task easier of accomplishment. . . . We should provide our southern neighbors, if they request it, with such engineer advisors for the construction of roads and bridges. Private interests should look with favor upon all reasonable loans sought by these countries to open main lines of travel. Such assistance should be given especially to any project for a highway designed to connect all the countries in this hemisphere and thus facilitate intercourse and closer relations among them.[53]

Coolidge's appeal soon prompted Representative Cole to revisit the matter anew. Once more he sought the counsel of MacDonald and the State Department, and together they decided to push for a resolution requesting

$50,000 to fund a reconnaissance survey that would help determine a fixed route for the proposed hemispheric highway. As Cole explained in a January report to the House,

> All that the United States Government is called upon to do is to cooperate, along the lines laid down by President Coolidge. . . . The passage of this resolution by this Congress will be an expression of the spirit of this cooperation, and it will do much to bring about the realization of a dream that is as old as Henry Clay. After a century of contemplation of such international connections and communications, it is hoped and believed that we can at last make them realizations and when so realized they will stand out as great international achievements, binding together the Republics of the American Continents in mutual trade and mutual good fellowship. . . . On his recent "good-will tour" President-elect Hoover made frequent references to this great Pan American project, and everywhere it met with the most enthusiastic support.

Cole's resolution placed ultimate responsibility for the work with the secretary of state, but the actual survey personnel were to be drawn from MacDonald's bureau as part of the "loan" program authorized the year earlier.[54]

The resolution quickly received strong endorsements from the State Department as well as the members of the Pan-American Confederation for Highway Education. Their enthusiasm helped fortify congressional support for the measure, even though some worried about the long-term consequences of embarking on such a survey. Cole ultimately mollified these concerns with assurances about the limited scope of the commitment, noting, "It is not contemplated that this country will invest out of the United States Treasury a dollar in building a mile of road outside of this country."[55]

A month after the hearings, both houses of Congress agreed to pass the measure. Coolidge then joyfully signed the bill into law as his final executive action. The *Los Angeles Times* noted, "The signing of the bill by Calvin Coolidge, the retiring President, was one of the dramatic events preceding the inauguration of President Hoover. The signature of the President was affixed to the resolution a few moments before he mounted the rostrum to hear his successor take the oath of office."[56]

*   *   *

The new resolution dovetailed with an effort that Rowe had initiated four months prior, when he had sent letters to the foreign ministers of Central America and Panama inquiring whether their countries would participate in a highway location survey overseen by his confederation, a body that he deemed "peculiarly equipped to undertake the task." His letter had assured that the confederation had already drafted a map showing a "tentative route" as far south as Panama. Rowe had proposed that the survey be completed before the convening of the Second Pan-American Highway Conference, planned for August 1929 in Rio de Janeiro. The letter further explained that Rowe had excluded Mexico from his inquiry because its government "had already formulated a comprehensive highway program" and that he hoped to expand the survey to South America but felt that insufficient time existed before the Rio conference for such an ambitious undertaking.[57]

Rowe's proposal, however, had generated little initial enthusiasm. One State Department official suggested in March 1929 that the lukewarm reaction owed to a strong feeling in Central America "that the whole [project] is partly devised to increase the sale of American automobiles, and partly a scheme to facilitate our own military intervention."[58]

The resistance nonetheless failed to discourage the project's US boosters, who seemed doubtful that any Latin American nations would ultimately oppose the Pan-American Highway. Many assumed that the upcoming Rio conference would bring about definite, positive action. Congress had once again appropriated $15,000 to fund a large contingent, and Hoover had chosen as delegates a number of the men most intimately involved with promoting the Pan-American Highway, notably MacDonald, Drake, and Representative Cole. As Drake explained to the secretary of commerce, "The delegates have been selected with reference to their representation of the groups who have primarily sponsored and assisted in the promotion of Pan American Highway development." Drake further noted, "The impetus given to this project by the sixth international conference of American states at Havana, the indorsement of our own Congress, the action of several other governments and the universal public interest in this highway are all factors driving in the direction of its fulfillment."[59]

For Rowe, the naming of delegates presented another opportunity to try to advance the survey to Panama. Shortly after Hoover announced the US delegation, Rowe dashed off a letter to the foreign minister of Panama suggesting that a special supplemental conference be held after Rio in Panama City. The US delegation, Rowe explained, would be stopping on the isthmus in early October following a brief tour of South America, and their presence would provide a unique opportunity to discuss the proposed reconnaissance work. Rowe further noted, "The governments of Guatemala and Nicaragua have already indicated their interest in having a reconnaissance survey made of the route across their territories, and Mexico and Salvador have stated that their portions of the projected Highway have been located and construction actually started." Rowe, sensitive to the concerns about US imperialism, imagined that if the invitations came directly from Panama and not from the US-led Pan-American Union, then the nations of Central America would be more willing to participate.[60]

Rowe's appeal found support from both the Panamanian minister of public works and from road builder Tomás Guardia. Together they managed to convince their government to take the lead in organizing a conference, and soon all the nations involved agreed to send representatives.[61]

At the end of July, the US delegation to Rio convened in Washington to make final preparations for their trip. Before departing, they met briefly with President Hoover, who told them that "the further development of highway transportation in and between the countries of the Pan American Union [was] a matter of first rate importance to the peoples in all of them." Hoover's last words to the delegation were: "I envy you."[62]

The Rio conference had arrived at a moment when a considerable number of Latin American nations were finally awakening to the possibilities of motor transport. Automobile ownership rates in the region had climbed steadily since the last highway conference, and many national governments had begun recognizing a duty to support modern road construction. By the time of the Rio meeting, multimillion-dollar, nationally sponsored road building programs had commenced in Chile, Colombia, Brazil, Peru, Uruguay, Mexico, Cuba, El Salvador, and Panama. In numerous instances, concrete highways had displaced the railroad as the preferred prestige projects for Latin American leaders, with financing handled through a combination of US loans and increased customs revenues from historically high commodity prices. The entire region seemed gripped by road building enthusiasm, and US banks and road building firms appeared eager to help facilitate the transformation—as the *Literary Digest* observed in the fall of 1929, "There is no valid reason why 'exporting highways' can not be made one of [the United States'] very best foreign industries."[63]

The sudden motorization of Latin America gave the delegates in Rio much to discuss. They addressed not only technical matters, but also the administrative and financial questions that the earlier conference had largely avoided. Their breakout sessions covered everything from gasoline taxes to uniform traffic laws, and they found much to agree upon, including the need for cars in the Western Hemisphere to drive on the right-hand side of the road. The resolutions passed at the conference ultimately stretched out for twenty-two pages.[64]

The Pan-American Highway itself, however, had proved to be one of the "most delicate subjects," according to a US official. Many countries felt that their domestic programs should take priority and feared that the adoption of an international route might force them to build highways through border regions with sparse populations. Divisions had also emerged over the road's potential location, especially among the South American delegates, who revived the old disagreements that had plagued the Pan-American Railway project. Moreover, the ever-present concerns about US imperialism lingered. In the end, despite the explicit instructions passed at Havana the year prior, the Rio conference's resolutions failed to make any direct reference to the Pan-American Highway. Drake, who had been so bullish on its prospects before departing for Rio, subsequently concluded that its construction "will depend upon the gradual merging together of links of locally needed roads rather than through any concentration of public funds on a single highway whose sole purpose is international in character."[65]

The US delegation, according to reports, hoped that "far more satisfactory and decisive conclusions" might be reached at the supplemental conference awaiting them in Panama.[66]

The reception that the delegates received upon arrival in Panama City suggested that their hopes were well founded. "[I]t is difficult to convey in words the depth of public interest in the . . . proposal," observed Pyke Johnson, who had traveled with the official delegation. According to Johnson, everyone he spoke with "immediately asked the question, 'When will the road be finished?'" The expectant mood was well captured by the president of the Panama Association of Commerce during his address to the delegates on the eve of the conference:

> Yes, Gentlemen, highly suggestive is this reunion of this October night in which you prepare for the execution of the gigantic work represented by a road traversing two great and most important sections of the American continent, because gathered together also on a night

like this, Christopher Columbus and his companions, filled with faith, optimism and the spirit of self-sacrifice, traced over unknown seas the luminous path which led to immortal glory on the 12th of October, 1492, and gave to the Old World a new world.[67]

The conference began the next morning with a welcome speech from the Panamanian minister of public works, who reaffirmed the delegates' high ambitions. As he explained, "We have come here to forge the links of a chain that shall unite our countries in what could well be called the first chapter of this American aspiration. . . . Our object is . . . the pursuit of a project of transcendental importance."[68]

The Panamanian minister, however, soon abandoned the lofty oratory for a more pragmatic concern. No highway agreement could be reached, he insisted, until the delegates agreed to provisions for the construction of a permanent bridge or tunnel across the canal. In his view, such a structure would be "an imperative necessity" so that the highway reached the Panamanian capital, which sat on the canal's far side. The United States, he suggested, owed his nation a bridge or tunnel since it was the construction of the canal in the first place that had separated Panama's capital from the northwestern half of the country.[69]

The minister's request rattled the US delegation. Neither Drake nor MacDonald felt that they had any authority to address the matter, especially given the enormous cost involved in such a project. The controversy threatened to upend the entire conference, but after several tense hours, one of the US delegates convinced the Panamanians to accept language that simply required a vehicular crossing of the canal "at all times adequate for traffic," something that could be achieved with a ferry service instead of an "impossible bridge."[70]

Once the canal crossing issue had been resolved, the conference resumed its work. Soon MacDonald and Guardia took the lead in drafting plans. After several days of discussion, the delegates agreed on a series of resolutions to guide the building of a road from the United States to the Panama Canal, which would henceforth be known as the Inter-American Highway. And the first step leading toward its construction, they decided, would be to carry out in Central America and Panama the reconnaissance survey that Congress had agreed to fund.[71]

The delegates predicted that, thanks to their cooperative effort, the road would likely be completed within five years. Drake proudly declared at the conclusion of the conference,

Up to the present time the construction of an inter-American highway has been considered only as a dream, but the meeting of this congress has introduced a fundamental change in things, and it can truly be said that the first great practical step has been taken to unite the peoples of America by means of a highway, thus initiating a new era for the countries of this continent.... [A]nd I believe that since the discovery of America nothing more interesting and more vitally important has been done than the work performed by this congress during the course of this week, which undoubtedly will be an historic week.[72]

Drake's triumphant attitude nonetheless obscured certain hesitations that still lingered in some of the Central American countries. Costa Rica, in particular, displayed strong resistance to the highway out of concerns over its likely cost and its imperialistic undertones. As one of the US delegates in Panama noted, "opposition writers ... had used the theme of Yankee Penetration; they had pressed on it.... Anything that they could do to emphasize the idea of Yankee Penetration was the theme they were following."[73]

Eventually news of this resistance reached congressmen on the House Appropriations Committee, who reacted with consternation. Early in 1930, they declared that they were delaying the release of the $50,000 "until a larger number of Governments involved in such a survey indicate that they are interested in the project."[74]

The postponement embarrassed both the US delegation and Guardia, who had already begun making preparations for the survey. By February 1930, Guardia was writing to Drake in frustration, "It seems to me ... that you people over at your end are taking too long to stir things up a little bit.... [W]e shall not be the ones to hold back the Panama Detroit highway.... You will find us ready to cooperate when the time comes, but it is up to you to start the ball rolling."[75]

The impasse in Congress continued until mid-March, when MacDonald and a sympathetic State Department official managed to persuade reluctant lawmakers to issue the funds, arguing "it would be a mistake to wait until all the governments agree, and ... what we ought to do is to cooperate with those governments between here and Panama with which we can cooperate."[76]

The $50,000 appropriation was finally released slightly more than two years after the subject of the Pan-American Highway had first appeared in Congress. Over the course of that period, the original campaign to create an independent Pan-American Peoples Great Highway Commission had gradually been taken over by MacDonald's bureau, while the grand plans to directly oversee construction for a highway the length of the hemisphere had been whittled down to the more modest goal of conducting a reconnaissance survey along fifteen hundred miles of land between the southern border of Mexico and the Panama Canal. Nonetheless, the appropriation marked a new phase for the United States in the ultimate quest to forge a transportation route between the three Americas. For the first time since the days of the Intercontinental Railway Commission, the US government would be sending its citizens abroad to locate an international travel corridor through the wilds of the Central American isthmus.

"A Pretty Little Comedy"

The proposed survey in Central America and Panama presented MacDonald with challenges unlike any his bureau had previously faced. The engineers he dispatched for the project would need to navigate not only a tropical environment but also the politics of up to half a dozen foreign countries. Should the wrong men be chosen, the survey might easily turn into a complete failure, an embarrassment for both the bureau and the US government. In MacDonald's view, the bureau had a duty to send only the "right type of engineers" with the "highest qualifications and broadest experience" so that "genuinely cooperative relationships" would be forged.[77]

MacDonald decided to place responsibility for the survey with Edwin Warley James, a fifty-two-year-old engineer who had been with the bureau for two decades. James possessed a combination of experience and pedigree that was unrivaled within the bureau. He was an alumnus of both Exeter Academy and Harvard University, where his classmates had included Robert Frost and Wallace Stevens. His formal education had been completed with graduate work at the Massachusetts Institute of Technology in highway engineering, a program whose existence owed to an initial donation from the "godfather" of the good roads movement, Colonel Albert Pope himself. When MacDonald had arrived at the bureau in 1919, James was already a veteran with ten years' worth of experience and a strong record of accomplishments. Over the course of the 1920s, the two men had grown close as they worked together to implement the burgeoning federal aid program. MacDonald had come to see James as a model of efficiency and professionalism, and in 1929 had even selected him to be the first engineer whom the bureau "loaned" to a Latin American nation as part of the

Pan-American good roads movement. James had subsequently spent several months working in Colombia to help design its national highway system. The time abroad gave James valuable exposure to Latin American work that MacDonald hoped would serve him well in managing the Inter-American Highway survey.[78]

During the spring of 1930, James worked with MacDonald and members of the State Department to put together a basic plan of operations. They concluded that the $50,000 appropriation would be sufficient to support a field team of three for an estimated two years of work. The first phase of the survey, they determined, would cover Panama, where Guardia had assured "such a hearty send-off that the neighboring countries would feel compelled to keep the ball rolling." James planned to oversee operations from Washington, DC, while his field team would use Panama City as a permanent base throughout the survey's duration.[79]

The process of selecting men for the three-man field team stretched out for several weeks, but eventually James managed to assemble a team that he considered "robust [and] in the prime of life." The group's leader would be Thomas A. Forbes, a consulting engineer whom James had met while in Bogota and who spoke Spanish fluently. James felt that Forbes had "considerable tropical experience" that would prove essential in negotiating the challenges of Central America. Assisting Forbes would be David Tucker Brown, a long-serving member of the bureau who was considered a gifted surveyor, and Marcel J. Bussard, one of the younger engineers in the bureau who also happened to speak Spanish.[80]

By the time the team was organized, James had already sketched out the rudiments of a proposed route in order to hopefully spare his engineers from having "all the continent to select from, from sea to sea." James's suggested line, in broadest terms, favored the Pacific side of the isthmus along its entire length. Of this decision he explained, "El Salvador could not be unceremoniously passed by, and that country alone has only one coastline, on the Pacific, and most of the population throughout the entire region seems to have strung itself along the highlands adjacent to the Pacific." The determination to exclude any potential Atlantic-side routes from the survey, James felt, "at once reduced the amount of exploratory work enormously."[81]

The initial preparations finally drew to a close on June 21, 1930, when the three engineers, their families, and James boarded the steamer *Virginia* destined for Panama. Several days later they arrived in Panama City and received a warm welcome from Guardia, who had arranged for the surveyors to occupy an office rent free in the Palacio Nacional. James remained with the group just long enough to see them settled and then departed, trusting that his men "would be able to carry on the work effectively, smoothly and with the rapidity necessary."[82]

James's faith in his team, however, was put to the test even before any actual surveying began. He soon learned that Bussard was "homesick and sensitive," while Forbes, though "good on paper," turned out to be "rough, brusque, short, and domineering." Moreover, Forbes's imperious behavior alienated Brown, who already harbored resentment over being placed in a subordinate position on the team. And compounding these problems was the frequent intermeddling of the State Department, which insisted on maintaining an active role in the survey and repeatedly sent instructions that conflicted with those of James.[83]

The situation deteriorated so rapidly that James was forced to return to Panama in early September to resolve "the biggest bit of administrative bungling I have ever seen." He subsequently spent several days allowing the three men to air their grievances, a move that seemed to help curtail the infighting. As he wrote in his journal on September 11, 1930, "Many of the sore points are cleared away and I feel that matters should move along smoothly."[84]

The fieldwork in Panama finally commenced two weeks after James's emergency intervention. Though the surveyors technically needed to cover the entirety of Panama above the canal, Guardia had already overseen the construction of a national road that extended more than three hundred miles northwest of Panama City. All that actually remained to be surveyed was a sixty-five-mile stretch between the city of David and the border with Costa Rica. This distance, however, contained a tangled mass of mountainous jungle, and the delays in getting the survey started meant that the men would be attempting to cross this difficult terrain at the height of the rainy season.[85]

The work quickly proved far more difficult than the surveyors had anticipated. As Brown explained, "The jungle growth is so thick that one walks all day without seeing any distant view at all." The torrential rains only amplified the frustration, soaking the men and turning the forested floor into a muddy soup. James later noted, "At places the poor mules actually dragged their bellies on the ground and how they scrambled through was incomprehensible." Adding to the surveyors' discomfort were the swarms of insects, especially one known as a je-jen. In the words of George Curtis Peck, a US commercial attaché who had accompanied the engineers on the survey, "There is more unadulterated hell concentrated in the infinitesimal carcass

of that vicious cuss than could be extracted from the Third International. . . .
I am not so sure but they can penetrate boilerplate. . . . No use to count
bites—they had fused into one."[86]

The surveyors eventually conceded defeat and returned to Panama City
chastened. A subsequent dispatch to James explained that the work "was
not completed due to the rainy season." James, already frustrated by the
team's constant bickering, expressed disappointment with the "very meager"
results of their efforts.[87]

The difficulties that the team experienced in northwestern Panama
nonetheless convinced James that traditional survey methods might be
insufficient. Soon he made arrangements for the US Army Air Corps to
fly special missions over Central America in order to prepare "photographic
mosaics" of the region.[88]

The surveyors remained in Panama City throughout the second half
of October to wait out the rainy season. James, back in Washington, spent
this time anxiously awaiting the arrival of Costa Rica's formal request for
survey help, something he needed if his team were to cover an unbroken
line northward from Panama. By the time November came, however, nothing had yet arrived from Costa Rica, forcing James to abandon his plans
for a continuous survey and focus instead on the three requests he had
already received from Guatemala, Honduras, and Nicaragua. James concluded that the survey should "treat each country as a unit and without
regard to order, advanc[ing] the field work wherever the authorities were
ready to proceed."[89]

James decided that the next destination should be Honduras, where he
expected the work to be "short and easy." The surveyors, based on his preliminary plans, would need to cover only a hundred miles of terrain that was
fairly level and featured mule trails between settlements. James's proposed
route, which offered the shortest line between El Salvador and Nicaragua,
curved through the lowlands surrounding the Gulf of Fonseca and avoided
the mountainous interior entirely. This approach promised to keep costs
to a minimum, though it meant that the line excluded the isolated, inland
capital of Tegucigalpa, an omission that understandably irked some local
politicians.[90]

The Honduran fieldwork, which began in early November 1930, only
managed to further expose the problems with James's survey team. Forbes,
for his part, simply refused to go altogether, claiming that he was receiving
conflicting instructions from the bureau and the State Department. As for
Brown and Bussard, they spent most of their time in Honduras arguing. At

one point, James received a message from Brown that insisted, "I do not believe [Bussard realizes] as yet of what a reconnaissance survey consists." Brown further complained to James that Bussard had forced them to pass on an invitation for an informal visit to tour El Salvador's road network because the young engineer "would not stay out over Christmas."[91]

The discord within the survey team prompted James to return to Panama City once more in mid-January 1931. When he arrived, he found Forbes and Bussard in full-scale revolt, claiming that they answered to the State Department and not James. Only Brown showed him any courtesy, asserting, "I am and expect to be absolutely loyal to the [bureau] regardless of what course the other members pursue. They can paddle their own canoes." The rebellious actions of Bussard and Forbes infuriated James, who contemplated firing them both outright for what seemed nothing short of mutiny. Such a radical step, however, could not be taken until MacDonald convinced the State Department to relinquish its authority. And although MacDonald had assured James before his departure that this would happen imminently, no word of a new agreement with the State Department had arrived by the end of January. At that point, James decided to leave "the pretty little comedy being played here" and headed to Costa Rica. A personal appeal, he hoped, might secure Costa Rica's consent before the convening of the Second Inter-American Highway Conference, scheduled for mid-March 1931 in Panama City.[92]

The source of Costa Rican resistance to the survey was no mystery to James. Several months earlier, he had learned from the US ambassador in San José the twofold nature of the problem. On the one hand, the Costa Rican president feared that agreeing to the survey would carry with it an obligation to actually build the road, something his country could not afford. On the other hand, some influential Costa Ricans felt that the United States was likely to construct a second canal in Nicaragua and would then be desperate for a strategic road to connect its twin interoceanic passages, a situation that would place the Costa Rican government "in a strategic position to demand a quid pro quo for permitting such a highway to pass through her territory." And along with these concerns also came staunch opposition from the political left—as the pro-socialist *Reportorio Americano* observed in 1931, "This road network is only necessary to serve the designs of the men who beat on the anvil of Empire."[93]

None of these arguments, however, seemed the least bit valid to James, who felt that he simply needed to find the right political ally in Costa Rica. Once in San José, he spent his time searching for such a partner and quickly landed upon Manuel Castro Quesada, the Costa Rican ambassador to the United States who happened to be back in his home country for a visit. Castro Quesada, James later recalled, was "a strong man politically, with presidential aspirations." James arranged to share a train ride with the ambassador and by its conclusion had secured a promise of cooperation, one that, unbeknownst to James, was owed in part to Castro Quesada's interest in having the Inter-American Highway pass by lands that he controlled near San José. Castro Quesada soon managed to override the political opposition to the reconnaissance survey. The formal Costa Rican request for aid arrived just in time for the Second Inter-American Highway Conference.[94]

The last obstacle to completing the survey appeared to be finally removed, but questions still lingered over the actual route that the highway should follow in Costa Rica. For James, the only cost-effective plan followed the Pacific lowlands and avoided the mountainous interior, even though such a course eliminated most of the population centers, including the capital of San José. James had left these details vague during his discussions with Castro Quesada, but had planned to unveil his proposal at the Second Inter-American Highway Conference with the hopes that the various delegations in attendance would pressure Costa Rica into complying. His strategy, however, quickly unraveled when the delegate from Costa Rica, a close confidant of Castro Quesada, exploded with indignation and declared it "impossible" to cooperate if the route skipped San José. James had no choice but to concede, knowing that this allowance would make immeasurably more difficult the work facing his team and would exponentially raise the cost of any future highway.[95]

The fight over the Costa Rican route nonetheless belied the general tenor of the Second Inter-American Highway Conference, which featured few disagreements and bristled with optimism. The delegates felt especially confident that loans for the highway would be forthcoming, particularly in light of evidence presented on progress in South America—a Colombian observer at the conference insisted, with only some exaggeration, "a Pan-American highway is already passable by automobile for almost the entire length of the west coast of South America." By the close of the proceedings, the Costa Rican delegate who had earlier protested so vigorously was informing a reporter, "[It was] predicted [that] the route will be completed within five years, and I will stick with that prediction."[96]

*   *   *

The survey, by this point, had moved on to its next destination, Guatemala. James's men had arrived there shortly before the conference began and were busily trying to select the best route from among the nation's four-thousand-mile wagon road network. Their options included a route through the populous highlands and one along the fertile lowlands. Ultimately the team settled on the upland course, in part to avoid upsetting the International Railways of Central America, Minor C. Keith's former company, which had already built a line along the flatter terrain near the Pacific Coast. As an internal bureau report later explained, "The International Railways of Central America are not nationally owned, but are just as vital to the welfare of the country as if they were. The road system must be developed in such a way as to not jeopardize the operation of any part of the railroad system."[97]

While the fieldwork in Guatemala had presented few challenges, hard work lay ahead. The survey's next planned stop, Costa Rica, contained vast stretches of jungle with few trails altogether. Moreover, the obligation to find a line into and out of San José was going to force the surveyors to fight their way through treacherous mountains that reached up to thirteen thousand feet in the region south of the capital. James, who had been studying the old Intercontinental Railway Commission reports for guidance, noted that parts of southern Costa Rica had been described by engineer Shunk as "harder to penetrate than [anything] found in the high Andes in Peru."[98]

The proposed fieldwork seemed so daunting that both Bussard and Forbes found ways to avoid going entirely. Only Brown remained, a circumstance that forced James into a frantic hunt for additional men. Eventually he tracked down four nearby Americans who were willing to go and who, in James's view, "were accustomed to taking care of themselves in the bush."[99]

The reconstituted survey team reached San José in late April 1931 with plans to first tackle the difficult southern zone and then cover the slightly less foreboding stretch north toward Nicaragua. Upon arrival, they were joined by a local Costa Rican engineer, and their ranks soon swelled to include a small army of porters, mules, and horses tasked with handling all the equipment and provisions. A member of the party noted, "one of the horses loaded with tripods and rods looked like a moving Christmas tree."[100]

The team decided initially to follow an old mule trail that headed into the heart of the continental divide and provided the only known connection between San José and the undeveloped southern interior. The trail, whose difficulty was legendary, culminated with a crossing of a summit more than eleven thousand feet high known as Cerro de la Muerte, or Mountain of Death. Of the first day's climb Brown observed, "Men have become exhausted and could not mount or dismount, horses have given out and fallen with and without rider." James later described the trail as being "dotted and striped with the skulls and ribs of dead animals that had passed that way only to stop and die in the cold or the wind." When the men finally reached the harsh summit, they concluded that an automobile highway would be nearly impossible to construct. James, upon reviewing their report, declared, "The Cerro de la Muerte region must be rejected at once."[101]

The shortcomings of the Cerro de la Muerte route compelled the men to drop down to a lower elevation in the hopes of finding an alternate passage. But the conditions they soon encountered were even worse than those around the Mountain of Death, with every move a contest against steep gorges and violent rivers. James described this lower clime as little more than "the treacherous slopes that come down from the central range" with "long ridges like bulky fingers." At one point the Costa Rican porters assisting the men threatened to quit, insisting that they had only agreed to work through "familiar trails" and not this "unknown jungle." Brown's subsequent report of his time spent searching for a lower passage convinced James that the region was "the roughest along the entire line to Panama and will not only be the most costly and difficult to build but will involve perplexing administrative matters."[102]

The southern survey endured for five weeks before the exhausted crew returned to San José. They had valiantly traversed some of the most difficult terrain anywhere on earth in the name of the Inter-American Highway, but their labors had ultimately amounted to little besides bruises, insect bites, and the knowledge that a road across southern Costa Rica, should it ever be built, would be tougher going than anything ever known in the United States.

After a week spent recovering in San José, the team headed out for the northern half of their Costa Rican survey. The subsequent journey presented fewer challenges than what they had experienced in the south, though seasonal rains had turned much of the terrain into what James described as a "plastic unstable slurry." James later observed that northwestern Costa Rica was "famed as a cattle country but [was] so badly in need of transportation facilities that cattle lose twenty five percent in weight between pasture and market."[103]

*   *   *

Back in Panama City, the situation between James and his two mutinous surveyors continued to deteriorate. While Brown was away in Costa Rica, James had learned that the other two men were capitalizing on the administrative confusion between the bureau and the State Department to collect inflated salaries. Their actions struck James as nothing short of a defrauding of the American people. In June 1931, James wrote in his journal, "I half expect when they are ordered back to Washington, that they refuse to come unless ordered back by the President!"[104]

James's frustrations with the two men grew with each passing month, until finally, late in the year, having managed to secure from the State Department the authority to take unilateral action, he fired both men. As his journal entry from the day of their dismissal in December noted,

> I have done all I can to save those two from themselves but it just can't be done! Their every next move makes the situation worse. Their incoming letters are the joke of the office—we refer to them as "just another laugh." It is a most interesting, astonishing, and disappointing case! Two men who had such an opportunity as probably they will never have again, simply failed on all points to rise to the occasion and have "made a flop" in the worst manner. Apparently men do not always rise to their responsibilities.[105]

The month after the firings, the reconnaissance survey moved on to the last remaining country, Nicaragua. James had delayed sending his men there out of concern over the ongoing anti-US Sandino rebellion, but further postponement seemed unwise given that no resolution to the conflict was in sight. The proposed line, which passed through Sandino-controlled lands in the northwest, corresponded closely to the original Intercontinental Railway Commission route, following the settled lowlands between the Pacific coast and the western shores of both Lake Nicaragua and Lake Managua.[106]

Brown, the only remaining original surveyor, led the fieldwork. He began in areas outside of Sandino's control and encountered few problems aside from a troublesome type of soil known as sonsocuite, which James described as "an extreme form of gumbo" that "has a consistency reminding one of liver." After several weeks, the survey headed into Sandino territory with trepidation, hoping that the Nicaraguan government would ensure their protection. Awaiting them, however, was a sixty-man ambush that Sandino had ordered. The survey team only avoided capture thanks to

Brown's serendipitous last-minute decision to pursue an alternate line in the northwest. This change of plans, in James's view, unquestionably saved the men's lives.[107]

The men faced further danger during their return stopover in San José, Costa Rica, where an attempted revolution was being carried out by James's old ally Castro Quesada. The coup ultimately failed, but not before the survey team came close to several gunfights. As Brown noted, "The American Legation was hit a number of times and the presidencia was shot full of holes."[108]

Brown arrived back in Panama in mid-February, during the peak of the dry season. The rains were not going to return for at least two months, and James wanted to capitalize on this window of clear weather, the last they would have before the survey reached its two-year deadline. Brown, ever faithful, soon agreed to embark on follow-up work in northwestern Panama and southern Costa Rica, the two regions that had caused the most problems. The subsequent fieldwork once more strained Brown and those accompanying him to the very limits of their endurance. At one point a guide fighting the underbrush accidentally hacked off his own toe with a machete, while an assistant engineer suffered a cerebral hemorrhage due to "exposure and overexertion."[109]

All of this sacrifice seemed worthwhile to those who believed in the dream of the Pan-American Highway, but the ranks of the faithful had thinned dramatically during the two years that had passed since the survey began.

The hemispheric through route, once seen as imminent, had become an impractical fantasy as the sobering effects of the Great Depression spread throughout the hemisphere. Many of the Latin American road loans that US banks had financed during the booming 1920s had ended up in default, and an irate US Congress had launched a full-scale investigation into the sale of these and other foreign securities. Under such circumstances, few congressmen wanted to press for the development of an overseas highway. Even President Hoover, a stalwart supporter of the great Pan-American road, had gradually lost interest in the project as he became preoccupied with trying to save the domestic economy.[110]

The inhospitable political climate caused James and MacDonald to delay the release of the survey report. James ultimately allowed Brown to spend more than a year synthesizing his field notes and organizing the mass of photographic data that the Army Air Corps had provided. In James's view, the likeliest outcome was that the report would simply "die a natural death."[111]

The multiyear effort to chart a course through Central America seemed to have reached a dead end, and the report appeared doomed to the same fate as the seven-volume study that the Intercontinental Railway Commission had produced thirty-five years earlier. However, just as the final revisions were being made to the report, the Inter-American Highway project would find its most powerful champion yet, Franklin Delano Roosevelt.

The First Million Is the Hardest

The elections of 1932 had channeled a wave of popular discontent with Hoover, the Republican Party, and their handling of the Great Depression. For the first time in a dozen years, the Democrats had regained control of both houses of Congress as well as the presidency. At the center of this dramatic reordering sat fifty-year-old Franklin Roosevelt, the newly elected commander in chief and the fifth cousin of a former one. Roosevelt had assured the American electorate that his administration would bring them a New Deal and finally end the crushing unemployment that the three-year-old economic crisis had brought about.[112]

Roosevelt's campaign had focused primarily on domestic policy, but the new president nonetheless saw his broad mandate as a chance to reorient the nation's international relations too. As he declared during his inaugural address, "I would dedicate this Nation to the policy of the good neighbor— the neighbor who resolutely respects ... the rights of others." Roosevelt's pronouncement, which came two months after the United States had finally given up its guerrilla war against Sandino, seemed to suggest a rejection of the interventionist policies that had inflamed anti-US sentiments throughout the hemisphere. And Roosevelt explicitly linked his new good neighbor policy with the goal of closer US–Latin American relations several weeks later, during an April speech celebrating Pan-America Day: "The essential qualities of a true Pan Americanism must be the same as those which constitute a good neighbor, namely, mutual understanding, and, through such understanding, a sympathetic appreciation of the other's point of view. It is only in this manner that we can hope to build up a system of which confidence, friendship, and good-will are the cornerstones."[113]

Roosevelt's firm embrace of Pan-Americanism gave MacDonald and James new hope that the Inter-American Highway project might be resuscitated. In July 1933, MacDonald managed to arrange a personal meeting with Roosevelt to discuss the survey work already completed as well as the path forward. The meeting did not last especially long, but MacDonald's appeal made a strong impression on Roosevelt. The president seemed immediately to conclude that the so-called highway of friendship could provide a concrete demonstration of the ideals contained in his good neighbor doctrine. Roosevelt even provided "various valuable suggestions" for how his administration might go about financing it.[114]

Over the next several months, Roosevelt's interest in both the Inter-American Highway and the larger Pan-American Highway intensified as he began thinking about the upcoming Seventh Pan-American Conference, scheduled for December 1933 in Montevideo, Uruguay. The conference offered his administration a chance to demonstrate its enlightened approach to hemispheric affairs, and the highway projects seemed perfect avenues for a "practical expression" of the good neighbor policy. A White House statement released the month before the gathering announced, "[N]o matter what advantageous arrangements are made [in Montevideo], such arrangements will lack full effectiveness in increasing neighborly contacts and trade unless there is betterment in the rapidity of communications and transportation.... The immediate program proposed by the United States therefore is to have a proper scientific survey made of the contemplated [Pan-American Highway] route at a cost of less than $500,000." Roosevelt assured that he would encourage Congress to "bear the entire immediate cost of this most important survey" throughout all of Latin America if the other nations agreed to participate. Roosevelt's close adviser Louis Howe soon informed a journalist, "I can think of nothing more likely to bring better understanding. Trains and boats and planes can't stop at the door while their occupant asks directions or begs some water for his parched throat or for his gas buggy's parched radiator. And that's the manner in which you really get to know your neighbors."[115]

Roosevelt's gesture to fund a survey, though magnanimous, was not entirely without political calculation. Like Coolidge five years earlier, some in his administration felt that an emphasis on transportation development could help direct the conference away from more controversial issues, which once again included talk of a binding agreement on nonintervention. Shortly before the conference began, Howe informed Cordell Hull, the newly appointed secretary of state and leader of the US delegation, "We don't think you need to undertake much down at Montevideo. Just talk to them about the Pan American highway from the United States down through Central and South America."[116]

Howe's advice, however, went entirely unheeded. Once in Montevideo, the secretary of state devoted almost no attention to the highway survey, which ultimately failed to gain any traction. Hull's focus instead went straight to the proposed nonintervention pact, which he soon decided to endorse. With his support, the last barrier to the agreement's enactment had been removed, and on the conference's sixteenth day the delegates passed the measure unanimously to much celebration and fanfare. One joyous member of the US delegation later recalled, "[That] afternoon . . . was the greatest hour in the history of the Inter-American movement since July 18, 1826, when the first treaty on Union, League, and Confederation was signed at Panama. . . . Here, finally, was an agreement upon the essential quality of a good neighbor—not to rush into the home of another in the middle of the night and begin to tell him how to manage his children." Though Hull's action had been taken without prior authorization, the president had no intention of countermanding his secretary of state and upsetting an entire hemisphere. Ten days after the agreement was issued, Roosevelt proclaimed, "The definite policy of the United States from now on is one opposed to one of armed intervention."[117]

The amity expressed in Montevideo made it easy to overlook the fact that the hemisphere's delegates had rejected Roosevelt's proposed Pan-American Highway survey. The nations of South America, in particular, had refused to see his proposition as a "practical expression" of the good neighbor policy. Rather, as the *New Republic* observed, they had feared "that this proposal to promote public works on a grand scale in Latin America would inevitably mean, in not the remote future, a renewal of 'yanqui imperialismo.'"[118]

Not all the nations of Latin America, however, shared this view. In Central America and Panama, the earlier reconnaissance survey had left the impression among some politicians that further US assistance would inevitably follow. As commercial attaché Peck had observed in July 1933, "Interest in Central America in this road is still very much alive, [but] none of these countries is likely to forward the work without the guidance and leadership of the United States." Shortly after Montevideo, Peck's sentiments received an official confirmation when the nations of Central America issued a special resolution that "urge[d] the Governments of the five republics to reach an understanding with the Government of the United States . . . in order to arrive at an agreement concerning the most rapid and efficient manner of completing that portion [of the Pan-American Highway] which interests those countries."[119]

For Roosevelt, this Central American resolution confirmed that the Inter-American Highway deserved his full support. Soon he decided that the US government should fund the project outright if possible. From the president's perspective, the highway would essentially be a good neighbor extension of a massive public works program his administration had inaugurated as part of the New Deal. Roosevelt even made an effort to get money directly from his newly created Public Works Authority, which had a multibillion-dollar budget for infrastructure projects, including road building. But this scheme collapsed in late March when Roosevelt learned that the underlying legislation only permitted spending on domestic projects. Undeterred, Roosevelt went directly to Congress in early May and asked for a $5 million appropriation as an initial investment in construction.[120]

Roosevelt's request was without precedent in US history. The earlier appropriations for both the Intercontinental Railway and the Inter-American Highway had merely covered survey work, not actual overseas construction. The only times the United States had previously embarked on construction projects abroad, they had taken place either in colonial possessions, in the Canal Zone, or as part of a military intervention. In all of those instances, however, effective political or military control had preceded any actual building. Roosevelt was seeking to embark upon a different type of overseas US government activity altogether: development work unrelated to a broader occupation. As James observed, it would be "an entirely new form of cooperative undertaking."[121]

The month after Roosevelt reached out to Congress, the proposal finally hit the Senate floor, where a passionate debate erupted, with strong opposition coming from several Republicans. One of them declared, "if we have $5,000,000 to 'blow' in Central America we might better 'blow' that money in the United States of America. . . . I think that if we pay $5,000,000 for somebody's goodwill, the goodwill will not be worth a rap." Another cautioned that the appropriation "puts the camel's nose under the tent" and questioned Congress's right to appropriate the money in the first place. The proposal nonetheless enjoyed unwavering support from Roosevelt's loyal Democratic majority, who accused their colleagues of rank partisanship and assured that the funds would only go to the purchase of US highway materials and equipment. Eventually, a prominent Republican senator known for his isolationist views suggested that he could support the measure were the money involved only $1 million. The Democrats, seeking to build consensus, immediately agreed to this reduction. A vote followed shortly thereafter, and, with ten more yeas than nays, the compromise measure managed to gain passage. The following day, the Democratic-majority House gave its approval as well. The appropriation finally became law on June 19, 1934. The United States, after more than forty years of discussions about a hemispheric transportation route, was at long last poised to help build one outside its borders.[122]

No action could be taken, however, until the other nations involved consented to this new type of development assistance. Soon the State Department took up the matter, instructing its legations in the region to find out whether the various governments would accept US aid and would approve the route laid out in the bureau's reconnaissance report. Their inquiries quickly received favorable responses from Guatemala, Honduras, and Panama, but resistance emerged from the other three countries on the route. For El Salvador, which had not participated in the original survey on the grounds that it had already mapped out its portion of the route, road building remained a strictly nationalist project. For Nicaragua and Costa Rica, meanwhile, the objections centered on the highway's potential to undercut nationally owned railways, whose receipts provided a major source of government revenue.[123]

The resistance nonetheless failed to discourage James and MacDonald, who had been given responsibility for the $1 million appropriation. They had faced similar obstacles with the survey several years earlier and believed that eventually all the nations would come around. As James observed,

> In spite of small beginnings, of inherent doubts whether there would be any continuity of effort, of obvious difficulties incident to operating in foreign states and to the retarding effects of selfish nationalistic policies, it seemed wise to adopt a course at the start that might well be dictated by such a transcendental motto as that which John Fiske, the historian, had inscribed over a fireplace in his study: "Plan your work as if you expected to live forever; Work your plan as if you expected to die tomorrow."[124]

During the fall of 1934, James and MacDonald outlined a proposal for the $1 million appropriation. Their plan focused on bridge building, which they felt would provide the most tangible results with the limited amount of money available. The United States, they decided, would design the bridges and provide all the cement and structural steel, while each host nation would contribute labor as well as lumber, sand, and gravel. This approach would allow both sides to prevent the exchange of funds, something James felt needed to be avoided at all costs based on his prior experience in the region. As he explained years later, "If we transferred funds to them, we could have no certain control of the expenditure of those funds. I knew personally of cases where bond issues raised for one purpose were diverted for other purposes. . . . If the countries should transfer funds to us, and we had the expenditure of them, we would constantly be under attack for misspending the money, defalcations, threats, or most anything else." [125]

After formulating their plan, James and MacDonald came to a disagreement over how best to proceed. For James, the next logical step would be that he visit the isthmus in order to select bridge sites in the three consenting countries and dialogue with the three holdout governments. But he faced staunch resistance from MacDonald, who insisted that every effort first be made to secure the participation of Mexico as well. MacDonald believed that the highway in Central America would be fundamentally compromised should Mexico fail to construct its portion of the through route in a timely manner. The only way to ensure that such an outcome did not come to pass, MacDonald felt, would be for the bureau to get directly involved. MacDonald had already embarked on informal discussions with some Mexican highway officials and seemed to feel certain that their assent would be forthcoming. However, the Mexican government remained wary of US involvement in its internal affairs as well as in those of Central America. Mexico had even secretly suggested to several Central American governments that they all band together to construct the Inter-American Highway as a toll road and therefore excise the United States from the project completely. A State Department official who learned of this rival plan in late January 1935 griped, "While we are patiently waiting for Mexico to come in with us on our plan to assist with the highway project, Mexico is going ahead in its own way to eliminate us from the picture." Mexico's effort ultimately unraveled two months later, and by that point the State Department had managed to persuade MacDonald that James should proceed to Central America without further delay. [126]

James's new round of highway advocacy finally commenced in April 1935, nearly a year after the $1 million appropriation had been issued. He planned to start in Panama and then work his way northward, with visits to each Central American capital along the way. "James was a good diplomat," observed a writer who covered him years later. "When he had to be he was inscrutable, polite, even icily polite, cajoling or pleasant. His organ had all the stops in the register, and he pulled them masterfully."[127]

The first stop on the trip, in Panama City, was a reunion with his old friend Guardia, who remained eager as ever. The two men soon agreed that Panama's initial portion of the congressional allocation would be used for an eight-hundred-foot-long suspension bridge spanning the Chiriquí River in the northwest of the country.[128]

James's next two destinations, Costa Rica and Nicaragua, offered cooler receptions. Both countries remained hostile to any project that threatened to diminish the revenue of their state-owned railways. As James explained, "They didn't want to destroy their security, their assets." In the end, James failed to secure consent from either nation.[129]

Following these setbacks, James headed to Honduras, which had already agreed to further US assistance. As James later recollected, "I knew that Honduras preferred a road through the mountains [to Tegucigalpa], but [it] would have been almost impossible . . . to finance. . . . So my urge was to get a major structure on the route of the reconnaissance and to tie it down." This time, James managed to get exactly what he sought, persuading the Honduran president to support construction of an eleven-hundred-foot-long suspension bridge on the Choluteca River.[130]

But James's good luck was not meant to last. At his subsequent call in El Salvador, the president rejected him flatly. James later explained, "He was very affable and frank [but insisted] that public opinion would not support him in accepting anything in the nature of a gift from the government of the United States."[131]

James's tour of Central America ended in Guatemala City, where he met with Jorge Ubico, a military general who had seized political power three years earlier and was continuing the tradition of brutal repression that Estrada Cabrera had perfected a generation earlier—among Ubico's personal vehicles was an armored car with machine guns attached. James and Ubico discussed several possible bridge locations, and the Guatemalan strongman eventually selected one on the Tamazulapa River, the last natural obstacle impeding car travel between the Guatemalan and Salvadoran capitals.[132]

James returned to Washington in June 1935. His trip had not been an unqualified success, but the three agreements he had secured offered a reason to move forward. Over the next month, he drafted a memorandum covering the bridges on the Chiriquí, Choluteca, and Tamazulapa Rivers. Soon the memo reached Roosevelt, who read it with "great interest," and in mid-August the president formally authorized the bureau to "take up the plan with the Republics concerned." James subsequently began arranging a special team of federal engineers. By October a new bureau field office had been set up in San José to coordinate the work on the bridges in Panama, Guatemala, and Honduras.[133]

James contemplated breaking ground in mid-December, but at the last moment an unforeseen obstacle arose in the form of John McCarl, the US comptroller. McCarl, a staunch Republican appointed during the Harding administration, opposed the New Deal and saw the Inter-American Highway appropriation as the latest example of profligate spending. His office had the power to review all federal expenditures, and he decided to read the language in the $1 million highway appropriation as narrowly as possible. No funds could be disbursed, he declared, until all the countries signaled their approval. The appropriation appeared doomed until Roosevelt personally intervened in March 1936 and declared McCarl's ruling inapplicable. "We have cut the ground from under Mr. McCarl's feet," James wrote in triumph to his wife. Nonetheless, McCarl's actions had cost James most of the dry season. He subsequently complained that the comptroller had "to an incalculable extent increased the cost of cooperation."[134]

Finally, in the spring of 1936, work commenced. The bureau had suddenly become an international construction agency, and the system of federal aid, originally designed to bring modern roads to the individual US states, had transformed into a mechanism for overseas development. As James noted, "Standard specifications of the Bureau of Public Roads were used and the standard United States Government contract and bond required.... [We followed] the usual process with respect to plans as has long been used in Federal Aid projects in the United States."[135]

The methods developed in the United States, however, had to be adapted to accommodate the challenges of work in Central America. James noted, "Lack of spare parts, the time and cost of obtaining them from the United States and occasionally even the absence of a supply of the simplest tools any where within reach ... gave us no end of trouble." James's men also confronted endless rains, swollen rivers, and work sites with practically no access points. James noted of Guatemala, "In one case, in order to deliver a bridge through the nearest and most convenient railroad point, we shipped it to the country of its final destination by ocean freight, entered it, loaded it on the railroad, shipped it to a point in the adjacent country which was on the railroad, unloaded it, put it on trucks and carried it back over the highway into the country of its destination, by what was actually the shortest road haul we could figure out." James encountered equally challenging circumstances in transporting some 2,330 tons of materials to Honduras: first his supplies had to be shipped to the small Pacific port of Amapala and loaded onto launches, then trucks had to carry everything until the poor dirt roads forced the use of oxcarts, and finally the goods were transferred to dugout canoes for the journey's last leg.[136]

Despite these challenges, the work progressed steadily and garnered wide admiration on the ground. A fawning November 1936 editorial in a Guatemalan paper declared of the half-constructed Tamazulapa Bridge,

> This colossal work, symbol of the psychology of the great North American people, was conceived in Washington through the powerful imagination of Mr. Roosevelt, President of that great nation, who has, with admirable touch and the inspiration of genius, turned the antipathy created by previous administrations into the great sympathy now felt toward North America—at last regarded as the big brother of the continent.... Hail, Tamazulapa Bridge, Hail.[137]

This newfound goodwill had arrived at a propitious moment for Roosevelt, who was seeking closer hemispheric relations as a bulwark against emerging threats from Germany. In January 1936, he had declared during his annual congressional message, "a point has been reached where the people of the Americas must take cognizance of growing ill-will, of marked trends toward aggression, of increasing armaments, of shortening tempers—a situation which has in it many of the elements that lead to the tragedy of general war." Later that month, Roosevelt issued a call for an "extra-ordinary inter-American conference" to discuss "the maintenance of peace among the American republics." The conference's ultimate goal, Roosevelt hoped, would be a mutual defense pact that treated any attack against one as an attack against all.[138]

The proposed conference finally convened eleven months later in Buenos Aires. Roosevelt attended in person, hoping that his presence would ensure the event's success. Once the conference began, the nations of Central America all lined up squarely behind Roosevelt and remained unshakable even in the face of intense pressure from the Argentine foreign minister, whose nation maintained close ties with Germany and remained ever wary of US intentions. One US diplomat who had attended the conference recalled, the Argentine Foreign Minister . . . informed [the Central Americans] flatly that they should immediately reject the proposals favored by the United States, inasmuch as they contained traps set for the unwary and were nothing more nor less than a means by which the United States hoped to extend its power and influence over the smaller nations of the hemisphere. The senior member of the Central American delegations, . . . speaking for all his associates, . . . made it clear that the Central American governments were in no need of advice as to the course they should follow. . . . [T]he practical application of the good neighbor policy had worked a material change in [their] sentiments.[139]

The delegates at Buenos Aires ultimately agreed that any attack in the hemisphere would trigger immediate consultation for "peaceful collaboration," significantly more than what Argentina had sought to allow. And the defense pact was not the only by-product of the goodwill engendered through Roosevelt's foreign policy: among the agreements reached at Buenos Aires was also the long-sought-after convention on the Pan-American Highway. It read, in part:

> The Governments represented at the Inter-American Conference for the Maintenance of Peace; [c]ognizant of the fact that the primary purpose of the Inter-American Conference is the strengthening of the bonds of friendship already existing between the countries of this Continent; [c]onvinced that direct and material contact between the American peoples necessarily would strengthen those bonds, consolidating therefore the peace of the Continent, [k]nowing that the general welfare will be greater when there is greater facility for the exchange of the products of said countries; [c]onsidering, finally, that one of the most adequate and efficient means for the attainment of the moral and material ends aimed at jointly by the American Republics, is the termination of a highway which establishes a permanent communication between their respective territories, . . . agree to collaborate, with all diligence and by all adequate means, in the speedy completion of a Pan American Highway, which will permit at all times the transit of motor vehicles.[140]

The issuance of the Pan-American Highway convention complemented work that James had continued to do on the isthmus. Over the course of

1936, he had managed to dramatically expand the scope of the cooperative labors there.

The first step in this direction had come during the spring with the negotiation of a second round of bridge projects in Guatemala, Honduras, and Panama. The three countries ultimately agreed to a total of eleven smaller structures that would complement the trio of large suspension bridges already under construction.[141]

James's efforts had then turned to Costa Rica, where the population's demand for good roads near San José had made the government willing to cooperate despite its concern over the highway's impact on the nationally owned railway. James had initially pushed for another bridge project, but the government's insistence on prioritizing construction near the capital had forced him to alter his designs and accept a proposal to jointly build twenty-five miles of the surveyed route in the tablelands around San José. As a result, actual road building, as opposed to bridgework, soon became part of the bureau's overseas activities.[142]

The final phase of James's 1936 highway advocacy had involved an appeal in November to Nicaragua's soon-to-be president Anastasio Somoza, a military general who was widely thought to have orchestrated the recent assassination of Sandino. Somoza, like Zelaya before him, appeared committed to both repressive tactics and infrastructure development. James's proposal of cooperation had immediately interested Somoza, though the Nicaraguan insisted that the route be revised to avoid competition with the nationally owned railroad. James soon agreed to this request, and, shortly after Somoza ascended to the presidency in December, the new leader officially authorized cooperation with the bureau on twenty-five miles of road building along the alternate line. Conveniently for Somoza, the revised route led directly to property that he controlled.[143]

By early 1937, the total scope of the bureau's work on the isthmus had ballooned to fourteen bridges and fifty miles of highway development, and the original $1 million had been fully budgeted. James and MacDonald, however, wanted to expand the work even further. Soon they put together a memorandum proposing an additional $1.5 million in support. This figure, they felt, represented the highest amount of US contributions that would still allow for the other governments to continue supplying sufficient labor and materials.[144]

Their request, though modest, nonetheless found few supporters. The free-spending Congress of the early thirties had grown increasingly frugal after the initial New Deal stimulus programs had failed to break the

Depression's grip on the economy, and Roosevelt, desperately focused himself on balancing the budget, seemed unwilling to intervene despite his personal fondness for the Inter-American Highway. By August 1937, an irate MacDonald was complaining to other federal officials that it would be "highly undesirable . . . from the standpoint of economy, the blow to the existing enthusiasm for road building, and the loss of the cordial public attitude toward the work, to permit this project to die for lack of further financial support."[145]

Over the next two years, while Congress remained impassive, James finished expending the funds from the original $1 million allocation. As he later reflected,

> In all we shipped 6,365 tons of equipment and materials to the several jobs. . . . The records show that of the million dollars, 74 percent was paid directly to American manufacturers for their products. Ninety percent was paid for American products, services and personnel. In other words, in expending the million dollars in cooperation with the countries of Central America, nine hundred thousand dollars went directly to the benefit of citizens of the United States. . . . The most gratifying matter, however, was the concrete evidence of a remarkable spirit of cooperation in all the countries. . . . In the construction accounts as a whole, distinguished from the engineering and overhead, the other governments contributed practically dollar for dollar with the United States.

The first project that James had arranged, the Chiriquí River Bridge in Panama, was the last major one to be completed. At its opening in March 1939, the Panamanian president declared,

> [A]bove its economic significance, [this bridge] responds in an unconscious but irrevocable manner to the highest, wisest, and most humane of the philosophical principles of modern times—the Good Neighbor Policy. When other continents tremble under the threats of aggressive nationalism, the voice of Franklin D. Roosevelt proclaims for our Americas a new creed of international relations inspired in reciprocal comprehension, and aspiring to place the human community on more noble and more sincerely Christian principles. . . . It is in this manner, gentlemen, that I wish to interpret the beautiful architecture of this bridge whose realization has made possible the joint labor of

two peoples distant in space, but closely united in the same ideal of peace and concord. The steel and concrete of this work which joins the two banks of the Chiriquí River are telling us that . . . the gold of the United States and the sweat of the Panamanian laborer complemented themselves to materially and spiritually bring closer the peoples of a continent; they tell us that the men of a united and strong America may pass freely, sure and cordially, in the most ample democratic community of the globe.[146]

Nearly fifteen years had now passed since the 1924 tour that sparked the Pan-American good roads movement.

Much had changed since Drake, Rowe, MacDonald, and their cohort had initiated the project. They had seen modern highways begin to displace railways throughout the hemisphere, and they had watched the Pan-American Highway evolve through two different phases of friendship, first a commercial relationship based around good roads, and then a broader social, cultural, and political bond with the good neighbor policy. Through these interlinked ideas of friendship, the Pan-American Highway had become an official hemispheric project and the Inter-American Highway had become the United States' largest overseas development initiative of the 1930s, the greatest practical expression of Roosevelt's foreign policy.

Nonetheless, the initial predictions from 1929 that the Inter-American Highway would be completed within five years had all proved wildly unrealistic. The work that James had overseen on the isthmus represented only a tiny fraction of what would be necessary to put a road through to the canal. Friendship ultimately had its limits.

For the United States, something more would be necessary to justify deeper involvement with the hemispheric highway project. However, a new rationale was about to surface: hemispheric defense.

The Inter-American Highway, conceived in friendship, was about to become a war road.

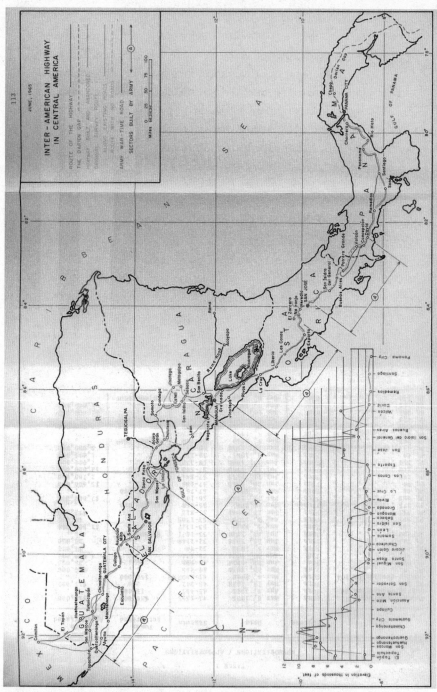

A map comparing the route of the Inter-American Highway with that of a World War II "pioneer" road. Note in the height map at the bottom the extreme rise in southern Costa Rica, a construction job completed in 1945 that the US chief federal highway engineer considered to be the hardest road building project ever undertaken.

CHAPTER SIX

The Far Western Front

The New Roosevelt Corollary

The specter of the future Axis powers—Germany, Italy, and Japan—loomed over the approaching Eighth Pan-American Conference, scheduled to convene in December 1938 at Lima, Peru. In the words of Samuel Guy Inman, one of the US delegates,

> Between 1936 and 1938 the threat to the American continent was in fact more critical than that from the Holy Alliance a century before. The three Axis powers had consolidated their forces and were driving hard against the League of Nations, then rapidly disintegrating. Axis propaganda in Latin America grew more menacing day by day. . . . Strong German colonies in Brazil, Argentina, and Chile were collaborating with reactionary, nationalistic groups. . . . A typical news dispatch of the time, coming out of Rome . . . , stated . . . that South America was the continent on which the United States and the Fascist powers were most likely to meet in mortal combat.[1]

Along with propaganda had also come economic infiltration. Trade between Latin America and the Nazi regime, in particular, had grown dramatically thanks to a combination of German export subsidies and a credit system—the aski mark—that limited debtor purchases to German-manufactured goods. The *Cincinnati Enquirer* observed shortly before the Lima conference, "Few Americans realize how keen and critical is the contest for Latin-American markets, or how directly this bears on the larger struggle for political influence there."[2]

For advocates of the Pan-American Highway, the threat of fascist diffusion offered a new rationale to advance their project. One California businessman who championed the highway wrote to Roosevelt in November 1938,

> It was by the transcontinental railroads that the United States was knit to the west and if we do not do the modern equivalent south of us will be what is rapidly becomming [sic] a nest of European and Japanese intrege [sic] most dangerous to our very safty [sic]. These roads built with U.S. loans never collected will cost vastly less than battleships and armaments which will not meet the need. . . . Things are developing so rapidly along medeaval [sic] lines and barbaric power is reaching out so rapidly that the need to combat it with positive action is very pressing if we are to avoid war. It may now be too late.

The businessman concluded with a plea for the upcoming Lima conference to take steps to advance the great Pan-American road project.[3]

The conference, however, paid little attention to the highway. The delegates instead focused on the question of "continental solidarity," the new watchwords for a hemisphere facing a chaotic world. The conversations in Lima echoed those that had taken place two years earlier in Buenos Aires, with the United States pushing hard for a mutual defense pact and Argentina leading the resistance. Once more, the nations of Central America all lined up behind the United States, and eventually the assembled conference agreed to a new declaration that significantly strengthened the hemisphere's commitment to its internal solidarity. The declaration's key language read: "[I]n case the peace, security or territorial integrity of any American Republic is . . . threatened by acts of any nature that may impair them, they proclaim their common concern and their determination to make effective their solidarity." Inman, the US delegate, later explained, "The Declaration of Lima . . . was a new continentalized Monroe Doctrine in its guarantee of the 'American System.' Its unanimous adoption by the greatest bloc of republics in the world notified the totalitarian states that Americans were still ready to sacrifice many other things for the precious possession of democracy."[4]

The "continentalization" of the Monroe Doctrine nonetheless failed to curtail fascist propaganda and economic pressure. Soon the Roosevelt administration concluded that the United States needed to make an even stronger commitment to Latin America through direct economic support.

The president announced the new policy during an April 1939 speech celebrating Pan-America Day, declaring,

> The American family is today a great cooperative group facing a troubled world in serenity and calm.... The American peace which we celebrate today has no quality of weakness in it! We are prepared to maintain it, and to defend it to the fullest extent of our strength, matching force to force if any attempt is made to subvert our institutions, or to impair the independence of any one of our group. Should the method of attack be that of economic pressure, I pledge that my country will also give economic support, so that no American Nation need surrender any fraction of its sovereign freedom to maintain its economic welfare. This is the spirit and intent of the Declaration of Lima: the solidarity of the continent.[5]

Roosevelt's proclamation, which was broadcast in multiple languages and carried on international stations, quickly reverberated around the world. England's *Manchester Guardian* described the speech as "one of the most important on foreign affairs that [Roosevelt] has ever made." The *Daily Boston Globe* noted the next day, "The Fascists in Rome referred to the speech as new evidence of 'provocative meddling' in the affairs of Europe. They reiterated a threat that unless the United States quit 'interfering,' Italy and Germany would mix in the affairs of the United States." The *New York Times* headlined its coverage of the speech, "The New Monroe Doctrine," noting, "As the President sees it, Pan-American relationships are entering upon a new phase.... Our good will toward South America and our resolve to defend South American freedom must be expressed not merely in thrilling language but in terms of bread and butter."[6]

Roosevelt's promise of economic support faced an early test the following month, when Nicaraguan president Anastasio Somoza traveled to Washington for a widely publicized state visit. Somoza had requested the meeting late the previous year and planned to ask Roosevelt for funding to support a wide array of public works projects. Somoza's most elaborate proposal involved the construction of a $9 million, 110-mile-long barge canal along the San Juan River to connect Lake Nicaragua with the Atlantic Ocean. The Nicaraguan leader believed that the United States owed his nation some form of canal development in return for the 1916 Bryan-Chamorro Treaty, which had granted the United States the exclusive right to build an interoceanic canal across Nicaragua.[7]

Somoza's argument for canal funding ultimately failed to persuade Roosevelt, but the president felt that his guest should not leave Washington empty-handed while Nazi pressure awaited in Nicaragua. The two men then came to discuss the Inter-American Highway, the second item on Somoza's wish list of public works projects. Somoza explained that he considered it vital to the future of his country, and Roosevelt, a longtime advocate for the highway, quickly offered his assistance.[8]

To manage the financing, the president turned to the Export-Import Bank of Washington. The bank had been established five years earlier as a New Deal program to support Americans involved in foreign trade, but administration officials had realized that they could stretch the bank's mandate to channel aid to Latin America without triggering new congressional action. Roosevelt's offer proved satisfactory to Somoza, who responded by complimenting the president on his "brilliant personality" and his "sincere and noble devotion to the ideals of Pan-Americanism." By late May, the Export-Import Bank had worked out the terms for a $2 million credit to Nicaragua.[9]

Roosevelt's renewed support for the Inter-American Highway inspired the project's champions within the federal government. Edwin Warley James and his State Department contacts soon began meeting to plan a strategy for finishing the road, only now they also included the Export-Import Bank directors in their discussions. In late June, the group submitted a letter to Roosevelt that called for the highway to be completed with Export-Import Bank funds that would be administered by the bureau, which had recently been renamed the Public Roads Administration.[10]

The president received the letter several days later and signaled his approval with an "OK" scrawled at the top of the page. The highway boosters in Washington, after several years spent waiting in vain for congressional support, had finally gained a new plan for their road to the canal.[11]

Two months after this development, on September 1, 1939, the war that the world had long been anticipating finally arrived in Europe.

The Western Hemisphere was an island of peace in a hostile world.

The effects of the war nonetheless rippled across the Americas as the transatlantic commercial trade collapsed. Without access to European markets, much of Latin America faced financial ruin.

This sudden vulnerability gave newfound importance to Roosevelt's earlier pledge of support, especially for Central America. As a subsequent message from Secretary of State Cordell Hull noted, "Most of the Central American countries are dependent upon bananas and coffee to meet their foreign exchange requirements, and with the European market practically closed to them for the present, it is to the mutual interest of the United States and of the Central American countries to take all practicable measures to maintain the economic structure in Central America."[12]

By the time the war began, the Export-Import Bank had already started negotiating the next loan related to the new Inter-American Highway plan. The $2.5 million credit was to help Panama defray the expense of laying a concrete surface along eighty-five miles of road heading northwest from the canal. The Panamanian government had already started a portion of this work using materials acquired through a nationwide "donate a bag of cement" campaign, but supplies were quickly exhausted. In December 1938, the Panamanian president, Arnulfo Arias, had appealed to Roosevelt for direct financial aid, arguing the United States must, at the very least, fund the concrete surfacing of the eighty-five miles northwest of the canal since that stretch reached a US air base at Rio Hato, and military vehicles traveling between the two locations caused excessive wear on the road. Arias's claim persuaded Roosevelt, who then brought the matter to Congress in January 1939. Congress, however, delayed passage of the measure until that July, when it appropriated $1.5 million for the concrete surfacing as a canal defense measure. Once Congress gave its approval, the Export-Import Bank stepped in to provide supplemental support, and the Panamanian government received the funds six months later, in February 1940.[13]

News of the Panama loan soon reached Costa Rica, where sentiment for modern roads also remained strong. The incoming Costa Rican president, Raphael Ángel Calderon Guardia, was particularly interested in connecting the capital of San José with the undeveloped, fertile lands of the General Valley in the south of the country. "To a progressive, far seeing administration in San José the course of action was obvious," observed a Public Roads Administration memorandum. "The valley had suddenly become valuable as it never had been before. Its slopes covered with hardwoods, its tobacco

lands that promise a production of the desirable 'bright' tobacco so exten-
sively used in the cigarette world, and its square miles of undeveloped land."
Between this rich valley and San José, however, stood Cerro de la Muerte.
The Costa Rican government had spent several years searching desperately
for an easier, lower passage, but by 1940 had concluded that the road must
go through Cerro de la Muerte, regardless of the construction challenges.
That April, two months after the issuance of the Panama loan, President
Calderon Guardia formally appealed to the Export-Import Bank for aid in
building a road south from San José. The Mountain of Death, it seemed,
would not deny the march of the automobile, as long as the Export-Import
Bank agreed.[14]

After receiving the request, the bank initially hesitated. The inherent
riskiness of financing such heavy construction in a poor, small country worried some of the bank's executives, who feared that the loan might ruin
Costa Rica's credit. But then, in July, Roosevelt issued a call for a major
increase in Latin American lending as a war relief measure. The president
explained,

> As a result of the war in Europe, far-reaching changes in world affairs
> have occurred, which necessarily have repercussions on the economic
> life of both the United States and of the other American Republics. . . .
> Until liberal commercial policies are restored and fair-trading on a
> commercial plane is reopened, distress may be continued. I therefore
> request that the Congress give prompt consideration to increasing the
> capital and lending power of the Export-Import Bank of Washington
> by $500,000,000. . . . [T]he directors of the Bank should have a free
> hand as to the purposes for which loans are authorized and the terms
> and conditions upon which they are made.

Roosevelt's request soon gained passage from a defense-minded Congress.[15]

The month after Roosevelt announced the $500 million lending pro-
gram, the bank finally opened formal negotiations with Costa Rica. The
Costa Rican government quickly dispatched its chief road engineer, Juan
Matamoros, to handle the matter, and the bank instructed him to confer
with James directly. Together, James and Matamoros concluded that they
could probably build the road with a minimum of $4.6 million in funding,
assuming that the Public Roads Administration handled the cost of engineering and design. James's subsequent assurances helped convince the bank

to support the loan, and in late September 1940 the $4.6 million credit was issued. The *New York Times* reported several days later,

> The local [San José] post office was flooded today with circulars warning against the "terrible dangers" inherent in the acceptance of a loan from the Export-Import Bank of the United States.... The press calls the circulars Nazi-Fascist-Communist propaganda, as the three groups work in close collaboration here. The circular refers to the people and the government of the United States in scurrilous terms and charges that they have an imperialistic plan to take over Costa Rica.[16]

The Costa Rican loan arrived at a moment when the State Department was starting to question the efficacy of trying to fund the Inter-American Highway through Export-Import Bank credits alone. As diplomat John Cabot explained,

> The policy of extending Export-Import credits had resulted in some progress, but it was quite evident that either sufficient money would not be made available or that the republics would borrow more than they could repay.... The respective republics simply did not have the resources to build and maintain a modern highway across their entire territory.... Even the desultory direct aid which the United States had [extended], notably in the construction of bridges, was likely to be lost either through failure to maintain these structures or through changes in the route which would bypass them.[17]

By September 1940, the shortcomings of the highway loan program were leading some in the State Department to consider making a new push for congressional appropriations. Such a request, however, seemed unlikely to succeed unless a new rationale emerged to justify the highway's funding. The project's boosters in the State Department thus seized on the issue of hemispheric defense. As diplomat Laurence Duggan explained in a mid-September letter to his supervisor, "Important among the reasons for a reconsideration seems to be the desirability from a defense point of view of having road communication between the United States and the Panama Canal." Duggan also noted that he had recently consulted with the War Department, which did not feel that the highway constituted "a vital link in the defense of the Canal" but nevertheless acknowledged "that [the high-way] has a certain value as an anchor to windward in case of difficulties in sea communication."[18]

The following month, State Department officials brought the matter to the president. The proposal intrigued Roosevelt, but he had reservations about the potential expense. According to Cabot, after the meeting, "The White House informally inquired as to the probable cost of such a program." The State Department then turned for an estimate to James, who subsequently put together a proposal that placed the total anticipated expenses for construction in Central America and Panama at roughly $60 million.[19]

James's new proposal reached the president early in 1941. After reading the memorandum, Roosevelt concluded that the expense was simply too great to allow for further US involvement. As Cabot explained, "The President said that he would not authorize a contribution of more than $20,000,000 on our part."[20]

Roosevelt's pronouncement forced the State Department to solicit a revised estimate from the Public Roads Administration. Over the next two months, James and MacDonald reverse-engineered a budget from a starting figure of $30 million, the combined amount of Roosevelt's proposed maximum grant and the Export-Import Bank loans. Gone were the plans for a first-class automobile highway, replaced by designs for a narrower road surfaced with local materials. As MacDonald later observed, "That $30,000,000 we represented would provide what we could call a transitable road."[21]

The revised proposal landed on the president's desk in mid-March. Roosevelt accepted the new estimate with little question and soon informed the State Department, "I approve the general program and you are requested to draft the necessary legislation to carry it into effect." Several weeks later, the State Department produced legislation calling for a $20 million appropriation to fund the completion of the Inter-American Highway. The new legislation, like its earlier 1934 incarnation, framed the project as a cooperative one and obliged each nation on the route to contribute a third of the total cost (presumably with funds loaned from the Export-Import Bank).[22]

The appearance of the legislation on May 1, 1941, prompted a new round of advocacy from the boosters of the Pan-American Highway. As James proclaimed several days later, "Conclusion of the Inter-American Highway will be equal in significance to the building of the Panama Canal or the completion of the Union Pacific Railroad." Nelson Rockefeller, the influential head of Roosevelt's new Office of the Coordinator of Inter-American

Affairs, added, "The enactment of this legislation will, in my opinion, be a real contribution to hemisphere defense, as well as to the program of this Office for strengthening the bonds between the United States and the other American Republics."[23]

The press largely treated the new legislation as a necessary step in the Roosevelt administration's quest to secure the hemisphere. The *New York Herald Tribune* observed, "The extension of the highway would be a part of the President's campaign to prevent Axis intrusion in South America." The Associated Press compared the project to the Burma Road, a vital military lifeline that the Chinese had recently carved from the jungles of Southeast Asia. The *Washington Post* simply declared in one early-May headline, "Pan American Highway Is America's 'Greatest Road Project.'"[24]

The $20 million measure quickly passed the Senate, but then faced resistance in the House Foreign Affairs Committee. The committee's chairman, Representative Sol Bloom of New York, remained skeptical of the road's true defense value and also wanted certainty that the other six nations involved would actually participate.[25]

Bloom's committee decided to hold hearings in June, and Bloom invited James and the chief of the State Department's Latin American Division to provide statements in person. Their subsequent testimony assured that the road would serve strategic purposes and that full participation was likely. These promises, however, failed to assuage the committee chair.[26]

Soon Bloom reached out directly to General George Marshall, the army's chief of staff, to gain his opinion on the matter. In mid-July, Marshall offered the following reply:

> The construction of this Inter-American highway cannot be supported
> by the War Department purely on the basis of its military importance
> as a supply or transit route in time of war for our garrison in Panama,
> for example. The value of the route to the national defense would
> result from its great influence on the development and maintenance of
> more friendly relations with the countries concerned. On that basis I
> urge ... enactment of [the legislation].

Marshall's qualified endorsement nonetheless remained insufficient for some of the skeptics in Congress, who continued to stall the legislation throughout the summer and fall.[27]

*   *   *

Five months after Marshall issued his letter, on December 7, 1941, war finally reached American shores when the Japanese bombed a naval base at Pearl Harbor, Hawaii, killing nearly twenty-five hundred people. The United States declared war against Japan the next day and officially joined the Allies in their struggle against the rest of the Axis powers three days later. Within a week, the nations of Central America and Panama had all joined the United States in the fight.[28]

These sudden developments helped to free the Inter-American Highway legislation from committee. The bill reached the broader House during the frenzied week that followed Pearl Harbor. The day it arrived, Marshall declared in a letter to Congress, "This road will be of great benefit from a military point of view. It will afford communication by land no matter what difficulties might be encountered by sea."[29]

When the legislation finally made it to the House floor, on December 16, 1941, several war-minded House members rushed to offer their support for Marshall's statement. As Representative Hamilton Fish of New York observed, "The highest authority in our Army, our Chief of Staff, says it is almost a war necessity, that it is for our national defense, and that we need it now. It must be self-evident to everybody today that we need direct communication with the Panama Canal not only by sea but by land, and we need it immediately." Representative Thomas Rolph of California joined Fish in praising the road's defense benefits, noting,

> The highway will . . . tend to make this portion of the Western Hemisphere well-nigh impregnable to invasion. The war in Europe has demonstrated that good roads for the movement of mechanized units are almost as important as are the different types of equipment. With the highway completed it would be possible for the United States to keep a moving wall of fighting machines along every inch of the continent and make almost impossible the massing of troops and equipment by any foreign enemy.

A final paean to the road's defense value came from Representative Wilburn Cartwright, a longtime proponent of the Pan-American Highway: "[It] is the Burma Road of the Western Hemisphere, an integral part of the defense mechanism of the North American Continent, and vital to the economy, safety, and well-being of the people of the New World."[30]

Not all the nation's legislators, however, accepted these defense claims.

Republican Charles Halleck of Indiana insisted, "the only real argument that can be advanced for this road as a defense measure is that it is expected it will tend to the social and economic stabilization of the countries to be traversed by the road and that it will develop a friendlier feeling toward us." Halleck's Republican colleague Earl Michener of Michigan went even further in his defense critique, adding,

> I am, therefore, wondering what our farmers and taxpayers are going to think when we tell them that we are spending millions of dollars of borrowed money to build scenic, cultural, and friendship highways hundreds of miles from home in foreign countries at this time. That is going to be a pretty hard thing to explain. . . . I am thoroughly convinced that this project has no real defense value other than the cultural value to which I have already referred.[31]

But "cultural value" alone was enough to persuade many of the congressmen who had already supported the project as a goodwill measure in the 1930s. Republican Charles Eaton of New Jersey noted on this point, "This road I have looked upon as an undertaking to open up an artery through which could flow back and forth the moral, the intellectual, and economic exchanges and influences which would place this Nation of ours in the position of recognized friendship and leadership on these continents, which position it must occupy if we fulfill our destiny and assist the other American nations to fulfill theirs."[32]

The combination of cultural and defense arguments ultimately won over a majority of representatives. "This is both a peace measure and a defense measure at the same time," observed Fish. He added for emphasis, "This House has no intention of voting down this measure." The approved bill reached Roosevelt several days later, and he signed it into law on December 26, 1941, less than three weeks after the nation had entered the war.[33]

By this point, the Inter-American Highway program at the Export-Import Bank had also expanded to include two more loans. One of these credits, for slightly more than $1 million, had gone to El Salvador, whose newfound embrace of highway loans cut against decades of resistance to US involvement in its road network in the name of nationalism. The other loan, for $40 million, had been given to Mexico, which had already completed its stretch of the Inter-American Highway as far as its capital but still needed to finish the southern half toward Guatemala.[34]

Three years had now elapsed since the Declaration of Lima. During that time, the rising concerns over hemispheric defense had reanimated US interest in the Inter-American Highway project. Between the Export-Import Bank loans and the new congressional appropriation, more than $65 million had been expended on the Inter-American Highway as the nation entered World War II. The new resources gave the Public Roads Administration a budget that dwarfed what had been available during the mid-1930s. But the wartime legislation raised a new question: If the road was so vital to defense, why was the military not directly involved?

The First Line of Defense

The idea that a highway to the canal should be a military project originated with General Brehon Somervell, the powerful commander of the army's Services of Supply. Somervell's duties included oversight of the army's Corps of Engineers, and he had long felt that his men should play a more prominent role in road building. James once noted of the Army Corps' rivalry with the Public Roads Administration, "[Somervell] . . . was for holding on to all they had and getting as much more as they could. During the last war—the First World War—the Engineering Corps was hopeful of getting into the road game and Somervell told me he thought they ought to have the Federal Aid work. They didn't succeed, however." [35]

Somervell's hard-charging attitude extended to all aspects of his mandate and had won him many admirers within the military during the 1930s. The *Washington Post* noted of Somervell, "he has the qualities of greatness with none of the pomp." Somervell, in summarizing his own philosophy, observed, "My ambition is to see the United States Army the best-equipped, the best-fed, the most mobile army on the face of the earth. Nobody's going to court-martial me if I give it too much. But if I should give it too little, then a court-martial would be too good for me." [36]

In Somervell's view, one of the army's most glaring supply deficiencies on the eve of war concerned the nation's two outlying continental possessions, the Canal Zone and Alaska. Neither location shared road or rail connections with the mainland United States, and ship transport seemed uncertain in the face of German and Japanese submarines.

Somervell's campaign to remedy this situation began in earnest following Pearl Harbor. He first pushed for a highway to Alaska, insisting that the Army Corps should build the road as an insurance policy against

Japanese submarine encroachment. General Marshall concurred with Somervell's assessment, and soon thereafter Canada, which had joined the Allied cause, agreed to cooperate. By February 1942, the Army Corps was at work planning the so-called Alcan Highway, running fifteen hundred miles from a railhead in Dawson Creek, British Columbia, to Fairbanks, Alaska. Somervell's attention next turned to the Canal Zone. On March 30, he instructed his chief of transportation, General Charles Gross:

> Please give immediate consideration to the desirability of completing the Pan American Highway as far as Panama as a military route.... Would it not be possible ... to select the parts of the highway which need improvement, so that if the worse comes to worst we could use it. If good for no other purpose, it would certainly serve to train some additional engineer regiments.

Gross later recalled,

> Those were dark days.... That was March 30, 1942.... The justification for [the highway's] construction was to meet a contingency in the future.... If the world became black, if Russia fell, if everything were lost in north Africa, if the Germans were to take Dakar, if they were to take that gap over to Natal, we then had a job of defending the Panama Canal. [The road] was some insurance to get solidarity and to secure readier consent to the establishment of airfields in Central America, and for their supply and defense.[37]

Somervell's request soon sent Gross to the Public Roads Administration. Within days, Gross was meeting with MacDonald directly. MacDonald estimated that it would take at least another five years under the current program to complete the road. However, the military, MacDonald acknowledged, did not need a route built to the planned standards of the Inter-American Highway, with scenic vistas and two lanes throughout. For military purposes, all that would be necessary was a so-called pioneer road, one with no surfacing, minimal width, high grades, and narrow curves, but nonetheless capable of handling army vehicles. After the meeting, Gross noted in an April 8 letter to Somervell, "From data available, completion of a pioneer road in two years appears to be feasible, provided Army personnel is utilized [and] construction equipment is made available."[38]

Somervell responded to Gross with instructions to halve the proposed timeline. Over the next month, Gross worked with top officials from the Public Roads Administration, the Army Corps, and the State Department to carry out Somervell's request. They concluded that the fastest results could be achieved if the Public Roads Administration and the Army Corps combined their efforts, with the former using its recent congressional appropriation to build permanent steel bridges and the latter handling new road construction with military funds. They also determined that construction in Mexico, which remained hostile to the idea of US-directed road building, would be unnecessary, since a standard-gauge railroad already extended all the way to the Guatemalan border and could be used for moving supplies. James, recently returned from a trip to Central America, estimated that the military could likely complete the remaining portion of the route from Guatemala to the canal for about $15 million. According to James's calculations, approximately a third of the fifteen hundred miles involved remained wholly unconstructed, another third required some form of improvement, and the final third—which included Panama's three-hundred-mile-long national road—was already built to sufficient standards. Gross wrote Somervell on May 9, after meeting with James, "[T]he best information from the Public Roads Administration ... indicates completion of an all-weather pioneer road in one year is possible, provided surveys are begun in early June and construction equipment is on the ground ready to begin work immediately at the end of the wet season (November 15)."[39]

Gross's revised plan earned the approval of Somervell, who sent it to the office of the army chief of staff. Two weeks later, the chief of staff consented to the program with reservations, explaining, "Although the need for the pioneer road at present or during the war may be questioned, it appears to be a desirable project which should be started at this time, subject to non-interference with more urgent construction projects."[40]

The chief of staff's halfhearted authorization prompted the delivery of the proposal to General Dwight D. Eisenhower, who commanded the army's Operations Division. Eisenhower, focused on prosecuting the war in Europe and Asia, responded with even greater skepticism than had the chief of staff. He questioned the road's practicality and feared that its construction would invariably pull resources from other, vital war initiatives. A June 4 letter that Eisenhower wrote to the chief of staff noted, "The Operations Division considers that the utility of the proposed road to the present war is problematical. Consequently, no justification exists for the diversion to this project of men or critical materials or equipment."[41]

Eisenhower's directive could easily have sidelined the pioneer road, but his letter had arrived at a moment of heightened paranoia. As diplomat Cabot explained,

> In the late spring of 1942, the military position of the [Western Hemisphere] reached its lowest ebb. The United States Pacific battle fleet had been largely paralyzed by the blow struck at Pearl Harbor. Japan was rapidly extending her conquest through the southwest Pacific.... Definite apprehension was felt among the military authorities in Washington that an attack on this hemisphere might be attempted. At the same time, the German submarine campaign on American shipping lanes had reached its height. Several ships a day were being sunk. In particular, the lanes between the United States ports and the Canal Zone were infested with German submarines. The United States was therefore in a position on the one hand of facing a possible attack on an area vital to American security and on the other of having very uncertain communications both on sea and on land to counter such an attack if it were made.

Cabot added, "Fears were even being expressed that because of the submarine campaign . . . our forces in the Canal Zone might literally starve."[42]

These threats drove Secretary of War Henry Stimson to override Eisenhower's protest. Soon Stimson agreed to authorize the pioneer road with the caveat that its construction not compete against other, more pressing military objectives. On June 10, he wrote to Secretary of State Hull to ask for assistance in acquiring consents from the countries along the route. The same day, Somervell instructed the chief of the Army Corps to "initiate and execute the necessary surveys." The Inter-American Highway was fast becoming a war route.[43]

The Army Corps assigned responsibility for the pioneer road survey to Colonel Edwin Kelton, a district engineer then overseeing airport construction and flood control in the Southwest. Kelton, a 1915 West Point graduate, had a strong record of service, though nothing in his past distinguished him for the job at hand. He had never been to Central America, he spoke no Spanish, and his entire experience in road building totaled barely a hundred miles of construction.[44]

Kelton found his new directive to be "very vague." As he later explained, "Preliminary instructions were limited to the statement that a pioneer all-weather highway would be provided between the Mexico-Guatemala boundary and Panama City, and that the work would be carried on in collaboration with the Public Roads Administration and the [army's] Transportation Service." Several days after receiving the orders, Kelton met with James to discuss his instructions. During the meeting, James laid out a bewildering array of tasks that needed to be handled before the dry season if work were to be completed in one year. James's list included bridge design, steel and timber acquisition, the securing of shipping space, the hiring of contractors, and the erection of work camps. Following the meeting with James, Kelton informed Somervell that the road could not be completed within one year unless the military immediately organized and funded a full-scale construction program.[45]

Kelton's plea led Somervell to take new action, appealing to the chief of staff for $15 million to fund construction. The chief of staff quickly consented and again sent the matter to Eisenhower's Operations Division. Eisenhower, however, was away from Washington when the request arrived. In his absence, his subordinates decided to sign off on his behalf. A June 19 letter from the Operations Division noted, "It is recommended that this project be approved, subject to the condition that no troops nor critical materials needed for essential military projects are committed to the undertaking." The following month, on July 16, Kelton learned that the project had been authorized, that the other nations involved had approved, and that he had been appointed Director, Pan-American Highway.[46]

Upon receiving the new instructions, Kelton immediately appealed to the Army-Navy Munitions Board for a high priority rating, a necessity at a moment when materials, construction equipment, and shipping space were in short supply. But the board only agreed to an A-1-a rating, the lowest level for any military construction. This minimal priority assignment reflected the board's desire to respect the Operations Division's demand that no "critical materials or troops" be committed to the project. Moreover, the army had categorized the Caribbean as a low importance zone, only outranking peripheral military targets such as Iceland and Greenland. Kelton griped that his priority rating was "not worth the paper it was written on." When James learned about the rating, he simply exclaimed, "The job can't be done under these conditions."[47]

By the time the rating had been issued, the military survey for the pioneer road had already commenced. Kelton had recruited nearly two hundred men to handle the work, a vast increase over the team of three that

MacDonald had sent a decade earlier to cover similar ground. Kelton later recalled of this new reconnaissance,

> Conditions under which the survey parties worked were exceedingly unpleasant to say the least.... It would be hard to exaggerate the difficulties encountered and the hardships suffered by many of the parties making this survey through a generally rugged and mountainous country, mostly covered with dense jungle, and under conditions of almost daily rainfall. Prevalence of malaria and other tropical diseases was an additional hazard.... For more than 200 miles, the jungle growth was so dense as to require the clearing of practically every foot of the line and of the cross-sections, before surveys could be made.[48]

The reconnaissance generally followed the imagined line of the Inter-American Highway, but Kelton made several major reorientations, mainly to avoid mountainous construction and shorten the total distance. In Guatemala, he chose the lowland route that James had earlier avoided out of concerns over upsetting the International Railways of Central America. In Nicaragua, he diverted the road away from the rugged lands near President Somoza's farm. In El Salvador, he bypassed a short detour that carried the Inter-American Highway past the Gulf of Fonseca. All these changes were accepted with little resistance by host nations content to gain additional free roads as part of their war effort.[49]

Kelton nonetheless soon faced pushback over the pioneer road from his own countryman Thomas MacDonald. MacDonald's concern, first raised in midsummer 1942, related to the "exceedingly steep mountain slopes and general roughness of the terrain" along the seventy-one-mile stretch around Cerro de la Muerte. As MacDonald explained,

> It is not feasible ... to build merely the Pioneer Road in these mountains.... The narrow cuts adequate for the Pioneer Road would hamper passing and repassing of heavy earth-moving equipment, and seriously retard the progress of construction; the work to be done later in widening the cuts would have to be done largely by hand; and widening the fills would result in serious slides and increase of quantities.... A road to serve any useful purpose must have width and curvature to make it safe, and to accomplish such construction [there] will be more costly than a mere Pioneer Road.

MacDonald ultimately insisted that the Public Roads Administration maintain control over the Cerro de la Muerte stretch. After a brief deliberation, Kelton decided to honor the request.[50]

Following this, Kelton turned to hiring contractors, the only way to secure labor since his instructions had prohibited using large numbers of troops. The project's low priority rating, however, discouraged most firms, who worried that supplies and shipping space would be exceedingly difficult to secure. As one army general noted, "Contractors were fearful that delays in obtaining men, materials, and equipment would tie up their organizations in an unprofitable enterprise during a period when construction was at a peak and contractors greatly in demand." Some firms also expressed concern over the risk the tropical climate posed for their equipment. In desperation, Kelton offered the few contractors who had shown interest exceptionally generous terms, including high machine rental fees that would continue even after the government paid enough to buy the equipment outright. By September, agreements had been reached with three US contractors as well as with several Central American highway departments, which received "the easier stretches," according to Kelton.[51]

Soon equipment and supplies destined for Central America began arriving in Los Angeles, where Kelton had his base of operations. But once more the low priority rating plagued Kelton and left him unable to secure shipping space for the estimated twenty-five thousand tons of materials, which piled up on the Los Angeles docks throughout the fall. Kelton worked desperately to resolve the problem, only to be rebuffed time and again. As one contractor noted, "everything in the world was against us." Almost no materials made it to Central America until November, when Kelton began shipping some of his supplies over the Mexican rails that American capitalists had built sixty years earlier. An army colonel involved with the pioneer road noted of this rail transportation, "[I]t was very rough and a lot of the equipment may have been damaged in shipment. . . . [I]n some of the equipment we sent by rail through Mexico we were obliged to send armed guards. . . . We had a lot of stuff stolen or . . . damaged on the way down."[52]

Despite the lack of supplies, the work proceeded. Throughout the fall, the contractors and governments assembled an army of laborers that eventually swelled to twenty thousand men. Most of the workers came from within Central America, where the pioneer road functioned as one of the largest wartime employment programs. The contractors, however, also brought in roughly three thousand Americans to assist with the job and handle many of the skilled and supervisory tasks.[53]

Construction began with the erection of work camps, which the army decided to segregate. For the Americans, the contractors built "[t]heater-of-operation type" housing. As Kelton noted, "All buildings were screened, electric light plants were installed, all water was boiled and/or chlorinated, proper bathing and latrine facilities were provided, and in most cases, wells were drilled or dug for the water supply and refrigerator space was provided for perishable foods." For the local laborers, in contrast, the contractors offered practically no living support beyond the barest essentials. Kelton observed of the barracks in Costa Rica and Panama, "Camps were . . . very primitive, often consisting of a palm-leaf roof supported by a pole frame with no walls or floor. Frequently no other facilities were provided." Kelton, for his part, rationalized the decision to segregate on the grounds that Central Americans "were accustomed to poor living conditions, lack of sanitary and cooking facilities, and little or no protection from the weather, insects, etc."[54]

The segregated housing was the most visible manifestation of a racism that pervaded the entire pioneer road operation. As a State Department dispatch noted,

> The attitude of the Americans, from top to bottom, seems to be "To hell with the natives—get your money, get the job done, and get out. . . ." [C]ertain officials . . . employed by the contractors habitually and pointedly draw a line between the Americans and "Latin Americans" of all social levels, classing the latter as inferiors.

In some instances, US workers hung "For Americans only" signs above parts of their camps.[55]

The American workforce distinguished itself not only through its racism, but also its debauched behavior. Locals complained to the government and to US embassies of constant drunkenness, widespread gambling, and heavy demand for prostitutes. A beleaguered State Department official noted, "The difficulty appears to be due to the 'tropical tramp' type of contractors or sub-contractors and to the riff-raff which they have employed (possibly because of the difficulty of finding more suitable personnel)." Another witness observed, "There are a number who are motivated by no impulses other than that of self-interest. Generally speaking, these men are morally and patriotically of a low standard. Many have paid little attention to what they do and less to what they say, particularly when under the influence of liquor." At one point, American behavior in Honduras grew so rowdy that

President Tiburcio Carías declared a form of martial law and sent a reported "notorious killer" to enforce the peace.[56]

The combination of poor US discipline and insufficient supplies ensured that very little construction took place during the first dry season. A frustrated Army Corps engineer complained to the press in July 1943, "It was a standing joke down there to ask for newspaper and magazine clippings on the progress of the highway so the men on the job could know how much they've done—it was the only way they could see their 'progress.'" In some parts of the isthmus, the contractors had spent the entire dry season simply working to clear access roads from the Pacific coast to the actual pioneer route so that supplies could be brought to the true work sites.[57]

The Public Roads Administration, during this period, had also encountered setbacks in its quest to tame Cerro de la Muerte. The contractor MacDonald had hired, Ralph E. Mills of Kentucky, was forced to spend most of his firm's resources building a thirty-five-mile-long access road from the tiny coast town of Dominical to San Isidro, a small settlement in the heart of the General Valley. Moreover, MacDonald and James had realized that their original cost projection for the Cerro de la Muerte stretch was woefully inadequate. In their view, the budget needed to be increased by $12 million, an amount the Costa Rican government could not possibly afford. Before the end of the dry season, MacDonald had begun actively seeking supplemental funding in the United States. As he explained in a May letter to the State Department, "This is the heaviest work ever undertaken by the Public Roads Administration in any of its projects."[58]

The delays at all levels compelled the army's leadership to extend the pioneer road's deadline and bolster its funding further. However, support for the project among top army officials was starting to wane as the nation's military position improved during the late spring of 1943. Diplomat John Cabot explained,

American naval superiority in the Pacific, shattered at Pearl Harbor, had been restored, and the Japanese threat to the Pacific side of the Western Hemisphere evaporated. Moreover, by [mid-]1943 the submarine warfare had swung sharply in favor of the [United States]. No longer was the shipping route from the United States to the Canal Zone precarious and inadequate. It became more and more evident that in all probability no military convoy would ever traverse the pioneer highway.[59]

An official reevaluation of the Inter-American Highway as a military route began in May 1943, when a committee from the army's chief of staff office initiated "a strategic survey of the world situation." One general involved with the assessment later explained, "In view of planned offensive operations and the progress of the war in the Mediterranean and the Pacific Ocean areas, a decision was reached to review and restudy the defense installations and projects in the Western Hemisphere with a view to their reduction." Following these meetings, in early July, the chief of staff instructed the Operations Division to study the Inter-American Highway "with a view to its curtailment or abandonment." The command prompted little protest from the Operations Division, which had never expressed much interest in the pioneer road. In late August, the Operations Division's report on the matter concluded, "The completion of the Pan-American Highway, even though it be accomplished in the next year, which is doubtful, will not assist in the conduct of the war. On the other hand, it may interfere by the diversion of critical materials to the project." The week after the report appeared, the secretary of war approved its conclusion to terminate the road. Kelton then learned of the decision by letter on September 14, fifteen months after he had first received the assignment.[60]

The military's decision to abandon the pioneer road provoked indignation from many in Central America, where the project remained a major employment program. For all its flaws, the road program had provided work for tens of thousands of men, and by the fall of 1943 much of the more flagrant American behavior had been brought under control. As the State Department noted in September, the local press "echoed public reaction to the effect that suspension of the work 'does not harmonize with the Good Neighbor policy and the policy of giving economic assistance to nations affected by the war.'" The president of Costa Rica even appealed directly to Roosevelt to rescind the military's order. The pressure to preserve US goodwill—from both Central American nations and from the secretary of state—ultimately prompted the military to give away millions of dollars' worth of US equipment to several nations as a way to save face.[61]

Work on the pioneer road finally drew to a close at the start of November 1943. In total, the army had spent over $30 million and employed more than twenty thousand men. The massive workforce had bulldozed countless acres of jungle, but the road to the canal still remained a distant dream. Only the governments of El Salvador and Nicaragua, which had the least challenging sections, completed their contracts outright. The portions allotted to the US contractors all stood less than half done. One US company had even been fired for "gross incompetence" and "lack of cooperation" halfway through after showing no progress whatsoever.[62]

In the end, Somervell's proposed road to the canal had turned into a debacle from start to finish. Kelton had been asked to do the impossible, and he had failed.

The termination of the military-sponsored pioneer road, however, did not mean the end of US wartime work on the Inter-American Highway. The Public Roads Administration retained control over the Cerro de la Muerte stretch as well as several smaller jobs. Moreover, the month before the army canceled the pioneer road program, Congress had approved special legislation granting the $12 million that MacDonald insisted would be necessary to advance construction in southern Costa Rica.[63]

The contractor on the Costa Rica job, Ralph E. Mills, was nearing completion of his access road to San Isidro, the southern gateway to Cerro de la Muerte, when Congress acted. The $12 million appropriation thus gave Mills much-needed resources at the very moment he was preparing to embark on the exceptionally heavy construction leading toward the Mountain of Death.[64]

To handle the work, Mills had recruited an army of laborers nearly five thousand strong. Most of the men were Costa Rican, but some came from the United States. Mills divided his workforce into two main groups, a northern half that started near Cartago and a southern half that began at San Isidro, with plans to converge around Cerro de la Muerte.[65]

The heaviest work commenced once the dry season began in November. Soon the men were forced to brave challenges greater than almost any previously witnessed in the history of road building. As a Public Roads Administration memorandum written during the construction explained,

In building the road ... the engineers and contractors are encountering extraordinary problems. Many are unique even for the men who have had wide experience in the Rockies and in the Sierras which rise to more than 14,000 feet. The size of the Costa Rica project is staggering. ... Because this enormous movement of earth results in cuts as much as 100 feet deep and fills up to 125 feet high, pressures develop and slides and collapses occur. Occasionally after a protracted tropical downpour, an apparently good fill will collapse as though made of stiff mush rather than of solid earth and rock, or a slide may bring enormous quantities of dirt down onto the highway.

The unstable mountain terrain tormented the laborers relentlessly. In the worst reported accident, a slide killed two men trying to drill through a boulder.[66]

The men also struggled to contend with the enormous oak trees that grew all along the Cerro de la Muerte route. According to the US foresters who discovered these trees in 1942, the oaks were on average the largest in the world. One forester noted, "The appearance of the forest is quite awe-inspiring, causing [us] to dub it 'the ancestral home of the gremlins,' an allusion to the weird light effects and swirling mists which give this type of cloud forest an almost unearthly and 'spooky' appearance." These ancient trees, however, were obstacles to progress for Mills's men. Any oaks that blocked their path were met with heavy explosives. James noted, "Dynamite is used freely to lift the huge trees with their buttressed roots, and often as much as 120 pounds of explosive are used for a single tree."[67]

With dynamite and determination, the work crews soldiered on. Mills kept his men on schedule and maintained high morale through expert administration. By the end of the first dry season, they had reached beyond the halfway point. The rainy months then slowed down progress somewhat, but construction returned to full strength once late November arrived. Two months later, in January 1945, Mills's men conquered Cerro de la Muerte. The final piece of earthmoving was handled directly by Costa Rican president Teodoro Picado. The US chargé d'affaires in Costa Rica, who participated in the ceremony, noted, "The President and I mounted a bulldozer which pushed aside the last bit of earth on the mountainside between it and another bulldozer coming northward. . . . The president personally informed me that he considered it one of the most significant events in recent years of Costa Rican history."[68]

The largest single geographic impediment to the Inter-American Highway—the Mountain of Death—had at last been tamed. James noted of the effort,

The 71 miles of construction require[d] the handling of about 17 million cubic yards of excavation or nearly 250,000 yards per mile as compared with 15,000 yards per mile on the Alaska Highway. . . . Nearly

half of the Costa Rica work [was] rock. . . . In the United States no
project on record has involved such large quantities per mile over anything like so long a distance.

MacDonald added, "The work of the Pan-American Highway in southern
Costa Rica is one of the most difficult engineering accomplishments so far
attempted in the world."[69]

The triumph over Cerro de la Muerte nonetheless came at a moment
when the broader Inter-American Highway program lacked momentum. James and MacDonald had seriously underestimated the amount of
money needed to complete the road, and the funds from the congressional
appropriations and Export-Import Bank loans were fast nearing exhaustion. According to a revised Public Roads Administration estimate, over
$70 million would be necessary to complete the road, a $40 million increase
from the March 1941 figure. Somehow all the work performed during the
war years had resulted in the outstanding budget more than doubling. Mac-
Donald delayed bringing this information to Congress, claiming fears that
it would distract from his proposed domestic highway legislation. But by
early 1945 the State Department began pressuring MacDonald, arguing
that increased appropriations were necessary as a goodwill measure. Mac-
Donald finally relented that May and agreed to draft new legislation to fund
the completion of the road.[70]

The timing of his request, however, could not have been more unfortunate, for scandal was about to engulf the Inter-American Highway.

"An Inexcusable Degree of Boneheadedness"

The fifteen-minute-long national radio broadcast began in the early evening
of June 4, 1945:

> Tonight, ladies and gentlemen, I'm ready to begin presenting to you
> this report on which I have been working here in Los Angeles for
> more than 2 weeks. . . . It's a story with tremendous ramifications, as
> you will find out from day to day, as it unfolds through this microphone.
> It's a story that involves untold millions of dollars of your money, and
> where those millions have gone and where they are going every day.
> [T]he topic [is] the Latin-American Highway, which was designed as
> a military transportation link between the United States proper and
> the Panama Canal Zone, in the early days of the present war, when the

possibility of a Japanese attack on the Canal and the stoppage of coast shipping by Japanese submarines was very threatening.

The voice in the broadcast belonged to forty-two-year-old Fulton Lewis Jr., a conservative radio host with an audience of millions. Lewis had decided to conduct an investigation into the Inter-American Highway after hearing rumors of widespread improprieties. His subsequent inquiries had unearthed enough salacious material to fill an entire week of programming.[71]

Lewis began his indictment of the highway with a series of testimonials concerning "petty and small-time fraud." His first guest, a former auditor on the pioneer road, told of how one supervisor on the job had colluded with local businessmen to overcharge the US government for supplies, the profits then being divided among all the parties involved. The same supervisor, the auditor noted, had also built an eight-mile diversion road to his personal hacienda. Lewis next turned to a second disgruntled auditor, who explained, "They had trucks to bring loads of liquor to their favorite saloons . . . and plenty of transportation to go into town for big nights; but I couldn't even thumb a ride out to the scene of construction, to check on pay rolls or equipment time, or anything else." A third witness on Lewis's program went so far as to assure that he had tried to present evidence of these frauds to the FBI but had been the subject of an anonymous intimidation campaign, noting, "one night . . . three men in zoot-suits grabbed me on the street . . . —just before I was to make a speech on the subject— and beat me up. They didn't take any money or other belongings, but they did steal my briefcase with all the papers. I spent months in a hospital with various broken bones."[72]

After setting the stage with these allegations, Lewis moved on "to the higher brackets where the stakes climb up into the millions." The heart of the fraud, Lewis explained, lay in the rental agreements that allowed the contractors to continue receiving payments on their equipment long after an amount equal to the purchase price had been expended in rental fees. "In these contracts which the Army made," Lewis fumed, "the contractors were paid profits on their equipment, the smallest of which was 110 percent per year, and in some cases it ran as high as 400 percent per year."[73]

Lewis's exposé concluded with a condemnation of the contractors' equipment, which he assured had arrived in terrible condition. The final witness on Lewis's multipart series noted, "It was one of the worst collections of junk I've ever seen." Lewis added, "In short . . . the contractor brought poor equipment on the job and drew full rental on every piece of it all through the job, until the Government repaired or rebuilt it to perfect working condition and returned it to the contractor at the end of the job."[74]

The week after the broadcasts, Republican senator Edward Robertson of Wyoming, a devoted Lewis listener, invited the radio host to present his findings directly to a small group of congressmen. The meeting that followed, according to Robertson, "removed any doubt in my mind—and I think also from the minds of other Senators that this is a matter of the gravest importance and one which should be the subject of immediate senatorial investigation." The day after the meeting, Robertson introduced a transcript of the Lewis broadcasts into the *Congressional Record* and demanded a formal inquiry by the Committee to Investigate the National Defense, also known as the Mead Committee, a Senate body that had been established in 1941 to look into wartime waste and profiteering.[75]

Robertson's request immediately found support from Senator Homer Ferguson of Michigan, the most aggressive member of the Mead Committee. Ferguson had built a reputation as "a one-man grand jury" during his years as a Detroit judge and had joined the Mead Committee upon entering the Senate in 1943. Ferguson's list of suspect wartime projects already included two other major Western Hemisphere initiatives, the Alcan Highway and the Canol Pipeline, constructed in 1943 to bring oil from Canada to Alaska. Ferguson not only endorsed Robertson's request for an investigation into the Inter-American Highway, he also pointed a finger at the attorney general for failing to initiate an inquiry of his own. Ferguson concluded,

> The people of the United States should expect that if there is any graft or corruption, they will know about it and the Department of Justice will take proper proceedings against those who are guilty [and] that no one who is guilty will go unpunished. . . . I hope we will receive the cooperation of the Army and various other agencies of Government, so that the people may be certain that they know the facts and so that they may know whether their bond dollars and tax dollars have been correctly spent or corruptly spent.[76]

The exchange on the Senate floor triggered a cascade of government responses. First, on June 16, the attorney general, reacting to Ferguson's indictment, opened a file on the charges raised during the Lewis broadcasts. Then, almost immediately thereafter, the army's War Frauds Department began a parallel inquiry. Next came the announcement of a full-scale investigation into the entire Inter-American Highway program by the Mead Committee. And finally, in early July, the House's Committee on Roads declared that it too would be formally looking into the matter.[77]

Public hearings before the Mead Committee commenced several weeks later. For the first round of testimony, the committee members invited half a dozen top military officials. Ferguson took the lead in the questioning and challenged the generals to explain what true defense purpose the road could serve. The generals tried to argue that the road seemed justified when the decision was made, but their rationales mattered little to Ferguson. Eventually, the Michigan senator, who had reviewed all the military correspondence, seized on Eisenhower's opposition as proof that a faulty command structure had resulted in the road being approved despite serving no military purpose. His interrogation culminated with the question, "And you used $38 million of [military funds] to provide this highway which General Eisenhower said wasn't of any value to the military for the winning of the war?" In response, one of the generals sheepishly replied, "Correct, sir." The *Washington Post* observed of this initial hearing, "In lifting the lid on the Pan-American Highway project, the Mead Committee appears to have uncovered a first-rate case of careless planning and performance.... Altogether, this undertaking appears to have involved an inexcusable degree of boneheadedness."[78]

At the time of the hearings, MacDonald's new $25 million Inter-American Highway request was stalled in committee, once again on account of Sol Bloom. The chair of the House Foreign Affairs Committee was concerned with the allegations against the road and frustrated with the Public Roads Administration's faulty estimates. Bloom had demanded assurances that the new $25 million request would be sufficient to complete the road, but James and MacDonald had consistently refused to provide such a guarantee. Bloom's opposition compelled the State Department to go directly to President Harry S. Truman, who agreed to endorse the appropriation in the late summer of 1945, shortly after the close of World War II. On September 9, Truman declared as part of a special message on public works, "Now that materials and manpower will become more plentiful, we should be prepared to undertake a program of useful public works.... I recommend that the Congress appropriate $25,000,000 to continue the construction of the Inter-American Highway through the Central America Republics to the Canal Zone."[79]

Truman's support nonetheless proved insufficient to free the appropriation request from committee. With both chambers of Congress pursuing formal investigations of the Inter-American Highway, Bloom faced little pressure to act. Moreover, the House Roads Committee had decided to conduct a preliminary fact-finding tour of the Inter-American Highway, which they scheduled for early the following year.

Five months later, in mid-February 1946, a group of six from the House Roads Committee assembled at New Orleans, where a steamer was waiting to take them to Panama. Joining them were MacDonald, James, and a handful of other federal and military officials. The tour brought the Public Roads Administration, for the first time, face-to-face with its inquisitors. One congressman told the press before departing, "There have been charges that the road cost too much money. I believe there have been expenditures that cannot be justified. We intend to find out." Another committee member added, "[I don't] want to prejudge the thing, but I'm curious where all that money went. Personally, I feel we came out of World War II on wings, and there isn't much need for the road." [80]

The inspection tour officially commenced several days later in Panama City. Almost immediately, however, the group encountered the first major obstacle to their progress: the canal. In order to cross, the men loaded their cars onto the Thatcher Ferry, which had opened in 1932 and had been funded through US legislation that grew out of the original Inter-American Highway Conference. The ferry then carried the men to a point on the far side of the canal that connected with the national highway Guardia had built in the 1920s and 1930s. Over the course of the next three hundred miles, the men had a chance to see firsthand what Guardia had accomplished with Panamanian and US funds. The eighty-five-mile stretch nearest the canal featured the concrete surfacing that US wartime grants had paid for, while a level, two-lane road carried them much of the remaining distance to David. But the road beyond David eventually turned into a one-lane dirt path that ceded entirely to jungle about twenty-five miles before the Costa Rican border. [81]

After arriving at David, the surveyors boarded a plane and headed direct to San José, Costa Rica. The flight allowed them to bypass several hundred miles of the Inter-American Highway that remained unconstructed between northwestern Panama and San Isidro, Costa Rica. The jungle still ruled this distance and had already clawed back much of the scattered clearing work that pioneer road crews had performed during the war. [82]

When the inspectors reached San José, they received an enthusiastic welcome from a government desperate for additional highway funds. President Picado personally greeted the group upon their arrival and then accompanied them on a tour of Cerro de la Muerte. One witness noted of the subsequent ceremony, "the military band of Cartago, waiting for the committee [near the summit], played the American and Costa Rican anthems. The Costa Rican and American flags crossed together at the top of a hill represented the joining of the two countries by this wonderful highway, which will be of mutual benefit to both countries if it is finished."[83]

The scene at Cerro de la Muerte captured the sense of promise that surrounded the Inter-American Highway. Such sentiments, however, conspicuously ignored the negative impacts that the road was already bringing to the broader landscape. As the *New York Times* noted shortly after the Cerro de la Muerte ceremony, "The new road has given access to the forest and has made it easy to transport . . . charcoal to market in Cartago and San José. Hundreds of ancient oak and other trees, many a hundred feet tall, have been chopped down and burned in the pits that smoke and smolder beside the highway. Erosion will soon join the charcoal burners in completing the picture of desolation." The vistas the engineers had carefully created were fast turning into landscapes of ruin.[84]

After touring Cerro de la Muerte, the inspectors resumed their journey northward. Thanks to the combined efforts of the Central American governments, the Public Roads Administration, and the US Army, the remaining portion of the road was passable by jeep throughout its entire length to the Mexican-Guatemalan border, at least in the dry season. The roughest stretches lay in northern Costa Rica and southern Nicaragua, both regions that Kelton had assigned to US contractors during the war. In those places, the road was often little more than a ten-foot-wide, partly cleared dirt path with only temporary bridgework at river crossings.

But other parts of the route, including large stretches in El Salvador and central Nicaragua, featured modern surfacing, permanent bridges, and broad clearances throughout.[85]

The tour concluded when the group reached the southern terminus of the Mexican railroad system. In total, the six congressmen from the Roads Committee had spent nearly two weeks inspecting the Inter-American Highway. They had seen firsthand the exceptional challenges overcome in constructing a road through the tropics. They had felt the heat of the jungle. For a majority of them, the time in Central America brought newfound respect for the project. One of the congressmen declared on the House floor soon after the trip,

> If the construction of the highway is not delayed by lack of funds or political difficulties, it can be completed within three years. I am favorably impressed with the work that has been done, and I believe the Public Roads Administration has, in general, done an excellent job.... We must do our share. We desire the cooperation and friendship of our neighbor. But true friendship sometimes consists of a hand extended to assist in self-help.

That April, the Roads Committee formally recommended approval of the $25 million appropriation request.[86]

Despite this endorsement, MacDonald urged that the appropriation be delayed further. Little congressional action, he felt, seemed likely with an active Senate investigation still under way. Moreover, talks had recently begun to contract out the difficult remaining Costa Rica portion of the road to "Subway" Sam Rosoff, a legendary and controversial builder who had worked on New York City's underground transportation system. Rosoff had offered to build the road and fund part of its construction if Costa Rica would agree to give him a large tract of land along the new highway for a proposed settlement of Jewish refugees. Rosoff's proposal had the potential to substantially reduce the cost remaining to the US government for completing the Inter-American Highway, though the State Department confidentially believed it "most improbable that the Costa Rican government would be interested." The small chance of success was nonetheless sufficient for MacDonald, who hoped that Rosoff's contribution would lower the overall budget enough to soften congressional resistance to new appropriations.[87]

In August, four months after the House Roads Committee endorsed the $25 million appropriation, the Mead Committee embarked on its own inspection of the Inter-American Highway. The subsequent trip followed the same general route that the House members had taken, but this time the senators also had to contend with a rainier climate, which worsened the condition of the roads and made some river crossings especially difficult. For Ferguson, the road's sharpest critic, the rough going only hardened his conviction that millions had been wasted. The *Chicago Daily Tribune* quoted

Ferguson during the trip as insisting that the road would require "plenty of explanation." The article further noted, "He said that at one place the road was so bad they actually 'wore out one jeep and had to take another.' [I]n Panama the party had come to one place where the highway ran into a mountainside and ended there. Elsewhere, he said, there appeared to be little or no relation between the road sections and it seemed difficult to figure out what purposes of defense they could have served."[88]

Following the trip, the Mead Committee held a second round of hearings. The new session drew from a much broader pool of witnesses, not only generals, but also contractors, Public Roads Administration officials, and Army Corps engineers.

The questioning began with Kelton, who had recently retired from the army. Kelton insisted that he was just trying to follow orders and could not be held responsible for the pioneer road's failings. At one point, he declared, "I received so many impossible directives during this war that it becomes the ordinary thing." In response, Ferguson asked, "[You] claim because you did not have the right to make the decisions that you are not to be criticized, that you were just following an order?"[89]

Ferguson's wrath next fell on several of the contractors. He seemed convinced that only outright fraud could explain their meager results in Central America. The contractors, however, insisted that they had acted patriotically under difficult circumstances. One of the project managers explained in frustration,

If you recall, we started with the jungle. We had to start off building our own shops. We got not one board foot of lumber from this country. We had to fly in sawmills, saw out our own lumber to build our shops. While that was going on we had some equipment down that was very difficult to maintain. By the time we built a shop one place the equipment would be down the road working somewhere else and we had to go through the same procedure.[90]

After berating the contractors for several hours, the Mead Committee turned to General Gross, Somervell's chief of transportation. Gross had been instrumental in getting the pioneer road project started, but under interrogation he confessed that he had never felt that the initiative served a strategic defense purpose aside from its general impact on goodwill. Gross's account nonetheless conflicted with one soon given by the diplomat Cabot, who testified that military defense had been his chief motivation for promoting the road. In response to this assertion, the Mead Committee's lead counsel declared, "Mr. Cabot, your statements now seem to leave the impression—I want to be sure that it is correct, as it goes into our record—that the State Department was concerned only about military advantages, whereas the War Department seems to have been concerned only with diplomatic advantage." None of the men facing the Mead Committee had a satisfactory rejoinder to this observation.[91]

Following Cabot's testimony, the committee brought in Edwin Warley James. The veteran engineer began his session with a cool demeanor, but eventually the committee's questions started to rattle him, and he struggled to explain why his estimations had fluctuated so much. During the interrogation, Ferguson scolded James,

> So it was represented to Congress we could build it for $30,000,000 and then the standards were changed. . . . [Y]ou obtained an appropriation for a certain standard of road, and then you did not build that road. You built one that will cost many, many times as much. And that is where we are today. That is what we will face in Congress, as in the past, but you have to keep your agreement. You started the road. You can't stop. That is why we are always in trouble.

James offered no response to this reproach.[92]

The committee members also demanded to know why there had not been better cooperation between the Public Roads Administration and the army. Neither Kelton nor James had satisfactory answers. They feuded over the reasons behind the route changes, over the projected timelines that guided the project, and over the fact that Kelton gave away millions in equipment to Central American governments instead of to the Public Roads Administration. Their back-and-forth led Ferguson to state, "In other words, there was a war (and we will not pass on who is to blame) between the Public Roads Administration and the Army as far as the erection of this road was concerned."[93]

After four days of hearings, the committee adjourned to review its findings and start preparing a summary report. Ferguson informed the press later that fall,

> The highway is a monumental $140,000,000 blunder and the Public Roads Administration should stop construction on it immediately. . . . For a combination of sheer extravagance, stupidity and blundering, this

highway project is without precedent in the waste of the taxpayers' dollars.... Despite all this expense, despite twelve years of work, and the intervention of the War Department to get it completed in 1942–1943, you still can't get in an automobile at Laredo, Texas, and drive to Panama City. There are gaps all along the way. At one point in Costa Rica the road ends with a gap of 110 miles of jungle.... It is time that we quit playing Santa Claus over this highway.[94]

The Mead Committee held its last hearing in March 1947. The main witness for this concluding round of questions was Thomas MacDonald. During his testimony, MacDonald attempted to explain his agency's suspect estimates, but nothing he said seemed to appease Ferguson, who mounted an interrogation for several hours. Following the hearing, one State Department official noted to a superior,

The record will disclose that Mr. MacDonald made a very poor showing. The senators were "out with hatchets" and openly and frankly told Mr. MacDonald that he might as well answer forthright (which he definitely was not doing) for the Committee was determined to get the facts of the situation. The attitude of the investigators all morning was one of conviction that they had something on [the Public Roads Administration].[95]

The Mead Committee finally released its formal report on the Inter-American Highway four months later, in early July 1947. The report opened bluntly, declaring, "The War Department should not have undertaken construction on the so-called Inter-American Highway in Central America as a war project. Thirty-six million dollars were added to the cost of World War II without contributing to the defense of the United States." Despite the strong introductory language, the report refrained from accusing anyone of outright fraud or gross incompetence. Kelton, James, MacDonald, Cabot, and Gross had all escaped formal censure. The report even included a measured endorsement of the highway as an ongoing aid project, noting, "if such a highway is to be built in the interest of the economic development of the American continents, to strengthen the commercial and political ties between the American nations and to promote the security and defenses of this hemisphere, then the committee believes that the manner in which this highway project is conceived and executed should be ... calculated to achieve the objectives stated."[96]

For all Ferguson's bluster, he had ultimately failed to find any concrete charges to lay against the Inter-American Highway program, and his luck had been little better with the investigations into the Alcan Highway and Canol Pipeline. The *Atlanta Constitution* noted in August 1947, shortly after the Inter-American Highway report appeared,

> Sen. Homer Ferguson, of Michigan, the ambling, awkward, bumbling Chairman of the Senate War Investigating Subcommittee, has turned out to be about the biggest flop as a public official Washington has seen in a long time. . . . He may have been a successful investigator of petty graft as a county court judge in Detroit. But here the situation is different. He now has to deal with smarter men and bigger issues. He is not the first man who has failed to measure up to his advance billing.[97]

By the time the Mead Committee closed its inquiry into the Inter-American Highway, the other governmental investigations had all concluded as well. None found criminal or civil wrongdoing. The scandal that the Lewis broadcasts prompted had finally run its course, but along the way much damage had been done to the reputation of the Inter-American Highway project. Many in Congress now saw the road as a boondoggle.[98]

The United States, however, would soon find a new strategic purpose for the road, one that overrode the lingering concerns from the scandal years. The road birthed in friendship and bolstered in war was about to become a "highway of freedom," a bulwark against the influence of international communism in the Western Hemisphere.

CHAPTER SEVEN

Freedom Road

"The Red Tide Has Touched the Western Hemisphere"

The war years had brought hemispheric cooperation to new heights, but circumstances had changed dramatically by the spring of 1948, when the Ninth Pan-American Conference convened in Bogota, Colombia. As US delegate and State Department official Sumner Welles noted, "The feeling against this country at the Bogota conference was more bitter than at any inter-American meeting since the Havana conference of 1928." The source of this bitterness was no longer intervention, as it had been at Havana, but the United States' handling of foreign aid.[1]

At the time of the Bogota conference, the United States was on the cusp of implementing the largest foreign aid project in history, a multibillion-dollar program of assistance known as the Marshall Plan. But the plan failed to include Latin America, concentrating all the resources on rebuilding Western Europe. For many Latin Americans, the total absence of aid for their region seemed an affront. They struggled to understand the reason that the Americas, which had contributed to the war effort almost without question, were now being overlooked entirely in favor of Europe. A *Chicago Tribune* reporter describing the situation wrote,

> "Why," our incredulous neighbors ask, "should the Americas be brushed off with such a diplomatic rebuff when sixteen European nations get the cream of United States productive efforts and don't have to worry about interest payments or amortization? Why won't your government lend us money to develop our commerce and industry? Aren't we a good long term financial risk? Or is the giving away of billions of dollars to Europe a better risk than helping Latin America?"[2]

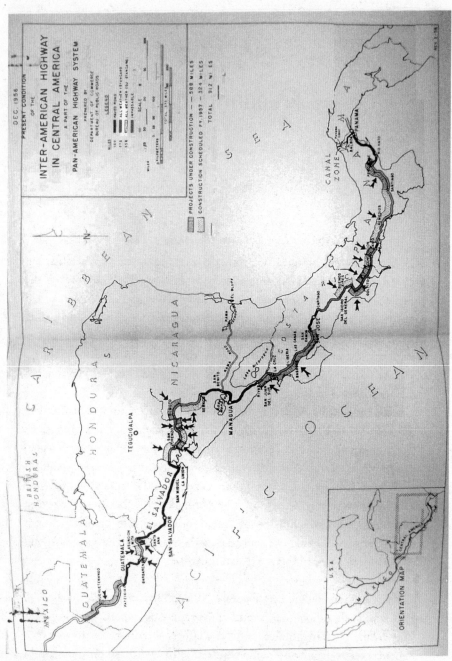

A map from 1956 showing the "present condition" of the Inter-American Highway. Note that two wholly impassable sections still remained, one in northern Guatemala and one at the Costa Rica–Panama border.

The Truman administration hoped that a strong showing in Bogota might combat some of these sentiments and thus dispatched ninety-three official delegates, the largest contingent ever sent to a Pan-American Conference. At the head of the delegation was Secretary of State George Marshall, the architect of the European relief package and the man now tasked with rescuing hemispheric relations. Marshall, the former army chief of staff, was more at home among generals than diplomats, but he was prepared to endure several weeks of pomp and ceremony in order to carry out his mission. Pan-Americanism, for Marshall, was less an end in itself than a tool in a new global fight against international communism, something that had become a preoccupation of the Truman administration in the postwar years. Latin America seemed fertile territory for the "red menace," and Marshall hoped to use the conference as a way to combat it through diplomacy. Delegate Samuel Guy Inman noted on this point, "the developing break between the Free World and its former ally, Communist Russia, began to be recognized as a threat to civilization itself. . . . The Washington government thought of [the conference] as an opportunity to convince the Latin Americans that all should give their primary interest to fighting Communism."[3]

The conference arrived at a difficult time for the host city of Bogota. Inflation had wrecked the local currency, the citizenry had been suffering food shortages, and basic services were being suspended in the weeks beforehand. The economic hardships added to the unpopularity of a Conservative government that had only gained power as the result of a three-way election. The Conservatives faced additional opposition from local Communists, whose voice had strengthened as the privations endured. The responsibility of hosting a major conference threatened to overburden the city entirely. As the *Washington Post* noted, "The gravity of this drain may be inferred from a Uruguayan delegate's plea not to abuse the hospitality of Colombia by unnecessarily prolonging the discussions over [nonurgent] issues."[4]

The fragility of the city's grip on order could be felt in the atmosphere that greeted the US delegation upon its arrival. Spread among the cheering throngs were several hundred policemen, an insurance policy against a rumored Communist demonstration. While the protest never materialized, a few Communists in the crowd held up signs proclaiming Marshall a Nazi.[5]

The signs were a reminder for Marshall that Communists could be found everywhere. His intelligence briefings on the conference had already warned him that local Communists viewed Pan-Americanism as a tool of US imperialism and planned to demonstrate. Marshall barely waited for the welcoming formalities to conclude before he made his feelings on communism known. During the organizing session preceding the first plenary meeting, he took to the floor and asked for the agenda to be amended "to permit discussion of the problem of foreign-inspired subversive activities directed against the institutions and the peace and security of the American republics." Marshall added for emphasis, "I am told that this is a subject of considerable concern to the countries represented here."[6]

Marshall's chance to formally address the hemisphere came two days later, on April 1, when he gave a speech before the assembled delegates in the capitol. Early in his remarks, Marshall once more raised the subject of communism, noting, "We have encountered, as you are aware, the determined and open opposition of one group of states. If the genuine co-operation of the Soviet Union could be secured, world recovery and peace would be assured. Until such co-operation is secured, we must proceed with our own efforts."[7]

After pausing to drive this point home, Marshall turned to the topic most on the minds of the assembled delegates: foreign aid. It was Marshall's own European recovery plan, after all, that was the source of so much animosity in Latin America. Marshall refused to apologize for his nation's actions, but he pled for understanding and cooperation. The nation, he explained, was reaching the limits of its power and could not afford to provide Latin Americans the aid they sought. As he noted,

> We must face reality. Allow me to talk to you frankly regarding the tremendous problems the United States is facing. . . . [M]y people find themselves today faced with the urgent necessity of meeting staggering and inescapable responsibilities—humanitarian, political, financial, and military, all over the world—in Western Europe, in Germany and Austria, in Greece and Turkey, in the Middle East, in China, Japan and Korea. Meeting these unprecedented responsibilities has demanded tremendous drafts on our resources and imposed burdensome taxes on our people. These are heavy exactions—far heavier than seems to be realized.

The *New York Herald Tribune*, in summarizing Marshall, wrote, "The expansion of communism and threats to democracy must be stopped. Money for Latin America, when the world was on the threshold of another war, was out of the question."[8]

Marshall's words were a sobering departure from the rhetoric of the

Good Neighbor years. It indeed sounded like Latin America was no longer a US priority. Marshall nonetheless assured at the end of his speech that his nation had not forgotten its New World neighbors. He explained that President Truman was eager to share technical expertise and was about to request an increase in Export-Import Bank lending to the region.[9]

The Truman administration believed that increased lending alone might assuage its critics in Latin America. Truman had decided to pledge $500 million of potential bank loans, the same amount that Roosevelt had called for nine years earlier to widespread acclaim. Truman's official request reached Congress soon after Marshall gave his speech, and when the news arrived in Bogota, the secretary of state insisted that it be read aloud at the conference's next plenary session. Marshall, however, had badly misjudged the room. As the *New York Times* noted, "There was not a single handclap or other reaction. . . . The United States delegation had had the Truman message put into Spanish in advance so as to get the maximum effect from the reading. But the fiasco was complete, and [the delegation] sat in uncomfortable silence as the session ended." Inman, who was present for the snub, later recalled, "Latin America's *dignidad* had been wounded. . . . The United Press reported that Washington suffered 'one of the coldest and most unanimous rebuffs in the history of Pan Americanism.'"[10]

The tension between the United States and the rest of the hemisphere over economic aid threatened to overwhelm the conference. Marshall's awkward attempts at conciliation had all fallen flat. But soon the delegates would be forced to put aside their differences, for Bogota was about to explode in violence.

At 1:00 p.m. on April 9, ten days after the Ninth Pan-American Conference began, four gunshots rang out across a plaza in downtown Bogota. As the gunman tried to flee the scene, a crowd formed around the dying body of Jorge Eliécer Gaitán, the leading opposition candidate in Colombia. Anger and confusion swept the gathering masses, which only grew further as news of the assassination spread on the radio. For many in the crowds, the death of Gaitán was the final blow, the last injustice following the inflation and the food shortages and the unpopular government. Before long, the mourners turned violent, the start of a riot that would quickly spread throughout the entire city.[11]

"There is complete anarchy," observed an eyewitness reporter. "Police and troops are firing in the streets. It is a flaming, full-fledged revolt." Another witness added, "I saw mobs of men brandishing razorlike machetes, swords, clubs, pistols and rifles surging through the streets of this once-beautiful capital. I saw thousands of men, women and children sweep through shop after shop, wrecking and looting." Joining in the riots were local Communists, who sought to capitalize on the chaos. Within an hour of the riot beginning, witnesses reported a red Communist flag flying before the capitol.[12]

The Pan-American Conference was in the middle of its daily sessions within that very capitol when rioters stormed through the doors. A woman trapped inside recounted, "For 20 minutes the mob worked its destructive way through the conference headquarters, breaking furniture and typewriters. The unarmed Capitol guard did not try to stop them. Soon 100 soldiers arrived and drove out the mob with rifles and bayonets. Delegates who were still in the building and conference personnel were herded up on the third floor for protection." In the midst of the rioting, the mob encountered the president of the conference, a much-disliked member of Colombia's ruling Conservative Party. They murdered him where he stood.[13]

When the rioting finally subsided later that night, downtown Bogota was in ruins. Fires still burned on the streets. In total, more than twelve hundred people died in the violence, some shot by government troops. It was among the deadliest urban riots in history. The delegates to the Pan-American Conference, huddled back in their hotels, agreed to suspend the proceedings until further notice.[14]

In the wake of the riots, the fate of the conference initially appeared doomed. One witness wrote on April 10, "At this moment there seems to be no possibility of restoring order and continuing the ninth International Conference of American States. There is belief in every delegation that the conference is over." The *New York Times* added two days later, "There is no doubt that the uprising has already dealt a serious blow to the prestige of the Conference, and if that was one of the purposes of the instigators of the violence they have succeeded."[15]

Many in the press accepted that the conference had indeed collapsed. The influential columnist Walter Lippmann greeted news of the conference's supposed demise as an appropriate wake-up call for Latin America. As he explained,

The conference showed, so I venture to think, the United States and the Latin-American republics, despite all their traditional bonds, do not constitute a viable community in the modern world, and their problems are becoming progressively more insoluble within the confines of the Western Hemisphere.... The reason for Secretary Marshall's going to Bogota at this immensely critical moment in history was to explain in person—what should have been explained carefully and persistently during the past year to the diplomats in Washington and in the Latin American capitals—that the Western Hemisphere must take its place in the larger community of the Western world, of which the Atlantic ocean is now the inland sea.[16]

Back in Bogota, with the conference suspended, the Conservative government rushed to blame local Communists for the riots. Though the hard proof available told an ambiguous story, the government made up for the lack of evidence with conviction. The New York Herald Tribune explained,

The government contends that the Communists followed standard Communist tactics by taking advantage of the situation. There was trouble, it says, and the Communists made it worse. It says the Communists had a plan to force termination of the conference and embarrass the Colombian government. They were waiting for an opportunity, the government holds, and when Mr. Gaitan was killed they infiltrated into the mobs which formed.[17]

The anti-Communist stance taken by the Colombian government found widespread support from the US contingent at Bogota. In the words of one US delegate, "Gentlemen, the red tide has touched the Western Hemisphere. This is war as truly as if we were opposed by armed might and a physical enemy." The Hartford Courant reported, "Every top member of the United States delegation is convinced beyond reasonable doubt that the Communists incited the uprising to break up the Pan-American Conference."[18]

On April 13, four days after the riots, Marshall became the first foreign dignitary in Bogota to publicly blame communism for the mob violence that had disrupted the conference. A spokesman for the State Department recounted that "the Secretary, in many 'salty remarks,'... stated that it was 'quite ridiculous to suppose that the twenty-one American republics should even consider being intimidated by the protestations of one kind or another from Communists, or anyone else.'" Marshall, sounding more like a general than a diplomat, reportedly insisted "that this conference must go on here in Bogota or a major battle in the 'cold war' will be lost."[19]

The other delegates heeded Marshall's call and agreed to reinstate the conference soon after his exhortation. A delegate who participated in the discussions explained that the decision had been reached "to show that the Communists can't kick us out" and "demonstrate that Pan-American relationships are not at the mercy of subversion." Marshall had finally started to find the unity that had proved so elusive before the conference's suspension. As diplomat Welles observed, "Bad as it is, the revolt at Bogota may prove to be a blessing in disguise. It will probably pull us together in taking effective defense measures. And it has at least postponed the open clash between the United States and the other republics which seemed inevitable before the rebellion occurred."[20]

The conference, once it reconvened, gave newfound attention to Marshall's chief concern: anti-communism. Within days, the delegates had rushed a strongly worded resolution through committee and brought it to the general assembly. When it reached the floor, it found broad support, though some delegates cautioned that anti-communism could easily be abused by regimes seeking to silence the opposition. As one Uruguayan protested, "[I] combat Communism as a regime of violence, but not as the doctrine of a political party." These concerns ultimately could not stop the measure from passing unanimously. The *New York Herald Tribune* summarized the resolution as "stating that international communism will not be tolerated in the Western Hemisphere and that any tentacles which have grasped American soil will be torn loose."[21]

The anti-Communist resolution that Marshall had shepherded was joined by a host of landmark decrees that passed in the closing weeks of the conference. There were agreements on human rights and women's civil rights, measures taken to hasten an end of colonialism, and the formation of a new hemispheric body, the Organization of American States, to serve as a regional agency of the United Nations. One US delegate declared on April 30, the last day of the conference, "I will be glad to challenge anyone who attempts to define this Bogota Conference as anything but a magnificent success and a great achievement in the spirit of American solidarity."[22]

Despite the violence, the conference had exceeded the expectations of Marshall and other State Department officials. They knew, however, that the underlying tension over foreign aid remained. The solidarity displayed in the wake of the riots had only masked the bitterness felt over the Marshall Plan. The Truman administration was in need of goodwill projects for Latin America. And, before long, some in the State Department and Congress would land, once more, upon the Inter-American Highway.

"It Is Now Time to Do Something for Latin America"

At the time of the Ninth Pan-American Conference, US funding for the Inter-American Highway was again nearing exhaustion. The last major US government appropriation for the program had taken place in 1943. During the intervening years, MacDonald and James had stretched the funds enough to avoid a complete shutdown of work, but the project badly needed new resources. Completion, they estimated, would require another $60 million to $70 million, assuming the United States continued paying two-thirds of the total cost.

The responsibility of bringing a new request to Congress ostensibly rested with MacDonald, but he showed little interest in now doing so. Memories of the congressional investigation were still fresh, and critics such as Senator Homer Ferguson remained. Moreover, both MacDonald and James feared that a Congress preoccupied with rebuilding Europe would have little interest in a road to the canal.[23]

A different attitude, however, prevailed among a number of Latin Americanists in the State Department. For them, the impending exhaustion of US funds for the Inter-American Highway posed a potential threat to the nation's relationship with Central America and Panama, where the project remained popular. By the fall of 1948, these diplomats had decided they needed to start pressuring MacDonald to get legislation before Congress. They went so far as to send MacDonald drafts of letters addressed to the congressional Foreign Affairs Committees promising that proposed legislation would be immediately forthcoming. The letters argued,

> Now that the United States appropriations are nearly exhausted, our government is in a situation where, if we do not make available at an early date the necessary additional funds to complete the project as originally intended, we are exposing ourselves to possible accusations of bad faith.... [I]f we do not continue our cooperation until this highway is finished, the prestige and reputation of the United States government will undoubtedly suffer in Central America and probably also in the other American Republics.[24]

The State Department's attempt to force the legislation forward was nonetheless deflected by MacDonald. He simply had it conveyed that no proposal could be put forth until his Public Roads Administration compiled a new estimate. It was the fault of "recent changes in prices," which demanded that his engineers "restudy" all the budgets. Several additional months, MacDonald assured, would be needed to accomplish this work.[25]

MacDonald's answer left the State Department with little choice but to wait. The diplomats sat by patiently until April 1949, when the prospect of an end to the congressional session prompted them to once more begin coercing MacDonald. This time, MacDonald relented. At the end of April, he submitted to the respective chairs of the congressional Foreign Affairs Committees proposed legislation calling for $64 million in new funds to be spent over eight years.[26]

The committee chairs, as MacDonald had feared, showed little interest in the new proposal. Space in their legislative calendar was at a premium with the United States now operating as a global power and requiring new laws to do it. The Inter-American Highway had to compete for attention not only with the European rebuilding and defense initiatives but also with Point Four, a new, ambitious program of technical assistance for Latin America, Africa, and Asia that Truman had asked of Congress in January, partly in response to the criticisms of US foreign aid at Bogotá. Point Four shared certain goals with the Inter-American Highway, but the two programs remained distinct from one another, leaving the highway without backers powerful enough to push MacDonald's proposal through committee.[27]

Despite the proposal's bleak prospects, it represented a step forward, one that was greeted eagerly on the isthmus. Perhaps the most vocal supporter of the measure was Tomás Guardia, still the chief road builder in Panama. Guardia had never stopped championing the highway. He also desperately needed new funds for his own road department, which was on the brink of bankruptcy. The $64 million proposal offered a solution to this dilemma and a chance to realize his twenty-nine-year-old dream.[28]

Guardia soon arranged with his government to embark upon a tour of Central America to drum up support for the project. The subsequent trip, which took place in early June, helped to align the various nations behind the $64 million proposal, a development that the State Department considered "probably ill advised" on account of the ongoing resistance in Congress.[29]

At the end of June, on Guardia's urging, the ambassadors from most of the nations involved formally called on the State Department in Washington to discuss the measure. They explained that they "were anxious to have the Department help in getting legislation enacted during the present session of Congress." The State Department responded with caution, noting that Congress had before it "very full schedules, including two extremely important items of legislation—the technical assistance or Point 4 program, and the military assistance program for Europe." One of the State Department officials nonetheless suggested that the ambassadors would be well served to get confirmation from their governments on four points: the provision of funds to meet a third of the construction cost; the prohibiting of taxes, tolls, or other charges on the road; the responsibility for ongoing maintenance; and an assurance that "the highway follow the most direct and economical route, so as to keep the total cost at a minimum." [30]

The meeting in Washington ultimately generated little enthusiasm, much to Guardia's chagrin. In the ensuing months, only two governments, those of Costa Rica and Guatemala, answered the State Department's request for confirmation on the four points. Even Guardia's own country of Panama had failed to respond, a consequence of internal political dissension. Guardia, however, remained optimistic and concluded that the US Congress might still be moved to action if he organized a new Inter-American Highway Conference, one that could demonstrate Central America's eagerness to cooperate. [31]

In November 1949, Guardia traveled to Washington and met with the State Department to discuss his plan. Guardia's hope was that the United States would agree to participate in the proposed conference. Though the department was unwilling to agree to this request, calling US participation "undesirable," department representatives acknowledged that "a conference of the six other countries might help toward the construction of the highway if it would result in assurances from those respective countries of their real interest in the project and their willingness to cooperate in an effective way toward its completion." This encouragement was all that Guardia needed to move forward. Days later, Panama sent out invitations to the public works ministers of all the Central American countries for a conference "to organize joint action looking toward early completion of the Inter-American Highway." [32]

Guardia's conference finally took place six months later, in March 1950. All the Central American nations agreed to participate except for Honduras, whose absence owed to mounting anger over the fact that the Inter-American Highway's route passed through every Central American capital except Tegucigalpa. During the conference, Guardia worked to build consensus around the State Department's demands on funding, maintenance, tolls, and routing. After a day of discussion, the attendees agreed to commit their nations to everything but the promise to provide a third of the construction costs. Guardia considered the meeting a landmark success and informed the press immediately afterward, "It's time now for the United States to put its shoulder to the wheel and complete the great Inter-American Highway."[33]

By the time of the conference, the highway had found a new backer in Congress, Senator Dennis Chávez of New Mexico. Chávez, the only US senator of Hispanic descent, supported the highway in part because he felt "it is now time to do something for Latin America since we have done so much for Europe."[34]

Chávez's first public pronouncement on the highway came several days after Guardia's conference, in a speech before the annual convention of the American Road Builders Association in Cincinnati. Chávez told the audience of one hundred that the $64 million proposal was assured of "certain success" and that he would personally intervene to secure it. After his speech, a fretful State Department official noted to a colleague, "Chávez add[ed] fuel to the flames of the expectations of the Latin Americans present for further financial aid from the United States. Certainly the Senator gave not the slightest hint of the very real difficulties which lie in the way of congressional approval of the Inter-American Highway bill."[35]

The daunting odds only seemed to inspire Chávez, a master of Senate procedure. Several weeks after the Cincinnati conference, he had the $64 million proposal reintroduced as a rider to the Federal Aid Highway Act, which was overseen by the Public Works Committee, of which Chávez was the chair. The transfer placed Chávez in control of the process, and soon after gaining this authority he arranged for hearings to be held on the subject so that the State Department could make its case.[36]

The subsequent hearings centered around testimony from Edward G. Miller, the assistant secretary of state for Inter-American Affairs. Miller had grown convinced of the highway's importance during a trip to Costa Rica and Panama the previous year and had become the department's lead spokesman for the road in the interim. It was Miller, in fact, who had first recruited Chávez for the project. Miller, in anticipation of the hearings, had prepared a lengthy list of reasons to support the highway beginning with "Because it is the announced intention of this Government to build a through road. This intention has been repeatedly expressed by the President, by the Secretary of State, and by Members of Congress." For Miller, there was little doubt that building the highway was settled policy of the United States, though he also insisted that its completion was necessary as a means to preserve goodwill abroad, noting, "There is no single matter in our relations with the six countries concerned which has a higher priority from their point of view."[37]

Miller's testimony left the Senate Public Works Committee divided. Chávez wanted immediate action, but some members still held reservations about spending public works funding abroad. The debate dragged out through the summer, until Chávez agreed to reduce the terms from a total of $64 million over eight years to $16 million over four years. The decision meant that the road would lack a meaningful timetable for completion, but $16 million was better than nothing, and Congress had been tightening expenditures as a result of the Korean War.[38]

By this point, Chávez had managed to build broad support for the measure in the House and Senate, both of which voted to approve the $16 million proposal in the final week of August. Miller wrote to a colleague shortly after the announcement, "Even regardless of the Korean situation we feel Senator Chávez has achieved a real personal victory getting the Highway proposal through Congress. . . . What should be emphasized is the positive advantage of having gotten as much as we have." Miller had even kinder words for Chávez directly, noting in a letter, "At the beginning of this session I did not think that we had very much of a chance of getting anything for the Highway and I am elated that we have done as well as we have. To me this is the most important thing that we can do in Central America and I deeply appreciate everything that you have done."[39]

But not everyone greeted the news as enthusiastically as Miller. Leaders across Central America were disappointed that the final bill was only a fourth the size of the original proposal. Among the critics was Nicaraguan dictator Anastasio Somoza, who played to US fears of Communist infiltration in his remarks on the subject. Somoza observed,

> The sum of sixteen million dollars is really very limited . . . if the Pan-American Highway is expected to be finished with a minimum of delay in view of the grave threat which hangs over the Continent—a threat which not only makes imperative a line of very close cooperation with the United States of America, but also an effective material contact with that country. No one now doubts that communism is invading

America, more every day, in the hidden manner which is characteristic of its tactics; in the meantime, interest in cutting down geographic distances on the Continent seems to have fallen off.[40]

Like Somoza, Miller was also beginning to see the highway as a potential tool in the Cold War. The diplomat started introducing references to communism in memos on the road written during the months in which the House Appropriations Committee debated when to release the first $4 million annual allotment of the new $16 million program. A November memorandum that Miller wrote noted,

> The outbreak of the Korean crisis has emphasized the need for a careful reassessment of the Latin American position with regard to the United States.... There is an important need for a positive United States program to demonstrate that the United States really has an interest in helping Latin America to improve their economies—to demonstrate that the Communists and other anti-United States elements are not correct when they assert the United States seeks only to exploit Latin America as "economic colonies" and to drain off their natural resources.

In December, before the House Appropriations Committee, Miller insisted further, "[The Inter-American Highway will] increase the ability of these countries ... to successfully resist the aggression of international communism." The month after Miller gave this testimony, the House Appropriations Committee finally released the first $4 million allotment.[41]

It had been a difficult two-year campaign to get new funds. The efforts of Guardia, Chávez, and Miller had kept support for the project alive, but the new appropriation only represented a small fraction of the outstanding budget. Completion seemed a long way off. It would not be funding alone, however, that kept the road from progressing in the short term. The highway that Miller thought could be a tool to help fight communism was instead about to become a hostage of Cold War diplomacy in Guatemala.

Trouble at the Selegua Gap

When the appropriation arrived, engineer Edwin Warley James was preoccupied with a problem that had arisen over the Inter-American Highway's route in northern Guatemala. He had already helped build the road there once, to a point on the Suchiate River that intersected with Mexico's National Railways line, but that road lay some fifty miles away from the newly completed southern terminus of the Inter-American Highway in Mexico, which had been rerouted inland during the mid-1940s to avoid competition with the National Railways. In rerouting the road, Mexico had placed the burden of completion back on Guatemala and also, indirectly, on James. The veteran engineer now considered this "Guatemala gap" his "top priority." It was all that stood between automobile through traffic from the United States to Costa Rica, twenty-five hundred miles away.[42]

The distance involved in closing the gap was not especially great, but the required engineering made it a major undertaking. Surveys had revealed that the only practical way to link the two road systems necessitated building for twenty-five miles through the valley of Guatemala's Selegua River, where narrow canyons and loose volcanic rock fields promised nightmarish construction. On a per mile basis, the amount of excavation the job demanded would rival what had taken place at Cerro de la Muerte in Costa Rica. "The [Selegua] canyon is deep," noted an article in *Popular Science* magazine, "but the marsh of international politics into which hopes for the road have sunk at this point is far deeper."[43]

The month after the new funds were appropriated, James traveled to Guatemala to study the problem on the ground. While there, he was unexpectedly brought into contact with a well-respected Mexican contractor who offered to build the Selegua section in less than a year for $3.6 million. The bid undercut James's own estimates by several million and made the project suddenly affordable within the annual budget that Congress had granted. James told the Guatemalan foreign minister before the trip concluded, "In view of the extremely favorable circumstances that now exist for closing the 25 mile gap in the Selegua valley, it is possible that a large portion of the $4,000,000 appropriation for the highway may be spent in Guatemala."[44]

Upon returning from his trip, James met with the State Department to discuss the new appropriation. The State Department initially proposed that the $4 million be spread widely among all the countries to maximize its geographic and political impact, but James impressed upon them the merits of conquering Selegua. If they failed to act, he assured, they risked losing the Mexican contractor and the price might climb again. One State Department official noted of James's appeal, "[We became] convinced that this was the most important single thing we could do on the Highway as a whole." Before the meeting ended, the men had agreed that the United States would prioritize funding for the Selegua Gap.[45]

The State Department's agreement on Selegua, however, had come with a caveat, one that had to do with the political situation in Guatemala. A new Guatemalan president, thirty-seven-year-old Jacobo Arbenz, had just been elected, and the State Department was unsure whether he was an ally or enemy in the fight against communism, a struggle that had only grown more paranoid in the three years since Marshall's appearance at Bogota. The department had already lost faith in Arbenz's predecessor and political ally Juan José Arévalo, a leftist politician who had gained power following a 1944 democratic revolution. Arévalo's greatest sin, for many in the State Department, was his maligning of United Fruit and its subsidiary the International Railways of Central America, two entities that Arévalo contended were suffocating his country through their control of land, labor, and transportation. It was an understandable complaint given the depth of US corporate control in Guatemala, but the State Department largely refused to see Arévalo's attacks on United Fruit and the International Railways of Central America as anything less than a Communist plot to destroy private capital. Department officials hoped that the newly elected Arbenz would reverse this trend, though they remained skeptical. As the State Department noted to James, "should the new administration prove to be far more radical than the present one, it might be necessary to revise this [highway funding]."[46]

The Arbenz administration, for its part, assumed that it was negotiating in good faith with the United States over Selegua. Arbenz himself was eager to complete the project, feeling that it would help Guatemala escape the transportation monopoly of the International Railways of Central America. In May 1951, two months after James met with the State Department, Guatemala informed department officials that it looked favorably upon the project and only had several reservations that could hopefully be dealt with easily. The greatest concern was the United States' cooperative requirement that Guatemala contribute a third of the cost, an amount the Arbenz administration felt its budget could not handle. The Arbenz administration also pointed out that Guatemalan labor laws would not allow a governmental project to use large amounts of foreign workers, something that seemed unavoidable should a Mexican contractor be employed. Once these matters were dealt with, Guatemala suggested, the work could proceed apace.[47]

By this point, the State Department was beginning to second-guess its decision to provide highway funds for Guatemala. The hoped-for warming of relations with Arbenz had failed to materialize, and department officials were considering a move to suspend the release of highway money in response. On May 14, the week after the Guatemalan appeal, the department informed James that they were leaning toward delaying the Selegua funds "in order to attain the maximum possible political advantage and leverage from [their] use." James and MacDonald protested, but their efforts only managed to get the department to agree to review the situation later that summer.[48]

The months that followed, however, saw the State Department's view harden further. It helped that United Fruit had undertaken a propaganda war to paint Arbenz as a Communist and had successfully enlisted the aid of many reporters. But there were troubling signs on the ground as well, including widespread anti-Communist riots that gripped the capital in early July and led to several deaths.[49]

During this period, the Arbenz regime continued to believe that negotiations over Selegua remained open. In August, an Arbenz representative made a revised appeal to the State Department in which Guatemala agreed to provide its one-third portion of the funding if the United States withdrew the provision allowing for the use of foreign labor. It was a good faith effort to advance the project but one that left the State Department wholly unmoved. A cynical State Department official noted in an internal memo summarizing the Guatemalan offer, "The decision has been made not to go ahead with any work in Guatemala for the time being for political reasons so it is to our advantage to keep the negotiations going."[50]

Guatemala only began to suspect that something was amiss later that month, when a US official from the Bureau of Public Roads (formerly the Public Roads Administration) let it slip that the State Department was planning to redistribute the funds earmarked for Selegua to other Central American countries. The news shocked the Arbenz administration and left them facing sharp criticism from within Guatemala for their failure to reach an agreement. The Guatemalan paper *El Impacto* declared, "The withdrawal is due to pure negligence on the part of the Guatemalan directors of the work.... Needless to say we have failed to take advantage of the benefits offered by North America ..., especially since the democracy of the north was determined to lend assistance in the construction of projects of definite utility for the use of the peoples of Latin America."[51]

The revelation about the Selegua funds left the Arbenz administration unsure how to proceed. The issue lay fallow for the better part of a year before Guatemala finally attempted to reopen negotiations through its newly appointed ambassador to the United States, Guillermo Toriello. In September 1952, Toriello met with the State Department and explained that negotiations over Selegua had been "very much mishandled" and were "unfortunately misunderstood." Not only was his government willing to contribute its one-third portion, he declared, it was now even amenable to allowing the foreign worker clause in the contract.[52]

Further evidence of Arbenz's desire to cooperate came several weeks later at a ceremony to dedicate a new stretch of paved highway in southern Guatemala. Arbenz had invited the US ambassador to Guatemala and used the ceremony to impress upon him Guatemala's commitment to working with the United States. The ambassador noted of the ceremony,

> [T]here was no note that could have jarred on an American ear but on the contrary, the speeches gave full recognition to the contribution of the United States to the development and financing of the Pan American Highway.... [T]his is the first instance in my 18 months here that the Guatemalan Government has made openly friendly public statements toward the United States, has broadcast them over the Guatemalan radio network and has publicized them in the Guatemalan press.[53]

The Guatemalan campaign to pressure the United States continued throughout the fall with Toriello repeatedly raising the issue before the State Department. But his efforts amounted to little aside from excuses. At first, the State Department placed blame for the delay with Congress. Department officials noted that Congress had decided to reduce the 1952 appropriation to only $1 million, an amount insufficient for the Selegua job. When that explanation failed to satisfy Guatemala, they attributed the inaction to the presidency. General Dwight D. Eisenhower, they explained, had just been elected president and needed a chance to review US foreign policy before embarking on any new projects. One State Department official noted of a November conversation with an Arbenz representative, "I replied that the present time was not especially propitious for negotiations.... As he well knew, the election period in any country is always a difficult time."[54]

In December, a frustrated Toriello brought his campaign directly to the Guatemalan press. Speaking before a throng of reporters, he made no mention of the State Department's reluctance to negotiate and assured that an agreement had been reached over Selegua. The State Department's report on the event noted, "[The] announcement . . . has been generally interpreted by the press, apparently following 'off the record' statements by Guatemalan officials as meaning that United States financial assistance for the completion of the Highway is now assured."[55]

Toriello's bold move nonetheless had little impact on the State Department in the short term. The majority of the department continued to view Arbenz as a potential Communist regardless of his appeals for cooperation. Arbenz, many felt, had shown his hand the year prior with the issuance of a land reform law that had faced manic opposition from United Fruit. Despite Arbenz's repeated assertions that he was not, in fact, a Communist, the State Department subscribed to the radical image of him pushed by the banana company. In January 1953, diplomat John Cabot, himself related to a United Fruit executive, told the vice president of the AAA, "given the present character of the Communist-dominated Government of Guatemala, the Department of State [is] not prepared to support any expenditures of funds for highway construction in that country."[56]

The department's resolve only stiffened with the arrival of Eisenhower's new secretary of state, John Foster Dulles, an anti-Communist crusader almost on a par with his contemporary Senator Joseph McCarthy. Dulles also had close ties to United Fruit—the lead sponsor of anti-Arbenz propaganda—through former business dealings and through his brother Allen, who had sat on the company's board and had recently been appointed director of the Central Intelligence Agency (CIA).[57]

The State Department's hard line on Selegua overwhelmed any resistance put forth by the Bureau of Public Roads. Both James and MacDonald, at this point, were over seventy years old and more focused on retirement than on interdepartmental squabbling. Shortly after Eisenhower's inauguration, MacDonald formally announced his intention to step down effective April 1, drawing to an end his thirty-four-year reign as chief. James followed MacDonald into retirement six months later. He had given more than forty years to the bureau and looked forward to a quieter life of reading history books and enjoying time in his DC home with his wife, Ethel. In July, James wrote appreciatively to MacDonald, "I wish to thank you especially for the unusual opportunity which you made it possible for me to take in entering the field of foreign work. . . . I naturally and rather logically went into the Inter-American Highway project in 1930 and I realize now what a wonderful opportunity it has been both professionally and intellectually."[58]

By the time James departed the scene, the United States' opposition to Arbenz was entering a new, far more serious phase. The State Department's policy of denying highway funds for Guatemala had failed to satisfy Secretary Dulles, who painted Arbenz as the single greatest threat to hemispheric security and argued that the only solution was to force his removal by covertly backing a coup d'état. It was a radical proposal but one that fit the feverish anti-Communist paranoia of the Eisenhower administration. Eisenhower had already shown a willingness to use covert force several months earlier when he authorized the CIA to carry out a coup against a left-leaning regime in Iran that was attempting to nationalize that nation's oil reserves. The success of that operation helped convince the president that covert tactics worked more effectively than diplomacy, and in August 1953, after a short discussion, the Eisenhower administration officially decided to move against Arbenz. As one administration official noted, "A word from one [Dulles] to the other substituted for weeks of inter- and intra-agency debate."[59]

The plot to depose Arbenz gradually took shape over the next eleven months. The CIA recruited a member of the Guatemalan military, Carlos Castillo Armas, to serve as the "liberator" and began funneling weapons and equipment to him at a base camp in Honduras. The long-planned attack finally commenced on June 18, 1954, when two CIA-funded planes started bombing targets in the capital. The CIA supported these sorties with a massive radio campaign assuring that an army of liberation was soon to march on Guatemala City. Arbenz tried to hold out, but the CIA propaganda left him unsure of the rebellion's true size and he struggled to rally his generals. After nine days of attacks, Arbenz took to the radio at 9:15 a.m. on June 27 to announce his resignation, declaring,

> Workers, peasants, patriots, my friends: people of Guatemala: Guatemala is enduring a most difficult trial. . . . The United Fruit Company, in collaboration with the governing circles of the United States, is responsible for what is happening to us. . . . They have used the pretext of anti-communism. The truth is very different. The truth is to be found in the financial interests of the fruit company and the other U.S. monopolies which have invested great amounts of money in Latin America. . . . After reflecting with a clear revolutionary conscience, I have made a decision that is of great importance for our country in the hope of containing this aggression and bringing peace back to Guatemala. . . . I say goodbye to you, my friends, with bitterness and pain, but remaining firm in my convictions.[60]

Once Arbenz resigned, the United States moved quickly to install Castillo Armas as the new president. The ten-year-old revolution that had brought Guatemala democratic leadership for the first time had been snuffed out, but the Eisenhower administration considered its covert operation a runaway success. Vice President Richard Nixon declared in early July, "[E]very Communist dictator sleeps less easily now [since the Guatemalan people] rose to throw off the Communist regime there. It is the first time in history that communism has received such a setback."[61]

Despite such public confidence, the Eisenhower administration feared that the new Guatemalan regime would require support to survive. They hoped to bolster Castillo Armas through generous foreign aid, and almost immediately attention landed on the nation's oldest development project: the Inter-American Highway. The State Department reopened discussions over Selegua the week after Castillo Armas assumed the presidency and carried them on throughout the fall. Finally, in mid-November, after a delay of more than three years, the two nations signed the long-overdue agreement to close the Selegua Gap.[62]

The coup's impact on the Inter-American Highway, however, extended beyond Selegua. It had also set in motion a chain of events that would lead the United States to recommit itself to completing the great road, once and for all.

The Final Push

Following the coup, the Eisenhower administration decided that it needed to make a public display of support for the new Guatemalan regime. Eisenhower and Dulles thus concluded in the fall of 1954 that Vice President Richard Nixon should embark upon a goodwill tour of Central America and the Caribbean to generate positive media coverage. In announcing the tour, scheduled for early February 1955, the *New York Herald Tribune* noted, "The United States Information Agency will carry the story of the Vice-President's trip to the free world and penetrate the Iron Curtain with it by means of press, radio, and motion pictures."[63]

The tour, as originally conceived, had little to do with the Inter-American Highway, but that soon changed thanks to Robert Woodward, the US ambassador to Costa Rica. Woodward had arrived at his post the year prior and had grown convinced that rapid completion of the highway was "the one action that the United States Government can take in Central America that will probably have the most far-reaching, the most beneficial, and the most mutually advantageous effects" on the region. Nixon's upcoming trip, Woodward felt, offered a unique opportunity to get the Eisenhower administration focused on this goal.[64]

Woodward began his promotional mission in mid-January 1955 with the drafting of a fourteen-page memorandum that laid out his thoughts on the Inter-American Highway. "It may be no exaggeration," he opened, "to state that nowhere in our foreign relations may we be able to gain so much so easily." Woodward dismissed as insufficient the current approach in Congress, which had continued to appropriate funds but only several million per year. As he noted, "At the rate this work has been budgeted for since 1950, it could be fifteen years or more before the highway is completed—despite the comparatively small amount left to be done." Woodward urged completion within three years.[65]

The ambassador marshaled a host of arguments to justify this goal, starting with the road's "ideological influence" on the region. Like Miller and Somoza four years earlier, Woodward had come to view the road as a key tool in the prosecution of the Cold War. "I am convinced," he wrote, "that [its] influence on the populations of Central America will work powerfully against the possibility of Communism ever getting a foothold again in this part of the world. . . . It is not impossible that this artery of influence could have been the factor to tip the scales away from Communism in the population of Guatemala—so paradoxically isolated while geographically close to the United States."[66]

Woodward's memo served as the opening salvo in a campaign that he carried out over the next several weeks to raise interest among his diplomatic colleagues on the isthmus. He had the memo sent to all the US embassies in the region and followed this up with personal letters to each US ambassador, begging their cooperation. Concerted action, he urged, "would be a very fine prelude to the visit by Vice President Nixon." Soon Woodward managed to align the entire diplomatic corps behind the goal of a completed Inter-American Highway within three years.[67]

When Nixon arrived in Guatemala on February 12 to begin his trip, he was inundated with pleas to push work on the highway. Woodward's memo seemed to be what everyone wanted to talk about. The appeals strongly impressed Nixon, who telegrammed Secretary Dulles from Guatemala that he was "exceedingly interested" in finishing the road. One State Department official who traveled with Nixon wrote Woodward from Guatemala, "I have the impression that he will be most insistent that steps be taken quickly to encourage the Congress to appropriate funds promptly."[68]

The campaign to enlist Nixon's support for the highway only intensified as he continued his journey south through Central America. Nearly every diplomat and official he encountered sang the praises of the road. As Nixon later observed, "Each of the Chiefs of State of the countries I have visited and each of our Ambassadors have emphasized that the Inter-American Highway, once completed, would make a greater contribution to the overall welfare of these individual nations than any other single thing the United States could do."[69]

This sustained lobbying left Nixon thoroughly convinced about the soundness of Woodward's plan by the time he reached Panama. He finally went public with his support on February 26 before a gathering of reporters in Panama City. He declared, "The present program for United States participation in the construction of the Pan American Highway is inadequate, uneconomical, and completely unrealistic. . . . There is no question about United States policy with regard to the highway. . . . Since the United States is committed to contribute its share of the cost of the highway eventually, we should move up the completion date." Nixon, like Woodward, framed the situation within the context of the Cold War, explaining, "Through an improved mutual understanding and increased economic activity many of the conditions which communism has exploited in Central America in the past would be eliminated." Following his remarks to the Panamanian press, Nixon cabled Dulles to have a request "prepared immediately to accomplish the objective of completing the highway within three years."[70]

Nixon's directive received prompt attention back in Washington. Officials from the State Department began holding meetings with the Bureau of Public Roads and the Export-Import Bank to respond to Nixon's "very anxious" appeal. The Bureau of Public Roads rushed to prepare a new estimate for an accelerated program and concluded in early March that "such a program will cost $112,000,000 of which $75,000,000 will have to be appropriated by the Congress on the usual two to one [terms]." Soon legislation calling for a $75 million appropriation over three years was put together on an "urgent basis." Upon receiving the legislation, Dulles offered his "complete support and cooperation," noting that the road would above all serve as a tool in fighting communism. As he explained to the secretary of commerce, "We must not fail to exert our every effort to see that communism does not return to the Americas. . . . The political stability resulting from early completion of the Inter-American Highway would increase the growing influence which these Central American countries and the other republics of this hemisphere are now exerting in world affairs."[71]

The draft legislation, on Nixon's urging, was next sent to President Eisenhower for review. Eisenhower had once strongly opposed the pioneer road when the rationale for its completion was hemispheric defense, but now that the Inter-American Highway was packaged as a tool to combat communism, his objections disappeared. The president had also become a huge booster of domestic highway construction generally, having called on Congress the year prior to fund a massive new network of federal aid roads, soon to be known as the Interstate System. The $75 million Inter-American Highway proposal won over Eisenhower so completely that he decided to lend it his personal support. On March 31, he issued a public letter to Speaker of the House Sam Rayburn that declared,

> I believe this would be the most significant single action the United States can take in Central America and Panama to bring about the most mutually advantageous results. . . . The stabilizing effect of [the road] will tend to bar any possible return of communism which was so recently and successfully defeated in this area. . . . I trust that Congress will give this proposal for accelerated completion of the Inter-American Highway its most favorable consideration.[72]

The publication of Eisenhower's letter pushed the Inter-American Highway back into the forefront of national politics for the first time since the postwar scandal. The *New York Herald Tribune* declared, "President Eisenhower's request . . . deserves speedy and whole hearted approval. . . . In an era of technical progress such as ours, it seems rather strange that an all-weather highway linking the American nations should not have come sooner." A retired Edwin Warley James wrote admiringly to Eisenhower in early April, "your recommendation of support . . . is just what has been needed for so long."[73]

The $75 million proposal quickly found broad backing from a Congress worried about the spread of communism. Representative Frank Bow of Ohio captured these sentiments when he declared on the House floor, "The highway, whose completion the President is strongly urging, will draw together the peoples of Central America. Through personal contact they will be able to spot more quickly subversive activities taking place. They will also be able to act in concert to defeat that force of evil which is international communism." Among those now praising the road's anti-Communist potential was longtime Inter-American Highway supporter Senator Dennis Chávez. His Public Works Committee report on the legislation noted, "[A]ccelerated construction of this highway will result in general development of stronger, more independent, and more durable economies in these countries. . . . It should follow that strengthened economies would result in higher living standards which is generally recognized as a strong safeguard against subversive influences."[74]

The anti-Communist crusaders joined with those preaching Pan-Americanism and easily carried the day against the critics who remembered when the road was considered a wartime boondoggle. The measure passed the House in June by a vote of 353 to 13. Senate approval came soon thereafter. And on July 1, barely three months since the legislative campaign began, the president signed the measure into law. After years of waffling, the United States had finally committed itself to complete the Inter-American Highway.[75]

But Eisenhower was not quite through with the road. The month after the legislation passed, he signed a treaty with Panama that pledged $20 million for the United States to build a permanent bridge over the canal as part of the Inter-American Highway. The treaty finally answered the grievance that Panama had raised at the original Inter-American Highway Conference of 1929. In consequence, by late summer 1955, the United States was poised to finish the road not just to the canal, but all the way to Panama City.[76]

The Bureau of Public Roads had little room for error or delay if the three-year completion deadline was to be met. As one federal engineer explained, "when the accelerated construction program began . . . [only] 548 miles [of 1,573] were completed to a paved surface status. This meant that construction work of one type or another was required on the remaining 1,025 miles, [of which] 769 miles required grading and drainage." Contained within this distance were also two wholly impassable sections: the 25-mile Selegua Gap in Guatemala, and a 110-mile gap in southern Costa Rica below San Isidro.[77]

Work was supposed to commence once the rains receded in November, but when the date arrived, the bureau found itself still awaiting the consent of Costa Rica, where the largest amount of construction remained. The delay owed to a group of Costa Rican congressmen who refused to approve a $10 million loan that the Export-Import Bank had granted for Costa Rica's one-third share of construction costs. The loan controversy dragged on for several months, until President José Figueres personally intervened. A witness to Figueres's act noted, "The President pointed out that the United States would pay for two thirds of the cost of the project and was providing the loan for the remaining one third. He observed that when 'a horse is a gift, one doesn't examine it down to the teeth.' . . . He noted that while the highway would benefit all the Americas, Costa Rica needed it even more than the United States." Costa Rica's consent finally arrived in mid-February, by which point more than half of the dry season had already passed.[78]

Much of the bureau's resources during that dry season went to the effort to close the Selegua Gap. Construction had started there in mid-1955 and had quickly proved overwhelming for the inexperienced bureau officers, most of whom were new to the job since James's retirement. As one engineer observed, "This is a much younger country and the geological formations are different than we are experiencing in most parts of the United States." An inspector who toured the site noted, "The construction of the road has been extremely difficult owing to the precipitous slopes of rock beds that prevail and the presence along the walls of the canyon of grand accumulations of rubble—deposits that are predisposed to slide . . . when their natural slopes are oversteepened by the excavation for the highway."[79]

The bureau's challenges with Selegua only deepened upon arrival of the rainy season. The worst rainstorms could set off slides that reached 100,000 cubic yards in mass, a small mountain of debris. Before the rainy season concluded, the bureau had recorded twenty major slides at Selegua, and several men had died. A March 1957 report on the region noted, "Approximately 800,000 cubic meters of material have been removed as a result of landslides and a conservative estimate, without the advantage of measurement, indicates that an additional volume of 500,000 to 800,000 cubic meters still needs to be removed in order to stabilize the existing slides. . . . Carrying this out under the prevailing conditions will be expensive and dangerous."[80]

By mid-1957, the bureau was far behind schedule and finding prices to be rising faster than expected. Federal engineers estimated that it would require another $10 million on top of the $75 million already authorized. In June, the bureau decided to submit draft legislation calling for this supplemental amount. The letter accompanying the legislation attributed the budget increase simply to "substantial and unpredictable rises in construction costs." After twenty-five years of operating in Central America, the bureau still could not produce a reliable estimate.[81]

The legislation finally reached the House floor nine months later. The coalition that had championed the road in 1955 came back together to support this supplemental bill. They put forward a range of well-worn arguments, old appeals to hemispheric unity, though the conversation ended up passing once more to the road's anti-Communist influence. In the words of Representative Jim Wright of Texas,

It must be remembered, Mr. Chairman, that this narrow but extremely critical connection between the great American land masses is under constant pressure from the Communists and political adventurers, both domestic and foreign. Nothing would be more pleasing to the Kremlin than to gain a foothold in this hemisphere. No area in the New World affords such a vulnerable lure as these undeveloped areas where a Communist state could effectively block any American land passage to the Panama Canal and to our South American friends and allies. . . . It certainly is in our own best interests, therefore, to promote the economic development and progress of all of the Western Hemisphere.

Soon after the floor discussion, the $10 million appropriation gained passage in both houses of Congress.[82]

The new funds temporarily solved the bureau's financial problems, but the construction woes endured. Selegua remained awash in rockslides. In Costa Rica, meanwhile, the surfacing along an eighty-mile section of road was reportedly disintegrating, its bituminous macadam not thick enough to withstand the wear from overloaded trucks. "The Disaster of the Inter-American Highway" declared a headline from the Costa Rican newspaper *La Nación*. The various construction setbacks ensured that the bureau was nowhere close to finished when the three-year deadline arrived in July 1958.[83]

The shortcomings of the highway were hard to overlook when the AAA sent a driver the following year to tour the uncompleted road. Upon concluding the journey, the harried driver deemed the route "not recommended at this time." He went on to explain,

The highway itself is in poor condition, accommodations and food service are inadequate, customs are still very annoying, and the points of interest, especially south of Guatemala, do not justify the effort and expense necessary. Only one-half the . . . miles of highway from Mexico south to Panama City are paved. . . . The remaining passable mileage is dirt, gravel or stone. Many stretches of the highway are so rough that frequent car repairs are necessary.[84]

The bureau's budget continued to swell as the road fell farther behind schedule. The 1955 estimate of $75 million had ballooned more than 50 percent by the time the new decade dawned. Each month that passed, the cost to completion seemed to rise faster. In mid-1961, with funds running low, the bureau decided to ask Congress for yet another appropriation, this time for $32 million.[85]

The familiar arguments for the road were once more dusted off, but State Department officials now also introduced a new one: the road's impact on the Alliance for Progress, President John F. Kennedy's newly inaugurated multibillion-dollar program of development aid for Latin America. The road, they argued, would provide the transportation infrastructure to support the broad economic development that the Alliance for Progress sought to achieve. One State Department official testified before the House, "It is clear that increased contact between the United States and the countries traversed by the highway, through tourism, commercial travel, and transport, could result in a variety of mutual benefits, the sum of which would be to strengthen our relations with those countries as they move forward under the Alliance for Progress."[86]

When the bill reached the full Senate in June 1962, the discussion turned toward the future and the question of maintenance. Many feared that the bureau would continue asking for money indefinitely and insisted that the United States not provide any funds for maintaining the highway once completed. As Ernest Gruening of Alaska declared, "Otherwise, this would become a bottomless pit into which to pour money for maintenance of roads all over the world. . . . Why should not the people of those countries do something to maintain the road? . . . I like the people south of the border so well that I want them to do their share. I want to permit them to help keep up the roads." The anti-maintenance crowd nonetheless accepted that the United States had an obligation to first complete the job. They ultimately supported the bureau's $32 million request, which passed in the fall.[87]

By this point, the bureau could finally see an end on the horizon. The new funds were approved just as another dry season was beginning, and engineers expected to have the road fully opened—if not fully paved—before the rains came the following April. After thirty-three years of planning and countless setbacks, the Inter-American Highway was almost a reality.

The opening of the road was set to be a momentous occasion. The State Department and Bureau of Public Roads decided to celebrate with a ceremonial caravan, one that would take the first "official" trip along the Inter-American Highway. The caravan, they determined, would start in Panama City in mid-April 1963 and continue all the way to Washington, DC. The final stop on the journey would be the Ninth Pan-American Highway Conference, which was meeting in the United States for the first time.[88]

When the morning of departure finally arrived, a grand send-off was arranged in Panama City. The president of Panama and the local archbishop both came to offer their personal support to the sixty highway officials and politicians from twenty-two countries who had been selected for the inaugural journey. Among the travelers was Bureau of Public Roads chief Rex Whitton, who declared that the road was "ready for the able, the hardy, and the venturesome." After the welcoming formalities, the officials boarded three air-conditioned General Motors intercity carrier buses for the start of their journey north. The *New York Times* observed, "Three silvery buses decorated with flags and the emblems of the Alliance for Progress left this morning on what was officially described as an 'adventurous, pioneering journey' ... over the inter-American section of the Pan-American Highway."[89]

The subsequent voyage north had been decades in the making. All the gaps in the road had finally been filled, even if paving remained to be done in some places. The road, by this point, also crossed the canal thanks to the $20 million Bridge of the Americas, which had opened to traffic in October 1962. The *Christian Science Monitor* observed at the caravan's departure, "Poor as the road is, especially in Costa Rica and Guatemala, the condition has less meaning than the fact that it is open at all, after 22 years of construction and many more years of hope." A Peruvian member of the caravan proclaimed the trip "the grand finale of a 35-year dream for linking the American countries by roads."[90]

The journey brought the caravan into contact with a spectacular variety of landscapes as it traveled through Central America. The *New York Times* reporter who covered the caravan wrote admiringly, "The trip ... meant a stunning range of scenery, from steamy lowlands to chilling summits. It meant a bewildering profusion of jungle, plantation and rocky river bed; of lush banana, coffee and cotton land rimmed by volcanoes." The captivating landscapes helped compensate for the discomfort of traveling along the road's poorer stretches. As the article in the *New York Times* explained,

It meant jouncing and rattling over unpaved sections in Panama, Costa Rica and Guatemala, and rolling around S-curves in the phantom mists of the Cerro de la Muerte. ... It also meant chunks of rock, stirred up by bus tires, dancing on the unfinished stretches and pounding the nether armor of the buses. ... And it meant the corrugated surface of a finished portion of the road in Nicaragua breaking down either the air-conditioner or the reverse gear system in the three buses.[91]

The shortcomings of the road, however, did not undermine its ultimate utility. International automobile transit was now possible between the United States and Panama. The effects of the road on the local economies could already be felt. The *Chicago Tribune* explained in April,

> As sections of the highway were completed in past years, commerce along it gradually increased. First it doubled, then it tripled, then it soared. In 1950, five countries—Guatemala, El Salvador, Honduras, Nicaragua, and Costa Rica—exchanged a total of 8 million dollars worth of goods. By 1960, the figure had risen to 37 million, and it is still climbing. The enormous increase is attributable almost solely to progress on the highway. Without it, Central America's fledgling Common Market would have bogged down because of inadequate transportation facilities.[92]

After a journey of two weeks, the caravan travelers arrived safely in Washington, just in time for the Ninth Pan-American Highway Conference. The conference organizers welcomed the travelers as conquering heroes. The *Washington Post* reported that all the participants "had warm words of praise for the recently completed highway and scorn for reports that some of the roads were dangerous and unfit for the ordinary tourist."[93]

The caravan's final engagement was an audience before President Kennedy, who greeted the group in the Rose Garden of the White House. "I want to express my admiration for your surviving [the trip]," Kennedy quipped. He then spoke of the importance he accorded the Pan-American Highway:

> I can't believe that we could concentrate our efforts on any great enterprise which has more significance, symbolically and actually, than the development of this highway. The more we can do to link the sister republics of this hemisphere in one great community, the stronger we'll all be, the greater we'll serve our national interests, and the more abundant we'll make the life of our people. This is a matter of consuming interest, consuming passion, of this government and this people in the United States in these days.[94]

Kennedy's words spoke to the great dream that the Pan-American Highway represented, a dream of the Americas united into one community. It was a dream as old as Henry Clay and Simón Bolívar. It was a dream that had inspired Franklin Roosevelt when he first pushed for a road to the canal thirty years earlier. It was a dream that endured even as the Cold War twisted the nation's Latin America policy into an anti-Communist frenzy. With the opening of the Inter-American Highway, a major step had been taken toward completing the hemispheric road that symbolized this great dream.

But one more obstacle remained: the last 250-mile break in the Pan-American Highway, the Darien Gap. A legendary wilderness, it sat at the exact spot where the two American landmasses touched. "Darien," wrote one reporter, "is the center piece, El Broche de Oro, the broach of gold that links the two continents. . . . It has been a source of rumor, legend and fable which have not made any easier the assaying of the actual road building problems it presents." Darien was all that stood in the way of through traffic between New York and Buenos Aires. Completion of the Pan-American Highway seemed tantalizingly close. However, in the jungles of Darien, the highway dream that Kennedy so eloquently described would face newfound resistance. And in the end, the dream of the road would come undone.[95]

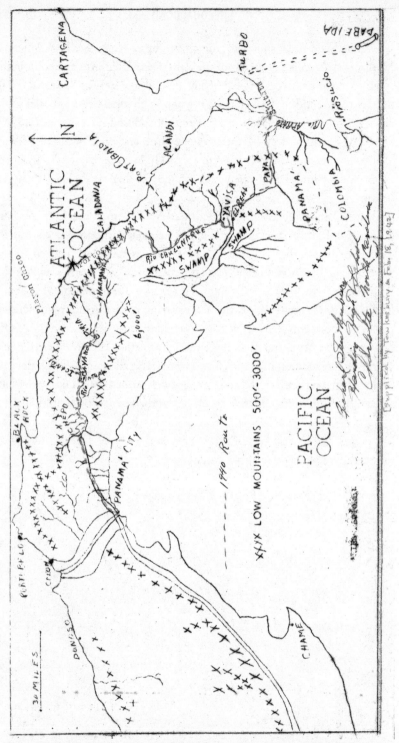

A map (c. 1940) showing the route that North Carolinian Richard Tewkesbury covered in what was considered the first crossing on foot of the legendary Darien Gap.

CHAPTER EIGHT

The Missing Link

"Richard A. Tewkesbury—Conqueror of the Jungles of Panama"
A quarter century before the dedication of the Inter-American Highway, on a chilly morning in mid-April 1939, officials at the Pan-American Union building received an unexpected visitor demanding to talk about the Darien wilderness and the Pan-American Highway. His name was Richard Tewkesbury, and the thirty-two-year-old had traveled there from Charlotte, North Carolina, where he was a high school mathematics teacher. He was seeking support for a feat he planned to undertake during the upcoming summer vacation, a feat that he insisted would have profound ramifications for the future of the hemispheric motor route.[1]

The origins of Tewkesbury's unusual feat could be found in an automobile pleasure trip he had taken with his wife two years earlier to tour the recently completed northern stretch of the Mexican Pan-American Highway. During the trip, Tewkesbury experienced a flash of insight after a passenger in a southbound car of young Americans shouted that they were going to Mexico City "or as far beyond as we can get." According to Tewkesbury, at that moment, "I started wondering what it would mean if those kids could keep right on going through the Latin American countries, right on to South America. If thousands like them could spend their vacations driving around down there and spreading good will. And if thousands of South Americans could drive up here and find out we are pretty decent folks after all."[2]

The dream of the Pan-American Highway had seduced Richard Tewkesbury like so many before him. He soon decided to spend the next summer on a solo trip following the proposed route of the Pan-American Highway as far south as possible. After a year spent saving up funds, Tewkesbury departed on his journey south in June 1938. The adventuresome part of the trip began once Tewkesbury got below Mexico City, as the road gave way in many places to mule trails, or footpaths, or simply impassable jungle. It was only several years earlier, after all, that the United States and Central America had begun cooperating on the Inter-American Highway. Nonetheless, by train, bus, plane, and any other means available, Tewkesbury made it as far as Panama City. He was prepared to proceed farther south, but when he told his plans to an engineer he had met there, the man pointed at the Darien region on a nearby map and laughed. "That is an insuperable barrier in the way of your highway," the engineer reportedly said. When Tewkesbury asked why, the man replied, "That jungle happens to have a worse reputation than any bush country in Africa, that's all. A dozen explorers have tackled it, but not one of them has gone through. They'll never push a road through this missing link." Tewkesbury concluded there was no point in going farther that summer, but his interest in the Pan-American Highway's development remained undimmed.[3]

The Darien region consumed Tewkesbury's thoughts in the months that followed. He recalled, "As an enthusiast for a true Pan Americanism, I foresaw that this break in the great chain of the Pan American Highway would deter the dreamed-of interchange of Americans between the two continents." Tewkesbury soon grew convinced that it was his mission to cross Darien during the upcoming summer as a symbolic scout for the Pan-American Highway. Only through such action would the myths about Darien be put to rest and the path of the highway assured. As one fawning reporter observed of Tewkesbury, "Some men devote themselves to writing plays or symphonies, others to discovering cures for diseases. Tooks decided to devote himself to making that dream of the Pan-American Highway come true."[4]

The last obstacle to the Pan-American Highway, somewhat ironically, sat at the exact spot where the Spanish conquest of the New World's *Tierra Firme* began.

It was in 1510 that a Spanish expedition established Santa María de la Antigua del Darién, the Americas' first mainland city, on the Gulf of Urabá, near the present-day Panama-Colombia border. Three years later, an exploratory mission led by the city's founder, Vasco Nuñez de Balboa, crossed the Darien isthmus and discovered the Pacific Ocean, revolutionizing Europe's understanding of world geography. Darien's time as the center of Spanish activity on the mainland lasted until 1519, when the man who displaced Balboa—and ultimately executed him on trumped-up charges of treason—decided to erect a settlement farther north and on the Pacific side of the isthmus, known as Panama City. Soon the pioneer settlement of Santa María de la Antigua del Darién was depopulated. Its end came in 1524, burned by local Cueva tribes who had suffered greatly beneath Spanish depredations in the quest for gold.[5]

In little less than fifteen years, Darien had gone from being the locus of Spain's mainland ambitions to a backwater region, a peripheral space between Panama City and Cartagena. At times in the centuries that followed the Spanish crown made moves to exert greater control over the region, but it had little overall success. Some of the resistance arose from the region's geography, a matrix of swamps and dense jungle growth, with rainfall among the highest anywhere on earth in its southernmost zone. But the greater issue was the non-Spanish populations who inhabited Darien, including escaped slaves, pirates, and the indigenous Cuna and Chocó peoples, all of whom, by and large, opposed state control.[6]

In certain respects, there had existed in Darien a prolonged low-intensity war between the Spanish and the Cuna, who possessed well-developed organizational structures that allowed for coordinated resistance. The Spanish crown initially tried to exert control over the Cuna through missionary work, achieving some success in the early 1600s before a major uprising in 1651. Over the course of the subsequent century, the Cuna allied with English, French, and Dutch pirates, who used the Darien region as a staging point for raids on Spanish vessels. The Spanish finally reached a peace accord with the Cuna in 1741, but barely ten years elapsed before another major revolt broke out. The Cuna's subsequent resistance to state control led the Spanish crown in 1783 to issue an order calling for the "extermination" of the rebellious natives. The ensuing ten years witnessed prolonged fighting, until Spain concluded that the effort was too costly and abandoned the forts that it had recently constructed in Darien. Tensions cooled somewhat in the nineteenth century, as the cause of New World liberation drew attention away from the centuries-long battle with the Cuna. Their territory eventually ended up within the state of Colombia, which paid them relatively little mind, but the situation changed with Panamanian independence in 1903. The Cuna suddenly found themselves living within the new Republic of Panama, whose leaders sought to exert greater control over the relatively stateless zone that began only forty miles from their capital, Panama City.

Soon police officers and missionaries began appearing in the Darien territory, much to the chagrin of some Cuna leaders. After two decades of rising
discontent, the Cuna finally launched a revolt with the aid of American
Richard Marsh, an anthropologist who had initially come to the region as
a rubber agent for Henry Ford and Harvey Firestone but who had quickly
come to sympathize with the Cuna's plight. The revolt gained the backing of the United States, which placed a gunboat off the Darien coast and
helped negotiate a peace between the Cuna and the Panamanian government in 1925. Thirteen years later, the Panamanian government officially
recognized the Cuna's right to control a portion of the Darien territory, a
major victory for the Cuna after more than three hundred years of intermit-
tent war.[7]

It was the same year as this Cuna triumph that Richard Tewkesbury first
learned of Darien, that zone of myths and strange beasts, a stretch of land
running from just south of Panama City into northern Colombia, a route
that reportedly no white man had ever crossed.

Tewkesbury, on the surface, was an unlikely candidate to traverse Darien.
He stood 5-foot-3 and weighed 112 pounds, with a young-looking face and
sandy blond hair. As the *Saturday Evening Post* once observed, "He didn't
play either football or Fancy Dan at Iowa State, where he went to college,
and he is neither bronzed, brawny nor blasé. Instead, he is modest, unassum-
ing, inclined to belittle his own exploits. In other words, he is the complete
antithesis of the articulate and shirt-open-at-the-throat explorers who do so
well on the lecture circuit."[8]

Tewkesbury nonetheless had the heart of an adventurer. He had grown
up hiking in the woods and spent the summers between school years on
international odysseys. His previous summer trips had included summits of
Mount Fuji in Japan and the onerous Popocatepetl in Mexico.[9]

In April 1939, after months of preparing for his Darien trek, Tewkesbury headed to the Pan-American Union to seek official support. The
headstrong schoolteacher was determined not to accept "no" for an answer,
even if his idea sounded preposterous on its face. Tewkesbury made his
initial pitch to Pan-American representative Colonel E. E. Valentini, who
nearly laughed his guest out of the building, but Tewkesbury's perseverance induced Valentini to bring the indomitable mathematics instructor to
his superior, Stephen James. Upon hearing Tewkesbury's proposal, James
responded even more skeptically than had Valentini, declaring,

Look, Mr. Tewkesbury. That stretch of jungle's got head-hunters in it. Head-hunters. Know what I mean? And swamps with every sort of fever we've ever heard about, and probably a few we haven't. And snakes—big ones. Weigh close to half-a-ton, they say. . . . I think you must be mad, clean off your rocker! You couldn't get through that jungle! Why, do you know, our army down in Panama, they don't care even about arming that section of the country, that's how sure they are nobody can get through![10]

James's tirade, despite its severity, had little impact on Tewkesbury. The schoolteacher replied defiantly, "Somebody's got to do it. . . . You won't help me?" James then attempted to put the matter to rest by refusing categorically to fund Tewkesbury, but the insistent teacher assured that he would pay his own way. Finally, exasperated, James agreed to provide a modicum of official support with a letter of introduction to Panamanian authorities. As soon as a triumphant Tewkesbury left the office, James bet Valentini a nickel that they would never see the schoolteacher again. James's subsequent letter to Panama read, "This will introduce Mr. Richard Tewkesbury, a reckless, stubborn young American who is ambitious to make the trip overland . . . to the Colombian border. I urge you to discourage him from this mad adventure. If, however, he will not be discouraged and persists in his announced intention to undertake this journey, will you please give him such advice and assistance as you reasonably can."[11]

Tewkesbury set off for Panama two and a half months after his meeting at the Pan-American Union during the early height of the Darien rainy season. He brought with him a moderately sized adventurer's pack that contained only the barest essentials for jungle survival. Twenty pounds of its contents were foods that had been chosen carefully by his wife, a professional dietician who supported her husband's adventuring. Tewkesbury's jungle diet would consist of a mix of dried potatoes, canned rice, dried apricots, salt, and tinned corned beef and roast beef. Tewkesbury carried no tent, preferring instead to trust his fate to improvised shelters and a waterproof sleeping bag made from a material resembling a shower curtain. Among Tewkesbury's most noteworthy supplies were the trinkets his students had collected to serve as tribal gifts, including plastic toy elephants, red bandanna scarves, postcards, and needles.[12]

Tewkesbury had a simple strategy for navigating Darien, one based on advice he had received from an engineer in the Canal Zone to stick to the rivers. His starting point was the town of Chepo, where the Pan-American

Highway ended, thirty-eight miles southeast of Panama City and near the mouth of the Bayano River, whose origins lay deep within Darien. Tewkesbury planned to travel fifty miles upriver on the Bayano to its headwaters, then go overland thirty miles to the headwaters of the Chucunaque River, which flowed in the opposite direction, and finally follow the Chucunaque southeast sixty miles to Yaviza, a town founded by Spanish missionaries in 1638 that lay thirty miles from the Colombian border and that Tewkesbury believed was connected through overland routes to Colombia's road network. By following the rivers, Tewkesbury would avoid the mountains, which some erroneously thought reached heights of more than fifteen thousand feet, snowcapped in the midst of the tropics. Geography, however, was not his only challenge: it was rumored that the fiercest tribe, potential headhunters, occupied the headwaters of the Chucunaque.[13]

On July 6, 1939, Tewkesbury arrived at Chepo to start his journey. He made for a strange sight in the outpost town with his hiking pack and his safari hat. After waiting for two days in the small settlement, he managed to secure passage on a canoe heading up the Bayano. As Tewkesbury recalled,

> For eight days . . . the Indians pushed their dugout canoes up the Bayano River, carrying me ever deeper into the dark portion of the jungle. At nights we would sleep on the banks of the stream or in the bottom of the boats, usually in a tropical downpour, I in a cellophane sleeping bag and the Indians carrying on ceremonies begging the heavens to cease the deluge. . . . Along the way I gathered bits of information that might be helpful in determining a route for the Pan-American Highway. I recorded the steepness of the hills, physical evidences of flood stages of the rivers, the type of soil, the attitude of the natives, gathered samples of rock from the streams and from the cordillera.

His journey up the Bayano ended at the Cuna village of Piria, where Tewkesbury was received cordially but told firmly that he could not cross to the Chucunaque, a decision he attributed to fear of the headwaters tribe. Tewkesbury pleaded, but the local chief refused and ultimately assigned two men to escort him out of their territory and onto the Caribbean shore, which sat on the far side of the Darien coastal range. Tewkesbury dutifully followed, only to have his guides suddenly and inexplicably abandon him while halfway up the mountain, in the midst of an unbroken maze of jungle. Alone in Darien, Tewkesbury was hopelessly lost. And his compass, the best chance for survival, had recently broken.[14]

Tewkesbury sat down to consider his fate. Finding his way back from where he came seemed impossible without a guide. Following the protracted ridgeline of the coastal range farther southeast to Colombia was certain death without more food, which he had nearly exhausted despite his wife's careful preparations. The only option, he figured, was to cross over the ridge of the coastal range, find a river, and pray that it led him to the Caribbean, whose shore was populated by Cuna villages. He grabbed his pack and started climbing through vegetation so dense that each step forward marked a small triumph. Eventually he found a stream. Hours passed as he waded, exhausted, through the waist-deep water. As night began to fall, he built a rough shelter along the riverbank. He ate a tin of corned beef and then tried to sleep while the mosquitoes swarmed.

When the daylight awoke him the next morning the air was cooler. Back into the stream he waded. Submerged logs hindered his steps. Three-foot-long black and brown snakes slithered along the banks as he plodded onward along the endless river bends.

Tewkesbury had been lost and alone for more than twenty-four hours when, in the distance, he spotted two Cuna boys in a canoe. He hastily splashed toward them. With gestures and a limited vocabulary, he explained that he sought the coast. The boys pointed him toward a nearby trail and continued on their way. Several more hours of hiking followed before Tewkesbury encountered another soul, this time a fisherman with a boat. Together they traveled to a nearby village on the coast, arriving at 4:00 p.m. on July 21, 1939.[15]

Tewkesbury had survived the jungle. But he had also abandoned his route, the reason he had come in the first place. For the moment, his quest to advance the Pan-American Highway had failed.

Tewkesbury made for a pitiful sight when he reached the coast. The journey through Darien had whittled his weight down even further than its usual 112 pounds and he was suffering the early stages of malaria. The coastal Cuna took mercy on Tewkesbury, feeding and housing him. They even brought him to meet the great leader Nele Kantule, who had played a central role in the 1925 Cuna revolt. According to Tewkesbury,

I at once realized that Nele was no ordinary Indian. No other chief so far had asked me such intelligent questions. . . . The Chief wanted to know what mathematics is, how much the President of the United States receives, what the daily income of the United States treasury is, what probably will be the next great invention, the names of some of

the large ships, where our airplanes are made, who invented his pho-
nograph, who the outstanding inventor of today is, whether we permit Jews to enter our country, how the Negroes got to America and
how many factories there are in the United States.... He desired to
know the population of the American Indians, whether the Philippines had their independence, whether the United States was enlarg-
ing the Panama Canal, and whether the highway would be built from
Panama City to Colombia. He was certain that a highway would be
built some day.

After meeting with the Cuna leader, Tewkesbury spent a month conva-
lescing on the Darien coast, taking several day trips back to the interior to
explore tributaries of the Chucunaque. Meanwhile, as Tewkesbury relaxed,
enjoying Cuna hospitality, several representatives from the interior Cuna
tribes traveled to Panama City to voice their discontent with the explorer.
As one supposed witness to the exchange observed,

> [T]hey [registered their] disapproval of Tewkesbury's coming to their
> country, on the grounds that he lacked ... knowledge of the jungle,
> and would not eat the food they offered. They were troubled because,
> they said, he might die and they be blamed by the Americans for his
> death.... [T]hey said Tewkesbury told them the road would be built
> whether they objected or not, that white men always did what they
> set out to do, which was a less friendly approach than they expected.[16]

Tewkesbury returned to Charlotte denied but not defeated. He was barely
recovered from malaria when he began planning a return trip for the following summer. The mistakes of the first attempt, he felt, were merely lessons
for its follow-up. Soon he reappeared at the Pan-American Union, much
to the surprise of Stephen James. His nickel bet had been lost. Tewkesbury
assured the audience at the Pan-American Union that he was confident
Darien was traversable and that he intended to prove it during the upcoming summer.[17]

Tewkesbury's conviction only deepened with the outbreak of World
War II in late 1939, a development, he believed, that added newfound
urgency to closing the highway gap in Darien. As Tewkesbury observed of
his second trip,

the immediate need for information about the [Darien] region [was required] even more so if "Hemisphere Defense" by land was to become a reality. Without the information, plans would be formulated to make a long detour for the Highway. When completed, troops, mechanized units, or the American public could motor south through Mexico and the Central American countries to the Panama Canal. But at the Canal they would have to begin a lengthy detour 1000 miles by boat to Venezuela, and another 1000 miles by the Bolivar Highway to Bogota, Colombia. In all a 2,082 mile detour, to get around the 250 miles of unknown Panamanian jungles.[18]

Tewkesbury at last returned to Panama in June 1940. He carried the same safari hat and a much larger pack, this time stuffed with nearly sixty pounds of food. He also had a new bundle of trinkets: "blue cotton cloth for skirts, red and yellow beads, post cards, [and] hundreds of toy dogs and elephants." Soon Tewkesbury's curious appearance and possessions, especially his maps, caught the attention of Panamanian police, who arrested him on suspicion of being a Nazi. While in custody, Tewkesbury wrote for help to engineer Edwin Warley James, who had taken an interest in the schoolteacher's work: "My maps, my passport, and personal letters were taken from me. . . . I would greatly appreciate a letter from you that would verify my reason for attempting to cross the Darien region." After nine anxious days, Tewkesbury was finally released and allowed to proceed on his way.[19]

Barely one week later Tewkesbury reached the Bayano's upriver village of Piria, where his progress had stalled the prior year. The locals seemed welcoming, and the chief explained that Tewkesbury had only been abandoned previously due to fear of a nearby ocelot, an explanation that Tewkesbury accepted, though he personally believed that the betrayal had occurred because he had lost the escorts' respect. Once more, the chief seemed to warn Tewkesbury of the fearsome tribe at the headwaters of the Chucunaque. Once more, Tewkesbury was pressured to return to the coast. And once more, Tewkesbury acceded. This familiar script played out for several days until Tewkesbury, back on the path to the Caribbean, suddenly changed tactics. Turning to his two escorts, he explained that he was tired and wanted to camp. They pressed to continue, but Tewkesbury, dissembling, insisted that he could be left alone and would find his way out to the ocean, just as he had done before. He handed them eight dollars and, upon their protests, some potatoes and half a sardine. The abandonee had become the abandoner.[20]

In the distance, thunder rumbled. The jungle now controlled Tewkesbury's fate. The next morning, with a compass as his only companion, he began trekking southeast along the cordillera toward Colombia, intending to follow the ridgeline far enough to get beyond the territory of the feared headwaters tribe, at which point he would turn inland toward the Chucunaque. The days that followed were "mental agony," his frayed psyche buoyed with images of "the shining stream of motor cars which one day would thread the jungle." After a week of navigating the cordillera, with his supplies and spirit nearly spent, he located a tiny Cuna community that lived on one of the Chucunaque tributaries he had explored the previous summer during his convalescence. It was a crucial breakthrough, but immediately fever gripped Tewkesbury for several days. When his stupor lifted, he made his way toward the Chucunaque River, where he eventually encountered a banana-laden canoe heading downstream whose pilots agreed to give him passage to Yaviza for $10. Four days later, a weary Tewkesbury disembarked at his long-sought end point. "Civilization at last," Tewkesbury wrote in his journal.[21]

He had made it through. And that, presumably, meant a road could too. While in Yaviza, he dashed off a letter to Stephen James: "There seems to be no physical barriers along this route. There are, however, many Indian tribes to deal with and centuries old customs among them that will have to be respected."[22]

Upon his return to Charlotte, Tewkesbury became a self-appointed spokesman for the Pan-American Highway, giving talks wherever he could find an audience. As he observed in 1941,

[I] have publicized the feasibility of such a route to whoever would listen to me. And I do not intend to stop until the first automobile travels freely over that great system from Buenos Aires to New York. It shall open for us a new era, the like of which this hemisphere has never experienced. . . . All I can see is the vision of a great highway and thinking about how valuable the highway would be for fostering the Good Neighbor policy, if it had no other advantage.[23]

Tewkesbury's self-promotion soon garnered the attention of the national media. "Tooks Tames the Jungle," declared *American Magazine* in early

1941, noting, "[His] feat was about as amazing as if a green bantamweight should jump in the ring with Joe Louis and lick the stuffing out of him." In the ensuing months, versions of his story appeared everywhere from *Time* magazine to *Reader's Digest* to *Scholastic*. He was offered a book deal, which he failed to pursue, and also became the subject of a *True Comics* issue titled "Jungle Trailblazer." There was even a national radio drama with voice actors playing Tewkesbury and Stephen James. At the broadcast's conclusion, James declared: "It's almost impossible to overestimate Tooks' contribution to the highway. He took the first step, always the hardest. He dispelled the fearful legends, four hundred years old. We know now that a road can and will be pushed through the jungle. When it is, millions of people in North and South America should be grateful to this heroic little school teacher." A subsequent radio broadcast on Tewkesbury went so far as to assure, "When the complete story of the Pan American Highway is told, it will tell of engineering genius, the surmounting of apparently insurmountable obstacles, of Pan American solidarity—union in a common endeavor, and it will contain a special chapter entitled "Richard A. Tewkesbury—Conqueror of the Jungles of Panama." [24]

Not everyone, however, felt that Tewkesbury deserved the credit he received. As Tewkesbury's fame rose, accounts began to emerge from others claiming to have been the first across Darien. The strongest denunciation came from James Price, known as "Jungle Jim," an American living in Panama who made his way giving adventure tours. At one point, Price wrote Edwin Warley James, fuming, "This article [on Tewkesbury] states that no white man [has] ever traveled between Central and South America overland. *This is wrong*.... There were quite a few newspaper 'writeups' about our trip through [in 1937]. It was known as a 'Jungle Jim' expedition." But Jungle Jim's rant ultimately failed to persuade James, who considered himself something of an expert on the subject of overland crossings along the route of the Pan-American Highway. None of the rival accounts, James felt, had truly covered the highway's proposed route, even if some, like that of Price, had dealt with a portion of it. James wrote to Tewkesbury at one point, "I am yet to be convinced that any white man had made the longitudinal trip until you did. Each new case as it comes to my attention ends up like 'Jungle Jim Price's.'" [25]

A semiofficial recognition of Tewkesbury's feat finally came in September 1941, when he was made an honored guest at the Fourth Pan-American Highway Conference, held in Mexico City. The delegates marveled at the diminutive Tewkesbury, who had taken off from school to attend the event. In the middle of the conference, Tewkesbury delivered a keynote address that recounted his adventures in Darien. "I am one," he declared,

> who ... has caught the vision and the spirit of freedom of travel between the New World Republics. There are hundreds of thousands of enthusiasts like I am in this New World. . . . You have gathered here for you believe, as I, in the future of mutual association between our nations through the medium of a roadway system. If my coming before you to tell of what lies in Darien has hurried that day forward for such a projected connecting road, then I consider that I have been amply rewarded.[26]

Tewkesbury's message received a warm reception from the room, but he was a man ahead of his time. It would be another thirteen years before Darien again became the subject of serious discussion at a Pan-American Highway Conference. And only then would a sustained movement to bridge Darien begin to form.

"The Most Noble Conquest Ever Attempted"

Around midday on July 12, 1954, at the Sixth Pan-American Highway Conference in Caracas, Venezuela, an audience gathered to hear a lecture titled "The Darien Link," the first address on Darien since Richard Tewkesbury's talk more than a dozen years prior. The speaker was thirty-nine-year-old Panamanian engineer Tommy Guardia Jr., whose name carried great weight as well as expectations. He was the son of Tomás Guardia, considered one of the two "godfathers" of the Inter-American Highway (alongside Edwin Warley James), but the audience could have been forgiven for failing to see a family resemblance. The younger Guardia was gallant and loquacious, standing well over six feet with a thick mane of black hair, a stark contrast to his revered father, laconic and unsparing, with thinning hair, a shorter build, and a face that rarely broke into a smile. But Tommy had inherited from his father a passion for the Pan-American Highway and now sought to complete his father's work by putting a road through Darien. As he told the audience, "The Pan-American Highway, that golden dream of a group of men of grand vision in each of our American states, which is fast approaching reality, must cross all the Republic of Panama, from east to west, in all its longitudinal extension."[27]

Guardia's speech had been highly anticipated by Rómulo O'Farrill, a Mexican multimillionaire at the conference who had been trying for several years to drum up interest in Darien. A newspaper magnate, O'Farrill was among the most influential men in his country. He had gotten his start as an auto mechanic and had initially grown rich through automobile distributorships, which perhaps explained his interest in the Pan-American Highway. O'Farrill had helped revive the Pan-American Highway Conference system after it had gone on hiatus during World War II and had begun lobbying for Darien as an international project in the early 1950s. He declared at one point in 1953, "This [Darien] section . . . offers a communication problem that is not only Panamanian but also continental. . . . [I] refer to the possibility that . . . all the American countries would concur to cover, with the authorization of the Republic of Panama, the expense of the road through multilateral conversations. . . . This . . . would give great prestige to the spirit of multilateral cooperation characteristic of the true Panamerican."[28]

O'Farrill and the two Guardias formed the core of an incipient lobbying movement coming together at the 1954 Caracas conference. No issue, they felt, warranted more attention than this last missing link in the highway, which they named the "Darien Gap" or "El Tapón del Darién." It became, according to Guardia Jr., "one of the main topics of discussion [in Caracas]," and before the conference concluded, they secured an official resolution from the four hundred assembled delegates calling for the "organization of a technical study, with the authorization and collaboration of Panama and Colombia, of a practicable route for the Pan American Highway through the isthmus of Darien." The resolution placed responsibility for the study with a newly created Permanent Executive Committee, to be chaired by O'Farrill.[29]

Channeling Tewkesbury, whose feat seemed to have faded into the forgotten past, Guardia Jr. soon decided that he must make a preliminary crossing of Darien to scout the route. As he later explained to a reporter, "We wanted to have a look at the country and to test out the attitude of the Indians who live in it." In late 1954, several months after the Caracas conference, Guardia Jr. and a companion set off by canoe into Darien, following the same route that Tewkesbury had taken fifteen years prior. It was easier going than Tewkesbury's first trip, which occurred in exceptionally rainy circumstances, but they still struggled with the jungle environment and, at one point, Guardia Jr. managed to find himself imprisoned in a native stockade. Despite this encounter, Guardia Jr. concluded that "the Indians . . . seemed receptive to the idea." The larger issue, he felt, was the geography:

"The terrain ... offers the main problem. There are rivers to be bridged, bogs to be crossed and dense forests to be penetrated." Guardia Jr. nonetheless determined that the difficulties were "surmountable." His single greatest concern, somewhat surprisingly, lay outside Panama. As he explained, "The most formidable obstacle lies just over the border in Colombia, where the great swamps of the Atrato River Valley will have to be traversed or circumvented."[30]

Guardia Jr. presented his findings that February in Mexico City to the first meeting of the seven-man Permanent Executive Committee. "His report," an assistant to Guardia Jr. later noted, "was the opening round in a battle to break down the myth of Darien—adventurers' tall tales of head-hunters who blow poison darts from the tree-tops, of swarming blood-sucking insects, of bottomless morasses, of ferocious jaguars and wild boars—which had led highway engineers to write off the feat as hopeless." O'Farrill, as committee president, fostered the sanguine conclusions of Guardia Jr. and helped arrange a consensus to "send an expedition of technicians 'as soon as possible' to determine the best route," which Panama and Colombia agreed to. The committee further called for a joint "Darien Subcommittee" to be formed among Panama, Colombia, and the United States to "draw up plans preparatory to the expedition." To many present, the active involvement of the United States seemed a foregone conclusion, a logical extension of the policy begun with the Inter-American Highway. The US delegate on the committee went so far as to pledge his country's financial support. As he explained to a reporter, "The United States will maintain and extend its technical and economic aid policy to help ... to eliminate these bottlenecks at the earliest possible [date]."[31]

Six months later, the newly formed Darien Subcommittee held its inaugural session in Panama City. The chairmanship was assigned to Guardia Sr., the crafty veteran who had endured more than twenty changes of Panamanian administrations in his time as that nation's chief road builder. The assignment nonetheless presented Guardia Sr. with challenges unlike any he had previously faced. "[We had] to confront," the subcommittee noted in its initial report, "no less than twenty thousand square kilometers of virgin jungle, unexplored in its majority, surrounded by legends and confused data. ... The few and confusing maps available showed, at each one of the possible passages, some characteristic which made their feasibility doubtful." The subcommittee's difficulties only deepened when its US member announced that his nation was not yet comfortable providing direct funding, as had earlier been suggested, but only technical support.

This announcement forced the subcommittee to reduce its proposed survey budget from nearly $500,000 to a mere $90,000, on the assumption that Panama and Colombia could each provide $30,000 and that a coalition of Latin American nations would cover the remaining third. While the budget was being settled, the subcommittee appointed Guardia Jr. as its technical executive director, with responsibility for carrying out the survey mission.[32]

The underfunded survey commenced the following April with plans to cover several possible routes across the Darien Gap. Guardia Jr. hoped to have recommendations ready in time for the Seventh Pan-American Highway Conference, scheduled for August 1957 in Panama City. Over the next several months, crews assisted by the US Army and armed with machetes "sweated blood" and traveled by helicopter as they began hacking out pioneer trails from Panama's Darien wilderness. Guardia Jr., working with an anthropologist, acted as diplomat to the Cuna and Chocó tribes. Of this work he concluded, "Though they were somewhat reserved and distrustful, the Indians responded to gifts and letters of official introduction and soon extended their hospitality and cooperation.... In time, the confidence of the Indians grew to the point that tribal spokesmen ... often came to the Darien Office in Panama for counsel and support." After more than a year of work, Guardia Jr. settled on the outlines of a proposed route through Panama, one that roughly followed the path Tewkesbury had originally plotted.[33]

The survey's preliminary work in Colombia, meanwhile, was just enough to confirm the younger Guardia's fear that the greatest challenge lay in that country. The shortest route between Yaviza and the existing Colombian road network ran right into the heart of the Atrato Swamp, which extended inland over two hundred miles from the Gulf of Urabá. As one reporter noted, "It ranks as one of the most desolate places on earth, an almost featureless expanse of eight-foot-high grass and brush, here and there interlaced with sluggish channels of turbid water, mantling a seemingly bottomless sea of muck and slime." Soundings of the swamp conducted during the survey revealed mud at least one hundred feet deep. Guardia Jr. was unsure whether it would even be technologically possible to build a road across the center of the Atrato, but the alternative was a huge detour through Colombia's Chocó Province that added more than 250 miles and passed by some of the wettest terrain anywhere on the globe.[34]

Guardia Jr. completed his report just in time for the Seventh Pan-American Highway Conference. After receiving the report, his father wrote O'Farrill on behalf of the Darien Subcommittee, "Within the limitations of our resources we've carried out [the selection of a practical route] in Panama. The myth of the Darien has been refuted. In regard to the 'adjoining areas' in Colombia . . . there still remains much to be explored. Nevertheless, we have come to the conclusion that in that country it is also possible to find a route which presents no unconquerable obstacles." The next step, the elder Guardia felt, was a full technical survey consisting of reconnaissance, preliminary alignments, studies of stream crossings, structural designs, prospective blueprints, volumetric and budget studies, and specifications for construction contracts. He estimated the cost at $2 million.[35]

The subcommittee report had reached O'Farrill while he recovered from a horrific automobile accident that had cost him his leg. But the recent amputation could not stop O'Farrill from attending the Panama City conference as a propagandist for Darien. Once there, O'Farrill caught the US delegation off guard with a call for a multinational, US-led $100 million fund to construct the so-called Darien Highway. Two-thirds of the cost, O'Farrill explained, should be borne by the United States, just as it had done with the Inter-American Highway. The remaining third would be split equally among Panama, Colombia, and a coalition of the other Pan-American countries. Seeking to bring pressure on the United States, O'Farrill declared to the press, "I am authorized to state that Mexico, within its economic resources, is ready to contribute not only towards the expenditures for the final study but towards the actual construction, within the scope of the equitable formula [I proposed]." O'Farrill's surprise proposal ultimately sank beneath resistance from the United States, but O'Farrill still managed to secure from the delegates of the twenty-one nations present approval for his Permanent Executive Committee to continue its Darien work. The Panamanian public works minister in attendance applauded O'Farrill as "the brain, the arm and the heart of these endeavors for Pan American unity," adding that the Mexican had achieved "'a bright new milestone' in the history of hemispheric communication and transport."[36]

In the wake of the conference, O'Farrill and the Guardias intensified their public lobbying, hoping to coax the United States into supporting the road. A subcommittee report summarizing this period noted, "Through press, radio, conferences, and magazine articles, in which we have counted on the enthusiastic collaboration of people and entities interested in the development of the Pan American Highway, we have spread word of Darien to all the Americas."[37]

The subcommittee also worked to pressure Panama and Colombia into designating an official route for the Darien Highway. Such a step seemed necessary before the subcommittee could embark on the full-scale survey that Guardia Sr. had recommended and that O'Farrill hoped the United States would underwrite. In Panama, Guardia Sr. used his influence to achieve a governmental consensus around the conclusions of the 1957 report. The formal Panamanian route approval came less than a year after the Panama City conference concluded. In Colombia, by contrast, an "intense and profound debate" had broken out, according to a Colombian engineer involved in the project. He explained that the choice between the short but uncertain Atrato option and the far longer Chocó one had left the country divided on both the route and the merits of the project, "not only within the bosom of Parliament, but in all the spheres—professional, technical and journalistic, etc." The subcommittee had to wait until mid-1959 before the Colombian government finally reached a decision, endorsing the Chocó route. Soon thereafter the presidents of Panama and Colombia issued a joint declaration on the highway, promising, "The ideal of all the peoples of the Americas to have land communication which will join them and intensify their cultural and economic relations is about to be fulfilled." [38]

By the time the route question had been settled, Guardia Jr. was making arrangements for another landmark Darien expedition, this time by automobile along the pioneer trails in Panama the preliminary survey had made. The scheme, more publicity stunt than technical study, would involve an eight-man crew and two vehicles. Guardia Jr. planned to start the trip in February 1960 from Chepo, with the ultimate goal of arriving that May at the Eighth Pan-American Highway Conference, which was being hosted in Bogota, Colombia. The subsequent journey stretched Guardia Jr. and his crew to their very limits as they struggled to drag and shove their jeep and Land Rover (dubbed *la cucaracha cariñosa*, or "the affectionate cockroach") through the unforgiving Panamanian jungle. They averaged less than three miles per day. As a subcommittee report explained, "They crossed 180 rivers and streams, and they had to improvise bridges over 125 of them, made of the trunks of palm trees that were hard and flexible. Three dangerous automotive upsets occurred, with no personal injury. The use of the winch for the vehicles was constant and sometimes very dangerous due to the breakage of the cable." After a journey of four months and twenty days, Guardia Jr. reached Bogota, triumphant. [39]

Once in Bogota, Guardia Jr. worked with O'Farrill to keep Darien at the top of the conference's agenda. O'Farrill's strategy, however, had changed from three years earlier in Panama City. He no longer asked for a $100 million US-led construction fund, but instead a more modest $3 million survey, following the terms Guardia Sr. had first laid out in 1957. O'Farrill's proposal called for the United States to finance two-thirds of the cost, with the rest of the budget divided among Panama, Colombia, and a Latin American coalition of nations. In the end, O'Farrill got the resolution he sought with unanimous approval and declared the conference a major victory, even though the United States refused any formal commitment to contribute its share. The *Christian Science Monitor* noted shortly after the resolution passed, "Success of the conference [now] depends on United States willingness to provide the $2,000,000." The paper added, "At a time when Washington's relations with Panama are strained, United States participation in closing the Darien gap would be an obviously friendly act. By helping open up 40 per cent of the country to fuller development it might be expected to mitigate tensions involving control of the Panama Canal."[40]

Despite such arguments, O'Farrill's proposed survey failed to gain much initial traction with the US government. The request had arrived with only months remaining in the second term of President Eisenhower, who was still waiting for the completion of the Inter-American Highway. And once the Kennedy administration assumed power, the Darien proposal got lost in the broader effort to create the Alliance for Progress, the president's expansive vision of aid and cooperation for the hemisphere. It was only during the summit launching the Alliance for Progress in August 1961 that the United States seemed to take O'Farrill's plan seriously, following a successful effort by Panama and Colombia to push through a resolution calling for the survey to be completed "as soon as possible." Six months later, the United States finally agreed that it would fund the survey as part of the Alliance for Progress. A vindicated O'Farrill declared soon thereafter, "The conquest of the Darien is definitely the most noble ever attempted [as] the leaders of this conquest do not seek gold or power. Theirs is a crusade with no other ambition than the desire to link the three portions of the Americas."[41]

With spirits high, O'Farrill and the Guardias turned to organizing the long-delayed survey. Their plans called for a private contractor to oversee the work, which they expected would require at least a year to carry out. More than eighty firms submitted bids for the project, and the subcommittee decided in September 1962 to select the massive US firm of Brown & Root. Joining the contractor in carrying out the survey would be the Bureau of Public Roads, whose leadership had agreed to provide additional oversight in early 1963, just as the contractor's teams were readying to enter the gap.[42]

The planning phase of the survey concluded shortly before the Ninth Pan-American Highway Conference, the same Washington gathering that had celebrated the arrival of the inaugural Inter-American Highway caravan. Guardia Jr. insisted on traveling personally to the conference on behalf of the survey despite suffering from a lymphatic cancer that those closest to him believed was somehow contracted in the jungles of Darien. In a speech before several US congressmen, the ailing Guardia Jr. declared, "[B]y now I can state that having passed the initial stages of organization ... the contractor is very much in the field, with five parties in Colombia and three parties in Panama. We know from the way that the work is organized that within 12 to 14 months they will have a stretch of road surveyed." His speech received a standing ovation from the room.[43]

The public assurances of Guardia Jr., however, stood in sharp contrast to the actual state of the survey on the ground. To begin with, several Latin American nations had failed to contribute their promised funds, and the United States, agreeing to participate only on a matching basis, withheld its corresponding portion in response. Adding to the budget woes were demands from the contractor that the fees for the Colombian work be increased by 35 percent to account for unforeseen difficulties in the soaked jungle terrain. The Panamanian government, meanwhile, prohibited the surveyors from carrying out their work in the Bayano region on the grounds that a planned hydroelectric dam there might compromise the route. And in the midst of these setbacks came news in mid-1964 that Guardia Jr. had succumbed to cancer at age forty-nine, leaving the survey without its functional leader. "To the extent that the younger Guardia's jungle exertions contributed to his death," observed one reporter, "he stands as a modern martyr of the Darien." The elder Guardia, who had survived his son and continued acting on behalf of the subcommittee, informed O'Farrill in 1965, "Our studies have not developed in the form we would have desired."[44]

Complicating matters further was a decision from the Bureau of Public Roads to survey the Atrato swamp, potentially reopening the Colombian route debate. Bureau officials felt that new technologies, including infrared photogrammetry, might allow them to locate areas in the swamp where the mud gave way to a solid subsurface. Of this effort a reporter explained,

From the photomosaic, technicians plotted five possible routes.... [The Bureau then] assigned engineers and specialists in research, geophysics, photogrammetry, soils and geology.... Where workers could, they went in by helicopter. Often this required hovering while a man went down a rope with a machete to cut the grass and form it in a mat atop the mulch as a landing pad for the helicopter. Where the helicopter couldn't go, men went by canoe, working their way in by rivers and back bayous.

After prolonged study, the bureau concluded that a route through was indeed possible and that it would cost $120 million less than the longer Chocó option that Colombia had already passed into law.[45]

Neither the tragic death of Guardia Jr. nor the complications and limitations of the survey, entering its third year in 1966, discouraged O'Farrill. He felt that the time had arrived to once more petition the United States for construction funding. His best opportunity, he believed, was an upcoming April trip that President Lyndon Johnson was making to Mexico for a presidential summit. O'Farrill had the ear of the Mexican president, who in turn would have the attention of Johnson. It was O'Farrill's hope that Johnson would come to embrace the highway just as his predecessor, President Kennedy, had done when he praised the road in mid-1963 as "a matter of consuming interest, consuming passion." O'Farrill was not to be disappointed. Before the meeting concluded, Johnson declared, "it is one ambition of my presidency to work with the other nations of this hemisphere for closing the several hundred miles of the Darien Gap that now exist."[46]

But Johnson's endorsement, O'Farrill soon learned, came with a caveat. As one US State Department official explained to O'Farrill, "[I]t would be difficult for the United States to consider financing the Pacific route in Colombia in view of the survey findings that the Atrato route was superior." The United States' stance meant that no funds would be forthcoming unless Colombia reversed the route decision it had enacted during mid-1959, after years of hard-fought debate.[47]

President Johnson hoped to overcome this dilemma through personal diplomacy at an upcoming hemispheric summit whose goal was to validate the Alliance for Progress, which had failed to live up to early expectations. In anticipation of the summit, scheduled for April 1967 in Punta del Este, Uruguay, the United States put forth a formal plan to Colombia calling for studies and financing of the Atrato route. The plan initially received a positive response from the Colombian president, but, in the face of political pressure, he reversed course on the eve of the Punta del Este gathering, informing the United States that an "undertaking of such magnitude should not be subject of public announcement [at the] summit." Despite this, Johnson dedicated himself to the topic of Darien in a brief toast he gave at a dinner held the night before the summit with the presidents of Central America and Panama. As he declared,

> It is easy to speak of "cooperation and partnership"—of "cooperation" and "unity." . . . But they will remain only words—only ideals—unless we take the actions that will give them meaning and power. You have been taking those actions: In building the great inter-American highway, and in developing a common market. . . . We want to move on to help you connect your highway with South America by closing the Darien Gap.

Johnson's appeal nonetheless had limited impact on the Colombian president, who insisted that the Darien project stay off the summit's official agenda.[48]

It was a disappointing development for O'Farrill, but the Mexican believed that Colombia was closer to accepting the Atrato option than the events at Punta del Este suggested. The shorter route had several powerful constituencies supporting it, including the city of Medellín, which wanted an overland connection to the Panama Canal, and United Fruit, which hoped to open up banana lands in the region near the Atrato. In July 1967, several months after the Punta del Este summit, O'Farrill traveled to Colombia to make his case personally to the president as well as to a new minister of public works, someone US officials felt "realize[d] the importance of accepting the short route." Soon O'Farrill succeeded where Johnson had failed, departing Colombia with a confidential pledge that the Atrato option would be accepted.[49]

Colombia's sudden reversal seemed to clear the way for US funding. Johnson's earlier assurances, however, had obscured sharp divisions within the federal government over the value of the Darien Highway. While the highway enjoyed the support of the Bureau of Public Roads, eager to prove that the Atrato could indeed be conquered, the project had yet to gain a constituency in Congress and faced active resistance in the State Department. One State Department official insisted in August 1967, "[The] closing of the Darien Gap is far from the top of the priority list in terms of the most economically desirable way to spend money on projects in Latin America." That November, the State Department went so far as to instruct the US delegates to the Tenth Pan-American Highway Conference to "refrain from taking any position which could give the impression that the United States is pressing for the closing of the Darien Gap; . . . give no encouragement concerning the possibility of the use of US resources to finance the completion of the highway."[50]

The interdepartmental stalemate within the federal government continued for more than a year, until the Bureau of Public Roads managed to recruit several congressmen to its side. In early June 1969, these legislators jointly submitted a bill calling for the United States to fund two-thirds of the cost of the Darien Highway, which the bureau estimated would require $150 million total. One of the bill's sponsors, Representative Don Clausen of California, assured during a speech announcing the measure, "[T]he Darien project could well prove to be the cornerstone for a new structure of international cooperation in the whole field of transport and communication."[51]

Congress finally held hearings on the bill six months later. It was the first time Congress had discussed the Pan-American Highway since the Kennedy-era debates nearly a decade earlier. The politicians had changed more than the underlying principles, with the bill's strongest backers singing dithyrambs to its impact on the long-sought but generally elusive goal of hemispheric unity. Even the specific claims about anti-communism remained, with Clausen stating, "And if there is no other reason than to check the threat of Castroism in this continent, it is to move in [this direction] rather than having to set the stage for military expenditures and all that sort of thing." For a few, the physical and technical demands alone were enough to justify the effort as a testament to US fortitude, with one enthusiastic congressman declaring, "the challenge of linking the two continents of the Western Hemisphere together will prove almost as exciting and certainly more personally rewarding to more people in our lifetimes than landing a man on the moon will."[52]

Joining the growing chorus of supporters was President Richard Nixon, who had played such a pivotal role in getting funds to finish the Inter-American Highway fourteen years earlier. Nixon had remained enthusiastic about the great road despite becoming somewhat disenchanted with Latin America following a chilling 1958 encounter in Caracas when an angry mob encircled his car during a state visit.[53]

Even before the hearings, Nixon had started to discuss the Darien Highway, promising the Colombian president in mid-June 1969 that he would see it through. His assurance had created fits within the State Department, which continued to have "mixed feelings" about the road. As one State Department official observed, "Nobody wanted to touch it with a ten foot pole. Everybody wanted to tell Nixon that it was a dumb idea. It didn't make any economic sense. . . . It took a couple of months to finally get a message to him [that] said it was a dumb idea. . . . This apparently infuriated Nixon." The president received a kinder appraisal from his closest adviser, the assistant for National Security Affairs, Henry Kissinger. Though often a hard-nosed realist, Kissinger approved of the road in relatively idealistic terms, noting in a memorandum to Nixon, "Closing the Gap would have historical significance in terms of the physical integration and ultimate development of the hemisphere. Although the immediate cost-benefit ratio may not be favorable, the potential economic and political effects which a completed Pan American Highway will have by the end of the century cannot be foreseen."[54]

Nixon finally made his feelings on Darien public in a letter written specifically to be read at the highway hearings. In it he stated, "Completion of the Pan American Highway is a goal I have long advocated and supported. Closing the final link in the great highway net between North, Central, and South America will have an immense economic effect for the nations of this hemisphere." The president let it be known that it was his goal to drive across the Darien Gap in 1976 to celebrate the bicentennial of US independence.[55]

Once the hearings concluded, Clausen and his cohort worked diligently to firm up support for the legislation, pushing back against those who questioned whether the project deserved a high priority. The Darien Subcommittee noted in mid-1970 that the legislation was "progressing through the U.S. Congress in a satisfactory manner and favorable action is anticipated leading toward authorization." Several months later Congress finally passed a version of the Clausen bill, which Nixon eagerly signed into law on December 31, 1970. The legislation stated, "The United States shall cooperate with [Panama and Colombia] in the construction of approximately two hundred and fifty miles of highway in . . . the location known as the 'Darien Gap.'. . . Funds [shall be] expended subject to the same terms . . . as are funds authorized by the Inter-American Highway."[56]

Following the legislation's enactment, the State Department negotiated terms with the governments of Colombia and Panama, both of which soon agreed in principle to contribute their allotted one-third shares and to work toward Nixon's ambitious five-year timeline to completion. The trilateral project finally became official in May 1971, with a signing ceremony among the three nations at the Pan-American Union building. In a letter read at the ceremony, President Nixon declared,

I welcome this development with the greatest enthusiasm—I believe that the completion of the Darien Gap portion over the next several years will constitute an historic milestone along the road to under-standing and unity within our hemisphere.... For a long time experts thought that this section could not be built: the "bottomless" Atrato Swamp which it must cross could not be conquered; the fact that this project will now be undertaken is a tribute not only to modern engi-neering but also to the determination of our countries to forge this final link in a great, unifying international project.... It will fulfill a dream which dates back, in the United States at least, to a proposal made in the Congress in 1884 to build a railroad connecting the coun-tries of North and South America.[57]

The signing ceremony marked a culmination of sorts for the lobbying campaign that had begun in 1954. The Guardias and O'Farrill had suc-cessfully championed an international crusade to get the Darien Highway funded. Of the three, only O'Farrill remained to enjoy the victory, as the elder Guardia had passed several years after his son. But their victory, like so many others in the quest to link the Americas, was to be short-lived, for lurking just on the horizon was a problem that neither O'Farrill nor any of his inner circle seemed to fully anticipate, one that would soon bring the highway's momentum grinding to a halt.

The Deadly Vector

The word "aftosa" was never spoken at the 1969 Darien Highway hearings. A similar omission could be found in the many reports from O'Farrill and the Guardias. No one involved in the project from Nixon on down, inten-tionally or otherwise, had ever seemed to want to utter a word about aftosa. One incredulous observer wrote to the State Department soon after the 1971 signing ceremony, "I am very much surprised [at the indifference] to the increased danger [of aftosa] from ... the Pan-American Highway."[58]

Aftosa, or foot-and-mouth disease, had once plagued the US farmer. Cattle infected with the disease developed high fevers and then ulcers in the mouth, between cloven hooves, and on their teats. They refused to eat and produced little milk. Cows in calf suffered high rates of miscarriages. The United States had fought major outbreaks of foot-and-mouth six times before finally eradicating it in 1929. The campaigns had included wholesale slaughtering of cattle, often using the "sanitary rifle." The domestic fight eventually turned into an international one, as the United States grew concerned about aftosa crossing into its borders from Latin America, where the disease remained prevalent. The United States began working with Mexico in 1928 and declared the effort there successful in 1954. Fourteen years later, after the disease had also been eradicated as far south as Panama, the United States entered into an aftosa control agreement with the nations of Central America. By that point, Darien had become the last natural barrier between the aftosa-free north and the aftosa-infected south. The gap was all that stood in the way of a possible pandemic, one that some estimated would cost the United States alone at least $10 billion.[59]

The Nixon administration first flagged the highway-aftosa threat as a serious problem around the time of the signing ceremony. Responsibility for handling the issue went to the Undersecretaries Committee of Nixon's National Security Council, which treated aftosa as a potential matter of homeland defense. The committee's first action was to convene a meeting to coordinate a strategy with representatives of the Departments of State, Agriculture, and Transportation. During this July meeting, the committee tasked the several departments with drafting a preliminary plan of action, an outline for preventing the disease's spread north once the highway was built.[60]

The subsequent study, handled largely by the Department of Agriculture, reached the council in late 1971. Its conclusions were daunting. The entire border zone, it declared, would have to be "livestock free" on both sides. In this region and those adjacent, the two countries would need to have inspection facilities, surveillance posts, and wildlife monitoring. Alongside these measures, especially in Colombia, would have to come a broader program of inoculation and eradication. But even with all these safety measures, until the disease was fully controlled in Colombia, there would still be "a constant threat of introduction [from] people travelling who were in recent contact with FMD infected animals [and] the deliberate or innocent smuggling of possibly infected animals and animal products through the border stations."[61]

The report's sobering conclusions left the Undersecretaries Committee concerned but not dispirited. By early 1972, the committee had approved the Department of Agriculture's plan and delivered it to President Nixon, who quickly endorsed its conclusions.[62]

Negotiations over the plan with Panama soon got off to a favorable start thanks in large part to Panamanian president Omar Torrijos, a left-leaning general who had come to power four years earlier. Torrijos wanted to incorporate the Darien region more fully into the Panamanian economy and saw the highway and planned Bayano hydropower dam as the keys to this vision. As he declared of the highway in 1972: "It is the most important project in this part of the world since the construction of the Panama Canal. . . ." He added, "We want to assimilate the Indians—not keep them in reservations like museum pieces." Fearing a delay in the highway project, the Torrijos administration readily assented to the United States' aftosa guidelines. The two nations signed a formal agreement on May 26, 1972, the same day that Panama received a $15 million, US-guaranteed loan from the First National Bank of Chicago to cover its initial portion of the Darien Highway's construction costs.[63]

The United States had a harder time selling its aftosa plan to Colombia. The scale and cost of the program itself seemed to dissuade some officials. Others felt that the problem could be handled by Panama alone. A number of the Colombian agencies involved also chafed at the idea of potential US oversight in their affairs. Negotiations had broken down so completely by late 1972 that Nixon decided to intervene personally. He wrote to his Colombian counterpart,

> [O]ne of the principal problems we have faced has been how to avoid the spread of foot-and-mouth disease into Panama and further northward as a result of constructing the highway. I understand that a solution to this exceedingly serious problem has been more difficult to achieve than we had earlier expected. . . . I assure you that the United States is prepared to assist in resolving the problems which might arise, in order that construction of the Darien Highway in Colombia can be continued.[64]

Nixon's letter received a pro forma response but no commitment from Colombia. This tacit rejection left the Nixon administration in a tricky situation, committed by law to build a highway but unable to do so without risking billions in livestock damages. The Undersecretaries Committee wrestled with this dilemma for much of the next year, debating whether Colombia might be induced to take aftosa action if actual road construction were to begin. Finally, in late 1973, the National Security Council reached a decision against construction, prohibiting any road building work in Colombia, at least, until the US Department of Agriculture "certifies that foot-and-mouth disease has been eliminated in a buffer zone between Panama and northwestern Colombia." As long as the aftosa threat remained unaddressed in Colombia, the Pan-American Highway would remain incomplete so far as the United States was concerned.[65]

Fear of aftosa spreading was not the only cloud looming over the Darien Highway. The road's potential negative impact on the landscape and on the indigenous communities living there had begun to attract international attention as well.

Among the first to sound a warning was a British expedition that had made a much-publicized motor crossing of Darien in mid-1972. During the trip, its members had seen firsthand the early phases of a Darien land rush brought about by settlers following the route of the planned road. One member of the team explained, "the forest has been completely cleared for a considerable distance on either side of the road. . . . This cleared area is being used for shifting cultivation and for cattle grazing. This is regrettable even on economic grounds. The return . . . is trivial by comparison with the value of the timber destroyed." Another member of the expedition stressed that these environmental changes would spell disaster for the indigenous communities of Darien. As he noted, "Their situation is particularly vulnerable because they do not benefit from the short-term gains of exploiting the jungle with which they have always lived in harmony. . . . [I]f it is removed, they are likely to die out. The only choice facing those concerned with the Indians' immediate future lies between protecting their territory and allowing them to be eliminated."[66]

Soon the fears that the British expedition expressed also gained voice in the United States. At the center of this incipient questioning of the Darien Highway was the Sierra Club, one of the oldest conservation organizations in the nation. Though traditionally focused on domestic issues, the organization felt that Darien fell within its purview since the US government was providing the majority of funds for the highway. The involvement of the United States, moreover, opened up the potential for the Sierra Club to mount effective legal challenges.[67]

The Sierra Club saw its greatest chance to protect Darien from the road in the National Environmental Policy Act of 1969 (NEPA). The three-year-old act, a landmark piece of legislation, required among other things that all federal construction projects first carry out a newly required Environmental Impact Statement, a thorough review of any potential environmental harms and of any less impactful alternatives. Such statements were required to be open to public comment, and NEPA's provisions gave private groups like the Sierra Club the right to contest the sufficiency of these statements, including through litigation. A finding against the government typically resulted in an injunction prohibiting future work until court-imposed conditions were met. It was not wholly certain whether NEPA applied to the Darien Highway, but the Sierra Club intended to find out.[68]

In November 1972, the Department of Transportation received the opening salvo in the Sierra Club's campaign, an informal petition for an environmental impact statement on the Darien Highway. The petition came at a time when the department was already mired in an internal debate over the need for a statement, confused about whether NEPA should apply to the highway at all. But the newfound pressure from the Sierra Club seemed to tip the balance toward compliance. In late December, the Departments of Transportation and State held a meeting to discuss the situation, concluding, "an environmental impact statement should be prepared on this project because of: (1) the spirit of NEPA; (2) the possible environmental effects on cattle in the U.S.; and (3) the effects of U.S. territorial interest in the Panama Canal Zone." The Department of Transportation informed the Sierra Club several weeks later that a statement would be forthcoming.[69]

Despite this assurance, the Department of Transportation remained wary of the assignment. The statement, if contested, threatened to disrupt all progress on the Darien Highway, including ongoing construction work in Panama and preliminary studies in Colombia, where the government remained stalled in debates with the United States over aftosa control. The department soon reduced the statement down to a mere "assessment" and then farmed out the work to a private contractor.[70]

This "assessment," which finally arrived in mid-1974, only fanned the flames of opposition. The highway's critics assured that the assessment's brevity alone indicated the superficial treatment the subject had received. The assessment faced particular scrutiny for its refusal to discuss alternate routes or conservation plans in light of its glib conclusion that the current route might lead to the "cultural extinction" of the Cuna and Chocó. The assessment's critics soon included the President's Council on Environmental Quality and the Environmental Protection Agency, which insisted that a full-scale statement was the "appropriate vehicle" for the Darien Highway.[71]

In June 1975, the Sierra Club finally took its case to court, leading a coalition composed of the National Audubon Society; Friends of the Earth,

Inc.; and the International Association of Game, Fish, and Conservation Commissioners. The complaint, filed with the District Court of Washington, DC, argued that the Department of Transportation had systematically failed to comply with NEPA in the two and a half years since the Sierra Club first petitioned for a statement. The complaint's conclusion explained that the Sierra Club sought two remedies: an order requiring the Department of Transportation to complete a full and satisfactory statement, and an injunction prohibiting the department "from entering into any contracts, obligating any funds, expending any funds, or taking any other action whatsoever in furtherance of construction of the Darien Gap Highway unless and until they have complied with the requirements of NEPA." The Sierra Club, in effect, was demanding that the entire operation be shut down for at least several years.[72]

The ruling on the case came out four months later and proved a decisive triumph for the Sierra Club. The judge all but ignored any concerns about whether NEPA fully applied to the Darien Highway or whether the Sierra Club had the standing to sue over the overseas issue in the first place. His decision instead focused on the assessment's shortcomings, assailing its failure to discuss aftosa sufficiently and its refusal to consider alternatives that "may present [opportunities] for avoiding the 'cultural extinction' so casually predicted by the Assessment." The judge ultimately granted the plaintiffs full relief, ordering that a new statement be drafted and enacting an immediate injunction against any work on the highway. It was a landmark decision with profound ramifications that stretched far beyond the Darien Highway. As one of the Sierra Club's representatives noted, "For the first time NEPA was found to apply to activities funded and carried out by the United States *overseas*. As a result of the decision, environmental impact statements, with resultant public input, may be required of all such US-funded projects."[73]

News of the injunction shocked the governments of Colombia and Panama. It seemed somewhat outlandish that a domestic court could force the United States to violate its sworn commitment to build a highway abroad. Panama argued to the State Department that the court had "illegally interfered" and acted for political reasons. Similar remonstrances came from the Colombian president, who had just visited the United States and discussed moving forward on aftosa control directly with President Gerald Ford. One State Department official observed in a confidential telex soon after the ruling,

Panama's speculation that the suit and consequent preliminary injunction were politically motivated is totally incorrect.... [The issue is only] "political" in a U.S. domestic sense, that is, environmental concerns are a major political issue in the U.S. It is not, however, directed in any way toward Panama or the [canal] negotiations. Panama is simply—but unfortunately—an incidental victim of the environmentalists' campaign to require the U.S. government to take their concerns for the environment into account.[74]

Two weeks after the ruling, a highway strategy meeting was held among the Departments of Transportation, State, Justice, and Agriculture. The State Department, which had earlier opposed the road, now argued that its continuation in Panama was necessary, a sign of good faith during a delicate period of negotiations over future control of the Panama Canal. The interdepartmental group concluded that the Department of Justice should petition the district court "for reconsideration of its refusal to balance the equities of this case." The most pressing concern, they agreed, was that the injunction be lifted on ongoing construction work in aftosa-compliant Panama.[75]

Soon the matter was back before the district court. The judge who had earlier sided so strongly with the plaintiffs now softened his stance in the face of the government's urgent appeals and talk of bilateral relations. Two months after the initial ruling, the court issued a revised opinion, lifting the injunction for Panama on preliminary construction. Only Colombia would remain fully enjoined, just as had been effectively the case since 1973 when the National Security Council resolved to prohibit construction there without a USDA-approved aftosa-compliance program in place.[76]

The revised ruling managed to satisfy neither the environmentalists nor the Department of Transportation. Their battle recommenced the following June, when the department finally produced a full-scale statement. Insisting that the statement fulfilled its obligation to the court, the department announced in July that it was planning to move forward with a new round of construction work in Panama. Soon, however, the Sierra Club pulled the department back to district court, arguing that the statement remained insufficient. And once more the judge agreed, pointing to the statement's apparent failings in its discussion of aftosa, indigenous culture, and alternate routes. He concluded, "the statement is indeed so deficient in certain respects that the injunction must be extended until those deficiencies are remedied." He added, "the defendants' compliance continues to reflect a minimalist approach to [NEPA's] requirements. While this may be due to their failure to recognize NEPA's applicability for literally years during the earlier phases of the project, that failure does not justify any relaxation of those requirements now."[77]

The new ruling greatly disappointed the Department of Transportation, which sincerely believed that its statement had directly spoken to the substantive issues that the judge had earlier found fault with. The department felt that its only choice was to appeal, hoping for a more sympathetic hearing from the DC circuit court. The longer the project remained delayed, the department worried, the higher the potential cost of the Darien Highway would rise, especially in a time of increased inflation. The department's case, which gained a hearing the following year, found greater favor among the three-judge appellate panel than it had with the district court's lone jurist. The appellate judges concluded that the environmentalists had indeed failed to prove the statement insufficient, even if the Department of Transportation repeatedly mishandled its execution. The appellate opinion of March 1978 declared,

> Accordingly, we vacate the preliminary injunction. However, because we have found evidence which indicates that the Government may be a bit too anxious to complete this project, we remand this case to the district court with the instruction that the Department of Agriculture certification with regard to aftosa control in Colombia be filed with the district court and the appellees prior to the initiation of any construction in that country.[78]

The decision effectively drew to a close the environmentalists' NEPA-based campaign to spare the Darien region from the highway. After a two-and-a-half-year legal battle, the injunction for Panama had been lifted and the ruling seemed likely to be upheld if appealed. There remained only the requirement of a certification from the USDA that aftosa was under control in Colombia, the same obligation that the National Security Council— seemingly unbeknownst to the Sierra Club—had enacted in 1973.

Aftosa, however, was a long way from being under control. The Colombian border region had witnessed a settlement rush in anticipation of the highway, and the government was disinclined to start displacing and regulating people in order to create the protected ecological zones the USDA plan required. By 1977, the Agriculture and State Departments were entirely demoralized, with one official noting, "The apparent lack of urgency with which [the Colombian president] views the FMD eradication effort confirms our doubts about the political commitment of the [government of Colombia] to a successful FMD control program and construction of the highway." The situation seemed set to continue like this even following the appellate court ruling, but then, that May, two months after the decision, a new Colombian president, Julio César Turbay, announced publicly that he was making the Darien Highway a top priority. According to one witness, Turbay "stated that by the end of his term in office in 1982, it was his firm aspiration to be able to travel to Panama by land."[79]

Suddenly, there was political will in Colombia to get aftosa under control. Six months after Turbay's announcement, Colombia notified the United States that it was allocating $1 million to aftosa control and ready to cooperate fully. One high-ranking Colombian official informed the US ambassador to Colombia in late 1978, "No doubt is left of the very high priority that the government assigns to the Darien project, with regard as much to its sanitary aspects as to [its] construction."[80]

But Colombia's newfound enthusiasm for the highway butted up against a reality where the project had lost much of its backing within the US government. The years of litigation had fully exposed the project's downsides, and the total cost had spiraled in the interim, nearly doubling to an estimated $285 million. When the Department of Transportation made a new $20 million appropriation request in mid-1978 for construction in Panama, it found few enthusiastic supporters in Congress, with some feeling that the nation had already been overly generous in President Carter's recent treaty giving eventual control of the canal to Panama. In the words of conservative congressman Robert Bauman of Maryland, who led the campaign to kill the appropriation,

> The point is not that there should not eventually be such a highway or even that the threat of the spread of hoof-and-mouth disease, as disastrous as that might be, is the main point, but, rather, that since 1971, when this project was originated and authorized by the Congress, the political and economic situation has changed materially. I do not think, in view of the impending transfer of an $8 billion capital plant, the Panama Canal, and the Canal Zone to Panama . . . that we should pay two-thirds of the money for a project that will be of principal benefit to Panama.

Bauman's arguments ultimately overran the old appeals to hemispheric unity. The appropriation was soon struck from the budget.[81]

This latest political impediment only convinced Colombia to increase its pleas to the United States. In November, Turbay wrote Carter personally, "Mr. President, . . . the aim of my Government is to overcome whatever problem has been presented in the past and to finish the highway that will unite Colombia with Panama and integrate the Americas." Turbay requested Carter's "personal intervention" to resolve the matter, "furthering thereby a monument in the path of progress and understanding among our peoples and governments."[82]

While Carter wrote Turbay an effusive response, he failed to include any funds for Darien construction in his administration's upcoming budget, citing concerns over aftosa. The explicit withdrawal of presidential support was, in some ways, the reversal of a policy that reached back to the days of Calvin Coolidge. For the Carter administration, the traditional arguments about hemispheric unity had lost their sway against the ongoing threat of aftosa, and Colombia's newly emphatic promises of compliance were not enough to convince the administration otherwise.[83]

Beneath the shadow of US inaction, Colombia began working directly with Panama to resolve the aftosa problem. The two neighboring nations soon reached an agreement reportedly "stepping up the fight against foot and mouth disease." The week of the August 1979 signing ceremony, Turbay publicly called on the United States "to put aside its negative attitude toward opening the Darien Gap." Turbay's efforts to inveigle the United States then continued late in the year with the expansion of Los Katios National Park, which sat at the Panamanian-Colombian border, on the route of the Darien Highway. The following year, Panama announced that it too would create a protected aftosa buffer zone—one much larger than Los Katios—on its side of the border, to be known as Darien National Park.[84]

In the midst of Turbay's aftosa maneuverings, President Jimmy Carter lost his reelection bid to Ronald Reagan, the former actor and Republican governor of California. Reagan had blamed Carter during the campaign for a "precipitous decline" in US–Latin American relations, one tied to "[his] Administration's economic and diplomatic sanctions linked to its undifferentiated charges of human rights violations." Turbay hoped that Reagan's agenda for improved relations might include reviving the Darien Highway, restoring the presidential leadership that Carter had withdrawn. Nine months after Reagan's inauguration, Turbay and his Panamanian counterpart issued a joint letter to the US president, imploring his help. The letter declared, "We feel that you, Mr. President, who have entered the White House inspired by projects of continental scope, surely want to link your government to the fulfillment of old commitments that will certainly create a new and promising situation in relations between North America and the rest of the countries of the hemisphere."[85]

But their plea would be in vain. The Reagan administration paid the road even less attention than the Carter administration had. When it came to Latin America, Reagan had other priorities.

"Central America is the most important place in the world for the United States today," declared Reagan's ambassador to the United Nations in 1981. The region, which had seemed relatively stable when the Inter-American Highway was completed in 1963, had exploded into revolutionary violence during the years leading up to Reagan's inauguration. In Guatemala and El Salvador, authoritarian regimes fought brutally to contain popular leftist uprisings. In Nicaragua, the long-lived Somoza family dynasty had fallen after prolonged fighting to the leftist Sandinistas, named for the general who had fought defiantly against the United States, and this regime change had provoked a guerrilla war of its own.[86]

Reagan had made his feelings about Central America known during the 1980 campaign, when he announced that the Caribbean was "rapidly becoming a Communist lake in what should be an American pond." Reagan's aggressive rhetoric soon transformed into a prolonged campaign of military and economic intervention in Central America in the name of anti-communism, promoting the authoritarians and combating the Sandinistas. It was a period defined by bloodshed, chaos, and terror.[87]

Even the Inter-American Highway, the result of thirty-five years' cooperation, fell victim to the violence, as all parties involved fought for control of the strategic route. Bombings became almost routine, some sponsored by the CIA. At one point in early 1982, a reported CIA-backed bombing of a bridge on the Inter-American Highway in Nicaragua prompted the Sandinista regime to declare martial law. That particular bombing had come shortly after Turbay requested Reagan's cooperation on the Darien Highway, an appeal that seemed almost absurd with the Inter-American Highway itself under siege. The United States was now destroying the very thing it had spent so many decades working to realize.[88]

When the Reagan administration left office in early 1989, Central America was in tatters but taking steps toward peace. The architect of the peace process, President Óscar Arias of Costa Rica, had helped push the United States to the side during the negotiations, which in part explained his success. The final tally of the violence during the Reagan years included hundreds of thousands of casualties.[89]

The calming of Central America allowed Reagan's successor, George Herbert Walker Bush, to shift the United States' focus toward a newfound preoccupation on the isthmus, President Manuel Noriega of Panama. A former general, Noriega had risen to power after Torrijos, the United States' negotiating partner in the canal transfer treaty, died in a mysterious plane accident, and the new leader had turned Panama into a military-backed authoritarian state. The United States, scheduled to begin transitioning canal control to Panama in the early 1990s, feared the consequences of giving the great infrastructure project to a figure like Noriega, one widely believed to be involved in drug trafficking, with processing facilities supposedly in Darien. Bush grew so alarmed that he authorized military action in December 1989. Soon US soldiers descended on Panama City, eventually taking Noriega prisoner. Reported figures of total casualties from the invasion ranged from the US military's tally of several hundred to some locals' accounts of several thousand, a body count that somewhat tempered the success of the operation, which ultimately restored democracy to Panama.[90]

Nearly a decade had passed, by this point, since Reagan had implicitly rejected Turbay's appeal for the Darien Highway. In the meantime, the highway, like Pan-Americanism itself, had largely fallen off the map of US policy. The Department of Transportation had long ago ceased asking about appropriations for Panamanian construction. Many of the congressmen who had supported highway funding in the late 1960s had retired. The last president to take serious interest in the road was Nixon. There were thus few left to celebrate the news that emerged in late 1991, almost ten years after Turbay's appeal, that the USDA had determined Colombia was aftosa-compliant.[91]

The End of the Road

At the time of the USDA announcement, barely sixty miles of the Darien Gap remained. The gap had shrunk gradually over the course of the 1970s and 1980s, with Colombia extending a small spur twenty miles northwest from a point on the Turbo–Medellín highway and with the government of Panama pushing a pioneer dirt road southeast from Chepo for nearly two hundred miles. Panama's extensive construction effort had included a crossing of the newly formed Lake Bayano, which sat upstream from the Bayano Hydropower Dam, and had continued as far as Yaviza, the terminus of Richard Tewkesbury's journey fifty years earlier. Rather remarkably, the "Darien Gap" of 1991—from Yaviza to the southern side of the Atrato swamp—bore no overlap with the route that Tewkesbury had explored a half century prior.[92]

The USDA's announcement on aftosa served to revitalize a Colombian campaign to close the Darien Gap that had been on hiatus for much of the 1980s. An official from the Colombian province of Antioquia, home to the city of Medellín, wrote the Department of Transportation in 1991, "[As t]he obstacle of foot and mouth disease has been eradicated from the zone included in the Darien Gap . . . , this is the moment to take the necessary steps to reactivate the [project] . . . with a look towards achieving the reasonable desire of the countries of the continent, American integration." Further support soon came directly from the Colombian president, who considered the road vital to both a regional development program, dubbed the Plan Pacífico, and a potential free trade agreement with Mexico and Venezuela. As one Colombian foreign affairs representative noted, "The highway . . . will facilitate trade of petroleum, cotton, cloth, iron, steel, and other goods between Mexico, Colombia and Venezuela." Another government official, speaking in 1992, summed up the Colombian sentiments thusly: "If the Berlin Wall fell, why can't the Darien Gap?"[93]

The Colombians who supported the road readily dismissed the broader concerns that had emerged in the 1970s about environmental harms. One former Colombian ambassador to the United States assured in 1992, "once the highway is built we could . . . send police to the border to guard against deforestation." The Colombian journal *El Espectador* went so far as to declare, "The idea that the road threatens the environment is nothing less than a distracting sophism. The only way to effectively avoid deforestation, which is constantly increasing due to the absence of control and surveillance, is the completion of . . . the route between Panama and Colombia."[94]

The Colombians' assurances, however, ignored the mounting evidence from the Darien Highway in Panama. The jungle that had once tormented Richard Tewkesbury had ceded to endless cow pastures, despite the Panamanian government's efforts to control deforestation. An official from one of Panama's largest conservation organizations lamented in 1992, "After they opened the route, the zone was devastated by an anarchic and uncontrolled deforestation." A *Washington Post* reporter who toured the highway observed that same year, "In spite of strict government regulations forbidding logging and the decimation of the jungle for cattle ranching, no one seems surprised by battered trucks hauling enormous loads of first-growth lumber out of the wilderness. Panama's land-hungry campesinos also see this as a promised land, a place to . . . wrench themselves free from Panama's poverty cycle."[95]

Environmental harm notwithstanding, Panama began cooperating with Colombia to push the highway forward shortly after the USDA announcement. The first step was a meeting between the presidents of the two nations in March 1992 to "revive" the Darien Highway project. Both governments subsequently appealed to the United States for support, though their efforts went nowhere. Undiscouraged, they agreed in late 1992 to bring the matter to the Inter-American Development Bank, a multilateral lending agency established in 1959. This appeal found greater success than had their earlier campaign before the US government, with the bank promising to study the highway, whose estimated cost now stood at $300 million. Months later, in August 1993, the public works ministers of Panama and Colombia jointly declared that their nations were each willing to pledge $50 million toward the highway "that will unite overland the American continent." They further assured,

> Our governments have made a strong commitment to preserve and improve the fragile environment and take all necessary measures to guarantee that the road will not be used as access to new land for colonization, but as a "bridge" to enable all people from the Americas to freely move through our Continent. . . . The Darien Gap Highway will improve the image held in the United States and our two countries of road builders so damaged by a history of lack of concern towards environmental issues and prove that development and environment are complementary, rather than antagonistic elements in any society whether developed or not.[96]

The renewed bilateral talk of closing the Darien Gap—despite these environmental promises—had set off alarms for the indigenous communities living beyond Yaviza. They had seen what the Darien Highway did to the neighboring lands toward Panama City, and they feared what a completed road would mean for their forests and their livelihood. By 1993, organized resistance was beginning to take shape among the Emberá and Wounaan, two subgroups of the so-called Chocó people. These groups had traditionally lived in isolated family units but had begun organizing into villages in the middle of the century and then assumed a relatively unified political voice, a development that led the government of Panama to grant them in 1983 two *comarcas* (autonomous indigenous zones), one near the Pacific Ocean and the other situated just north of the Darien National Park and almost bordering on Yaviza. This eastern comarca, unlike the Pacific comarca or the Cuna ones farther north and along the coast, lay directly in a possible path of the Pan-American Highway.[97]

Fears about the highway led the Emberá-Wounaan in late 1993 to call for an Indigenous Pan-American Highway Commission. That December, over five hundred delegates from various Emberá-Wounaan communities gathered to discuss the next steps. One delegate declared, "the construction of the Pan-American highway through our territories would cause irreparable damage to our forests, rivers, flora and farms upon which depend our brothers and sisters the animals and our river culture. The wounds caused by the recent construction of the Pan-American highway to Yavisa are still fresh." Another insisted, "We are demanding our legal rights to consultation regarding any plans the government has for our ancestral lands." The conference ended up passing a resolution stating its "rejection of the Pan-American Highway's construction through Indigenous territories in Panama."[98]

The Emberá-Wounaan found common cause with an international environmental movement that had grown dramatically since the 1970s. The year before the indigenous highway congress, Brazil had hosted a major UN environmental summit in Rio de Janeiro that many saw as the start of a new era. The United Nations, for its part, had already taken several steps to protect the Darien National Park, designating it a Biological and Cultural World Heritage Site in 1981 and a Biosphere Reserve in 1983. Originally created as an aftosa buffer zone, the park was now one of only two dozen locations on earth to hold both UN distinctions. The Darien Gap, noted one contemporary writer, had become "a crucial testing ground for the Earth Summit Conventions on Biological Diversity and Climate Change [signed at Rio]." The month after the indigenous highway conference, in January 1994, the International Union for the Conservation of Nature, based out of Switzerland, passed a resolution declaring the protection of Darien "a priority for all humanity."[99]

To many environmentalists, Darien's location at the crossing point of two continents gave it immeasurable importance. Archibald Carr, a biologist with the New York–based Wildlife Conservation Society, observed in 1994, "If the Darien is a biological plug, a barrier to a biological upheaval that could affect both major continents in the region, then it achieves greater conservation significance than any other forest." Others noted that its position and geography had made it a hot spot of biodiversity, something that the Rio summit had focused on. The Darien Gap, observed one report, "is one of the most ecologically diverse regions in the world because it acts as a land bridge where species from both continents intermingle." Scientists estimated that the region contained over four hundred species and subspecies of birds alone. More than seven thousand species of vascular plants, many endemic, were thought to exist there as well. The area also hosted a number of endangered animal species, including cougars, harpy eagles, jaguars, macaws, spectacled bears, and tapirs. A 1994 UN-sponsored environmental report criticizing the highway project noted, "The Darien is a living laboratory and perhaps one of the planet's epicentres with the most genetic flow."[100]

The concerns that environmental and indigenous groups raised proved difficult for the Inter-American Development Bank to ignore. The bank noted in a 1994 report that the Darien Gap was "critical for ecosystem conservation" and that indigenous groups there "oppose[d] development of the Panamerican Highway through their lands." Soon the bank's conclusions led it to abandon its planned road assessment in favor of a less politically charged regional development study. One bank official reportedly observed in mid-1995, "the [bank will] provide no financing for either the construction or renovation of roads in the Darien Gap."[101]

The bank's apparent withdrawal from the highway provoked little outcry in Panama, where feelings toward the project had cooled. Some of this diminished enthusiasm stemmed from the same concerns that had troubled the bank, but the erosion of support also owed to increasing fear about problems spilling over from Colombia. Though Colombian highway boosters rarely emphasized it, their portion of the Darien Gap was a battleground in two worsening internal wars—and corresponding humanitarian crises for the Emberá-Wounaan tribes and Afro-Colombians living there—that promised to complicate any road building projects. The first war concerned cocaine operations inside Colombia, the world's lead supplier of the illegal drug, with some coca fields around Darien. The second war involved a Marxist separatist group known as the Revolutionary Armed Forces of Colombia (FARC), which had units stationed amid the Darien Gap's jungles. The violence had first crossed over into Panama in January 1993, when armed FARC guerrillas attacked the village of Púcuro, on the Panamanian side of the Darien Gap, and took four missionaries hostage. After that, tensions along the border in Panama remained high as the twin wars raged.

The highway meant to promote hemispheric unity seemingly threatened to further inflame two intractable, brutal Colombian conflicts, with uncertain consequences for adjacent Panama. The highway's Panamanian critics also pointed to the potential issue of unchecked immigration from unstable Colombia, a nation with ten times the population of its northern neighbor.[102]

Panama's increasing ambivalence toward the highway was nonetheless ignored by the project's die-hard proponents. In 1995, the Colombian transportation minister, echoing a century of highway dreamers, declared, "I think it is outrageous that in this day and age there is still no road to connect the Americas. I am going to keep pressing the issue because it is a necessity. To say it can't be done is easy. We have to say, let's find a way for the road to be built." Later that year, there was even a quixotic push in the United States to get the highway going by Representative Thomas Petri of Wisconsin, who convinced Congress to approve a $200,000 Darien Highway study that ultimately went nowhere. A *Washington Post* reporter who covered this ill-fated study quipped, "First the missile gap, then the credibility gap, then the generation gap and finally the gender gap. Next: the Darien Gap, in which the U.S. government mulls the feasibility of building a 65-mile stretch of paved highway through the rain forest between Panama and Colombia."[103]

But the remaining Darien Highway champions soon confronted a Panamanian government that had evolved from ambivalence to hostility. The president of Panama made these sentiments known in August 1996, when he bluntly declared, "there will be no highway built through the Darien during my [term]." It was the first time a president of either Panama, Colombia, or the United States had ever unambiguously opposed the road in public.[104]

The Panamanian president instead supported a new proposal from the Inter-American Development Bank for a holistic Darien development plan, one that included paving the existing road to Yaviza but no further work in the gap. The proposal also called for mechanisms to ensure indigenous participation in the planning process. "What we are doing in Darien," declared the president of the bank in 1998, "will be a model for all of Latin America." A US activist who had worked with the Indigenous Pan-American Highway Commission noted of the new bank agreement, which went into effect in 1999, "This is a huge step for the indigenous people of the Darien. . . . For the first time, they will get the chance to show how you can do development while respecting people's rights and the environment."[105]

The announcement of the landmark bank loan came eight years after the

USDA had declared Colombia aftosa-compliant. In that time, the Darien Highway project had reemerged only to collapse once more, perhaps permanently. The dream of the highway, by this point, had transformed into something of a nightmare. The road represented a threat to indigenous livelihood and cattle health as well as the potential destruction of a forest unique in the world. Completion of the great "highway of friendship" would also allow for the possible transmission of Colombian violence into Panama and the spread of illegal drugs into the United States. This was hardly the vision that Tommy Guardia Jr. and Rómulo O'Farrill had fought so hard for.[106]

Panama's opposition to the road only grew stronger in the years after the bank loan. The multiple arguments against the road that had come to the fore in the 1990s continued to outweigh the long-standing appeals for hemispheric unity and economic integration. One bank official noted in 2004 of Panama, "They like the gap." Even in the face of prolonged pressure from Colombian president Álvaro Uribe, who served from 2002 to 2010 and marshaled a raft of arguments extolling the benefits of the "transcendental[ly] importan[t]" road, the Panamanian government remained largely steadfast in its resolve. Resistance to the project had become enshrined in Panamanian policy.[107]

It appears, for the moment, that the Darien Gap is safe from the road.

Conclusion

A century and a half has now passed since Hinton Rowan Helper first asked his immortal question "Why not by rail?" and began the quest to link the Americas. Over the course of that period, his dream of hemispheric connectivity took on a remarkable life. It snaked its way through more than a century of US–Latin American relations, much like the Pan-American Highway would snake its way through the hemisphere. It had inspired US presidents from Benjamin Harrison to Richard Nixon and Latin American leaders from Porfirio Díaz to Omar Torrijos. It had shaped wars and revolutions. It had birthed modern US overseas development in the era of the Good Neighbor and eventually cost the United States billions in aid, factoring inflation.

It was a dream that appeared inevitable until suddenly it was not.

The end of the quest in the United States seemed, in some ways, like a symbolic conclusion to the greater Pan-American movement with which it was inextricably bound up. The movement of "true" Pan-Americanism that had inspired Andrew Carnegie and Franklin Roosevelt and Richard Tewkesbury had gradually faded as a relic of the twentieth century. After the Cold War years had undermined Pan-Americanism's nonintervention principles, a rising discourse of globalization had displaced the need for a hemispheric ideology altogether. The United States had come to see Latin America not as part of a larger Pan-American region but as a piece of the "developing world" or "global south." US policy became more focused on keeping drugs and migrants from Latin America out and less on working toward broader political, cultural, or economic projects cooperatively with the Americas. The strengthening during this post–Cold War period of regional ties in Europe—a continent that had fought so catastrophically during the twentieth century—offered a stark counterpoint to the Americas, which could get no further in these same years than an aborted hemispheric free trade agreement. Even as the United States' own population has grown increasingly Hispanicized over the past three decades, the nation's public policy has paradoxically reflected minimal interest in the idealism of a Pan-American movement that had prospered in an earlier time. The great imagined hemispheric infrastructure project in the era of President Donald Trump is no longer a road to connect the Americas but a wall to divide them.

The Pan-American Highway, though incomplete, remains today a reminder that it was not always this way. The road is a monument to a forgotten path.

Acknowledgments

I have amassed more debts in the service of this book than I can ever hope to repay. These acknowledgments offer only the barest accounting.

It would have been a hopeless task to try to reconstruct the events contained herein without the assistance of a small battalion of librarians and archivists. I was fortunate to have at my disposal throughout the duration of this project Yale University's library system and its exceptionally helpful staff. It would also have been impossible to navigate the holdings at the National Archives, the single-most consequential repository for this project, without the assistance of several archivists, notably transportation specialist David Pfeiffer, who repeatedly located boxes unlisted in the finding aids. Several essential records there, moreover, were only unearthed due to Victor Wagher, the records officer at the Federal Highway Administration—and for putting us in touch I must additionally thank Richard Weingroff, historian at the Federal Highway Administration. Finally, my deepest gratitude to the librarians and archivists in Costa Rica and Panama who took mercy on a foreigner desperately searching for all records on the *carretera panamericana*.

The later chapters of the book benefited immensely from the dozens of people in multiple countries who agreed to sit with me and share their recollections and analysis. They all have my most heartfelt appreciation and are listed in the sources, but I would be remiss if I did not acknowledge several who went far beyond what could ever have been expected: Edilberto Dogirama, president of the Congreso General Emberá, who provided me with authorization papers for my research trip to Yaviza, Panama; the Guardia family, who established a living link to characters in the book reaching back to the 1920s; Roberto Pacheco, who shared materials from the 1950s and 1960s that he had saved; Michel Puech, owner of Panama Exotic Adventures, who proved indefatigable in the pursuit of some half dozen people he knew with specialized knowledge of Darien; and Rodolfo Silva Vargas, a former Costa Rican Minister of Public Works, who contacted several retired government officials with direct knowledge of the Inter-American Highway.

The book further relied on generous support from several institutions. The Yale History Department provided a dissertation fellowship as well as travel and research grants. Additional assistance came from Yale's Macmillan Center, its Agrarian Studies program, and its International Security Studies program (specifically, the Smith Richardson Foundation fellowship). The American Historical Association also aided my research through its Albert J. Beveridge Grant. And I was fortunate to receive a year of writing funding from the Society for Historians of American Foreign Relations. Lastly, I must thank the Ucross Foundation in Wyoming for a two-week writer's residency.

The Longest Line on the Map would never have been realized without encouragement from a number of individuals who nurtured and shaped the book from its earliest phases. My PhD co-advisers, Glenda Gilmore and Gil Joseph, each of whom I first worked with nearly twenty years ago, introduced me to the profession of history as an undergraduate. Thanks also go to Paul Sabin, who helped me navigate the twists and turns that inevitably accompany a PhD. Literary agent Eric Lupfer embraced the project as it was first taking shape, and I've long counted on the aid and counsel of Eric Simonoff at WME. Scribner's editor in chief, Colin Harrison, a modern-day Maxwell Perkins, trusted my vision as it first came into focus and, as with *American Canopy*, assembled a production team without parallel.

Finally, my thanks (and apologies) go to my friends and family, who patiently spent years hearing about nothing but trees only to be rewarded with endless talk of roads and a mysterious quest. Particular debts of gratitude go to my college roommates, the old Thursday clubhouse crew, the Uvita/Flutterby community, and the Living Library. If patience were money, no one would be wealthier than Elizabeth Herman, who lived with this project as much as with me.

Without all of this support, *The Longest Line on the Map* could not have been completed. That being said, the omissions and errors—both the inevitable and the avoidable—are mine and mine alone.

Notes

Chapter 1: The Magnificent Conception

1. "The Three Americas Railway," *Washington Post*, April 20, 1899, p. 6; Helper, "Railway Communication Between North and South America," October 12, 1882 (hereinafter, *Helper 1882 Letter*), enclosed in Helper to Secretary of State Bayard, November 3, 1885, National Archives II at College Park, Maryland (hereinafter, *NARA*), Record Group 59, Central Files 1789–1906—Miscellaneous Letters (File M-179, Microfilm Reel 689, Frame 0079).
2. Stewart Holbrook, *The Lost Men of American History* (Macmillan, 1946), p. 175.
3. Savoyard, *In the Pennyrile of Old Kentucky* (Sudwarth, 1911), p. 118; see also David Brown, *Southern Outcast* (LSU, 2006), pp. 20–24.
4. Helper, *Land of Gold* (Henry Taylor, 1855), pp. 188–197.
5. See Brown, *Southern Outcast*, p. 70.
6. Helper, *The Impending Crisis of the South* (Burdick Brothers, 1857), preface.
7. See Holbrook, *The Lost Men of American History*, p. 172; Brown, *Southern Outcast*, pp. 137–142 and 157–175; see also *Congressional Globe* (December 5, 1859), 36th Cong., 1st sess., p. 3, and *Congressional Globe* (December 7, 1859), 36th Cong., 1st sess., p. 30. See also Horace Greeley, *The American Conflict*, vol. 1 (O. D. Case, 1865), pp. 304–306; and John Sherman, *Recollections of Forty Years*, vol. 1 (Werner, 1895), pp. 169–180.
8. See Brown, *Southern Outcast*, pp. 179–184.
9. See "Hinton Rowan Helper's Railroad," *Jackson Daily Citizen* (Michigan), December 24, 1884, p. 6; see also Brown, *Southern Outcast*, pp. 192–195.
10. See "The Three Americas Railway," *Washington Post*, April 20, 1899, p. 6; "Projected Intercontinental Railway Through the Three Americas," S.Doc. 504 (June 25, 1906), 59th Cong., 1st sess., pp. 4–5; see also Brown, *Southern Outcast*, p. 196.
11. Helper to Seward, July 13, 1863, NARA, RG 59, Despatches from United States Consuls in Buenos Aires, vol. 11 (M70), quoted in Brown, *Southern Outcast*, p. 203.
12. Helper to Seward, August 21, 1866, NARA, RG 59, Despatches from United States Consuls in Buenos Aires, vol. 12 (M70), quoted in Brown, *Southern Outcast*, p. 209.
13. On this period in Helper's life generally, see Brown, *Southern Outcast*, pp. 195–212.
14. Helper to Theodore Roosevelt, November 7, 1901, p. 7., enclosed in Helper to John Hay, November 23, 1901, NARA, RG 59, Central Files 1789–1906, Miscellaneous Letters (File M-179, Roll 1118, Frame 0604); and Helper 1882 Letter, 11. On the extent of Helper's patriotism, see Helper 1882 Letter, pp. 9–10; see also "Projected Intercontinental Railway Through the Three Americas," S. Doc. 504 (June 25, 1906), 59th Cong., 1st sess., pp. 10–11.

15. "A Great Enterprise," *Baltimore Sun*, December 27, 1889, p. 1.

16. See Randolph Campbell, "The Spanish-American Aspect of Henry Clay's American System," *Americas* 24 (1967): 3–17.

17. Ibid., pp. 3–17.

18. Henry Clay, "Mission to South America," May 10, 1820, in Daniel Mallory, ed., *The Life and Speeches of Henry Clay*, vol. 1 (Bixby, 1844), p. 429; see also Campbell, p. 8.

19. "Message from the President of the United States," H. Doc. 2 (December 2, 1823), 18th Cong., 1st sess., p. 14.

20. Simón Bolívar, "Reply of a South American to a Gentleman of This Island [Jamaica]," September 6, 1815, in Vincente Lecuna, comp., *Selected Writings of Bolívar, 1810–1822* (Colonial Press, 1951), p. 118; and "Circular from Simón Bolívar," December 7, 1824, in *International American Conference, Historical Appendix*, Sen. Ex. Doc. 232, Part 4 (1890), 51st Cong., 1st sess., pp. 159–161; see also Andrew N. Cleven, "The First Panama Mission and the Congress of the United States," *Journal of Negro History* 13 (1928): 225–254.

21. Cleven, p. 225 and general; see also Ralph Sanders, "Congressional Reaction in the United States to the Panama Congress of 1826," *Americas* 11 (1954): 141–154.

22. See Samuel Inman, *Inter-American Conferences, 1826–1954* (University Press of Washington, DC, and Community College Press, 1965), pp. 1–19.

23. Ibid., pp. 20–32; see also Mark Van Aken, *Pan-Hispanism: Its Origin and Development to 1866* (University of California Press, 1959); and *International American Conference— Historical Appendix*, Sen. Ex. Doc. 232, Part 4 (1890), 51st Cong., 1st sess. On mid-twentieth-century historical interpretations of US hemispheric imaginings in the United States, see Herbert Bolton, "The Epic of Greater America," *American Historical Review* 38 (1933): 448–474; and Arthur P. Whitaker, *The Western Hemisphere Idea* (Cornell University Press, 1954).

24. Helper, *Noonday Exigencies in America* (Bible Brothers, 1871), p. 198; see also Helper to Roosevelt, November 7, 1901, p. 17, enclosed in Helper to John Hay, November 23, 1901, NARA, RG 59, Central Files 1789–1906, Miscellaneous Letters (File M-179, Roll 1118, Frame 0604). On this period in Helper's life generally, see Brown, *Southern Outcast*, pp. 213–251.

25. Helper to Dom Pedro II, May 9, 1877, in Helper, *Oddments of Andean Diplomacy* (W. S. Bryan, 1879), p. 378; see also *Oddments*, 337–438, and Brown, *Southern Outcast*, 251–254.

26. "Projected Intercontinental Railway Through the Three Americas," S. Doc. 504 (June 25, 1906), 59th Cong., 1st sess., p. 15.

27. See Brown, *Southern Outcast*, pp. 254–256.

28. "Money to Throw Away," *Baltimore Sun*, January 17, 1881, p. 2.

29. "The Great Backbone Road," *New York Times*, May 31, 1880; and "Money to Throw Away," *Baltimore Sun*, January 17, 1881. Details of this early promotion and the prize-winning essays can be found in Helper, *The Three Americas Railway* (W. S. Bryan, 1881).

30. Helper 1882 Letter, pp. 4–5, and generally see "Helper's 'The Three Americas Railway,'" H. Rep. 1750 (July 28, 1882), 47th Cong., 1st sess.; see also Brown, *Southern Outcast*, p. 259.

31. Helper explained his bill and some of the ideas it conveyed in Helper 1882 Letter, pp. 7–16.

32. "Another Open Letter to Mr. Sherman," *Washington Post*, April 11, 1884, p. 2; "Commercial Relations with South and Central America," H. Rep. 1445 (May 7, 1884), 48th Cong., 1st sess., p. 5.

33. "South American Trade," *St. Louis Post-Dispatch*, July 10, 1884, p. 7.

34. On Blaine, see David Muzzey, *James G. Blaine* (Dodd, Mead, 1934).

35. Blaine to John Henderson, July 15, 1884, in Blaine, *Political Discussions, 1856–1886* (Henry Bill, 1887), p. 429. On Blaine's views toward Latin America, see David Healy, *James G. Blaine and Latin America* (University of Missouri Press, 2001), and A. Curtis

Wilgus, "James G. Blaine and the Pan American Movement," *Hispanic American Historical Review* 5 (1922): 662–708.

36. George Hoar, "Some Political Reminiscences," *Scribner's Magazine* XXV (1899): 457; see also Healy, p. 4.

37. "Speech of Mr. Ingersoll," *Proceedings of the Republican National Convention* (Republican Press Association, 1876), p. 74; Conkling quoted in Harry Peck, *Twenty Years of the Republic, 1885–1905* (Dodd, Mead, 1920), p. 42; see also Muzzey, pp. 287–325.

38. On Elkins's New Mexican activities, see Gustavus Myers, *History of the Great American Fortunes*, vol. III (Charles Kerr, 1910), pp. 311–337; see also John Williams, "Davis and Elkins of West Virginia" (Ph.D. diss., Yale University, 1967). On Kerens, Blaine, and the Star Route Frauds, see J. Martin Klotsche, "The Star Route Cases," *Mississippi Valley Historical Review* 22 (1935): 407–418.

39. See Muzzey, pp. 287–325.

40. Ibid., pp. 326–360; see also Healy, pp. 120–137.

41. Gail Hamilton, *The Biography of James G. Blaine* (Henry Bill, 1895), p. 439; see also Healy, p. 16; and Russell Bastert, "A New Approach to the Origins of Blaine's Pan American Policy," *Hispanic American Historical Review* 39 (1959): 377–379.

42. See Healy, pp. 54 and 17–119.

43. Bastert, p. 405. On Garfield's assassination, see Ira Rutkow, *James A. Garfield* (Times Books, 2006).

44. Blaine to President Arthur, February 3, 1882, in Blaine, *Political Discussions*, p. 409; see also Bastert, p. 380, and Healy, p. 94.

45. Blaine, "Withdrawal of Invitations to a Peace Congress," in *Political Discussions*, pp. 407–410; see also "American Peace Congress," House Ex. Doc. 174 (April 18, 1882), 47th Cong., 1st sess. For a discussion of which countries accepted the invitations, see Blaine, *Political Discussions*, p. 406.

46. *International American Conference—Historical Appendix*, Sen. Ex. Doc. 232, Part 4 (1890), 51st Cong., 1st sess., pp. 295–296. On Blaine's friendship with Morgan, see Edward Crapol, *James G. Blaine* (SRI, 2000), p. 64.

47. See *International American Conference—Historical Appendix*, Sen. Ex. Doc. 232, Part 4 (1890), 51st Cong., 1st sess., p. 302.

48. "South American Trade," *New-York Tribune*, July 29, 1885, p. 2. See also "Report from the Central and South American Commissioners," House Ex. Doc. 226 (February 13, 1885), 48th Cong., 2nd sess.; and James Vivian, "The South American Commission to the Three Americas Movement" (Ph.D. diss., American University, 1971).

49. See *International American Conference—Historical Appendix*, Sen. Ex. Doc. 232, Part 4 (1890), 51st Cong., 1st sess., pp. 312–313. According to one recent study, the British minister in Washington believed that the approval of the conference "reflected a political maneuver by which the Democratic majority in the House had backed it in the name of freer trade, while the Republican majority in the Senate supported [it] to help alleviate pressure against the protective system [of tariffs]." Joseph Smith, "The First Conference of American States (1889–1890) and the Early Pan American Policy of the United States," in David Sheinin, ed., *Beyond the Ideal: Pan Americanism in Inter-American Affairs* (Greenwood Press, 2000), p. 22. See also Intercontinental Railway Commission, *A Condensed Report*, vol. I, part I (GPO, 1898), pp. 10–15.

50. "The Plumed Knight," *Los Angeles Times*, February 4, 1893, p. 11; see also Muzzey, pp. 361–391.

51. "Story of the Nomination," *New-York Tribune*, June 27, 1888, p. 1; see also "The Blaine Men Did It," *St. Louis Post-Dispatch*, June 25, 1888, p. 2; "Harrison and Elkins," *Chicago Daily Tribune*, June 21, 1888, p. 3; H. Wayne Morgan, *From Hayes to McKinley* (Syracuse University Press, 1969), p. 289; and Healy, p. 140.

52. See Healy, pp. 138–139; and David Nasaw, *Andrew Carnegie* (Penguin Books, 2006), p. 328.

53. Harrison to Blaine, January 17, 1889, in Albert Volwiler, ed., *The Correspondence*

Between Benjamin Harrison and James G. Blaine, 1882–1893 (APS, 1940), p. 44. On Harrison's attitude toward political appointments, see Morgan, *From Hayes to McKinley*, pp. 320–326.

54. On the Republican delegates, see Thomas McCann, *Argentina, the United States, and the Inter-American System, 1880–1914* (Harvard University Press, 1957), pp. 130–131.

55. On Davis, see, e.g., Williams, *Davis and Elkins of West Virginia*; Charles M. Pepper, *The Life and Times of Henry Gassaway Davis, 1823–1916* (Century, 1920); and John Caruso, "Henry Gassaway Davis and the Pan American Railway" (Ph.D. diss., West Virginia University, 1949). On the mixed business interests of Davis, Blaine, Elkins, and Kerens, see also "Trouble at a Railroad Meeting," *Chicago Daily Tribune*, January 29, 1890, p. 6; "The Elkins-Blaine Road," *New York Times*, January 27, 1892, p. 2; "Accused of Fraud in Railway Management," *New York Times*, October 18, 1892, p. 2; "Reported Consolidation of Elkins-Kerens-Davis Interests in West Virginia," *Washington Post*, August 5, 1899, p. 4; Davis to Mrs. James G. Blaine, May 2, 1901, West Virginia and Regional History Center, Morgantown, WV, Papers of Henry Gassaway Davis (hereinafter, *Davis Papers*), Letter Books.

56. José Martí, "Congreso Internacional de Washington (November 3, 1889)," *La Nación* (Buenos Aires, Argentina), December 19, 1889, p. 1; and see Matías Romero, "The Pan-American Conference I," *North American Review* 151 (1890): 357–358. See also William Eleroy Curtis, *Trade and Transportation Between the United States and Spanish America* (GPO, 1889).

57. Charles Flint, *Memories of an Active Life* (Putnam's, 1923), p. 151.

58. See Romero, "The Pan-American Conference II," *North American Review* 151 (1890): 410 and 418–419; see also McCann, pp. 130–164.

59. See Blaine, "Address to the International American Conference," draft dated 1889, Library of Congress, Washington, DC, Papers of James G. Blaine, Reel 12; see also Inman, pp. 40–41.

60. See "Claims He Is the Author," *Chicago Daily Tribune*, January 20, 1890, p. 2. According to Davis's close friend and biographer Charles Pepper, "It is probable that the interest of Henry G. Davis had been awakened . . . possibly through Richard A. Parsons, a distinguished Virginia engineer and railway builder who had sought to put the enterprise on a practical basis." Pepper, *The Life and Times of Henry Gassaway Davis*, p. 122. Pepper, whose association with Davis only began after 1900, almost certainly confused the name "Richard A. Parsons" with that of Davis's actual friend Colonel H. C. Parsons. Davis's enthusiasm for the railway likely also stemmed from the same economic concerns that Helper had expressed earlier. Davis wrote in his diary, several months after the conference, "Trade is now against us. Europe can successfully compete with water, but not with rail." Quoted in Pepper, p. 124.

61. See "Report of the Committee on Railroads," February 21, 1890, *Davis Papers*, Box 186, Folder C. See also *International American Conference—Reports of Committees*, Sen. Ex. Doc. 232, Part 1 (1890), 51st Cong., 1st sess., pp. 93–102.

62. Domingo de Pantoja and Victor Galvez (Vicente Gregorio Quesada), *Los Estados Unidos y La América del Sur* (J. Peuser, 1893), p. 360 (author's translation). Romero, "The Pan-American Conference II," p. 421. Root quoted in *International American Conference—Excursion Appendix*, Sen. Ex. Doc. 232, Part 3 (1890), 51st Cong., 1st sess., p. 293. For a brief history of the term "Pan-American" in the context of international diplomacy, see Inman, p. 79.

63. "Continental Railway to Connect American Nations," H. Rep. 2243 (May 29, 1890), 51st Cong., 1st sess.; see also *Congressional Record—Senate*, June 24, 1890, pp. 6429–6433.

64. Blaine to Harrison, July 22 and September 2, 1890; and Harrison to Blaine, September 4 and 15, 1890, in Volwiler, pp. 111, 123, and 126.

65. *Minutes of the Intercontinental Railway Commission* (Washington, DC, 1891), pp. 3–4.

66. Technically, the Commercial Bureau of American Republics, the other organization

to emerge from the conference, began concurrently. However, the Commercial Bureau remained an almost entirely US affair for the first several years. See "The Pan American Union, 1890–1940," in *Bulletin of the Pan American Union* LXXIV (April 1940): 201.

67. See *Minutes*, p. 3; see also, translation of "Letter from Dr. Don Miguel Tedin," *La Nación* (Buenos Aires), April 25, 1891, NARA, RG 43, Intercontinental Railway Commission (hereinafter, *IRC Papers*), Private Papers of the Surgeon Attached to Corps, no. 2, 1892–1896.

68. *Minutes*, p. 15.

69. See "Report of the Committee on Railroads," February 21, 1890, *Davis Papers*, Box 186, Folder C.

70. On these matters, see generally, *Minutes*, pp. 22 and 35; and Helper to Cassatt, April 22, 1891, enclosed in Helper to Blaine, April 23, 1891, *IRC Papers*, Private Papers of the Surgeon Attached to Corps, no. 2, 1892–1896.

71. See *Minutes*, pp. 22–103. On Argentine-US relations generally in this period, see McCann, pp. 165–187.

72. Helper, *The Three Americas Railway*, p. 6; and John Bacon to unknown, June 21, 1887 (discussing a South American route proposed by a Professor Posada), *IRC Papers*, Private Papers of the Surgeon Attached to Corps, no. 2, 1892–1896; see also Bacon to Department of State, January 11, 1888, in "Continental Railway to Connect American Nations," H. Rep. 2243 (May 29, 1890), 51st Cong., 1st sess., pp. 4–5.

73. See "Report of the Committee on Railroads," February 21, 1890, *Davis Papers*, Box 186, Folder C. See also *Report of the International American Conference Relative to an Intercontinental Railway Line* (GPO, 1890), appendix, pp. 83–200.

74. Ibid., pp. 168–171.

75. Details of these activities can be found in *Minutes*, p. 21, and throughout.

76. *Minutes*, pp. 61–62.

77. Ibid., p. 98.

78. Ibid., p. 102. See also R. M. G. Brown, "The Great Storm at Samoa," *United Service* (March 1903): 999–1000.

79. *Minutes*, p. 93.

80. See *Minutes*, pp. 110–116. See also Merle Curti and Kendall Birr, *Prelude to Point Four* (University of Wisconsin Press, 1954), pp. 11–37.

81. Intercontinental Railway Commission, *Report of Surveys and Explorations Made by Corps No. 1*, vol. I, part II (GPO, 1898), p. 16; "Work on the Pan-American Railway Progressing," *Times-Picayune*, November 16, 1891, p. 2; and Shunk to Cassatt, May 19, 1891, *Davis Papers*, Box 186, Folder S.

82. Cassatt and Davis to Blaine, May 5, 1891; Miller to Cassatt, May 23, 1891; Shunk to Cassatt, May 19, 1891; and Kelley to Brown, February 7, 1892, *Davis Papers*, Box 186 (Folders I and S).

83. Frederick Ogden to Brown, October 3, 1891, *IRC Papers*, Letters and Reports Received from Survey Corps, 1891–1894: Box 1, Folder: Letters, Feb.–Dec. 1891; and James Parker to Brown, January 4, 1892, *Davis Papers*, Box 186, Folder S. On US culture in the era of scientific racism, see, e.g., Gail Bederman, *Manliness & Civilization* (University of Chicago Press, 1995).

84. Shunk to Cassatt, July 12, 1891; Kelley to Brown, January 3, 1892; and Shunk to Cassatt, January 3, 1892, *Davis Papers*, Box 186 (Folders I and S).

85. Shunk to Helper, January 10, 1892, *Davis Papers*, Box 186, Folder S.

86. Shunk to Cassatt, May 18, 1892; Shunk to Cassatt, January 19, 1892; Kelley to Brown, April 6, 1892; and Kelley to Brown, April 13, 1892, *Davis Papers*, Box 186 (Folders I and S).

87. Cassatt to Brown, March 28, 1892, *IRC Papers*, Letters Received by the Secretary from the President of the Commission, 1890–1899, Folder: Letters from Pres.

88. "Resigned," *St. Louis Post-Dispatch*, June 4, 1892, p. 1; "Forced to Resign," *Chicago Daily Tribune*, June 6, 1892, p. 9; see also Muzzey, pp. 471–474.

89. *Congressional Record—House*, July 6, 1892, p. 5809.

90. Ibid., pp. 5811 and 5815.

91. See Brown to Cassatt, July 8, 1892, *Davis Papers*, Box 186, Folder C; "An act making appropriations for the diplomatic and consular service of the United States," 27 Stat. 223 (July 16, 1892); Helper to Friend, July 20, 1892, *IRC Papers*, Private Papers of the Surgeon Attached to Corps, no. 2, 1892–1896, Folder: From Mr. Helper.

92. Shunk to Cassatt, May 18, 1892, *Davis Papers*, Box 186, Folder S; and Macomb to Brown, December 25, 1892, *Davis Papers*, Box 186, Folder B.

93. Shunk to Cassatt, January 16, 1893; Shunk to Brown, April 16, 1893; and Macomb to Brown, April 4, 1893, *Davis Papers*, Box 186, Folder S.

94. "James G. Blaine's Funeral," *New-York Tribune*, January 31, 1893, p. 1; see also *Nicaragua Canal—Reports of the Committee of Foreign Relations in the Senate* (GPO, 1894); "Nicaragua Canal," H. Rep. 226 (December 19, 1893), 53rd Cong., 2nd sess.; and "Col. Parsons Killed," *Washington Post*, June 30, 1894, p. 1.

95. See Patricia Davis, *End of the Line: Alexander J. Cassatt and the Pennsylvania Railroad* (Neale Watson, 1978), pp. 114–125; see also "Retires Because of Injuries Received in the Service," *Daily Boston Globe*, December 13, 1894, p. 3.

96. Cassatt to E. Z. Steever, June 7, 1898, *IRC Papers*, Letters Received Concerning Reports of the Commission, 1892–1899, Folder: Letters on Various Subjects; see also J. D. Garrison, "From Baltimore to Buenos Aires by Rail," *Baltimore Sun*, December 17, 1922, p. AN6; and "The Pan-American Railway Surveys" (c. October 1892), in *IRC Papers*, Private Papers of the Surgeon Attached to Corps, no. 2, 1892–1896, Folder: Clippings for Scrap-Book.

97. Hay to Cassatt, January 21, 1899, *IRC Papers*, Letters Received Concerning Reports of the Commission, 1892–1899, Folder: Letters on Various Subjects; Helper to Cassatt, November 28, 1898, *IRC Papers*, Misc. Letters Received, 1891–1899, Folder: H–K; Cassatt to Steever, March 14, 1899, *IRC Papers*, Letters Received by the Secretary from the President of the Commission, 1890–99, Folder: Letters from Pres.

98. See Walter Hamm, "Great Engineering Projects," *Cosmopolitan* XXVIII (1899–1900): 162–163; see also *Report of the Nicaragua Canal Commission* (Lord Baltimore Press, 1899); Helper to Steever, November 6, 1898, *IRC Papers*, Misc. Letters Received, 1891–1899, Folder: H–K; and "The Nicaragua Canal," *New York Times*, November 6, 1898, p. 23. On the idea that the Intercontinental Railway had once far exceeded an isthmian canal as a national priority, see, e.g., "That Pan-American Railway," *Wall Street Journal*, May 12, 1916, p. 1.

99. Quoted in John Blum, *The Republican Roosevelt* (Harvard University Press, 1954), p. 1.

100. On the Rough Riders and Roosevelt, see Edmund Morris, *The Rise of Theodore Roosevelt* (Ballantine Books, 1979), pp. 593–661; see also Roosevelt, *The Rough Riders* (Charles Scribner's Sons, 1902).

101. On the origins of the war, see, e.g., Louis Pérez Jr., *The War of 1898* (UNC Press, 1998); Thomas Schoonover, *Uncle Sam's War of 1898 and the Origins of Globalization* (University Press of Kentucky, 2003); and Kristin Hoganson, *Fighting for American Manhood: How Gender Politics Provoked the Spanish–American and Philippine–American Wars* (Yale University Press, 1998).

102. Charles Pepper, "They Are Lionized," *Arizona Republican*, September 26, 1898, p. 8.

103. Roosevelt, *An Autobiography* (Macmillan, 1913), pp. 8, 17, and 59. On Roosevelt's early years, see also Morris, *The Rise of Theodore Roosevelt*, pp. 32–103.

104. Roosevelt, *Autobiography*, p. 62.

105. Ibid., p. 103.

106. Quoted in Frederick Wood, ed., *Roosevelt as We Knew Him* (John C. Winston, 1927), p. 456. On Roosevelt's life in this period, see Morris, *The Rise of Theodore Roosevelt*, pp. 481–515.

107. Alfred Thayer Mahan, *The Influence of Sea Power Upon History* (Little, Brown, 1890), preface; review, "The Influence of Sea Power Upon History," *Atlantic Monthly* LXVI

(1890): 567. See also Richard W. Turk, *The Ambiguous Relationship* (Greenwood Press, 1987), p. 16.

108. Roosevelt, *Autobiography*, pp. 224 and 230.

109. Ibid., pp. 237 and 275.

110. Arthur Dunn, *From Harrison to Harding* (Putnam, 1922), p. 335.

111. *Official Proceedings of the Democratic National Convention* (Logansport, IN, 1896), pp. 226–234; Roosevelt, *Autobiography*, p. 322.

112. Interview with General James Rufling from November 21, 1899, reprinted as "Interview with President McKinley," *Christian Advocate* 78 (January 22, 1903), p. 137.

113. On differing views regarding the historical development of US empire, see Samuel Flagg Bemis, *The Latin American Policy of the United States* (Harcourt, Brace, 1943); William Appleman Williams, *The Tragedy of American Diplomacy* (World, 1959); and Walter LaFeber, *The New Empire* (Cornell University Press, 1963).

114. José Rodó (F. J. Stimson, trans.), *Ariel* (Houghton Mifflin, 1922), p. 90.

115. On civilizing missions and US culture, see, e.g., Mary Renda, *Taking Haiti* (UNC Press, 2001).

116. "Latest Speech of President M'Kinley," *Chicago Daily Tribune*, September 7, 1901, p. 6.

117. Quoted in H. H. Kohlsaat, "From McKinley to Roosevelt," *Saturday Evening Post*, July 22, 1922, p. 44.

118. Quoted in Wood, *Roosevelt as We Knew Him*, 91; see also Roosevelt, *Autobiography*, p. 381.

119. Roosevelt to Mahan, February 14, 1900, Library of Congress, Washington, DC, Papers of Theodore Roosevelt (hereinafter, *Roosevelt Papers*), Series 2, Reel 323; see also Turk, *The Ambiguous Relationship*, pp. 41–48 and 126. For a general discussion of the history of the canal, see, e.g., David McCullough, *The Path Between the Seas* (Simon & Schuster, 1977).

120. Roosevelt, *Autobiography*, p. 389.

121. See Inman, pp. 49–54.

122. Quoted in "Second International Conference of American States," S. Doc. 330 (April 29, 1902), 57th Cong., 1st sess., pp. 32–33 (italics added). On Roosevelt's views of international law, see Roosevelt, *Autobiography*, pp. v and 419.

123. On the relationship between railroads and development in Latin America, see John H. Coatsworth, *Growth Against Development* (Northern Illinois University Press, 1981); see also Stephen Haber, "Financial Markets and Industrial Development: A Comparative Study of Government Regulation, Financial Innovation, and Industrial Structure in Brazil and Mexico, 1840–1930," in Haber, ed., *How Latin America Fell Behind* (Stanford University Press, 1997), pp. 146–178.

124. *Informe que La Delegación de México Presenta a La Segunda Conferencia Pan-Americana* (Palacio Nacional, 1901), p. 16 (author translation); J. B. Calvo, "The Intercontinental Railway," *Monthly Bulletin of the International Bureau of American Republics* XII (May 1902): 1145 and 1148; see also Inman, pp. 54–55.

125. On Reyes generally, see Eduardo Lemaitre, *Rafael Reyes* (Intermedio, rev. 2002); see also David Bushnell, *The Making of Modern Colombia* (University of California Press, 1993), pp. 156–161.

126. See introduction in Ramon de S. N. Araluce, ed., *Across the South-American Continent: Explorations of the Brothers Reyes* (Mexico City: n.p., 1902), pp. 3–13.

127. Ibid., p. 8; and Reyes, "Narrative of the Journeys of Exploration Made by General Rafael Reyes and His Brothers," in *Across the South-American Continent*, p. 20; see also Reyes, *Memorias, 1850–1885* (Fondo Cultural Cafetero, 1986), pp. 109–178.

128. Reyes, "Narrative of the Journeys of Exploration," pp. 21 and 32.

129. Ibid., p. 31.

130. See John Noel, *History of the Second Pan-American Congress* (Guggenheimer, Weil, 1902), pp. 268–270.

131. Ibid., pp. 149–155; see also "Second International Conference of American States," S. Doc. 330 (April 29, 1902), 57th Cong., 1st sess.

132. Quoted in Nasaw, p. 586.
133. See Davis to Carnegie, March 5, 1902, and Davis to Cassatt, March 5, 1902, *Davis Papers*, Letter Books; "Proposed Intercontinental Railway," S. Doc. 144 (January 28, 1903), 57th Cong., 2nd sess., p. 4; see also Davis to Helper, February 4, 1902; Davis to Hay, March 27, 1902; and Davis to Roosevelt, March 27, 1902, *Davis Papers*, Letter Books; see also Hay to Roosevelt, April 1, 1902, *Roosevelt Papers*; "Pan-American Railway," S. Doc. 314 (April 22, 1902), 57th Cong., 1st sess.
134. Davis to Cockrell, February 5, 1903, *Davis Papers*, Letter Books.
135. See Davis to Carnegie, March 3, 1903, *Davis Papers*, Letter Books.
136. "Pan-American Railroad," *New-York Tribune*, March 12, 1903, p. 1; "The Intercontinental Project," *Baltimore Sun*, March 13, 1903, p. 4; Reyes quoted in "Trusts the United States," *Washington Post*, March 18, 1903, p. 1; Helper, "From Alaska to Patagonia," *Washington Post*, March 19, 1903, p. 5; see also "Met Morgan in Cuba," *Washington Post*, March 9, 1903, p. 4. On Morgan being the "central figure," see "Carnegie Millions for Intercontinental Road," *St. Louis Post-Dispatch*, March 22, 1903, p. B1.
137. See "'All Aboard for Buenos Aires!'" undated clipping (c. April 1903); and "Pan-American Rail Feared by Germans," *New York Herald*, April 5, 1903, *Davis Papers*, Box 146, Folder: QR.
138. Davis to Pepper, May 12, 1902; Davis to Pepper, May 24, 1902; Davis to Hay, June 9, 1902; and Davis to Carnegie, April 15, 1903, *Davis Papers*, Letter Books; "Intercontinental Railroad Plan," *New-York Tribune*, April 14, 1903, p. 2. Helper appealed for a spot in a 1903 letter to Congress, see "Proposed Intercontinental Railway," S. Doc. 144 (January 28, 1903), 57th Cong., 2nd sess., p. 6.

Chapter 2: The Eagle and the Octopus

1. "Grant Speaks on Mexico," *New York Times*, November 12, 1880, p. 2; see also Matías Romero, *Informe de Matías Romero* (Filomeno Mata, 1881). For a sample 1880 Delmonico's menu, see "Fine Dinners in New York," *New York Times*, November 10, 1895, p. 21.
2. On Huntington generally, see David Lavender, *The Great Persuader* (Doubleday, 1970).
3. See Richard Orsi, *Sunset Limited* (University of California Press, 2005), p. 7; see also "Mr. Huntington's Career," *New-York Tribune*, August 15, 1900, p. 2.
4. See, e.g., Lewis Haney, *A Congressional History of Railways in the United States, vol. II* (Democrat Printing, 1910), pp. 49–75; see also Richard White, *Railroaded* (Norton, 2011), pp. xxiii–xxix and 17.
5. Testimony of Huntington, "Government Debt of the Pacific Railroads," S. Rep. No. 778 (May 1, 1896), 54th Cong., 1st sess., p. 49.
6. Ibid., p. 38.
7. See Lavender, pp. 92–114; Orsi, p. 9; and Haney, pp. 62–63.
8. Lavender, p. 391, n. 5; testimony of Huntington, p. 54; see also Lavender, pp. 114–175; Haney, pp. 63–64 and 78–81; Orsi, pp. 13–17; and White, pp. 18–31; see also Julius Grodinsky, *Transcontinental Railway Strategy, 1869–1893* (University of Pennsylvania Press, 1962), pp. 2–4.
9. On railroad strategy generally, see White, pp. 140–169; see also Grodinsky, pp. 10–13, 104–106; and Orsi, p. 18.
10. See Lavender, pp. 210–224 and 254–270; Orsi, pp. 18–19.
11. Frank Norris, *The Octopus* (Doubleday, 1901), p. 104.
12. *How Congressmen Are Bribed—The Colton Letters* (n.p., n.d.), pp. 3, 4, and 7; see also Grodinsky, pp. 30–32, 42–45, and 53.
13. See Haney, pp 114–141. On the battles to control the southern transcontinental line in the 1870s, see White, pp. 118–130; and Grodinsky, pp. 8–9, 26, 57–68, and 126.
14. "Commerce Between the United States and Mexico," H. Ex. Doc. No. 86 (February 8, 1884), 48th Cong., 1st sess., p. 8; see also Haney, p. 150.

15. On Mexican topography and railroads, see generally Fred Powell, *The Railroads of Mexico* (Stratford, 1921), pp. 83–89; see also Alfred Conkling, "Mexico: Her Physical Geography and Resources," *Journal of the American Geographical Society of New York* 15 (1883): 319–348.

16. See Maury Klein, *The Life and Legend of Jay Gould* (Johns Hopkins University Press, 1986).

17. See ibid., p. 12; "Mr. Huntington's Career," *New-York Tribune*, August 15, 1900, p. 2. For an example of early hagiography, see Henry Northrup, *Life and Achievements of Jay Gould* (S. M. Southard, 1892).

18. Quoted in "C. P. Huntington Dead," *New York Times*, August 15, 1900, p. 1; and George Miles, "Collis P. Huntington," *New York Times*, February 13, 1898. See also Klein, *Gould*, p. 393.

19. See Klein, *Gould*, pp. 137–159 and 225. On the failures of 1873 and Gould's subsequent involvement, see White, pp. 77–87 and 188–197; see also Grodinsky, pp. 70–82.

20. *Report of the Committee of the Senate upon the Relations between Labor and Capital*, vol. I, *Testimony* (GPO, 1885), p. 1067; see also Klein, *Gould*, p. 128.

21. "On to Mexico," *St. Louis Post-Dispatch*, December 25, 1880, p. 9; see also Klein, *Gould*, pp. 249 and 264.

22. See Klein, *Gould*, 250; Walther Brandt, "The Railway Invasion of Mexico" (Master's Thesis, University of Wisconsin, 1917), pp. 7–8; and Grodinsky, pp. 20–21.

23. See Brandt, pp. 5–7; and Keith L. Bryant, *History of the Atchison, Topeka and Santa Fe Railway* (Macmillan, 1974).

24. On Palmer, see John Fisher, *A Builder of the West* (Caston Printers, 1939). On Palmer's mentor Rosencrans, see David Pletcher, "General William S. Rosencrans and the Mexican Transcontinental Railroad Project," *Mississippi Valley Historical Review* 38 (1952): 657–678.

25. See Cy Warman, "The Grand Canyon War," *Santa Fe Magazine* XVII (January 1923): 59–65; see also Grodinsky, pp. 96–98.

26. For a summary of US views toward Mexican investment up to this point, see Powell, pp. 115–121.

27. See David Pletcher, "The Building of the Mexican Railway," *Hispanic American Historical Review* 30 (1950): 26–52; Brandt, pp. 1–3; Powell, pp. 1 and 99–108. On US rail lines in 1876, see Susan Carter et al., eds., *Historical Statistics of the United States* (Cambridge University Press, 2006), table Df874–881: Railroad Mileage and Equipment: 1830–1890.

28. Matías Romero, *Railways in Mexico* (Washington, DC: n.p., 1882), p. 14. On Romero's views of the United States generally, see Harry Bernstein, *Matías Romero, 1837–1898* (Fondo de Cultural Económica, 1973).

29. Powell, pp. 103–104; "Opposition to American Railroads in Mexico" (speech of Alfred Chavero, May 22, 1878), in *Papers Relating to the Foreign Relations of the United States*, vol. I (GPO, 1879), p. 794. On the unconfirmed Lerdo quote, see Frank Knapp Jr., *The Life of Sebastián Lerdo de Tejada* (University of Texas Press, 1951), pp. 135–136.

30. "Opposition to American Railroads in Mexico," p. 795; see also Powell, pp. 110–111; and Romero, *Informe*, p. 21.

31. See "Affairs in Mexico," *New York Times*, December 30, 1877, p. 1. On the history of these failed concessions, see Brandt, pp. 13–22; Powell, pp. 99–113; and White, pp. 51–55; see also Knapp Jr., "Precursors of American Investment in Mexican Railroads," *Pacific Historical Review* 21 (1952): 43–64; and Robert Gorsuch, *The Republic of Mexico and Railroads* (Hosford & Sons, 1881). On the link between railroads and Díaz's revolution, see Gilbert Haven, *Our Next-Door Neighbor* (Harper, 1875), p. 76; and David Pletcher, "General William S. Rosencrans," p. 676.

32. Romero, *Mexico and the United States*, vol. I (Putnam, 1898), pp. 117–118; see also Powell, p. 1; Brandt, p. 55; and David Pletcher, "Mexico Opens the Door to American Capital, 1877–1880," *Americas* 16 (1959): 1–14.

33. Quoted in "Dinner to General Grant," *New-York Tribune*, November 12, 1880, p. 5; see also Osgood Hardy, "Ulysses S. Grant: President of the Mexican Southern Railroad," *Pacific Historical Review* 24 (1955): 111–120; and Brandt, pp. 27–32.

34. Romero, *Speech of Señor Don Matías Romero Read on the 65th Anniversary of the Birth of General Ulysses S. Grant* (New York: n.p., 1887), pp. 9–10; see also Brandt, pp. 31–32.

35. *British Parliamentary Papers*, 1881, LXXXIX (c. 2944): 393, quoted in Brandt, p. 31, n. 68. See "Mexican International and Interoceanic Railroad Act," reproduced in Mexican Central Railway Co. Limited, *Introductory Report* (n.p., 1881), pp. 58–63, Yale University, Manuscripts and Archives, New Haven, CT; and Powell, p. 128.

36. See Mexican Central, *Introductory Report*, p. 3; see also Brandt, pp. 59–78.

37. See *Concession to the Mexican National Construction Company* (Gazette, 1880); "Mexican Millions in Subsidy," *Washington Post*, October 17, 1880, p. 1; see also Brandt, pp. 79–80; "Mexico Opens the Door to American Capital," p. 12.

38. Romero, *Informe*, p. 39 (author's translation).

39. Ibid., p. 9 (author's translation). See also Romero, *Speech Read on . . . Grant*, pp. 10–12.

40. Romero, *Informe*, pp. 7, 25, and 29 (author's translation).

41. "Russell Sage's Career," *Washington Post*, January 28, 1883, p. 6; see also "Gen. G. M. Dodge Dies in Iowa," *Hartford Courant*, January 4, 1916, p. 18, and "Sidney Dillon's Career," *Washington Post*, April 27, 1884, p. 6.

42. See Romero, *Informe*, pp. 28–29.

43. On the fragility of cooperation and railroaders' inevitable tendency toward competition and overbuilding, see White, pp. 212–214; see also Grodinsky, pp. 113–119.

44. See "Railway Matters," *Detroit Free Press*, November 18, 1880, p. 2; "Gould's Latest Purchase," *New York Times*, December 21, 1880, p. 3; see also Klein, *Gould*, pp. 257 and 274–275; Brandt, pp. 8–9; and Romero, *Informe*, p. 33.

45. "On to Mexico!" *Chicago Daily Tribune*, December 24, 1880, p. 2.

46. See Romero, *Informe*, pp. 9–35, 36, and 39; and Brandt, pp. 112–120; see also "The Mexican Railway Scheme," *Hartford Daily Courant*, November 20, 1880, p. 2.

47. See Brandt, pp. 118–119.

48. See "Holland's Letter," *Wall Street Journal*, August 30, 1910, p. 1; see also "The Three Americas Railway," *Washington Post*, December 2, 1903, p. 5.

49. See "The Mexican Railway Project," *New York Times*, July 22, 1881, p. 5; see also William Schell Jr., *Integral Outsiders* (SRI, 2001), p. 2; Klein, *Gould*, pp. 274–275; and Brandt, pp. 112 and 116.

50. "Gould and Huntington Agree," *New York Times*, November 17, 1881, p. 5.

51. "The Gould-Huntington Alliance," *Atlanta Constitution*, November 24, 1881, p. 4; see also "Railroad Work and Plans," *New York Times*, March 28, 1882, p. 2; "Grabbing a Land Grant," *New York Times*, February 19, 1883, p. 1; Ex-Gov. Lionel A. Sheldon, "How Jay Gould and Collis P. Huntington Waged Railroad War When the State Was Young," *Los Angeles Herald*, April 8, 1906; see also Klein, *Gould*, pp. 269–272; Grodinsky, pp. 172 and 214–215; and Orsi, p. 22.

52. "What It All Means," *San Francisco Chronicle*, February 2, 1882, p. 1; see also "Once More to the Breach," *St. Louis Post-Dispatch*, January 26, 1882, p. 1; "Purchased by Gould and Huntington," *New-York Tribune*, January 26, 1882, p. 1; "Jay Gould's Latest Move," *New York Times*, January 29, 1882, p. 7; and "Gould and the Atchison System of Railroads," *New York Times*, January 31, 1882, p. 1; see also Grodinsky, pp. 166–167.

53. On Mexican Central construction, see Brandt, pp. 82–83; see also "Mexican Railway Plans," *New York Times*, March 4, 1881, p. 2. On the connection between rails and forests in the United States during the nineteenth century, see Eric Rutkow, *American Canopy* (Scribner, 2012), pp. 99–105.

54. Mexican Central, *Introductory Report*, p. 6; Cy Warman, *The Story of the Railroad* (D. Appleton, 1906), pp. 217–218; see also Sandra Ficker, "Economic Backwardness and Firm Strategy: An American Railroad Corporation in Nineteenth-Century Mexico," *Hispanic American Historical Review* 80 (2000): 267–298.

55. "How the Boston Party Were Entertained in Mexico," *St. Louis Post-Dispatch*, May 29, 1884, p. 4; see also Brandt, pp. 91–92; and "Mexico to Chicago," *Chicago Daily Tribune*, March 29, 1884, p. 15.

56. "The Mexican Central Railway," *Washington Post*, March 10, 1884, p. 2; "Mexican Railways," *San Francisco Chronicle*, August 3, 1884, p. 1; "Mexican Railways," *New-York Tribune*, July 12, 1885, p. 6; see also Brandt, pp. 96–100; and Powell, pp. 125 and 130.

57. See "Affairs of a Mexican Company," *New-York Tribune*, December 17, 1881, p. 5; "The Mexican National Construction Company Waters Its Stock," *Chicago Daily Tribune*, February 24, 1882, p. 7; "The Modern El Dorado," *St. Louis Post-Dispatch*, March 8, 1882, p. 5; "Reported Sale of the Palmer and Sullivan Railroad to an English Syndicate," *Chicago Tribune*, April 27, 1883, p. 6; "The Mexican Central Railway," *Washington Post*, March 10, 1884, p. 2; see also Brandt, pp. 100–104 and 112; and Powell, pp. 133–134.

58. Quoted in *Speech of Señor Don Matías Romero*, p. 16; see also "Aid for General Grant," *Washington Post*, May 11, 1884, p. 1.

59. "Grant and Gould," *Chicago Tribune*, January 14, 1883, p. 3; "General Grant's Mexican Roads," *Hartford Daily Courant*, May 29, 1883, p. 3; see also Brandt, pp. 116–120; Klein, *Gould*, p. 306; "Concessions Granted to the Mexican Southern Railroad Company," reproduced in "Commerce Between the United States and Mexico," pp. 57–59; and "An Unprofitable Scheme," *New York Times*, June 11, 1885, p. 5. On rumors of Gould's ongoing schemes, see "Jay Gould's Influence in Mexico," *San Francisco Chronicle*, July 14, 1885, p. 8; "Jay Gould in Mexico," *San Francisco Chronicle*, July 16, 1885, p. 4; and Powell, p. 119.

60. See "Railway Management," *New York Times*, January 11, 1888, p. 2; "Short Route to Mexico," *New York Times*, October 24, 1888, p. 2; "Completion of Another Line of Railway Between the United States and the City of Mexico," *Scientific American* LIX (November 3, 1888): 273; see also Brandt, pp. 109 and 112–115; and Powell, pp. 137–138.

61. See John Coatsworth, "Railroads, Landholding, and Agrarian Protest in the Early Porfiriato," *Hispanic American Historical Review* 54 (1974): 48–71; see also Coatsworth, *Growth Against Development* (Northern Illinois University Press, 1981), pp. 149–174; see also Powell, pp. 189–194.

62. "Discussed by Jay Gould," *Chicago Daily Tribune*, April 29, 1890, p. 2; see also "George J. Gould at Home Again," *New-York Tribune*, April 4, 1890, p. 3; "Mr. Gould Praising Texas and Mexico," *New-York Tribune*, April 12, 1890, p. 5; "Gould's Southern Trip," *New York Times*, March 8, 1892, p. 2; "Gould the Schemer," *San Francisco Chronicle*, March 26, 1892, p. 3; "Huntington and Gould Sign a Paper," *New York Times*, April 2, 1892, p. 3; "Meeting of Gould and Huntington at El Paso," *St. Louis Post-Dispatch*, April 2, 1892, p. 6.

63. See "Jay Gould Dead," *San Francisco Chronicle*, December 3, 1892, p. 1. On Gould's net worth, see Klein, *Gould*, p. 484.

64. Quoted in "Jay Gould's Career Ended," *New York Times*, December 3, 1892, p. 1.

65. See "The Big Deal Just Made by Huntington," *San Francisco Chronicle*, November 7, 1892, p. 3; "Huntington Will Succeed Geo. Gould," *Chicago Tribune*, June 1, 1893, p. 11; "Mr. Huntington's Guatemala Road," *Wall Street Journal*, October 27, 1894, p. 2; Klein, *Gould*, pp. 451 and 455; "C. P. Huntington's Mexican Line," *San Francisco Chronicle*, April 28, 1896, p. 8; "For a Mexican Railway," *San Francisco Chronicle*, May 13, 1896, p. 2; "Railways in Guatemala," *New York Times*, March 11, 1899, p. 5; and "Railroad Interests," *New-York Tribune*, April 4, 1899, p. 8.

66. See "Mr. Huntington's Career," *New-York Tribune*, August 15, 1900, p. 2; see also "Jay Gould Dead," *San Francisco Chronicle*, December 3, 1892, p. 1.

67. See John Hart, *Empire and Revolution* (University of California Press, 2002), pp. 129–130; and Hart, *Revolutionary Mexico* (University of California Press, 1987), pp. 133–134 and 177–182; see also Andrew Barlow, "United States Enterprises in Mexico," in *Com-*

mercial Relations of the United States with Foreign Countries, vol. I (GPO, 1903), pp. 433–503. The Díaz quotation, though widely reproduced in the historiography, lacks confirmed sourcing. See, e.g., Paul Garner, *Porfirio Díaz* (Longman, 2001), p. 137. See also Myra Wilkins, *The Emergence of Multinational Enterprise* (Harvard University Press, 1970), pp. 114–115.

68. Powell, pp. 191–192; and White, p. 462; see also Grodinsky, pp. 401 and 422–428. For an excellent discussion of disastrous rate competition among the various US lines in this period, see also Arturo Grunstein, "Railroads and Sovereignty" (Ph.D. diss., UCLA, 1994), pp. 49–92.

69. "Sage Remarks Upon Gould," *Los Angeles Times*, March 27, 1901, p. 2; see also Klein, *The Life & Legend of E. H. Harriman* (UNC Press, 2000), p. 65; Huntington quoted in Earl Berry, "The Men That Control the Railroads," *Ainslee's Magazine* VII (May 1901): 311; and Harriman's mustache described in Frank A. Vanderlip, *From Farm Boy to Financier* (D. Appleton-Century, 1935), p. 144.

70. Klein, *Harriman*, pp. 130 and 445.

71. Ibid., pp. 111, 118–119, and 135–136.

72. Quoted in George Kennan, *E. H. Harriman*, vol. I (Houghton Mifflin, 1922), p. 241; see also Klein, *Harriman*, pp. 214–224.

73. "Reported Visit of Mr. Harriman to Mexico," *Mexican Herald*, February 26, 1902, p. 5. On Pierce's Mexican interests and purchase of the former Atchison line, see Jonathan Brown, *Oil and Revolution in Mexico* (University of California Press, 1993), pp. 13–16. On Speyer, see Gene Hanrahan, *The Bad Yankee*, vol. I (Documentary Publications, 1985), pp. 121–123.

74. Burton Hendrick, "The Passing of a Great Railroad Dynasty," *McClure's Magazine* XXXVIII (March 1912): 488; see also "Gould and Harriman Interests," *Boston Globe*, September 12, 1901, p. 9; and Klein, pp. 264–265.

75. On other rivals for Central America in this period, see, e.g., "Building Road to Guatemala," *Idaho Statesman*, November 14, 1903, p. 2.

76. "Long Chain's Mighty Link," *Los Angeles Times*, April 5, 1903, p. 8.

77. See "President Diaz Will Not Sell the Tehuantepec Road," *Los Angeles Times*, July 12, 1892, p. 3; Edward Glick, "The Tehuantepec Railroad," *Pacific Historical Review* 22 (1953): 373; Powell, pp. 149–152; and White, p. 408.

78. Fremont Everett, *Some of the Everetts* (Portland, OR: n.p., 1916), p. 116, Yale University, Beinecke Rare Book and Manuscript Library; see also Valente Molina Pérez, *Por Los Rieles de Chiapas: Construcción del Ferrocarril Panamericano* (Gobierno de Chiapas, 2006), pp. 19–35.

79. "Uniting Continents with Steel Bands," *Los Angeles Times*, October 18, 1901, p. A1; see also "Road Through Diaz's Domain," *San Francisco Call*, May 7, 1903.

80. "Uniting Continents with Steel Bands"; see also "John M. Neeland," *New York Times*, April 9, 1933, p. 30; "Neeland v. The State," *Reports of Cases Argued and Determined in the Supreme Court of the State of Kansas* XXXIX (Kansas Publishing, 1888), pp. 154–163. On Kansas railroading in the 1880s, see White, p. 211.

81. Quoted in "Long Chain's Might Link," *Los Angeles Times*, April 5, 1903, p. 8; "Among Men of Action," *Los Angeles Times*, December 31, 1905, p. VI6; see also Mark Wasserman, "Enrique Creel: Business and Politics in Mexico, 1880–1930," *Business History Review* 59 (1985): 645–662. On the *Mexican Herald*'s importance during the Porfiriato, see Schell, *Integral Outsiders*, pp. 14–17.

82. Everett, p. 115.

83. Ibid.; see also "1904 Intercontinental Railway Map," contained in "Pan-American Railway," S. Doc. No. 206 (March 15, 1904), 58th Cong., 2nd sess.

84. Everett, pp. 115–117; see also "A New Concession," *Mexican Herald*, September 3, 1901, p. 2.

85. Everett, pp. 117, 124.

86. "Uniting Continents with Steel Bands," *Los Angeles Times*, October 18, 1901, p. A1; see

also "An Extended Tour," *Mexican Herald*, April 24, 1901, p. 2; and "Articles of Incorporation," reproduced in Molina Pérez, 47.

87. "A New Concession," p. 2; see also Molina Pérez, pp. 46–51.

88. "Manager Neeland of the Pan-American Road Here," *Mexican Herald*, November 21, 1901, p. 8; see also "Concessionaires Are Sad," *Mexican Herald*, October 28, 1901, p. 8; and "Court Denies Claim Against Pan-American Railway," *Los Angeles Herald*, July 27, 1910.

89. Henry Lane Wilson, *Diplomatic Episodes in Mexico, Belgium, and Chile* (Doubleday, Page, 1927), p. 173; "Construction in Mexico," *Dallas Morning News*, March 1, 1902, p. 3; see also José Limantour, *Apuntes Sobre Mi Vida Pública* (Editorial Porrúa, 1965); and Robert Randall, "Mexico's Pre-Revolutionary Reckoning with Railroads," *Americas* 42 (1985): 24–28.

90. Everett, pp. 126, 142, and 144; see also Schell, "Banco de Chiapas: A License to Print Money," *SECOLAS Annals* 24 (1993): 58–68; "Chiapas New Bank," *Mexican Herald*, March 21, 1902, p. 5; "Contrato para el establecimiento de un Banco de emisión en Tuxtla Gutiérrez, Estado de Chiapas," in *Memoria de Hacienda y Crédito Público correspondiente al año económico de 10 de Julio de 1901 a 30 de Julio de 1902* (Mexico City: n.p., 1905), pp. 163–164 (Document 78); Molina Pérez, pp. 53 (containing a reproduction of a banknote) and 62.

91. Everett, pp. 117 and 149.

92. "Among the Railroads," *Mexican Herald*, December 23, 1902, p. 5; James Parsons Jr., Consular Dispatch No. 124, Subject: Southern Mexico Trip—Pan American Land and Colonization Company, April 21, 1905, p. 6, NARA, RG 59, Despatches from US Consuls in Mexico City, 1822–1906, M296, Reel 15; see also Despatches of April 27, May 5, May 15, May 29, June 2, June 13, and July 7, 1905, M296, Reel 15; see also Schell, "American Investment in Tropical Mexico, 1897–1913," *Business History Review* 64 (1990): 217–254.

93. Everett, pp. 156–158; see also "Pan-American Railroad Projector Is Hopeful," *San Francisco Call*, April 13, 1903.

94. See "Contract Is Awarded," *Mexican Herald*, May 18, 1904, p. 2; "Pan-American Railroad Sold by St. Louisans," *St. Louis Post-Dispatch*, August 26, 1909, p. 2; see also Alexander McConachie, "The 'Big Cinch': A Business Elite in the Life of a City, St. Louis, 1895–1915" (Ph.D. diss., Washington University, 1976), p. 101. George Gould owned some portion of the new syndicate as well, though his role remained minor.

95. Everett, pp. 157–158; see also "Railroad Construction," *Railroad Gazette*, May 27, 1904, p. 412.

96. See "Millions for Improvement," *Los Angeles Times*, October 30, 1904, p. D7.

97. See "The Pan-American Railway Company Incorporated," *San Francisco Chronicle*, October 29, 1891, p. 2; and "Two-Continent Railroad," *New York Times*, August 25, 1903, p. 2.

98. "Remarkable Journey of Chas. M. Pepper," *Dallas Morning News*, January 18, 1904, p. 6.

99. "Pan-American Railway," S. Doc. No. 206 (March 15, 1904), 58th Cong., 2nd sess., pp. 11, 16, 36–37, and 41.

100. Ibid., p. 55.

101. Ibid., p. 10; Roosevelt, *An Autobiography* (Macmillan, 1913), p. 592.

102. "Pan-American Railway," *Wall Street Journal*, April 20, 1904, p. 1; see also "El Ferrocarril Panamericano," *El Imparcial*, March 17, 1904, p. 3.

103. C. M. Hendley to Pepper, August 1, 1904, *Davis Papers*, Letter Books. On Davis's selection as vice president, see Arthur Dunn, *Gridiron Nights* (Frederick A. Stokes, 1915), p. 152; Pepper, *The Life and Times of Henry Gassaway Davis*, pp. 166–180; and Edmund Morris, *Theodore Rex* (Random House, 2001), pp. 339–343.

104. On the 1904 campaign, see Morris, *Theodore Rex*, pp. 339–364.

105. On Harriman and the Northern Securities Case, see Klein, *Harriman*, pp. 238–240 and 308–316; Roosevelt to Hamlin Garland, May 5, 1902, in Elting Morison, ed., *The*

Letters of Theodore Roosevelt, vol. 4 (Harvard University Press, 1951), pp. 590–591; and "E. H. Harriman," *Hartford Courant*, September 11, 1909, p. 8.

106. Letter from Theodore Roosevelt, November 4, 1904, in Roosevelt, *Presidential Addresses and State Papers*, vol. III (Review of Reviews, 1910), p. 100; see also Morris, pp. 359–360.

107. Carnegie, Letter to the Pan-American Railway Committee, March 16, 1905, Library of Congress, Washington, DC, Papers of Andrew Carnegie (hereinafter, *Carnegie Papers*), Box 112; see also Davis to Carnegie, January 3 and February 27, 1905, *Davis Papers*, Letter Books; and "Pan-American Railway: Remarks of the Chairman, Hon. H. G. Davis" (Gibson Brothers, 1905).

108. Carnegie to Roosevelt, March 11, 1904, *Roosevelt Papers* on microfilm, S1, Reel 42.

109. On the general debates between Carnegie and Roosevelt in this period, see "Philippine Independence," *New-York Tribune*, December 9, 1904; Carnegie to Mrs. Charles Lowell, January 31, 1905, Carnegie to Roosevelt, February 5, 1905, Roosevelt to Carnegie, February 6, 1905, Roosevelt to Carnegie, February 8, 1905, and Carnegie to Roosevelt, February 9, 1905, *Carnegie Papers*, container 111.

110. "Carnegie and the Monroe Doctrine," *New-York Tribune*, March 26, 1905, p. C1. On Roosevelt's view toward Carnegie, see Nasaw, *Andrew Carnegie*, p. 747; see also Roosevelt, *Autobiography*, foreword.

111. See, e.g., Davis, "The Pan-American Railway: Its Business Side," *North American Review* 182 (1906): 709–720.

112. Davis to Roosevelt, October 23, 1905, *Davis Papers*, Letter Books; Roosevelt to Davis, October 31, 1905, *Davis Papers*, Box 146, Folder: QR.

113. "Intercontinental Railway Through the Three Americas," S. Doc. No. 92 (December 18, 1905), 59th Cong., 1st sess., pp. 3 and 5.

114. Davis to Root, January 16, 1906, *Davis Papers*, Letter Books; Davis, "The Pan-American Railway: Its Business Side"; and Davis, *Report of the Permanent Pan-American Railway Committee to the Third International Conference of the American States* (GPO, 1906).

115. See *Report of the United States Delegates to the Third International Conference of the American States* (GPO, 1907).

Chapter 3: The Route of Volcanoes

1. See "Revolutionary Movement Begun in Guatemala . . . ," *Mexican Herald*, May 29, 1906, p. 1; see also "Ocos Is Abandoned by Revolutionists," *Mexican Herald*, May 30, 1906, p. 1.

2. "Ocos Is Abandoned . . ."

3. "Revolutionary Movement Begun . . ."; see also "A Formidable Uprising," *Baltimore Sun*, May 30, 1906, p. 2.

4. William Sands, *Our Jungle Diplomacy* (UNC Press, 1944), pp. 85, 95. On Estrada Cabrera's tyranny, see also "Sever All Relations," *Mexican Herald*, July 3, 1906, p. 2; "Tales of Veritable Reign of Terror Told by Persons Coming Here from Guatemala," *Mexican Herald*, May 10, 1907, p. 1; "Estrada Cabrera," *New York Times*, May 12, 1907, p. SM5; Emilio de Leon to Ambassador Thompson, May 10, 1907, and Statement of Dr. A. M. Mansanto (n.d., but c. May 1907), NARA, RG 59, Central Files 1906–1910—Numerical and Minor Files (M-862), Roll 448, No. 550 (Conditions of Affairs in Guatemala).

5. On Estrada Cabrera's military, see "War Declared by Honduras," *Washington Post*, July 15, 1906, p. 1, and Sands, p. 91. On Estrada Cabrera's belligerent view toward El Salvador, see "Revolutionary Junta Springs a Sensation," *New Orleans Times-Picayune*, July 9, 1906, p. 2, and Telegram from Minister Combs to the Secretary of State, June 1, 1906, *Foreign Relations of the United States* (hereinafter, *FRUS*), 1906, part I, p. 834.

6. Edward Butler, "To Equator by Pullman," *Los Angeles Times*, June 24, 1906, p. VI10; see also "Seeks Concessions in Central America," *Mexican Herald*, June 25, 1906, p. 1.

7. "Seeks Concessions . . ."; see also "Sever All Relations."

8. Roosevelt to President Escalón (El Salvador), July 13, 1906, *FRUS* 1906, part I, p. 837.

9. Roosevelt quoted in Schell, *Integral Outsiders*, pp. 139–140; see also *FRUS* 1906, part I, p. 836, and Memorandum from the Department of State, April 23, 1910, p. 2, *NARA*, RG 59, Records Relating to the Internal Affairs of Central America, 1910–1929 (M672), Roll 2. On Mexico's policies toward Central America generally in this period, see Jürgen Buchenau, *In the Shadow of the Giant* (University of Alabama Press, 1996).

10. *FRUS* 1906, part I, pp. 835–837; "Will Mediate," *Detroit Free Press*, July 16, 1906, p. 1; see also Frederick Palmer, "Smallest American Republic," *New York Times*, February 27, 1909, p. 8, and "Marblehead at Hand," *New-York Tribune*, July 17, 1906, p. 1.

11. Sands, pp. 178–179. On Marblehead generally, see also "Reconciling the Enemies," *Los Angeles Times*, July 20, 1906, p. I6; *FRUS* 1906, part I, pp. 842–852; and "Peace in Central America," *Baltimore Sun*, August 17, 1906, p. 2.

12. See "Award of the Nobel Peace Prize to President Roosevelt," *FRUS* 1906, part II, pp. 1191–1193.

13. See Emilio de Leon to Ambassador Thompson, May 10, 1907, p. 5.

14. "Reconciling the Enemies"; "Bonds Are in Demand," *Mexican Herald*, July 29, 1906, p. 4.

15. "The Pan-American Conference," *Advocate of Peace* 68 (August 1906): 165–166.

16. Sands, p. 11; see also *Report of the Delegates of the United States to the Third International Conference of American States* (GPO, 1907), p. 24. On US relations with Latin America generally in this period, see Thomas O'Brien, *Making the Americas* (University of New Mexico Press, 2007), pp. 75–96.

17. *Report of the Delegates*, pp. 23, 62, and 65. On perceptions of Root in Latin America, see also Schell, p. 143, and Sands, p. 12.

18. See *Report of the Delegates*, pp. 12–14, 29–40, 57, and 135–136; see also "Drago Doctrine Discord," *Washington Post*, August 17, 1906, p. 3.

19. Quoted in Frederick Lynch, *Personal Recollections of Andrew Carnegie* (Revell, 1920), p. 82.

20. *Report of the Delegates*, p. 43.

21. Ibid., pp. 22 and 153–154; see also "The Railway to Link the Two Americas," *Baltimore Sun*, August 27, 1906, p. 4, and "The Pan-American Railway," *New York Times*, August 11, 1906, p. 6.

22. See *Conferencia de paz Centro-Americana* (Tipografía Nacional, 1906).

23. José Santos Zelaya, *Manifiesto que Dirige a Los Nicaragüenses* (Tipografía y Encuadernación Nacional, 1906), p. 21. On the history of efforts at Central American Union see Alberto Herrarte, *La Unión de Centroamérica* (Centro Editorial José de Pineda Ibarra, 1963); and Thomas L. Karnes, *The Failure of Union* (University of North Carolina Press, 1961).

24. Sands, p. 83; William Merry to Root, December 20, 1906, NARA, RG 59, Central Files 1906–1910—Numerical and Minor Files (M-862), Roll 355; see also Frederick Palmer, "Zelaya and Nicaragua," *Outlook*, December 18, 1909, pp. 855–859.

25. "A Formidable Uprising," *Baltimore Sun*, May 30, 1906, p. 2.

26. Walter LaFeber, *Inevitable Revolutions* (Norton, 1983), p. 42; see also Frederick Palmer, "Honduras Wants Intervention," *New York Times*, March 1, 1909, p. 8.

27. Merry to Root, December 20, 1906; see also Palmer, *Central America and Its Problems* (Moffat, Yard, 1910), pp. 182–183.

28. *FRUS* 1907, Part II, 607; see also "Zelaya The Ambitious," *Baltimore Sun*, July 25, 1908, p. 11.

29. Zelaya to Roosevelt, February 13, 1907, in *FRUS* 1907, part II, p. 619; see also ibid., pp. 607–634; "Hondurans Defeated," *Washington Post*, February 20, 1907, p. 1; and Nicaragua, Ministerio de Relaciones Exteriores, *Documentos oficiales referentes a la guerra entre Nicaragua y Honduras de 1907* (Compañía tip. internacional, 1907).

30. "El Gobierno de Guatemala arroja la máscara," *El Dictamen*, May 6, 1907, p. 1 (author's translation). See also "Estrada Cabrera," *New York Times*, May 12, 1907, p. SM5; "Diaz

Massing Mexican Army on the Border," *Atlanta Constitution*, May 21, 1907, p. 1; "Prepares for Emergencies," *Los Angeles Times*, June 30, 1907, p. III3; and "Gen. Toledo Would Invade Guatemala," *St. Louis Post-Dispatch*, May 6, 1907, p. 3.

31. Palmer, *Central America and Its Problems*, p. 298; Neeland to Ambassador Thompson, May 14, 1907, NARA, RG 59, Central Files 1906–1910—Numerical and Minor Files (M-862), Roll 448, No. 550 (Conditions of Affairs in Guatemala).

32. "Neeland Is with Zelaya," *Mexican Herald*, June 16, 1907, p. 3.

33. "Plan Union by War in Central America," *Los Angeles Times*, June 10, 1907, p. I2; "Plot to Merge States of Central America," *San Francisco Call*, June 11, 1907; see also "Neeland Entertains," *Mexican Herald*, June 18, 1907, p. 5; "Peace Will Follow These Steel Rails," *Los Angeles Times*, June 29, 1907, p. II1; see also "Man-Birds Mourn Deaths of Fliers," *San Jose Mercury News*, January 1, 1911, p. 3.

34. "Nicaragua Opens War," *Washington Post*, June 12, 1907, p. 1; see also "War Cloud over Central America," *New York Times*, June 15, 1907, p. 4.

35. See, e.g., "Isthmian War Near," *Los Angeles Times*, June 17, 1907, p. I1; see also "Cancelación de la contrata para el Ferrocarril Pan-Americano," *Diario del Salvador*, July 24, 1907, p. 1.

36. Honduran Minister to the Secretary of State, August 18, 1907, Roosevelt to Díaz, August 25, 1907, and Díaz to Roosevelt, August 27, 1907, in *FRUS* 1907, Part II, pp. 636–638; see also "Pleads for Honduras," *Baltimore Sun*, June 19, 1907, p. 9.

37. "Address of Elihu Root when calling the [Washington] Conference to Order on November 14, 1907," in William Buchanan, *The Central American Peace Conference* (GPO, 1908), p. 26 and generally; Acting Secretary of State Robert Bacon to the Costa Rican Minister, October 2, 1907, in *FRUS* 1907, part II, p. 653. See also "Peace Proposal Liked," *New-York Tribune*, September 2, 1907, p. 3; and "W. I. Buchanan Chosen," *Baltimore Sun*, November 9, 1907, p. 2.

38. Address of Root, in Buchanan, p. 27.

39. "Argument Supporting the Honduras Project for a Central American Union" and "Argued Vote of the Minority," in Buchanan, 90–97.

40. See Buchanan, pp. 6–7 and 11; "Report of the Members of the Committee Against the Honduran Project," in Buchanan, pp. 10–11. On Guatemala's initial intentions, see "Memorandum Submitted by the Delegation from Guatemala," November 18, 1907, in Buchanan, pp. 8–9. See also Karnes, *The Failure of Union*.

41. "Report of the Members of the Committee Against the Honduran Project," in Buchanan, p. 10. See also *Notes on a Railway Through Central America Presented by the Delegation of Costa Rica* (Washington, DC: n.p., November 1907); J. B. Calvo, "Proposed Intercontinental Railway," *Washington Post*, April 27, 1902, p. 26.

42. "Continental Railway to Connect American Nations," H. Rep. No. 2243 (May 29, 1890), 51st Cong., 1st sess., p. 3; "Convention on Communications," in Buchanan, pp. 77–80; see also Buchanan, p. 16.

43. "Convention for the Establishment of a Central American Court of Justice," in Buchanan, pp. 43–53. For an example of court-focused media coverage, see "Peace Assured in Central America," *New-York Tribune*, December 15, 1907, p. 1.

44. Root to Buchanan, May 23, 1908, in *FRUS* 1908, pp. 231–232.

45. "Address of the Secretary of State . . . Declaring the Central American Peace Conference of Washington Closed," December 20, 1907, in Buchanan, p. 90.

46. See "Report of William I. Buchanan," in *FRUS* 1908, pp. 221–222.

47. Ibid., pp. 228 and 246; see also "On Peace Mission," *Washington Post*, April 4, 1908, p. 1.

48. Sands, p. 183. See also Hermann Deutsch, *The Incredible Yanqui* (Longmans, Green, 1931); and Dana Munro, *The Five Republics of Central America* (Oxford University Press, 1918), pp. 217–219.

49. Quoted in Karnes, pp. 194–195; see also "The First Case Before the Central American Court of Justice," *American Journal of International Law* 2 (October 1908): 835–841; and "Central America Quieter," *New York Times*, July 17, 1908, p. 7.

50. "Latin-American Politics," *Los Angeles Times*, July 17, 1908, p. II4; see also "El Ferrocarril Panamericano en Guatemala," *Diario del Salvador*, July 22, 1908, p. 1.

51. Deputy Consul-General Owen to the Assistant Secretary of State, July 25, 1908, NARA, RG 59, Central Files 1906–1910—Numerical and Minor Files (M-862), Roll 912.

52. Neeland to Root, June 2, 1908, NARA, RG 59, Central Files 1906–1910—Numerical and Minor Files (M-862), Roll 448.

53. See Morris, *Theodore Rex*, pp. 519–521.

54. F. M. Huntington Wilson, *Memoirs of an Ex-Diplomat* (Bruce Humphries, 1945), pp. 199, 208, 213, and 243; Anonymous, *The Mirrors of Washington* (Putnam, 1921), pp. 203 and 205.

55. See "Will Force Zelaya to Terms" and "Letter Foretold Many Troubles," *Mexican Herald*, March 14, 1909, p. 1; "Mexico to Support Action in Nicaragua," *New York Times*, March 15, 1909, p. 4; and Frederick Palmer, "The Growing Problem of Central America," *New York Times*, March 21, 1909, p. SM11.

56. See Walter Scholes, "Los Estados Unidos, México y América Central en 1909," *Historia Mexicana* 10 (1961): p. 621 and generally.

57. See Consul Moffat to the Secretary of State, October 9 and 12, 1909, in *FRUS* 1909, p. 452.

58. On Merry's involvement, see Zelaya, *The Revolution of Nicaragua and the United States* (Bernardo Rodriguez, 1910), pp. 28–29 and 33; see also "Merry to Leave Nicaragua," *Chicago Daily Tribune*, March 13, 1907, p. 10, and "Says Zelaya Is Truculent," *Los Angeles Times*, March 23, 1907, p. I2. On the involvement of US corporations, see Zelaya (1910), p. 54. Estrada Cabrera also provided aid to the revolutionaries; see Zelaya (1910), pp. 34–36. For a description of the revolution from the perspective of a Nicaraguan contemporary opposed to Zelaya, see Macario Alvarez Lejarza, *Impresiones y Recuerdos de la Revolución de 1909 a 1910* (Escuela Tipografía Salesiana, 1945).

59. See Zelaya (1910), pp. 139–167. For an account of how the United States viewed the executions, see *FRUS* 1909, pp. 446–451.

60. The Secretary of State to the Nicaraguan Chargé, December 1, 1909, in *FRUS* 1909, p. 456; see also Scholes, "Los Estados Unidos, México y América Central en 1909," and Harim Guitiérrez, *Una alianza fallida: México y Nicaragua contra Estados Unidos, 1909–1910* (Instituto Mora, 2000).

61. See Zelaya (1910), pp. 58 and 115–116.

62. See ibid., especially pp. 59–117; see also Zelaya, *Refutación al Presidente Taft* (Brussels: n.p., 1911).

63. Philip Brown to the Secretary of State re: An Account in a Local Paper of an Incident Between the Secretary of State and Mr. Carnegie, February 2, 1910, with enclosures, NARA, RG 59, Records Relating to the Internal Affairs of Central America, 1910–1929 (M-672), Roll 2.

64. See Arturo Grunstein, "Railroads and Sovereignty: Policy-making in Porfirian Mexico" (Ph.D. diss., UCLA, 1994), pp. 93–112.

65. "Railroad Changes," *Mexican Herald*, March 29, 1901, p. 2; see also Grunstein, pp. 113–128, and Klein, *Harriman*, pp. 205–207.

66. On Harriman's visit to Mexico, see Klein, *Harriman*, p. 264, and Grunstein, pp. 128–138.

67. Limantour, "Informe presentado al Presidente de la República . . . (Documento Número 156)," in *Memoria de Hacienda y Crédito Público, Julio de 1903 a Junio de 1904* (Tipografía de la Oficina Impresora de Estampillas, 1909), pp. 414–415 (author's translation); Limantour, *Apuntes Sobre Mi Vida Pública, 1892–1911* (Editorial Porrua, S.A., 1965), p. 86 (author's translation).

68. Sands, p. 196; Consul General to Herbert H. D. Pierce, June 6, 1903, NARA, RG 59, Despatches from US consuls in Mexico City (M-296), Roll 14. For a summary of Limantour's actions from 1902 to 1904, see also Grunstein, pp. 139–166.

69. See Grunstein, pp. 172–209 and 217–221.

70. Limantour, *Apuntes*, p. 88 (author's translation); see also Grunstein, pp. 227–232.

71. For Limantour's full report on his efforts to create the National Railways, see Ambassador Thompson to the Secretary of State re: Railway Merger of Mexican Central and National Lines, December 22, 1908, NARA, RG 59, Central Files 1906–1910—Numerical and Minor Files (M-862), Roll 308. For US criticism of the deal Limantour negotiated, see Hart, *Revolutionary Mexico*, p. 139.

72. Mexico's success in nationalizing its transportation infrastructure pushes against the dominant development narrative in Latin America historiography, often known as "dependency theory." See, e.g., Fernando Henrique Cardoso and Enzo Faletto, *Dependency and Development in Latin America* (University of California Press, 1979); see also Immanuel Wallerstein, *World-Systems Analysis* (Duke University Press, 2004); but see also Coatsworth, *Growth Against Development*, p. 176.

73. "New Mexican Railway," *Daily Consular and Trade Reports*, June 20, 1908, p. 5.

74. "El Ferrocarril Panamericano," *Heraldo de Chiapas*, September 1, 1907, p. 1 (author's translation) (The Mexican Revolution Microfilm Series 1900–1929, Sterling Library, Yale University, New Haven, CT); "Un Servicio Pésimo," *Dictamen*, December 16, 1908, p. 2 (author's translation); Hugh Pollard, *A Busy Time in Mexico: An Unconventional Record of Mexican Incident* (Constable, 1913), pp. 56–57 and 61.

75. Edward Butler, "Valuable Concession," *Los Angeles Times*, August 27, 1905, p. VI12.

76. On the Mexican government's control of routes south of Mexico City, see Grunstein, pp. 162–166.

77. "Harriman Is After Railroad to Panama," *Mexican Herald*, November 13, 1908, p. 1; see also Robert Trennert Jr., "The Southern Pacific Railroad of Mexico," *Pacific Historical Review* 35 (1966): 265–284.

78. On concerns over Díaz's retirement, see Alan Knight, *The Mexican Revolution*, vol. I, (Cambridge University Press, 1986), pp. 48–55; see also Hart, *Revolutionary Mexico*, pp. 100–104. On the saga of Doak's divorce, see "Divorce Suit Is Social Shock," *Los Angeles Times*, August 24, 1909, p. II1; "Banker Gives Up Wife for Affinity," *Morning Oregonian*, August 26, 1909, p. 1; and "Double Love Now Divorce," *Los Angeles Times*, April 12, 1910, p. II1.

79. "Pan-American Railway Sold to David Thompson," *Los Angeles Times*, August 15, 1909, p. II11.

80. On Thompson generally, see "Thompson on Trail of Invader Cortes," *Omaha World Herald*, December 12, 1909, p. 13; and "From Brakeman to United States Senator," *San Francisco Chronicle*, March 20, 1901, p. 2. For a useful but fawning portrait of Thompson, see Sands, pp. 123–128, 133–134, and 148–151. On Knox's dismissal of Thompson, see "The American Embassy," *Mexican Herald*, March 14, 1909, p. 1; "Thompson to Retire," *New York Times*, July 4, 1909, p. 7; and Schell, p. 169.

81. "Confidence in Mexico," *Mexican Herald*, August 27, 1909, p. 1; "Harriman's Gall," *Los Angeles Herald*, August 27, 1909.

82. "Not Harriman's Agent," *New-York Tribune*, August 27, 1909, p. 2; "Harriman Line to Panama," *Baltimore Sun*, September 9, 1909, p. 2. On Harriman's death, see Klein, *Harriman*, pp. 434 and 440. On Harriman's dreamed-of world-spanning transportation system, see Klein, *Harriman*, pp. xiv, 182, 285, 300, and 416.

83. "Ambassador Has Pan-American," *Los Angeles Times*, September 22, 1909, p. I16.

84. See "Pan-American Railway Names Its Directors," *St. Louis Post-Dispatch*, October 31, 1909, p. A7; "People Met in Hotel Lobbies," *Washington Post*, February 8, 1910, p. 6.

85. Sands to Thompson, April 27, 1910, NARA, RG 59, Central Decimal Files 1910–1929, 810.77/65 (4440/65).

86. Harry Franck, *Tramping Through Mexico, Guatemala, and Honduras* (Century, rev. 1921), pp. 253–254; see also Brickwood to Secretary of State, November 5, 1910, NARA, RG 59, Central Decimal Files 1910–1929, 810.77/68; "Thompson Says Guatemala Bars Pan-American," *Mexican Herald*, December 21, 1911, p. 1.

87. See "Takes Over Two Roads," *New-York Tribune*, August 28, 1910, p. 5; and "New Property Acquisitions by National Railways of Mexico," *Wall Street Journal*, September 20, 1910, p. 8. On the celebrations of 1910, see Enrique Krauze (Hank Heifetz, trans.), *Mexico: Biography of Power* (HarperPerennial, 1997), pp. 1–16.

88. See "New Property Acquisitions by National Railways of Mexico," and Krauze, p. 255.

89. On Madero's political emergence and revolution, see Knight, pp. 55–77, and Krauze, pp. 245–256.

90. Quoted in Krauze, p. 241, Knight, p. 218, and Hart, p. 237. On Madero's revolutionary actions and triumph over Díaz, see Knight, pp. 171–218.

91. "Road Connecting Buenos Aires and This City Likely," *St. Louis Post-Dispatch*, June 29, 1911, p. 3. On the political situation in the months following Díaz's resignation, see Knight, pp. 247–257.

92. Quoted in Desmond Young, *Member for Mexico: A Biography of Weetman Pearson, First Viscount Cowdray* (Cassell, 1966), p. 154. On Pearson's influence in Mexico and Pierce's resulting discontent, see Jonathan Brown, *Oil and Revolution in Mexico* (University of California Press, 1993), pp. 47–55, 61–65, and 175; Paul Garner, *British Lions and Mexican Eagles* (Stanford University Press, 2011); and "Investigation of Mexican Affairs," S. Doc. 285 (1920), 66th Cong., 2nd sess., vol. II, pp. 2520–2574 (testimony of Sherburne G. Hopkins).

93. See John Skirius, "Railroad, Oil, and Other Foreign Interests in the Mexican Revolution, 1911–1914," *Journal of Latin American Studies* 35 (2003): 33–37. On Madero's view of the *científicos* on National Railways, see testimony of Sherburne G. Hopkins, pp. 2553–2557 and 2560.

94. On Madero's rise and fall, see Krauze, pp. 245–273. On Pearson's supposed funding of the coup, see Skirius, p. 36.

95. For a general overview of the relationships among US investment, anti-Americanism, and the Mexican Revolution, see Hart, *Revolutionary Mexico*; see also Sands, pp. 143–144.

96. "Investigation of Mexican Affairs," vol. I, p. 1790 (statement of Mr. Edward N. Brown). On Huerta's reign generally, see Michael Meyer, *Huerta* (University of Nebraska Press, 1972).

97. On Carranza, see Krauze, pp. 334–341.

98. Wilson quoted in Robert Quirk, *An Affair of Honor* (University Press of Kentucky, 1962), p. 18, and Samuel Blythe, "Mexico: The Record of a Conversation with President Wilson," in James Brown Scott, ed., *The Foreign Policy of President Wilson* (Oxford University Press, 1918), p. 337; see also *Oil and Revolution*, p. 192; and "Huerta Takes Charge of All the Railroads," *Tampa Tribune*, April 28, 1914, p. 1. For an assessment of the Pan-American Railroad at this time, see J. W. Kendrick, "A Report upon the Pan-American Railroad" (New York: n.p., March 1914), Gordon Library—Manuscripts and Archives, Worcester Polytechnic Institute, Worcester, MA.

99. See "Interest of 'Big Business' in Mexican Affairs Is Shown by Amazing Correspondence," *Washington Post*, June 28, 1914, p. 1; and "Rebel Leader Stirred," *Boston Globe*, June 29, 1914, p. 8. On Carranza's triumph over Huerta, see Krauze, pp. 341–347.

100. For an excellent summary of the circumstances leading to Carranza's ultimate confiscation, see Skirius, pp. 48–51 and general.

101. Statement of Mr. Edward Brown, "Investigation of Mexican Affairs," 1795–1796; ibid., 1937 (testimony of Wallace Thompson). See also John McNeely, "The Railways of Mexico," *Southwestern Studies* 2 (Spring 1964): 3–56; and Osgood Hardy, "The Revolution and the Railroads of Mexico," *Pacific Historical Review* 3 (1934): 249–269.

102. William McAdoo, *Crowded Years* (Houghton Mifflin, 1931), p. 351.

103. B. C. Forbes, "Wake Up, United States!" *New York American*, August 7, 1914, in Library of Congress, Washington, DC, the Papers of William McAdoo (hereinafter, *McAdoo Papers*), Box 136.

104. For a helpful summary of the arguments concerning the need for the United States

to capture South American trade written several years before the outbreak of war, see John Barrett, "South America—Our Manufacturers' Greatest Opportunity," *Annals of the American Academy of Political and Social Science* 34 (November 1909): 82–93.

105. On McAdoo's early life, see *Crowded Years*, 17–108, and Douglas Craig, *Progressives at War* (Johns Hopkins University Press, 2013), pp. 12–18.

106. "Trolley Tunnel Open to Jersey," *New York Times*, February 26, 1908, p. 3. On construction of the Hudson rail tunnels generally, see Craig, pp. 26–38.

107. *Crowded Years*, pp. 105 and 109. On McAdoo's progressivism, see Craig, pp. 84–91.

108. On McAdoo's relationship with Wilson in this period, see Craig, pp. 67–77, and *Crowded Years*, pp. 109–176. On McAdoo's segregation, see Craig, pp. 119–123.

109. Quoted in *Crowded Years*, p. 178. On McAdoo's involvement with the Federal Reserve Act's implementation, see Craig, pp. 126–136, and *Crowded Years*, pp. 177–289. On McAdoo's relationship with Wilson's daughter, see especially *Crowded Years*, pp. 272–277. For a masterful summary of the impact of 1907, see William Silber, *When Washington Shut Down Wall Street* (Princeton University Press, 2007), pp. 42–65.

110. For a discussion of McAdoo's actions during 1914, see Silber, pp. 66–172; see also Craig, pp. 136–137 and *Crowded Years*, pp. 290–307. On the origins of McAdoo's interest in Latin America, see *Crowded Years*, pp. 8–9, and Craig, pp. 137–138.

111. On McAdoo's role in leading the Pan-American Financial Conference, see *Crowded Years*, pp. 351–353; see also Craig, p. 138. On McAdoo's physical exhaustion, see McAdoo to the Uruguayan Minister, May 15, 1915, and McAdoo to Fuller, May 17, 1915, *McAdoo Papers*, Box 136. See also materials generally in Boxes 136, 137, and 544, *McAdoo Papers*; and "Act for 18 Republics," *Washington Post*, May 24, 1915, p. 3.

112. Santiago Marín Vicuña, "The Pan American Railroad," *La Razón*, April 10, 1916, in *McAdoo Papers*, Box 544; see also "For Pan-American Railway," *Washington Post*, April 12, 1916, p. 10. On McAdoo's 1916 trip, see *Crowded Years*, pp. 353–360. Much media commentary in Latin America cheered the efforts of the 1916 conference, but for a critical take, see "The Failure of the Financial Conference," *La Union* (Chile), April 11, 1916, *McAdoo Papers*, Box 157. On McAdoo, the 1916 conference, and his subsequent South American tour generally, see Boxes 157 and 158, *McAdoo Papers*.

113. McAdoo, press release, May 4, 1916, *McAdoo Papers*, Box 158; see also "Ships, M'Adoo Slogan—For Pan-American Railway," *Washington Post*, May 5, 1916, p. 1.

114. Frederick Palmer, "Industrial Preparedness," *New York Times*, January 30, 1916, p. SM1; Roosevelt, "The Mexican Iniquity (October 21, 1916)," in *Americanism and Preparedness* (*Mail and Express*, 1917), p. 101. See also "Through Sleepers from Nome to Cape Horn," *Popular Mechanics Magazine* 22 (November 1914): 646–648.

115. "Report of the United States Section of the International High Commission," H. Doc. No. 1788 (December 20, 1916), 64th Cong., 2nd sess., pp. 39–42; see also McAdoo, "The International High Commission and Pan American Cooperation," *American Journal of International Law* 11 (1917): 778–779.

116. Davis to Francis Loomis, April 5, 1907, *Davis Papers*, Letter Books; see also Hendley to Pepper, June 17, 1907, Davis to Roosevelt, September 27, 1907, Davis to Root, September 30, 1907, and Davis to Root, November 1, 1907, all in *Davis Papers*, Letter Books; "Say He Will Wed," *Baltimore Sun*, December 7, 1907, p. 11.

117. "Weary of Failure," *Washington Post*, March 10, 1909, p. 1.

118. Davis to Taft, January 4, 1910, Davis to Knox, January 4, 1910, and Davis to Carnegie, January 31, 1910, all in *Davis Papers*, Letter Books; and Carnegie to Davis, February 3, 1910, *Davis Papers*, Box 146, Folder C.

119. Quoted in Pepper, *The Life and Times of Henry Gassaway Davis*, p. 133; Davison to Davis, February 24, 1910, *Davis Papers*, Box 146, Folder B. On the role of the Pan-American Railway at the Fourth Pan-American Conference, see "Fourth International Conference of American States," S. Doc. 744 (January 16, 1911), 61st Cong., 3rd sess., pp. 11–13.

120. Hendley to Pepper, August 11, 1913, and Davis to Pepper, August 26, 1914, *Davis*

Papers, Letter Books. See also "Henry G. Davis to Retire," *New York Times*, December 12, 1912, p. 3; and "Rails to Link Nations," *Washington Post*, February 5, 1913, p. 16.

121. See "Henry G. Davis, Ex-Senator, Dies," *New York Times*, March 11, 1916, p. 11; see also Pepper, *Life and Times of Davis*, pp. 304–307.

122. On Wilson's frustration with McAdoo's international activities, see Craig, pp. 108–109. On McAdoo's relationship with Wilson, see also *Crowded Years*, p. 341. On Wilson's Pan-Americanism and Latin American policy generally, see Mark Gilderhus, *Pan American Visions* (University of Arizona Press, 1986).

123. See "Seek Only Nation's Peace," *New York Times*, June 23, 1916, p. 1; see also Craig, pp. 141–145, and Gilderhus, pp. 62–65 and 75–77.

124. On McAdoo's role in the 1916 election, see *Crowded Years*, pp. 363–365. On McAdoo's move to supporting US entry into the European war, see Craig, pp. 146–147, and *Crowded Years*, pp. 368–372.

125. *Crowded Years*, p. 369. On the Zimmerman telegram, see Friedrich Katz, *The Secret War in Mexico* (University of Chicago Press, 1981), pp. 350–383. On the US entry to World War I generally, see David Kennedy, *Over Here: The First World War and American Society* (Oxford University Press, 1980).

126. On McAdoo's early wartime activities, see *Crowded Years*, pp. 315–316 and 372–445.

127. James Speyer, "Fair Play for Investors in Stocks and Bonds of American Railways," *Railway Review* 61 (December 22, 1917): 766; "Government Control of Railroads," S. Doc. 159 (1918), 65th Cong., 2nd sess., p. 4; and "McAdoo Most Powerful Man in America Next to President," *New-York Tribune*, November 23, 1918, p. 2. On McAdoo's role as administrator of US railroads, see Craig, pp. 196–207; see also *Crowded Years*, pp. 57 and 446–498.

128. See Craig, p. 5; see also generally, Kennedy, *Over Here*.

129. On McAdoo's relationship to these changes, see generally Silber. On the beginnings of US national bank penetration into Latin America, see Edward Hurley, Vice Chairman, Federal Trade Commission, to McAdoo, May 25, 1915, *McAdoo Papers*, Box 136; and "Federal Reserve Banks in Latin America," *Bankers' Magazine* 91 (October 1915): 470. On the ascendance of the merchant marine, see Edward Hurley, *The New Merchant Marine* (Century, 1920). For a summary of some of these changes in hemispheric relations, see Inman, *Inter-American Conferences*, pp. 88–89; Gilderhus, pp. 37 and 132; Burton Kaufman, "United States Trade and Latin America: The Wilson Years," *Journal of American History* 58 (1971): 342–363; and Clarence Jones, "The United States and Its Chief Competitors in South American Trade," *Economic Geography* 3 (October 1927): 409–433.

130. *Crowded Years*, p. 499. On McAdoo's post-resignation career, see Craig, pp. 240–243, 246–249, 252–258, 266–279, 353–369, and 390–398; see also *Crowded Years*, pp. 498–529. On McAdoo's interest in Mexican railroads, see "William G. McAdoo Shall Receive the National Railroads," *El Excelsior*, December 28, 1920, and "Mexican Matters," n.d., *McAdoo Papers*, Box 544.

131. See Vincent Charles Peloso, "The Politics of Federation in Central America, 1885–1921" (Ph.D. diss., University of Arizona, 1969), pp. 172–209; and Karnes, p. 211.

132. On Thompson, see "Ex-Diplomat Takes a Bride," *Los Angeles Times*, June 16, 1921, p. Il1.

133. B. C. Forbes, *Men Who Are Making America* (B. C. Forbes, 1917), p. 224.

134. Quoted in Forbes, p. 225; see also John Keith Hatch, *Minor C. Keith* (n.p., 1962), pp. 1–12. See also Watt Stewart, *Henry Meiggs* (Duke University Press, 1946).

135. Sands, p. 98; see also Hatch, pp. 14–27, and Watt Stewart, *Keith and Costa Rica* (University of New Mexico Press, 1964), pp. 33–47.

136. Quoted in Hatch, p. 30; see also *Keith and Costa Rica*, pp. 144–159.

137. Samuel Crowther, *The Romance and Rise of the American Tropics* (Doubleday, Doran, 1929), p. 209; see also Hatch, pp. 35 and 48–49.

138. Hatch, p. 60; see also Crowther, p. 170. For a concise contemporary description of popular views toward United Fruit, see Sands, p. 97.

139. Walter Lippmann, *Men of Destiny* (University of Washington Press, 1927), p. 113. On Guatemalan railway development generally, see Delmer Ross, *Development of Railroads in Guatemala and El Salvador, 1849–1929* (Edwin Mellen Press, 2001).

140. See Ross, pp. 27–69; see also "Guatemala Railroad Done," *Washington Post*, May 17, 1908, p. A2.

141. Quoted in Forbes, p. 230; and Hatch, p. 61.

142. See "El Ferrocarril de La Unión a Guatemala," *Diario del Salvador*, June 16, 1908, p. 4. On the link between Keith's Guatemala work and the Pan-American Railway, see also Dosal, pp. 48–49.

143. See Hitt to Secretary of State, January 26, 1912, NARA, RG 59, Records Relating to the Internal Affairs of Guatemala, 1910–1929 (M-655), Roll 35 (814.77/23); see also Hatch, pp. 64–66; and "America Owns Guatemalan Railways," *Daily Boston Globe*, January 5, 1913, p. SM3. During 1912, Keith also acquired a concession to construct Honduras's portion of the Pan-American Railway. See W. Rodney Long, *Railways of Central America and the West Indies* (GPO, 1925), p. 13.

144. Sands quoted in Dosal, p. 61; and Deputy Consul-General Owen to the Assistant Secretary of State, July 25, 1908, NARA, RG 59, Central Files 1906–1910—Numerical and Minor Files (M-862), Roll 912. On the obstacles that International Railways faced, see also Chargé d'Affaires Wilson to Secretary of State, November 26, 1912 (with enclosures), NARA, RG 59, Records Relating to the Internal Affairs of Guatemala, 1910–1929 (M-655), Roll 35 (814.77/31).

145. Williamson to Estrada Cabrera, February 6, 1913, NARA, RG 59, Records relating to the internal affairs of Guatemala 1910–1929 (M-655), Roll 36, 814.77/56; and Wilson to the Secretary of State, April 20, 1913, NARA, RG 59, Records relating to the internal affairs of Guatemala 1910–1929 (M-655), Role 35, 814.77/34; and untitled editorial, *La Campaña*, April 19, 1913, NARA, RG 59, Records relating to the internal affairs of Guatemala 1910–1929 (M-655), Roll 35, 814.77/37.

146. B. C. Gleason, "The International Railways of Central America," *Maintenance of Way Bulletin* 7 (June 10, 1918): 94; see also Crowther, pp. 163–165; letter to Minister Bianchi, March 15, 1922, M-655, Roll 37 (814.77/97); and Policarpo Bonilla (former president of Honduras), "The Wilson Doctrine" (New York: n.p., 1914).

147. See "Report of George W. Davis, Original," NARA, RG 59, Records relating to the internal affairs of Guatemala 1910–1929, M-655, Roll 36 (814.77/45); and Guatemalan Consul to Secretary of State, April 6, 1914 (special mission of General Davis to Guatemala), M-655, Roll 36 (814.77/47). See also Keith to Minister of Fomento, April 22, 1921, enclosure 4, in Lansing and Woolsey to Secretary of State, August 23, 1921, M-655, Roll 36 (814.78); and "Report of Boaz Long," May 6, 1922, in Boaz Long to Keith, May 6, 1922, p. 29, M-655, Roll 37 (814.77/114); and Geissler to Secretary of State, February 19, 1923, M-655, Roll 39 (814.77/192).

148. See Karnes, *Failure of Union*, pp. 219–222. See "Report of Boaz Long," pp. 22, 24, 30. See also Richard Southgate to Secretary of State, May 16, 1922, NARA, RG 59, Records relating to the internal affairs of Guatemala 1910–1929, M-655, Roll 37 (814.77/118); Keith to Lansing and Woolsey, June 15, 1922, M-655, Roll 37; letter to White re: Pacific Mail Steamship Co. and Zacapa Ry. concession, December 28, 1922, M-655, Roll 39 (814.77/186); and Long to Lansing and Woolsey, January 5, 1923, NARA, RG 59, Records relating to the internal affairs of Guatemala 1910–1929, M-655, Roll 39 (814.77/211).

149. Letter to the Secretary of State re: The International Railways Question in Guatemala, September 27, 1922, NARA, RG 59, Records relating to the internal affairs of Guatemala 1910–1929, M-655, Roll 39 (814.77/184); see also Henry Fletcher to Charles Curtis, February 6, 1922, M-655, Roll 37 (814.77/94); and Munro to White, January 22, 1923, M-655, Roll 39 (814.77/190); and Memo of Consul General Holland re: Control of the International Railways, April 6, 1927, NARA, RG 84, pre-1936 Guatemalan consular reports, v. 261.

150. See Santiago Marín Vicuña, *Política Ferroviaria de la América* (Santiago de Chile: Imprenta Universitaria, 1927) and *El Ferrocarril Panamericano* (Santiago de Chile: Imprenta Cervantes, 1917), Columbus Memorial Library, Washington, DC. See also *Report of the Delegates of the United States of America to the Fifth International Conference of American States* (GPO, 1924), pp. 167–169 (appendix 39); and "Supplemental Report on Steps Taken by the Pan American Union in Fulfillment of the Conventions and Resolutions Adopted by the Fifth International Conference of American States" (n.p., June 2, 1924), p. 6.

151. See "Latin America—Pan American Railroad," *Time*, July 14, 1924, p. 13; Pan-American Railway Committee, minutes, August 7, 1924, and April 28, 1927, in Pan-American Railway Committee, "Miscellaneous Documents, Minutes of Meetings," binder (n.d.) (hereinafter, *Committee Binder*), Columbus Memorial Library, Washington, DC.

152. Juan Briano, *Ferrocarril Intercontinental Panamericano—Sus Nuevas Orientaciones* (Buenos Aires: Talleres Gráficos de la Guía "Expreso," 1919) in unnamed binder (containing materials from Briano) (hereafter, *Unnamed Binder*), October 17, 1950, Columbus Memorial Library, Washington, DC. See also *Report of the Delegates of the United States to the Third International Conference of American States*, p. 22.

153. See "Biographical Notes Relative to the Persons Suggested as Members of the Pan American Railway Committee" (n.d. but late 1923), in *Committee Binder*.

154. Havens to Rowe, February 4, 1923, *Committee Binder*; and "Memorandum by Mr. Havens," June 13, 1928, *Committee Binder*.

155. Pan-American Railway Committee minutes, October 7, 1925, *Committee Binder*.

156. See International Railways of Central America, *Annual Report for the Year Ended December 31, 1924*, p. 7; *Annual Report for the Year Ended December 31, 1925*, p. 10. See also Hewes to Secretary of State, March 10, 1924, NARA, RG 59, Records Relating to the Internal Affairs of Guatemala, 1910–1929, M-655, Roll 39 (814.77/267); and "Memorandum of Mr. Minor C. Keith," May 19, 1925, *Committee Binder*. See also Robert S. Platt, "Central American Railways and the Pan-American Route," *Annals of the Association of American Geographers* 16 (March 1926): 12–21.

157. F. J. Lisman, "Central America's Largest Railroad American-Owned, Part I," *Railway Age* 77 (August 30, 1924), p. 377; Keith quoted in *Annual Report for the Year Ended December 31st, 1926*, pp. 4–5. On rail labor statistics, see International Railways of Central America, *Annual Report for the Year Ended December 31st, 1925*, p. 6.

158. "International Rys. Expects Profit Gain," *Wall Street Journal*, July 25, 1928, p. 9; and Alberto Ibarra M., "International Railways Company of Central America," *Bulletin of the Pan American Union* LXI (January 1927): 50.

159. Munro to White, June 5, 1929, NARA, RG 59, Central American Internal Affairs, 1910–1929 (M-672) (813.77/25); see also International Railways, *Annual Report for the Year Ended December 31st 1928*, p. 5. See also "New Central American Rail Link Opened," *Railway Age* 88 (January 18, 1930): 216.

160. Quoted in "Minor C. Keith Dies," *New York Times*, June 15, 1929, p. 8; see also Pepper, "Minor C. Keith," *New York Herald Tribune*, June 22, 1929, p. 12.

161. "Doubts Pan-American Line," *New York Times*, June 16, 1929, p. N9; see also "Lavis Discusses Inter'l Railways," *Wall Street Journal*, June 17, 1929, p. 20.

162. See "C. M. Pepper Dies," *New York Times*, November 5, 1930, p. 21; see also "Cover Letter," October 17, 1950, *Unnamed Binder*; and "Summary of Attempts to Secure Financial Assistance for the Committee" (n.d. but c. 1935), *Committee Binder*. On the termination of the Pan-American Railway Committee, see Caruso, "The Pan-American Railway," *Hispanic American Historical Review* 31 (1951): 638–639.

163. "Carretera en Vez de Ferrocarril Panamericano," *El Mercurio* (Santiago, Chile), May 6, 1927 (author's translation), *Committee Binder*.

Chapter 4: Out of the Muck

1. Quoted in Gaillard Hunt and James Scott, eds., *The Debates in the Federal Convention of 1787* (Oxford University Press, 1920), pp. 563–564 (debates of Tuesday, September 14, 1787). On the history of internal improvements in the early United States, see generally John Larson, *Internal Improvement* (UNC Press, 2001); Victor Albjerg, "Internal Improvements Without a Policy, 1789–1861," *Indiana Magazine of History* 28 (1932): 168–179; and Ellis Armstrong, *History of Public Works in the United States 1776–1976* (American Public Works Association, 1976).

2. Alexander Hamilton, "Examination of Jefferson's Message to Congress," in John Hamilton, ed., *The Works of Alexander Hamilton*, vol. VII (John F. Trow, 1856), p. 755; see also "Federal Aid in the Construction of Rural Post Roads," Senate Report No. 250 (March 10, 1916), 64th Cong., 1st sess., p. 9; and Larson, pp. 35–36, 39, and 45–50.

3. See Joseph Harrison, "'Sic Et Non': Thomas Jefferson and Internal Improvement," *Journal of the Early Republic* 7 (1987): 335–349; and Drew McCoy, *The Elusive Republic* (UNC Press, 1980). On the National Road, see, e.g., Theodore Sky, *The National Road and the Difficult Path to Sustainable National Investment* (University of Delaware Press, 2011).

4. See Sky, pp. 15–28.

5. See *Report of the Secretary of the Treasury, on the Subject of Public Roads and Canals* (R. C. Weightman, 1808); see also Larson, pp. 59–63; and Nicholas Dungan, *Gallatin* (NYU Press, 2010).

6. See Brian Schoen, "Calculating the Price of Union: Republican Economic Nationalism and the Origins of Southern Sectionalism, 1790–1828," *Journal of the Early Republic* 23 (2003): 173–206.

7. John C. Calhoun, "Internal Improvement," in Frank Moore, ed., *American Eloquence*, vol. II (D. Appleton, 1880), p. 480; see also Larson, pp. 63–67.

8. James Madison, "Veto Message of March 3, 1817," in *Journal of the House of Representatives of the United States* (William A. Davis, 1816), p. 535. See also Stuart Leibiger, ed., *A Companion to James Madison and James Monroe* (Wiley-Blackwell, 2013), pp. 203–206.

9. See Larson, pp. 126–139. On the scope and history of the general welfare clause, see Theodore Sky, *To Provide for the General Welfare: A History of the Federal Spending Power* (University of Delaware Press, 2003).

10. James Monroe, "Special Message to the House of Representatives," May 4, 1822, online by Gerhard Peters and John T. Woolley, *The American Presidency Project*; see also Sky, *National Road*, pp. 39–43 and 48; and Leibiger, pp. 442–446.

11. James Monroe, "Seventh Annual Message," December 2, 1823, *The American Presidency Project*. Monroe's position would subsequently help guide federal highway policy in the twentieth century as well. See Sky, *National Road*, pp. 46 and 80.

12. See Larson, pp. 183–185; Sky, pp. 58–59; and Senate Report No. 250, p. 10. See also Carlton Jackson, "The Internal Improvement Vetoes of Andrew Jackson," *Tennessee Historical Quarterly* 25 (1966): 261–279.

13. See Sky, *National Road*, 52, 59–67; see also Thomas Agg and John Brindley, *Highway Administration and Finance* (McGraw-Hill, 1927), p. 19.

14. *Speeches of Mr. Randolph* (Gales & Seaton, 1824), p. 25; see also Daniel Walker Howe, *What Hath God Wrought* (Oxford University Press, 2007), p. 222.

15. Quoted in Albjerg, p. 177.

16. See Agg, pp. 20–21.

17. On US transportation in this period generally, see Caroline MacGill, *History of Transportation in the United States before 1860* (Carnegie Institute, 1917).

18. See Charles Dearing, *American Highway Policy* (Brookings, 1941), pp. 44–45.

19. N. S. Shaler, "The Common Roads," *Scribner's Magazine* VI (October 1889): 477. On road building practices in the United States in the nineteenth century, see Charles Wixom, *Pictorial History of Roadbuilding* (American Road Builders Association, 1975); and Clemens Herschel, *The Science of Road Making* (Engineering News, 1890).

20. Memorandum, "Object Lesson Roads" (n.d., but c. December 1897), NARA, RG 30 (Bureau of Public Roads), Letters Sent by the Bureau, 1893–1904 (hereinafter, *Early Bureau Letters*).

21. "To Test Auto Wear," *New-York Tribune*, May 16, 1909, p. 11. See generally John Loudon McAdam, *Remarks on the Present System of Road Making* (J. M. Gultch, 1816).

22. McAdam, *Remarks on the Present System of Road Making* (Longman, Hurst, Rees, Orme, & Brown, 1823), preface to the seventh ed., p. v.

23. Horace Bushnell, *The Day of Roads* (Elihu Geer, 1846), p. 13.

24. Charles Dickens, *American Notes for General Circulation*, vol. II (Chapman & Hall, 1842), p. 162. On corduroy roads, see MacGill, pp. 299–305.

25. *Report of the Commissioner of Agriculture for the Year 1868* (GPO, 1869), p. 353; "Shall Farm Laborers Work on the Road," *Southern Planter* (February 1, 1884): 68–69; "A Slough of Despond," *Southern Cultivator* 50 (June 1892): 294; Selim Peabody to Albert Pope in Pope, *Road Making as a Branch of Instruction in Colleges* (Albert A. Pope, 1892), p. 7; and *Report of the Commissioner of Agriculture, 1888* (GPO, 1889), p. 47.

26. "Good Dirt Roads," *Southern Cultivator* 41 (June 1883): 4. On early agricultural good roads advocacy, see generally Howard Preston, *Dirt Roads to Dixie* (University of Tennessee Press, 1991); and Philip Mason, "The League of American Wheelmen and the Good Roads Movement, 1880–1905" (Ph.D. diss., University of Michigan, 1957), pp. 68–69. Jingle quoted in Wayne Fuller, *RFD* (Indiana University Press, 1964), p. 181.

27. James Beaver, "Why We Have So Few Good Roads," *Forum*, August 1892, pp. 776–777.

28. "Jersey Country Roads," *New York Times*, December 26, 1888, p. 2; "Improved County Roads," *New York Times*, March 30, 1890, p. 19; see also Mason, pp. 208–210.

29. See generally Linda Gross and Theresa Snyder, *Philadelphia's 1876 Centennial Exposition* (Arcadia, 2005).

30. John McClintock, "Colonel Albert A. Pope," *Granite Monthly* IX (August 1886): 220. On early bicycles and Pope generally, see Stephen Goddard, *Colonel Albert Pope and His American Dream Machines* (McFarland, 2000).

31. Mark Twain, *What Is Man and Other Essays* (Harper & Brothers, 1917), p. 296.

32. See "How the L.A.W. Was Organized," *Bicycling World* XXXIX (August 10, 1899): 548–552 (reproduced from *Bicycling World*, June 12, 1880), in Beinecke Library, Yale University, New Haven, CT, *Scrapbook of Amos Batchelder*, vol. II (hereinafter, *Batchelder Scrapbooks*).

33. See Mason, pp. 47 and 64–82.

34. Ibid., pp. 83–90; see also "Working for Good Roads," *Los Angeles Times*, November 11, 1890, p. 3. On Potter's background and rise as a Wheelman, see "What Bicyclists Have Done," *New York Times*, September 11, 1892, p. 12.

35. Isaac Potter, *The Gospel of Good Roads* (League of American Wheelmen, 1891), pp. 55, 59, and general. For a further summary of good roads arguments, see Archer Hulbert, *The Future of Road-making in America* (Arthur H. Clark, 1905), pp. 81–169.

36. See Mason, pp. 83–123; "The Wheelman's Duty," *Outing* 16 (May 1890): 156; and George Perkins, "The Growth and Condition of the Roads Question," *Good Roads* 3 (January 1, 1893): 4.

37. "What Bicyclists Have Done," *New York Times*, September 11, 1892, p. 12; see also "Wheelmen in Session," *Daily Boston Globe*, February 17, 1891, p. 10.

38. Pope, "Highway Improvement" (n.p., October 17, 1889).

39. Stone to Reid, July 21, 1892, NARA, RG 30, General Correspondence 1893–1916, Box 2, Folder 1 (Old Public Roads Corres 1893). See also "A National Highway Commission," *New-York Tribune*, July 11, 1892, p. 6; "Better Roads Demanded," *New-York Tribune*, July 17, 1892, p. 5; and Mason, pp. 124–149. See also Richard Weingroff, *Portrait of a General* (Federal Highway Administration, 1993).

40. Harrison quoted in "What Bicyclists Have Done," *New York Times*, September 11, 1892, p. 12. Roy Stone, "Urging National Road Improvement," *New-York Tribune*, August 25, 1892, p. 4; see also Mason, pp. 128–129.

41. James Dunn to Stone, July 27, 1892, NARA, RG 30, General Correspondence 1893–1916, Box 2, Folder 1 (Old Public Roads Corres 1893).

42. See "The Omaha Platform," *World Almanac and Bureau of Information* (Press Publishing, 1892), pp. 83–85. On the populists generally, see Charles Postel, *The Populist Vision* (Oxford University Press, 2007).

43. Charles Crisp, "A Letter from Speaker Crisp," *Baltimore Sun*, July 30, 1892, p. 6. Stone quoted in Mason, p. 242. See also Mason, pp. 133–135.

44. See *National League for Good Roads: Proceedings of the Convention*, vol. 1, no. 1 (Chicago: n.p., November 1892), pp. 1–5; see also Roy Stone, "Good Roads and How to Get Them," in *Proceedings of the National Good Roads Convention* (Office of Public Roads Inquiries, Bulletin No. 26) (GPO, 1903), p. 46; see also Mason, pp. 136–138.

45. Stone, "Opening Address," in *The National League for Good Roads: Proceedings of the Convention*, p. 6.

46. Ibid., p. 14.

47. See "Would a Road Department Help?" *New-York Tribune*, November 13, 1892, p. 6.

48. "At Work for Good Roads," *New York Times*, November 20, 1892, p. 14. See also Pope, "A Memorial to Congress on the Subject of a Road Department" (n.p., n.d., but c. March 1893).

49. See *Proceedings of a Convention of the National League for Good Roads and Hearing by the Committee of Agriculture* (Department of Agriculture, Office of Experiment Stations, Bulletin No. 14) (GPO, 1893), p. 86; see also Mason, p. 145.

50. *Proceedings of a Convention of the National League for Good Roads*, pp. 23 and 87–88.

51. See "For Improved Roads," *Baltimore Sun*, December 11, 1893, p. 2.

52. Pope, "National Road Department," *Southern Cultivator*, March 1893, p. 125; see also Goddard, p. 120, and Mason, p. 141.

53. "Work for Good Roads," *Hartford Courant*, December 19, 1896, p. 3.

54. See Stone to Morton, September 7, 1895, *Early Bureau Letters*.

55. See "'Gen' Coxey's Waterloo,'" *Daily Boston Globe*, May 2, 1894, p. 1. On Coxey's march generally, see, e.g., Jerry Prout, "Coxey's Challenge in the Populist Moment" (Ph.D. diss., George Mason University, 2012).

56. "Response of Gen. Stone," *Proceedings of the National Road Conference* (Office of Road Inquiry, Bulletin No. 10) (GPO, 1894), pp. 7–9; and Stone to Charles Manderson, July 10, 1894, *Early Bureau Letters*.

57. See generally, Office of Road Inquiry Bulletins Nos. 1–21. See also Bruce Seely, *Building the American Highway System* (Temple University Press, 1987), pp. 11–16. On state-level developments, see "Good Roads Movement," *St. Louis Post-Dispatch*, January 21, 1895, p. 4; and Stone to Morton, September 7, 1895, *Early Bureau Letters*.

58. Stone, "The National Government and Good Roads," *Independent* (New York), February 6, 1896, p. 4; and Stone to Wilson, September 1, 1897, *Early Bureau Letters*.

59. "Object Lesson Roads," c. December 1897, *Early Bureau Letters*. On Stone's earlier efforts to experiment with object lesson roads, see Stone to Morton, November 9, 1895, *Early Bureau Letters*; see also Mason, p. 158.

60. "The Road of the Future," *Clay Record* 9 (August 12, 1896): 18; see also Stone's comments in "United for Good Roads," *New-York Tribune*, February 4, 1900, p. 10. On Wilson's resistance to push for appropriations, see Maurice Eldridge to Thomas MacDonald, June 3, 1939, Cushing Memorial Library, Texas A&M University, College Station, TX, the Papers of Thomas MacDonald (hereinafter, *MacDonald Papers*), Box 21 (Folder 22).

61. "Good Roads the Topic," *St. Louis Post-Dispatch*, November 22, 1897, p. 2; "In the Cycling World," *New-York Tribune*, December 19, 1897, p. B2; and "Gossip of the Cyclers," *New York Times*, February 20, 1898, p. 6.

62. See "Taking of Adjuntas," *Daily Boston Globe*, August 14, 1898, p. 4.

63. "No Roads in Puerto Rico," *New York Times*, November 4, 1898, p. 5; see also "Good

Roads in Cuba," *New-York Tribune*, August 25, 1898, p. 6; and Stone, "Puerto Rico's Needs: A Practical Suggestion," *Outlook* 63 (December 30, 1899): 1023–1025.

64. See "Untitled Biographical Sketch of Martin Dodge," c. January 1900, *Early Bureau Letters*. See also Eldridge to Wilson, October 30, 1899, *Early Bureau Letters*.

65. "Untitled Memo," c. January 1900, *Early Bureau Letters*.

66. "Promotes Good Roads," *Detroit Free Press*, July 21, 1900, p. 4; see also Fuller, *RFD*, p. 182 and general; and *Rural Free Delivery* (GPO, 1899).

67. See "To Get Good Roads," *St. Louis Post-Dispatch*, September 10, 1897, p. 7; and "Have a New Name," *St. Louis Post-Dispatch*, November 23, 1898, p. 10.

68. See "Push the Good Roads," *St. Louis Post-Dispatch*, May 22, 1899, p. 5; and "Apostles of Good Roads," *Omaha World Herald*, September 1, 1899, p. 8.

69. "Apostles of Good Roads," *St. Louis Post-Dispatch*, February 4, 1900, p. A9; and Dodge to Wilson, July 16, 1900, *Early Bureau Letters*.

70. See "Good Roads Convention," *New-York Tribune*, November 20, 1900, p. 8; and "A Good Roads Congress," *Toronto Globe and Mail*, December 1, 1900, p. 5.

71. See "Good Roads Committee Acts," *New York Times*, November 27, 1900, p. 12; and Dodge to Wilson, November 27, 1900, *Early Bureau Letters*.

72. Quoted in Pope, *Wagon Roads as Feeders to Railways* (Albert A. Pope, 1892), p. 4; and Moore, "History and Purposes of the Good Roads Movement," *Proceedings of the National Good Roads Convention* (Office of Public Road Inquiries, Bulletin No. 26) (GPO, 1903), p. 11.

73. Dodge to Wilson, July 2, 1901, *Early Bureau Letters*; see also Moore, "History and Purposes of the Good Roads Movement," pp. 10–11; and Dodge, "The Good Roads Train," *Brick*, March 1, 1902, p. 156.

74. Quoted in Seely, p. 18.

75. "Statement of Mr. M. O. Eldridge," in *Interstate Highway System—Hearings Before the Committee on Post Offices and Post Roads, United States Senate* (GPO, 1921), p. 536.

76. On Dodge's authorship, see "Statement of Mr. Martin Dodge," ibid., p. 196. On New York's road legislation, see E. A. Bonney, "Roads of New York," *Good Roads XVII* (February 22, 1919): 73–76.

77. See Walter Brownlow, "National Aid to Road Improvement," *Cosmopolitan XXXIV* (January 1903): 355–358.

78. Untitled memorandum, c. April 1893, and Dodge to Moore, December 12, 1902, *Early Bureau Letters*. Eighty-year-old quoted in "National Aid Coming Soon" (n.d., but c. 1903), NARA, RG 30, General Correspondence 1893–1916, Box 4 (National Aid to Road Building 1892–1912, Brownlow Bill).

79. G. Russell Taggart to James Abbott, February 14, 1903, *Early Bureau Letters*.

80. "'Good Roads' His Slogan," *Los Angeles Times*, March 28, 1903, p. A1.

81. "Workers for Good Roads Hold Notable Convention," *St. Louis Post-Dispatch*, May 3, 1903, p. 6B.

82. Stone, "Good Roads and How to Get Them," *Proceedings of the National Good Roads Convention* (Office of Public Road Inquiries Bulletin, No. 26), p. 46.

83. Theodore Roosevelt, "Good Roads as an Element in National Greatness," ibid., p. 79; see also Eldridge to Cassatt, May 28, 1903, *Early Bureau Letters*.

84. Eldridge to Dodge, October 24, 1903, NARA, RG 30, General Correspondence 1893–1916, Box 4 (National Aid to Road Building 1892–1912, Brownlow Bill); "For Good Roads," *Los Angeles Times*, November 24, 1903, p. 6.

85. Dodge to Moore, February 29, 1904, *Early Bureau Letters*; "Better Than the Brownlow Scheme," *Washington Post*, January 31, 1903, p. 6; "Here It Is Again," *Washington Post*, May 5, 1903, p. 6; "Stupendous Paternalism," *Washington Post*, January 27, 1904, p. 6; "Congress and the Brownlow Scheme," *Washington Post*, April 22, 1904, p. 6; and "Why Not Interplanetary Transportation?" *Washington Post*, August 25, 1904, p. 6.

86. See Dodge to Moore, February 29, 1904, *Early Bureau Letters*; and Moore to Stuyvesant

Fish, February 9, 1903, and Eldridge to F. M. Simmons, January 31, 1903, NARA, RG 30, General Correspondence 1893–1916, Box 2, Folder 2 (Old Public Roads Corres— Establishment of Good Roads Bureau 1900–1908).

87. "Zeal Cost Them Office," *New-York Tribune*, February 24, 1905, p. 3. On Dodge's questionable behavior in this period, see Seely, pp. 18–20.

88. Page to John King, May 21, 1907, NARA, RG 30, General Correspondence 1893–1916, Box 4 (National Aid to Road Building 1892–1912, Brownlow Bill); Page, "Road Legislation," Address delivered December 4, 1906, NARA, RG 30, General Correspondence 1893–1916, Box 75, Folder 326 II; and Page also quoted in Seely, p. 26.

89. On Page's background, see "Secretary Williams' Tribute to Mr. Page," *Road-Maker* 13 (January 1919): 44–48; and "Logan Waller Page," *Transactions of the American Society of Civil Engineers* 83 (1919): 2305–2309. On the birth of road building education in colleges, see Pope, *Road Making as a Branch of Instruction in Colleges.*

90. "Statement of Logan W. Page," *Agricultural Appropriation Bill Hearings*, December 15, 1911, NARA, RG 30, General Correspondence 1893–1916, Box 4, Folder 3 (Work of Office in General); and Nathaniel Shaler, *American Highways* (Century, 1896), p. 235.

91. Quoted in "News from the Classes, 1895," *Harvard Graduates' Magazine* 27 (March 1919): 412.

92. John Goodell, "Logan Waller Page," *Engineering News-Record*, December 12, 1918, p. 1095; and Thomas MacDonald, "The Engineer's Relation to Highway Transportation for the Sixth Salzberg Memorial Lecture," April 1954, p. 34, *MacDonald Papers*, Box 4, Folder 19.

93. Quoted in "Logan Waller Page," *Transactions of the American Society of Civil Engineers* 83 (1919): 2305.

94. Page, "The Selection of Materials for Macadam Roads," in *Yearbook of the Department of Agriculture for 1901* (GPO, 1902), pp. 349–352; and Page, *The Testing of Road Materials, Bureau of Chemistry Bulletin* 79: 4 and general (GPO, 1903).

95. See "Work of the Office of Public Road Inquiries," July 24, 1902, NARA, RG 30, General Correspondence 1893–1916, Box 3, Folder 2-3 (Work of Office in General 1896–1906).

96. Page to Hon. W. B. Lamar, June 6, 1906, NARA, RG 30, General Correspondence 1893–1916, Box 3, Folder 2-3 (Work of Office in General 1896–1906); and "Statement of L. W. Page," c. May 1905, NARA, RG 30, General Correspondence 1893–1916, Box 3, Folder 1 (Old Bureau Corres—Work of Office in General 1896–1899).

97. "The Auto and the Highway Problem," *Hartford Courant*, April 27, 1908, p. 14.

98. Charles Sorensen, *My Forty Years with Ford* (Wayne State University Press, 2006), p. 109; and Charles Duryea, "Racing Came First," January 3, 1914, p. 8, *Batchelder Scrapbooks*, vol. I.

99. On the advance of the automobile, see Curt McConnell, *Coast to Coast by Automobile* (Stanford University Press, 2000).

100. "Names the Commission to French Road Congress," *Augusta Chronicle*, June 8, 1908, p. 10; see also H. M. Chittenden, "Oil as a Road-builder," c. 1906, NARA, RG 30, General Correspondence 1893–1916, Box 75, Folder 326 II.

101. Page, "Dust Preventives," *Yearbook of the United States Department of Agriculture* 1907 (GPO, 1908), p. 257. Page additionally quoted in William Judson, *Road Preservation and Dust Prevention* (Engineering News Publishing, 1908), p. 11.

102. See "Dustless Road of Molasses," *New-York Tribune*, September 20, 1908, p. C4; see Judson, *Road Preservation*, generally.

103. Rose Wilder Lane, "Grandpa's Fiddle," in William Anderson, ed., *A Little House Sampler* (University of Nebraska Press, 1988), p. 81; see also I. B. Holley Jr., "Blacktop: How Asphalt Paving Came to the Urban United States," *Technology and Culture* 44 (2003): 703–733.

104. See Holley, pp. 721–722; and Judson, generally.

105. See Allerton Cushman, "Oiling and Tarring Roads," c. 1909, NARA, RG 30, General

Correspondence 1893–1916, Box 75, Folder 326 I; see also "Report of the Director of the Office of Public Roads for 1910," c. July 1910, NARA, RG 30, General Correspondence 1893–1916, Box 8, Folder 23 (Reports 1906–1911); "Terms Used in Bituminous Road Work," *Municipal Journal and Engineer* XXX (March 15, 1911): 359; "Dustless Road of Molasses"; Clifford Richardson, *Asphalt Construction for Pavements and Highways* (McGraw-Hill, 1913); and Holley, pp. 716–717, 729, and 731.

106. See Robert Lesley, *History of the Portland Cement Industry in the United States* (International Trade, 1924), foreword; Page, "The Possibilities of Portland Cement as a Road Material," *Cement Age* 10 (January 1, 1910): 37–40; "Statement of Logan W. Page," *Agricultural Appropriation Bill Hearings*, December 15, 1911, p. 164; "Inventors Who Take No Profit from Their Work," *New York Times*, December 4, 1910, p. SM9; "Government Helps Road Preservation," *New York Times*, July 2, 1911, p. C8; and Page, "Concrete Roads," *Cement Age* 14 (June 1, 1912): 280–281.

107. Quoted in "Automobile Gossip," *Washington Post*, August 23, 1908, p. S3.

108. Page, "Report of the American Delegation to the First International Road Congress," c. November 1908, NARA, RG 30, General Correspondence 1893–1916, Box 74 (International Road Congresses 1908–1912); see also "The Auto and the Highway Problem," *Hartford Courant*, April 27, 1908, p. 14.

109. Page to Charles E. Hughes, July 16, 1908, NARA, RG 30, General Correspondence 1893–1916, Box 74 (International Road Congresses 1908–1912); see also "Names the Commission to French Road Congress," *Augusta Chronicle*, June 8, 1908, p. 10.

110. "Road Builders of World in Conference," *San Jose Mercury News*, December 2, 1908, p. 6; and "Report of the American Delegation to the First International Road Congress."

111. "For a Bureau of Good Roads," *Los Angeles Times*, November 29, 1908, p. I7; "International Roads Bureau," *New-York Tribune*, November 29, 1908, p. C7. On Page's experiences in Europe, see "Autoists Want Horses Barred from Highways," *St. Louis Post-Dispatch*, December 6, 1908, p. A5.

112. Quoted in "International Roads Bureau." On the highway statistics, see "The World's Conquerors," *Arizona Republican*, December 22, 1908, p. 12; and "U.S. Is Behind in Road Work," *Detroit Free Press*, November 7, 1909, p. 20.

113. Quoted in "The World's Conquerors." See also "Report and Comments of the Secretary of Agriculture on Senate Bill No. 174, p. 7, NARA, RG 30, General Correspondence 1893–1916, Box 2, Folder 3 (Old Public Roads Corres—Establishment of Good Roads Bureau 1909–1912).

114. "Automobiles on Public Roads," *Southern Cultivator*, December 1, 1904, p. 10; and "Has the Good Roads Movement Petered Out?" *Los Angeles Times*, February 2, 1906, p. I14.

115. Taft quoted in "Taft Says States Should Build Roads," *New York Times*, December 21, 1911, p. 2. On Dodge's 1908 campaign, see "Good Roads Is Their Cry," *Kansas City Star*, June 8, 1908, p. 4; "The National Good Roads Congress," *Good Roads Magazine*, July 1908, p. 243; "Road Congress Coming," *Baltimore Sun*, March 11, 1909, p. 9; and "Spend More for Roads," *Baltimore Sun*, May 23, 1909, p. 5.

116. See "Legislative and Good Roads Convention at Buffalo," *Good Roads Magazine*, August 1908, pp. 247–255. On Grange support, see "Good Roads the Cry," *New-York Tribune*, September 12, 1909, p. 11.

117. Quoted in "Legislative and Good Roads Convention at Buffalo," pp. 247 and 252; see also "Good Roads Men Reach Cleveland," *Cleveland Plain Dealer*, September 19, 1909, p. 1; and "5000 Delegates to Talk Good Roads Here Next Month," *St. Louis Post-Dispatch*, August 28, 1910, p. 4S.

118. Quoted in "Motoring, 'New York Press,'" c. late 1910, *Batchelder Scrapbooks*, vol. I. On Batchelder's background, see "Hoo's Hoo and Wat's Wat in Gasolene," n.d., and "The A.A. of America," *Motor Trader*, December 18, 1912, p. 1034, *Batchelder Scrapbooks*, vol. I.

119. "Autoists' Slogan Is 'Good Roads,'" *Oregonian*, June 30, 1912, *Batchelder Scrapbooks*, vol. I.

120. "Batchelder Here for Good Roads," *Seattle Post-Intelligencer*, n.d., but c. March 1911, *Batchelder Scrapbooks*, vol. I.

121. Page quoted in "For Better Roads," *Washington Post*, November 23, 1910, p. 1; and "Response by Logan Waller Page," *Papers, Addresses and Resolutions before the American Road Congress* (American Association for Highway Improvement, 1912), p. 8. On the origin of Page's organization, see "Wants Uniform Road System," *New-York Tribune*, August 21, 1910, p. 11; "For United National Highway Improvements," *Automobile Topics* XXI (December 3, 1910): 558–559; and "Secretary Williams' Tribute to Mr. Page," *Road-Maker* 13 (January 1919): 46. On Page as a reform progressive, see Seely, pp. 16–45.

122. "Plans Extensive Road Improvement," *New York Times*, July 9, 1911, p. C8; see also "Spending Money for Good Roads," *New York Times*, July 30, 1911, p. C8; and "Co-operate in Good Roads," *Detroit Free Press*, September 24, 1911, p. C8.

123. "Plans Extensive Road Improvement." See also "Federal Aid for Roads in Dispute," *Atlanta Constitution*, November 21, 1911, p. 1; "Pushed Good Roads," *Washington Post*, November 26, 1911, p. R2; and *Papers, Addresses and Resolutions before the American Road Congress*, generally.

124. Batchelder, "National Aid for Better Highways," *New York Times*, January 7, 1912, *Batchelder Scrapbooks*, vol. I; see also "Must Unite for Roads," *Washington Post*, January 17, 1912, p. 2; and *Federal Aid for Good Roads: Proceedings of First National Convention* (Washington, DC: n.p., 1912).

125. See "States in Road Fight," *Washington Post*, January 15, 1912, p. 5; and "US Aid for Roads," *Washington Post*, April 11, 1912, p. 4.

126. Edwin Warley James to Bill Reid, March 21, 1963, American Heritage Center, University of Wyoming, Laramie, WY, Papers of Edwin Warley James (hereinafter, *James Papers*), Box 4; and James to Cron, February 21, 1967, *James Papers*, Folder B-J232-ew; see also "Government Aids Good Roads Plan," *Chicago Daily Tribune*, August 30, 1912, p. 5.

127. See "Much Good Roads Work in 1912," *Horseless Age* 31 (January 1, 1913): 30.

128. "Build Roads by Auto Tax Says Batchelder," n.d. but c. fall 1912, *Batchelder Scrapbooks*, vol. I; and Page to A. G. Spalding, May 2, 1912, NARA, RG 30, General Correspondence 1893–1916, Box 50, Folder 141 (Trans-Continental Hwys 1897–1911). On the growth of these various highway movements generally, see ibid.

129. See, e.g., Charles Davis, *National Highways to Bring About Good Roads Everywhere* (National Highways Association, 1913). On the organization's self-interest in promoting highways, see "Millions for Roads," *New York Times*, August 2, 1913, p. 6.

130. "'Pork Barrel' Bill Author on Defense" (n.d., but c. 1914), *Batchelder Scrapbooks*, vol. I.

131. Quoted in "Congress Fight for Good Road Aid Is Told," *San Francisco Call*, July 7, 1916, *Batchelder Scrapbooks*, vol. II; see also "Let Uncle Sam Do It" (n.d., but c. 1916), *Batchelder Scrapbooks*, vol. II.

132. Quoted in "Secretary Williams' Tribute to Mr. Page," *Road-Maker* 13 (January 1919): 46; see also *Proceedings of the Fourth American Road Congress* (American Highway Association, 1915).

133. "American Highway Officials Are Now Organized," *World* (WV), August 22, 1916, *Batchelder Scrapbooks*, vol. II (see also Batchelder's handwritten annotation to the article); see also "State Road Officials Form an Association," *Atlanta Constitution*, December 13, 1914, p. 5.

134. Batchelder, "Government May Aid States with Road Appropriation," n.d., *Batchelder Scrapbooks*, vol. II; and "Ask $25,000,000 a Year," *Baltimore Sun*, December 6, 1915, p. 2.

135. On the congressional fight, see "Action on Roads Bill," *Washington Post*, February 20, 1916, p. 11; "Hope to Merge Good Roads Bill and Win," *New York Times*, April 30, 1916, p. XX2; and "Good Roads," S. Doc. 474 (June 26, 1916), 64th Cong., 1st sess.

136. "President Used Four Pens" (n.d., but c. July 1916), *Batchelder Scrapbooks*, vol. II.

137. Page to Atlee Pomerene, April 13, 1918, NARA, RG 30, Classified Central Files 1912–1950, Box 1956, Folder 481 (Federal Aid System 1917–1918).

138. James to Cron, February 21, 1967, *James Papers*, Folder B-J232-ew; "Road Work Delayed by Doubt About Law," *Atlanta Constitution*, February 27, 1917, p. 10; and "Time to Do Something!" *Atlanta Constitution*, May 25, 1917, p. 8.

139. Page, "One Year's Experience in the Federal Aid Road Law," *Good Roads*, December 22, 1917, p. 326, in *MacDonald Papers*, Box 7, Folder 87.

140. "State Highway Officials Take Vigorous Action at Richmond Convention," *Contractor* 24 (December 21, 1917): 553–554.

141. Ibid.

142. "To Haul Freight Over Highways," *New-York Tribune*, November 10, 1917, p. 15.

143. "A Baby Automobile," *New-York Tribune*, November 7, 1901, p. 5. On Chapin's life, see J. C. Long, *Roy D. Chapin* (Wayne State University Press, 2004); see also B. C. Forbes, *Automotive Giants of America* (B.C. Forbes, 1926), pp. 14–29.

144. See "Car Makers Do Highway Work," *New York Times*, October 11, 1914, p. XX5; see also Long, pp. xvii and 40.

145. Chapin to Batchelder, July 11, 1916, *Batchelder Scrapbooks*, vol. II; see also Chapin, "The Automobile Manufacturer in Relation to Good Roads," c. 1913, enclosed in Pyke Johnson to MacDonald, February 4, 1929, *MacDonald Papers*, Box 20, Folder 24. On state automobile taxes and road building, see "Build Roads by Auto Tax Says Batchelder" (n.d., but c. June 1912), *Batchelder Scrapbooks*, vol. I; "Auto Fees of $16,000,000 Spent for Road Building," *Christian Science Monitor*, July 22, 1916, p. 8; Long, pp. 139–140; and Agg, pp. 116–117.

146. Chapin quoted in Long, p. 143; see also Long, p. 147.

147. Quoted in Long, p. 146; see also "President Chapin Heads New War Committee," *Hudson Triangle* VII (November 24, 1917): 2.

148. Long, p. 152.

149. "War Motors Coming to Ports Overland," *New York Times*, December 14, 1917, p. 13; see also Long, pp. 155–157.

150. Quoted in "Plan Truck Express from Farm," *Atlanta Constitution*, March 31, 1918, p. D9; and Chapin, "Shipping Via the Highways," *Outlook*, August 7, 1918, p. 568; see also "Trucks Connect Farms with Washington," *Outlook*, June 5, 1918, p. 234; and Long, p. 161.

151. Quoted in "Auto Transport Era Will Boom America, Roy Chapin Predicts," *Detroit Free Press*, January 5, 1919, p. C11; see also Chapin, *The New Way to Market* (n.p., 1918).

152. "A. G. Batchelder of Three A's Talks to the Motor Club," *Tropical Sun* (FL), March 1, 1918, *Batchelder Scrapbooks*, vol. II; see also "Declares States Delay Highways," *Washington Post*, September 20, 1918, p. 4.

153. MacDonald, "The Man with an Idea," enclosed in MacDonald to G. Donald Kennedy, November 13, 1956, *MacDonald Papers*, Box 8, Folder 34; attendee quote in William Mertz, "Origins of the Interstate," unpublished manuscript, April 4, 1986, p. 8, Cushing Memorial Library, Texas A&M University, College Station, TX, Papers of Francis Turner (hereinafter, *Turner Papers*), Box 15, Folder 22; see also "50,000-Mile National Highway Proposed at Chicago Conference," *Automotive Industries* XXXIX (December 12, 1918): 1018; and "Significance of the Chicago Highway Congress," *Road-Maker* 13 (January 1919): 42–44.

154. Page quoted in "Urge Immediate Road Work," *Baltimore Sun*, November 30, 1918, p. 14; see also "Status of Federal Aid-Road Projects," *Road-Maker* 13 (January 1919): 40–42.

155. Page quoted in "Urge Immediate Road Work."

156. Quoted in "Has National Roads Plan," *Boston Transcript*, February 13, 1919, NARA, RG 30, Classified Central Files 1912–1950, Box 1955.

157. "Secretary Williams' Tribute to Mr. Page" and "By the Association," *Road-Maker* 13 (January 1919): 44 and 48; see also "Logan Waller Page," *Highway Magazine* X (February 1919): 11.

158. Quoted in Mertz, p. 8.

159. Pyke Johnson, partial biography of Thomas MacDonald, unpublished manuscript, p. 31, enclosed in Johnson to Francis C. Turner, August 22, 1967, *Turner Papers*, Box 15, Folder 1.

160. See J. C. Welliver to H. S. Fairbank, and enclosure, April 10, 1942, *MacDonald Papers*, Box 1, Folder 16; see also William Lind, "Thomas H. MacDonald" (master's thesis, American University, 1966); and "Thomas H. MacDonald," March 20, 1953, *MacDonald Papers*, Box 1, Folder 29.

161. "An American You Should Know," *Evening Star*, October 14, 1937, and "A Chapter of History," n.d., *MacDonald Papers*, Box 1, Folder 15.

162. Quoted in Welliver to Fairbank.

163. On MacDonald's demeanor, see C. H. Claudy, "At His Nod Millions Move," *Motor Life*, June 1922, *MacDonald Papers*, Box 1.

164. Lind, p. 27; and Welliver to Fairbank.

165. "To Direct Federal-Aid Road Work," *Engineering News-Record*, April 3, 1919, *MacDonald Papers*, Box 1, Folder 3; and "Memorandum to Mr. Harrison," April 10, 1919, NARA, RG 30, Classified Central Files 1912–1950, Box 1955; see also H. G. Shirley to MacDonald, March 21, 1919, *MacDonald Papers*, Box 1, Folder 2; "Ask $25,000,000 a Year," *Baltimore Sun*, December 6, 1915, p. 2; and Mertz, p. 8.

166. See "$500,000,000 for Roads, New Government Plan," *Chicago Daily Tribune*, February 16, 1919, p. D8.

167. See "This Road Bill Merits Attention," *Atlanta Constitution*, April 6, 1919, p. A7; "Federal Highways Council Aims to Coordinate Plans," *Detroit Free Press*, April 27, 1919, p. D9; "Highways Urged to Boost Rural Trade," *San Francisco Chronicle*, May 11, 1919, p. A8; and "Townsend Bill Is Well Supported," *Detroit Free Press*, August 17, 1919, p. D1.

168. Secretary of War quoted in John Weeks to the Secretary of Agriculture, October 14, 1922, NARA, RG 30, Classified Central Files 1912–1950, Box 1955; and "Motor Convoy Trip Presages National Highway System," *San Francisco Chronicle*, September 7, 1919, p. A1.

169. See Seely, pp. 51–59.

170. Quoted in Seely, p. 61. On MacDonald and Johnson's friendship, see, e.g., MacDonald to Kennedy, November 13, 1956, *MacDonald Papers*, Box 8, Folder 34; and Johnson to Turner, August 22, 1967, *Turner Papers*, Box 15, Folder 1.

171. Quoted in "Auto Makers Pleased with Harding's Attitude," *Wall Street Journal*, April 21, 1921, p. 9; see also Seely, p. 61. On the two plans' different maintenance requirements, see "Pending Road Legislation," June 18, 1921, NARA, RG 30, Classified Central Files 1912–1950, Box 4261, Folder (July 1, 1919, to June 30, 1921).

172. Quoted in "Guarantee of the Upkeep of Roads Constructed with Federal Aid Is Desired," *St. Louis Post-Dispatch*, May 22, 1921, p. A1; see also Mertz, pp. 9–14.

173. See "$75,000,000 Is Voted to Highways by Senate," *Baltimore Sun*, August 20, 1921, p. 2; "Signs Good Roads Bill," *Baltimore Sun*, November 10, 1921, p. 2; see also Seely, pp. 59–62.

174. Townsend quoted in "$75 Million Is Released for Nation's Roads," *New-York Tribune*, November 13, 1921, p. A6; and "New Highway Law a Step Forward, Chapin Declares," *Detroit Free Press*, November 20, 1921, p. A1; see also "A. G. Batchelder Fathered Federal Good Roads Plan," *Washington Post*, June 12, 1921, p. 24.

175. Quoted in Mertz, p. 11; MacDonald, "Federal Aid Facts and Figures," *Constructor*, April 1922, *MacDonald Papers*, Box 6, Folder 27; and "At His Nod Millions Move"; see also "Deluge of Dollars Is Poured Out in US for Auto Highways," *Toronto Globe and Mail*, February 12, 1925, p. 1.

176. "Address of President Warren G. Harding in Accepting the Gift of the Zero Milestone," in *Zero Milestone Souvenir of Dedication*, June 4, 1923, p. 10, American Heritage Center, University of Wyoming, Laramie, WY, Papers of J. Walter Drake, Box 3, vol. 1 (2 of 2); see also "Caravan Ends Trip at Zero Ceremony," *Washington Post*, June 5, 1923, p. 5.

177. S. M. Johnson, "How the Zero Milestone Came About," in *Zero Milestone Souvenir of Dedication*, p. 3.

Chapter 5: Good Roads Make Good Neighbors

1. "Address of Charles Evans Hughes," in *Highways of Friendship* (Highway Education Board, 1924), p. 6.
2. Ibid.
3. See Edwin Warley James, introduction in Roger Stephens, *Down That Pan American Highway* (Ganis & Harris, 1948), pp. 14–15.
4. Manuel Gonzales, "Latin America Restricted Truck Market," *Automotive Industries* XXXVII (July 26, 1917): 159. On highways and motor transport in Latin America during this period, see Frank Curran, *Motor Roads in Latin America* (GPO, 1925); *Facts and Figures of the Automobile Industry* (National Automobile Chamber of Commerce, 1923); and "A Pan-American Highway," *Christian Science Monitor* (August 6, 1928), p. 16.
5. "Latin America Has Few Excess Stocks," *Automotive Industries* XLVII (September 14, 1922): 547; see also Curran, pp. 10, 115, and 117; and Memorandum from the Department of Commerce—Transportation Division, "Good Roads Movement in Latin America," April 13, 1925, NARA, RG 151 (Bureau of Foreign and Domestic Commerce), General Records, 1914–1958, File 532.1, Box 2446.
6. See *Report of the Delegates of the United States of America to the Fifth International Conference of American States* (GPO, 1924), p. 14; and "Promoting the Pan American Highway: The Commission of 1924," unpublished memorandum, p. 4, *James Papers*, Box 15, pamphlets.
7. Quoted in "Find Trade Growing with South America," *New York Times*, May 29, 1923, p. 16. On the conference proceedings, see Edwin Warley James, "The Inter-American Highway: History of the First Ten Years, 1929–1938," unpublished manuscript (hereinafter, *James Manuscript*), pp. 33 and 37, *James Papers*, Box 14; James to Maury Baker, September 29, 1962, *James Papers*, Box 13 (Correspondence); "Promoting the Pan American Highway: The Commission of 1924," p. 5; and *Verbatim Record of the Plenary Sessions of the Fifth International Conference of American States* (Imprenta Universitaria, 1925), pp. 548–550 (vol. 1) and 209 (vol. 2).
8. On Rowe, see Gustav Sallas, "Leo S. Rowe" (Ph.D. diss., George Washington University, 1956).
9. E. S. Gregg to Julius Klein, July 16, 1923, NARA, RG 151, General Records, 1914–1958, File 532.1, Box 2445; see also Drake to the Secretary of State, January 14, 1925, NARA, RG 40 (Department of Commerce), General Records of the Department of Commerce Office of the Secretary, General Correspondence, Box 541.
10. See MacDonald, "Turning Back the Clock Twenty Years," n.d., *MacDonald Papers*, Box 25, Folder 35.
11. See Ellis Hawley, "Herbert Hoover, the Commerce Secretariat, and the Vision of an 'Associative State,' 1921–1928," *Journal of American History* 61 (1974): 116–140; see also Louis Kemp, "Highway Diplomacy: The United States and the Inter-American Highway, 1923–1955" (Ph.D. diss., George Washington University, 1989), pp. 29–31; Mary Kniseley, "Highway Diplomacy" (Ph.D. diss., Texas A&M University, 1992), pp. 167–169; "U.S. Will Help Market Autos," *Detroit Free Press*, December 18, 1921, p. 1; and "Walter Drake Tells How Department of Commerce Aids Business at Home and Abroad Through Cooperation," *Washington Post*, January 20, 1924, p. EA16.
12. See Kemp, p. 38. On Drake's biography and interest in exports, see *Drake's Scrapbook*, vol. 1, part 2, articles from May 1923, in *Drake Papers*, Box 3; and James Ward, *Three Men in a Hupp* (Stanford University Press, 2003). On Drake's role in getting "motor transport" onto the Santiago conference agenda, see Pyke Johnson, "Memorandum to Mr. MacDonald," November 14, 1922, *MacDonald Papers*, Box 20, Folder 16; Kniseley, p. 172; and Stephens, pp. 14–15.

13. "Autos Create Demand for Roads, Ford Declares at Highway Conference," *Atlanta Constitution*, September 8, 1929, p. E3. On the motor industry's attitude toward exports in this period, see Kemp, pp. 21–29.

14. See Drake to S. T. Henry, November 3, 1923, NARA, RG 40, General Records of the Department of Commerce Office of the Secretary, General Correspondence, Box 541.

15. Drake to A. J. Brosseau, November 30, 1923, NARA, RG 40, General Records of the Department of Commerce Office of the Secretary, General Correspondence, Box 541; and "Latin Americans Will Study Roads in U.S.," *Drake Scrapbook*, vol. 1, part 2, p. 63, *Drake Papers*, Box 3.

16. *James Manuscript*, p. 28; see also Kemp, pp. 40–42; and P. J. Croghan to George McLeod, March 2, 1925, NARA, RG 151, General Records, 1914–1958, File 532.1, Box 2446. On the Highway Education Board's genesis, see James to Maury Baker, May 10, 1961, *James Papers*, Box 13 (Correspondence).

17. Julius Klein to Pyke Johnson, December 8, 1923, and E. S. Gregg to Edward Feely, January 18, 1924, NARA, RG 151, General Records, 1914–1958, File 532.1, Box 2445.

18. Gregg to Klein, April 17, 1924, NARA, RG 151, General Records, 1914–1958, File 532.1, Box 2445; testimony of General George Barnett from October 24, 1921, in US Senate Select Committee on Haiti and Santo Domingo, *Inquiry into Occupation and Administration of Haiti and Santo Domingo*, vol. 1 (GPO, 1922), p. 448.

19. See *Highways of Friendship*, pp. 57–59.

20. Argentine delegate quoted in "Promoting the Pan American Highway: The Commission of 1924," p. 18; Coolidge quoted in *Highways of Friendship*, p. 1.

21. Quoted in *Highways of Friendship*, pp. 5–6 and 32; see also Kemp, p. 47.

22. Quoted in *Highways of Friendship*, pp. 4 and 9; and "Promoting the Pan-American Highway: The Commission of 1924," pp. 21–22.

23. "Pan-American Roads Benefit by US Tour," *New York Herald*, July 20, 1924, p. B15.

24. MacDonald to Chapin, July 10, 1924, *MacDonald Papers*, Box 25, Folder 30.

25. Quoted in Kemp, p. 55; see also "Promoting the Pan-American Highway: The Commission of 1924," p. 24; and Kemp, pp. 52–53. James suggested that it was during these post-tour meetings that the idea of a Pan-American Highway first took distinct shape. See E. W. James, "The Present Status of the Inter-American Highway," *Bulletin of the Pan American Union* LXV (1931): 719, fn. 1.

26. See S. T. Henry to Drake, January 20, 1925, *MacDonald Papers*, Box 25, Folder 14; see also *The Pan-American Confederation for Highway Education: Its Aims and Purposes* (Pan-American Confederation for Highway Education, c. 1928).

27. See Pyke Johnson, memorandum, "Dr. Rowe Urges Latin American Governments to Send Delegates to Road Congress," January 27, 1925, *MacDonald Papers*, Box 25, Folder 8; Edward Feely, Memorandum, "Pan-American Highway Conference," February 26, 1925, NARA, RG 151, General Records, 1914–1958, File 532.1, Box 2446; and "Pan American Highways Congress," S. Doc. No. 189 (January 22, 1925), 68th Cong., 2nd sess.

28. Quoted in *Congressional Record—House*, March 3, 1925, p. 5380; see also "Drake to Lead US Road Group to South America," *Washington Post*, April 13, 1925, p. 10. For a historical analysis of the highway that supports the "junket" critique as the main motive and extends this argument further, see J. Fred Rippy, "The Inter-American Highway," *Pacific Historical Review* 24 (1955): 287–298.

29. Quoted in memorandum, May 25, 1925, *MacDonald Papers*, Box 25, Folder 23; see also letter of March 10, 1925, NARA, RG 151, General Records, 1914–1958, File 532.1, Box 2446.

30. Quoted in H. H. Rice to Everett Sanders, August 28, 1925, *MacDonald Papers*, Box 25, Folder 24; see also *James Manuscript*, p. 39/48.

31. Pyke Johnson, "New Roads for Old," unpublished manuscript, p. 3, *MacDonald Papers*, Box 25, Folder 7. On Panamanian road building, see Curran, 31–36. On Guardia, see Rogelio Villalaz, "Tomás Guardia, el ingeniero que unió el país," *La Prensa* (Panama),

March 30, 2003, p. 3. On Guardia's largely successful attempts to free his office from politics in this period, see Guardia to Ricardo Alfaro, December 28, 1928, Museo, Biblioteca y Archivo Ricardo J. Alfaro, Panama City, Panama.

32. "New Roads for Old," Peru Section, 8; and "Peru to Follow Example of US in Good Roads," *New York Herald*, September 27, 1925, p. A12.

33. "New Roads for Old," Chile Section, Part One, p. 4.

34. Ibid., Argentina Section, pp. 3–4.

35. MacDonald, "Our International Relations as Shown by the Pan American Road Congress at Buenos Aires," November 19, 1925, p. 329, *MacDonald Papers*, Box 6, Folder 65. See also *First Pan American Congress of Highways: General Minutes* (Buenos Aires: J. Hays Bell & Cía, 1925); and Kemp, p. 58.

36. *Pan American Congress of Highways: Report of the Delegates of the United States* (GPO, 1928), p. 2, *Drake Papers*, Box 5/6 (vol. IV); see also Kemp, p. 59; "New Roads for Old," Argentina Section, pp. 3–5; and *James Manuscript*, p. 36/45.

37. "Experts Say Great Highway Through Latin Republics Can Be Built," *New York Times*, October 23, 1927, p. XX13. On the continuing work of the confederation, see "Scrapbook of the 1920s Tours," *MacDonald Papers*, Box 28, Folder 13.

38. See Michel Gobat, *Confronting the American Dream* (Duke University Press, 2005), pp. 205–231; and Lester Langley, *The Banana Wars* (University Press of Kentucky, 1983), pp. 181–203.

39. "Mr. Coolidge's Address," *New York Herald Tribune*, January 17, 1928, p. 1; see also William Hard, "Pan-Americanism," *New York Herald Tribune*, January 15, 1928, p. SM1A.

40. *Report of the Delegates of the United States of America to the Sixth International Conference of American States* (GPO, 1928), pp. 31, 36, 263, and 282; see also "Intervention Issue Grips Whole Parley," *New York Times*, February 7, 1928, p. 5; "Intervention Foes Divided at Havana," *New York Times*, February 8, 1928, p. 4; "Fletcher Sees Pan-American Air and Rail Net," *New York Herald Tribune*, March 9, 1928, p. 9; Samuel Inman, "Results of the Pan-American Congress," *Current History* 28 (April 1, 1928): 97–108; and *James Manuscript*, pp. 47/56 and 60/69–61/70.

41. *James Manuscript*, 47/56–48/57.

42. "La Gran Carretera Panamericana," *El Mundo* V (February 1927) (Panama) (author's translation), Biblioteca Nacional Ernesto J. Castillero R., Panama City, Panama, Carretera Panamericana Vertical File.

43. *Congressional Record—Senate*, January 3, 1927, pp. 967–969; and *Congressional Record—House*, January 12, 1927, pp. 1539–1540; see also J. L. Jenkins, "Pan-American Highway Link Plan Launched," *Chicago Daily Tribune*, January 21, 1927, p. 22.

44. *Congressional Record—House*, March 2, 1927, pp. 5418–5419.

45. See Kemp, pp. 103–104.

46. *Congressional Record—House*, March 30, 1928, pp. 5697–5698.

47. Ibid., p. 5696.

48. Quoted in "Pan-American Views on Highway Sought," *Automotive Industries* LVIII (February 11, 1928): 218; see also Kemp, pp. 105–106.

49. Quoted in Kemp, p. 108.

50. See *Congressional Record—Senate*, May 23, 1928, pp. 9569–9571; and "Joint Resolution Authorizing Assistance in the Construction of an Inter-American Highway on the Western Hemisphere," Pub. Res. No. 40/H. J. Res. 259 (May 4, 1928), 70th Cong., 1st sess.

51. "Inter-American Highway: Report of the Committee on Foreign Affairs," H. Doc. No. 329 (May 28, 1928), 70th Cong., 1st sess., pp. 6 and 8; see also *Congressional Record—House*, April 4, 1928, pp. 5899–5900; and *James Manuscript*, p. 55/64.

52. "All-America Highway," *Washington Post*, January 2, 1929, p. 6; and Will Irwin, "Sees Motor Line from Quebec to the Horn," *Daily Boston Globe*, January 18, 1929, p. 29; see also *James Manuscript*, p. 49/58.

53. Coolidge, "Sixth Annual Message," December 4, 1928, *The American Presidency Project*.

54. "Inter-American Highway or Highways," H. Rep. No. 2296 (January 30, 1929), 70th

Cong., 2nd sess., pp. 3–4; see also "Inter-American Highway Survey Favored in Bill," *Christian Science Monitor*, December 19, 1928, p. 4.

55. *Congressional Record—House*, February 18, 1929, p. 3685; see also US Congress, House, Committee on Foreign Affairs, "Inter-American Highway or Highways—Hearings" (January 30, 1929), 70th Cong., 2nd sess. (GPO, 1929); "Pan-American Highway Funds Are Sanctioned," *Christian Science Monitor*, January 31, 1929, p. 3; and Kemp, p. 113.

56. "Formal Recognition Given Great International North and South Highway," *Los Angeles Times*, March 31, 1929, p. F1; see also "Joint Resolution Authorizing the Appropriation of the Sum of $50,000 . . . ," Pub. Res. 104/H. J. Res. 355 (March 4, 1929), 70th Cong., 2nd sess.

57. "Pan-American Highway Seen Nearer Realization," *Washington Post*, November 18, 1928, p. A6; see also *James Manuscript*, pp. 58/67–59/68; and "Urges Highway Plan Upon Latin-Americans," *New York Times*, March 21, 1929, p. 13.

58. Quoted in Kemp, p. 116.

59. Drake to Secretary of Commerce, June 26, 1929, *MacDonald Papers*, Box 25, Folder 58; "American Highway Held Symbolical," *Washington Post*, August 4, 1929, p. A6; see also "Delegates to Pan-American Highway Congress Named," *New York Herald Tribune*, June 17, 1929, p. 8; and "Pan-American Highway Work Will Be Urged," *New York Herald Tribune*, July 14, 1929, p. B12.

60. Rowe to Ricardo Alfaro, July 9, 1929, *MacDonald Papers*, Box 26, Folder 1; see also *James Manuscript*, p. 60/69.

61. See Kemp, p. 122; and *James Manuscript*, 61/70–62/71.

62. Johnson, untitled account of the 1929 trip to South America, *MacDonald Papers*, Box 25, Folder 60, p. 2.

63. "Our Next Job—Exporting Highways," *Literary Digest* CIII (October 26, 1929): 60; see also A. W. Childs to P. M. Stelle, June 12, 1928, NARA, RG 151, General Records, 1914–1958, File 532.1, Box 2447; "New Roads in South America," *Baltimore Sun*, January 19, 1930, p. 84; and "Latin America Pushes Roads in Vast Development Program," *New York Herald Tribune*, April 13, 1930, p. C2.

64. See *Second Pan American Highway Congress: Report of the Delegation from the United States of America* (GPO, 1930), *MacDonald Papers*, Box 25, Folder 43.

65. Ibid., p. 5; and Department of Commerce, "Special Circular No. 1122—Automotive Division, the Second Pan-American Highway Congress," November 7, 1929, p. 4, *MacDonald Papers*, Box 25, Folder 62; see also *James Manuscript*, p. 67/76; and *Drake Papers*, Box 4/5 (vol. III).

66. "Delegates Arrive for Pan-American Conference Here," *James Papers*, Box 2 (personal clippings, June 1929 to March 1931).

67. Johnson, "Panama and the Inter-American Highway" (n.d. but c. October 1929), pp. 1–2, *Drake Papers*, Box 5/6 (vol. IV); "Canal Crossing . . . Discussed—Committees to Be Appointed to Urge Immediate Action," c. October 1929, *James Papers*, Box 2 (personal clippings, June 1929 to March 1931).

68. L. F. Clement, "Discurso—Conferencia de la Carretera Interamericana" (Panama, October 7, 1929), pp. 9–10, Biblioteca Nacional de Panamá, Panama City, Panama.

69. Ibid., p. 13.

70. *James Manuscript*, p. 109/588.

71. See "Inter-American Highway Conference: Minutes and Resolutions of the Meeting in Panama City," *MacDonald Papers*, Box 25, Folder 65; see also Kemp, p. 122; and Johnson to Tasker Oddie, December 28, 1929, *MacDonald Papers*, Box 26, Folder 1.

72. Quoted in *Congressional Record—Senate*, March 12, 1930, pp. 5040–5041.

73. James, "Transcripts from the Tapes," pp. 5–6, *James Papers*, Box 14 (manuscripts).

74. *Congressional Record—House*, February 20, 1930, p. 4017.

75. Guardia to Drake, February 13, 1930, *Drake Papers*, Box 6/7 (vol. V).

76. US Congress, Senate, Committee on Appropriations, "First Deficiency Appropriation Bill for 1930—Hearings . . . on H. R. 9979," 71st Cong., 2nd sess., p. 21.

77. Quoted in Kemp, pp. 109 and 124.

78. On James's biography, see Miscellaneous Biographical Materials, *James Papers*, File B-J232-ew; see also "Ol' Man River, He Just Keeps Rollin' Along," n.d. (listing James's Harvard classmates), *James Papers*, Box 4.

79. Guardia to Rowe, February 22, 1930, and Secretary of Agriculture to Secretary of State, June 7, 1930, NARA, RG 30, Classified Central Files 1912–1950, File 713, Box 4165; see also "Agreement Between the Department of State and the Department of Agriculture Relating to Reconnaissance Survey of Feasible Routes for an Inter-American Highway," Inter-American Highway Binder, *MacDonald Papers*, Box 25, Folder 2.

80. *James Manuscript*, pp. 7/161 and 16/167.

81. Ibid., p. 15/166.

82. Ibid., p. 8/162; see also "Engineers Arrive for Start on Pan-American," *James Papers*, Box 2 (personal clippings, June 1929 to March 1931).

83. Diary of Edwin Warley James (hereinafter, *James Diary*), August 6, August 22, and August 28, 1930, *James Papers*, Box 6. On tensions between the State Department and the bureau, see Davis to Forbes, September 6, 1930, Brown to McNeir, December 3, 1930, Brown to James, December 5, 1930, and James to MacDonald, December 3, 1930, NARA, RG 30, Classified Central Files 1912–1950, File 713, Box 4164; and *James Diary*, January 11, 1935.

84. *James Diary*, September 11–12, 1930.

85. *James Manuscript*, pp. 16/167–22/173.

86. Brown to James, October 29, 1930, NARA, RG 30, Classified Central Files 1912–1950, File 713, Box 4164; *James Manuscript*, p. 21/172; Peck quoted in *James Manuscript*, pp. 29/180–30/181.

87. James to Forbes, November 25, 1930, and Forbes to James, December 9, 1930, NARA, RG 30, Classified Central Files 1912–1950, File 713, Box 4164.

88. *James Manuscript*, pp. 35/186–36/187; see also Dunlap to Secretary of State, November 29, 1930, NARA, RG 30, Classified Central Files 1912–1950, File 713, Box 4164; and E. W. James and D. Tucker Brown, "The Inter-American Highway Reconnaissance in Central America," *Geographical Review* XXIV (July 1934): 353–370, in *James Papers*, Box 12.

89. *James Manuscript*, p. 36/187.

90. Ibid., pp. 37/188–43/194; see also Kemp, p. 131.

91. Brown to James, November 25, 1930, NARA, RG 30, Classified Central Files 1912–1950, File 713, Box 4164; and *James Diary*, February 11, 1931; see also Kemp, pp. 127–128; and "The Honduran Reconnaissance," c. January 1931, NARA, RG 30, Classified Central Files 1912–1950, File 713, Box 4164, Folder: Highway Transportation—Costa Rica, 1930–1940.

92. Brown quoted in Kemp, p. 128; *James Diary*, January 28, 1931.

93. Peck to Childs, February 27, 1931, NARA, RG 151, General Records, 1914–1958, File 532.1, Box 2441, Folder: Highway Transportation—Costa Rica, 1930–1940; Juan del Camino, "La 'carretera panamericana,' otro de los funestos negocios del imperialismo yanqui," *Reportorio Americano* (Costa Rica) XII (April 25, 1931): 235, Biblioteca Nacional de Costa Rica, San José, Costa Rica; see also *James Manuscript*, "The Case of Costa Rica," p. 3; and *James Diary*, September 25, 1930.

94. *James Manuscript*, "The Case of Costa Rica," pp. 4 and 6/160; see also Rowe to White, March 11, 1931, NARA, RG 30, Classified Central Files 1912–1950, File 713, Box 4164; and Kemp, pp. 131–132.

95. "Pan-American Route Fails to Please All," *New York Times*, March 17, 1931, p. 14; see also Kemp, 132.

96. "Financial Step for Road Taken," *Los Angeles Times*, March 19, 1931, p. 3; "Sees Complete Highway in Three Years," March 19, 1931, *MacDonald Papers*, Box 26, Folder 8.

97. "Report on location of the proposed Suchiate River Bridge," July 1936, *James Papers*, Box 20, Research Notes (IAH Misc 1936–1951); see also Kemp, p. 135; US Congress, Senate, Special Committee Investigating the National Defense Program, "Investigation of the National Defense Program—Hearings . . . Pursuant to S. Res. 55, Part 37, Inter-American Highway," 80th Cong. (1947), p. 21476; Melvin L. Bohan, "Memorandum for Highway Files: Roads—Guatemala," February 20, 1929, *MacDonald Papers*, Box 27, Folder 49; and *James Manuscript*, pp. 43/194–55/206.

98. James and Brown, "Aerial Reconnaissance Map of the Inter-American Highway," c. 1934, pp. 9–10, *James Papers*, Box 11, Reports (Folder 1).

99. *James Manuscript*, p. 58/210.

100. Ibid., p. 60/212.

101. Brown to James, May 4, 1931, NARA, RG 30, Classified Central Files 1912–1950, File 713, Box 4164; *James Manuscript*, pp. 72/224, 106/258, and, generally, 59/211–75/227.

102. *James Manuscript*, pp. 95/247, 100/252, 107/259, and 119/271.

103. James, "Construction of the Inter-American Highway," November 1952, p. 13, *James Papers*, Box 14, Manuscripts; *James Manuscript*, p. 28/338.

104. *James Diary*, June 1, 1931.

105. Ibid., November 28, 1931.

106. *James Manuscript*, pp. 111/263–112/264.

107. "Construction of the Inter-American Highway," p. 12; *James Manuscript*, p. 113/265.

108. Quoted in Kemp, p. 132; see also *James Manuscript*, pp. 113/265–114/266.

109. *James Manuscript*, pp. 116/268–117/269 and 123/275.

110. On the foreign securities scandal, see Jay Hall, "The Motorization of Central America" (Ph.D. diss., University of Chicago, 1953), pp. 107–111. On the 1920s boom in securities selling for Latin American projects, see J. Fred Rippy, "A Bond-Selling Extravaganza of the 1920s," *Journal of Business of the University of Chicago* 23 (1950): 238–247. On Hoover's attitude, see Drake to Pyke Johnson, July 2, 1931, *Drake Papers*, Box 6/7 (vol. V).

111. *James Manuscript*, p. 127/278; see also Kemp, pp. 138–139.

112. See Arthur M. Schlesinger Jr., *The Crisis of the Old Order, 1919–1933* (Houghton Mifflin, 1957).

113. Roosevelt, "Inaugural Address," March 4, 1933, *The American Presidency Project*; "Speech Celebrating Pan American Day," April 12, 1933, p. 2, Franklin D. Roosevelt Presidential Library and Museum, Hyde Park, NY, The Master Speech File, 1898–1945.

114. Letter to Marvin McIntyre, July 31, 1933, Roosevelt Presidential Library, President's Official File 1933–1945, OF 608—Inter-American Highway; see also Kemp, pp. 141–143.

115. Roosevelt, "Statement on the Conference of American States," November 9, 1933, *The American Presidency Project*; Howe quoted in Kemp, p. 149.

116. Quoted in Julius Pratt, *The American Secretaries of State and Their Diplomacy*, vol. 1, *Cordell Hull, 1933–1944* (Cooper Square Publishers, 1964), p. 154.

117. Inman, *Inter-American Conferences*, p. 157; see generally pp. 133–159.

118. "Yanqui Imperialismo," *New Republic*, December 6, 1933, p. 90.

119. "US-Panama Road Urged by G. C. Peck," *New York Times*, July 14, 1933, p. 11; resolution quoted in US Congress, House Committee on Appropriations, "Additional Appropriation for Emergency Purposes—Hearing" (May 16, 1934), 73rd Cong., 2nd sess. (1934), p. 257.

120. Roosevelt to Harold Ickes, April 7, 1934, Roosevelt Presidential Library, President's Official File 1933–1945, OF 608—Inter-American Highway; see also "Survey and Construction of the Inter-American Highway: Communication from the President of the United States," S. Doc. No. 218 (June 13, 1934), 73rd Cong., 2nd sess.; and Kemp, pp. 153–154.

121. *James Manuscript*, p. 6/487.

122. *Congressional Record—Senate*, June 15, 1934, pp. 11613–11624; see also *James Manuscript*, pp. 2/483–5/486.

123. *James Manuscript*, pp. 9/431–11/432, 24/440; see also Kemp, p. 160.

124. *James Manuscript*, p. 12/493.

125. James, "Transcripts from the Tapes," p. 9; see also *James Manuscript*, p. 10/491.

126. Quoted in Kemp, p. 196; see also *James Diary*, January 27 and February 12, 1935; and Kemp, pp. 184–198.

127. O. R. Bruce, "The Inter-American Highway," September 13, 1954, *James Papers*, Box 3 (personal clippings, January 1947 and later); see generally letters from James to Mrs. James, April 10, 1935–June 6, 1935, *James Papers*, Box 4.

128. *James Manuscript*, pp. 20/435 and 92/571.

129. "Investigation of the National Defense Program," p. 21219; see also *James Manuscript*, pp. 21/436–27/443.

130. James, "Transcripts from the Tapes," pp. 13–14; see also *James Manuscript*, pp. 27/443–29/445.

131. Quoted in Kemp, p. 164; see also *James Manuscript*, pp. 29/445–31/447.

132. See *James Manuscript*, pp. 33/448–36/450; see also Crede Calhoun to E. A. Lyman, October 29, 1935, American Heritage Center, Laramie, WY, Papers of Crede Calhoun, Box 4, Rodezno-Salvador. On Ubico generally, see Kenneth Grieb, *Guatemalan Caudillo* (Ohio University Press, 1979).

133. Roosevelt to Secretary of State, August 19, 1935, Roosevelt Presidential Library, President's Official File 1933–1945, OF 608—Inter-American Highway; see also *James Manuscript*, pp. 36/450, 42/456, and 13/494–17/498.

134. James to Mrs. James, March 21, 1936, *James Papers*, Box 4; *James Manuscript*, 33/514–37/518; see also J. R. McCarl to Hull, January 13, 1936, McCarl to Hull, February 7, 1936, and Roosevelt to Hull, March 19, 1936, Roosevelt Presidential Library, President's Official File 1933–1945, OF 608—Inter-American Highway.

135. *James Manuscript*, pp. 30/511 and 91/570.

136. Ibid., pp. 44/525, 66/547, and 101/580; James to Baker, May 13, 1961, *James Papers*, Box 13 (correspondence).

137. Reginaldo Menedez, "The Tamazulapa Bridge," *La Feria de Jutiapa*, November 1936, Supplemental document (e), Roosevelt Presidential Library, President's Official File 1933–1945, OF 608—Inter-American Highway.

138. Roosevelt, "Annual Message to Congress," January 3, 1936, and "Letter Suggesting an Inter-American Conference to Advance American and World Peace," January 30, 1936, *The American Presidency Project*; see also Inman, *Inter-American Conference for the Maintenance of Peace* (Friends' Peace Committee, October 1936), pp. 15–16. The importance that Roosevelt placed on the Inter-American Highway in this period can be seen through a fawning article in *Collier's Magazine* that he requested be written. See George Creel, "Rolling Down to Rio," *Collier's* XCIX (February 27, 1937): 55; and Kemp, pp. 176–177.

139. Sumner Welles, *The Time for Decision* (Harper & Brothers, 1944), pp. 207–208.

140. *Inter-American Conference for the Maintenance of Peace—Proceedings* (Buenos Aires: Imprenta del Congreso Nacional, 1937), p. 756. For an Argentinian perspective on interest in the Pan-American Highway written during this era, see Carlos Anesi, *La Carretera Panamericana* (Talleres gráficos de la Compañía general fabril financiera, 1938).

141. *James Manuscript*, pp. 74/555–75/556.

142. Ibid., "The Case of Costa Rica," pp. 23–26; Juan Matamoros to Brown, October 20, 1936, *James Papers*, Box 20, Research Notes (IAH Misc. 1936–1951).

143. See Kemp, pp. 235–237 and 240; "Investigation of the National Defense Program," p. 21221; and *James Manuscript*, "The Case of Costa Rica," pp. 26 and 65/476. On Sandino's death, see Paul Clark Jr., *The United States and Somoza, 1933–1956* (Praeger, 1992), pp. 10–11.

144. "Progress Report of Operations—Inter-American Highway, 1937" (Supplementary Document [(b)], p. 4, Roosevelt Presidential Library, President's Official File 1933–

1945, OF 608—Inter-American Highway; see also James, "Construction of the Inter-American Highway," November 1952, p. 6, *James Papers*, Box 14, manuscripts.

145. Quoted in Kemp, p. 290; see also Kemp, pp. 278–279; and "Cut in Road Aid Again Is Urged by Roosevelt," *Baltimore Sun*, December 23, 1937, p. 1.

146. *James Manuscript*, pp. 95/574–97/576; Panamanian president quoted in Frank Corrigan to Hull, March 25, 1939, NARA, RG 59, Central Decimal Files, 1930–1939, Box 4678 (File 810.154); see also "Sees 'Good Neighbor' Gain," *New York Times*, March 20, 1939, p. 6.

Chapter 6: The Far Western Front

1. Samuel Inman, *Inter-American Conferences, 1826–1954* (University Press of Washington, DC, and Community College Press, 1965), p. 180.

2. "Battle for Latin America," *Cincinnati Enquirer*, November 20, 1938, in Frank Switalski to Cordell Hull, November 25, 1938, NARA, RG 59, Central Decimal Files 1930–1939, Box 4678 (File 810.154); see also Thomas Leonard and John Bratzel, eds., *Latin America During World War II* (Rowman & Littlefield, 2007), pp. 9 and 42–43.

3. Jehiel Davis to Roosevelt, November 16, 1938, NARA, RG 59, Central Decimal Files 1930–1939, Box 4678 (File 810.154).

4. Inman, pp. 192 and 194. On US efforts to combat Nazism in Latin America generally, see Max Paul Friedman, *Nazis & Good Neighbors* (Cambridge University Press, 2005).

5. Roosevelt, "Address to the Governing Board of the Pan-American Union," April 14, 1939, *The American Presidency Project*.

6. "Roosevelt on Europe," *Manchester Guardian*, April 15, 1939, p. 13; "F. D.'s Peace Plea Vexes Axis," *Daily Boston Globe*, April 15, 1939, p. 1; and "The New Monroe Doctrine," *New York Times*, April 15, 1939, p. 18; see also Uwe Lübken, "'Americans All': The United States, the Nazi Menace, and the Construction of a Pan-American Identity," *Amerikastudien/American Studies* 48 (2003): 389–409.

7. See Clark, pp. 52–65.

8. See Department of State Press Bulletin, "Text of Letters Exchanged Today Between President Roosevelt and His Excellency Anastasio Somoza," May 22, 1939, *James Papers*, Box 20, Research Notes (IAH Misc., 1936–1951); see also "Discussions to Be Held with President Somoza of Nicaragua," May 1, 1939, Roosevelt Library, Series III, Diplomatic Correspondence, Box 45 (Nicaragua).

9. Somoza to Roosevelt, May 22, 1939, Roosevelt Library, Materials from President's Personal File (PPF 5913—Somoza, Anastasio); see also minutes of the Executive Committee of the Export-Import Bank for May 17, 1939, in *Meetings of the Board of Trustees and Executive Committee*, vol. III, NARA, RG 275 (Export-Import Bank); and Kemp, pp. 297–305. On the Export-Import Bank and Latin America generally, see Edward Elsasser, "The Export-Import Bank and Latin America, 1934–1945" (Ph.D. diss., University of Chicago, 1954).

10. See Sumner Welles to Roosevelt, June 29, 1939, Roosevelt Library, President's Official File, 1933–1945 (OF 608—Inter-American Highway, 1938–1939); see also Department of State Memorandum, "Participation of the United States in the Construction of the Inter-American Highway," May 4, 1939, and "United States Participation in the Construction of the Inter-American Highway to Panama," May 31, 1939, NARA, RG 59, Central Decimal Files 1930–1939, Box 4678 (File 810.154); and James to MacDonald, June 15, 1939, *MacDonald Papers*, Box 25, Folder 2.

11. Sumner Welles to Laurence Duggan, July 5, 1939 (containing an enclosure with Roosevelt's sign-off), NARA, RG 59, Central Decimal Files 1930–1939, Box 4678 (File 810.154).

12. "Roosevelt Plans Road to Panama," *New York Times*, May 2, 1941, p. 12. On US strategic objectives in Latin America during the war, see Edgar S. Furniss, "American Wartime Objectives in Latin America," *World Politics* 2 (1950): 373–389.

13. See "Roosevelt Tours Canal Zone Area," *New York Times*, August 6, 1938, p. 1; *Con-*

gressional Record—Senate, May 19, 1939, pp. 5787 and 5822–5823; "Supplemental Estimate of Appropriation, War Department, 1940," H. Doc. No. 444 (July 24, 1939), 76th Cong., 1st sess.; "Memorandum, Basis of Understanding Between the Republic of Panama and the United States," March 23, 1940, *MacDonald Papers,* Box 26, Folder 39; "Agree on Road at Canal," *New York Times,* April 6, 1940, American Heritage Center, Laramie, WY, Papers of Crede Calhoun (hereinafter, *Calhoun Papers*), Box IV (Scrapbook—Panama II); "Memorandum for Mr. Bonsal re: Chorrera—Río Hato Road," January 18, 1941, NARA, RG 59, Central Decimal Files 1930–1939, Box 4678 (File 810.154); and Kemp, pp. 315–325.

14. Public Roads Administration, "Untitled Memorandum," c. January 1941, *James Papers,* Box 11 (Reports—Folder 2); see also Matamoros to James, January 26, 1940, NARA, RG 30, Classified Central Files, 1912–1950, File 713, Box 4148; "Construction of the Pan American Highway," Cross Reference File Note, April 24, 1940 (noting Calderon Guardia's formal request), NARA, RG 59, Central Decimal Files, 1940–1944, Box 3370 (File 810.154); and Kemp, pp. 309–311.

15. Roosevelt, "Message to Congress on Assistance for Other American Republics in Marketing Surplus Products," July 22, 1940, *The American Presidency Project;* "Loan Hazards Seen in Latin American Field," *New York Herald Tribune,* September 30, 1940, p. 23; see also Elsasser, p. 152; and Kemp, pp. 312–313.

16. "Costa Rica Warned on U.S.," *New York Times,* October 21, 1940, *Calhoun Papers,* Box 2 (Scrapbook—Costa Rica); "Costa Rica Obtains Loan of $4.6 million," *Baltimore Sun,* September 25, 1940, p. 9; Department of State Memorandum, "Loans to Costa Rican Government for Construction of Inter-American Highway," September 9, 1940, "Memorandum for Mr. Duggan," October 1, 1940, "Memorandum for Mr. Bonsal re: Costa Rica Project," January 18, 1941, and untitled letter to Bursley et al., January 25, 1941, NARA, RG 59, Central Decimal Files, 1940–1944, Box 3370 (File 810.154).

17. John Cabot, "The Inter-American Highway, 1941–1943," p. 1, NARA, RG 59, Central Decimal Files, 1940–1944, Box 3374 (File 810.154).

18. Duggan to Welles, September 11, 1940, NARA, RG 59, Central Decimal Files, 1940–1944, Box 3370 (File 810.154); see also "The Watch on Our Life Line," *New York Times,* September 15, 1940, p. 110.

19. See Cabot, "The Inter-American Highway," p. 2; and US Congress, Senate, Special Committee Investigating the National Defense Program, "Investigation of the National Defense Program—Hearings . . . Pursuant to S. Res. 55, Part 37, Inter-American Highway," 80th Cong. (GPO, 1947), pp. 21432, 21483, and 21507 (hereinafter, *Highway Hearings*).

20. *Highway Hearings,* p. 21432.

21. Ibid., p. 21507.

22. Roosevelt to Secretary Hull, March 27, 1941, NARA, RG 59, Central Decimal Files, 1940–1944, Box 3370 (File 810.154); Public Roads Administration, "Memorandum to the Director of the Budget re: Inter-American Highway," February 1941, *MacDonald Papers,* Box 26, Folder 43; and "Proposed Inter-American Highway: Message from the President of the United States," H. Doc. No. 197 (May 1, 1941), 77th Cong., 1st sess.

23. James quoted in "Pan American Highway Is America's 'Greatest Road Project,'" *Washington Post,* May 4, 1941, p. B6; Rockefeller quoted in US Congress, House, Committee on Foreign Affairs, "Inter-American Highway—Hearings" (June 3, 1941), 77th Cong., 1st sess., pp. 27–28.

24. "Roosevelt Asks Inter-American Road Extension," *New York Herald Tribune,* May 2, 1941, p. 12A; "Congress Asked to Build 'Burma Road' to the Canal," *Hartford Courant,* May 2, 1941, p. 8; and "Pan American Highway Is America's 'Greatest Road Project,'" *Washington Post,* May 4, 1941, p. B6.

25. See "Memorandum for Mr. Duggan," May 2 and 6, 1941, NARA, RG 59, Central Decimal Files, 1940–1944, Box 3370 (File 810.154); "Memorandum for Mr. Bonsal," May 26, 1941, NARA, RG 59, Central Decimal Files, 1940–1944, Box 3374 (File

810.154); and "Inter-American Highway," S. Rep. No. 354 (May 23, 1941), 77th Cong., 1st sess.; see also Kemp, p. 354.

26. See "Inter-American Highway—Hearings" (June 3, 1941), 77th Cong., 1st sess.

27. Marshall to Bloom, July 16, 1941, in *Highway Hearings*, appendix, p. 21732 (Exhibit No. 2061).

28. "'West Front' of Americas Is Steel Wall," *Hartford Courant*, February 1, 1942, p. C7.

29. Quoted in US Congress, House, Committee on Roads, "The Inter-American Highway—Interim Report" (December 18, 1946) (GPO, 1946), p. 4; see also Kemp, p. 359.

30. *Congressional Record—House*, December 16, 1941, pp. 9871, 9876, and 9878.

31. Ibid., pp. 9869 and 9872.

32. Ibid., p. 9874.

33. Ibid., pp. 9870–9871; "Inter-American Highway Fund Bill Is Signed," *Washington Post*, December 27, 1941, p. 13.

34. See Statement of Mr. Hawthorne Arey, Vice President and General Counsel, Export-Import Bank of Washington, in *Highway Hearings*, appendix, pp. 21771–21773.

35. James, "Reflections," August 3, 1945, pp. 23–24, *James Papers*, Box 10.

36. "Man of War," *Washington Post*, November 3, 1942, p. B7; "Gen. Brehon Somervell Dies Chatting with His Wife," *Baltimore Sun*, February 14, 1955, p. 1.

37. Quoted in *Highway Hearings*, pp. 21351–21352 and 21769; see MacDonald, "Construction Activities of the Public Roads Administration . . . on the Canadian-Alaska Military Highway," January 20, 1943, *MacDonald Papers*, Box 7, Folder 29; and Harold Richardson, "Alcan—America's Glory Road," in Waldo Bowman et al., *Bulldozers Come First* (McGraw-Hill, 1944), pp. 118–135; see also Kemp, p. 371.

38. Gross to Somervell, April 8, 1942, in *Highway Hearings*, appendix, pp. 21769–21770.

39. Gross to Somervell, May 9, 1942, in ibid., pp. 21770–21771; see also Kemp, p. 374; and "Memorandum for Mr. Duggan," May 11, 1942, NARA, RG 59, Central Decimal Files, 1940–1944, Box 3372 (File 810.154). On the status of the highway in mid-1942, see Army Corps of Engineers, "Design and Construction of Pan-American Highway—Final Project Report" (April 1944), pp. 10–11.

40. Quoted in Army Corps of Engineers, "Design and Construction of Pan American Highway—Appendices to Final Report," vol. 1 (April 1944), p. A-11.

41. Eisenhower to the Chief of Staff, June 4, 1942, in *Highway Hearings*, appendix, p. 21512.

42. Quoted in *Highway Hearings*, p. 21414; and Cabot, "The Inter-American Highway," p. 40.

43. See "Memorandum for the Chief of Engineers re: Pan American Highway," June 10, 1942, and Secretary of War to Secretary of State, June 10, 1942, in "Appendices to Final Report," pp. A13–A15.

44. See Kemp, p. 381; "Army Engineer Given Advancement," *Los Angeles Times*, July 5, 1941, p. A3; "New Army District Engineer Takes Over Duties Today," *Los Angeles Times*, September 1, 1939, p. A12; and *Highway Hearings*, p. 21102.

45. Army Corps of Engineers, "Final Project Report," p. 115; James to Kelton, June 15, 1942, NARA, RG 30, Classified Central Files, 1912–1950, File 713, Box 4145; and *Highway Hearings*, p. 21378.

46. Quoted in *Highway Hearings*, appendix, pp. 21513–21514; and "Memorandum to Kelton," July 16, 1942, in Army Corps, "Final Project Report," p. 4. On Eisenhower's absence when the pioneer road was approved, see *Highway Hearings*, p. 20929.

47. Kelton quoted in Kemp, p. 384; James quoted in *Highway Hearings*, p. 21232. On the Caribbean's low priority, see *Highway Hearings*, p. 20982.

48. Army Corps of Engineers, "Final Project Report," p. 132; see also ibid., pp. 23, 123, and 131–133.

49. See *Highway Hearings*, pp. 21221–21223, 21251, and 21451–21452.

50. MacDonald to Milo Perkins, Board of Economic Warfare, November 5, 1942, *MacDonald Papers*, Box 27, Folder 45; see also James to Bonsal, October 13, 1942, NARA, RG 59, Central Decimal Files, 1940–1944, Box 3372 (File 810.154); "Statement of

the Causes Which Have Increased the Cost of the Inter-American Highway, Particularly on the Cartago–San Isidro Section in Costa Rica," n.d., NARA, RG 59, Central Decimal Files, 1940–1944, Box 3373 (File 810.154); and Memorandum re: The Inter-American Highway, September 28, 1942, NARA, RG 84, Costa Rica Consular Reports—Classified General Records, 1938–1961, Box 18 (File 815.4).

51. Quoted in *Highway Hearings*, p. 20922; see also Army Corps of Engineers, "Final Project Report," pp. 17–18 and 36; *Highway Hearings*, pp. 20922 and 21171–21172; and Kemp, pp. 389–390 and 395–396.

52. Quoted in *Highway Hearings*, 21181 and 21284; see also Kemp, pp. 401–405; Army Corps of Engineers, "Final Project Report," pp. 39–55; and "Mexico-Guatemala Bridge Opens Torpedo Proof Route to Panama," *Daily Boston Globe*, November 2, 1942, p. 3.

53. On employment figures, see "Summary of Personnel Employed on Pan-American Highway," in Army Corps of Engineers, "Design and Construction of Pan-American Highway—Plates" (April 1944), appendix E, plate 1. For an eyewitness account of the construction, see A. N. Carter, "Building the Inter-American Highway," *Engineering News-Record*, July 29 and August 12 and 26, 1943, NARA, RG 406, Accession No. 406-05-0028, Box 1, Folder: Pan-American Highway Study (4).

54. Quoted in Army Corps of Engineers, "Final Project Report," pp. 98–102.

55. Quoted in untitled summary of dispatches related to American conduct in Honduras (n.d. but c. May 1943), and John Lockwood to Trowbridge vom Baur, "Special Report on Pioneer Road Workers in Honduras," June 15, 1943, p. 5, NARA, RG 229 (Office of Inter-American Affairs), Box 637 (Conduct of Americans); see also "Comprobada la situación de desventaja de los costarricenses en la carretera Panamericana," *Diario de Costa Rica*, March 31, 1943, *James Papers*, Box 19 (Research Notes—IAH Clipping 1938–1944).

56. "Summary of Dispatches"; and John Erwin to Secretary of State, May 14 and August 10, 1943, NARA, RG 59, Central Decimal Files, 1940–1944, Box 3373 (File 810.154).

57. "Public Fooled on Pan-American Highway Progress, Former US Employee Charges," July 25, 1943, *James Papers*, Box 20 (research notes—newspaper clippings: army); see also Army Corps of Engineers, "Final Project Report," pp. 39 and 91–98.

58. MacDonald to Bonsal, May 26, 1943, p. 4, NARA, RG 59, Central Decimal Files, 1940–1944, Box 3373 (File 810.154); Department of State Memorandum of Conversation, "Discussion with Mr. James Concerning Inter-American Highway and Related Matters," March 22, 1943, NARA, RG 84, Costa Rica Consular Reports—Classified General Records, 1938–1961, Box 27 (File 815.4); see also Army Corps of Engineers, "Final Project Report," pp. 183; and *Highway Hearings*, pp. 21495–21496.

59. Cabot, "The Inter-American Highway," p. 48; see also Kelton, "Changed Conditions on Pan-American Highway Due to Lack of Ocean Shipping and Increased Work," January 20, 1943, in "Appendices to Final Report," B-1; and *Highway Hearings*, pp. 21204–21206 and 21636–21637 (on military increasing the timeline and funding).

60. *Highway Hearings*, pp. 20937, 20947, 20957–20958, 21658–21659, and 21662–21664.

61. Trueblood to Secretary of State, September 16 and 30, 1943, NARA, RG 84, Costa Rica Consular Reports—Classified General Records, 1938–1961, Box 27 (File 815.4); Acting Secretary to Roosevelt, September 29, 1943, Roosevelt Library, President's Official File 1933–1945 (OF 608—Inter-American Highway); Erwin to Secretary of State re: Stoppage of Pioneer Highway Work, September 20, 1943, NARA, RG 59, Central Decimal Files, 1940–1944, Box 3373 (File 810.154); Cabot to Boaz Long, September 22, 1943, NARA, RG 59, Central Decimal Files, 1940–1944, Box 3374 (File 810.154); and "Pan-American Highway—Plan of Termination," September 16, 1943, in "Appendices to Final Report," R-1.

62. See Army Corps of Engineers, "Final Project Report," pp. 187, 261–275, and generally; "Memorandum to Mr. Bonsal," February 11, 1943 (on the firing of the Foundation Company), NARA, RG 59, Central Decimal Files, 1940–1944, Box 3372 (File 810.154); and "Army Reports on Pan American Highway," *Civil Engineering* 13

(November 1943): 515–521, in *James Papers*, Box 19 (research notes). For a Central American critique of the army program, see also Alvaro Facio, "Forty-Million-Dollar Lesson," *Inter-American* (March 1944): 10–12 and 46–47, in *James Papers*, Box 19 (Research Notes—IAH clippings, 1938–1944).

63. See "Estimate of Appropriation—Federal Works Agency," S. Doc. No. 77 (June 25, 1943), 78th Cong., 1st sess.

64. See Army Corps of Engineers, "Final Project Report," p. 184.

65. On construction of this stretch generally, see Kemp, pp. 491–496.

66. Public Roads Administration, "Inter-American Highway" (July 1944), pp. 3–4, NARA, RG 30, Classified Central Files, 1912–1950, File 713, Box 4143; and Kemp, p. 493.

67. William Dayton, "Copey Oak in Costa Rica," *Agriculture in the Americas* IV (July 1944): 134–135, in *James Papers*, Box 20 (research notes—IAH 1950); and James to Robert Tomlin, July 19, 1943, p. 5, *James Papers*, Box 11 (Reports—Folder 1); see also Arthur Bevan, "Giant Oaks of Costa Rica," *American Forests* 49 (October 1943): 486–487.

68. Walter Washington to Secretary of State, January 18, 1945, NARA, RG 59, Central Decimal Files, 1940–1944, Box 4330 (File 810.154).

69. James quoted in "Inter-American Highway" (July 1944), p. 3; and MacDonald quoted in "The Ocular Inspection of the Inter-American Highway in Costa Rica Has Been Terminated," *La Tribuna* (Costa Rica), March 1, 1946, translation, NARA, RG 30, Classified Central Files, 1912–1950, File 713, Box 4143.

70. "Proposed Request to Congress for Appropriations to Complete the Inter-American Highway and Rama Road," February 1, 1947, p. 11, NARA, RG 59, Central Decimal Files, 1940–1944, Box 3373 (File 810.154); see also Kemp, pp. 545–547; "Confidential Memorandum re: Exhaustion of Funds," March 23, 1945, NARA, RG 84, Costa Rica Consular Reports—Classified General Records, 1938–1961, Box 41 (File 815.4); "Memorandum re: Problems of Public Roads Administration in CCA Countries," March 14, 1945; "Memorandum re: Inter-American Highway Bill Introduced," May 10, 1945; "Memorandum re: Proposed Agreement with Public Roads Administration," April 23, 1945; Cochran to Warren, August 13, 1945, NARA, RG 59, Central Decimal Files, 1940–1944, Box 4330 (File 810.154); and W. P. Cochran Jr., "The Inter-American Highway, January 1, 1944 to June 30, 1946," August 1946, p. 2, NARA, RG 59, Central Decimal Files, 1940–1944, Box 4331 (File 810.154).

71. Lewis broadcast reproduced in *Congressional Record—Senate*, June 14, 1945, pp. 6099–6104; see also "Fulton Lewis Jr. Is Dead at 63," *New York Times*, August 22, 1966, p. 33.

72. Reproduced in *Congressional Record—Senate*, June 14, 1945, p. 6101.

73. Ibid., p. 6104.

74. Ibid.

75. Ibid., p. 6097.

76. Ibid., p. 6099; see also "Ferguson to Put Fire in Congress," *Washington Post*, December 27, 1942, p. B7; "Truman Committee Assails Somervell for Canol Project," *Baltimore Sun*, January 9, 1944, p. 3; "Alcan Road, Like Canol, Faces US Abandonment," *Atlanta Constitution*, April 8, 1945, p. 7A; and "Wasted Billions," *Chicago Daily Tribune*, March 16, 1945, p. 16.

77. See "Biddle Orders Probe of Pan-American Road Charges," *Austin American*, June 17, 1945, p. 12; "Mead Committee Begins Probe of Canol, Highway," *Washington Post*, June 20, 1945, p. 11; "House Approves New Probe of Highway Costs," *Chicago Daily Tribune*, July 4, 1945, p. 3; and "Memorandum re: Pan-American Highway—Fraud Against the Government," August 23, 1945, in *Highway Hearings*, appendix, pp. 21784–21787.

78. *Highway Hearings*, p. 20974; "Pan-American Highway," *Washington Post*, July 21, 1945, p. 4.

79. "Excerpts from President Truman's Message to Congress Recommending Public Works," September 6, 1945, *James Papers*, Box 20 (research notes—IAH 1945–1946); see also "Memorandum re: Inter-American Highway," September 17, 1945, NARA,

RG 59, Central Decimal Files, 1940–1944, Box 4330 (File 810.154); and Kemp, pp. 542–543.

80. Quoted in "Pan-Am Highway Probers in City," February 17, 1946, *James Papers*, Box 20 (research notes—IAH 1945–1946).

81. US Congress, House, Committee on Roads, "The Inter-American Highway—Interim Report" (December 18, 1946) (GPO, 1946), pp. 13–14.

82. Ibid.

83. "The Ocular Inspection of the Inter-American Highway in Costa Rica has been Terminated," *La Tribuna* (Costa Rica), March 1, 1946, translation, NARA, RG 30, Classified Central Files, 1912–1950, File 713, Box 4143; see also "Triunfal Recibimiento," *La Tribuna* (Costa Rica), February 27, 1946, *James Papers*, Box 20 (research notes—IAH 1945–1946).

84. "Costa Ricans Ruin Highway Beauty," *New York Times*, September 24, 1946, in *James Papers*, Box 20 (research notes—IAH congressional trip 1946).

85. See House Committee on Roads, "Interim Report," pp. 14–21.

86. Hon. Albert Cole, "Rolling Down to Rio," statement printed in the *Congressional Record*, April 8, 1946, NARA, RG 30, Classified Central Files, 1912–1950, File 713, Box 4142; see also "Expects Argentina to End Trade Curb," *New York Times*, April 12, 1946, p. 31.

87. "Memorandum re: Costa Rica—Sam Rosoff—Completion Inter-American Highway," September 4, 1946, NARA, RG 84, Costa Rica Consular Reports—Classified General Records, 1938–1961, Box 51 (File 815.4); see also Kemp, pp. 561–562.

88. "Army's Roads in Central America Rile Sen. Ferguson," *Chicago Daily Tribune*, August 28, 1946, p. 6.

89. *Highway Hearings*, pp. 21168 and 21183.

90. Ibid., p. 21197.

91. Ibid., p. 21416.

92. Ibid., p. 21434.

93. Ibid., p. 21392.

94. Quoted in "American Highway a 'Colossal Mess,'" *New York Times*, December 27, 1946, p. 12.

95. "Memorandum re: Hearing by Senate Special War Investigating Committee," March 31, 1947, NARA, RG 59, Central Decimal Files, 1940–1944, Box 4330 (File 810.154).

96. "Investigation of the National Defense Program—Inter-American Highway," S. Rep. No. 440 (July 7, 1947), 80th Cong., 1st sess., pp. 1 and 4.

97. "Ferguson's Miserable Failure," *Atlanta Constitution*, August 16, 1947, p. 4.

98. See Kemp, p. 470.

Chapter 7: Freedom Road

1. Sumner Welles, "Bogota's Lesson," *Washington Post*, April 20, 1948, p. 11; see also "Problems at Bogota," *New York Times*, March 30, 1948, p. 22; and Samuel Inman, *Inter-American Conferences, 1826–1954* (University Press of Washington, DC, and Community College Press, 1965), pp. 232–251.

2. "Tells Why US Loses Hold on Latin America," *Chicago Daily Tribune*, August 1, 1948, p. 24; see also "Bogota Talks May Center on US Aid," *Hartford Courant*, March 30, 1948, p. 22.

3. Inman, p. 235.

4. "Behind the Bogota Revolt," *Washington Post*, April 25, 1948, p. B4.

5. "Delegates Arrive for Conference," *Washington Post*, March 30, 1948, p. 7; "Marshall Gets Bogota Ovation; Red Demonstration Called Off," *New York Herald Tribune*, March 30, 1948, p. 1.

6. "US Asks Bogota to Act on Communism," *Christian Science Monitor*, March 31, 1948, p. 1; "Marshall Scoffed at Early Warnings on Reds in Bogota," *New York Times*, April 16, 1948, p. 1.

7. "Marshall's Address and Remarks at Bogota Conference of American States," *New York Herald Tribune*, April 2, 1948, p. 28.
8. Ibid.; "Marshall Tells Bogota: Aid to Europe Is First," *New York Herald Tribune*, April 2, 1948, p. 1.
9. See "Marshall Tells Bogota: Aid to Europe Is First"; and "Marshall's Address and Remarks."
10. "No Bogota Applause for US Half Billion," *New York Times*, April 9, 1948, p. 1; Inman, p. 247; see also "Truman Asks Export-Import Loans to Latins," *New York Herald Tribune*, April 9, 1948, p. 6.
11. "Revolt Erupts in Bogota," *New York Herald Tribune*, April 10, 1948, p. 1.
12. "Anarchy Grips Bogota, Says Eyewitness," *Washington Post*, April 10, 1948, p. 1; and "Eyewitness Describes Mob Violence in Bogota," *Los Angeles Times*, April 12, 1948, p. 1; see also "Communism in Latin America," *New York Herald Tribune*, April 21, 1948, p. 26.
13. "Anarchy Grips Bogota"; and "Revolt Erupts in Bogota."
14. "Fatalities at Bogota," *Christian Science Monitor*, April 22, 1948, p. 8.
15. "Revolt Erupts in Bogota"; and "The Warning of Bogota," *New York Times*, April 12, 1948, p. 20.
16. Walter Lippmann, "Latin America and the Future," *Daily Boston Globe*, April 13, 1948, p. 16.
17. "Bogota Restoring Order," *New York Herald Tribune*, April 11, 1948, p. 1.
18. "Marshall Scoffed at Early Warnings on Reds in Bogota," *New York Times*, April 16, 1948, p. 1; and "Marshall Blames Reds for Colombia Uprising, Sees 'Cold War' Battle," *Hartford Courant*, April 13, 1948, p. 1.
19. "Marshall Scoffed at Early Warnings"; and "Marshall Blames Reds."
20. "Bogota Talks to Be Resumed There Today," *Baltimore Sun*, April 14, 1948, p. 1; and Welles, "Bogota's Lesson."
21. Quoted in "Anti-Communism Resolution Passed at Bogota Meeting," *Washington Post*, April 23, 1948, p. 10; "Bogota Pact Signed, New Union Set Up," *New York Herald Tribune*, May 1, 1948, p. 1; see also "Anti-Red Measure Passed in Bogota," *New York Times*, April 23, 1948, p. 1.
22. "Bogota Conference Concludes Pacts of Wide Range," *Christian Science Monitor*, April 30, 1948, p. 10.
23. See Memorandum, "Inter-American Highway," April 6, 1949, NARA, RG 59, Central Decimal Files 1945–1949, Box 4332 (File 810.154).
24. Enclosed in Paul C. Daniels to Philip B. Fleming, October 26, 1948, NARA, RG 59, Central Decimal Files 1945–1949, Box 4332 (File 810.154). For a Latin American perspective on the highway's beneficial impact on inter-American relations in this era, see Diego Suarez, "The Pan-American Highway and Inter-American Relations" (n.p., October 1952), p. 40.
25. Fleming to Daniels, November 15, 1948, NARA, RG 59, Central Decimal Files 1945–1949, Box 4332 (File 810.154).
26. See James Webb to Fleming, April 18, 1949, and Ernest Gross to Frank Pace, May 5, 1949, NARA, RG 59, Central Decimal Files 1945–1949, Box 4332 (File 810.154).
27. See Webb to Embassy, June 18, 1949, NARA, RG 84, Costa Rica Consular Reports—Classified General Records, 1938–1961, Box 75 (File 504.12); and Department of State Memorandum, "Inter-American Highway," June 30, 1949, NARA, RG 59, Central Decimal Files 1945–1949, Box 4332 (File 810.154); see also "Point Four and Latin America," *Christian Science Monitor*, May 25, 1949, p. 13; and Department of State, *World Economic Progress Through Cooperative Technical Assistance, the Point Four Program* (GPO, 1949).
28. Informe Sobre la Seccion de Caminos, Calles y Muelles presentado al Ingeniero David Samudio, Ministro de Obras Públicas, por Tomás Guardia, Ingeniero Jefe, Carretera Interamericana, Agosto de 1949, pp. 171–177, Archivo Nacional de Panama, Panama

City, Panamá, Registro Público de Panamá; Sección: Administración del Estado; Año: 1948–1949; No. 3.9.1; Procedencia: Ministerio de Obras Publicas; Caja: 135; Exp: 397.

29. Department of State Airgram, June 23, 1949, and see Davis to Secretary of State, June 16, 1949, NARA, RG 59, Central Decimal Files 1945–1949, Box 4332 (File 810.154); see also "Delegado de Panamá Visita a Guatemala," *El Imparcial* (Guatemala), June 2, 1949, and "La Carretera a Costa Rica y La Opinion Publica," *Panamá America,* June 11, 1949, p. 2, *James Papers,* Box 20 (research notes—IAH 1949).

30. Department of State Memorandum, "Inter-American Highway," June 30, 1949, NARA, RG 59, Central Decimal Files 1945–1949, Box 4332 (File 810.154).

31. Department of State Memorandum, "Inter-American Highway," November 8, 1949, NARA, RG 84, Costa Rica Consular Reports—Classified General Records, 1938–1961, Box 75 (File 504.12).

32. Ibid.; Foreign Service Dispatch, "Conference in Panama of Minister of Public Works in Central America," November 18, 1949, NARA, RG 59, Central Decimal Files 1945–1949, Box 4332 (File 810.154); see also Foreign Service Dispatch, "Inter-American Highway and Rama Road," March 2, 1950, NARA, RG 59, Central Decimal Files 1950–1954, Box 4382 (File 810.2612); and Tomás Guardia to David Samudio, November 17, 1949, pp. 168–170, Archivo Nacional de Panama, Registro Público de Panamá; Sección: Administración del Estado; Año: 1948–1949; No. 3.9.1; Procedencia: Ministerio de Obras Publicas; Caja: 135; Exp: 397.

33. Quoted in "Si a Nosotros Nos Conviene Que Se Termine La Interamericana, a Los Estados Unidos Tambien," *Diario de Costa Rica,* May 13, 1950 (author's translation), *James Papers,* Box 20 (research notes—IAH 1950); see also Foreign Service Dispatch, "Resolutions of Public Works Ministers' Conference on the Inter-American Highway, March 23, 1950, NARA, RG 59, Central Decimal Files 1950–1954, Box 4560 (File 820.2612); and Mario Echandi to Dean Acheson, April 26, 1950, NARA, RG 59, Central Decimal Files 1950–1954, Box 4543 (File 818.2612).

34. Quoted in Department of State Memorandum, "Report on Trip to Cincinnati," March 15, 1950, NARA, RG 59, Central Decimal Files 1950–1954, Box 4382 (File 810.2612). On Chávez generally, see Rosemary Díaz, "El Senador, Dennis Chávez," (Ph.D. diss., Arizona State University, 2006).

35. "Report on Trip to Cincinnati."

36. Heins to Bennett, March 31, 1950 (noting Chávez's proposal), and Barber to Mann (noting Chávez's "very effective handling" of the legislation), NARA, RG 59, Central Decimal Files 1950–1954, Box 4382 (File 810.2612).

37. Testimony of Edward Miller, in US Congress, Senate, Committee on Public Works, "Federal Aid Highway Act of 1950—Hearings," 81st Cong., 2nd sess., pp. 248 and 250; see also Department of State Memorandum, "Inter-American Highway Legislation," December 13, 1949, RG 84, Costa Rica Consular Reports—Classified General Records, 1938–1961, Box 75 (File 504.12).

38. "Senate Committee Slashes Appropriation for Constructing Inter-American Highway," August 19, 1950, *James Papers,* Box 20 (Research Notes—IAH 1950).

39. Miller to Williams, August 28, 1950, NARA, RG 59, Central Decimal Files 1950–1954, Box 4382 (File 810.2612); and Miller to Chávez, August 30, 1950, NARA, RG 59, Central Decimal Files 1950–1954, Box 4560 (File 820.2612).

40. "Statement Issued by President Anastasio Somoza Regarding the Inter-American Highway and Rama Road," August 25, 1950, enclosed in Foreign Service Dispatch, "Inter-American Highway and Rama Road," August 25, 1950, NARA, RG 59, Central Decimal Files 1950–1954, Box 4382 (File 810.2612).

41. Miller to Elmer Staats, November 20, 1950, NARA, RG 59, Central Decimal Files 1950–1954, Box 4498 (File 813.2612); and testimony of Miller in US. Congress, House, Committee on Appropriations, "Second Supplemental Appropriation Bill for 1951—Hearings," 81st Cong., 2nd sess. (1950), p. 396.

42. Department of State Memorandum, "Inter-American Highway," September 14, 1950, NARA, RG 59, Central Decimal Files 1950–1954, Box 4382 (File 810.2612).

43. "The Wonderful Road We Never Finished," *Popular Science Monthly* (January 1954), p. 102.

44. Quoted in Foreign Service Despatch, "Interview with Mr. E. W. James," February 23, 1951, NARA, RG 59, Central Decimal Files 1950–1954, Box 4560 (File 820.2612); and see Ernest Siracusa to Capus Waynick, April 25, 1951, NARA, RG 59, Central Decimal Files 1950–1954, Box 4382 (File 810.2612).

45. Siracusa to Waynick, April 25, 1951.

46. Department of State Memorandum, "Tentative Allocation for Inter-American Highway," March 5, 1951, NARA, RG 59, Central Decimal Files 1950–1954, Box 4560 (File 820.2612). On US-Guatemalan relations generally in this period, see Stephen Schlesinger and Steven Kinzer, *Bitter Fruit* (Harvard University Press, 2005).

47. Ernest Siracusa to Ambassador Nufer, May 9, 1951, NARA, RG 59, Central Decimal Files 1950–1954, Box 4560 (File 820.2612).

48. Department of State Memoranda, "Inter-American Highway," May 14, 1951, "Use of Inter-American Highway for Bargaining Purposes," March 7, 1951, and "Conversation with Mr. James," May 15, 1951, NARA, RG 59, Central Decimal Files 1950–1954, Box 4498 (File 813.2612); see also Siracusa to Waynick, May 24, 1951, NARA, RG 59, Central Decimal Files 1950–1954, Box 4382 (File 810.2612).

49. "Anti-Red Riot Injures Scores," *Washington Times-Herald*, July 13, 1951, and "Communists in Guatemala," *New York Times*, July 14, 1951, *James Papers*, Box 20 (Research Notes—IAH 1950); see also *Bitter Fruit*, pp. 86–87.

50. Department of State Memoranda, "Inter-American Highway in Guatemala," August 6, 1951, and "Inter-American Highway Agreement," August 13, 1951, NARA, RG 59, Central Decimal Files 1950–1954, Box 4382 (File 810.2612).

51. Enclosed in Department of State Despatch, "Press Reaction to Reports," September 12, 1951, and see Department of State Memorandum, "Visit of E. W. James," August 28, 1951, NARA, RG 59, Central Decimal Files 1950–1954, Box 4509 (File 814.2612).

52. Department of State Memorandum, "Conversation with Ambassador Toriello," September 11, 1952, NARA, RG 59, Central Decimal Files 1950–1954, Box 4383 (File 810.2612).

53. Quoted in Foreign Service Despatch, "Inauguration of Paved Stretch of Pan American Highway," September 23, 1952, NARA, RG 59, Central Decimal Files 1950–1954, Box 4383 (File 810.2612).

54. Department of State Memoranda, "Inter-American Highway Agreement," November 13, 1952, "Inter-American Highway Agreement with Guatemala," October 9, 1952, "Courtesy Call of New Guatemalan Ambassador," October 6, 1952, "Inter-American Highway Agreement with Guatemala," October 31, 1952, "Inter-American Highway Agreement," November 3, 1952, and William Krieg to Edward Clark, October 17, 1952, NARA, RG 59, Central Decimal Files 1950–1954, Box 4383 (File 810.2612).

55. Foreign Service Despatch, "Guatemalan Press Expects Immediate Resumption of US Aid," December 24, 1952, NARA, RG 59, Central Decimal Files 1950–1954, Box 4383 (File 810.2612).

56. Department of State Memorandum, "Construction of the Inter-American Highway," January 21, 1954, NARA, RG 59, Central Decimal Files 1950–1954, Box 4383 (File 810.2612).

57. See *Bitter Fruit*, p. 106; and generally, Stephen Kinzer, *The Brothers* (Times Books, 2013).

58. E. W. James to Thomas MacDonald, July 14, 1953, *McDonald Papers*, Box 8, Folder 44.

59. Quoted in *Bitter Fruit*, p. 108.

60. Ibid., pp. 199–200; see also Nick Cullather, *Secret History* (Stanford University Press, 1999).

61. "Guatemala First Big Defeat for Reds, Nixon Asserts," *Atlanta Constitution*, July 7, 1954, p. 2. On the United States' pursuit of the Cold War in Latin America generally, see Stephen Rabe, *The Killing Zone* (Oxford University Press, 2011).

62. Department of State Telegram, July 8, 1954, and Foreign Service Despatch, "Signature of Inter-American Highway Agreements," November 19, 1954, NARA, RG 59, Central Decimal Files 1950–1954, Box 4383 (File 810.2612).

63. "Nixon Off Today for Caribbean," *New York Herald Tribune*, February 6, 1955, p. 8; and see "Central American Tour Is Arranged for Nixon," *New York Herald Tribune*, December 31, 1955, p. 1.

64. Robert Woodward, "Recommendation for Urgent Revision in Budgeting for Completion of Inter-American Highway," January 12, 1955, p. 1, NARA, RG 84, Costa Rica Consular Reports—Classified General Records, 1938–1961, Roads for 1953–1955 (504.12), Box 92.

65. Ibid.

66. Ibid., p. 4.

67. Woodward to John Ohmans, January 14, 1955, NARA, RG 84, Costa Rica Consular Reports—Classified General Records, 1938–1961, Roads for 1953–1955, Box 92 (File 504.12).

68. Ohmans to Woodward, February 18, 1955, NARA, RG 84, Costa Rica Consular Reports—Classified General Records, 1938–1961, Roads for 1953–1955, Box 92 (File 504.12).

69. Quoted in "Stepping Up US Aid to Inter-American Highway," May 1955, reprint from Department of State Bulletin of April 11, 1955, Publication 5829, Nettie Lee Benson Latin American Collection, University of Texas, Austin, TX.

70. Ibid.; and Philip A. Ray to J. C. Allen, May 23, 1955, NARA, RG 30, General Correspondence and Related Records, 1912–1965, Box 184 (Inter-American Highway).

71. Department of State Memorandum, "Inter-American Highway," March 18, 1955, *Foreign Relations of the United States 1955–1957*, vol. VI, *American Republics*, Document 58; Department of State Memorandum, "Inter-American Highway," March 7, 1955, NARA, RG 59, Central Decimal Files 1955–1959, Box 4075 (File 810.2612); and John Foster Dulles to Sinclair Weeks, April 1, 1955, enclosed in Weeks to Richard Nixon, April 15, 1955, NARA, RG 30, General Correspondence and Related Records, 1912–1965, Box 184 (Inter-American Highway).

72. Quoted in "Authorizing Certain Sums to Be Appropriated Immediately for the Completion of the Construction of the Inter-American Highway," H. Rep. No. 611 (May 23, 1955), 84th Cong., 1st sess., p. 4.

73. "Highway for the Americas," *New York Herald Tribune*, April 4, 1955, p. 16; and James to Eisenhower, April 8, 1955, *James Papers*, Box 13 (correspondence). For a sharp critique of the road that likely arose in response to Eisenhower's action, see Rippy, "The Inter-American Highway," *Pacific Historical Review* 24 (1955): 287–298.

74. H. Rep. No. 611, 3; and *Congressional Record—House*, April 19, 1955, p. 4737.

75. See "House Passes Highway Bill," *Washington Post*, June 9, 1955, p. 1; and "President Signs Road Bill," *New York Times*, July 2, 1955, p. 24.

76. See "Panama Treaty Signed," *New York Times*, August 18, 1955, p. 4.

77. Quoted in "Authorizing an Additional $10 Million for the Completion of the Inter-American Highway," H. Rep. No. 959 (July 31, 1957), 85th Cong., 1st sess., p. 3.

78. Foreign Service Despatch, "Passage of the Inter-American Regional Project," March 2, 1956, NARA, RG 59, Central Decimal Files 1955–1959, Box 4076 (File 810.2612); and see "Costa Rica Spurs Big Highway Task," *New York Times*, February 19, 1956, *James Papers*, Box 19 (research notes—clippings, 1953).

79. Quoted in US Congress, House, Committee on Public Works, "Report on the Inter-American Highway and Rama Road—Hearing" (August 30, 1962), 87th Cong., 2nd sess. (GPO, 1962), p. 29; and untitled Assessor report on Selegua, March 26, 1957, NARA, RG 59, Central Decimal Files 1955–1959, Box 4076 (File 810.2612).

80. Untitled Assessor report, pp. 4–5.

81. Quoted in H. Rep. No. 959, p. 4.

82. *Congressional Record—House*, March 13, 1958, p. 4338; see also "Road Fund Approved," *New York Times*, May 27, 1958, p. 21.

83. "El desastre de la Carretera Interamericana," *La Nacion* (Costa Rica), December 19, 1958, p. 6.

84. Quoted in "Finds Highway of Americas in Bad Condition," *Chicago Daily Tribune*, May 10, 1959, p. 25.

85. Department of State Airgram, October 26, 1961, NARA, RG 59, Central Decimal Files 1960–1963, Box 2248 (File 810.2612).

86. Quoted in "Report on the Inter-American Highway and Rama Road—Hearing" (August 30, 1962), p. 3.

87. *Congressional Record—Senate*, June 6, 1962, p. 9873.

88. See Edward Martin to Carl Richards, June 4, 1962, NARA, RG 59, Central Decimal Files 1960–1963, Box 2248 (File 810.2612).

89. "60 Begin 2,600 Mile Trip on Pan-American Highway," *New York Times*, April 17, 1963, p. 5; and "America's Route Is for the Hardy," *New York Times*, April 28, 1963, p. 20.

90. "Mirror of World Opinion—Long Bus Ride," *Christian Science Monitor*, April 16, 1963, p. 16; and "Group Reaches D.C. After 1st Trip Over Pan-American Road," *Washington Post*, May 5, 1963, p. A25. Some of the US congressmen involved in the caravan apparently complained that the road was a "bottomless pit" of funds. See interview with Roberto Pacheco, March 2014, San José, Costa Rica. On the bridge opening, see "Thatcher Ferry Bridge Dedication Program," October 12, 1962, Biblioteca de la Autoridad del Canal de Panamá Roberto F. Chiari, Panama City, Panama; and *Congressional Record Appendix—House*, "Panama Bridge Ceremonies Marred by Mob Tactics," March 28, 1963, pp. A1822–A1823.

91. Milton Bracker, "Dream Come True," *New York Times*, May 12, 1963, p. XXI.

92. "Inter-American Road Nears Opening," *Chicago Tribune*, April 14, 1963, p. A3. On Central American political economy generally, see Victor Bulmer-Thomas, *The Political Economy of Central America Since 1920* (Cambridge University Press, 1987); and William Cline and Enrique Delgado, eds., *Economic Integration in Central America* (Brookings Institution Press, 1978).

93. "Group Reaches D.C. After 1st Trip Over Pan-American Road," *Washington Post*, May 5, 1963, p. A25.

94. John F. Kennedy, "Remarks to Delegates to the Pan-American Highway Congress," May 7, 1963, accession number WH-180-008, John F. Kennedy Presidential Library, Boston, MA.

95. Ben Grauer, "The Break in the Golden Brooch," c. 1951, *James Papers*, Box 19 (reprints).

Chapter 8: The Missing Link

1. See Richard Tewkesbury, "The Darien and the Pan-American Highway," May–June 1943, p. 81, *James Papers*, Box 19 (research notes).

2. William Birnie, "Tooks Tames the Jungle," *American Magazine* (April 1941): 45, Papers of Richard Tewkesbury (hereinafter, *Tewkesbury Papers*), Iowa State University Library, Ames, Iowa, Box 1, Folder 10; see also Tewkesbury, "There's Drama in Mexico," *The Car Owner* XVI (January–February 1938), *Tewkesbury Papers*, Box 1, Folder 9.

3. Birnie, "Tooks Tames the Jungle," pp. 45 and 66.

4. Tewkesbury, "The Darien and the Pan-American Highway," p. 81; and "Tooks Tames the Jungle," p. 45.

5. See generally, Carl Ortwin Sauer, *The Early Spanish Main* (University of California Press, 1966).

6. See generally, Joaquín García Casares, *Historia del Darién* (Editorial Universitaria, 2008).

7. Ibid.; see also Erland Nordenskiold, *An Historical and Ethnological Survey of the Cuna Indians* (Goteborg, Sweden: Goteborgs Museum, Entografiska Avdelningen, 1938); and James Howe, *A People Who Would Not Kneel: Panama, the United States, and the San Blas Kuna* (Smithsonian Institution Press, 1998).

8. Milton MacKaye, "Tewkesbury Conquers the Jungle," *Saturday Evening Post*, December 27, 1941, and "Tooks Takes a Trip," *Time*, June 19, 1941, *Tewkesbury Papers*, Box 1, Folder 10.

9. Tewkesbury, "The Darien and the Pan-American Highway," p. 81; see also MacKaye, "Tewkesbury Conquers the Jungle."

10. "Listen America" broadcast transcript, November 30, 1941, pp. 2–3, *Tewkesbury Papers*, Box 1, Folder 11.

11. Ibid., p. 3; and Stephen James to Jaén Guardia, June 19, 1939, *Tewkesbury Papers*, Box 1, Folder 7.

12. See "Tewkesbury equipment list," February 18, 1942, *Tewkesbury Papers*, Box 1, Folder 8; WSOC broadcast, November 25, 1941, p. 5, *Tewkesbury Papers*, Box 1, Folder 11; and "An Explorer Sets Forth," *Pan-American Magazine I* (July–September 1940): 27–29, *Tewkesbury Papers*, Box 1, Folder 9; see also Brodie Burnham, "At the Crossroads," *Panama American*, June 14, 1941, *Tewkesbury Papers*, Box 1, Folder 10.

13. See Tewkesbury, "The Darien and the Pan-American Highway," *Florida Public Works*, May 1943, p. 10, *James Papers*, Box 19 (research notes). On myths about Darien mountains, see Gordon Gould and Carl Turk, "When Can You Drive . . . to South America?" *Chicago Daily Tribune*, December 4, 1960.

14. Tewkesbury, "Jungle Journey for a Hemisphere Highway," *Scholastic*, May 18, 1942, *Tewkesbury Papers*, Box 1, Folder 9. See also "Transcript of Tewkesbury's 1939 Notes," pp. 10–11 and 17, *Tewkesbury Papers*, Box 1, Folder 7; and MacKaye, "Tewkesbury Conquers the Jungle."

15. "Transcript of Tewkesbury's 1939 Notes," pp. 17–18.

16. Tewkesbury quoted in "An Explorer Sets Forth," pp. 27–29; Cuna quoted in Fred McKim, "Some Comments on the Tewkesbury Exploit," p. 3, *Tewkesbury Papers*, Box 1, Folder 12.

17. See E. W. James, "Memorandum," September 23, 1939, *Tewkesbury Papers*, Box 1, Folder 7.

18. "Jungle Journey for a Hemisphere Highway."

19. Tewkesbury, "Explorations in the Unknown Darien Jungle in Contribution to the Pan-American Highway," *Washington Evening Star*, September 1, 1940, *Tewkesbury Papers*, Box 1, Folder 9; and Tewkesbury to E. W. James, June 27, 1940, *Tewkesbury Papers*, Box 1, Folder 8; see also Tewkesbury, "The Diary of Richard Tewkesbury on His Second Trip into the Darién Region of Panama: Notes in Brief," *Tewkesbury Papers*, Box 1, Folder 8; and "WSOC Broadcast transcription," November 25, 1941, p. 4.

20. "The Diary of Richard Tewkesbury on His Second Trip," pp. 5 and 7. On Tewkesbury's fearing he'd lost the Cuna's respect, see MacKaye, "Tewkesbury Conquers the Jungle," p. 56.

21. "The Diary of Richard Tewkesbury on His Second Trip," p. 14; and Tewkesbury, "Friendly Indians Are Found in Wilds Highway Will Pierce," *Washington Evening Star*, September 3, 1940, p. B8, *Tewkesbury Papers*, Box 1, Folder 9.

22. Tewkesbury to Stephen James, July 27, 1940, *Tewkesbury Papers*, Box 1, Folder 8.

23. Tewkesbury, "Darien and the Pan-American Highway," *Panama Star & Herald*, October 17, 1941, *Tewkesbury Papers*, Box 1, Folder 9; and "WSOC broadcast transcription," November 25, 1941, p. 3.

24. Quoted in Birnie, "Tooks Tames the Jungle," *American Magazine*, 44; Stephen James quoted in "Listen America" broadcast transcript, November 30, 1941, p. 7; second radio quote from "The Americas Speak" broadcast transcript, February 22, 1942, pp. 2–3, *Tewkesbury Papers*, Box 1, Folder 11; see also "Tooks Takes a Trip," *Time*, June 19, 1941, "'Tooks' Tames the Jungle," *Reader's Digest*, June 1941, "Jungle Journey for a Hemi-

sphere Highway," *Scholastic*, May 18–23, 1942, and "Jungle Trailblazer," *True Comics*, July 1942, *Tewkesbury Papers*, Box 1. On the book offer, see Myron L. Boardman to Tewkesbury, June 30, 1941, *Tewkesbury Papers*, Box 1, Folder 10.

25. James Price to E. W. James, November 5, 1940, *Tewkesbury Papers*, Box 1, Folder 12; and E. W. James to Tewkesbury, March 14, 1941, *Tewkesbury Papers*, Box 1, Folder 10; see also "Claimant and Contradictor," *Saturday Evening Post*, January 31, 1942, p. 4, *Tewkesbury Papers*, Box 1, Folder 12.

26. Tewkesbury, "Darien and the Pan American Highway," Speech at the Fourth Pan-American Highway Conference, pp. 1 and 8, *Tewkesbury Papers*, Box 1, Folder 9.

27. Tommy Guardia Jr., "El Eslabón de Darién," July 1954, p. 1, *James Papers*, Box 15 (pamphlets). On Guardia generally, see *Tommy Guardia, in Memoriam* (Instituto Geográfico Nacional "Tommy Guardia," August 1981), author's collection; and interview with Betty de Guardia, May 2015, Panama City, Panama.

28. Quoted in Darien Subcommittee, *The Darien Gap Project—Historical Review* (Panama, October 1965), p. 47. On O'Farrill's background, see Jose March, *El Mito del Darién* (Editorial Comoval, S.A., 1960), pp. 110–111.

29. Guardia Jr. quoted in Darien Subcommittee, *Explorations in the Darien Gap* (Panama, August 1957), p. 87; and "Report of the United States Delegation—Sixth Pan-American Highway Congress," September 1, 1954, p. 8, *James Papers*, Box 21 (research notes—Sixth Pan-American Highway Congress).

30. Guardia Jr. quoted in A. T. Steele, "Plans for the Darien Gap to Link Two Continents," *New York Herald Tribune*, February 5, 1955, p. 8. On Guardia Jr.'s imprisonment, see US Congress, House, Committee on Public Works, "The Final Link—Report on the Darien Gap," Committee Print No. 2, 88th Cong., 1st sess. (GPO, 1963), p. 15; and interview with Tomás "Pancho" Guardia, May 2015, Panama City, Panama.

31. Guardia Jr. assistant quoted in "Exploring for Highway Route to Link Americas," *Panama Star & Herald*, July 28, 1957, p. 2, *James Papers*, Box 21 (research notes—Seventh Pan-American Highway Congress); Arthur Marley, "Closing Gaps in the Pan American Highway," *New York Times*, March 6, 1955, p. X19; and US delegate quoted in Marion Wilhelm, "Wild Panama Area to Get Road Survey," *Christian Science Monitor*, March 25, 1955, p. 9; see also Tommy Guardia Jr., "Report on Explorations for a Road Through Darien" (February 1955), *James Papers*, Box 19 (research notes—articles by various persons).

32. Subcommittee initial report quoted in Darien subcommittee, *The Darien Gap Project—Historical Review*, p. 52; see also *Explorations in the Darien Gap*, p. 41.

33. "Sweated blood" quoted in "Now It's the Colombia Gap," n.p., n.d., *James Papers*, Box 21 (research notes—Seventh Pan-American Highway Congress); Guardia Jr. quoted in *Explorations in the Darien Gap*, pp. 48 and 56; see also William Ellett, "Darien Gap Beckons Road Builders to Close Span," *Christian Science Monitor*, c. 1958 (describing the survey), American Heritage Center, Laramie, WY, Papers of William Ellett, Box 1, Folder 1.

34. Reporter quoted in "A Route Found to Close Darien Gap," c. April 1963, in Memorandum, "Pan American Highway—Darien Gap," February 14, 1967, NARA, RG 398 (Department of Transportation), Office of Secretary—General Correspondence, 1967–1972, 1967 Subject File for IAH and PAH (6043), Box 47. On the Atrato soundings, see *Explorations in the Darien Gap*, p. 60. On the cost of the two Colombian routes, see Darien subcommittee, *Final Conclusions and Recommendations* (1968), p. 5, NARA, RG 406 (Federal Highway Administration), accession number 406-05-0025, Box 2.

35. Guardia Sr. to O'Farrill, July 1957, and Guardia Sr. to Isaac Fabrega, February 28, 1957, in *Explorations in the Darien Gap*, pp. 5 and 99.

36. On O'Farrill's accident, see March, *El Mito del Darién*, p. 113. O'Farrill quoted in "Darien Road Plan Gets Boost from Mexico," n.p., n.d., *James Papers*, Box 21 (research notes—Seventh Pan-American Highway Congress); Panamanian Public Works minister quoted in "Hopes High for Early Start on Darien Road," n.p., n.d., *James Papers*,

Box 21 (research notes—Seventh Pan-American Highway Congress); see also "Report of the US Delegation—Seventh Pan-American Highway Congress," 1957, *James Papers*, Box 18 (Reports II); and "Darien Highway Project Formally Endorsed," *Panama Star & Herald*, August 9, 1957, in Foreign Service Dispatch, "Continuation of Darien Project Approved by Seventh Pan-American Highway Congress," August 9, 1957, NARA, RG 59, Central Decimal Files 1955–1959, Box 4076 (File 810.2612).

37. Subcomité del Darién, *Informe y Anexos del Octavo Congreso Panamericano de Carreteras* (Washington, DC, 1960), pp. 8 and 20, *James Papers*, Box 21 (research notes—PAH 1960).

38. Colombian engineer quoted in *The Darien Gap Project—Historical Review*, p. 57; joint declaration in "Darien Highway Supported by Presidents," *World Highways* XI (May 1, 1960), p. 1, *James Papers*, Box 15 (Periodicals—World Highways); see also "Tapón del Darién—50 años de conflicto," *Panama American*, September 13, 2004; and *Informe y Anexos*, p. 11.

39. *The Darien Gap Project—Historical Review*, pp. 84–85; see also "Final Link," p. 10; and Richard E. Bevir, "We Built Our Own Road Through the Darien Gap," *Popular Mechanics* 116 (August 1961): 128.

40. Bertram Johansson, "Americas Road Link Pushed," *Christian Science Monitor*, May 25, 1960, p. 9; and "Closing the Darien Gap," *Christian Science Monitor*, May 31, 1960, p. 14; see also "Pan-American Road Pushed," *Christian Science Monitor*, June 21, 1960, p. 12.

41. O'Farrill quoted in "Executive Committee Details Darien Plan," *World Highways* XIII (August 1962), p. 2; see also "Punta del Este Agreement Calls for Darien Action," *World Highways* XII (September 1, 1961): 1; and "Pan-American Road Gets US Boost," *Christian Science Monitor*, March 22, 1962, p. 2.

42. See "Final Link," p. 20; and "Aid Given Pan-Am Highway," *New York Times*, March 6, 1963, p. 9.

43. Guardia quoted in "Joint Meeting of the Committees on Public Works of the Senate and House of Representatives and Delegates to the Ninth Pan-American Highway Congress" (May 13, 1963), Committee Print No. 3, 88th Cong., 1st sess., p. 15. On Guardia's contraction of cancer, see interview with Tommy "Pancho" Guardia, May 2015, Panama City, Panama.

44. Reporter quoted in "A Route Found to Close Darien Gap," c. April 1963; Guardia Sr. quoted in "Untitled Memorandum to O'Farrill," n.d., p. 24 (author translation), *James Papers*, Box 18 (Reports II). On survey problems see generally ibid.; and Ministerio de Obras Publicas de Panama, *Memoria Annual*, October 1, 1966, pp. 1–2, Library of the Instituto Geográfico Nacional "Tommy Guardia," Panama City, Panama.

45. Reporter quoted in "A Route Found to Close Darien Gap." On cost savings, see F. C. Turner to Alan Boyd, January 11, 1967, in packet dated June 9, 1967, NARA, RG 398, Office of Secretary—General Correspondence 1967–1972, 1967 Subject File for IAH and PAH (6043), Box 47. On the Atrato survey generally, see Darien Subcommittee, *Final Conclusions* (1968), pp. 21–23.

46. Johnson quoted in "Pan-American Highway Fate Up in the Air," *Los Angeles Times*, June 6, 1966, p. B10.

47. Alan Boyd to F. C. Turner, January 11, 1967, p. 3, NARA, RG 406, accession number 406-06-0003, Box 3 (Agreements Folder).

48. Lyndon Johnson, "The President's Toast at the Dinner in Punta del Este, Uruguay," April 11, 1967, *The American Presidency Project*; Colombian president Lleras quoted in F. C. Turner to Alan Boyd, May 19, 1967, p. 3, in packet dated August 21, 1967, NARA, RG 398, Office of Secretary—General Correspondence 1967–1972, 1967 Subject File for IAH and PAH (6043), Box 47.

49. Boyd to Turner, January 11, 1967, and see A. F. Ghiglione to Robert Tarr, June 9, 1967, in packet dated August 21, 1967; see also A. F. Ghiglione, "Summary Foreign Trip Report," July 1967 (noting the O'Farrill-Lleras meeting that resulted in the policy

change), in packet dated August 8, 1967, NARA, RG 398, Office of Secretary—General Correspondence 1967–1972, 1967 Subject File for IAH and PAH (6043), Box 47; Darien Subcommittee, *Final Conclusions* (1968), pp. 26–27; and "Hemisphere Link for Road Chosen," *New York Times*, March 9, 1969, p. 90.

50. Memorandum of Conversation, "Darien Gap," August 17, 1967, in packet dated August 21, 1967; and Position Paper, "Pan American Highway System International Projects: Darien Gap," November 24, 1967, in Donald G. Agger to Covey Oliver, November 28, 1967, NARA, RG 398, Office of Secretary—General Correspondence 1967–1972, 1967 Subject File for IAH and PAH (6043), Box 47.

51. Don Clausen, "The Darien Gap," *Congressional Record—House*, June 10, 1969, p. 15352; see also A. F. Ghiglione to Representative George H. Fallon, January 4, 1968, NARA, RG 398, Office of Secretary—General Correspondence, 1967–1972, 1968 Subject File for Inter-American and Pan-American Highways (6043), Box 8; and O'Farrill to Ghiglione, June 18, 1969, NARA, RG 406, accession number 406-06-0003, Box 3 (Materials from Agreements, 1966–1974).

52. US Congress, House, Committee on Public Works, Subcommittee on Roads, "Darien Gap Highway—Hearing" (December 10, 1969), 91st Cong., 1st sess. (GPO, 1970), pp. 13 and 20.

53. See "Caracas Mobs Peril US Visitor," *Chicago Daily Tribune*, May 14, 1958, p. 1.

54. State Department official quoted in Joseph Winder Oral History, August 23, 1999, p. 12, Association for Diplomatic Studies and Training, Arlington, VA, Foreign Affairs Oral History Collections; Kissinger quoted in "Memorandum to President Nixon," October 2, 1969, *Foreign Relations of the United States, 1969–1976*, vol. E-10, Documents on American Republics, 1969–1972, no. 10. On State Department's "mixed feelings," see memorandum from Lowell K. Bridewell re: Darien Gap, June 8, 1967, in packet dated August 21, 1967, NARA, RG 398, Office of Secretary—General Correspondence, 1967–1972, 1967 Subject File for Inter-American and Pan-American Highways (6043), Box 47. On Nixon's interest, see "Nixon Considers Aid for the Pan-American Highway," *La Estrella de Panamá*, July 23, 1969, in NARA, RG 406, accession number 406-06-0003, Box 3 (Materials from Agreements, 1966–1974); and "Memorandum of Meeting Between Nixon and Lleras Restrepo," June 12, 1969, in *Foreign Relations of the United States, 1969–1976*, vol. E-10, Documents on American Republics, 1969–1972, no. 150.

55. Nixon quoted in "Darien Gap Highway—Hearing," December 10, 1969, p. 34. On Nixon's interest in inaugurating the road, see "Paving the Gap in Pan-American Road," *Christian Science Monitor*, June 4, 1973, p. 4; and "Pan-American Road Put Off Indefinitely," *New York Times*, September 18, 1973, p. 18.

56. *Report of the Darien Subcommittee*, February 1969 to May 1970, p. 32, NARA, RG 406, accession number 406-05-0025, Box 2; and 23 USC §216 (1970).

57. Nixon, "Statement About Agreements with Panama and Colombia to Complete the Pan American Highway," May 6, 1971, *The American Presidency Project*; see also "Memorandum re: Signing Ceremony for Agreements with Colombia and Panama on the Darien Gap Highway Project," April 3, 1971, NARA, RG 59, Subject Numeric Files, (1970–1973) Panama—Inland Transport, Box 1368.

58. Roger Soles, "The Proposed Location of the Pan-American Highway Through Panama and Colombia," June 1971, p. 7, NARA, RG 398, Office of Secretary—General Correspondence 1967–1972, 1971 Subject File for IAH and PAH (6143), Box 46 (packet re: Darien Gap).

59. See Manuel Machado Jr., *Aftosa* (SUNY Press, 1969), pp. xii–xiii and generally. On the 1968 Central American agreement, see US Comptroller General, "Linking the Americas—Progress and Problems of the Darien Gap Highway" (February 23, 1978), p. 2. On the potential cost to the cattle industry, see "Colombia–Panama Road Runs into Snags," *Los Angeles Times*, October 26, 1975, p. I2.

60. See NSC Undersecretaries Committee, "Memorandum—The Pan American Highway

and the Darien Gap," November 8, 1971, NARA, RG 398, Office of Secretary—General Correspondence 1967–1972, 1971 Subject File for IAH and PAH (6143), Box 46.

61. "Plan for the Prevention of Introduction of Foot-and-Mouth Disease from Colombia into Panama," December 20, 1971, p. 10 and generally, NARA, RG 59, Subject Numeric Files (1970–1973), Panama—Inland Transport, Box 1368.

62. See "Memorandum for the President—The Pan American Highway and the Darien Gap," January 22, 1972, and "Memorandum for the President—Report to the President on Foot-and-Mouth Disease Control," December 21, 1971, NARA, RG 59, Subject Numeric Files (1970–1973), Panama—Inland Transport, Box 1368.

63. Torrijos quoted in "Pan-American Road Pushed by Panama," *Los Angeles Times*, November 12, 1972, p. D11. On the highway loan and aftosa control signing, see Embassy Memorandum, "Darien Highway Loan and Aftosa Commission Agreement Signing," May 31, 1972, NARA, RG 59, Subject Numeric Files (1970–1973), Panama—Inland Transport, Box 1368. Torrijos's enthusiasm for the road likely had more to do with a desire to open up Darien for resettlement of northwestern campesinos than with making an overland connection to Colombia. On the idea that Torrijos was primarily interested in national development and not Pan-American connections, see interviews with Ulises Lay, May 2015, and Stanley Heckadon-Moreno, June 2015, Panama City, Panama.

64. Nixon to Colombian president Andrés Pastrana, November 7, 1972, *Foreign Relations of the United States*, 1969–1976, vol. E-10, Documents on American Republics, 1969–1972, no. 166.

65. NSC conclusion quoted in William Lipford and Stephen Thompson, "The Pan-American Highway: The Incomplete Highway Linking North, Central, and South America" (Congressional Research Service, October 4, 1979), p. 9; see also Pastrana to Nixon, December 5, 1972, *Foreign Relations of the United States*, 1969–1976, vol. E-10, Documents on American Republics, 1969–1972, no. 167. For an argument that the aftosa threat might have been overblown, see interview with Alberto Alemán, June 2015, Panama City, Panama.

66. P. J. K. Burton, "Impact of the Pan-American Highway," *Geographical Journal* 139 (February 1973): 49; and A. R. Hanbury-Tenison, "The Indian Dilemma," *Geographical Journal* 139 (February 1973): 49.

67. On the Sierra Club's general opposition to road building, see Jason Schultz, "To Render Inaccessible" (master's thesis, University of Maryland, 2008).

68. See A. Dan Tarlock, "The Application of the National Environmental Policy Act of 1969 to the Darien Gap Highway Project," *NYU Journal of International Law and Policy* 7 (1974): 459–473.

69. M. F. Maloney to James Beggs re: Darien Gap Highway, December 27, 1972, NARA, RG 398, Office of Secretary—General Correspondence 1967–1972, 1972 Subject File for IAH and PAH (6143), Box 42; see also *Sierra Club et al.*, "Complaint for Declaratory Judgment and Injunctive Relief," June 27, 1975, p. 11, NARA, RG 406, accession number 406-06-0003, Box 1 (materials related to court injunction).

70. See Department of State Telegram, "Darien Highway—Battelle Memorial Institute," June 04, 1973, NARA, RG 59, Subject Numeric Files (1970–1973), Panama—Inland Transport, Box 1368.

71. "Cultural extinction" discussed in *Sierra Club v. Coleman* (October 17, 1975), 405 F. Supp. 56; "appropriate vehicle" discussed in *Sierra Club et al.*, "Complaint for Declaratory Judgment and Injunctive Relief," June 27, 1975, p. 12.

72. *Sierra Club et al.*, "Complaint," p. 13.

73. *Sierra Club v. Coleman* (October 17, 1975), 405 F. Supp. 53; Sierra Club representative quoted in Eugene Coan and Michael Moss, "The Darién Gap Highway: Manifest Destiny Revisited," *Environmental Policy and Law* 2 (1976): 121.

74. Quoted in Department of State telex, "District of Columbia Court Injunction on Darien Gap Highway," October 24, 1975, aad.archives.gov; "illegally interfered"

quoted in Department of Transportation, "Briefing Paper: Meeting with Panamanian Officials—Darien Gap Highway," March 3, 1977, NARA, RG 406, accession number 406-05-0025, Box 2 (materials from Darien Gap folder). On Colombian aftosa negotiations, see Gerald Ford, "Joint Communiqué Following Discussions with President Lopez of Colombia," September 26, 1975, *The American Presidency Project*.

75. Department of State telex, "Darien Highway Problem," November 6, 1975, aad.archives.gov.

76. Department of State telex, "Darien Gap Highway Injunction," December 24, 1975, aad.archives.gov.

77. *Sierra Club v. Coleman* (September 23, 1976), 421 F. Supp. 63; see also Federal Highway Administration, *Darien Gap Highway—Draft Environmental Impact Statement* (March 1, 1976), Biblioteca Nacional de Panamá, Panama City, Panamá; and Department of State telex, "Court Injunction and Darien Gap Highway," August 13, 1976, NARA, RG 406, accession number 406-06-0003, Box 2 (materials related to court injunction).

78. *Sierra Club v. Adams* (March 14, 1978), 578 F. 2d 389, 397.

79. Official quoted in Department of State telex, "Foot-and-Mouth Disease/Darien Gap Highway," June 23, 1977, aad.archives.gov; witness quoted in Department of State telex, "Darien Gap Highway," August 30, 1978, aad.archives.gov.

80. Quoted in Department of State telex, "Foot-and-Mouth Disease," December 19, 1978, aad.archives.gov.

81. *Congressional Record—House*, June 9, 1978, p. 16988.

82. Turbay to Carter, November 3, 1978, NARA, RG 406, accession number 406-06-0003, Box 1 (correspondence from May 1970 to December 1978).

83. Carter to Turbay, December 8, 1978, NARA, RG 406, accession number 406-06-0003, Box 1 (correspondence from May 1970 to December 1978); see also Department of Transportation memorandum, "Information and Action: Darien Gap Highway—F. Y. 1980 Budget Amendment," February 2, 1979, NARA, RG 406, accession number 406-06-0003, Box 1 (Darien Gap Highways).

84. Agreement discussed and Turbay quoted in Department of State telex, "Pan-American Highway: Turbay Asks US to Change Negative Attitude Toward Darien Gap Highway," August 27, 1979, aad.archives.gov. On Los Katios National Park, see Ministerio de Obras Publicas y Transporte (Colombia), "Carretera Tapon del Darien: Informe a la XI Reunion del Comite Consultivo del Proyecto Cooperativo ICA-USDA" (Bogota, February 28, 1980), p. 5, Biblioteca Nacional de Panamá, Panama City, Panamá. On Darien National Park, see Ministerio de Obras Publicas (Panamá), "Incidencia de la Fiebre Aftosa en la Terminacion de la Carretera del Tapon del Darien" (October 1986), p. 9, Library of the Ministry of Public Works (Albrook Building), Panama City, Panamá.

85. Letter to Reagan quoted in "Pan-American Highway Needs Cash to Close Gap," *Hartford Courant*, January 10, 1982, p. A15. Reagan quoted in LaFeber, *Inevitable Revolutions* (Norton, 1993), p. 274.

86. Quoted in LaFeber, p. 5.

87. Ibid., p. 274. On this period in Central America generally, see Kinzer, *Blood of Brothers* (Harvard University Press, 1991).

88. See "Managua Suspends Individual Rights," *New York Times*, March 16, 1982, p. A1. On other accounts of bridges being attacked, see Department of State telex, "After Action Report on the FMLN Attack on the Honduran Border Town of El Amatillo," May 11, 1983, Digital National Security Archive, George Washington University, Washington, DC; Department of State telex, "Bridge Hit in Sebaco," August 1, 1985, Digital National Security Archive; "Around the World—El Salvador Insurgents Press Drive in East," *New York Times*, November 8, 1981, p. 5; and Lawrence Cohen Oral History, July 12, 2007, p. 44, Association for Diplomatic Studies and Training, Foreign Affairs Oral History Collections.

89. See generally William LeoGrande, *Our Own Backyard* (UNC Press, 2000); and Philip Travis, *Reagan's War on Terrorism in Nicaragua* (Lexington Books, 2016), pp. 184–187.

90. See Patricia Pizzurno Gelós and Celestino Andrés Araúz, *Estudios Sobre el Panamá Republicano, 1903–1989* (Panama City: Manfer, S.A. 1996), pp. 641–644. On Noriega's Darién drug operations, see John Dinges, "The Case Against Noriega," *Washington Post*, January 28, 1990, p. w13.

91. See Indra Sofia Candanedo Díaz, "Closing the Darien Gap" (master's thesis, University of Maryland, 1997), p. 14, Biblioteca Nacional de Panamá.

92. See Peter Herlihy, "Opening Panama's Darien Gap," *Journal of Cultural Geography* 9 (1989): 42–59. On the Colombian spur road see Pascal Girot, "The Darien Region Between Colombia and Panama: Gap or Seal?" in Lyuba Zarsky, ed., *Human Rights and the Environment* (Earthscan, 2002), p. 180.

93. Governor Gilberto Echeverri Mejia to Dr. Larson, February 23, 1991, Greg Speier, trans., NARA, RG 406, accession number 406-06-0003, Box 3 (Darien general correspondence); Colombian foreign affairs representative quoted in Alicia Korten, "Closing the Darien Gap?" *Abya Yala News* 9 (June 30, 1994): 29; "Berlin Wall" quote taken from Girot, p. 179; see also Daniel Suman, "Globalization and the Pan-American Highway," *University of Miami Inter-American Law Review* 38 (2006–2007): 577.

94. Ambassador quoted in Candanedo Díaz, "Closing the Darien Gap," p. 21; Gustavo Gaviria Gonzalez, "Integracíon americana: El Tapón del Darién," *El Espectador* (Colombia), February 26, 1993, p. 2A, NARA, RG 406, accession number 406-05-0025, Box 2 (Darien Gap 1993).

95. Conservation official quoted in "Ambientalistas adversan conclusión de ruta," *Semanario Universidad*, September 11, 1992, p. 20, Biblioteca Nacional de Costa Rica, San José, Costa Rica; David Yeadon, "Panama Gap: Into the Heart of Darien, by Boat and on Foot," *Washington Post*, August 16, 1992, p. E1; see also Stanley Moreno and Alberto McKay, eds., *Colonization y Destruccion de bosques en panama* (Asociación Panameña de Antropología, 1984); and interview with Ulises Lay, May 2015, Panama City, Panama.

96. "Cien Millones de Dólares para Terminar la Vía Panamericana," *El Tiempo* (Colombia), August 14, 1993, digital archive (author trans.); public works ministers quoted in Girot, p. 195; presidential meeting discussed in "Across a Gap in Darien," *Economist*, November 21, 1992, p. 57; see also "Asfalto en la Selva," *Viva* (revista diaria de *La Nación*) (Costa Rica), February 10, 1994, p. B1, Biblioteca Nacional de Costa Rica.

97. See generally Peter Herlihy, "A Cultural Geography of the Embera and Wounan (Choco) Indians of Darien, Panama" (Ph.D. diss., Louisiana State University, 1986); Julie Velasquez Runk, "And the Creator Began to Carve Us of Cocobolo" (Ph.D. diss., Yale University, 2005); and interview with Franklin Mezua, June 2015, Panama City, Panama.

98. Quotes from Korten, "Closing the Darien Gap?"; see also interview with Korten, April 2015, via Skype; and interview with Hector Huertas, May 2015, Panama City, Panama.

99. Girot, p. 189; IUCN resolution quoted in "Asfalto en la Selva," B1 (author trans.); see also Center for Popular Legal Assistance, "Summary Report: Closing the Darien Gap: The Pan-American Highway's Last Link," March 1996, p. 3, NARA, RG 406, accession number 406-05-0028, Box 1, Pan-American Highway Study 4.

100. Carr quoted in Korten, "Paving the Pan-American Gap," *Multinational Monitor* 16 (November 1995); "ecologically diverse" quote from "Summary Report: Closing the Darien Gap," 1996; UN report quoted in Logan Ward, "Road Impact on Rain Forest Studied," *Toronto Globe and Mail*, July 15, 1995.

101. Bank report quoted in US Congress, Senate, Committee on Appropriations, "Foreign Operations, Export Financing, and Related Programs Appropriations for Fiscal Year 1995—Hearings" (GPO, 1995), p. 1062; bank official paraphrased in Alicia Korten and Dialis Ehrman, "Indigenous Peoples Speak Out to Save Ancestral Lands," *Mesoamérica* 14 (October 1995): 91–92.

102. See Suman, pp. 566–572; and Ed Culberson, "The Ever-Dangerous Darien," *South American Explorer* 36 (1995): 13–15.

103. Colombian public works minister quoted in "Parkland Route of Pan-American Highway Sets Off Storm," *New York Times*, March 21, 1995, p. C4; Guy Gugliotta, "Gap Could Be Paved with Good Intentions," *Washington Post*, October 22, 1996, p. A17. On Colombian actions in this period see Suman, pp. 578–580.

104. Quoted in Candanedo Díaz, "Closing the Darien Gap," p. 18.

105. Bank president quoted in Inter-American Development Bank, "Nuevo Rumbo para una Frágil Frontera: Gente del Darién Ayuda a Preparar un Proyecto," bank press briefing, July 1, 1998, iadb.org; American activist quoted in Mark Schapiro, "Panama Jungle Saved from Pavers," *Conde Nast Traveler*, c. 1997, NARA, RG 406, accession number 406-05-0028, Box 1, Pan-American Highway Study 2; see also "$88m to Improve Border Area," *Financial Times* (London), February 23, 1999, p. 5; and Inter-American Development Bank, "Panamá y BID firman préstamo para desarrollo sostenible del Darién," bank press briefing, February 21, 1999, iadb.org.

106. See Suman, pp. 592–607.

107. Bank official quoted in "Minding the Gap," *Economist* 373 (September 30, 2004): 38; Uribe quoted in Suman, p. 585. On Panamanian resistance in the face of pressure from Uribe, see "Tapón del Darién no se abrirá, Gobierno," *Panamá América*, November 27, 2004, www.panamaamerica.com.pa; "Carretera por Darién no Está en la Agenda del Gobierno," *Panamá América*, December 2, 2005; "Panama Envoy to Colombia Says Darien Gap to Remain Closed," *La Prensa* (Panama), August 27, 2009, www.prensa .com; "Revive polémica por el tapón del Darién," *La Estrella de Panamá*, www.laestrella .com.pa, March 10, 2011; interview with Ulises Lay Pérez, May 2015, Panama City, Panama (noting that a preliminary binational meeting in 2004 failed to reach any agreement); and interview with Juan Manuel Leaño, May 2015, Panama City, Panama. On Uribe's campaign, see Suman, pp. 580–586; and interview with Pancho Guardia, May 2015, Panama City, Panama.

Sources

Archives and Repositories

American Heritage Center at the University of Wyoming, Laramie, Wyoming
    Papers of Crede Calhoun
    Papers of Joseph R. Drake
    Papers of J. Walter Drake
    Papers of William Ellett
    Papers of Edwin Warley James
The American Presidency Project, at the University of California, Santa Barbara, California, www.presidency.ucsb.edu
Archivo Nacional de Costa Rica, San José, Costa Rica
Archivo Nacional de Panamá, Panama City, Panama
Beinecke Library and Manuscripts and Archives at Yale University, New Haven, Connecticut
Biblioteca de la Autoridad del Canal de Panamá Roberto F. Chiari, Panama City, Panama
Biblioteca del Ministerio de Obras Públicas y Transporte, San José, Costa Rica
Biblioteca del Ministerio de Obras Públicas y Transporte (Albrook Building), Panama City, Panama
Biblioteca del Ministerio de Ralaciones Exteriores (Cancillería), Panama City, Panama
Biblioteca Nacional Ernesto J. Castillero R., Panama City, Panama
Biblioteca Nacional "Miguel Obregón Lizano," San José, Costa Rica
Biblioteca Simón Bolívar at the Universidad de Panamá, Panama City, Panama

Columbus Memorial Library, Organization of American States, Washington, DC

Cushing Memorial Library at Texas A&M University, College Station, Texas

Papers of Thomas H. MacDonald

Papers of Francis C. Turner

Foreign Affairs Oral History Collections at the Association for Diplomatic Studies and Training, Arlington, Virginia, adst.org/oral-history/

Franklin D. Roosevelt Library and Museum, Hyde Park, New York

Gordon Library—Manuscripts and Archives at Worcester Polytechnic Institute, Worcester, Massachusetts

Instituto Geográfico Nacional "Tommy Guardia," Panama City, Panama

Iowa State University Library, Ames, Iowa

Papers of Richard Tewkesbury

John F. Kennedy Presidential Library & Museum, Boston, Massachusetts

Library of Congress, Washington, DC

Papers of James G. Blaine

Papers of Andrew Carnegie

Papers of William Gibbs McAdoo

Papers of Theodore Roosevelt

Museo, Biblioteca y Archivo Ricardo J. Alfaro, Panama City, Panama

National Archives II, College Park, Maryland

Record Group 30 (Bureau of Public Roads)

Record Group 40 (Department of Commerce)

Record Group 43 (International Conferences, Commissions, and Expositions)

Record Group 59 (Department of State)

Record Group 84 (Foreign Service Posts of the Department of State)

Record Group 151 (Bureau of Foreign and Domestic Commerce)

Record Group 229 (Office of Inter-American Affairs)

Record Group 275 (Export-Import Bank)

Record Group 398 (Department of Transportation)

Record Group 406 (Federal Highway Administration)

The National Security Archive at George Washington University, Washington, DC, nsarchive.gw.edu

Nettie Lee Benson Latin American Collection at the University of Texas, Austin

New York Public Library, New York, New York

Map Division

Sterling Memorial Library at Yale University, New Haven, Connecticut
West Virginia and Regional History Center, Morgantown, West Virginia
    Papers of Henry Gassaway Davis

Oral Histories

Alemán Zubieta, Alberto, former CEO of the Autoridad del Canal de Panamá (1996–2012), June 2015, Panama City, Panama.

Baltodano Guillén, Federico, former chief engineer of the Junta Nacional de Carreteras and the Departamento de Construcciones de la Secretaría de Fomento (1940s and 1950s) and former chief engineer of the Rafael Herrera construction firm, which worked on the Inter-American Highway (1957–1967), March 2014, San José, Costa Rica.

Bethancourt Rojas, Bernardo, former head school instructor in Yaviza, Panama (1954–1986), June 2015, Yaviza, Panama.

de Guardia, Betty, widow of Tommy Guardia, May 2015, Panama City, Panama.

Dogirama, Edilberto, president of the Congreso General Emberá, May 2015, Panama City, Panama.

Echandi Zurcher, Ricardo, former Ministro de Obras Públicas y Transportes, Costa Rica (1962–1966), February 2014, San José, Costa Rica.

Espinosa, Carlos, forestry specialist for the World Wildlife Fund in Panama, June 2015, Panama City, Panama.

Filós, Alberto, civil engineer, president of Tecnipan, S.A., and former president of the Colegio de Ingenieros Civiles de la Sociedad Panameña de Ingenieria y Arquitectura (Panama), May 2015, Panama City, Panama.

Grahales, Feliciano, commissioner of the Yaviza station of the Servicio Nacional de Fronteras (Senafront), June 2015, Yaviza, Panama.

Guardia, Tomás "Pancho," son of Tommy Guardia Jr. and grandson of Tomás Guardia, May 2015, Panama City, Panama.

Heckadon-Moreno, Stanley, anthropologist and staff scientist emeritus, Smithsonian Tropical Research Institute, June 2015, Panama City, Panama.

Huertas, Hector (Ubiliguiña), lead attorney for the Coordinadora Nacional de Pueblos Indigenas de Panama and former legal adviser for the Comisión Indígena Carretera Pan-Americana/Centro de Asistencia Legal Popular (1990s), May 2015, Panama City, Panama.

Korten, Alicia, former adviser for the Comisión Indígena Carretera Pan-

Americana/Centro de Asistencia Legal Popular (1990s), April 2015, via Skype.

Lay Pérez, Ulises, civil engineer, former president of the Colegio de Ingenieros Civiles de la Sociedad Panameña de Ingenieros y Arquitectos (Panama), May 2015, Panama City, Panama.

Leaño, Juan Manuel, transportation specialist for the Inter-American Development Bank, May 2015, Panama City, Panama.

McFarlane, Zacariah, former tractor operator involved in construction of the Inter-American Highway (1950s), February 2014, La Cruz, Costa Rica.

McNish, Brian, transportation specialist for the Inter-American Development Bank, May 2015, Panama City, Panama.

Mezua, Franklin, Emberá elder, June 2015, Panama City, Panama.

Monge, Sarita, quality control engineer of highway maintenance for the Consejo Nacional de Vialidad (CONAVI), March 2014, San José, Costa Rica.

Pacheco Gurdián, Roberto, former chief engineer for the Inter-American Highway in Costa Rica (1950s and 1960s), March 2014, San José, Costa Rica.

Puech, Michel, owner of Panama Exotic Adventures (specializing in tours of Darien), June 2015, Panama City, Panama.

Quirós Castro, Teodoro (don Yoyo), former Ministro de Agricultura, Costa Rica (1957–1958), February 2014, San Pedro del General, Perez Zeledón, Costa Rica.

Rubinoff, Annabela, daughter of Tommy Guardia and granddaughter of Tomás Guardia, May 2015, Panama City, Panama.

Silva Vargas, Rodolfo, former Ministro de Obras Publicas y Transporte, Costa Rica (1970–1974), February 2014, San José, Costa Rica.

Torres Alvarado, Eduardo, engineer with the Ministerio de Obras Publicas y Transporte (Costa Rica) in San Isidro, who worked on the Inter-American Highway in the 1960s, December 2013, San Isidro, Costa Rica.

Webber, Richard, retired auto mechanic whose family immigrated to San Isidro, Costa Rica, in the 1950s by following the route of the Inter-American Highway to what was then its terminus, January 2014, San Isidro, Costa Rica.

Image and Map Credits

Interior Maps

P. viii: Library of Congress

P. 6: West Virginia & Regional History Center, Papers of Henry Gassaway Davis

P. 54: Promotional brochure for the National Railways of Mexico (1913), Sterling Memorial Library, Yale University

P. 90: International Railways of Central America, Annual Report (1926)

P. 144: National Archives

P. 202: *The Christian Science Monitor*

P. 250: William Hilburn, "The Highway Without End: The Inter-American Highway," master's thesis, University of Texas, 1965

P. 286: American Heritage Center, Papers of Edwin Warley James

P. 316: Iowa State University Library, Papers of Richard Albert Tewkesbury

Insert Photographs

1–2: *Intercontinental Railway Commission, Report of Surveys and Explorations*, vol. I, part II, Washington, 1898

3: Library of Congress

4, 22, 31, 42: Author's collection

5: *The Bankers Magazine*, LXXX (1910)

6: *Mexican Herald*, November 1, 1908

7: *El Imparcial* (Mexico), February 9, 1909

8: American Heritage Center, Papers of J. R. Drake

9, 10: F. J. Lisman, *International Railways of Central America*, Sterling Memorial Library, Yale University

11: International Railways of Central America, *Annual Report* (1926)

12: Isaac B. Potter, *The Gospel of Good Roads* (New York, 1891)

13–14: Archer B. Hulbert et al., *The Future of Road-Making in America* (Cleveland: Arthur H. Clark Company, 1905)

15–16, 21: Cushing Memorial Library, Papers of Thomas H. MacDonald

17: American Heritage Center, Papers of J. Walter Drake

18, 19, 23–26, 29–30, 32–33, 36–37, 41, 43: American Heritage Center, Papers of Edwin Warley James

20. Franklin D. Roosevelt Presidential Library and Museum

27: Archivo Nacional, San José, Costa Rica

28: National Archives

34: *Baltimore Sun*

35: Personal collection of Roberto Pacheco

38–39: Iowa State University Library, Papers of Richard Albert Tewkesbury

40: Wikimedia Commons

44–45: Courtesy of the author

Index

About the Author

Eric Rutkow is an assistant professor of history at the University of Central Florida in Orlando. His first book, *American Canopy: Trees, Forests, and the Making of a Nation* (2012), received the Association of American Publishers' PROSE Award for US history and was named one of the top books of the year by *Smithsonian* magazine. He earned his BA and PhD from Yale and his JD from Harvard.